THE
American
Polity
Reader

Ann G. Serow

W. Wayne Shannon

Everett Carll Ladd

THE
American
Polity
Reader

W · W · NORTON & COMPANY

NEW YORK · LONDON

THE TEXT OF THIS BOOK *is composed in Bembo, with display type set in
Garamond Old Style. Composition and manufacturing by Arcata Graphics Kingsport.
Cover photograph by Steve Liss /* Time Magazine. *Book design by Marjorie J. Flock.*

FIRST EDITION

Since this page cannot legibly accommodate all the copyright notices, pages 703–
709 constitute an extension of the copyright page.

Library of Congress Cataloging-in-Publication Data
The American polity reader / edited by Ann G. Serow, W. Wayne Shannon,
Everett Carll Ladd.
    p.   cm.
    1. United States—Politics and government.   I. Serow, Ann Gostyn.
II. Shannon, W. Wayne.   III. Ladd, Everett Carll.
JK21.A466   1990
320.973—dc20   89–70981

ISBN 0-393-95612-1

W.W. Norton & Company, Inc., 500 Fifth Avenue, New York, N.Y. 10110
W.W. Norton & Company Ltd., 37 Great Russell Street, London WC1B 3NU

2 3 4 5 6 7 8 9 0

To our students

CONTENTS

PART THREE

Democracy, 87

PART FOUR

Separation of Powers and Federalism, 124

Contents

PART FIVE

Congress, 169

PART SIX

The Presidency, 217

PART SEVEN

The Executive Branch, 315

Contents   xi

PART EIGHT
The Judiciary, 339

PART NINE
Public Opinion, 382

PART TEN

Interest Groups, 416

PART ELEVEN

Voting and Elections, 442

PART FIFTEEN

The Political Economy, 595

PART SIXTEEN

Public Welfare, 645

PART SEVENTEEN

Foreign and Defense Policy, 675

PREFACE

WHAT MAKES THE United States the kind of country it is? Friends and critics alike have long puzzled over this and offered a great variety of answers.

Some of them mingle the serious and the facetious. Gertrude Stein, a writer often critical of American life, who chose to spend most of her adult years in Paris, once opined that the country's sheer size and relative emptiness did much to shape it. "In the United States," she wrote, "there is more space where nobody is than where anybody is. That is what makes America what it is."

Edmund Wilson, the literary critic, managed to blend praise and sarcasm in noting America's historic penchant for practical technology: "I have derived a good deal more benefit of the civilizing kind as well as of the inspirational kind from the admirable American bathroom than I have from the cathedrals of Europe. ... I have had a good many more uplifting thoughts, creative and expansive visions—while soaking in comfortable baths or drying myself after bracing showers—in well-equipped American bathrooms than I have ever had in any cathedral."

Others have waxed poetic—as did Philip James Bailey, in describing the key part played by unparalleled immigration to the United States in shaping the nation's character. He called America "half-brother of the world / With something good and bad of every land." Henry Wadsworth Longfellow was one of many, especially in the late eighteenth and nineteenth centuries, who saw the United States distinguished by a special role and mission. He told the country: "Humanity with all its fears / With all its hopes of future years / Is hanging breathless on thy fate." And in the great prose poem that he delivered at the cemetery in Gettysburg on November 19, 1863, Abraham Lincoln saw the essence of America in the political ideas on which it was established—"a new nation, conceived in Liberty, and dedicated to the proposition that all men are created equal."

The American Polity Reader is designed for introductory courses in American government. It might accompany a basic textbook on the subject (the current edition of *The American Polity*, by Everett Ladd, among them), or perhaps a briefer core text. For some instructors, the selections here might provide enough reading for the course. *The American Polity Reader* could stand alone as the basic text in such cases. However the *Reader* might be used, many of the selections address the question of what, *politically or governmentally*, distinguishes the United States. Some of the analysts whose work we sample come to praise, others to criticize. But among them there is little disagreement that America *is different* politically, significantly so, from other nations. By exploring where and why, we come to understand better the essence of our system. Many of the readings that we offer here probe from contrasting perspectives the fundamental features of America's polity—its distinctive ideas, constitution, governmental institutions, partisan divisions, and public policy choices.

We need to see this enduring structure, and to understand why it has endured. But American government is hardly static; the polity continues to grow and change. We present here over a hundred separate readings. It is a great advantage of so wide a selection that contemporary developments—in the presidency, Congress, and the Supreme Court, in political campaigns and the role of the press, and in Washington's policy debates, from the budget deficit to how black Americans' needs are best met—can be amply covered, even as the things that really don't change are thoroughly reviewed.

This essential coverage of the old and the new can be combined in a reader of reasonable price and length only one way—by tightly editing some of the most important work of leading analysts with the practical needs of introductory-course students in mind. Students' time for reading is limited. This volume brings them a vital core of commentary and assessment. Because of the time and care we gave not just to selecting material but as well to abridging it, we are confident that the *Reader*'s excerpts throughout faithfully represent the argument of the books and articles from which they are derived.

We are indebted to the political science faculty—especially, Christopher J. Bosso, Northeastern University; James Carter, Sam Houston State University; James Chalmers, Wayne State University; Euel Elliott, Virginia Polytechnic Institute and State University; Christopher Foreman, Jr., University of Maryland; Michael W. Gant, University of Tennessee-Knoxville; Kenneth L. Hill, La Salle University; Jon Hurwitz, University of Pittsburgh; Walfred Peterson, Washington State University; H. Mark Roelofs, New York University; Wallace H. Spencer, Pacific Lutheran University; Jonathan Tompkins, University of Montana; Robert Weber, Saint John's University—who reviewed our choices and helpfully criticized them. We also thank our students, to whom we have dedicated this book, for they have been the willing testers of other readers and of pre-publication sections of this reader. Finally, when it came time to make sure everything was in place, a proofreading army—Morgan Shipway, Michael D'Amato, Stergios Lazos, Richard Dale; Laurie Sullivan and Kathleen Buckley (in the Cave at Trinity); Betty D'Amato; and Kingswood-Oxford students Megan Fitzpatrick, Lee Gold, Jesse Cooner, Sue Decker, Jim Moore, Kim Karp, Carrie Dorr, and Joanne Marks—all came to the rescue.

THE
American
Polity
Reader

PART ONE

American Ideology

NATIONS, Alexis de Tocqueville observed a century and a half ago, inevitably "bear some marks of their origin." What the great American scholar, Louis Hartz, called "the storybook truth about American history: that America was settled by men who fled from the feudal and clerical oppressions of the Old World" has left an indelible mark on American political thought. As Hartz saw more clearly than anyone else, a contrast with Europe is essential if we are to understand the structure of American political ideas.

In a nutshell, what makes American political thought virtually unique among the Western democracies is that it is wholly contained within the boundaries of one part of European thought that is called liberalism. If the class for which you are studying now were being taught anywhere in Europe, your lectures and readings would stress the importance of at least *three* great ideological traditions and their sequential evolution since the seventeenth century: conservatism (in large part a defense of aristocratic institutions); liberalism (predominantly a middle-class or "bourgeois" attack on aristocratic privileges in favor of free economic markets, constitutionalism, and extension of the suffrage); and, finally, socialism (a

"working-class" vision of truly egalitarian socio-political arrangements characterized by common ownership of the economy and
complete political democracy). European politics from the seventeenth to the twentieth century would be conceptualized as a monumental struggle between these ideologies and the social classes
supporting them. Such an approach covers the European story
pretty well.

The dynamic of American political thought has been entirely
different. The "exceptionalism" of American thought stands out
clearly against the European contrast. It is no accident that many
of the most insightful commentaries on it are by Europeans. Two
of the three great European ideological traditions are plainly missing in the American case. Aristocratic conservatism, with its emphasis on natural inequality and the necessity for permanent class
divisions in the social order (some born to rule, others to obey),
spoke a language that Americans simply could not understand.
By the 1840s the rudimentary efforts made to plant it here had become hopeless failures. Socialism, a vigorous popular movement
throughout Europe in the nineteenth and twentieth centuries,
would root no more successfully here. Socialism in America has
amounted to little more than a subject of intricate doctrinal disputes
among leaders who have tried to import various versions of the
ideology from its native European ground; it simply did not find a
receptive mass audience here. By the time of the American Revolution liberalism had become the universal language of American
politics, and it has remained so to the present day. In Hartz's
language America has had a "liberal consensus"—one ideology
that is *the* ideology of the whole society.

Cut off as we are from Europe, it has been difficult for us to
understand the American ideology in comparative context. Like
Molière's Monsieur Jourdain, who spoke prose naturally without
knowing what it was called, we have spoken liberalism, often
without recognizing it as such. So intuitively in tune with the
consensual liberal ideology are we that we often think of ourselves
as nonideological. Nothing could be farther from the truth; we are
in fact the most ideological people in the Western world. Liberalism, as Hartz saw, is hard to recognize when its tenets are accepted
by everyone. Europeans have always seen us more clearly. Since
Tocqueville, they have been fascinated with "the American democrat," who, knowing no feudal past, appeared as a new kind of

person on the world stage, articulating the "commonsensical" elements of a robust and populistic American liberalism—liberty, equality, individualism, economic opportunity, and, above all else, an unembarrassed argument in favor of the worth and dignity of the cómmon man. Like it or not, European observers recognized "Americanism" as a set of beliefs held by all Americans as if no other political ideas were even worth consideration.

Each of the following readings offers a perspective on the American ideology. We begin with an excerpt from Tocqueville's classic, *Democracy in America*. Note clearly his argument that American political ideas follow from the "eminently democratic" social condition of Americans. What he means in simple terms is that American society had no aristocracy and no peasantry. There were surely substantial gradations of property, but by European standards Americans were pretty much alike. There were no fixed social strata. Americans would think alike because they were social equals. The selection from Hartz's *The Liberal Tradition in America* builds on Tocqueville's insight. Our having been "born free" (knowing no feudal past, and needing no revolution against it) has made us a homogeneously liberal community. Our political thought is exclusively (in fact, intolerantly) liberal. Such a liberal consensus can appear quite oppressive to those outside it. Both aristocratic conservatives and socialists have often found themselves in just this fix in America. In Europe they are as common as garden vegetables, easily recognized for what they are. Here, as it were, they have appeared to be freakish exceptions to the American Creed—at least odd, and at most dangerous. Often misunderstood, Hartz's commentary on American exceptionalism portrays it as a mixed blessing. Not understanding how and why we are different from the rest of the world, Americans, he fears, will be intolerant of domestic dissenters and simpleminded on the world stage.

G. K. Chesterton's essay from *What I Saw in America* began with an experience that has often baffled European visitors to the United States. In order to get his passport cleared he had to answer questions about his political beliefs, including whether he was in favor of overthrowing the government by force or violence. Chesterton, a seasoned traveller, thought this very odd. In his travels to many exotic places, he tells us, nothing like this had happened before. A lesser intellect would have left the matter at that, but

Chesterton was moved to think it out. The result is a brilliant essay. America, he concludes, is a most "peculiar" nation. It is the only nation in the world built on a creed—a system of ideas set forth with "dogmatic theological lucidity" in one of its great founding documents, the Declaration of Independence. All citizens are expected to believe it. As intolerant as the Spanish Inquisition, the American Creed is at the same time entirely universalistic and egalitarian in that it pays no attention to such factors as ethnicity, race, or social background. Anyone can be "Americanized" immediately by affirming the Creed, allowing assimilation of immigrants from wildly disparate backgrounds. The Creed, Chesterton concludes, is the very essence of American nationalism.

Daniel Boorstin, much more than Hartz an American celebrationist, argues that Americans do not need to think out what to Europeans have been difficult questions of political theory, because our ideas seem to us to have been "given" at the outset. We have the sense that our political ideas were developed fully for all time in the mind of our founders. Our political history seems to us a unity. Thus, we can look back to the founders as if they were contemporaries. Our politicians (Ronald Reagan is a perfect example) cite the founders constantly and use their ideas to support or criticize current policies. For better or worse, Boorstin is surely onto something. It would certainly not occur to anyone in the United Kingdom, for example, to ask if Locke or Burke would favor the National Health System. In America it does not seem in the least odd to ask if the framers would be for or against this or that aspect of the welfare state.

Michael Kammen's and Samuel Huntington's pieces stress the paradoxes of American ideology. Kammen is struck by our unabashed affirmation of jarringly incompatible concepts with no sense of contradiction (for example, majority rule and minority rights, and equality and individualism). The promises of the American Creed, he thinks, have often been sharply contradicted by social reality. Huntington develops this theme insightfully in *American Politics: The Promise of Disharmony*. So idealistic is the Creed that it can never be realized in actual institutions. Thus, there will always be an "IvI gap"—a disjunction between our ideas and our actual socio-political arrangements. Because our hopes are so high, America will always be a disappointment to those who take the Creed most seriously.

David Riesman, more than the other authors presented here, emphasizes change in the American "social character" over time. In *The Lonely Crowd* he argues that "other direction" (the shaping of individuals by peer pressure and mass media) is replacing an older "inner direction." Much has been made of this argument in recent years. We are struck, however, by Riesman's comment that the modern American is strikingly similar to the social and political animal described by Tocqueville more than a hundred and fifty years ago. We doubt that there has really been that much change at the deeper levels of American values.

Our readings on American ideology conclude with a brief excerpt from a book by the young socialist immigrant, Leon Samson, published during the depression some fifty years ago. Samson, like many other writers, is fascinated with our virtually unique lack of a socialist tradition. Why, he asks, does "the socialist argument fall so fruitlessly on the American ear?" The universal acceptance of the Creed, he thinks, is the culprit. "Americanism" (stop and think about the oddity of the concept; "Italianism?" "Irishism?" "Argentinism?") is a substitute for socialism, Samson argues. Although American society is characterized by considerable economic inequality, Americans do not think in terms of social class. Individualism and economic opportunity are universal values. Americans regard capitalism in an odd kind of socialistic way, believing that "everybody can become a capitalist." Liberalism, a "bourgeois" phenomenon in Europe, has been a robust, popular ideology in America. Indeed, it has been the only show in town. Other socialists have offered alternative explanations for the failure of socialism in the United States (mainly, either American capitalists' shrewd creation of "false consciousness" among workers or their use of force to repress socialist sentiment), but we think Samson's analysis, consistent with a line of explanation running from Tocqueville to Hartz, is much more persuasive. We should not forget that Tocqueville, long before the industrialization of America, noted our universal hope for economic success and our profound "contempt ... for the theory of the permanent equality of property."

I

ALEXIS DE TOCQUEVILLE

Origin and Democratic Social Conditions of the Anglo-Americans

From *Democracy in America*

———

AFTER THE BIRTH of a human being, his early years are obscurely spent in the toils or pleasures of childhood. As he grows up, the world receives him, when his manhood begins, and he enters into contact with his fellows. He is then studied for the first time, and it is imagined that the germ of the vices and the virtues of his maturer years is then formed. This, if I am not mistaken, is a great error. We must begin higher up; we must watch the infant in his mother's arms; we must see the first images which the external world casts upon the dark mirror of his mind, the first occurrences which he witnesses; we must hear the first words which awaken the sleeping powers of thought, and stand by his earliest efforts,—if we would understand the prejudices, the habits, and the passions which will rule his life. The entire man is, so to speak, to be seen in the cradle of the child.

The growth of nations presents something analogous to this; they all bear some marks of their origin. The circumstances which accompanied their birth and contributed to their development affect the whole term of their being. If we were able to go back to the elements of states, and to examine the oldest monuments of their history, I doubt not that we should discover in them the primal cause of the prejudices, the habits, the ruling passions, and, in short, of all that constitutes what is called the national character. We should there find the explanation of certain customs which now seem at variance with the prevailing manners; of such laws as conflict with established principles; and of such incoherent opinions as are here and there to be met with in society, like those fragments of broken chains which we sometimes see hanging from the vaults of an old edifice, and supporting nothing. This might explain the destinies of certain nations which seem borne on by an unknown force to ends of which they themselves are ignorant. But hitherto facts have been wanting to researches of this kind: the spirit of inquiry has only come upon communities in their latter days; and when they at length contemplated their origin, time had already obscured it, or ignorance and pride adorned it with truth-concealing fables.

America is the only country in which it has been possible to witness the natural and tranquil growth of society, and where the influence exercised on the future condition of states by their origin is clearly distinguishable.... America, consequently, exhibits in the broad light of day the phenomena which the ignorance or rudeness of earlier ages conceals from our researches. Near enough to the time when the states of America were founded, to be accurately acquainted with their elements, and sufficiently removed from that period to judge of some of their results, the men of our own day seem destined to see further than their predecessors into the series of human events. Providence has given us a torch which our forefathers did not possess, and has allowed us to discern fundamental causes in the history of the world which the obscurity of the past concealed from them. If we carefully examine the social and political state of America, after having studied its history, we shall remain perfectly convinced that not an opinion, not a custom, not a law, I may even say not an event, is upon record which the origin of that people will not explain. The readers of this book will find in the present chapter the germ of all that is to follow, and the key to almost the whole work.

The emigrants who came at different periods to occupy the territory now covered by the American Union differed from each other in many respects; their aim was not the same, and they governed themselves on different principles. These men had, however, certain features in common, and they were all placed in an analogous situation. The tie of language is, perhaps, the strongest and the most durable that can unite mankind. All the emigrants spoke the same tongue; they were all offsets from the same people. Born in a country which had been agitated for centuries by the struggles of faction, and in which all parties had been obliged in their turn to place themselves under the protection of the laws, their political education had been perfected in this rude school; and they were more conversant with the notions of right, and the principles of true freedom, than the greater part of their European contemporaries. At the period of the first emigrations, the township system, that fruitful germ of free institutions, was deeply rooted in the habits of the English; and with it the doctrine of the sovereignty of the people....

Another remark, to which we shall hereafter have occasion to recur, is applicable not only to the English, but to ... all the Europeans who successively established themselves in the New World. All these European colonies contained the elements, if not the development, of a complete democracy. Two causes led to this result. It may be said generally, that on leaving the mother country the emigrants had, in general, no notion of superiority one over another. The happy and the powerful do not go into exile, and there are no surer guaranties of equality among men than poverty and misfortune. It happened, however, on several occasions, that persons of rank were driven to America by political and religious quarrels. Laws were made to establish a gradation of ranks; but it was soon found that the soil of America was opposed to a territorial aristocracy. To bring that refractory land into cultivation, the constant and interested exertions of the owner himself were necessary; and when the ground was prepared, its produce was found to be insufficient to enrich a proprietor and a farmer at the same time. The land was then naturally broken up into small portions, which the proprietor cultivated for himself. Land is the basis of an aristocracy, which clings to the soil that supports it; for it is not by privileges alone, nor by birth, but by landed property handed down from generation to generation, that an aristocracy is constituted. A nation may present immense fortunes and extreme wretchedness; but unless those fortunes are territorial, there is no true aristocracy, but simply the class of the rich and that of the poor....

In virtue of the law of partible inheritance, the death of every proprietor brings about a kind of revolution in the property; not only do his possessions change hands, but their very nature is altered, since they are parcelled into shares, which become smaller and smaller at each division. This is the direct, and as it were the physical, effect of the law. It follows, then, that, in countries where equality of inheritance is established by law, property, and especially landed property, must constantly tend to division into smaller and smaller parts.... But the law of equal division exercises its influence not merely upon the property itself, but it affects the minds of the heirs, and brings their passions into play. These indirect consequences tend powerfully to the destruction of large fortunes, and especially of large domains....

Great landed estates which have once been divided never come together again; for the small proprietor draws from his land a better revenue, in proportion, than the large owner does from his; and of course, he sells it at a higher rate. The calculations of gain, therefore, which decide the rich man to sell his domain, will still more powerfully influence him against buying small estates to unite them into a large one. What is called family pride is often founded upon an illusion of self-love. A man wishes to perpetuate and immortalize himself, as it were, in his great-grandchildren. Where family pride ceases to act, individual selfishness comes into play. When the idea of family becomes vague, indeterminate, and uncertain, a man thinks of his present convenience; he provides for the establishment of his next succeeding generation, and no more. Either a man gives up the idea of perpetuating his family, or at any rate, he seeks to accomplish it by other means than by a landed estate....

I do not mean that there is any lack of wealthy individuals in the United States; I know of no country, indeed, where the love of money has taken stronger hold on the affections of men, and where a profounder contempt is expressed for the theory of the permanent equality of property. But wealth circulates with inconceivable rapidity, and experience shows that it is rare to find two succeeding generations in the full enjoyment of it....

...The social condition of the Americans is eminently democratic; this was its character at the foundation of the colonies, and it is still more strongly marked at the present day.... America, then, exhibits in her social state an extraordinary phenomenon. Men are there seen on a greater equality in point of fortune and intellect, or, in other words, more equal in their strength, than in any other country of the world, or in any age of which history has preserved the remembrance.

The political consequences of such a social condition as this are easily deducible. It is impossible to believe that equality will not eventually find its way into the political world, as it does everywhere else. To conceive of men remaining forever unequal upon a single point, yet equal on all others, is impossible; they must come in the end to be equal upon all....

2

LOUIS HARTZ
The Concept of a Liberal Society

From *The Liberal Tradition in America*

———

THE ANALYSIS which this book contains is based on what might be called the storybook truth about American history: that America was settled by men who fled from the feudal and clerical oppressions of the Old World. If there is anything in this view, as old as the national folklore itself, then the outstanding thing about the American community in Western history ought to be the non-existence of those oppressions, or since the reaction against them was in the broadest sense liberal, that the American community is a liberal community. We are confronted, as it were, with a kind of inverted Trotskyite law of combined development, America skipping the feudal stage of history as Russia presumably skipped the liberal stage.... One of the central characteristics of a nonfeudal society is that it lacks a genuine revolutionary tradition, the tradition which in Europe has been linked with the Puritan and French revolutions: that it is "born equal," as Tocqueville said....

Surely, then, it is a remarkable force: this fixed, dogmatic liberalism of a liberal way of life. It is the secret root from which have sprung many of the most puzzling of American cultural phenomena....

At bottom it is riddled with paradox. Here is a Lockian doctrine which in the West as a whole is the symbol of rationalism, yet in America the devotion to it has been so irrational that it has not even been recognized for what it is: liberalism. There has never been a "liberal movement" or a real "liberal party" in America: we have only had the American Way of Life, a nationalist articulation of Locke which usually does not know that Locke himself is involved; and we did not even get that until after the Civil War when the Whigs of the nation, deserting the Hamiltonian tradition, saw the capital that could be made out of it. This is why even critics who have noticed America's moral unity have usually missed its substance. Ironically, "liberalism" is a stranger in the land of its greatest realization and fulfillment. But this is not all. Here is a doctrine which everywhere in the West has been a glorious symbol of individual liberty, yet in America its compulsive power has been so great that it has posed a threat to liberty itself. Actually Locke has a hidden conformitarian germ to begin with, since natural law tells equal people equal things, but when this germ is fed by the explosive power of modern nationalism, it mushrooms into something pretty remarkable. One can reasonably wonder about the liberty one finds in Burke.

I believe that this is the basic ethical problem of a liberal society: not the danger of the majority which has been its conscious fear, but the danger of unanimity, which has slumbered unconsciously behind it: the "tyranny of opinion" that Tocqueville saw unfolding. ... When Tocqueville wrote that the "great advantage" of the American lay in the fact that he did not have "to endure a democratic revolution," he advanced what was surely one of his most fundamental insights into American life. However, while many of his observations have been remembered but not followed up, this one has scarcely even been remembered. Perhaps it is because, fearing revolution in the present, we like to think of it in the past, and we are reluctant to concede that its romance has been missing from our lives. Perhaps it is because the plain evidence of the American revolution of 1776, especially the evidence of its social impact that our newer historians have collected, has made the comment of Tocqueville seem thoroughly enigmatic. But in the last analysis, of course, the question of its validity is a question of perspective. Tocqueville was writing with the great revolutions of Europe in mind, and from that point of view the outstanding thing about the American effort of 1776 was bound to be, not the freedom to which it led, but the established feudal structure it did not have to destroy. . . .

Thus the fact that the Americans did not have to endure a "democratic revolution" deeply conditioned their outlook on people elsewhere who did; and by helping to thwart the crusading spirit in them, it gave to the wild enthusiasms of Europe an appearance not only of analytic error but of unrequited love. Symbols of a world revolution, the Americans were not in truth world revolutionaries. There is no use complaining about the confusions implicit in this position, as Woodrow Wilson used to complain when he said that we had "no business" permitting the French to get the wrong impression about the American revolution. On both sides the reactions that arose were well-nigh inevitable. But one cannot help wondering about something else: the satisfying use to which our folklore has been able to put the incongruity of America's revolutionary role. For if the "contamination" that Jefferson feared, and that found its classic expression in Washington's Farewell Address, has been a part of the American myth, so has the "round the world" significance of the shots that were fired at Concord. We have been able to dream of ourselves as emancipators of the world at the very moment that we have withdrawn from it. We have been able to see ourselves as saviors at the very moment that we have been isolationists. Here, surely, is one of the great American luxuries that the twentieth century has destroyed.... When the Americans celebrated the uniqueness of their own society, they were on the track of a personal insight of the profoundest importance. For the nonfeudal world in which they lived shaped every aspect of their social thought: it gave them a frame of mind that cannot be found anywhere else in the eighteenth century, or in the wider history of modern revolutions.... The issue of history itself is deeply involved here. On this score, inevitably, the fact that the revolutionaries of 1776 had inherited the freest society in the world shaped their thinking in an intricate way. It gave them, in the first place, an appearance of outright conservatism.... The past had been good to the Americans, and they knew it....

Actually, the form of America's traditionalism was one thing, its content quite another. Colonial history had not been the slow and glacial record of development that Bonald and Maistre loved to talk about.* On the contrary, since the first sailing of the *Mayflower,* it had been a story of new beginnings, daring enterprises, and explicitly stated principles—it breathed, in other words, the spirit of Bentham himself. The result was that the traditionalism of the Americans, like a pure freak of logic, often bore amazing marks of antihistorical rationalism. The clearest case of this undoubtedly is to be found in the revolutionary constitutions of 1776, which evoked, as Franklin reported, the "rapture" of European liberals everywhere. In America, of course, the concept of a written constitution, including many of the mechanical devices it embod-

---

*Louis Bonald and Joseph de Maistre were prominent French conservative political theorists of the early nineteenth century. Both were inveterate enemies of the radical and rationalistic ideas associated with the French Revolution. They were leading figures in the European Reaction.—EDS.

ied, was the end-product of a chain of historical experience that went back to the Mayflower Compact and the Plantation Covenants of the New England towns: it was the essence of political traditionalism. But in Europe just the reverse was true. The concept was the darling of the rationalists—a symbol of the emancipated mind at work....

But how then are we to describe these baffling Americans? Were they rationalists or were they traditionalists? The truth is, they were neither, which is perhaps another way of saying that they were both. For the war between Burke and Bentham on the score of tradition, which made a great deal of sense in a society where men had lived in the shadow of feudal institutions, made comparatively little sense in a society where for years they had been creating new states, planning new settlements, and, as Jefferson said, literally building new lives.* In such a society a strange dialectic was fated to appear, which would somehow unite the antagonistic components of the European mind; the past became a continuous future, and the God of the traditionalists sanctioned the very arrogance of the men who defied Him.

This shattering of the time categories of Europe, this Hegelian-like revolution in historic perspective, goes far to explain one of the enduring secrets of the American character: a capacity to combine rock-ribbed traditionalism with high inventiveness, ancestor worship with ardent optimism. Most critics have seized upon one or the other of these aspects of the American mind, finding it impossible to conceive how both can go together. That is why the insight of Gunnar Myrdal is a very distinguished one when he writes: "America is ... conservative.... But the principles conserved are liberal and some, indeed, are radical." Radicalism and conservatism have been twisted entirely out of shape by the liberal flow of American history....

What I have been doing here is fairly evident: I have been interpreting the social thought of the American revolution in terms of the social goals *it did not need to achieve*. Given the usual approach, this may seem like a perverse inversion of the reasonable course of things; but in a world where the "canon and feudal law" are missing, how else are we to understand the philosophy of a liberal

*Edmund Burke, an eighteenth-century English political theorist, is perhaps the most artful defender of tradition in the history of political theory. Jeremy Bentham, an English theorist of the late eighteenth and early nineteenth centuries, was as rationalistic as Burke was traditionalistic. While Burke generally saw virtues in inherited institutions, Bentham generally advocated their reform.—EDS.

revolution? The remarkable thing about the "spirit of 1776," as we have seen, is not that it sought emancipation but that it sought it in a sober temper; not that it opposed power but that it opposed it ruthlessly and continuously; not that it looked forward to the future but that it worshiped the past as well. Even these perspectives, however, are only part of the story, misleading in themselves. The "free air" of American life, as John Jay once happily put it, penetrated to deeper levels of the American mind, twisting it in strange ways, producing a set of results fundamental to everything else in American thought. The clue to these results lies in the following fact: the Americans, though models to all the world of the middle class way of life, lacked the passionate middle class consciousness which saturated the liberal thought of Europe. . . .

But this is not all. If the position of the colonial Americans saved them from many of the class obsessions of Europe, it did something else as well: it inspired them with a peculiar sense of community that Europe had never known. . . . Amid the "free air" of American life, something new appeared: men began to be held together, not by the knowledge that they were different parts of a corporate whole, but by the knowledge that they were similar participants in a uniform way of life—by that "pleasing uniformity of decent competence" which Crèvecoeur loved so much. The Americans themselves were not unaware of this. When Peter Thacher proudly announced that "simplicity of manners" was the mark of the revolutionary colonists, what was he saying if not that the norms of a single class in Europe were enough to sustain virtually a whole society in America? Richard Hildreth, writing after the leveling impact of the Jacksonian revolution had made this point far more obvious, put his finger directly on it. He denounced feudal Europe, where "half a dozen different codes of morals," often in flagrant contradiction with one another, flourished "in the same community," and celebrated the fact that America was producing "one code, moral standard, by which the actions of all are to be judged. . . ." Hildreth knew that America was a marvelous mixture of many peoples and many religions, but he also knew that it was characterized by something more marvelous even than that: the power of the liberal norm to penetrate them all.

Now a sense of community based on a sense of uniformity is a deceptive thing. It looks individualistic, and in part it actually is. It cannot tolerate internal relationships of disparity, and hence can easily inspire the kind of advice that Professor Nettels once imagined a colonial farmer giving his son: "Remember that you are as good as any man—and also that you are no better." But in another sense it is profoundly anti-individualistic, because the common standard is its very essence, and deviations from that standard inspire it with an irrational fright. The man who is as good as his neighbors is in a tough spot when he confronts all of his neighbors combined. Thus William Graham Sumner looked at the other side of Professor Nettels's colonial coin and did not like what he saw: "public opinion" was an "impervious mistress.... Mrs. Grundy held powerful sway and Gossip was her prime minister."

Here we have the "tyranny of the majority" that Tocqueville later described in American life; here too we have the deeper paradox out of which it was destined to appear. Freedom in the fullest sense implies both variety and equality.... At the bottom of the American experience of freedom, not in antagonism to it but as a constituent element of it, there has always lain the inarticulate premise of conformity.... American political thought, as we have seen, is a veritable maze of polar contradictions, winding in and out of each other hopelessly: pragmatism and absolutism, historicism and rationalism, optimism and pessimism, materialism and idealism, individualism and conformism. But, after all, the human mind works by polar contradictions; and when we have evolved an interpretation of it which leads cleanly in a single direction, we may be sure that we have missed a lot. The task of the cultural analyst is not to discover simplicity, or even to discover unity, for simplicity and unity do not exist, but to drive a wedge of rationality through the pathetic indecisions of social thought. In the American case that wedge is not hard to find....

It is this business of destruction and creation which goes to the heart of the problem. For the point of departure of great revolutionary thought everywhere else in the world has been the effort to build a new society on the ruins of an old one, and this is an experience America has never had. We are reminded again of Tocqueville's statement: the Americans are "born equal."

That statement, especially in light of the strange relationship which the revolutionary Americans had with their admirers abroad, raises an obvious question. Can a people that is born equal ever understand peoples elsewhere that have become so? Can it ever lead them? ... America's experience of being born equal has put it in a strange relationship to the rest of the world.

3

G. K. CHESTERTON

What Is America?

From *What I Saw in America*

———

[My purpose here is to] inquire what it really is which makes America peculiar, or which is peculiar to America. In short, it is to get some ultimate idea of what America *is;* and the answer to that question will reveal something much deeper and grander and more worthy of our intelligent interest.

It may have seemed something less than a compliment to compare the American Constitution to the Spanish Inquisition. But oddly enough, it does involve a truth; and still more oddly perhaps, it does involve a compliment. The American Constitution does resemble the Spanish Inquisition in this: that it is founded on a creed. America is the only nation in the world that is founded on a creed. That creed is set forth with dogmatic and even theological lucidity in the Declaration of Independence; perhaps the only piece of practical politics that is also theoretical politics and also great literature. It enunciates that all men are equal in their claim to justice, that governments exist to give them that justice, and that their authority is for that reason just. It certainly does condemn anarchism, and it does also by inference condemn atheism, since it clearly names the Creator as the ultimate authority from whom these equal rights are derived. Nobody expects a modern political system to proceed logically in the application of such dogmas, and in the matter of God and Government it is naturally God whose claim is taken more lightly. The point is that there is a creed, if not about divine, at least about human things.

Now a creed is at once the broadest and the narrowest thing in the world. In its nature it is as broad as its scheme for a brotherhood of all men. In its nature it is limited by its definition of the nature of all men.... America invites all men to become citizens; but it implies the dogma that there is such a thing as citizenship.... nothing like this idea exists anywhere except in America. This

idea is not internationalism; on the contrary it is decidedly nationalism. The Americans are very patriotic, and wish to make their
new citizens patriotic Americans. But it is the idea of making a
new nation literally out of any old nation that comes along. In a
word, what is unique is not America but what is called Americani-
sation. We understand nothing till we understand the amazing
ambition to Americanise the Kamskatkan and the Hairy Ainu.
    ...America is the one place in the world where this process,
healthy or unhealthy, possible or impossible, is going on. And the
process, as I have pointed out, is *not* internationalisation. It would
be truer to say it is the nationalisation of the internationalised. It is
making a home out of vagabonds and a nation out of exiles. This
is what at once illuminates and softens the moral regulations which
we may really think faddist or fanatical. They are abnormal; but
in one sense this experiment of a home for the homeless is abnormal. In short, it has long been recognised that America was an
asylum. It is only since Prohibition that it has looked a little like a
lunatic asylum.... there are some things about America that a
man ought to see even with his eyes shut.... It is the thing called
abstraction or academic logic. It is the thing which such jolly people
call theory; and which those who can practise it call thought. And
the theory or thought is the very last to which English people are
accustomed, either by their social structure or their traditional
teaching. It is the theory of equality. It is the pure classic conception
that no man must aspire to be anything more than a citizen, and
that no man should endure to be anything less. It is by no means
especially intelligible to an Englishman, who tends at his best to
the virtues of the gentleman and at his worst to the vices of the
snob. The idealism of England, or if you will the romance of
England, has not been primarily the romance of the citizen. But
the idealism of America, we may safely say, still revolves entirely
round the citizen and his romance. The realities are quite another
matter, and we shall consider in its place the question of whether
the ideal will be able to shape the realities or will merely be beaten
shapeless by them. The ideal is besieged by inequalities of the
most towering and insane description in the industrial and economic field. It may be devoured by modern capitalism, perhaps
the worst inequality that ever existed among men. Of all that we
shall speak later. But citizenship is still the American ideal; there is
an army of actualities opposed to that ideal; but there is no ideal
opposed to that ideal. American plutocracy has never got itself

respected like English aristocracy. Citizenship is the American ideal; and it has never been the English ideal. But it is surely an ideal that may stir some imaginative generosity and respect in an Englishman, if he will condescend to be also a man. In this vision of moulding many peoples into the visible image of the citizen, he may see a spiritual adventure which he can admire from the outside....

...He need not set himself to develop equality, but he need not set himself to misunderstand it. He may at least understand what Jefferson and Lincoln meant, and he may possibly find some assistance in this task by reading what they said. He may realise that equality is not some crude fairy tale about all men being equally tall or equally tricky; which we not only cannot believe but cannot believe in anybody believing. It is an absolute of morals by which all men have a value invariable and indestructible and a dignity as intangible as death. He may at least be a philosopher and see that equality is an idea; and not merely one of these soft-headed sceptics who, having risen by low tricks to high places, drink bad champagne in tawdry hotel lounges, and tell each other twenty times over, with unwearied iteration, that equality is an illusion.

In truth it is inequality that is the illusion. The extreme disproportion between men, that we seem to see in life, is a thing of changing lights and lengthening shadows, a twilight full of fancies and distortions. We find a man famous and cannot live long enough to find him forgotten; we see a race dominant and cannot linger to see it decay. It is the experience of men that always returns to the equality of men; it is the average that ultimately justifies the average man. It is when men have seen and suffered much and come at the end of more elaborate experiments, that they see men as men under an equal light of death and daily laughter; and none the less mysterious for being many. Nor is it in vain that these Western democrats have sought the blazonry of their flag in that great multitude of immortal lights that endure behind the fires we see, and gathered them into the corner of Old Glory whose ground is like the glittering night. For veritably, in the spirit as well as in the symbol, suns and moons and meteors pass and fill our skies with a fleeting and almost theatrical conflagration; and wherever the old shadow stoops upon the earth, the stars return.

4

DANIEL BOORSTIN

Why a Theory Seems Needless

From *The Genius of American Politics*

———

Now I SHALL BEGIN by trying to explain what I have called the first axiom of "givenness": the idea that values are a gift from our past. Here we face our conscious attitude toward our past and toward our way of inheriting from it. This particular aspect of the "givenness" idea may be likened to the obsolete biological notion of "preformation." That is the idea that all parts of an organism pre-exist in perfect miniature in the seed. Biologists used to believe that if you could look at the seed of an apple under a strong enough microscope you would see in it a minute apple tree. Similarly, we seem still to believe that if we could understand the ideas of the earliest settlers—the Pilgrim Fathers or Founding Fathers—we would find in them no mere seventeenth- or eighteenth-century philosophy of government but the perfect embryo of the theory by which we now live. We believe, then, that the mature political ideals of the nation existed clearly conceived in the minds of our patriarchs. The notion is essentially static. It assumes that the values and theory of the nation were given once and for all in the very beginning.

What circumstances of American history have made such a view possible? The first is the obvious fact that, unlike western European countries, where the coming of the first white man is shrouded in prehistoric mist, civilization in the United States stems from people who came to the American continent at a definite period in recent history....

The facts of our history have thus made it easy for us to assume that our national life, as distinguished from that of the European peoples who trace their identity to a remote era, has had a clear purpose. Life in America—appropriately called "The American Experiment"—has again and again been described as the test or the proof of values supposed to have been clearly in the minds of the Founders. While, as we shall see, the temper of much of our thought has been antihistorical, it is nevertheless true that we have leaned heavily on history to clarify our image of ourselves....

The notion of "givenness," as I have explained, has three aspects.... The first which I have been dealing with until now was the axiom that our values were the gift of our past, and actually of a particular period in the past. The second, to which I shall now turn, is that our values and our theory are the gift of the present: not of any particular men in the seventeenth and eighteenth centuries, but of the peculiarly fortunate conditions of life in America.

The first axiom is the one which I have just described and called by the name of the "preformation" ideal. It is the notion that, in the beginning and once and for all, the Founding Fathers of the nation gave us a political theory, a scheme of values, and a philosophy of government. As we have seen, it is an ideal, a static kind of "givenness"—a gift of orthodoxy, the gift of the past.

The second axiom is similar, in that it, too, is an excuse or a reason for not philosophizing. It is the notion that a scheme of values is given, not by traditions, theories, books, and institutions, but by present experience. It is the notion that our theory of life is embodied in our way of life and need not be separated from it, that our values are given by our condition. If this second part of the idea of "givenness" seems, in strict logic, contradictory to the first, from the point of view of the individual believer it is actually complementary. For, while the first axiom is ideal and static in its emphasis, the second is practical and dynamic. "Preformation" means that the theory of community was given, once and for all, in the beginning; the second sense of "givenness" means that the theory of community is perpetually being given and ever anew.

Taken together with the idea of preformation, this second "givenness" makes an amazingly comprehensive set of attitudes. The American is thus prepared to find in *all* experience—in his history and his geography, in his past and his present—proof for his conviction that he is equipped with a hierarchy of values, a political theory. Both axioms together encourage us to think that we need not invent a political theory because we already possess one. The idea of "givenness" as a whole is, then, both as idealistic as a prophet's vision and as hardheaded as common sense.

This second face of "givenness" is at once much simpler and much more vague than the concept of preformation. It is simply the notion that values are implicit in the American experience. The idea that the American landscape is a giver of values is, of course, old and familiar. It has long been believed that in America the community values would not have to be sought through books, traditions, the messianic vision of prophets, or the speculative schemes of philosophers but would somehow be the gift of the continent itself....

Our belief in the mystical power of our land has in this round-about way nourished an empirical point of view; and a naturalistic approach to values has thus, in the United States, been bound up with patriotism itself. What the Europeans have seen as the gift of the past, Americans have seen as the gift of the present. What the European thinks he must learn from books, museums, and churches, from his culture and its monuments, the American thinks he can get from contemporary life, from seizing peculiarly American opportunities....

The unspoiled grandeur of America helped men believe that here the Giver of values spoke to man more directly—in the language of experience rather than in that of books or monuments.

Our immigrant character has been an incentive toward this point of view. The United States has, of course, been peopled at widely distant times and for the most diverse reasons.... If American ideals are not in books or in the blood but in the air, then they are readily acquired; actually, it is almost impossible for an immigrant to avoid acquiring them. He is not required to learn a philosophy so much as to rid his lungs of the air of Europe.

The very commonness of American values has seemed their proof: they have come directly from the hand of God and from the soil of the continent....

The character of our national heroes bears witness to our belief in "givenness," our preference for the man who seizes his God-given opportunities over him who pursues a great private vision. Perhaps never before has there been such a thorough identification of normality and virtue. A "red-blooded" American must be a virtuous American; and nearly all our national heroes have been red-blooded, outdoor types who might have made the varsity team. Our ideal is at the opposite pole from that of a German Superman or an irredentist agitator in his garret. We admire not the monstrous but the normal, not the herald of a new age but the embodiment of his own. In the language of John Dewey, he is the well-adjusted man; in the language of Arthur Miller's Salesman, Willy Loman, he is the man who is not merely liked but *well-liked*. Our national heroes have not been erratic geniuses like Michelangelo or Cromwell or Napoleon but rather men like Washington and Jackson and Lincoln, who possessed the commonplace virtues to an extraordinary degree....

The third part of the idea of "givenness," as I have said, is actually a kind of link between the two axioms which I have already described: the notion that we have an ideal given in a particular period in the past (what I have called the idea of "preformation") and the idea that the theory of American life is always being given anew in the present, that values are implicit in the American experience. The third aspect to which I now turn helps us understand how we can at once appeal to the past and yet be fervently unhistorical in our approach to it.

By this I mean the remarkable continuity or homogeneity of American history. To grasp it, we must at the outset discard a European cliché about us, namely, that ours is a land without continuity or tradition....

The impression which the American has as he looks about him is one of the inevitability of the particular institutions, the particular kind of society in which he lives. The kind of acceptance of institutions as proper to their time and place which tyrants have labored in vain to produce has in the United States been the result of the accidents of history. The limitations of our history have perhaps confined our philosophical imagination; but they have at the same time confirmed our sense of the continuity of our past and made the definitions of philosophers seem less urgent. We Americans are reared with a feeling for the unity of our history and an unprecedented belief in the normality of our kind of life to our place on earth.

We have just been observing that our history has had a continuity: that is, that the same political institutions have persisted throughout our whole national career and therefore have acquired a certain appearance of normality and inevitableness. No less important is the converse of this fact, namely, that our history has *not* been *dis*continuous, has not been punctuated by the kind of internal struggles which have marked the history of most of the countries of western Europe....

...The important fact is what De Tocqueville observed a century ago, namely, that America somehow has reaped the fruits of the long democratic revolution in Europe "without having had the revolution itself." This was but another way of saying that the prize for which Europeans would have to shed blood would seem the free native birthright of Americans.

During these last one hundred and seventy-five years the history of the United States has thus had a unity and coherence unknown in Europe. Many factors—our geographical isolation, our special opportunities for expansion and exploitation within our own borders, and our remoteness from Europe—have, of course, contributed....

...The United States, with a kind of obstinate provincialism, has enjoyed relatively calm weather. While European politics became a kaleidoscope, political life in the United States has seemed to remain a window through which we can look at the life envisaged by our patriarchs. The hills and valleys of European history in the nineteenth century have had no real counterpart in the history of the United States. Because our road has been relatively smooth, we have easily believed that we have trod no historical road at all. We seem the direct beneficiaries of our climate, our soil, and our mineral wealth.

5

MICHAEL KAMMEN

The Contrapuntal Civilization

From *People of Paradox*

———

We have met the enemy and he is us.
—POGO

...OUR INHERITANCE has indeed been bitter-sweet, and our difficulty in assessing it just now arises from the fact that American institutions have had too many uncritical lovers and too many unloving critics. We have managed to graft pride onto guilt— guilt over social injustice and abuses of power—and find that pride and guilt do not neutralize each other, but make many decisions seem questionable, motives suspect, and consciences troubled.

Perhaps so many American shibboleths seem to generate their very opposites because they are often half-truths rather than the wholesome verities we believe them to be. Perhaps we ought to recall Alice in Wonderland playing croquet against herself, "for this curious child was very fond of pretending to be two people. 'But it's no use now,' thought poor Alice, 'to pretend to be two people! Why, there's hardly enough of me left to make one respectable person!' "...

This dualistic state of mind may be found also in the domestic political values subscribed to by most Americans. We are comfortable believing in both majority rule and minority rights, in both consensus and freedom, federalism and centralization. It may be perfectly reasonable to support majority rule with reservations, or minority rights with certain other reservations. But this has not been our method. Rather, we have tended to hold contradictory ideas in suspension and ignore the intellectual and behavioral consequences of such "doublethink."...

Americans have managed to be both puritanical and hedonistic, idealistic and materialistic, peace-loving and war-mongering, isolationist and interventionist, conformist and individualist, consensus-minded and conflict-prone. "We recognize the American," wrote Gunnar Myrdal in 1944, "wherever we meet him, as a practical idealist."...

Americans expect their heroes to be Everyman and Superman simultaneously. I once overheard on an airplane the following fragment of conversation: "He has none of the virtues I respect, and none of the vices I admire." We cherish the humanity of our past leaders: George Washington's false teeth and whimsical orthography, Benjamin Franklin's lechery and cunning. The quintessential American hero wears both a halo *and* horns.

Because our society is so pluralistic, the American politician must be all things to all people. Dwight Eisenhower represented the most advanced industrial nation, but his chief appeal rested in a naïve simplicity which recalled our pre-industrial past. Robert Frost once advised President Kennedy to be as much an Irishman as a Harvard man: "You have to have both the pragmatism and the idealism." The ambivalent American is ambitious and ambidextrous; but the appearance of ambidexterity—to some, at least—

suggests the danger of double-dealing and deceit. The story is told of a U.S. senator meeting the press one Sunday afternoon. "How do you stand on conservation, Senator?" asked one panelist. The senator squirmed. "Well, I'll tell you," he said. "Some of my constituents are for conservation, and some of my constituents are against conservation, and I stand foresquare behind my constituents."...

Raymond Aron, the French sociologist, has remarked that a "dialectic of plurality and conformism lies at the core of American life, making for the originality of the social structure, and raising the most contradictory evaluations." Americans have repeatedly reaffirmed the social philosophy of individualism, even making it the basis of their political thought. Yet they have been a nation of joiners and have developed the largest associations and corporations the world has ever known. Nor has American respect for the abstract "individual" always guaranteed respect for particular persons.

There is a persistent tension between authoritarianism and individualism in American history. The genius of American institutions at their best has been to find a place and a use for both innovators and consolidators, rebellious dreamers and realistic adjudicators. "America has been built on a mixture of discipline and rebellion," writes Christopher Jencks, "but the balance between them has constantly shifted over the years." Our individualism, therefore, has been of a particular sort, a collective individualism. Individuality is not synonymous in the United States with singularity. When Americans develop an oddity they make a fad of it so that they may be comfortable among familiar oddities. Their unity, as Emerson wrote in his essay on the New England Reformers, "is only perfect when all the uniters are isolated."

How then can we adequately summarize the buried historical roots of our paradoxes, tensions, and biformities? The incongruities in American life are not merely fortuitous, and their stimuli appear from the very beginning. "America was always promises," as Archibald MacLeish has put it. "From the first voyage and the first ship there were promises." Many of these have gone unfulfilled—an endless source of ambiguity and equivocation....

Above all other factors, however, the greatest source of dualisms in American life has been unstable pluralism in all its manifold forms: cultural, social, sequential, and political. *E pluribus unum* is a misbegotten motto because we have *not* become one out of many. The myth of the melting pot is precisely that: a myth. Moreover, our constitutional system seems to foster fragmentation of power while our economic-technological system seems to encourage consolidation of power. Thus the imperatives of pluralism under conditions of large-scale technology commonly conflict with principles and practices of constitutional democracy....

It has been the impulse of our egalitarianism to make all men American and alike, but the thrust of our social order and intolerance to accentuate differences among groups. We have achieved expertise at both xenophobia and self-hate! At several stages of our history, population growth has outstripped institutional change. The result in many cases has been violence, vigilante movements, or economic unrest, all with the special coloration of unstable pluralism. Because there are significant variations in state laws regulating economic enterprise, taxation, and welfare payments, people and corporations move to tax-sheltered states and to those with the most generous welfare provisions. In this way mobility becomes a function of pluralism.

I do not argue that pluralism is a peculiarly American phenomenon. But I do believe that unstable pluralism on a scale of unprecedented proportion is especially American....

There is a sense in which the super-highway is the most appropriate American metaphor. We have vast and anonymous numbers of people rushing individually (but simultaneously) in opposite directions. In between lies a no-man's-land, usually landscaped with a barrier of shrubs and trees, so that we cannot see the road to Elsewhere, but cannot easily turn back either. Indeed, the American experience in some spheres has moved from unity to diversity (e.g., denominationalism), while in other areas it has flowed in the opposite direction, from diversity to unity (e.g., political institutions). Along both roads we have paused from time to time in order to pay substantially for the privilege of traveling these thoroughfares.

There have always been Americans aware of unresolved contradictions between creed and reality, disturbed by the performance of their system and culture. Told how much liberty they enjoy, they feel less free; told how much equality they enjoy, they feel less equal; told how much progress they enjoy, their environment seems even more out of control. Most of all, told that they should be happy, they sense a steady growth in American unhappiness. Conflicts *between* Americans have been visible for a very long time, but most of us are just beginning to perceive the conflicts *within* us individually.

It is a consequence of some concern that our ambiguities often appear to the wider world as malicious hypocrisies. As when we vacillate, for example, between our missionary impulse and our isolationist instinct. From time to time we recognize that the needs of national security and the furtherance of national ideals may both be served by our vigorous but restrained participation in world affairs. At other times these two desiderata tug in opposite directions. However much we desperately want to be understood, we are too often misunderstood. . . .

Because of our ambivalent ambiance, we are frequently indecisive. "I cannot be a crusader," remarked Ralph McGill, "because I have been cursed all my life with the ability to see both sides." Our experience with polarities provides us with the potential for flexibility and diversity; yet too often it chills us into sheer inaction, or into contradictory appraisals of our own designs and historical development. Often we are willing to split the difference and seek consensus. "It is this intolerable paradox," James Reston writes, "of being caught between the unimaginable achievements of men when they cooperate for common goals, and their spectacular failures when they divide on how to achieve the simple decencies of life, that creates the present atmosphere of division and confusion." . . .

We have reached a moment in time when the national condition seems neither lifeless nor deathless. It's like the barren but sensuous serenity of the natural world in late autumn, before Thanksgiving, containing the promise of rebirth and the potential for resurrection. On bare branches whose leaves have fallen, buds bulge visibly in preparation for spring. Along the roadside, goldenrod stands sere and grizzled, and the leafless milkweed with its goosehead pods strews fluff and floss to every breeze, thereby seeding the countryside with frail fertility. The litter of autumn becomes the mulch, and then the humus, for roots and tender seeds. So it was, so it has been, and so it will be with the growth of American Civilization.

6

SAMUEL HUNTINGTON

Ideals and Institutions: IvI Gap

From *American Politics: The Promise of Disharmony*

———

As is His wont, God did not dare. Although it had showered the night before, the morning of the second Thursday in June 1969 dawned warm and sun-drenched. Steamy vapors rose from the soaking grass and dripping chairs, carefully ordered in their rows in the Yard, promising a hot and humid day for Harvard's 318th commencement. But although the University authorities maintained their usual casual optimism about the cooperation of the Almighty, there was considerable concern that less godly creatures might dare to be less accommodating. Turmoil, protest, and violence were reaching new peaks on American campuses that spring. The previous year, Columbia University had erupted into chaos. In April 1969 had come Harvard's turn, with the seizure of University Hall, the police bust, the student strike, the disruption of classes, and the endless mass meetings and bullhorns, demonstrations and demands, caucuses and resolutions. The night before commencement, prolonged negotiations among university officials, student leaders, and SDS (Students for a Democratic Society) extremists had produced an agreement that the normal order of ceremony would be interrupted to permit one of the SDS revolutionaries to speak briefly to the throng of ten thousand.* Before dawn a contingent of younger and presumably somewhat more robust faculty members had been quietly admitted through the locked gates of the Yard and had surrounded and occupied the platform—a preemptive measure to head off others with more disruptive intentions.

---

*The SDS (Students for a Democratic Society) was the leading student radical group of the 1960s. After its Port Huron Statement (1962), which offered an idealistic, social democratic critique of American institutions, chapters quickly formed in many universities and colleges. By the late sixties (the period about which Huntington is writing) the majority of SDS followers thought of themselves as revolutionaries in the tradition of Marxism-Leninism.—EDS.

As it turned out, such precautions were unnecessary. Overt revolutionary challenges to civil and academic authority during the two-hour ceremony were minimal. The SDS speaker "blew it," as one student said, with a tedious, uncompromising monologue which elicited loud boos from the audience. The protest walkout from the ceremonies drew less than two hundred students. The revolutionary impulse was limited to a clenched-fist greeting to university president Nathan Pusey by the graduating seniors, serving along with the clenched fists stenciled on their academic gowns as a lingering reminder of the upheavals earlier in the spring.

The revolutionary challenge to established authority thus fizzled in Harvard Yard, as it has always fizzled in American society. But one major challenge to established authority was posed in the Yard that day, and in traditional American pattern it came not from the fringes but from the mainstream. In appropriate Harvard fashion, it was posed intellectually rather than physically. It was to be found in the English Oration delivered by Meldon E. Levine, a native of Beverly Hills, California, and a graduate student in law. "What is this protest all about?" Levine asked. Addressing himself to the alumni, faculty, and parents and presuming to speak for his fellow students, he answered this question briefly—and accurately. Our protest, he said, is not an effort "to subvert institutions or an attempt to challenge values which have been affirmed for centuries. We are NOT," he emphasized, "...conspiring to destroy America. We are attempting to do precisely the reverse: we are affirming the values which you have instilled in us and which you have taught us to respect. You have told us repeatedly that trust and courage were standards to emulate. You have convinced us that equality and justice were inviolable concepts. You have taught us that authority should be guided by reason and tempered by fairness. AND WE HAVE TAKEN YOU SERIOUSLY." We have tried to put into practice your principles, Levine told the older generation, and you have frustrated us and obstructed us. "You have given us our visions and then asked us to curb them." We want to do what you have taught us is right to do, but "you have made us idealists and then told us to go slowly." All we ask is that "you allow us to realize the very values which you have held forth."...

This gap between political ideal and political reality is a continuing central phenomenon of American politics in a way that is not true of any other major state. The importance of the gap stems from three distinctive characteristics of American political ideals.

First is the *scope* of the agreement on these ideals. In contrast to most European societies, a broad consensus exists and has existed in the United States on basic political values and beliefs. These values and beliefs, which constitute what is often referred to as "the American Creed," have historically served as a distinctive source of American national identity. Second is the *substance* of those ideals. In contrast to the values of most other societies, the values of this Creed are liberal, individualistic, democratic, egalitarian, and hence basically antigovernment and antiauthority in character. Whereas other ideologies legitimate established authority and institutions, the American Creed serves to delegitimate any hierarchical, coercive, authoritarian structures, including American ones. Third is the changing *intensity* with which Americans believe in these basic ideals, an intensity that varies from time to time and from group to group. Historically, American society seems to evolve through periods of creedal passion and of creedal passivity. . . .

The basic ideas of the American Creed—equality, liberty, individualism, constitutionalism, democracy—clearly do not constitute a systematic ideology, and they do not necessarily have any logical consistency. At some point, liberty and equality may clash, individualism may run counter to constitutionalism, and democracy or majority rule may infringe on both. Precisely because it is not an intellectualized ideology, the American Creed can live with such inconsistencies.

Logically inconsistent as they seem to philosophers, these ideas do have a single common thrust and import for the relations between society and government: all the varying elements in the American Creed unite in imposing limits on power and on the institutions of government. The essence of constitutionalism is the restraint of governmental power through fundamental law. The essence of liberalism is freedom from governmental control—the vindication of liberty against power, as Bernard Bailyn summed up the argument for the American Revolution. The essence of individualism is the right of each person to act in accordance with his own conscience and to control his own destiny free of external restraint, except insofar as such restraint is necessary to ensure comparable rights to others. The essence of egalitarianism is rejection of the idea that one person has the right to exercise power over another. The essence of democracy is popular control over government, directly or through representatives, and the responsiveness of governmental officials to public opinion. In sum, the distinctive aspect of the American Creed is its antigovernment character. Opposition to power, and suspicion of government as the most dangerous embodiment of power, are the central themes of American political thought.

...In his classic study of race relations in the United States, Gunnar Myrdal brilliantly pinpointed "an American dilemma" that existed between the deep beliefs in the concepts of liberty, equality, and individualism of the American Creed and the actual treatment of black people in American society. He probed, however, only one manifestation (albeit the most dramatic one) of the widespread gap between American political ideals and institutions—referred to here as "the IvI gap." What he termed "an" American dilemma is really "the" American dilemma, the central agony of American politics.

American liberal and democratic ideas form a standing and powerful indictment of almost all political institutions, including American ones. No government can exist without some measure of hierarchy, inequality, arbitrary power, secrecy, deception, and established patterns of superordination and subordination. The American Creed, however, challenges the legitimacy of all these characteristics of government. Its ideas run counter to the nature of government in general. They run counter to the nature of highly bureaucratized and centralized modern government. They run counter to both the original and inherited nature of American government.

Therein lies the dilemma. In the United States, government is legitimate to the extent to which it reflects the basic principles of the American Creed. Government can never, however, reflect those principles perfectly, and it is therefore illegitimate to the extent to which people take seriously the principles of the American Creed. If people try to make government more legitimate by bringing political practice more into accord with political principle, they will weaken government rather than strengthen it. Because of the inherently antigovernment character of the American Creed, government that is strong is illegitimate, government that is legitimate is weak.

In practice, in comparison with European societies, government has always been weak in America. This weakness originally was the product of the fact that no need existed in the United States to centralize power and establish a strong government in order to overthrow feudalism. In this sense, as Tocqueville pointed out, Americans "arrived at a state of democracy without having to endure a democratic revolution, and ... are born equal instead of becoming so." The absence of feudalism thus eliminated a major negative impetus to strong government. The presence in its place of a pervasive consensus on liberal and democratic values furnished an additional, positive incentive to limit government. In the absence of a consensus, strong government would have been necessary; as Hartz pointed out, it is only because the images that the framers of the Constitution had of American society were erroneous that the system of divided and checked government that they created was able to last. The fact of consensus thus made possible weak political institutions. The content of the consensus reinforced the weakness of those institutions....

...One function of an ideology in a political system is to legitimate rule, to furnish a persuasive and compelling answer to the question: Why obey? The American Creed, however, provides the rationale for restraints on rule. It is a much more fruitful source of reasons for questioning and resisting government than for obedience to government.

Political ideas do play a role in America—a purgative role that is not characteristic of other societies. In countries in which there are a variety of ideologies and belief systems, there are a variety of sources of challenge to governmental institutions, accompanied almost invariably by a variety of defenses for these institutions. Tradition and social structure furnish a basis for the legitimacy of some institutions, and particular ideologies and political theories can be used to legitimize individual institutions. Attacks on one set of institutions from the perspective of one ideology generate equally intense defenses from the perspective of other ideologies. In the United States, on the other hand, the consensus is basically antigovernment. What justification is there for government, hierarchy, discipline, secrecy, coercion, and the suppression of the claims of individuals and groups within the American context? In terms of American beliefs, government is supposed to be egalitarian, participatory, open, noncoercive, and responsive to the demands of individuals and groups. Yet no government can be all these things and still remain a government. "Credibility gaps" develop in American politics in part because the American people believe that government ought not do things it must do in order to be a government and that it ought to do things it cannot do without

AMERICAN RESPONSES TO THE IvI GAP

INTENSITY OF BELIEF IN IDEALS	PERCEPTION OF GAP	
	CLEAR	UNCLEAR
High	Moralism (eliminate gap)	Hypocrisy (deny gap)
Low	Cynicism (tolerate gap)	Complacency (ignore gap)

undermining itself as a government.

The ideological challenge to American government thus comes not from abroad but from home, not from imported Marxist doctrines but from homegrown American idealism. The stability of political institutions is threatened not by deep-rooted cleavages but by deeply felt consensus. Americans cannot be themselves unless they believe in the Creed, but they also must be against themselves if they believe in the Creed. The more intensely Americans commit themselves to their national political beliefs, the more hostile or cynical they become about their political institutions. As a result of the IvI gap, the legitimacy of American government varies inversely with belief in American political ideals. . . .

What are the ways in which Americans cope with their national cognitive dissonance? Consensus and stability have generally characterized American political values, and the IvI gap is always present. Variations do occur, however, in the intensity with which groups of Americans hold to their beliefs in American political ideals—that is, the level of creedal passion in American society— and in the clarity with which Americans perceive the gap to exist. Differences in these two variables can yield the four major responses set forth in the table.

1. *Moralism.* If Americans intensely believe in their ideals and clearly perceive the IvI gap, they moralistically attempt to *eliminate* the gap through reforms that will bring practice and institutions into accord with principles and beliefs.

2. *Cynicism.* If intensity of belief is low and perception of the gap is clear, Americans will resort to a cynical willingness to *tolerate* the gap's existence.

3. *Complacency.* If intensity of belief is low and their perception of the gap is unclear, Americans can attempt to *ignore* the existence of the gap by in effect reducing its cognitive importance to themselves through complacent indifference.

4. *Hypocrisy.* If they are intensely committed to American ideals

and yet *deny* the existence of a gap between ideals and reality, they can alter not reality but their perceptions of reality through an immense effort at "patriotic" hypocrisy.[*]

At various times social critics, including foreign observers of the American scene, have seized upon one or another of these four responses as *the* typical American response. In fact, however, all four have been present throughout most of American history, interacting with one another in mutually reinforcing and mutually counterbalancing ways. Complacency is probably the most prevalent response, but it is also the least noted and least notable one. The others have all left a definite mark on American culture....

The propensity of American society as a whole to resort to one response or another, or some combination of responses, varies. The national mood can at different times be described as predominantly one of complacency, hypocrisy, moralism, or cynicism. Experience suggests that recourse to one of these responses may generate consequences that encourage recourse to another response. No one response, however, provides a lasting satisfactory solution to the problem of cognitive dissonance. Each is tried for a while and then abandoned in a never-ending search for a way out of the national dilemma. The logical dynamics of such a cyclical pattern of response are as follows.

1. *Moralistic reform (eliminating the gap)*. Since cognitive dissonance cannot be eliminated by changing fundamental principles, changes must occur in institutions and behavior. The moralistic response occurs when people feel intensely committed to American political values, clearly perceive the gap between ideals and reality, and attempt to restructure institutions and practices to reflect these ideals. The combination of intensity and perception furnishes the moral motive to reform. "The history of reform," Emerson said, "is always identical; it is the comparison of the idea with the fact." Major groups in American society become obsessed with the facts of inequality, lack of freedom, arbitrary power. They dramatize those facts and force them upon the public consciousness, making

---

[*]Some may observe that the labels I have given these four responses all carry unfavorable connotations—and this is certainly true. One could, perhaps, find euphemisms and talk about morality rather than moralism, realism rather than cynicism, satisfaction rather than complacency, and patriotism rather than hypocrisy. Yet these pleasant alternative labels obscure the critical point: that each response is, in some measure, unsatisfactory and cannot be maintained for long by substantial numbers of people. They tend to hide the problem of the gap rather than to highlight it.

it impossible for decision makers and the attentive public to ignore the extent to which the actuality of political life contradicts American beliefs. The moral indignation of the few stimulates public outrage from the many. Institutions and practices that had been accepted as part of the way things are lose their legitimacy. Demands for curtailing power and reforming the system sweep to the top of the political agenda: reality must be made to conform to the ideal. During such creedal passion periods, the latent disharmonic qualities of American society come to the surface.

2. *Cynicism (tolerating the gap)*. Large bodies of people can sustain high levels of moral indignation for only limited periods of time. The unveiling of evil, which was first the instrument by which moralism laid bare hypocrisy, later furnishes the vindication of cynicism against moralism. The perception of the IvI gap remains, but the expectation that anything can be done to close the gap dwindles. Those who had expounded the Creed in order to change reality find themselves increasingly divorced from reality. The exposers of hypocrisy become the exemplars of hypocrisy.

Reform begins with the assumption that the elimination of evil can be achieved by the elimination of evil men-in-power. It moves on to the assumption that some restructuring of institutions is necessary. It comes to an end with the realization that neither of these will suffice. Some reformers conclude that the "system" itself must be totally changed and advocate revolution. Others let the intensity of their commitment to reform values decline and lapse into at least temporary cynical toleration of the gap. The feeling that the gap must be eliminated is replaced by the feeling that nothing can be changed. Moral indignation is replaced by moral helplessness. All politicians are crooks, all institutions corrupt. The gap must be accepted—and perhaps even enjoyed, as its role in American humor suggests.

3. *Complacency (ignoring the gap)*. Cynicism is an effort to live with cognitive dissonance. But just as most people cannot maintain moral intensity indefinitely, neither can they indefinitely sustain toleration of the gap between ideal and practice. "Cognitive dissonance is a noxious state," and the "severity or the intensity of cognitive dissonance varies with the importance of the cognitions involved and the relative number of cognitions standing in dissonant relation to one another." Whereas the escape from creedal passion to cynicism involves a dulling of moral sensibility, the escape from cynicism to complacency involves a dulling of percep-

tual clarity. The importance of the dissonant cognitions is reduced simply by turning attention to other matters. During such periods of creedal passivity and perceptual opaqueness, Americans may, if compelled to do so, admit the existence of a gap between ideal and reality—as they did for years with respect to the role of black people in American life—but then shunt it off into a back corner of their consciousness and simply not become terribly concerned about it. The dilemma, as Myrdal argued, exists but it does not trouble people nor lead them to become intensely and passionately concerned with resolving it. Cognitive dissonance lurks uneasily beneath the surface of conscience but is not sufficiently commanding to trouble people seriously. There is no intense concern with American ideals or with the discrepancy between ideal and reality.

4. *Hypocrisy (denying the gap)*. The ideological nature of their national identity means that Americans cannot indefinitely eschew the affirmation of the basic values and principles of the national Creed. Responding to the need to articulate these values, however, they may still be reluctant to acknowledge the existence of the IvI gap. They may then view themselves through filtering lenses. American institutions are seen to be open and democratic; America is the land of opportunity; the equality of man is a fact in American life; the United States is the land of the free and the home of the brave; it is the embodiment of government of the people, by the people, and for the people. During these periods, Americans so shape their perceptions that they cannot see any gap between the unpleasant facts of political institutions and power in the United States and the values of the American Creed. Reality is hailed as the ideal. The discrepancies are strained out and avoided. The United States not only should be the land of liberty, equality, and justice for all; it actually is.

In due course, however, the intense assertion of American ideals leads to renewed perception of the IvI gap. New individuals and groups begin to use the affirmation of the ideals as a means not of glorifying the American way of life but of exposing it. The hypocritical identification of reality with ideal gives way to the moralistic denunciation of reality in terms of the ideal. The way is cleared for another wave of creedal passion directed toward reform....

...The question now is: Will the IvI gap and the responses to it continue to play the same role in American politics in the future that they have in the past? Or are there changes taking place or likely to take place in American political ideals, political institutions,

tions, and the relation between them that will make their future significantly different from their past?

Three possibilities exist. The relation between ideals and institutions, first, could continue essentially unchanged; second, it could be altered by developments within American society; and, third, it could be altered by developments outside American society and by American foreign involvements. Domestic developments within American society or changes in the international environment could alter the relation between American political ideals and institutions in four ways: the content of the ideals could change; the scope of agreement on the ideals could change; the nature of American political institutions could more closely approximate American ideals, thereby reducing the gap between them; and American political institutions could be significantly altered in an illiberal, undemocratic, anti-individualistic direction; or some combination of these developments could take place. . . .

The continued existence of the United States means that Americans will continue to suffer from cognitive dissonance. They will continue to attempt to come to terms with that dissonance through some combination of moralism, cynicism, complacency, and hypocrisy. The greatest danger to the IvI gap would come when any substantial portion of the American population carried to an extreme any one of these responses. An excess of moralism, hypocrisy, cynicism, or complacency could do in the American system. A totally complacent toleration of the IvI gap could lead to the corruption and decay of American liberal-democratic institutions. Uncritical hypocrisy, blind to the existence of the gap and fervent in its commitment to American principles, could lead to imperialistic expansion, ending in either military or political disaster abroad or the undermining of democracy at home. Cynical acceptance of the gap could lead to a gradual abandonment of American ideals and their replacement either by a Thrasymachusian might-makes-right morality or by some other set of political beliefs.* Finally, intense moralism could lead Americans to destroy the freest institutions on earth because they believed they deserved something better.

---

*Thrasymachus, a character in Plato's *The Republic* (fourth century B.C.) argues against Socrates that justice is nothing more than "the interest of the stronger party." Plato, of course, has Socrates refute the blunt, realistic argument. It reappears, however, again and again in the history of political theory. Its classic formulation is by Niccolò Machiavelli in *The Prince* (about 1513).—EDS.

To maintain their ideals and institutions, Americans have no recourse but to temper and balance their responses to the IvI gap. The threats to the future of the American condition can be reduced to the extent that Americans:

• continue to believe in their liberal, democratic, and individualistic ideals and also recognize the extent to which their institutions and behavior fall short of these ideals;

• feel guilty about the existence of the gap but take comfort from the fact that American political institutions are more liberal and democratic than those of any other human society past or present;

• attempt to reduce the gap between institutions and ideals but accept the fact that the imperfections of human nature mean the gap can never be eliminated;

• believe in the universal validity of American ideals but also understand their limited applicability to other societies; and

• support the maintenance of American power necessary to protect and promote liberal ideals and institutions in the world arena, but recognize the dangers such power could pose to liberal ideals and institutions at home.

Critics say that America is a lie because its reality falls so far short of its ideals. They are wrong. America is not a lie; it is a disappointment. But it can be a disappointment only because it is also a hope.

7

DAVID RIESMAN

Character and Society

From *The Lonely Crowd*

———

THIS IS A BOOK about social character and about the differences in social character between men of different regions, eras, and groups. It considers the ways in which different social character types, once they are formed at the knee of society, are then deployed in the work, play, politics, and child-rearing activities of society. More particularly, it is about the way in which one kind of social character, which dominated America in the nineteenth century, is gradually being replaced by a social character of quite a different sort.... Character, in this sense, is the more or less permanent socially and historically conditioned organization of an individual's drives and satisfactions—the kind of "set" with which he approaches the world and people.

"Social character" is that part of "character" which is shared among significant social groups and which, as most contemporary social scientists define it, is the product of the experience of these groups. The notion of social character permits us to speak, as I do throughout this book, of the character of classes, groups, regions, and nations....

My concern in this book is with two revolutions and their relation to the "mode of conformity" or "social character" of Western man since the Middle Ages. The first of these revolutions has in the last four hundred years cut us off pretty decisively from the family- and clan-oriented traditional ways of life in which mankind has existed throughout most of history; this revolution includes the Renaissance, the Reformation, the Counter-Reformation, the Industrial Revolution, and the political revolutions of the seventeenth, eighteenth, and nineteenth centuries. This revolution is, of course, still in process, but in the most advanced countries of the world, and particularly in America, it is giving way to another sort of revolution—a whole range of social developments associated with a shift from an age of production to an age of consumption....

One of the categories I make use of is taken from demography, the science that deals with birth rates and death rates, with the absolute and relative numbers of people in a society, and their distribution by age, sex, and other variables, for I tentatively seek to link certain social and characterological developments, as cause and effect, with certain population shifts in Western society since the Middle Ages....

It would be very surprising if variations in the basic conditions of reproduction, livelihood, and chances for survival, that is, in the supply of and demand for human beings, with all these imply for change in the spacing of people, the size of markets, the role of children, the society's feeling of vitality or senescence, and many other intangibles, failed to influence character. My thesis is, in fact, that each of these three different phases on the population curve appears to be occupied by a society that enforces conformity and molds social character in a definably different way.

The society of high growth potential develops in its typical members a social character whose conformity is insured by their tendency to follow tradition: these I shall term *tradition-directed* people and the society in which they live *a society dependent on tradition-direction*.

The society of transitional population growth develops in its typical members a social character whose conformity is insured by their tendency to acquire early in life an internalized set of goals. These I shall term *inner-directed* people and the society in which they live *a society dependent on inner-direction*.

Finally, the society of incipient population decline develops in its typical members a social character whose conformity is insured by their tendency to be sensitized to the expectations and preferences of others. These I shall term *other-directed* people and the society in which they live one *dependent on other-direction*.

High Growth Potential: Tradition-directed Types

...Since the type of social order is relatively unchanging, the conformity of the individual tends to reflect his membership in a particular age-grade, clan, or caste; he learns to understand and appreciate patterns which have endured for centuries, and are modified but slightly as the generations succeed each other. The important relationships of life may be controlled by careful and rigid etiquette, learned by the young during the years of intensive socialization that end with initiation into full adult membership. Moreover, the culture, in addition to its economic tasks, or as part of them, provides ritual, routine, and religion to occupy and to orient everyone. Little energy is directed toward finding new solutions of the age-old problems, let us say, of agricultural technique or medicine, the problems to which people are acculturated....

In societies in which tradition-direction is the dominant mode of insuring conformity, relative stability is preserved in part by the infrequent but highly important process of fitting into institutionalized roles such deviants as there are. In such societies a person who might have become at a later historical stage an innovator or rebel, whose belonging, as such, is marginal and problematic, is drawn instead into roles like those of the shaman or sorcerer. That is, he is drawn into roles that make a socially acceptable contribu-

tion, while at the same time they provide the individual with a
more or less approved niche....

Transitional Growth: Inner-directed Types

...Such a society is characterized by increased personal mobility, by a rapid accumulation of capital (teamed with devastating
technological shifts), and by an almost constant *expansion:* intensive
expansion in the production of goods and people, and extensive
expansion in exploration, colonization, and imperialism. The
greater choices this society gives—and the greater initiatives it demands in order to cope with its novel problems—are handled by
character types who can manage to live socially without strict and
self-evident tradition-direction. These are the inner-directed
types....

As the control of the primary group is loosened—the group
that both socializes the young and controls the adult in the earlier
era—a new psychological mechanism appropriate to the more open
society is "invented": it is what I like to describe as a psychological
gyroscope. This instrument, once it is set by the parents and other
authorities, keeps the inner-directed person, as we shall see, "on
course" even when tradition, as responded to by his character, no
longer dictates his moves. The inner-directed person becomes capable of maintaining a delicate balance between the demands upon
him of his goal in life and the buffetings of his external environment....

Incipient Decline of Population: Other-directed Types

...The type of character I shall describe as other-directed seems
to be emerging in very recent years in the upper middle class of
our larger cities: more prominently in New York than in Boston,
in Los Angeles than in Spokane, in Cincinnati than in Chillicothe.
Yet in some respects this type is strikingly similar to the American,
whom Tocqueville and other curious and astonished visitors from
Europe, even before the Revolution, thought to be a new kind of
man. Indeed, travelers' reports on America impress us with their
unanimity. The American is said to be shallower, freer with his
money, friendlier, more uncertain of himself and his values, more
demanding of approval than the European.... My analysis of the
other-directed character is thus at once an analysis of the American

and of contemporary man. Much of the time I find it hard or impossible to say where one ends and the other begins. Tentatively, I am inclined to think that the other-directed type does find itself most at home in America, due to certain unique elements in American society, such as its recruitment from Europe and its lack of any feudal past. As against this, I am also inclined to put more weight on capitalism, industrialism, and urbanization—these being international tendencies—than on any character-forming peculiarities of the American scene....

What is common to all the other-directed people is that their contemporaries are the source of direction for the individual—either those known to him or those with whom he is indirectly acquainted, through friends and through the mass media. This source is of course "internalized" in the sense that dependence on it for guidance in life is implanted early. The goals toward which the other-directed person strives shift with that guidance: it is only the process of striving itself and the process of paying close attention to the signals from others that remain unaltered throughout life. This mode of keeping in touch with others permits a close behavioral conformity, not through drill in behavior itself, as in the tradition-directed character, but rather through an exceptional sensitivity to the actions and wishes of others....

Much of our ideology—free enterprise, individualism, and all the rest—remains competitive and is handed down by parents, teachers, and the mass media. At the same time there has been an enormous ideological shift favoring submission to the group, a shift whose decisiveness is concealed by the persistence of the older ideological patterns. The peer-group becomes the measure of all things; the individual has few defenses the group cannot batter down. In this situation the competitive drives for achievement sponsored in children by the remnants of inner-direction in their parents come into conflict with the cooperative demands sponsored by the peer-group. The child therefore is forced to rechannel the competitive drive for achievement, as demanded by the parents, into his drive for approval from the peers. Neither parent, child, nor the peer-group itself is particularly conscious of this process. As a result all three participants in the process may remain unaware of the degree to which the force of an older individualistic ideology provides the energies for filling out the forms of a newer, group-oriented characterology....

I turn in this part of the book to an introductory effort to apply to American politics the theory of character developed in the preceding part. First, however, the problems and limitations of this sort of approach to politics must be pointed out. My general thesis is that the inner-directed character tended and still tends in politics to express himself in the style of the "moralizer," while the other-directed character tends to express himself politically in the style of an "inside-dopester." These styles are also linked with a shift in political mood from "indignation" to "tolerance," and a shift in political decision from dominance by a ruling class to power dispersal among many marginally competing pressure groups. Some of these shifts may be among the causative factors for the rise of other-direction. . . .

The typical style of the inner-directed person in nineteenth-century American politics is that of the moralizer. Since the inner-directed man is work driven and work oriented, his profoundest feelings wrapped up in work and the competence with which work is done, when he turns to politics he sees it as a field of work—and judges it accordingly. Presented with a political message, he sees a task in it, and, far from seeking to demonstrate his knowledge of its meaning in terms of personalities, he responds with emotional directness and often naïveté. (Of course not all inner-directed people are responsive to politics and not all who are, are moralizers.)

One variant of the moralizer projects on the political scene his characterological tendency toward self-improvement: he wants to improve all men and institutions. . . .

The inner-directed man, when he approaches politics, has a tendency to underestimate the values of easygoing looseness of political articulation. He does not look to politics for intellectual orientation in a confusing world, and generally he does not see it as a game to be watched for its human interest. Rather, he turns to politics to protect his vested interests, and whether these are of a "practical" or an "ideal" sort, he feels little ambivalence about them. . . .

In conclusion, when we think of the inner-directed man's political style, we must always think of the interests he brought to the political sphere. He participated not because he felt obliged to further a highly cooperative group life but because he had something specific at stake: a responsibility to himself or to others or both. In general, and despite its partial compartmentalization, the political sphere served to further the interests of his class position, class aspirations, or class antagonisms. Since politics was regarded as a forum for satisfying needs other than amusement and psychic escape, it was felt to react passively to the pressure of those needs; men were masters of their politics. Conversely, politics could not and did not invade a man's privacy, since it could only touch him so far as he felt that it was responding, or refusing to respond, to the pressure of what he was sure were his interests....

The spread of other-direction has brought to the political scene the attitude of the inside-dopester, originating not in the sphere of work but of consumption....

The other-directed man possesses a rich store of social skills— skills he needs in order to survive and move about in his social environment; some of these he can deploy in the form of political skills. One of these is his ability to hold his emotional fire, which he tries hard to do because of the cooperative pattern of life to which he is committed. This skill is related to his inescapable awareness, lacking in the inner-directed man, that in any situation people are as important as things.

The inside-dopester may be one who has concluded (with good reason) that since he can do nothing to change politics, he can only understand it. Or he may see all political issues in terms of being able to get some insider on the telephone. That is, some inside-dopesters actually crave to *be* on the inside, to join an inner circle or invent one; others aim no higher than to *know* the inside, for whatever peer-group satisfactions this can bring them.

The inside-dopester of whatever stripe tends to know a great deal about what other people are doing and thinking in the important or "great-issue" spheres of life; he is politically cosmopolitan rather than parochial. If he cannot change the others who dominate his political attention, his characterological drive leads him to manipulate himself in order not to change the others but to resemble them. He will go to great lengths to keep from looking and feeling like the uninformed outsider. Not all other-directed people are inside-dopesters, but perhaps, for the lack of a more mature model, many of them aspire to be.

The inside-dopester is competent in the way that the school system and the mass media of communication have taught him to be competent. Ideology demands that, living in a politically saturated milieu, he know the political score as he must know the score in other fields of entertainment, such as sports....

Politics, indeed, serves the inside-dopester chiefly as a means for group conformity. He must have acceptable opinions, and where he engages in politics he must do so in acceptable ways. In

the upper class, as among radical groups, the influence of the moral-
izing style is still strong, and many people who set the cultural
patterns carry on with an ideology of political responsibility; they
act as if politics were a meaningful sphere for them. The college
student or young professional or businessman of the upper middle
class may take up politics as he takes up golf or any other acceptable
hobby: it is a fulfillment of social role and in addition it is good
fun, good business, and a way to meet interesting people. It happens, of course, that people who enter politics, on one or another
level, with inside-dopester motivations, may find themselves becoming emotionally involved, and stay for quite other reasons.
More common, probably, are those inside-dopesters who use their
political experience to justify their emotional anemia, drawing on
their acquaintance with the inside story to look down on those
who get excited. . . .

Is it conceivable that these economically privileged Americans
will some day wake up to the fact that they overconform? Wake
up to the discovery that a host of behavioral rituals are the result,
not of an inescapable social imperative but of an image of society
that, though false, provides certain secondary gains for the people
who believe in it? Since character structure is, if anything, even
more tenacious than social structure, such an awakening is exceedingly unlikely—and we know that many thinkers before us have
seen the false dawns of freedom while their compatriots stubbornly
continued to close their eyes to the alternatives that were, in principle, available. . . .

If the other-directed people should discover how much needless
work they do, discover that their own thoughts and their own
lives are quite as interesting as other people's, that, indeed, they
no more assuage their loneliness in a crowd of peers than one can
assuage one's thirst by drinking sea water, then we might expect
them to become more attentive to their own feelings and aspirations.

This possibility may sound remote, and perhaps it is. But undeniably many currents of change in America escape the notice of
the reporters of this best-reported nation on earth. We have inadequate indexes for the things we would like to find out, especially
about such intangibles as character, political styles, and the uses of
leisure. America is not only big and rich, it is mysterious; and its
capacity for the humorous or ironical concealment of its interests
matches that of the legendary inscrutable Chinese. By the same

token, what my collaborators and I have to say may be very wide
of the mark. Inevitably, our own character, our own geography,
our own illusions, limit our view.

But while I have said many things in this book of which I am
unsure, of one thing I am sure: the enormous potentialities for
diversity in nature's bounty and men's capacity to differentiate
their experience can become valued by the individual himself, so
that he will not be tempted and coerced into adjustment or, failing
adjustment, into anomie. The idea that men are created free and
equal is both true and misleading: men are created different; they
lose their social freedom and their individual autonomy in seeking
to become like each other.

8

LEON SAMSON

Americanism as Surrogate Socialism

From *Toward a United Front*

———

WHEN WE EXAMINE the meaning of Americanism, we
discover that Americanism is to the American not a tradition or a
territory, not what France is to a Frenchman or England to an
Englishman, but a doctrine—what socialism is to a socialist. Like
socialism, Americanism is looked upon not patriotically, as a personal attachment, but rather as a highly attenuated, conceptualized,
platonic, impersonal attraction toward a system of ideas, a solemn
assent to a handful of final notions—democracy, liberty, opportunity, to all of which the American adheres rationalistically much
as a socialist adheres to his socialism—because it does him good,
because it gives him work, because, so he thinks, it guarantees
him happiness. Americanism has thus served as a substitute for
socialism. Every concept in socialism has its substitutive counter-
concept in Americanism, and that is why the socialist argument
falls so fruitlessly on the American ear.

America is, for all intents and ambitions, a capitalist civilization.
It has all the earmarks of capitalism: a strong political state—a

profit-wages system of imperial dimensions—a religion—a navy—
all the features in fact of a capitalist community. And yet, in the
mind of its inhabitants, in their manner, their rhythm, their style
of life, this American civilization appears to be in no sense capitalistic, appears, on the contrary, socialistic, proletarian, "human," at
any rate far from imperialistic. It is this socialistic fantasy in the
mind of the American that acts as an anticlimax to the socialist
agitation. The American does not want to listen to socialism, since
he thinks he already has it....

...The American is an individualist for the same reason and in
the same way that his neighbor is an individualist. Individualism
is in America a social style. It is a collective individualism. Bourgeois individualism is a bird of a different color. It is confined to
the bourgeoisie. In America everybody is an individualist, but the
ideal of universal individualism is a socialist conception of individualism. "And behold the result. Look down at that crowd on the
Avenue. Nothing but straw hats—and all exactly alike. Not a
shadow of variety. They even fix a day to change to straw hats in
the spring, and everyone must comply with the custom. Clothes
are all the same, too, as if they had come from the hand of the
same tailor. Get down among them and you will find that their
faces are all the same. I tell you, the American people are the most
docile, the most easily led, the least individualistic people in the
world."...

Opportunity is a key word in the dictionary of American idealism. But opportunity is not, strictly speaking, a capitalist concept.
It is, strictly speaking, a socialist or rather a "socialistic" concept.
Opportunity is the bourgeois concept of competition as it is re-
fracted by Americanism, that is to say, as it is brought down from
its bourgeois base to the broadest layers of the population—and so
is made to take on a social-democratic meaning. The idea that
everybody can become a capitalist is an American conception of
capitalism. It is a socialist conception of capitalism....

They relate themselves to capitalism socialistically. Only under
socialism does system take precedence over class. Socialism is a
system minus a class. This minus the American assumes. But why
does he assume it?

Because the classlessness of the American is the origin of his
Americanism. The very act of coming to America is an act of
escaping classes. It was those elements in European society that
have refused to participate in the class struggle that have, and

during periods of the sharpest class struggles, fled hot-haste away from it all in order to enter, and without struggle, into the classless state. Americans from the very beginning have thus been the "lumps" of the world, the declassed mass, those who have stood on the border line between the classes, in that twilight zone of social transition where nothing is sociologically fixed and final and so nothing is ideologically fixed and final, wherein everything hangs in a state of socio-neurotic doubt and indetermination....

Mass, as against class, this is an American preference—and one that has done much to discourage class theory and struggle in America. It may in fact be said that by far the most virulent of the substitutes that Americanism holds out against socialism, the one that more than any other has dulled the sharp edge of proletarian thought and struggle, has been precisely this concept mass. This concept is an ideological staple with Americans....

This phenomenon of mass accounts also for the amazing uniformity of American thought. Ideas in America spread very fast because Americans are of one mind, and they are of one mind because they are, in their consciousness at least, of one class. It is this feeling of classlessness, ahistoric though it be, that brings about the marvelous homogeneity of the American mind. And of the American emotion. The American feels—just "human." He has arrived, in his mind, at a state of classlessness, i.e., of humanity, and so is touched off by those sentiments only that are universal, uniform, "human."...

...This is precisely the point I want to make: the American is an unconscious socialist. And that is why, though he acts capitalistically, he speaks and thinks pseudo-socialistically....

Anyone who has tried to talk socialism to Americans must have had this strange experience. The American will follow the argument of class and class struggle, get it, and agree with it. Logically, the argument is as clear to him as to anyone else. But not psychologically. For the moment he is through admitting the correctness of the Marxian thesis is the very moment he will burst forth with a sudden and upsetting "but there are no classes in America," a sentiment he utters with the decisiveness of a sudden revelation. This phrase, "there are no classes in America," is not an idea—as an idea it has no legs to stand on—but an idiom. As such it must express, as to idioms, an unconscious wish. It is as if the American really wished there were no classes and class struggles, so that he as well as everyone else might be liberated from capitalist class competition and be placed on the happy hunting ground of socialist competitivism.

The American, then, is a socialist, but unconsciously so. Unconscious socialism is something to be reckoned with in understanding the resistance the American offers to the socialist agitation. His socialism is unconscious for the reason that the socialistic instincts in him, coming into conflict with the capitalistic institutions and ideas that surround him, are repressed.

PART TWO

The Constitution

THE CONSTITUTION of 1787 (the second American constitution, succeeding the ill-fated Articles of Confederation) has served as our fundamental law for two centuries. During that time it has undergone remarkably little change. As Michael Kammen argues in this section, the Constitution has provided a degree of "stability and continuity" to our politics that would no doubt amaze the framers themselves. If they could have returned for the bicentennial celebration in 1987, they would have had some pretty difficult adjusting to do to feel comfortable with the products of two hundred years of wrenching social change, but they would surely have immediately recognized and felt at home with their Constitution. In all of that time its basic architecture had not been altered.

Why has the Constitution worn so well? Why, especially since its separation-of-powers/checks-and-balances features have been so often criticized by scholars for more than a century now? The short life of the Articles of Confederation belies one explanation heard frequently in recent years—that Americans are simply constitution worshippers. This, we think, gets the story of the Constitution's longevity pretty nearly backwards. We scrapped one constitution inside a decade, because it came to be widely regarded as a bad basic law; we kept another for two hundred years because it has been widely regarded as a good one.

The Constitution has survived, we think, because it fits the way Americans think about government like a glove. A careful reading of Clinton Rossiter's description of American political thought on the eve of the Revolution and a few minutes of reflection on contemporary American political thought should convince you that not much has changed. As Rossiter points out, by 1776 Americans spoke a universal language of liberalism, and they still do. The Constitution is a product of this ideology. It is thoroughly republican, broadly based on the principle of popular sovereignty and wholly committed to the notion that "good government is limited government—limited in purpose, competence and duration." If Americans had changed their political thinking very much, they would undoubtedly also come to question the basic architecture of the Constitution. As it happens, they have done neither. As Rossiter put it in 1953, they have continued to think very much as they did two hundred years ago, and they have continued to venerate the Constitution.

Getting the story of the framers' political mind right has not been an easy job. Charles Beard and many other progressive historians of the early twentieth century saw the main actors at the convention as reactionaries out to undo the radical, democratic theories of the Declaration of Independence. Although nearly all historians now consider this view discredited by compelling evidence, it is still often presented to students. Similarly, the framers are often portrayed as possessed of a hopelessly pessimistic view of human nature—one utterly lacking in trust of the common people. Such a view is simply wrong. The framers were classical liberals. They emphasized both the "flaws" in human nature (especially self-interest) *and* the capacity of the people for self-government. This is a view that is easily misunderstood. They key to understanding it, as Richard Hofstadter points out, is the Madisonian logic underlying the special architecture of the Constitution, a logic that stresses setting "ambition against ambition" to prevent abuses of power. Federalism (dividing authority between national and state governments), separation of powers (creating three branches of the national government with independent powers), and checks and balances (giving the three branches the powers and motivations to oppose one another) are the three basic principles of the Constitution. If, as Hofstadter argues, there is a dilemma inherent in believing at the same time that "men are not angels" and that good government must be republican, it has worried Americans hardly at all. While critics for a century now have argued at regular intervals that the Constitution's extensive division of authority makes coherent government virtually impossible, there is precious little evidence that Americans want what the critics prefer—a more unified, parliamentarized national government. Rather, they think instinctively in Madisonian terms, wanting both popular rule and dispersed power.

There is no better way to appreciate the framers' classical liberalism than to encounter it firsthand. Thus, we present here Madison's *Federalist Paper* 10, the most famous part of the one American book that is considered a world-class contribution to political theory. You may also want to read Madison's *Federalist Paper* 51 now, although we have put it in Part Four. Because Madison's English is sometimes archaic, you will have to read him very carefully, sometimes translating his words into more modern language. But, you will find there a fascinating expression of the framers' political mind. What we have called classical liberalism stands out on every page. It is nothing less than amazing that Madison could pack so much into what was originally a short newspaper article. Make sure that you understand each of the following points: (1) the inevitability of faction in free societies, (2) his rejection of authoritarian solutions to the problems posed by faction, (3) his rejection of "pure democracy" (unlimited majority rule), and (4) his defense of federalism and social pluralism in a large republic. Divided and limited government, he argues, is a "republican remedy for the diseases most incident to republican government." Here, in a nutshell, is the theory of the American Constitution.

In the next selection, Garry Wills discusses Jefferson's Declaration of Independence and the Constitution, rejecting the familiar argument that one is a radical democratic statement of the rights of man and the other is a defense of property. There is no evidence that the framers saw such a distinction. Note that he also rejects G. K. Chesterton's understanding of the Declaration that we presented in Part One.

Michael Kammen recounts the many ways that various commentators have understood the Constitution over the years. He reminds us that the Constitution is a general basic law. From the beginning there has been vigorous argument over its meaning. It does not offer specific answers to such questions as the appropriate division of authority between the nation and the states or the exact division of authority between the president and Congress. The general principles of the Constitution are consensual, but their exact meaning has been the subject of vigorous disagreements that continue to this very day.

Robert Goldwin's commentary on the latest in a long series of poll findings to the effect that Americans display a remarkable ignorance of the Constitution's provisions contends that this approach is simpleminded. Goldwin argues that understanding the Constitution is not the stuff of a pop quiz. "Americans may not have the text of the Constitution in their heads, but they have the meaning of it in their hearts and in their bones." In other words, they instinctively agree with its basic principles.

9

CLINTON ROSSITER

From *Seedtime of the Republic*

CONSERVATISM, we are told, is the worship of dead revolutionists. If this is true, then Americans are conservatives twice over. Not only do we worship long-dead revolutionists, responding with religious fervor to the cadences of the great Declaration in which they appealed to a candid world, but the Revolution itself was as respectful of the past as a geniune revolution can be. Not only does our political faith stem directly from that of the American Revolution, but the latter reached back through the colonial past almost to the beginning of Western political thought. The Americans of 1776 were among the first men in modern history to defend rather than seek an open society and constitutional liberty; their political faith, like the appeal to arms it supported, was therefore surprisingly sober. . . .

. . . We must again recall that the Revolution produced neither a universal thinker nor a definitive book. The political theory of this great crisis was a popular creed that hundreds of gifted, hopeful leaders shouted in the midst of combat and tens of thousands of less gifted but no less hopeful followers took to their hearts. But if one able Revolutionist had set himself consciously to express the political consensus of his time, to cast the principles of 1776 in a pattern for later ages to inspect and ponder, this might well have been the outline he would have chosen to follow—this was the political theory of the American Revolution. . . .

Government—that is to say, good government—is a free association of free and equal men for certain well-defined purposes. It is not a necessary evil for which men can blame their moral insufficiencies, but a necessary blessing for which they can thank wise providence. Government is clearly necessary to the happiness of men, for only through the collective techniques that it provides can they order their relations with one another and do for themselves what they cannot do as individuals or in family groups.

Government is both a natural and mechanistic institution. It is natural in the sense that it is founded in the necessities of human nature: Man, a social and political animal, cannot exist without its protection and encouragement. It is mechanistic in the sense that he and his equal fellows have some control over its structure and complete control over its personnel. Though men are forced into government by their wants, they enter it on terms satisfactory to their interests and respectful of human nature. Good government is the result of a voluntary contract, which is another way of saying that good government is based on the consent of the governed. . . .

There is no one form of government good for all men at all times. Different communities may adopt different political systems yet reach the same level of liberty, prosperity, and happiness. A constitution is to be judged not by its logic or symmetry but by its ability to fulfill the great purposes for which all good governments are instituted. Yet if men are entirely free to adopt whatever form they desire, history and reason teach that most successful governments have exhibited the same characteristics and organs. Some structural rules for good government are:

1. Government must be plain, simple, and intelligible. The common sense of the common man should be able to comprehend its structure and functioning. Too often have governments been

made unnecessarily complex by elites or tyrants bent on enslaving the mass of the people.

2. Government must be republican; that is to say, representative and nonhereditary. Not only is simple democracy—government by the people directly—impractical in any community larger than a New England town or Swiss canton, but history demonstrates that representatives of the people, wise men chosen by the community and accountable to it, make more sensible day-to-day decisions than the people themselves. At the same time, there is no reason why these wise men, or one particular wise man as head of state, should occupy positions of decision by accident of birth. A virtuous, alert, liberty-loving people have no need of a king or hereditary aristocracy. They do have need of gifted, accountable leaders.

3. Government must be kept as near to the people as possible, chiefly through frequent elections and rotation-in-office. Frequent elections based on equal representation are the one sure means of keeping rulers responsible, of reminding them that they are servants not masters of the people. Rotation, which is secured by constitutional provisions forbidding indefinite re-eligibility, is an equally sure check against demagoguery or insolence in office. Another method of keeping government near to the people is, of course, to insist that they never delegate any task to government that they can do just as well for themselves.

4. Government must be constitutional, an empire of laws and not of men. The discretion and whim of all those in power must be reduced to the lowest level consistent with effective operation of the political machinery. The rule of law demands the existence of a written constitution, to be acknowledged and administered as law superior to the acts of the legislature, decrees of the judiciary, and ordinances of the executive. It demands, too, the inclusion in this constitution of a specific declaration of natural and civil rights. Only thus can liberty be secured against defections of weak rulers and designs of strong. A true constitution has three sound claims to obedience and even adoration: It is the command of the people, an original compact expressing their unalienable sovereignty; the handiwork of the wisest men in the community; and an earthly expression of the eternal principles of the law of nature. And a true constitution is a constant reminder that the only good government is limited government—limited in purpose, competence, and duration.

5. The one organ essential to free government is a representative legislature. The basic function of this organ—to serve as instrument of consent through which the people tax and restrict themselves—is evidence of its intrinsic character. Free government is difficult without an executive or judiciary; it is impossible without a representative assembly.

6. The fact of legislative primacy does not mean, however, that full, unchecked authority should be lodged in the representative assembly. The most successful and trustworthy governments are those in which the totality of political power is divided among three separate branches: a legislature, preferably bicameral; an executive, preferably single; and a judiciary, preferably independent. In turn, these branches should be held in position by a system of checks and balances. Divided and balanced government is something of a retreat from the principle that government must be plain, simple, and intelligible. A unified government—a one-chambered, unrestrained assembly—would certainly be easier to run and understand. Yet the advantages to be gained from separation and balance far outweigh those to be gained from union. Liberty rather than authority, protection rather than power, delay rather than efficiency must be the prime concern of constitution-makers. "The nature of man is such as to make free government possible but far from inevitable." Balanced government, which leads to rule by a persistent and undoubted majority, is most likely to strike the proper balance between liberty and authority....

The major characteristics of Revolutionary political thought would seem to have been these: individualism, since it placed man rather than the community at the center of political speculation, emphasizing his rights, his happiness, and his power to make and unmake government; optimism, since it chose to stress the good and equal in men rather than the evil and unequal; toughmindedness, since it refused to carry this optimism to extravagant lengths and insisted on calling attention to pitfalls in the way of free government; idealism, since it set out goals for all mankind that few men, even Americans, could hope to attain in their lives on earth; pragmatism, since it tempered this idealism about ends with a refusal to be doctrinaire about means; and morality, since it insisted that free government, and therefore human liberty, is essentially a problem in practical ethics.

Perhaps the most remarkable characteristic of this political theory was its deep-seated conservatism. However radical the principles of the Revolution may have seemed to the rest of the world, in the minds of the colonists they were thoroughly preservative and respectful of the past. Indeed, for generations to come Americans would be conservatives at home and radicals abroad. The explanation of this paradox lies in a decisive fact of history: By 1765 the colonies had achieved a society more open, an economy more fluid, and a government more constitutional than anything Europeans would know for years to come. Americans had secured and were ready to defend a condition of freedom that other liberty-minded men could only hope for in the distant future or plot for in the brutal present. The political theory of the American Revolution, in contrast to that of the French Revolution, was not a theory designed to make the world over. The world—at least the American corner of it—had already been made over as thoroughly as any sensible man could imagine. Americans had never known or had long since begun to abandon feudal tenures, a privilege-ridden economy, centralized and despotic government, religious intolerance, and hereditary stratification. Their goal therefore was simply to consolidate, then expand by cautious stages, the large measure of liberty and prosperity that was part of their established way of life. More than 150 years ago Americans took up their unique role of the world's most conservative radicals, the world's most sober revolutionists. They, like their descendants, spurned the attractive nostrums of both the Enlightenment and Romanticism for a system and philosophy dedicated realistically to individual liberty within a context of communal stability.

Present-day Americans have inherited all characteristics and most principles of Revolutionary political thought. They continue to attack problems of political structure and authority with a thought-process that combines individualism, optimism, tough-mindedness, idealism, pragmatism, morality, and conservatism— and thus they continue to horrify philosophers, doctrinaires, and absolutists of right and left. . . .

What is especially amazing about modern American political thought is not that it continues to employ the idiom and exhibit the mood of the Revolution, but that both idiom and mood seem adequate to deal with many present-day problems. Perhaps this is a huge mistake. Perhaps Americans could achieve a larger measure of liberty and prosperity and build a more successful government if they were to abandon the language and assumptions of men who lived almost two centuries ago. Yet the feeling cannot be downed that rude rejection of the past, rather than levelheaded respect for it, would be the huge mistake. Americans may eventually take the advice of their advanced philosophers and adopt a political theory that pays more attention to groups, classes, public opinion, power-elites, positive law, public administration, and other realities of twentieth-century America. Yet it seems safe to predict that the people, who occasionally prove themselves wiser than their philosophers, will go on thinking about the political community in terms of unalienable rights, popular sovereignty, consent, constitutionalism, separation of powers, morality, and limited government. The political theory of the American Revolution—a theory of ethical, ordered liberty—remains the political tradition of the American people.

10

RICHARD HOFSTADTER

The Founding Fathers:
An Age of Realism

From *The American Political Tradition*

———

...THE MEN who drew up the Constitution in Philadelphia during the summer of 1787 had a vivid Calvinistic sense of human evil and damnation and believed with Hobbes that men are selfish and contentious. They were men of affairs, merchants, lawyers, planter-businessmen, speculators, investors. Having seen human nature on display in the marketplace, the courtroom, the legislative chamber, and in every secret path and alleyway where wealth and power are courted, they felt they knew it in all its frailty. To them a human being was an atom of self-interest. They did not believe in man, but they did believe in the power of a good political constitution to control him.

This may be an abstract notion to ascribe to practical men, but it follows the language that the Fathers themselves used. General

Knox, for example, wrote in disgust to Washington after the Shays Rebellion that Americans were, after all, "men—actual men possessing all the turbulent passions belonging to that animal." Throughout the secret discussions at the Constitutional Convention it was clear that this distrust of man was first and foremost a distrust of the common man and democratic rule....

And yet there was another side to the picture. The Fathers were intellectual heirs of seventeenth-century English republicanism with its opposition to arbitrary rule and faith in popular sovereignty. If they feared the advance of democracy, they also had misgivings about turning to the extreme right. Having recently experienced a bitter revolutionary struggle with an external power beyond their control, they were in no mood to follow Hobbes to his conclusion that any kind of government must be accepted in order to avert the anarchy and terror of a state of nature....

Unwilling to turn their backs on republicanism, the Fathers also wished to avoid violating the prejudices of the people. "Notwithstanding the oppression and injustice experienced among us from democracy," said George Mason, "the genius of the people is in favor of it, and the genius of the people must be consulted." Mason admitted "that we had been too democratic," but feared that "we should incautiously run into the opposite extreme." James Madison, who has quite rightfully been called the philosopher of the Constitution, told the delegates: "It seems indispensable that the mass of citizens should not be without a voice in making the laws which they are to obey, and in choosing the magistrates who are to administer them." James Wilson, the outstanding jurist of the age, later appointed to the Supreme Court by Washington, said again and again that the ultimate power of government must of necessity reside in the people. This the Fathers commonly accepted, for if government did not proceed from the people, from what other source could it legitimately come? To adopt any other premise not only would be inconsistent with everything they had said against British rule in the past but would open the gates to an extreme concentration of power in the future....

If the masses were turbulent and unregenerate, and yet if government must be founded upon their suffrage and consent, what could a Constitution-maker do? One thing that the Fathers did not propose to do, because they thought it impossible, was to change the nature of man to conform with a more ideal system.

They were inordinately confident that they knew what man always had been and what he always would be. The eighteenth-century mind had great faith in universals....

...It was too much to expect that vice could be checked by virtue; the Fathers relied instead upon checking vice with vice. Madison once objected during the Convention that Gouverneur Morris was "forever inculcating the utter political depravity of men and the necessity of opposing one vice and interest to another vice and interest." And yet Madison himself in the *Federalist* number 51 later set forth an excellent statement of the same thesis:[*]

> Ambition must be made to counteract ambition.... It may be a reflection on human nature that such devices should be necessary to control the abuses of government. But what is government itself, but the greatest of all reflections on human nature? If men were angels, no government would be necessary.... In framing a government which is to be administered by men over men, the great difficulty lies in this: you must first enable the government to control the governed; and in the next place oblige it to control itself.

...If, in a state that lacked constitutional balance, one class or one interest gained control, they believed, it would surely plunder all other interests. The Fathers, of course, were especially fearful that the poor would plunder the rich, but most of them would probably have admitted that the rich, unrestrained, would also plunder the poor....

In practical form, therefore, the quest of the Fathers reduced primarily to a search for constitutional devices that would force various interests to check and control one another. Among those who favored the federal Constitution three such devices were distinguished.

The first of these was the advantage of a federated government in maintaining order against popular uprisings or majority rule. In a single state a faction might arise and take complete control by force; but if the states were bound in a federation, the central government could step in and prevent it....

The second advantage of good constitutional government resided in the mechanism of representation itself. In a small direct democracy the unstable passions of the people would dominate lawmaking; but a representative government, as Madison said,

[*]See selection 20.—Eds.

would "refine and enlarge the public views by passing them through the medium of a chosen body of citizens.". . .

The third advantage of the government ... [was that] each element should be given its own house of the legislature, and over both houses there should be set a capable, strong, and impartial executive armed with the veto power. This split assembly would contain within itself an organic check and would be capable of self-control under the governance of the executive. The whole system was to be capped by an independent judiciary. The inevitable tendency of the rich and the poor to plunder each other would be kept in hand. . . .

It is ironical that the Constitution, which Americans venerate so deeply, is based upon a political theory that at one crucial point stands in direct antithesis to the mainstream of American democratic faith. Modern American folklore assumes that democracy and liberty are all but identical, and when democratic writers take the trouble to make the distinction, they usually assume that democracy is necessary to liberty. But the Founding Fathers thought that the liberty with which they were most concerned was menaced by democracy. In their minds liberty was linked not to democracy but to property.

What did the Fathers mean by liberty? What did Jay mean when he spoke of "the charms of liberty"? Or Madison when he declared that to destroy liberty in order to destroy factions would be a remedy worse than the disease? Certainly the men who met at Philadelphia were not interested in extending liberty to those classes in America, the Negro slaves and the indentured servants, who were most in need of it, for slavery was recognized in the organic structure of the Constitution and indentured servitude was no concern of the Convention. Nor was the regard of the delegates for civil liberties any too tender. It was the opponents of the Constitution who were most active in demanding such vital liberties as freedom of religion, freedom of speech and press, jury trial, due process, and protection from "unreasonable searches and seizures." These guarantees had to be incorporated in the first ten amendments because the Convention neglected to put them in the original document. Turning to economic issues, it was not freedom of trade in the modern sense that the Fathers were striving for. Although they did not believe in impeding trade unnecessarily, they felt that failure to regulate it was one of the central weaknesses of

the Articles of Confederation, and they stood closer to the mercan-
tilists than to Adam Smith. Again, liberty to them did not mean
free access to the nation's unappropriated wealth. At least fourteen
of them were land speculators. They did not believe in the right of
the squatter to occupy unused land, but rather in the right of the
absentee owner or speculator to preempt it.

The liberties that the constitutionalists hoped to gain were
chiefly negative. They wanted freedom from fiscal uncertainty and
irregularities in the currency, from trade wars among the states,
from economic discrimination by more powerful foreign governments, from attacks on the creditor class or on property, from
popular insurrection. They aimed to create a government that
would act as an honest broker among a variety of propertied interests, giving them all protection from their common enemies and
preventing any one of them from becoming too powerful. The
Convention was a fraternity of types of absentee ownership. All
property should be permitted to have its proportionate voice in
government. Individual property interests might have to be sacrificed at times, but only for the community of propertied interests.
Freedom for property would result in liberty for men—perhaps
not for all men, but at least for all worthy men. Because men have
different faculties and abilities, the Fathers believed, they acquire
different amounts of property. To protect property is only to protect men in the exercise of their natural faculties. Among the many
liberties, therefore, freedom to hold and dispose [of] property is
paramount. Democracy, unchecked rule by the masses, is sure to
bring arbitrary redistribution of property, destroying the very essence of liberty. . . .

A cardinal tenet in the faith of the men who made the Constitution was the belief that democracy can never be more than a transitional stage in government, that it always evolves into either a
tyranny (the rule of the rich demagogue who has patronized the
mob) or an aristocracy (the original leaders of the democratic elements). . . .

What encouraged the Fathers about their own era, however,
was the broad dispersion of landed property. The small land-own-
ing farmers had been troublesome in recent years, but there was a
general conviction that under a properly made Constitution a *modus
vivendi* could be worked out with them. The possession of moderate plots of property presumably gave them a sufficient stake in
society to be safe and responsible citizens under the restraints of

balanced government. Influence in government would be proportionate to property: merchants and great landholders would be dominant, but small property-owners would have an independent and far from negligible voice. It was "politic as well as just," said Madison, "that the interests and rights of every class should be duly represented and understood in the public councils," and John Adams declared that there could be "no free government without a democratical branch in the constitution."...

...At the very beginning contemporary opponents of the Constitution foresaw an apocalyptic destruction of local government and popular institutions, while conservative Europeans of the old regime thought the young American Republic was a dangerous leftist experiment. Modern critical scholarship, which reached a high point in Charles A. Beard's *An Economic Interpretation of the Constitution of the United States,* started a new turn in the debate. The antagonism, long latent, between the philosophy of the Constitution and the philosophy of American democracy again came into the open. Professor Beard's work appeared in 1913 at the peak of the Progressive era, when the muckraking fever was still high; some readers tended to conclude from his findings that the Fathers were selfish reactionaries who do not deserve their high place in American esteem. Still more recently, other writers, inverting this logic, have used Beard's facts to praise the Fathers for their opposition to "democracy" and as an argument for returning again to the idea of a "republic."

In fact, the Fathers' image of themselves as moderate republicans standing between political extremes was quite accurate. They were impelled by class motives more than pietistic writers like to admit, but they were also controlled, as Professor Beard himself has recently emphasized, by a statesmanlike sense of moderation and a scrupulously republican philosophy. Any attempt, however, to tear their ideas out of the eighteenth-century context is sure to make them seem starkly reactionary. Consider, for example, the favorite maxim of John Jay: "The people who own the country ought to govern it." To the Fathers this was simply a swift axiomatic statement of the stake-in-society theory of political rights, a moderate conservative position under eighteenth-century conditions of property distribution in America. Under modern property relations this maxim demands a drastic restriction of the base of political power. A large portion of the modern middle class—and it is the strength of this class upon which balanced government depends—is propertyless; and the urban proletariat, which the Fathers so greatly feared, is almost one half the population. Further, the separation of ownership from control that has come with the corporation deprives Jay's maxim of twentieth-century meaning even for many propertied people. The six hundred thousand stockholders of the American Telephone & Telegraph Company not only do not acquire political power by virtue of their stock-ownership, but they do not even acquire economic power: they cannot control their own company.

From a humanistic standpoint there is a serious dilemma in the philosophy of the Fathers, which derives from their conception of man. They thought man was a creature of rapacious self-interest, and yet they wanted him to be free—free, in essence, to contend, to engage in an umpired strife, to use property to get property. They accepted the mercantile image of life as an eternal battleground, and assumed the Hobbesian war of each against all; they did not propose to put an end to this war, but merely to stabilize it and make it less murderous. They had no hope and they offered none for any ultimate organic change in the way men conduct themselves. The result was that while they thought self-interest the most dangerous and unbrookable quality of man, they necessarily underwrote it in trying to control it. . . .

II

JAMES MADISON
A Safeguard Against Domestic Faction

From *Federalist Paper* 10

———

No. 10: Madison

AMONG the numerous advantages promised by a well-constructed Union, none deserves to be more accurately developed than its tendency to break and control the violence of faction. The friend of popular governments never finds himself so much alarmed for their character and fate as when he contemplates their propensity to this dangerous vice. He will not fail, therefore, to set a due value on any plan which, without violating the principles to which he is attached, provides a proper cure for it. The instability, injustice, and confusion introduced into the public councils have, in truth, been the mortal diseases under which popular governments have everywhere perished, as they continue to be the favorite and fruitful topics from which the adversaries to liberty derive their most specious declamations. The valuable improvements made by the American constitutions on the popular models, both ancient and modern, cannot certainly be too much admired; but it would be an unwarrantable partiality to contend that they have as effectually obviated the danger on this side, as was wished and expected. Complaints are everywhere heard from our most considerate and virtuous citizens, equally the friends of public and private faith and of public and personal liberty, that our governments are too unstable, that the public good is disregarded in the conflicts of rival parties, and that measures are too often decided, not according to the rules of justice and the rights of the minor party, but by the superior force of an interested and overbearing majority. However anxiously we may wish that these complaints had no foundation, the evidence of known facts will not permit us to deny that they are in some degree true. It will be found, indeed, on a candid review of our situation, that some of the distresses under which we labor have been erroneously charged on the operation of our governments; but it will be found, at the same time, that other causes will not alone account for many of our heaviest misfortunes; and, particularly, for that prevailing and increasing distrust of public engagements and alarm for private rights which are echoed from one end of the continent to the other. These must be chiefly, if not wholly, effects of the unsteadiness and injustice with which a factious spirit has tainted our public administration.

By a faction I understand a number of citizens, whether amounting to a majority or minority of the whole, who are united and actuated by some common impulse of passion, or of interest, adverse to the rights of other citizens, or to the permanent and aggregate interests of the community.

There are two methods of curing the mischiefs of faction: the one, by removing its causes; the other, by controlling its effects.

There are again two methods of removing the causes of faction:

the one, by destroying the liberty which is essential to its existence; the other, by giving to every citizen the same opinions, the same passions, and the same interests.

It could never be more truly said than of the first remedy that it was worse than the disease. Liberty is to faction what air is to fire, an aliment without which it instantly expires. But it could not be a less folly to abolish liberty, which is essential to political life, because it nourishes faction than it would be to wish the annihilation of air, which is essential to animal life, because it imparts to fire its destructive agency.

The second expedient is as impracticable as the first would be unwise. As long as the reason of man continues fallible, and he is at liberty to exercise it, different opinions will be formed. As long as the connection subsists between his reason and his self-love, his opinions and his passions will have a reciprocal influence on each other; and the former will be objects to which the latter will attach themselves. The diversity in the faculties of men, from which the rights of property originate, is not less an insuperable obstacle to a uniformity of interests. The protection of these faculties is the first object of government. From the protection of different and unequal faculties of acquiring property, the possession of different degrees and kinds of property immediately results; and from the influence of these on the sentiments and views of the respective proprietors ensues a division of the society into different interests and parties.

The latent causes of faction are thus sown in the nature of man; and we see them everywhere brought into different degrees of activity, according to the different circumstances of civil society. A zeal for different opinions concerning religion, concerning government, and many other points, as well of speculation as of practice; an attachment to different leaders ambitiously contending for pre-eminence and power; or to persons of other descriptions whose fortunes have been interesting to the human passions, have, in turn, divided mankind into parties, inflamed them with mutual animosity, and rendered them much more disposed to vex and oppress each other than to co-operate for their common good. So strong is this propensity of mankind to fall into mutual animosities that where no substantial occasion presents itself the most frivolous and fanciful distinctions have been sufficient to kindle their unfriendly passions and excite their most violent conflicts. But the most common and durable source of factions has been the various and unequal distribution of property. Those who hold and those who are without property have ever formed distinct interests in society. Those who are creditors, and those who are debtors, fall under a like discrimination. A landed interest, a manufacturing interest, a mercantile interest, a moneyed interest, with many lesser interests, grow up of necessity in civilized nations, and divide them into different classes, actuated by different sentiments and views. The regulation of these various and interfering interests forms the principal task of modern legislation and involves the spirit of party and faction in the necessary and ordinary operations of government.

No man is allowed to be a judge in his own cause, because his interest would certainly bias his judgment, and, not improbably, corrupt his integrity. With equal, nay with greater reason, a body of men are unfit to be both judges and parties at the same time; yet what are many of the most important acts of legislation but so many judicial determinations, not indeed concerning the rights of single persons, but concerning the rights of large bodies of citizens? And what are the different classes of legislators but advocates and parties to the causes which they determine? Is a law proposed concerning private debts? It is a question to which the creditors are parties on one side and the debtors on the other. Justice ought to hold the balance between them. Yet the parties are, and must be, themselves the judges; and the most numerous party, or in other words, the most powerful faction must be expected to prevail. Shall domestic manufacturers be encouraged, and in what degree, by restrictions on foreign manufacturers? are questions which would be differently decided by the landed and the manufacturing classes, and probably by neither with a sole regard to justice and the public good. The apportionment of taxes on the various descriptions of property is an act which seems to require the most exact impartiality; yet there is, perhaps, no legislative act in which greater opportunity and temptation are given to a predominant party to trample on the rules of justice. Every shilling with which they overburden the inferior number is a shilling saved to their own pockets.

It is in vain to say that enlightened statesmen will be able to adjust these clashing interests and render them all subservient to the public good. Enlightened statesmen will not always be at the helm. Nor, in many cases, can such an adjustment be made at all without taking into view indirect and remote considerations, which will rarely prevail over the immediate interest which one party may find in disregarding the rights of another or the good of the whole.

The inference to which we are brought is that the *causes* of faction cannot be removed and that relief is only to be sought in the means of controlling its *effects*.

If a faction consists of less than a majority, relief is supplied by the republican principle, which enables the majority to defeat its sinister views by regular vote. It may clog the administration, it may convulse the society; but it will be unable to execute and mask its violence under the forms of the Constitution. When a majority is included in a faction, the form of popular government, on the other hand, enables it to sacrifice to its ruling passion or interest both the public good and the rights of other citizens. To secure the public good and private rights against the danger of such a faction, and at the same time to preserve the spirit and the form of popular government, is then the great object to which our inquiries are directed. Let me add that it is the great desideratum by which alone this form of government can be rescued from the opprobrium under which it has so long labored and be recommended to the esteem and adoption of mankind.

By what means is this object attainable? Evidently by one of two only. Either the existence of the same passion or interest in a majority at the same time must be prevented, or the majority, having such coexistent passion or interest, must be rendered, by their number and local situation, unable to concert and carry into effect schemes of oppression. If the impulse and the opportunity be suffered to coincide, we well know that neither moral nor religious motives can be relied on as an adequate control. They are not found to be such on the injustice and violence of individuals, and lose their efficacy in proportion to the number combined together, that is, in proportion as their efficacy becomes needful.

From this view of the subject it may be concluded that a pure democracy, by which I mean a society consisting of a small number of citizens, who assemble and administer the government in person, can admit of no cure for the mischiefs of faction. A common passion or interest will, in almost every case, be felt by a majority of the whole; a communication and concert results from the form of government itself; and there is nothing to check the inducements to sacrifice the weaker party or an obnoxious individual. Hence it is that such democracies have ever been spectacles of turbulence and contention; have ever been found incompatible with personal security or the rights of property; and have in general been as short in their lives as they have been violent in their deaths. Theoretic politicians, who have patronized this species of government, have erroneously supposed that by reducing mankind to a perfect equality in their political rights, they would at the same time be perfectly equalized and assimilated in their possessions, their opinions, and their passions.

A republic, by which I mean a government in which the scheme of representation takes place, opens a different prospect and promises the cure for which we are seeking. Let us examine the points in which it varies from pure democracy, and we shall comprehend both the nature of the cure and the efficacy which it must derive from the Union.

The two great points of difference between a democracy and a republic are: first, the delegation of the government, in the latter, to a small number of citizens elected by the rest; secondly, the greater number of citizens and greater sphere of country over which the latter may be extended.

The effect of the first difference is, on the one hand, to refine and enlarge the public views by passing them through the medium of a chosen body of citizens, whose wisdom may best discern the true interest of their country and whose patriotism and love of justice will be least likely to sacrifice it to temporary or partial considerations. Under such a regulation it may well happen that the public voice, pronounced by the representatives of the people, will be more consonant to the public good than if pronounced by the people themselves, convened for the purpose. On the other hand, the effect may be inverted. Men of factious tempers, of local prejudices, or of sinister designs, may, by intrigue, by corruption, or by other means, first obtain the suffrages, and then betray the interests of the people. The question resulting is, whether small or extensive republics are most favorable to the election of proper guardians of the public weal; and it is clearly decided in favor of the latter by two obvious considerations.

In the first place it is to be remarked that however small the republic may be the representatives must be raised to a certain number in order to guard against the cabals of a few; and that however large it may be they must be limited to a certain number in order to guard against the confusion of a multitude. Hence, the number of representatives in the two cases not being in proportion to that of the constituents, and being proportionally greatest in the small republic, it follows that if the proportion of fit characters be not less in the large than in the small republic, the former will present a greater option, and consequently a greater probability of a fit choice.

In the next place, as each representative will be chosen by a greater number of citizens in the large than in the small republic, it will be more difficult for unworthy candidates to practise with success the vicious arts by which elections are too often carried; and the suffrages of the people being more free, will be more likely to center on men who possess the most attractive merit and the most diffusive and established characters.

It must be confessed that in this, as in most other cases, there is a mean, on both sides of which inconveniencies will be found to lie. By enlarging too much the number of electors, you render the representative too little acquainted with all their local circumstances and lesser interests; as by reducing it too much, you render him unduly attached to these, and too little fit to comprehend and pursue great and national objects. The federal Constitution forms a happy combination in this respect; the great and aggregate interests being referred to the national, the local and particular to the State legislatures.

The other point of difference is the greater number of citizens and extent of territory which may be brought within the compass of republican than of democratic government; and it is this circumstance principally which renders factious combinations less to be dreaded in the former than in the latter. The smaller the society, the fewer probably will be the distinct parties and interests composing it; the fewer the distinct parties and interests, the more frequently will a majority be found of the same party; and the smaller the number of individuals composing a majority, and the smaller the compass within which they are placed, the more easily will they concert and execute their plans of oppression. Extend the sphere and you take in a greater variety of parties and interests; you make it less probable that a majority of the whole will have a common motive to invade the rights of other citizens; or if such a common motive exists, it will be more difficult for all who feel it to discover their own strength and to act in unison with each other. Besides other impediments, it may be remarked that, where there is a consciousness of unjust or dishonorable purposes, communication is always checked by distrust in proportion to the number whose concurrence is necessary.

Hence, it clearly appears that the same advantage which a republic has over a democracy in controlling the effects of faction is enjoyed by a large over a small republic—is enjoyed by the Union over the States composing it. Does this advantage consist in the substitution of representatives whose enlightened views and virtuous sentiments render them superior to local prejudices and to schemes of injustice? It will not be denied that the representation of the Union will be most likely to possess these requisite endowments. Does it consist in the greater security afforded by a greater variety of parties, against the event of any one party being able to outnumber and oppress the rest? In an equal degree does the increased variety of parties comprised within the Union increase this security? Does it, in fine, consist in the greater obstacles opposed to the concert and accomplishment of the secret wishes of an unjust and interested majority? Here again the extent of the Union gives it the most palpable advantage.

The influence of factious leaders may kindle a flame within their particular States but will be unable to spread a general conflagration through the other States. A religious sect may degenerate into a political faction in a part of the Confederacy; but the variety of sects dispersed over the entire face of it must secure the national councils against any danger from that source. A rage for paper money, for an abolition of debts, for an equal division of property, or for any other improper or wicked project, will be less apt to pervade the whole body of the Union than a particular member of it, in the same proportion as such a malady is more likely to taint a particular county or district than an entire State.

In the extent and proper structure of the Union, therefore, we behold a republican remedy for the diseases most incident to republican government. And according to the degree of pleasure and pride we feel in being republicans ought to be our zeal in cherishing the spirit and supporting the character of federalists.   *Publius*

I2

GARRY WILLS

... no part of our constitution ...

From *Inventing America*

———

AMERICANS LIKE, at intervals, to play this dirty trick upon themselves: Pollsters are sent out to canvass men and women on certain doctrines and to shame them when these doctrines are declared—as usually happens—unacceptable. Shortly after, the results are published: Americans have, once again, failed to subscribe to some phrase or other from the Declaration of Independence. The late political scientist Willmoore Kendall called this game "discovering America." He meant to remind us that running men out of town on a rail is at least as much an American tradition as declaring unalienable rights. A good point; but *should* that be our heritage? Shouldn't we, as Americans, subscribe to the creed that (we are told) *made* us Americans?...

...When many, or even most, refuse to agree with the Declaration's teaching, we are urged to fear that something has gone wrong with America; that it has ceased in part to be itself—i.e., to think as it ought....

It is not surprising that we should misunderstand the Declaration. It is written in the lost language of the Enlightenment. It is dark with unexamined lights....

Useful falsehoods are dangerous things, often costing something down the road. We can already tot up some of the things this myth has cost us. To begin with, the cult of the Declaration as our mystical founding document led to a downgrading of the actual charter that gives us our law. The Constitution has often been treated as a falling off from the original vision of 1776, a betrayal of the Revolution—a compromising of the *proposition* to which (after being conceived in liberty) we were dedicated. That view of things was bad history and has been revealed as such. But the surprising thing is that even scholars held and taught that view for so long—long enough for it to persist in the popular mind.

That shows the power of our favored myth to distort facts.

There are subtler and more important results of the myth. A belief in our extraordinary birth, outside the processes of time, has led us to think of ourselves as a nation apart, with a special destiny, the hope of all those outside America's shores....

If there is an American *idea,* then one must subscribe to it in order to be an American. One must sort out one's *mental* baggage to "declare" it on entry to the country. To be fully American, one must adopt this idea wholeheartedly, proclaim it, prove one's devotion to it. Unless we know what our fellows *think,* we do not know whether they are American at all, much less whether they are *truly* American. Indeed, since the idea is so pure and abstract, we must all be constantly striving toward it, trying to become *more* American. A Chesterton might well be shocked to find himself put under inquest before touching these religious shores; he had never been accused, at home, of "un-English activities."* But here, to tell someone "That is not the American way" is to say, in effect, that the person addressed is not entirely American—not worthy of citizenship; a kind of second-class American or disguised interloper. Uncovering heresy under such disguises was the aim of America's loyalty oaths, security tests, black lists. Even the questions asked by pollsters who quiz Americans on their dedication to the Declaration are a politer kind of loyalty oath. The implication is that those who answer "wrong" prove that we are not inculcating our creed well enough. This very activity leans back toward the tradition Willmoore Kendall described. It rides the unorthodox out on a rail, of ridicule at least, if not of actual violence.

This whole way of thinking would, on many grounds, have been alien to Thomas Jefferson. He was not, like Lincoln, a nineteenth-century romantic living in the full glow of transcendentalism (that school of faintly necrophiliac spirituality). He was an eighteenth-century empiricist, opposed to generalizations and concentrating on particular realities. With Locke, he had rejected innate ideas. He considered Plato's self-existent Ideas the great delusion of Western history. He did not believe one could "embalm" an idea in a text, lay it away in some heaven of the mind, for later generations to be constantly aspiring after. He denied that a spiritual ideal could be posed over-against some fleshly struggle toward it.

*See our excerpt from G. K. Chesterton's "What Is America?" (selection 3). —EDS.

He did not think material circumstances an obstacle to Reality. They, and they alone, *were* reality for him. He would not have accepted Lincoln's mystique of national union as a transcendentally "given" imperative.

He would never encourage people to yearn back toward some ideal of perfection delivered to their forebears. He opposed "entailing" opinions on a later generation; he wanted constitutions revised often, since accumulated knowledge must make later generations wiser than that which drew up *any* old document....

To the extent that Chesterton read the Declaration as "dogmatic and even theological," he was misreading it. Jefferson would take such terms as an insult if applied to his draft....

...For him, the highest test of a thing was its immediate practicality to the living generation.... The Declaration is not only part of our history; we are part of its history. We have cited it, over the years, for many purposes, including the purpose of deceiving ourselves; and it has become a misshapen thing in our minds. Jefferson never intended it for a spiritual Covenant; but it has traveled in an Ark that got itself more revered the more it was battered.

The best way to honor the spirit of Jefferson is to use his doubting intelligence again on his own text. Only skepticism can save him from his devotees, return us to the drier air of his scientific maxims, all drawn with the same precision that went into his architectural sketches. The pollster on the street wants us to "endorse" Jefferson's Declaration. But Jefferson would be the first to ask what such an exercise could mean. Despite his hostility to Plato, he liked Socrates and thought the unexamined life not worth living. Even more, the unexamined document is not worth signing. The Declaration has been turned into something of a blank check for idealists of all sorts to fill in as they like. We had better stop signing it (over and over) and begin reading it. I do not mean seeing it. I mean reading it....

It is not easy to understand today why since Civil War days intelligent Americans should so strangely have confused the Declaration of Independence and the Constitution, and have come to accept them as complementary statements of the democratic purpose of America. Their unlikeness is unmistakable: the one a classical statement of French humanitarian democracy, the other an organic law designed to safeguard the minority under republican rule.

—Vernon L. Parrington

Scholars long ago demolished Parrington's thesis that American history has been "largely a struggle between the spirit of the Declaration of Independence and the spirit of the Constitution, the one primarily concerned with the rights of man, the other more practically concerned with the rights of property." Yet the notion of antagonism between the documents lingers in the popular mind....

The Constitution had the virtue, for its contemporaries, of specificity. They liked their machinery well-made. The propaganda effort of Madison and Hamilton stressed the Constitution's complexity and predictability of function. But that first strength became a later liability. When things did not work well, or did not work as expected, the Constitution could be blamed for causing things it merely countenanced. The problem of slavery, for instance, had to be deferred to accomplish any kind of constitution. But then it was used as a bulwark for state authority to enslave. Its powerlessness looked like complicity.

The Declaration did not labor under those particular disadvantages. It did not (any more than the Constitution would) express a desire or form a plan to end slavery in America. That was even less thinkable to the delegates in 1776 than in 1789 (and it would have run up against just that *agrarian* power Beard tried to call the source of democracy). But the Declaration did say "all men are created equal," and that could be used as a pledge of future actions....

The Declaration, as it was passed and as it is generally read, looks just as vague as the Constitution looks concrete. Even its defenders and admirers think there is some virtue to its vagueness, its idealism, its general statement of nice goals, unencumbered by too precise and transient instructions over the means to be taken to such ends. Liberal apologists for an active presidency saw in "the pursuit of happiness" a general mandate for strong government measures that could promise happiness to those affected. "Self-evident truths"—ill-defined as their grounds might be—conveniently became any speaker's favorite truths of the moment.

In time it became psychically important for men to keep the Declaration vague. When the Constitution or some part of the actual government had to be criticized, this reality could be contrasted with the ideal. One could oppose the American government without becoming un-American. After all, what is more American than the Declaration of Independence? So radicals of the 1960s read the Declaration at gatherings meant to end in acts of civil disobedience. One could repudiate the mere *letter* of the law, the Constitution, in the name of a higher law, containing the *spirit* of America....

Jefferson has been made a vague idealist despite himself, despite his empiricism and love of precision. This has made him hard to understand but easy to use. It has made him and his Declaration a touchstone by which other men and ideas are found wanting.

13

MICHAEL KAMMEN

From *A Machine That Would Go of Itself*

———

THE [metaphor], the notion of a constitution as some sort of machine or engine, had its origins in Newtonian science. Enlightened philosophers, such as David Hume, liked to contemplate the world with all of its components as a great machine. Perhaps it was inevitable, as politics came to be regarded as a science during the 1770s and '80s, that leading revolutionaries in the colonies would utilize the metaphor to suit their purposes. In 1774 Jefferson's *Summary View* mentioned "the great machine of government."...

Over the next one hundred years such imagery did not disappear. But neither did it notably increase; and hardly anyone expressed apprehension about the adverse implications of employing mechanistic metaphors. Occasionally an observer or enthusiast might call the Constitution "the best national machine that is now in existence" (1794); or, at the Golden Jubilee in 1839, John Quincy Adams could comment that "fifty years have passed away since the first impulse was given to the wheels of this political machine."

James Fenimore Cooper uttered one of the few expressions of concern couched in this language between 1787 and 1887. "The boldest violations of the Constitution are daily proposed by politicians in this country," he observed in 1848, "but they do not produce the fruits which might be expected, because the nation is so accustomed to work in the harness it has placed on itself, that nothing seems seriously to arrest the movement of the great national car." Although his metaphors are ridiculously muddled, the message is clear enough. Exactly forty years later James Russell Lowell articulated this same apprehension much more cogently in an address to the Reform Club of New York. The pertinent passage marks the apogee of the metaphor, and remains today as profound a warning as it was in 1888.

After our Constitution got fairly into working order it really seemed as if we had invented a machine that would go of itself, and this begot a faith in our luck which even the civil war itself but momentarily disturbed. Circumstances continued favorable, and our prosperity went on increasing. I admire the splendid complacency of my countrymen, and find something exhilarating and inspiring in it. We are a nation which has *struck ile* [sic], but we are also a nation that is sure the well will never run dry. And this confidence in our luck with the absorption in material interests, generated by unparalleled opportunity, has in some respects made us neglectful of our political duties.

That statement epitomizes not merely the main historical theme of this book, but the homily that I hope to convey as well. Machine imagery lingered on for fifty years, casually used by legal scholars, journalists, civics textbooks, even great jurists like Holmes, and by Franklin D. Roosevelt in his first inaugural address. On occasion, during the 1920s and '30s especially, conservatives would declare that the apparatus, being more than adequate, should not be tampered with, whereas reformers insisted that "the machinery of government under which we live is hopelessly antiquated" (a word they loved) and therefore "should be overhauled."

In the quarter century that followed Lowell's 1888 lament, a cultural transition took place that leads us to the last of the major constitutional metaphors. We may exemplify it with brief extracts from three prominent justices: Holmes, who wrote in 1914 that "the provisions of the Constitution are not mathematical formulas ... they are organic living institutions"; Cardozo, who observed in 1925 that "a Constitution has an organic life"; and Frankfurter, who declared in 1951 that "the Constitution is an organism."

Unlike the other analogies that have been discussed, which were not mutually exclusive, this shift was not merely deliberate but intellectually aggressive at times. The quarter century is punctuated by the declarations of two political scientists deeply involved in public affairs. At the close of the 1880s, A. Lawrence Lowell wrote that "a political system is not a mere machine which can be constructed on any desired plan.... It is far more than this. It is an organism ... whose various parts act and react upon one another." In 1912, when Woodrow Wilson ran for the presidency, a key passage in his campaign statement, *The New Freedom,* elaborated upon Lowell's assertion. "The makers of our Federal Constitution," in Wilson's words, "constructed a government as they would have constructed an orrery,* —to display the laws of nature. Politics in their thought was a variety of mechanics. The Constitution was founded on the law of gravitation. The government was to exist and move by virtue of the efficacy of 'checks and balances.'"

Lowell and Wilson had obviously responded to the same current of cultural change; but they were not attempting to be intellectually trendy by explaining government in terms of evolutionary theory. The word-concept they both used in condemning a Newtonian notion of constitutionalism was "static." Wilson spelled out the implications: "Society is a living organism and must obey the laws of life, not of mechanics; it must develop. All that progressives ask or desire is permission—in an era when 'development,' 'evolution,' is the scientific word—to interpret the Constitution according to the Darwinian principle; all they ask is recognition of the fact that a nation is a living thing and not a machine."...

I would describe the basic pattern of American constitutionalism as one of *conflict within consensus.* At first glance, perhaps, we are more likely to notice the consensus....

The volume of evidence is overwhelming that our constitutional conflicts have been consequential, and considerably more revealing than the consensual framework within which they operate. When Americans have been aware of the dynamic of conflict within consensus, most often they have regarded it as a normative pattern for a pluralistic polity....

There is ... a ... closely linked aspect of American constitutionalism about which there has been no consensus: namely, whether our frame of government was meant to be fairly unchanging or flexible. Commentators are quick to quote Justice Holmes's "theory of our Constitution. It is an experiment, as all life is an experiment." Although much less familiar, and less eloquent, more Americans have probably shared this sentiment, written in 1936

---

*An apparatus for representing the motions ... of the planets....

by an uncommon common man, the chief clerk in the Vermont Department of Highways: "I regard the Constitution as of too much value to be experimented with."

The assumption that our Constitution is lapidary has a lineage that runs, among the justices, from Marshall and Taney to David J. Brewer and George Sutherland. It has been the dominant assumption for most of our history, and provided the basis for Walter Bagehot, Lord Bryce, and others to regard the U.S. Constitution as "rigid" by comparison with the British. The idea that adaptability was desirable emerged gradually during the mid-nineteenth century, appeared in some manuals aimed at a popular audience by the 1880s, and achieved added respectability in 1906 when Justice Henry Billings Brown spoke at a dinner in his honor. The Constitution, he said, "should be liberally interpreted—interpreted as if it were intended as the foundation of a great nation, and not merely a temporary expedient for the united action of thirteen small States.... Like all written Constitutions, there is an underlying danger in its inflexibility." For about a generation that outlook slowly gained adherents, until the two contradictory views were essentially counterpoised in strength by the 1930s.

Meanwhile, a third position appeared during the early decades of the twentieth century—one that might be considered a compromise because it blended facets of the other two. This moderately conservative, evolutionary position was expressed in 1903 by James Ford Rhodes, a nationalistic businessman-turned-historian. The Constitution, in his mind, "is rigid in those matters which should not be submitted to the decision of a legislature or to a popular vote without checks which secure reflection and a chance for the sober second thought, [yet] it has proved flexible in its adaptation to the growth of the country."...

Admittedly, our strict constructionists have on occasion stretched the Constitution, as Jefferson did in 1803 to acquire the vast Louisiana Territory. Lincoln, Wilson, and FDR each stood accused of ignoring constitutional restraints; yet each one could honestly respond that, within the framework of a Constitution intended to be flexible in an emergency, his goal had been to preserve the Union, to win a war fought for noble goals, or to overcome the worst and most prolonged economic disaster in American history. In each instance their constitutional critics spoke out clearly, a national debate took place, and clarification of our constitutional values occurred. Sometimes that clarification has come from the Supreme Court; sometimes from a presidential election campaign; sometimes from a combination of the two; and sometimes by means of political compromise. Each mode of resolution is a necessary part of our democratic system. I am led to conclude that Americans have been more likely to read and understand their Constitution when it has been controversial, or when some group contended that it had been misused, than in those calmer moments when it has been widely venerated as an instrument for all time. . . .

During the later 1950s, Robert M. Hutchins and his colleagues at the Center for the Study of Democratic Institutions, located in Santa Barbara, California, began to discuss the desirability of far-reaching constitutional changes. In 1964, following a series of seminars modestly entitled "Drafting a New Constitution for the United States and the World," Hutchins invited Rexford G. Tugwell, once a member of FDR's "Brain Trust," to direct a reassessment of the Constitution. Tugwell accepted and spent two years conferring with hundreds of jurists, politicians, and scholars. . . .

During the 1970s the Center's primary concerns shifted away from constitutionalism; Tugwell's two major volumes (1974 and 1976) received little attention aside from scholarly journals. When Tugwell died in 1979 at the age of eighty-eight, the *New York Times*'s appreciative editorial did not even mention the revised constitution on which he labored for more than a decade. The *Times* apparently did not regard it as a fitting culmination for a distinguished career in scholarship and public service.

The negligible impact of this seasoned planner's constitutional vision provides a striking contrast with an extremely tradition-oriented interpolation of the U.S. Constitution in science fiction. One popular episode of the television series "Star Trek," written in 1966, received hundreds of reruns during the many years when Tugwell labored over his revision. Millions of Americans watched "The Omega Glory" and recognized its affirmation of the good old Constitution that continued to function even though space, time, and ignorance shrouded its meaning.

Reducing the saga to its ideological essence, Captain Kirk and the starship *Enterprise* land on a planet where the inhabitants are guided by a Prime Directive that must not be violated. Those inhabitants are called Yangs (presumably the descendants of colonizers once known as Yanks), and possess "a worn parchment document" that is "the greatest of holies." Kirk and his crew encounter a bizarre political situation that is not so very different from the one criticized by James Russell Lowell in 1888. The Yangs worship "freedom" but do not understand what it means. Through the ages it has become a ritualized "worship word." The Yangs believe that their ancestors must have been very superior people; they swear an oath to abide by all regulations in the Prime Directive; and they can recite the opening lines of the Prime Directive, but "without meaning."

Following a primitive court scene, complete with jury, it becomes clear that institutions of justice are amazingly resilient—capable of enduring even though their rationale has suffered badly from neglect and amnesia. At the culmination Captain Kirk informs the Yangs that they revere a sacred document without understanding what it is all about. Kirk faces Cloud William, chief of the Yangs, and explains the meaning of the Prime Directive's preamble. Enlightenment then occurs and the great question—is the Prime Directive still operative, and does it apply to this planet?—achieves a satisfactory resolution. To use the language of yesteryear, "constitutional morality" would surely be restored.

Unlike Rexford Tugwell's new constitution, which kept "emerging" for so long that after a while no one cared, "Star Trek" had a constitutional homily with a happy ending. Americans like happy endings. Hence many younger Americans can still narrate "The Omega Glory" (Old Glory? Ultimate Glory?) flawlessly. How much of the homily got through, however, is another matter....

Ultimately, however, for better and for worse, it is ideological conflict that most meaningfully calls attention to the Constitution. We are then reminded that all Americans do not agree about the most appropriate division of authority: federalism tilting toward states' rights or federalism leaning toward national authority? We are then reminded that we still have broad and strict constructionists, followers of Hamilton and followers of Madison. And we are then reminded that we have had two complementary but divergent modes of constitutional interpretation: a tradition of conflict within consensus....

It is instructive to recall that the founders did not expect their instrument of government to achieve utopia: "merely" national cohesion, political stability, economic growth, and individual liberty. Despite abundant setbacks and imperfections, much of that agenda has been fulfilled for a great many Americans. During the past generation social justice got explicitly added to the agenda as a high priority, and the American Constitution, interpreted by the Supreme Court, was adapted accordingly. For a society to progress toward social justice within a constitutional framework, even by trial and error, is a considerable undertaking. To do so in good faith, more often than not, is equally commendable. If from time to time we require the assistance of gadflies, what flourishing political culture does not? Senator Lowell P. Weicker of Connecticut, for example, has played that role rather well on occasion. As he thundered in 1981, during debate over a legislative amendment to endorse organized prayer in public schools: "To my amazement, any time the word constitutionalism comes up it's looked upon as a threat. A threat! It shouldn't be; it's what holds us all together."

That has been true more often than not. Perhaps those who feel threatened by constitutionalism do not fully understand it. People frequently feel threatened by the unfamiliar. Perhaps it has not been fully understood because it has not been adequately explained. Perhaps it has perplexed us because aspects of its meaning have changed over time. Back in 1786 Benjamin Rush believed it "possible to convert men into republican machines. This must be done if we expect them to perform their parts properly in the great machine of the government of the state." His contemporaries not only took Rush at his word, but regarded the conversion of men into republican machines as a national imperative. . . .

More than a century later, Woodrow Wilson presented a piece of wisdom that tacked the other way. Call it constitutional revisionism if you like. He declared that if the real government of the United States "had, in fact, been a machine governed by mechanically automatic balances, it would have had no history; but it was not, and its history has been rich with the influences and personalities of the men who have conducted it and made it a living reality." Walter Lippmann chose to quote that sentence in 1913 when he wrote *A Preface to Politics*. But he promptly added that "only by violating the very spirit of the constitution have we been able to preserve the letter of it." What Lippmann had in mind was the role played by that palpable reality the Progressives called "invisible government": political parties, interest groups, trade unions, and so on.

Lippmann's remark was not meant to be as cynical as it might sound. It reflects the Progressive desire to be realistic and tough-minded. It also reflects the fact that Americans have been profoundly ambivalent in their feelings about government. Then, too, it reflects the discovery by three overlapping generations of Americans—represented by James Russell Lowell, Wilson, and Lippmann—that the U.S. Constitution is not, and was not meant to be, a machine that would go of itself.

Above all, Lippmann wanted to build upon his excerpt from Wilson and establish the point that there has been more to the story of constitutionalism in American culture than the history of the Constitution itself. The latter is a cherished charter of institutions and a declaration of protections. The former, constitutionalism, embodies a set of values, a range of options, and a means of resolving conflicts within a framework of consensus. It has supplied stability and continuity to a degree the framers could barely have imagined.

14

ROBERT GOLDWIN

What Americans Know about the Constitution

"AMERICANS today have a confused understanding of many of the Constitution's basic tenets and provisions" and "a poor grasp of some elemental American history." This was the finding of a national survey conducted by Research & Forecasts and sponsored by the Hearst Corporation in late 1986. Entitled "The American Public's Knowledge of the U.S. Constitution," the survey led its analysts to conclude that American ignorance of the Constitution is "a problem in need of a remedy."

These poll results were reported widely and with considerable editorial dismay. Apparently considered most alarming was that 45 percent of the American public think that the Constitution includes the phrase, "From each according to his ability, to each according to his need," the egalitarian Marxist formulation directly opposed to the idea of monetary incentives. Other examples are: only 34 percent know approximately how many constitutional amendments there are; 64 percent think the Constitution establishes English as the national language; only 41 percent identify the Bill of Rights as the first ten amendments to the original Constitution; 60 percent "incorrectly say the president, acting alone, can appoint a justice to the Supreme Court"; and only 43 percent know that William Rehnquist is the chief justice.

These answers confirmed what most of us might have guessed without a national survey—if you give adult Americans a high-school style quiz on the text of the Constitution or on dates and facts of any other aspect of American history, they will not score well. . . .

The Hearst poll reports that "nearly half (45 percent) say the Marxist declaration 'From each according to his ability, to each according to his need' is found in the Constitution." Can it be that Americans are unable to distinguish American constitutionalism from Marxism? Let's take a closer look.

The respondents were answering a question that was posed as a combination of true/false and multiple choice, in this fashion: "True or false: The following phrases are found in the U.S. Constitution." There followed five phrases, three from the Declaration of Independence, one from the Gettysburg Address, and one from Karl Marx. None of the phrases offered is from the Constitution. The correct answer to all five phrases was "false."

But respondents, reacting as they might to a high-school American history quiz, apparently were looking for "the right answer." They went strongly for "Of the people, by the people, for the people" (82 percent); "All men are created equal" (80 percent); "Life, liberty, and the pursuit of happiness" (77 percent); and "The consent of the governed" (52 percent). Marx came in last, well behind Abraham Lincoln and Thomas Jefferson.

How many of the 45 percent who answered "true" to "From each according to his ability ..." would have volunteered that phrase as part of the Constitution without prompting? We have no way to be certain from what the survey tells us, but my educated guess is, not one in thousands.

As for what the survey report calls the American public's "confusion" of the Declaration of Independence with the Constitution, it seems to me not at all a bad thing that Americans associate our Constitution with phrases such as "consent of the governed" and "all men are created equal." They might be "the wrong answers" on a quiz, but as a citizen's view of our governing principles, it seems to me all to the good.

In fact, there are serious constitutional scholars who argue, as I do, that the principles of the Declaration are embedded (without being mentioned explicitly) in the Constitution. The rights we enjoy under the Constitution are individual rights, ours because we are human beings, not because we belong to any particular group. There is no mention in the original Constitution of any group identified by race, color, religion, nationality, sex, language, or whatever. Because the rights of all are protected as "persons" or "citizens" without any other identification, the message is that no one is left out, that we are all included on the basis of equality. (The proof of this principle is best seen in the only exception: Indians. They *are* mentioned for the purpose of *excluding* them.)

For anyone who has trouble accepting that there are principles included in the Constitution that are not mentioned, consider this partial list: federalism, separation of powers, judicial review, separation of church and state, and checks and balances. All of these are certainly "embedded" in the Constitution; none of them is mentioned.

And so one should be very hesitant to say that it is "incorrect" to think that some principle is not really part of the Constitution just because it is not stated explicitly in the text. They may not always have the texts straight, but I don't see the evidence in this survey that the American public is "confused" about how much of the Declaration of Independence is in the Constitution. . . . Only if you think of the Constitution as a homework assignment to quiz kids on the next day would you design a survey as Hearst did. If, instead, you think of the Constitution more broadly, as the framework of government that guides and shapes our national life, you will not judge the American people as "confused" because they think the Constitution includes the phrases "of the people, by the people, for the people," and "all men are created equal."

In sum, I do not share the alarm of the Hearst Corporation about the American public's "ignorance" of the Constitution. Their answers, even when wrong on a strictly textual basis, are far from being "incorrect." Americans may not have the text of the Constitution in their heads, but they have the meaning of it in their hearts and in their bones.

PART THREE

Democracy

HOW DEMOCRATIC is American politics? Could there be much disagreement on so seemingly simple a question? The honest answer is yes, indeed. Part of the difficulty here lies in the meaning we choose to give a word that has meant many things since it was first used in the Greek city-states some twenty-five hundred years ago. Today, democracy means *something* to people everywhere. But what? Every government in the world now claims to be democratic, but surely, unless the word is to become meaningless, this cannot be. At a minimum most political scientists would insist that democracy requires a free press, freedom of association, and elections in which citizens have reasonably frequent opportunities to choose representatives from a field of competing candidates. Beyond these simple criteria, however, there is not much agreement on the meaning of the concept.

Another part of the difficulty is rooted in the nature of the social sciences. The bigger the question, it seems, the more difficult is the answer. Here we have a very big question. As our readings will show, answering such questions brings out the often disguised elements of ideology and normative political theory that lurk within us. Ultimately, thinking about democracy is an exercise in political theory—a classical exercise in which the elements of both science and philosophy are always present. If American social scientists often fail to recognize this, it is because they, like most Americans, unthinkingly accept liberal principles, which often enter their work as unarticulated major premises. As we will see, those who question the reality of American democracy are looking at the same facts from different ideological perspectives. A bit confusing? Yes, but that is what is going on.

C. Wright Mills's selection from his book, *The Power Elite,* pictures the modern American citizen as more acted upon than acting. Real ability to decide the most important public questions lies with a ruling elite composed of corporate chieftains, high political executives, and the military establishment. Together, they defend the values and position of a national business aristocracy. The public never sees the reality of its plight because the trappings of democracy are carefully observed, and democratic symbols are cleverly manipulated through advertising and public relations. The elite, possessing power but not legitimacy, must always make it appear that the people "really make the decision," but in reality they do not. Election campaigns are trivial, and largely concerned with phony "issues" created to manipulate the public. Mills is clearly outraged by what he sees as the hollowness of American democracy in the 1950s. In the tradition of Thomas Paine he cries out for a politics in which active and informed citizens take charge to create a new public order. His words did not fall on deaf ears. *The Power Elite* and other of his writings had great impact on the student New Left in the 1960s.

Robert Dahl's selection from *Who Governs?* presents a very different interpretation of American democracy. In his classic study of politics in New Haven, Connecticut, Dahl argues that American politics is pluralistic. New Haven politics moved historically from dominance by a patrician, Congregationalist, Federalist elite to a system in which several different groups have the ability to make policy in different issue-areas. There is a political stratum in New Haven, but it is open and divided by party and issues. Policy-making elites are significantly influenced by the public through elections. While the public may play a less active role than that envisioned by "classical democratic theory," an acceptable version of democracy is achieved that allows leaders to be influenced by the public. Dahl's analysis is in line with many other "realist" theories of modern democracy. The people can't and don't rule, but they make meaningful choices to select those who do, and broadly influence what they do as they make policy.

Michael Parenti, the author of our next selection, sees American democracy as "democracy for the few." His argument is similar to Mills's, but it is more overtly socialist. In Europe this perspective is common, but it is clearly not at all common in the United States. Parenti argues that American liberal politics allows wealth to confer great political advantages. "Anticapitalist dissidents," he argues, are systematically prevented from gaining positions of prominence in government, the labor movement, the news media, academe, or the entertainment community. Wealth controls both education and communications, and thus dominates recruitment to positions of influence and socializes Americans to accept capitalism. Parenti calls for the creation of a democratic socialist movement to offer citizens choices that are foreclosed in our present system. Again, we meet the question of why there has been no viable socialist tradition in America. Parenti, like most others who work in the socialist tradition, is not persuaded by the argument that Americans reject socialism on rational grounds. His argument is that the socialist alternative is prevented from ever getting a fair hearing. Just why the United States should be so different from Europe in this respect he does not say.

Benjamin Barber's piece from his book *Strong Democracy* finds the trouble with American democracy in our "thin" concept of citizenship and participation. Barber, a political theorist, places the blame squarely on the Lockean roots of American political thought. In this way of looking at things, the state is a limited public order created to protect life, liberty, and property. Satisfaction of the deepest human needs is to be found in the private realm, not the public. This kind of individualistic liberalism sees society as nothing but individuals occupying private spaces. Such ideas, Barber thinks, can never provide a "firm theory of citizenship, participation, public goods or civic virtue." The "strong democracy" that he advocates must be based on something more than a calculation of private interests. Politics must take place in a larger public space in which citizens engage in an active, common quest for the public good. The practiced eye will see here the ideas of the great Swiss-French theorist, Jean-Jacques Rousseau. Locke, looking at modern America, would see democracy fulfilled; Rousseau would see a citizenship so weak as to merit contempt. At bottom, this is what most arguments over American democracy are really about. They cannot be settled by facts alone, however well those facts are understood. They are arguments between theorists (often unwitting ones) who hold very different visions of what popular government should be.

We end this section with a selection from Bernard Crick's *In Defence of Politics*. Crick is a British political scientist, who happens both to be a practicing democratic socialist and a keen student of American politics. Democracy is only one part of the kind of political system that exists in both Great Britain and the United States. As different as these two systems are, they both exemplify the notion of politics that derives from the ancient Aristotelian idea of polity—a mixed and balanced government combining experience, skill, and knowledge with popular consent. Crick in the troubled times of the 1960s wanted to defend "politics" as a special form of activity that could take place only in a polity. This form of activity, manifestly imperfect, often needs the "most unpopular of all defences: historical analysis applied against the vagueness of popular rhetoric." Should you have gained the impression by now that thinking about democracy is a subtle business, you have taken our point.

15

C. WRIGHT MILLS

From *The Power Elite*

———

THE POWERS of ordinary men are circumscribed by the everyday worlds in which they live, yet even in these rounds of job, family, and neighborhood they often seem driven by forces they can neither understand nor govern. "Great changes" are beyond their control, but affect their conduct and outlook none the less. The very framework of modern society confines them to projects not their own, but from every side, such changes now press upon the men and women of the mass society, who accordingly feel that they are without purpose in an epoch in which they are without power.

But not all men are in this sense ordinary. As the means of information and of power are centralized, some men come to occupy positions in American society from which they can look down upon, so to speak, and by their decisions mightily affect, the everyday worlds of ordinary men and women. They are not made by their jobs; they set up and break down jobs for thousands of others; they are not confined by simple family responsibilities; they can escape. They may live in many hotels and houses, but they are bound by no one community. They need not merely "meet the demands of the day and hour"; in some part, they create these demands, and cause others to meet them. Whether or not they profess their power, their technical and political experience of it far transcends that of the underlying population. What Jacob Burckhardt said of "great men," most Americans might well say of their elite: "They are all that we are not."

The power elite is composed of men whose positions enable them to transcend the ordinary environments of ordinary men and women; they are in positions to make decisions having major consequences. Whether they do or do not make such decisions is less important than the fact that they do occupy such pivotal positions: their failure to act, their failure to make decisions, is itself an act that is often of greater consequence than the decisions they do make. For they are in command of the major hierarchies and organizations of modern society. They rule the big corporations. They run the machinery of the state and claim its prerogatives. They direct the military establishment. They occupy the strategic command posts of the social structure, in which are now centered the effective means of the power and the wealth and the celebrity which they enjoy.

The power elite are not solitary rulers. Advisers and consultants, spokesmen and opinion-makers are often the captains of their higher thought and decision. Immediately below the elite are the professional politicians of the middle levels of power, in the Congress and in the pressure groups, as well as among the new and old upper classes of town and city and region. Mingling with them, in curious ways which we shall explore, are those professional celebrities who live by being continually displayed but are never, so long as they remain celebrities, displayed enough. If such celebrities are not at the head of any dominating hierarchy, they do often have the power to distract the attention of the public or afford sensations to the masses, or, more directly, to gain the ear of those who do occupy positions of direct power. More or less unattached, as critics of morality and technicians of power, as spokesmen of God and creators of mass sensibility, such celebrities and consultants are part of the immediate scene in which the drama of the elite is enacted. But that drama itself is centered in the command posts of the major institutional hierarchies.

The truth about the nature and the power of the elite is not some secret which men of affairs know but will not tell. Such men hold quite various theories about their own roles in the sequence of event and decision. Often they are uncertain about their roles, and even more often they allow their fears and their hopes to affect their assessment of their own power. No matter how great their actual power, they tend to be less acutely aware of it than of the resistances of others to its use. Moreover, most American men of affairs have learned well the rhetoric of public relations, in some cases even to the point of using it when they are alone, and thus coming to believe it. The personal awareness of the actors is only one of the several sources one must examine in order to understand the higher circles. Yet many who believe that there is no elite, or at any rate none of any consequence, rest their argument upon what men of affairs believe about themselves, or at least assert in public.

There is, however, another view: those who feel, even if vaguely, that a compact and powerful elite of great importance does now prevail in America often base that feeling upon the historical trend of our time. They have felt, for example, the domination of the military event, and from this they infer that generals and admirals, as well as other men of decision influenced by them, must be enormously powerful. They hear that the Congress has again abdicated to a handful of men decisions clearly related to the issue of war or peace. They know that the bomb was dropped over Japan in the name of the United States of America, although they were at no time consulted about the matter. They feel that they live in a time of big decisions; they know that they are not making any. Accordingly, as they consider the present as history, they infer that at its center, making decisions or failing to make them, there must be an elite of power.

On the one hand, those who share this feeling about big historical events assume that there is an elite and that its power is great. On the other hand, those who listen carefully to the reports of men apparently involved in the great decisions often do not believe that there is an elite whose powers are of decisive consequence.

Both views must be taken into account, but neither is adequate. The way to understand the power of the American elite lies neither solely in recognizing the historic scale of events nor in accepting the personal awareness reported by men of apparent decision. Behind such men and behind the events of history, linking the two, are the major institutions of modern society. These hierarchies of state and corporation and army constitute the means of power; as such they are now of a consequence not before equaled in human history—and at their summits, there are now those command posts of modern society which offer us the sociological key to an understanding of the role of the higher circles in America.

Within American society, major national power now resides in the economic, the political, and the military domains. Other institutions seem off to the side of modern history, and, on occasion, duly subordinated to these. No family is as directly powerful in national affairs as any major corporation; no church is as directly powerful in the external biographies of young men in America today as the military establishment; no college is as powerful in the shaping of momentous events as the National Security Council. Religious, educational, and family institutions are not autonomous centers of national power; on the contrary, these decentralized areas are increasingly shaped by the big three, in which developments of decisive and immediate consequence now occur.

Families and churches and schools adapt to modern life; governments and armies and corporations shape it; and, as they do so, they turn these lesser institutions into means for their ends. Religious institutions provide chaplains to the armed forces where they are used as a means of increasing the effectiveness of its morale to kill. Schools select and train men for their jobs in corporations and their specialized tasks in the armed forces. The extended family has, of course, long been broken up by the industrial revolution, and now the son and the father are removed from the family, by compulsion if need be, whenever the army of the state sends out the call. And the symbols of all these lesser institutions are used to legitimate the power and the decisions of the big three.

The life-fate of the modern individual depends not only upon the family into which he was born or which he enters by marriage, but increasingly upon the corporation in which he spends the most alert hours of his best years; not only upon the school where he is educated as a child and adolescent, but also upon the state which touches him throughout his life; not only upon the church in which on occasion he hears the word of God, but also upon the army in which he is disciplined.

If the centralized state could not rely upon the inculcation of nationalist loyalties in public and private schools, its leaders would promptly seek to modify the decentralized educational system. If the bankruptcy rate among the top five hundred corporations were as high as the general divorce rate among the thirty-seven million married couples, there would be economic catastrophe on an international scale. If members of armies gave to them no more of their lives than do believers to the churches to which they belong, there would be a military crisis.

Within each of the big three, the typical institutional unit has become enlarged, has become administrative, and, in the power of its decisions, has become centralized. Behind these developments there is a fabulous technology, for as institutions, they have incorporated this technology and guide it, even as it shapes and paces their developments.

The economy—once a great scatter of small productive units in autonomous balance—has become dominated by two or three hundred giant corporations, administratively and politically interrelated, which together hold the keys to economic decisions.

The political order, once a decentralized set of several dozen states with a weak spinal cord, has become a centralized, executive establishment which has taken up into itself many powers previously scattered, and now enters into each and every cranny of the social structure.

The military order, once a slim establishment in a context of distrust fed by state militia, has become the largest and most expensive feature of government, and, although well versed in smiling public relations, now has all the grim and clumsy efficiency of a sprawling bureaucratic domain.

In each of these institutional areas, the means of power at the disposal of decision makers have increased enormously; their central executive powers have been enhanced; within each of them modern administrative routines have been elaborated and tightened up.

As each of these domains becomes enlarged and centralized, the consequences of its activities become greater, and its traffic with the others increases. The decisions of a handful of corporations bear upon military and political as well as upon economic developments around the world. The decisions of the military establishment rest upon and grievously affect political life as well as the very level of economic activity. The decisions made within the political domain determine economic activities and military programs. There is no longer, on the one hand, an economy, and, on the other hand, a political order containing a military establishment unimportant to politics and to money-making. There is a political economy linked, in a thousand ways, with military institutions and decisions. On each side of the world-split running through central Europe and around the Asiatic rimlands, there is an ever-increasing interlocking of economic, military, and political structures. If there is government intervention in the corporate economy, so is there corporate intervention in the governmental process. In the structural sense, this triangle of power is the source of the interlocking directorate that is most important for the historical structure of the present.

The fact of the interlocking is clearly revealed at each of the points of crisis of modern capitalist society—slump, war, and boom. In each, men of decision are led to an awareness of the interdependence of the major institutional orders. In the nineteenth century, when the scale of all institutions was smaller, their liberal integration was achieved in the automatic economy, by an autonomous play of market forces, and in the automatic political domain, by the bargain and the vote. It was then assumed that out of the imbalance and friction that followed the limited decisions then possible a new equilibrium would in due course emerge. That can no longer be assumed, and it is not assumed by the men at the top of each of the three dominant hierarchies.

For given the scope of their consequences, decisions—and indecisions—in any one of these ramify into the others, and hence top decisions tend either to become co-ordinated or to lead to a commanding indecision. It has not always been like this. When numerous small entrepreneurs made up the economy, for example, many of them could fail and the consequences still remain local; political and military authorities did not intervene. But now, given political expectations and military commitments, can they afford to allow key units of the private corporate economy to break down in slump? Increasingly, they do intervene in economic affairs, and as they do so, the controlling decisions in each order are inspected by agents of the other two, and economic, military, and political structures are interlocked.

At the pinnacle of each of the three enlarged and centralized domains, there have arisen those higher circles which make up the economic, the political, and the military elites. At the top of the economy, among the corporate rich, there are the chief executives; at the top of the political order, the members of the political directorate; at the top of the military establishment, the elite of soldier-statesmen clustered in and around the Joint Chiefs of Staff and the upper echelon. As each of these domains has coincided with the others, as decisions tend to become total in their consequence, the leading men in each of the three domains of power—the warlords, the corporation chieftains, the political directorate—tend to come together, to form the power elite of America.

The conception of the power elite and of its unity rests upon the corresponding developments and the coincidence of interests among economic, political, and military organizations. It also rests upon the similarity of origin and outlook, and the social and personal intermingling of the top circles from each of these dominant hierarchies. This conjunction of institutional and psychological forces, in turn, is revealed by the heavy personnel traffic within and between the big three institutional orders, as well as by the rise of go-betweens as in the high-level lobbying. The conception of the power elite, accordingly, does *not* rest upon the assumption that American history since the origins of World War II must be understood as a secret plot, or as a great and co-ordinated conspiracy of the members of this elite. The conception rests upon quite impersonal grounds.

There is, however, little doubt that the American power elite—which contains, we are told, some of "the greatest organizers in the world"—has also planned and has plotted. The rise of the elite, as we have already made clear, was not and could not have been caused by a plot; and the tenability of the conception does not rest upon the existence of any secret or any publicly known organization. But, once the conjunction of structural trend and of the personal will to utilize it gave rise to the power elite, then plans and programs did occur to its members and indeed it is not possible to interpret many events and official policies of the fifth epoch without reference to the power elite. "There is a great difference," Richard Hofstadter has remarked, "between locating conspiracies *in* history and saying that history *is,* in effect, a conspiracy ..."

The structural trends of institutions become defined as opportunities by those who occupy their command posts. Once such opportunities are recognized, men may avail themselves of them. Certain types of men from each of the dominant institutional areas, more far-sighted than others, have actively promoted the liaison before it took its truly modern shape. They have often done so for reasons not shared by their partners, although not objected to by them either; and often the outcome of their liaison has had consequences which none of them foresaw, much less shaped, and which only later in the course of development came under explicit control. Only after it was well under way did most of its members find themselves part of it and become gladdened, although sometimes also worried, by this fact. But once the co-ordination is a going concern, new men come readily into it and assume its existence without question.

So far as explicit organization—conspiratorial or not—is concerned, the power elite, by its very nature, is more likely to use existing organizations, working within and between them, than to set up explicit organizations whose membership is strictly limited to its own members. But if there is no machinery in existence to ensure, for example, that military and political factors will be balanced in decisions made, they will invent such machinery and use it, as with the National Security Council. Moreover, in a formally democratic polity, the aims and the powers of the various elements of this elite are further supported by an aspect of the permanent war economy: the assumption that the security of the nation supposedly rests upon great secrecy of plan and intent. Many higher events that would reveal the working of the power elite can be withheld from public knowledge under the guise of secrecy. With the wide secrecy covering their operations and decisions, the power elite can mask their intentions, operations, and further consolidation. Any secrecy that is imposed upon those in positions to observe high decision-makers clearly works for and not against the operations of the power elite.

There is accordingly reason to suspect—but by the nature of the case, no proof—that the power elite is not altogether "surfaced." There is nothing hidden about it, although its activities are not publicized. As an elite, it is not organized, although its members often know one another, seem quite naturally to work together, and share many organizations in common. There is nothing conspiratorial about it, although its decisions are often publicly unknown and its mode of operation manipulative rather than explicit.

It is not that the elite "believe in" a compact elite behind the scenes and a mass down below. It is not put in that language. It is just that the people are of necessity confused and must, like trusting children, place all the new world of foreign policy and strategy and executive action in the hands of experts. It is just that everyone knows somebody has got to run the show, and that somebody usually does. Others do not really care anyway, and besides, they do not know how. So the gap between the two types gets wider.

16

ROBERT DAHL

The Ambiguity of Leadership

From *Who Governs?*

———

In a political system where nearly every adult may vote but where knowledge, wealth, social position, access to officials, and other resources are unequally distributed, who actually governs?

The question has been asked, I imagine, wherever popular government has developed and intelligent citizens have reached the stage of critical self-consciousness concerning their society. It must have been put many times in Athens even before it was posed by Plato and Aristotle.

The question is peculiarly relevant to the United States and to Americans.... Americans espouse democratic beliefs with a fervency and a unanimity that have been a regular source of astonishment to foreign observers ... [such as] Tocqueville and Bryce....

Now it has always been held that if equality of power among citizens is possible at all—a point on which many political philosophers have had grave doubts—then surely considerable equality of social conditions is a necessary prerequisite. But if, even in America, with its universal creed of democracy and equality, there are great inequalities in the conditions of different citizens, must there not also be great inequalities in the capacities of different citizens to influence the decisions of their various governments? And if, because they are unequal in other conditions, citizens of a democracy are unequal in power to control their government, then who in fact does govern? How does a "democratic" system work amid inequality of resources? These are the questions I want to explore by examining one urban American community, New Haven, Connecticut.... In the course of the past two centuries, New Haven has gradually changed from oligarchy to pluralism. Accompanying and probably causing this change—one might properly call it a revolution—appears to be a profound alteration in the way political resources are distributed among the citizens of New Haven. This silent socioeconomic revolution has not substituted equality for inequality so much as it has involved a shift from cumulative inequalities in political resources ... to noncumulative or dispersed inequalities. This point will grow clearer as we proceed.

The main evidence for the shift from oligarchy to pluralism is found in changes in the social characteristics of elected officials in New Haven since 1784, the year the city was first incorporated after a century and a half as colony and town....

In the political system of the patrician oligarchy, political resources were marked by a cumulative inequality: when one individual was much better off than another in one resource, such as wealth, he was usually better off in almost every other resource—social standing, legitimacy, control over religious and educational institutions, knowledge, office. In the political system of today, inequalities in political resources remain, but they tend to be *noncumulative*. The political system of New Haven, then, is one of *dispersed inequalities*.

The patrician-Congregationalist-Federalist elite that ruled New Haven prior to 1840 was a tiny group that combined the highest social standing, education, and wealth with key positions in religion, the economy, and public life. The entrepreneurs drove a wedge into this unified elite; social standing and education remained with the patricians, but wealth and key positions in corporate and public life went to the new men of industry. With the rise of the ex-plebes there occurred a further fragmentation of political resources. Rising out of the newly created urban proletariat, of immigrant backgrounds and modest social standing, the ex-plebes had one political resource of extraordinary importance in a competitive political system: they were popular with the voters. Popularity gave them office, and office gave them other political resources, such as legality and city jobs. Office, legality, and jobs gave the ex-plebes influence over government decisions.

Within a century a political system dominated by one cohesive set of leaders had given way to a system dominated by many different sets of leaders, each having access to a different combination of political resources. It was, in short, a pluralist system. If the pluralist system was very far from being an oligarchy, it was also a long way from achieving the goal of political equality advocated by the philosophers of democracy and incorporated into the creed of democracy and equality practically every American professes to uphold.

An elite no longer rules New Haven. But in the strict democratic sense, the disappearance of elite rule has not led to the emergence of rule by the people. Who, then, rules in a pluralist democracy? . . .

One of the difficulties that confronts anyone who attempts to answer the question, "Who rules in a pluralist democracy?" is the ambiguous relationship of leaders to citizens.

Viewed from one position, leaders are enormously influential—so influential that if they are seen only in this perspective they might well be considered a kind of ruling elite. Viewed from another position, however, many influential leaders seem to be captives of their constituents. Like the blind men with the elephant, different analysts have meticulously examined different aspects of the body politic and arrived at radically different conclusions. To some, a pluralistic democracy with dispersed inequalities is all head and no body; to others it is all body and no head.

Ambiguity in the relations of leaders and constituents is generated by several closely connected obstacles both to observation and to clear conceptualization. To begin with, the American creed of democracy and equality prescribes many forms and procedures from which the actual practices of leaders diverge. Consequently, to gain legitimacy for their actions leaders frequently surround their covert behavior with democratic rituals. These rituals not only serve to disguise reality and thus to complicate the task of observation and analysis, but—more important—in complex ways the very existence of democratic rituals, norms, and requirements of legitimacy based on a widely shared creed actually influences the behavior of both leaders and constituents even when democratic norms are violated. Thus the distinction between the rituals of power and the realities of power is frequently obscure.

Two additional factors help to account for this obscurity. First, among all the persons who influence a decision, some do so more directly than others in the sense that they are closer to the stage where concrete alternatives are initiated or vetoed in an explicit and immediate way. Indirect influence might be very great but comparatively difficult to observe and weigh. Yet to ignore indirect influence in analysis of the distribution of influence would be to exclude what might well prove to be a highly significant process of control in a pluralistic democracy.

Second, the relationship between leaders and citizens in a pluralistic democracy is frequently reciprocal: leaders influence the decisions of constituents, but the decisions of leaders are also determined in part by what they think are, will be, or have been the preferences of their constituents. Ordinarily it is much easier to observe and describe the distribution of influence in a political system where the flow of influence is strongly in one direction (an asymmetrical or unilateral system, as it is sometimes called) than in a system marked by strong reciprocal relations. In a political system with competitive elections, such as New Haven's, it is not unreasonable to expect that relationships between leaders and constituents would normally be reciprocal....

In New Haven, as in other political systems, a small stratum of individuals is much more highly involved in political thought, discussion, and action than the rest of the population. These citizens constitute the political stratum.

Members of this stratum live in a political subculture that is partly but not wholly shared by the great majority of citizens. Just as artists and intellectuals are the principal bearers of the artistic, literary, and scientific skills of a society, so the members of the political stratum are the main bearers of political skills. If intellectuals were to vanish overnight, a society would be reduced to artistic, literary, and scientific poverty. If the political stratum were destroyed, the previous political institutions of the society would temporarily stop functioning. In both cases, the speed with which the loss could be overcome would depend on the extent to which the elementary knowledge and basic attitudes of the elite had been diffused. In an open society with widespread education and training in civic attitudes, many citizens hitherto in the apolitical strata could doubtless step into roles that had been filled by members of the political stratum. However, sharp discontinuities and important changes in the operation of the political system almost certainly would occur.

In New Haven, as in the United States, and indeed perhaps in all pluralistic democracies, differences in the subcultures of the political and the apolitical strata are marked, particularly at the extremes. In the political stratum, politics is highly salient; among the apolitical strata, it is remote. In the political stratum, individuals tend to be rather calculating in their choice of strategies; members of the political stratum are, in a sense, relatively rational political beings. In the apolitical strata, people are notably less calculating; their political choices are more strongly influenced by inertia, habit, unexamined loyalties, personal attachments, emotions, transient impulses. In the political stratum, an individual's political beliefs tend to fall into patterns that have a relatively high degree of coherence and internal consistency; in the apolitical strata, political orientations are disorganized, disconnected, and unideological. In the political stratum, information about politics and the issues of the day is extensive; the apolitical strata are poorly informed. Individuals in the political stratum tend to participate rather actively in politics; in the apolitical strata citizens rarely go beyond voting and many do not even vote. Individuals in the political stratum exert a good deal of steady, direct, and active influence on government policy; in fact some individuals have a quite extraordinary amount of influence. Individuals in the apolitical strata, on the other hand, have much less direct or active influence on policies.

Communication within the political stratum tends to be rapid and extensive. Members of the stratum read many of the same newspapers and magazines; in New Haven, for example, they are likely to read the *New York Times* or the *Herald Tribune,* and *Time* or *Newsweek.* Much information also passes by word of mouth. The political strata of different communities and regions are linked in a national network of communications. Even in small towns, one or two members of the local political stratum usually are in touch with members of a state organization, and certain members of the political stratum of a state or any large city maintain relations with members of organizations in other states and cities, or with national figures. Moreover, many channels of communication not designed specifically for political purposes—trade associations, professional associations, and labor organizations, for example—serve as a part of the network of the political stratum.

In many pluralistic systems, however, the political stratum is far from being a closed or static group. In the United States the political stratum does not constitute a homogeneous class with well-defined class interests. In New Haven, in fact, the political stratum is easily penetrated by anyone whose interests and concerns attract him to the distinctive political culture of the stratum. It is easily penetrated because (among other reasons) elections and competitive parties give politicians a powerful motive for expanding their coalitions and increasing their electoral followings.

In an open pluralistic system, where movement into the political stratum is easy, the stratum embodies many of the most widely shared values and goals in the society. If popular values are strongly pragmatic, then the political stratum is likely to be pragmatic; if popular values prescribe reverence toward the past, then the political stratum probably shares that reverence; if popular values are oriented toward material gain and personal advancement, then the political stratum probably reflects these values; if popular values are particularly favorable to political, social, or economic equality, then the political stratum is likely to emphasize equality. The apolitical strata can be said to "govern" as much through the sharing of common values and goals with members of the political stratum as by other means. However, if it were not for elections and competitive parties, this sharing would—other things remaining the same—rapidly decline.

Not only is the political stratum in New Haven not a closed group, but its "members" are far from united in their orientations and strategies. There are many lines of cleavage. The most apparent and probably the most durable are symbolized by affiliations with different political parties. Political parties are rival coalitions of leaders and subleaders drawn from the members of the political stratum. Leaders in a party coalition seek to win elections, capture the chief elective offices of government, and insure that government officials will legalize and enforce policies on which the coalition leaders can agree.

In any given period of time, various issues are salient within the political stratum. Indeed, a political issue can hardly be said to exist unless and until it commands the attention of a significant segment of the political stratum. Out of all the manifold possibilities, members of the political stratum seize upon some issues as important or profitable; these then become the subject of attention within the political stratum. To be sure, all the members of the political stratum may not initially agree that a particular issue is worthy of attention. But whenever a sizable minority of the legitimate elements in the political stratum is determined to bring some question to the fore, the chances are high that the rest of the political stratum will soon begin to pay attention....

In any durable association of more than a handful of individuals, typically a relatively small proportion of the people exercises relatively great direct influence over all the important choices bearing on the life of the association—its survival, for example, or its share in such community resources as wealth, power, and esteem, or the way these resources are shared within the association, or changes in the structure, activities, and dominant goals of the association, and so on. These persons are, by definition, the leaders....

The goals and motives that animate leaders are evidently as varied as the dreams of men. They include greater income, wealth, economic security, power, social standing, fame, respect, affection, love, knowledge, curiosity, fun, the pleasure of exercising skill, delight in winning, esthetic satisfaction, morality, salvation, heroism, self-sacrifice, envy, jealousy, revenge, hate—whatever the whole wide range may be. Popular beliefs and folklore to the contrary, there is no convincing evidence at present that any single common denominator of motives can be singled out in leaders of associations. We are not compelled, therefore, to accept the simple view that Moses, Jesus, Caligula, Savanarola, St. Ignatius, Abraham Lincoln, Boss Tweed, Mahatma Ghandi, Carrie Chapman Catt, Huey Long, and Joseph Stalin all acted from essentially the same motives.

To achieve their goals, leaders develop plans of action, or strategies. But actions take place in a universe of change and uncertainty; goals themselves emerge, take shape, and shift with new experiences. Hence a choice among strategies is necessarily based more on hunch, guesswork, impulse, and the assessment of imponderables than on scientific predictions. Adopting a strategy is a little bit like deciding how to look for a fuse box in a strange house on a dark night after all the lights have blown.

Ordinarily the goals and strategies of leaders require services from other individuals. (Both Christ and Lenin needed disciples to increase and rally their followers.) To perform these services more or less regularly, reliably, and skillfully, auxiliaries or subleaders are needed. The tasks of subleaders include aid in formulating strategies and policies; carrying out the dull, routine, time-consuming or highly specialized work of the eternal spear bearers, the doorbell ringers, the file clerks; recruiting and mobilizing the following; and, in a country like the United States where there exists a strong democratic ethos, helping by their very existence to furnish legitimacy to the actions of the leaders by providing a democratic façade.

To secure the services of subleaders, leaders must reward them in some fashion. Here too the range of rewards seems to be as broad as the spectrum of human motives. However, some kinds of rewards are easier to manipulate than others. In business organizations, the rewards are mainly financial ones, which are probably the easiest of all to manipulate. In many other kinds of associations—and evidently to some extent even in business—either financial rewards are too low to attract and hold subleaders capable of performing the tasks at the minimum levels required by the leaders, or within a certain range other kinds of rewards are more important to the auxiliaries than financial ones. Leaders may therefore contrive to pay off their auxiliaries with nonfinancial rewards like social standing, prestige, fun, conviviality, the hope of salvation, and so on.

Thus the survival of an association of leaders and subleaders depends on frequent transactions between the two groups in which the leaders pay off the subleaders in return for their services. To pay off the subleaders, leaders usually have to draw on resources available only outside the association. Sometimes leaders can obtain these resources from outside by coercion, particularly if they happen to control the single most effective institution for coercion: the government. This is one reason—but by no means the only one—why government is always such an important pawn in struggles among leaders. Ordinarily, however, the association must produce something that will appeal to outsiders, who then contribute resources that serve, directly or indirectly, to maintain the association. Probably the most important direct contribution of these outsiders—let us call them constituents—is money; their most important indirect contribution is votes, which can be converted into office and thus into various other resources. . . .

It is easy to see why observers have often pessimistically concluded that the internal dynamics of political associations create forces alien to popular control and hence to democratic institutions. Yet the characteristics I have described are not necessarily dysfunctional to a pluralistic democracy in which there exists a considerable measure of popular control over the policies of leaders, for minority control by leaders within associations is not necessarily inconsistent with popular control over leaders through electoral processes.

For example, suppose that (1) a leader of a political association feels a strong incentive for winning an election; (2) his constituents comprise most of the adult population of the community; (3) nearly all of his constituents are expected to vote; (4) voters cast their ballot without receiving covert rewards or punishments as a direct consequence of the way they vote; (5) voters give heavy weight to the overt policies of a candidate in making their decision as to how they will vote; (6) there are rival candidates offering alternative policies; and (7) voters have a good deal of information about the policies of the candidates. In these circumstances, it is almost certain that leaders of political associations would tend to choose overt policies they believed most likely to win the support of a majority of adults in the community. Even if the policies of political associations were usually controlled by a tiny minority of leaders in each association, the policies of the leaders who won elections to the chief elective offices in local government would tend to reflect the preferences of the populace. I do not mean to suggest that any political system actually fulfills all these conditions, but to the extent that it does the leaders who directly control the decisions of political associations are themselves influenced in their own choices of policies by their assumptions as to what the voting populace wants.

Although this is an elementary point, it is critical to an understanding of the chapters that follow. We shall discover that in each of a number of key sectors of public policy, a few persons have great *direct* influence on the choices that are made; most citizens, by contrast, seem to have rather little direct influence. Yet it would be unwise to underestimate the extent to which voters may exert *indirect* influence on the decisions of leaders by means of elections.

In a political system where key offices are won by elections, where legality and constitutionality are highly valued in the political culture, and where nearly everyone in the political stratum publicly adheres to a doctrine of democracy, it is likely that the political culture, the prevailing attitudes of the political stratum, and the operation of the political system itself will be shaped by the role of elections. Leaders who in one context are enormously influential and even rather free from demands by their constituents may reveal themselves in another context to be involved in tireless efforts to adapt their policies to what they think their constituents want.

To be sure, in a pluralistic system with dispersed inequalities, the direct influence of leaders on policies extends well beyond the norms implied in the classical models of democracy developed by political philosophers. But if the leaders lead, they are also led. Thus the relations between leaders, subleaders, and constituents produce in the distribution of influence a stubborn and pervasive ambiguity that permeates the entire political system.

17

MICHAEL PARENTI

From *Democracy for the Few*

—————

A GLANCE at the social map of this country reveals a vast agglomeration of groups and governing agencies. If by pluralism we mean this multiplicity of private and public groups, then the United States is a pluralistic society. But then so is any society of size and complexity, including allegedly totalitarian ones like the Soviet Union with its multiplicity of regional, occupational, and ethnic groups and its party, administrative, and military factions all competing over policies.

But the proponents of pluralism presume to be saying something about how *power* is distributed and how *democracy* works. Supposedly the desirable feature of a pluralistic society is that it works through democratic means and produces democratic outputs. Policies not only are shaped by competing groups but also benefit the human needs of the populace....

Power in America "is plural and fluid," claims Max Lerner. In reality, power is distributed among heavily entrenched, well-organized, well-financed politico-economic conglomerates that can reproduce the social conditions needed for continued elite hegemony. Of the various resources of power, wealth is the most crucial, and its distribution is neither "plural" nor "fluid." Not everyone with money chooses to use it to exert political influence, and not everyone with money need bother to do so. But when they so desire, those who control the wealth of society enjoy a persistent and pervasive political advantage.

...The political advantage enjoyed by the moneyed class is fortified by a variety of institutional and governmental arrangements. The pluralists have not a word to say about the pervasive role of political repression in American society, the purging and exclusion of anticapitalist dissidents from government, the labor movement, the media, academia, and the entertainment world, along with the surveillance and harassment of protest groups and sometimes even mild critics. Nor do the pluralists give any recognition to the way that the moneyed power controls the communication industry and most other institutions of society, setting the terms for the socialization, indoctrination, and recruitment of governmental and nongovernmental elites. Pluralists seem never to allude to the near-monopoly control of ideas and information which is the daily fare of the news and entertainment sectors of the mass media, creating a climate of opinion favorable to the owning-class ideology at home and abroad. Nor are the pluralists much troubled by the rigged monopoly rules under which the two major political parties operate, and an electoral system that treats private money as a form of free speech, and vast sums of it as a prerequisite for office.

...The pluralists make much of the fact that wealthy interests do not always operate with clear and deliberate purpose. To be sure, elites, like everyone else, make mistakes and suffer confusions as to what might be the most advantageous tactics in any particular situation. But if they are not omniscient and infallible, neither are they habitual laggards and imbeciles. If they do not always calculate rationally in the pursuit of their class interests, they do so often and successfully enough. It is also true that the business community is not unanimous on all issues.

...Is then the American polity ruled by a secretive, conspiratorial, omnipotent, monolithic power elite? No, the plutocracy, or ruling class, does not fit that easily refuted caricature. First of all, it cannot get its way on all things at all times. No ruling class in history, no matter how autocratic, has ever achieved omnipotence. All have had to make concessions and allow for unexpected and undesired developments. In addition, the ruling elites are not always secretive. They rule from legitimized institutions. The moneyed influence they exercise over governing bodies is sometimes overt—as with reported campaign contributions and control of investments, and sometimes covert—as with unreported bribes and deals. The ruling class controls most of the institutions and jobs of this society through corporate ownership and by control of management positions, interlocking directorates, and trustee-ships, the elite membership of which, while not widely advertised, is well-documented public knowledge. However, these elites do often find it desirable to plan in secret, to minimize or distort the flow of information, to deny the truth, to develop policies that sometimes violate the law they profess to uphold. Instances of this have been treated in this book.

...American government is not ruled by a monolithic elite. There are serious differences in tactics, differences in how best to mute class conflict and maintain the existing system at home and abroad. Differences can arise between moderately conservative and extremely conservative capitalists, between large and not-as-large investor interests, and between domestic and international corpora-tions—all of which lends an element of conflict and indeterminacy to policies. But these conflicts seldom take into account the interests of the public. Given the wide-ranging interests of the corporate class, policy is dictated by a variety of elites that cut across various financial circles and governing agencies. When push comes to shove, what holds them together is their common interest in pre-serving a system that assures their continued accumulation of wealth and enjoyment of social privilege....

One might better think of ours as a dual political system. First, there is the *symbolic* political system centering around electoral and representative activities including campaign conflicts, voter turn-out, political personalities, public pronouncements, official role-playing, and certain ambiguous presentations of some of the public issues that bestir presidents, governors, mayors, and their respec-tive legislatures. Then there is the *substantive* political system, in-volving multibillion-dollar contracts, tax write-offs, protections, rebates, grants, loss compensations, subsidies, leases, giveaways, and the whole vast process of budgeting, legislating, advising, regulating, protecting, and servicing major producer interests, now bending or ignoring the law on behalf of the powerful, now apply-ing it with full punitive vigor against heretics and "troublemakers." The symbolic system is highly visible, taught in the schools, dis-sected by academicians, gossiped about by news commentators. The substantive system is seldom heard of or accounted for....

We might ask: Why doesn't the future arrive? Why is funda-

mental change so difficult to effect? Why is social justice so hard
to achieve? The answer is twofold: First, because the realities of
power militate against fundamental reform, and second, because
the present politico-economic system could not sustain itself if such
reforms were initiated. Let us take each of these in turn:

...Quite simply, those who have the interest in fundamental
change have not yet the power, while those who have the power
have not the interest, being disinclined to commit class suicide. It
is not that decision makers have been unable to figure out the
steps for change; it is that they oppose the things that change
entails. The first intent of most officeholders is not to fight for
social change but to survive and prosper. Given this, they are
inclined to respond positively not to group *needs* but to group
demands, to those who have the resources to command their attention. In political life as in economic life, needs do not become
marketable demands until they are backed by "buying power" or
"exchange power," for only then is it in the "producer's" interest
to respond. The problem for many unorganized citizens and workers is that they have few political resources of their own to exchange. For the politician, the compelling quality of any argument
is determined less by its logic and evidence than by the strength of
its advocates. The wants of the unorganized public seldom become
marketable political demands—that is, they seldom become imperatives to which officials find it in their own interest to respond,
especially if the changes would put the official on a collision course
with those who control the resources of the society and who see
little wrong with the world as it is.

Most of the demands for fundamental change in our priorities
are impossible to effect within the present system if that system is
to maintain itself. The reason our labor, skills, technology, and
natural resources are not used for social needs and egalitarian purposes is that they are used for corporate gain. The corporations
cannot build low-rent houses and feed the poor because their interest is not in social reconstruction but in private profit. For the
state to maintain a "healthy" economy within the present capitalist
structure, it must maintain conditions that are favorable to investment, that is, it must guarantee high-profit yields. Were the state
instead to decide to make fundamental changes in our economic
priorities, it would have to redistribute income, end deficit spending by taxing the financial class from whom it now borrows, stop
bribing the rich to get still richer with investment subsidies and

other guarantees, and redirect capital investments toward not-for-profit public goals. But if the state did all this, investment incentives would be greatly diminished, the risks for private capital would be too high, many companies could not survive, and unemployment would reach disastrous heights. State-supported capitalism cannot exist without state support, without passing its immense costs and inefficiencies on to the public. The only way the state could redirect the overall wealth of society toward egalitarian goals would be to exercise democratic control over capital investments and capital return, but that would mean, in effect, public ownership of the means of production—a giant step toward *socialism*. . . .

But can socialism work? Is it not just a dream in theory and a nightmare in practice? Can the government produce anything of note? . . . Various private industries (defense, railroads, satellite communication, aeronautics, and nuclear power, to name some) exist today only because the government funded the research and development and provided most of the risk capital. We already have some socialized services and they work quite well if given sufficient funds. Our roads and water supplies are socialized as are our bridges and ports, and in some states so are our liquor stores, which yearly generate hundreds of millions of dollars in state revenues. And there are the examples of "lemon socialism" in which governments in this and other countries have taken over industries ailing from being bled for profits, and nursed them back to health, testimony to the comparative capacities of private and public capital. . . .

How do we get to socialism? Only time will tell. Better to know where we want to go and not yet be able to get there, than to go full speed ahead without knowing where we are going—which is the modus operandi of capitalism. Capitalism is a system without a soul and without a direction. It has nowhere to go, for it has nothing it wants to accomplish except the reproduction and expansion of its own capital accumulation process.

Whether socialism can be brought about within the framework of the existing modern capitalist state or by a revolutionary overthrow of that state is a question unresolved by history. So far there have been no examples of either road to socialism in modern industrial society. But because something has never occurred in the past does not mean it cannot happen in the future. In the late nineteenth century, knowing persons, relying on the fact that a successful workers' revolution had never taken place, concluded that one never would. Yet early in the next century the Bolshevik revolution exploded upon the world. And bourgeois pundits scoffed at the idea that "native" peoples could overthrow modern colonial powers and achieve self-rule, yet such things have happened.

The question of what kind of socialism we should struggle for deserves more extensive treatment than can be given here. American socialism cannot be modeled on the Soviet Union, China, Cuba, or other countries with different historical, economic, and cultural developments. But these countries ought to be examined so that we might learn from their accomplishments and problems. Whatever else one wants to say about existing socialist societies, they have achieved what capitalism cannot and has no intention of accomplishing: adequate food, housing, and clothing for all; economic security in old age; free medical care; free education at all levels; and the right to a job—in countries that are not as rich as ours but which use productive resources in more rational ways than can be done under capitalism.

The destructive and unjust effects of capitalism upon our nation, the pressures of competition between capitalist nations, the growing discontent and oppression of the populace, the continual productive growth within socialist nations, the new revolutionary victories against Western imperialism in the Third World, all these things make objective conditions increasingly unfavorable for capitalism. Yet people will not discard the system that oppresses them until they see the feasibility of an alternative one. It is not that they think society *should* be this way, but that it *must* be. It is not that they don't want things to change, but they don't believe things *can* change—or they fear that whatever changes might occur would more likely be for the worse.

What is needed is widespread organizing not only around particular issues but for a socialist movement that can project both the desirability of an alternative system and the *possibility* and indeed the great *necessity* for democratic change. Throughout the world and at home, forces for change are being unleashed. There is much evidence—some of it presented in this book—indicating that Americans are well ahead of the existing political elites in their willingness to embrace new alternatives, including public ownership of the major corporations and worker control of production. With time and struggle, as the possibility for progressive change becomes more evident and the longing for a better social life grows stronger, people will become increasingly intolerant of the monumental injustices of the existing capitalist system and will move toward a profoundly democratic solution. We can be hopeful the day will come, as it came in social orders of the past, when those who seem invincible will be shaken from their pinnacles. `

There is nothing sacred about the existing system. All economic and political institutions are contrivances that should serve the interests of the people. When they fail to do so, they should be replaced by something more responsive, more just, and more democratic. Marx said this, and so did Jefferson. It is a revolutionary doctrine, and very much an American one.

18

BENJAMIN BARBER

From *Strong Democracy*

———

LIBERAL DEMOCRACY has been one of the sturdiest political systems in the history of the modern West. As the dominant modern form of democracy, it has informed and guided several of the most successful and enduring governments the world has known, not least among them that of the United States.

Liberal democracy has in fact become such a powerful model that sometimes, in the Western world at least, the very future of democracy seems to depend entirely on its fortunes and thus on the American system of government and its supporting liberal culture. This perceived monopoly not only limits the alternatives apparent to those seeking other legitimate forms of politics but leaves Americans themselves with no standard against which to measure their own liberal politics and with no ideal by which to modify them, should they wish to do so.

Furthermore, succesful as it has been, liberal democracy has not always been able to resist its major twentieth-century adversaries: the illegitimate politics of fascism and Stalinism or of military dictatorship and totalism. Nor has it been able to cope effectively with its own internal weaknesses and contradictions, many of which grow more intractable as the American system ages and as its internal contradictions gradually emerge.

It is the central argument of the first part of this book that many of these problems stem from the political theory of liberal democracy itself. Liberal democracy is based on premises about human nature, knowledge, and politics that are genuinely liberal but that are not intrinsically democratic. Its conception of the individual and of individual interest undermines the democratic practices upon which both individuals and their interests depend.

Liberal democracy is thus a "thin" theory of democracy, one whose democratic values are prudential and thus provisional, optional, and conditional—means to exclusively individualistic and private ends. From this precarious foundation, no firm theory of citizenship, participation, public goods, or civic virtue can be expected to arise. Liberal democracy, therefore, can never lead too far from Ambrose Bierce's cynical definition of politics as "the conduct of public affairs for private advantage." It can never rise far above the provisional and private prudence expressed in John Locke's explanation that men consent to live under government only for "the mutual preservation of their lives, liberties and estates." And it can never evade the irony of Winston Churchill's portrait of democracy as "the worst form of government in the world, except for all the other forms." A democracy that can be defended only by mordant skepticism may find it difficult to combat the zealotry of nondemocrats.

In fact, Churchill's remark suggests that liberal democracy may not be a theory of political community at all. It does not so much provide a justification for politics as it offers a politics that justifies individual rights. It is concerned more to promote individual liberty than to secure public justice, to advance interests rather than to discover goods, and to keep men safely apart rather than to bring them fruitfully together. As a consequence, it is capable of fiercely resisting every assault on the individual—his privacy, his property, his interests, and his rights—but is far less effective in resisting assaults on community or justice or citizenship or participation. Ultimately, this vulnerability undermines its defense of the individual; for the individual's freedom is not the precondition for political activity but rather the product of it.

This is not to say that there is anything simple about liberal democracy. It is an exotic, complex, and frequently paradoxical form of politics. It comprises at least three dominant *dispositions,* each of which entails a quite distinctive set of attitudes, inclinations, and political values. The three dispositions can be conveniently called *anarchist, realist,* and *minimalist. . . .*

The American political system is a remarkable example of the coexistence—sometimes harmonious, more often uncomfortable—of all three dispositions. Americans, we might say, are anarchists in their values (privacy, liberty, individualism, property, and rights); realists in their means (power, law, coercive mediation, and sovereign adjudication); and minimalists in their political temper (tolerance, wariness of government, pluralism, and such institutionalizations of caution as the separation of powers and judicial review).

The anarchist, realist, and minimalist dispositions can all be regarded as political responses to *conflict,* which is the fundamental condition of all liberal democratic politics. Autonomous individuals occupying private and separate spaces are the players in the game of liberal politics; conflict is their characteristic mode of interaction. Whether he perceives conflict as a function of scarce resources (as do Hobbes and Marx), of insatiable appetites (as do Russell and Freud), or of a natural lust for power and glory (as does Machiavelli), the liberal democrat places it at the center of human interaction and makes it the chief concern of politics.

While the three dispositions may share a belief in the primacy of conflict, they suggest radically different approaches to its amelioration. Put very briefly, anarchism is *conflict-denying,* realism is *conflict-repressing,* and minimalism is *conflict-tolerating.* The first approach tries to wish conflict away, the second to extirpate it, and the third to live with it. Liberal democracy, the compound and real American form, is conflict-denying in its free-market assumptions about the private sector and its supposed elasticity and egalitarianism; it is conflict-repressing and also conflict-adjusting in its prudential uses of political power to adjudicate the struggle of individuals and groups; and it is conflict-tolerating in its characteristic liberal-skeptical temper. . . .

Liberal democracy's three dispositions, while distinct in their concerns and inclinations, are nevertheless linked in a single circle of reasoning that begins as it ends in the natural and negative liberty of men and women as atoms of self-interest, as persons whose every step into social relations, whose every foray into the world of Others, cries out for an apology, a legitimation, a justification. For all three dispositions, politics is prudence in the service of *homo economicus*—the solitary seeker of material happiness and bodily security. The title of Harold Lasswell's early classic, *Politics: Who Gets What, When, How?* could stand as the epigraph of each disposition. In these stark terms, democracy itself is never more than an artifact to be used, adjusted, adapted, or discarded as it suits or fails to suit the liberal ends for which it serves as means.

The uninspired and uninspiring but "realistic" image of man as a creature of need, living alone by nature but fated to live in the company of his fellows by enlightened self-interest combines with the cynical image of government as a provisional instrument of power servicing these creatures to suggest a general view of politics as zoo-keeping. Liberal democratic imagery seems to have been fashioned in a menagerie. It teems with beasts and critters of every description: sovereign lions, princely lions and foxes, bleating sheep and poor reptiles, ruthless pigs and ruling whales, sly polecats, clever coyotes, ornery wolves (often in sheep's clothing), and, finally, in Alexander Hamilton's formidable image, all mankind itself but one great Beast.

From the perspective of this political zoology, civil society is an alternative to the "jungle"—to the war of all against all that defines the state of nature. In that poor and brutish war, the beasts howl in voices made articulate by reason—for zoos, for cages and trainers, for rules and regulations, for regular feeding times and prudent custodians. Like captured leopards, men are to be admired for their proud individuality and for their unshackled freedom, but they must be caged for their untrustworthiness and antisocial orneriness all the same. Indeed, if the individual is dangerous, the species is deadly. Liberal democracy's sturdiest cages are reserved for the People. "Democracy is more vindictive than Cabinets," warned Churchill, a prudent custodian if ever there was one: "the wars of peoples will be more terrible than those of kings."

Although they vary in their portraits of human nature, all three dispositions share a belief in the fundamental inability of the human beast to live at close quarters with members of its own species. All three thus seek to structure human relations by keeping men apart rather than by bringing them together. It is their mutual incompatibility that turns men ·into reluctant citizens and their aggressive solitude that makes them into wary neighbors. . . .

What we have called "thin democracy," then, yields neither the pleasures of participation nor the fellowship of civic association, neither the autonomy and self-governance of continuous political activity nor the enlarging mutuality of shared public goods—of mutual deliberation, decision, and work. Oblivious to that essential human interdependency that underlies all political life, thin democratic politics is at best a politics of static interest, never a politics of transformation; a politics of bargaining and exchange, never a politics of invention and creation; and a politics that conceives of women and men at their worst (in order to protect them from themselves), never at their potential best (to help them become better than they are)....

Strong democracy is a distinctively modern form of participatory democracy. It rests on the idea of a self-governing community of citizens who are united less by homogeneous interests than by civic education and who are made capable of common purpose and mutual action by virtue of their civic attitudes and participatory institutions rather than their altruism or their good nature. Strong democracy is consonant with—indeed it depends upon—the politics of conflict, the sociology of pluralism, and the separation of private and public realms of action. It is not intrinsically inimical to either the size or the technology of modern society and is therefore wedded neither to antiquarian republicanism nor to face-to-face parochialism. Yet it challenges the politics of elites and masses that masquerades as democracy in the West and in doing so offers a relevant alternative to what we have called thin democracy—that is, to instrumental, representative, liberal democracy in its three dispositions....

The theory of strong democracy offers a different and more vigorous response: it envisions politics not as a way of life but as a way of living—as, namely, the way that human beings with variable but malleable natures and with competing but overlapping interests can contrive to live together communally not only to their mutual advantage but also to the advantage of their mutuality.

Because democratic politics makes possible cooperation and an approximation of concord where they do not exist by nature, it is potentially a realm of unique openness, flexibility, and promise....

The stress on transformation is at the heart of the strong democratic conception of politics. Every politics confronts the competition of private interests and the conflict that competition engenders. But where liberal democracy understands politics as a means of eliminating conflict (the anarchist disposition), repressing it (the realist disposition), or tolerating it (the minimalist disposition), strong democracy also aspires to transform conflict through a politics of distinctive inventiveness and discovery. It seeks to create a public language that will help reformulate private interests in terms susceptible to public accommodation; and it aims at understanding individuals not as abstract persons but as citizens, so that commonality and equality rather than separateness are the defining traits of human society.

Open to change and hospitable to the idea of individual and social transformation, strong democracy can overcome the pessimism and cynicism, the negativity and passivity that, while they immunize liberalism against naïve utopianism and the tyranny of idealism, also undermine its cautious hopes and leave its theory thin and threadbare and its practice vulnerable to skepticism and dogmatism. Under strong democracy, politics is given the power of human promise. For the first time the possibilities of transforming private into public, dependency into interdependency, conflict into cooperation, license into self-legislation, need into love, and bondage into citizenship are placed in a context of participation. There they are secure from the manipulation of those bogus communitarians who appeal to the human need for communion and for a purpose higher than private, material interests only in order to enslave humankind. . . .

In strong democracy, politics is something done by, not to, citizens. Activity is its chief virtue, and involvement, commitment, obligation, and service—common deliberation, common decision, and common work—are its hallmarks. . . .

. . . The creation of community here becomes a concomitant of the creation of public goods and public ends. Conversely, the creation of public ends depends on the creation of a community of citizens who regard themselves as comrades and who are endowed with an enlarging empathy. Community, public goods, and citizenship thus ultimately become three interdependent parts of a single democratic circle whose compass grows to describe a true public. . . .

. . . Strong democratic theory begins but does not end with conflict: it acknowledges conflict but ultimately transforms rather than accommodates or minimizes it. . . .

. . . Politics in the participatory mode does not choose between or merely ratify values whose legitimacy is a matter of prior record. It makes preferences and opinions earn legitimacy by forcing them to run the gauntlet of public deliberation and public judgment.

They emerge not simply legitimized but transformed by the processes to which they have been subjected. . . .

. . . Where voting is a static act of expressing one's preference, participation is a dynamic act of imagination that requires participants to change how they see the world. Voting suggests a group of men in a cafeteria bargaining about what they can buy as a group that will suit their individual tastes. Strong democratic politics suggests a group of men in a cafeteria contriving new menus, inventing new recipes, and experimenting with new diets in the effort to create a public taste that they can all share and that will supersede the conflicting private tastes about which they once tried to strike bargains. Voting, in the bargaining model, often fixes choices and thereby stultifies the imagination; judging, in the model of strong democracy, activates imagination by demanding that participants reexamine their values and interests in light of all the inescapable others—the public.

19

BERNARD CRICK

A Defence of Politics Against Democracy

From *In Defence of Politics*

THERE ARE THOSE who would tell us that democracy is *the* true form of politics. Some would even say that it *is* politics, or that it is clearly and always a form a government, value or activity superior to mere politics. But politics needs to be defended even against democracy, certainly in the sense that any clear and practical idea needs defending against something vague and imprecise. We will argue that while democracy as a social movement must exist in nearly all modern forms of political rule, yet, if taken alone and as a matter of principle, it is the destruction of politics.

Democracy is perhaps the most promiscuous word in the world of public affairs. She is everybody's mistress and yet somehow retains her magic even when a lover sees that her favours are being, in his light, illicitly shared by many another. Indeed, even amid our pain at being denied her exclusive fidelity, we are proud of her adaptability to all sorts of circumstances, to all sorts of company. How often has one heard: "Well, at least the Communists claim to be democratic"? But the real trouble is, of course, that they do not pretend to be democratic. They are democratic. They are democratic in the sound historical sense of a majority consenting to be ruled in a popular way.

So while democracy has most often been used to mean simply "majority rule" (which at the size of a state can only mean majority consent), all kinds of special meanings have arisen (many to refute rather than to refine this common view). Perhaps its primary meaning to most people at the moment is no more than "all things bright and beautiful," or some such rather general sentiment. Then others hold that, surprisingly enough, democracy "really means" liberty, even liberalism, or even individualism, even to defend the (democratic) individual against the (democratic) majority—this is certainly an amiable view. . . .

The word can be used, as De Tocqueville used it, as a synonym for equality, or, as Andrew Carnegie used it, to mean a highly mobile free-enterprise society with great (Darwinian) differences in station and wealth. Or it may be seen as a political system which places constitutional limitations even upon a freely elected (democratic) government (the most sought-after use, but the most historically implausible and rhetorical); or, on the contrary, as the "will of the people," or the "general will," triumphing over these "artificial" restraints of constitutional institutions. To many democracy means little more than "one man, one vote"—to which others would hopefully add: "plus real choices." And in broad terms embracing all of these usages, democracy can be seen as a particular recipe of institutions, or as a "way of life," some style of politics or rule, as when it is said that the "spirit of democracy" is more important than any institutional arrangements, or a democracy is where people behave democratically in their speech, dress, amusements, etc. . . .

Majoritarian democracy appears in its most unsatisfactory and unpolitical form in the famous doctrine of the "Sovereignty of the People" (which people?). . . .

The democratic doctrine of the sovereignty of the people threatens, then, the essential perception that all known advanced societies are inherently pluralistic and diverse, which is the seed and the root of politics. Few have understood more clearly than Alexis De Tocqueville the importance of group loyalties intermediate between "society" and the State. He was the first to see clearly why "the species of oppression by which democratic nations are menaced is unlike anything that ever before existed in the world ... I seek in vain for an expression that will accurately convey the whole of the idea I have formed of it; the old words *despotism* and *tyranny* are inappropriate: the thing itself is new ..." Thus he wrote even in his *Democracy in America* in which he sought to show that there were diversifying institutions in American society which *could* mitigate the danger of a "tyranny of the majority." In his *L'Ancien Régime et la Revolution* he christens this new thing "Democratic Despotism" and characterises it thus: "No gradations in society, no distinctions of classes, no fixed ranks—a people composed of individuals nearly alike and entirely equal—this confused mass being recognised as the only legitimate sovereign, but carefully deprived of all the faculties which could enable it either to direct or even to superintend its own government. Above this mass, a single officer, charged to do everything in its name without consulting it. To control this officer, public opinion, deprived of its organs; to arrest him, revolutions, but no laws. In principle a subordinate agent; in fact, a master."

That the word "democratic" can now be used to describe what earlier writers would have termed "mixed-government" (which is a clearer interpretive translation of Aristotle's *politeia* than simply "polity"), is a dangerous loss to political understanding. The older tradition of political theory in using the term "democracy" had exemplified Aristotle's tri-partite usage: democracy as, intellectually, the doctrine of those who believe that because men are equal in some things, they should be equal in all; constitutionally, the rule of the majority; sociologically, the rule of the poor. Democracy he saw as a necessary element in polity or mixed-government, but alone it was destructive of the political community, attempting the impossible feat of the direct rule of all—which in fact meant the unrestrained power of those who were trusted by most. Democracies were particularly prone to fall by "the insolence of demagogues" into tyrannies. Modern experience seems to bear out Aristotle's precise description of democracy rather than that of those who would have it stand for "all things bright and beautiful."

...Take the case of the United States. Here indeed must be an uncontested example of a political system which can be clearly, and by popular usage must be, characterised as democratic. But even here it is necessary to remind oneself that the word came to be applied very late to the system as a whole, rather than to these parts of it which were uniquely and from the beginning democratic—the franchise (with the great Negro exception) and what was, certainly by comparison with any other country, the broad equality of social conditions. Not until this century have all Americans, except political eccentrics, called American government unequivocally a democracy. The old Aristotelian distinction, well understood by the Founding Fathers, between democracy as a force on its own and democracy as one element in mixed-government, long survived the attacks of democratic rhetoric....

...The dispute continues between those Americans who regard their system as too democratic to provide effective government— if not in the domestic field, at least in the great jungle of foreign affairs—and those who regard it as not democratic enough—popular democracy is still frustrated by the checks and balances of the Constitution, the division of powers, particularly the Senate, on occasion the Supreme Court. American writers can still be found in abundance who are simply naïve democrats. The business of government to them is simply to find out the wishes of the people. "Democracy," as Mr. Justice Holmes said sarcastically, "is what the crowd wants." "Populist" direct democracy is one of the great animating myths of American politics for both left and right. Nearly half the States of the American Union, for instance, have provision in their constitutions for popular initiative, referendum and recall. They forget that the first business of government is to govern—which may at times, even in America, call for the deliberate endurance of unpopularity....

So if democracy is best understood as one element in free government, not as a characteristic of the whole system, then it will always be possible to argue that *more* or *less* democratic institutions or democratic spirit is needed in any particular circumstance. Once again, Aristotle more clearly defined the relationship between politics and democracy than the usually over-complicated, or purely ideological, writings of modern authors. The best form of government was to him political rule-'polity' or mixed-government. Such a government combined the aristocratic principle and the democratic; good government is a matter of experience, skill and knowledge—not just opinion, but is subject to the consent of the governed. If there is no democratic element, a state will be oligarchic or despotic; if democracy alone prevails, the result is anarchy—the opportunity of demagogues to become despots. Democracy, then, is to be appreciated not as a principle of government on its own, but as a political principle, or an element within politics. As an intellectual principle, the belief that because men are equal in some things they are equal in all, it can be disastrous to the skill and judgement needed to preserve any order at all, let alone the special difficulties of a conciliatory political order. . . .

Democracy, then, if we give the word the fairest meaning we may want to give it—if we value liberty, free choice, discussion, opposition, popular government, all of these things together—is still but one form of politics, not something to be hoped for at every stage of a country's development or in every circumstance. Politics is often settling for less than what we want, because we also want to live without violence or perpetual fear of violence from other people who want other things. But democracy, in its clearest historical and sociological sense, is simply a characteristic of modern governments both free and unfree. If industrial societies need governments of unparalleled strength, activity and energy, they must be based upon active consent.

So while democracy can be compatible with politics, indeed politics can now scarcely hope to exist without it, yet politics does need defending on many occasions against the exclusive claims of many concepts of democracy which can lead to either the despotism of People's Democracies or the anarchy of the Congo. But perhaps it needs most of all that most unpopular of defences: historical analysis applied against the vagueness of popular rhetoric. Democracy is one element in politics; if it seeks to be everything, it destroys politics, turning "harmony into mere unison," reducing "a theme to a single beat."

PART FOUR

Separation of Powers and Federalism

HOW TO HANDLE "the problem of power" is a dominant concern of all serious theories of government. The Constitution of 1787, unlike the Articles of Confederation, vested impressive powers in a national government. While the framers saw such powers as necessary to meet domestic and foreign problems threatening the new nation, they were aware that they could easily be abused. And, of course, the Antifederalist opponents of the Constitution, who saw no need for the new powers in the first place, were certain they would be abused. The framers' answer to "the problem of power" that both Federalists and Antifederalists perceived is what Madison calls the compound republic. First, powers would be divided between two distinct levels of government, national and state. Then, the portion allocated to the national government would be subdivided into three separate and distinct departments each of which would have independent powers and a will of its own.

The devices of the compound republic—federalism, separation of powers, and checks and balances—are the basic architectural principles of the Constitution. They have given a special quality to American politics for two hundred years. In no other democratic polity are the powers of government so thoroughly dispersed. The federal principle has proved attractive to quite a few other nations, among them Canada, Australia, West Germany, and India. Nowhere else, however, is there anything like the dispersion of power that the Constitution builds into our *national* government. Our unique separation-of-powers system is seen in Europe as something of an oddity—"good perhaps for Americans, but not for us." Even the hardiest admirers of the United States, such as the editors of the British liberal magazine, *The Economist,* shy from recommending its adoption at home. They admire elements of the Madisonian system, but fear that it would not export successfully. The standard European governmental arrangement is a unitary national government fusing executive and legislative powers. A prime minister and cabinet exercise all of the authority of government as long as they are supported by a parliamentary majority. The European answer to "the problem of power" is majority rule through parliamentary government.

The case for divided national government is nowhere more elegantly stated than in *Federalist Paper* 51. Popular control of government through elections is necessary, Madison argues, but "experience has taught mankind the necessity of auxiliary precautions." The Constitution, he explains, is designed to give "those who administer each of the departments the necessary constitutional means and personal motives to resist encroachments of the others.... Ambition must be made to counteract ambition." The president, Congress, and the national judiciary are thus invited to struggle over the determination of public policy. That is not all. Since the legislature is expected to be the strongest branch, it ought to be divided into two houses based on different principles of representation. "The problem of power" is solved by ensuring that no one part of government will ever be entirely in control of public policy.

While we argue that the vast majority of Americans have always been instinctively in tune with this Madisonian logic, it has not been without its critics. A small, but articulate minority of constitutional commentators has consistently stated the case for the superiority of parliamentary government. We have chosen to represent this tradition here by presenting the granddaddy of all these arguments, Woodrow Wilson's in *Congressional Government*. In fact, nothing essential has changed in these arguments all the way down to their most current articulation by Lloyd Cutler and others associated with the Committee on the Constitutional System. The essence of this point of view is that the framers' "piecing of authority, the cutting of it up into small bits" creates a government at odds with itself, incapable of prompt, coherent action. Such a government, the argument runs, lacks accountability. The public cannot determine whom to reward or blame. Today, the Committee on the Constitutional System asserts, the president and Congress are more often than not deadlocked over fiscal policy (taxing and spending), strategic nuclear policy, and such matters as whether to aid the Nicaraguan Contras. The prescription (as always from Wilson's time to the present) is to import at least some of the features of parliamentary government.

Our selections from the reports of the Iran-Contra committees and from a recent journalistic account of the dispute over the *Grove City College* case illustrate the Madisonian system in action at age 200. For better or worse it is immediately understandable in the language of *Federalist Paper* 51. In each case there is a vigorous struggle between the branches of the national government for control of policy. The Constitution does not determine the substantive outcome of such struggles, but it does ensure that they will occur. Note that the Majority and Minority Reports on Iran-Contra interpret the constitutional powers and roles of the president and Congress quite differently. The Majority Report finds clear evidence that the Reagan administration sought to negate the Constitution's mandate that the president and Congress share equally in determining foreign policy. The Minority Report argues that the president must "have the primary role of conducting the foreign policy of the United States," blaming the affair on Congress, which is seen as having usurped the president's role as chief diplomat. Whoever one thinks has the best of this argument (the editors, themselves, disagree on the matter), we would point out that the president and Congress have been engaged in similar struggles over foreign policy since the administration of George Washington. Both branches have "the constitutional means and personal motivations" to assert their will. Note that neither report sees the episode as evidence that we need constitutional reform. Many contemporary "Wilsonians" interpret Iran-Contra as evidence of the need for reform, but, as usual, their arguments have fallen on deaf ears. Most of those who feel that the Reagan administration violated the norms of American constitutionalism in Iran-Contra have celebrated the Madisonian system's capacity to ferret out the wrongdoing and expose it to public scrutiny and judicial action.

The dispute over the *Grove City College* case is a nearly perfect illustration of policy-making in the American compound Republic. The argument is all about how much power the central government should exercise to promote equality. Congress has passed in recent years a number of laws mandating equal access to federally funded facilities. The Supreme Court in *Grove City College v. Bell* (1984) interpreted these statutes in a way Congress did not like. Congress passed another statute, saying in effect, "let us be quite clear about what we mean." The president then vetoed the law. Then, Congress overrode his veto. Confused? Nobody ever argued that the Madisonian system is simple. "Wilsonians" argue that episodes like this are messy, protracted, and confusing. They are right. Yet, the best evidence is that Americans do not want what Wilson admired so much about Britain—"one supreme ultimate head," to settle policy disputes quickly and authoritatively. They remain so suspicious of concentrated power that they are willing to pay a considerable price to avoid it.

Our selections on federalism illustrate the ongoing process of sorting out the Constitution's fuzzy division of powers between the nation and the states. Madison outlines the framers' original conception of "dual federalism" in which the nation and the states have different spheres of authority. A strong nationalist at the time of this writing, he no doubt gilds the lily a bit in reassuring the Antifederalists that Americans will continue to hold their first allegiance to the states. Daniel Elazar, writing in the 1960s when many thought the role of the states was being eroded by new federal policies, reminds us of the many reasons why the states will always play an important role in American politics. Writing at the end of the Reagan era, David Walker summarizes the status of federalism today. The Reagan administration's efforts to reverse the expansion of the federal government and empower the states has had some effect, but the changes are well short of the rhetorical claims of a "Reagan Revolution." Finally, a recent journalistic account shows state and local officials trying to cope a bit more for themselves in an era of federal fiscal stringency.

20

JAMES MADISON

Separation of the Departments of Power

From *Federalist Paper* 51

————

No. 51: Madison

TO WHAT EXPEDIENT, then, shall we finally resort, for maintaining in practice the necessary partition of power among the several departments as laid down in the Constitution? The only answer that can be given is that as all these exterior provisions are found to be inadequate the defect must be supplied, by so contriving the interior structure of the government as that its several constituent parts may, by their mutual relations, be the means of keeping each other in their proper places. Without presuming to undertake a full development of this important idea I will hazard a few general observations which may perhaps place it in a clearer light, and enable us to form a more correct judgment of the principles and structure of the government planned by the convention.

In order to lay a due foundation for that separate and distinct exercise of the different powers of government, which to a certain extent is admitted on all hands to be essential to the preservation of liberty, it is evident that each department should have a will of its own; and consequently should be so constituted that the members of each should have as little agency as possible in the appointment of the members of the others. Were this principle rigorously adhered to, it would require that all the appointments for the supreme executive, legislative, and judiciary magistracies should be drawn from the same fountain of authority, the people, through channels having no communication whatever with one another. Perhaps such a plan of constructing the several departments would be less difficult in practice than it may in contemplation appear. Some difficulties, however, and some additional expense would attend the execution of it. Some deviations, therefore, from the principle must be admitted. In the constitution of the judiciary department in particular, it might be inexpedient to insist rigorously on the principle: first, because peculiar qualifications being essential in the members, the primary consideration ought to be to select that mode of choice which best secures these qualifications; second, because the permanent tenure by which the appointments are held in that department must soon destroy all sense of dependence on the authority conferring them.

It is equally evident that the members of each department should be as little dependent as possible on those of the others for the emoluments annexed to their offices. Were the executive magistrate, or the judges, not independent of the legislature in this particular, their independence in every other would be merely nominal.

But the great security against a gradual concentration of the several powers in the same department consists in giving to those who administer each department the necessary constitutional means and personal motives to resist encroachments of the others. The provision for defense must in this, as in all other cases, be made commensurate to the danger of attack. Ambition must be made to counteract ambition. The interest of the man must be connected with the constitutional rights of the place. It may be a reflection on human nature that such devices should be necessary to control the abuses of government. But what is government itself but the greatest of all reflections on human nature? If men were angels, no government would be necessary. If angels were to govern men, neither external nor internal controls on government would be necessary. In framing a government which is to be administered by men over men, the great difficulty lies in this: you must first enable the government to control the governed; and in the next place oblige it to control itself. A dependence on the people is, no doubt, the primary control on the government; but experience has taught mankind the necessity of auxiliary precautions.

This policy of supplying, by opposite and rival interests, the defect of better motives, might be traced through the whole system of human affairs, private as well as public. We see it particularly displayed in all the subordinate distributions of power, where the constant aim is to divide and arrange the several offices in such a manner as that each may be a check on the other—that the private interest of every individual may be a sentinel over the public rights.

These inventions of prudence cannot be less requisite in the distribution of the supreme powers of the State.

But it is not possible to give to each department an equal power of self-defense. In republican government, the legislative authority necessarily predominates. The remedy for this inconveniency is to divide the legislature into different branches; and to render them, by different modes of election and different principles of action, as little connected with each other as the nature of their common functions and their common dependence on the society will admit. It may even be necessary to guard against dangerous encroachments by still further precautions. As the weight of the legislative authority requires that it should be thus divided, the weakness of the executive may require, on the other hand, that it should be fortified. An absolute negative on the legislature appears, at first view, to be the natural defense with which the executive magistrate should be armed. But perhaps it would be neither altogether safe nor alone sufficient. On ordinary occasions it might not be exerted with the requisite firmness, and on extraordinary occasions it might be perfidiously abused. May not this defect of an absolute negative be supplied by some qualified connection between this weaker department and the weaker branch of the stronger department, by which the latter may be led to support the constitutional rights of the former, without being too much detached from the rights of its own department?

If the principles on which these observations are founded be just, as I persuade myself they are, and they be applied as a criterion to the several State constitutions, and to the federal Constitution, it will be found that if the latter does not perfectly correspond with them, the former are infinitely less able to bear such a test.

There are, moreover, two considerations particularly applicable to the federal system of America, which place that system in a very interesting point of view.

First. In a single republic, all the power surrendered by the people is submitted to the administration of a single government; and the usurpations are guarded against by a division of the government into distinct and separate departments. In the compound republic of America, the power surrendered by the people is first divided between two distinct governments, and then the portion allotted to each subdivided among distinct and separate departments. Hence a double security arises to the rights of the people. The different governments will control each other, at the same time that each will be controlled by itself.

Second. It is of great importance in a republic not only to guard the society against the oppression of its rulers, but to guard one part of the society against the injustice of the other part. Different interests necessarily exist in different classes of citizens. If a majority be united by a common interest, the rights of the minority will be insecure. There are but two methods of providing against this evil: the one by creating a will in the community independent of the majority—that is, of the society itself; the other, by comprehending in the society so many separate descriptions of citizens as will render an unjust combination of a majority of the whole very improbable, if not impracticable. The first method prevails in all governments possessing an hereditary or self-appointed authority. This, at best, is but a precarious security; because a power independent of the society may as well espouse the unjust views of the major as the rightful interests of the minor party, and may possibly be turned against both parties. The second method will be exemplified in the federal republic of the United States. Whilst all authority in it will be derived from and dependent on the society, the society itself will be broken into so many parts, interests and classes of citizens, that the rights of individuals, or of the minority, will be in little danger from interested combinations of the majority. In a free government the security for civil rights must be the same as that for religious rights. It consists in the one case in the multiplicity of interests, and in the other in the multiplicity of sects. The degree of security in both cases will depend on the number of interests and sects; and this may be presumed to depend on the extent of country and number of people comprehended under the same government. This view of the subject must particularly recommend a proper federal system to all the sincere and considerate friends of republican government, since it shows that in exact proportion as the territory of the Union may be formed into more circumscribed Confederacies, or States, oppressive combinations of a majority will be facilitated; the best security, under the republican forms, for the rights of every class of citizen, will be diminished; and consequently the stability and independence of some member of the government, the only other security, must be proportionally increased. Justice is the end of government. It is the end of civil society. It ever has been and ever will be pursued until it be obtained, or until liberty be lost in the pursuit. In a society under the forms of which the stronger faction can readily unite and oppress

the weaker, anarchy may as truly be said to reign as in a state of
nature, where the weaker individual is not secured against the
violence of the stronger; and as, in the latter state, even the stronger
individuals are prompted, by the uncertainty of their condition, to
submit to a government which may protect the weak as well as
themselves; so, in the former state, will the more powerful factions
or parties be gradually induced, by a like motive, to wish for a
government which will protect all parties, the weaker as well as the
more powerful. It can be little doubted that if the State of Rhode
Island was separated from the Confederacy and left to itself, the
insecurity of rights under the popular form of government within
such narrow limits would be displayed by such reiterated oppressions of factious majorities that some power altogether independent
of the people would soon be called for by the voice of the very
factions whose misrule had proved the necessity of it. In the extended republic of the United States, and among the great variety
of interests, parties, and sects which it embraces, a coalition of a
majority of the whole society could seldom take place on any
other principles than those of justice and the general good; whilst
there being thus less danger to a minor from the will of a major
party, there must be less pretext, also, to provide for the security
of the former, by introducing into the government a will not
dependent on the latter, or, in other words, a will independent of
the society itself. It is no less certain than it is important, notwithstanding the contrary opinions which have been entertained, that
the larger the society, provided it lie within a practicable sphere,
the more duly capable it will be of self-government. And happily
for the *republican cause,* the practicable sphere may be carried to a
very great extent by a judicious modification and mixture of the
federal principle.   *Publius*

21

WOODROW WILSON

From *Congressional Government*

———

I KNOW OF few things harder to state clearly and within
reasonable compass than just how the nation keeps control of policy

in spite of these hide-and-seek vagaries of authority. Indeed, it is doubtful if it does keep control through all the roundabout paths which legislative and executive responsibility are permitted to take. It must follow Congress somewhat blindly; Congress is known to obey without altogether understanding its Committees: and the Committees must consign the execution of their plans to officials who have opportunities not a few to hoodwink them. At the end of these blind processes is it probable that the ultimate authority, the people, is quite clear in its mind as to what has been done or what may be done another time? Take, for example, financial policy,—a very fair example, because, as I have shown, the legislative stages of financial policy are more talked about than any other congressional business, though for that reason an extreme example. If, after appropriations and adjustments of taxation have been tardily and in much tribulation of scheming and argument agreed upon by the House, the imperative suggestions and stubborn insistence of the Senate confuse matters till hardly the Conference Committees themselves know clearly what the outcome of the disagreements has been; and if, when these compromise measures are launched as laws, the method of their execution is beyond the view of the Houses, in the semi-privacy of the departments, how is the comprehension—not to speak of the will—of the people to keep any sort of hold upon the course of affairs? There are no screws of responsibility which they can turn upon the consciences or upon the official thumbs of the congressional Committees principally concerned. Congressional Committees are nothing to the nation; they are only pieces of the interior mechanism of Congress. To Congress they stand or fall. And, since Congress itself can scarcely be sure of having its own way with them, the constituencies are manifestly unlikely to be able to govern them. As for the departments, the people can hardly do more in drilling them to unquestioning obedience and docile efficiency than Congress can. Congress is, and must be, in these matters the nation's eyes and voice. If it cannot see what goes wrong and cannot get itself heeded when it commands, the nation likewise is both blind and dumb.

This, plainly put, is the practical result of the piecing of authority, the cutting of it up into small bits, which is contrived in our constitutional system. Each branch of the government is fitted out with a small section of responsibility, whose limited opportunities afford to the conscience of each many easy escapes. Every suspected culprit may shift the responsibility upon his fellows. Is Congress rated for corrupt or imperfect or foolish legislation? It may urge

that it has to follow hastily its Committees or do nothing at all
but talk; how can it help it if a stupid Committee leads it unawares
into unjust or fatuous enterprises? Does administration blunder
and run itself into all sorts of straits? The Secretaries hasten to
plead the unreasonable or unwise commands of Congress, and
Congress falls to blaming the Secretaries. The Secretaries aver that
the whole mischief might have been avoided if they had only been
allowed to suggest the proper measures; and the men who framed
the existing measures in their turn avow their despair of good
government so long as they must intrust all their plans to the
bungling incompetence of men who are appointed by and responsible to somebody else. How is the schoolmaster, the nation, to
know which boy needs the whipping?

Moreover, it is impossible to deny that this division of authority
and concealment of responsibility are calculated to subject the government to a very distressing paralysis in moments of emergency.
There are few, if any, important steps that can be taken by any
one branch of the government without the consent or cooperation
of some other branch. Congress must act through the President
and his Cabinet; the President and his Cabinet must wait upon the
will of Congress. There is no one supreme, ultimate head—whether
magistrate or representative body—which can decide at once and
with conclusive authority what shall be done at those times when
some decision there must be, and that immediately. Of course this
lack is of a sort to be felt at all times, in seasons of tranquil rounds
of business as well as at moments of sharp crisis; but in times of
sudden exigency it might prove fatal,—fatal either in breaking
down the system or in failing to meet the emergency. Policy cannot
be either prompt or straightforward when it must serve many
masters. It must either equivocate, or hesitate, or fail altogether. It
may set out with clear purpose from Congress, but get waylaid or
maimed by the Executive.

If there be one principle clearer than another, it is this: that in
any business, whether of government or of mere merchandising,
somebody must be trusted, in order that when things go wrong it
may be quite plain who should be punished. In order to drive
trade at the speed and with the success you desire, you must confide
without suspicion in your chief clerk, giving him the power to
ruin you, because you thereby furnish him with a motive for serving you. His reputation, his own honor or disgrace, all his own
commercial prospects, hang upon your success. And human nature

is much the same in government as in the dry-goods trade. *Power and strict accountability for its use* are the essential constituents of good government. A sense of highest responsibility, a dignifying and elevating sense of being trusted, together with a consciousness of being in an official station so conspicuous that no faithful discharge of duty can go unacknowledged and unrewarded, and no breach of trust undiscovered and unpunished,—these are the influences, the only influences, which foster practical, energetic, and trustworthy statesmanship. The best rulers are always those to whom great power is entrusted in such a manner as to make them feel that they will surely be abundantly honored and recompensed for a just and patriotic use of it, and to make them know that nothing can shield them from full retribution for every abuse of it.

It is, therefore, manifestly a radical defect in our federal system that it parcels out power and confuses responsibility as it does. The main purpose of the Convention of 1787 seems to have been to accomplish this grievous mistake. The "literary theory" of checks and balances is simply a consistent account of what our constitution-makers tried to do; and those checks and balances have proved mischievous just to the extent to which they have succeeded in establishing themselves as realities. It is quite safe to say that were it possible to call together again the members of that wonderful Convention to view the work of their hands in the light of the century that has tested it, they would be the first to admit that the only fruit of dividing power had been to make it irresponsible....

It was something more than natural that the Convention of 1787 should desire to erect a Congress which would not be subservient and an executive which could not be despotic. And it was equally to have been expected that they should regard an absolute separation of these two great branches of the system as the only effectual means for the accomplishment of that much desired end. It was impossible that they could believe that executive and legislature could be brought into close relations of cooperation and mutual confidence without being tempted, nay, even bidden, to collude. How could either maintain its independence of action unless each were to have the guaranty of the Constitution that its own domain should be absolutely safe from invasion, its own prerogatives absolutely free from challenge? "They shrank from placing sovereign power anywhere. They feared that it would generate tyranny; George III. had been a tyrant to them, and come what might they would not make a George III." They would conquer, by dividing, the power they so much feared to see in any single hand....

The natural, the inevitable tendency of every system of self-government like our own and the British is to exalt the representative body, the people's parliament, to a position of absolute supremacy.... Our Constitution, like every other constitution which puts the authority to make laws and the duty of controlling the public expenditure into the hands of a popular assembly, practically sets that assembly to rule the affairs of the nation as supreme overlord. But, by separating it entirely from its executive agencies, it deprives it of the opportunity and means for making its authority complete and convenient. The constitutional machinery is left of such a pattern that other forces less than that of Congress may cross and compete with Congress, though they are too small to overcome or long offset it; and the result is simply an unpleasant, wearing friction which, with other adjustments, more felicitous and equally safe, might readily be avoided....

The dangers of this serious imperfection in our governmental machinery have not been clearly demonstrated in our experience hitherto; but now their delayed fulfillment seems to be close at hand. The plain tendency is towards a centralization of all the greater powers of government in the hands of the federal authorities, and towards the practical confirmation of those prerogatives of supreme overlordship which Congress has been gradually arrogating to itself. The central government is constantly becoming stronger and more active, and Congress is establishing itself as the one sovereign authority in that government. In constitutional theory and in the broader features of past practice, ours has been what Mr. Bagehot has called a "composite" government.* Besides state and federal authorities to dispute as to sovereignty, there have been within the federal system itself rival and irreconcilable powers. But gradually the strong are overcoming the weak. If the signs of the times are to be credited, we are fast approaching an adjustment of sovereignty quite as "simple" as need be. Congress is not only to retain the authority it already possesses, but is to be brought again and again face to face with still greater demands upon its energy, its wisdom, and its conscience, is to have ever-

---

* Walter Bagehot (1826–1877), British economist, political theorist, and journalist, wrote *The English Constitution,* a book that had great influence on the young Woodrow Wilson. The idealized picture of the virtues of the British polity that informs *Congressional Government* is straight out of Bagehot.—EDS.

widening duties and responsibilities thrust upon it, without being granted a moment's opportunity to look back from the plough to which it has set its hands.

The sphere and influence of national administration and national legislation are widening rapidly. Our populations are growing at such a rate that one's reckoning staggers at counting the possible millions that may have a home and a work on this continent ere fifty more years shall have filled their short span. The East will not always be the centre of national life. The South is fast accumulating wealth, and will faster recover influence. The West has already achieved a greatness which no man can gainsay, and has in store a power of future growth which no man can estimate. Whether these sections are to be harmonious or dissentient depends almost entirely upon the methods and policy of the federal government. If that government be not careful to keep within its own proper sphere and prudent to square its policy by rules of national welfare, sectional lines must and will be known; citizens of one part of the country may look with jealousy and even with hatred upon their fellow-citizens of another part; and faction must tear and dissension distract a country which Providence would bless, but which man may curse. The government of a country so vast and various must be strong, prompt, wieldy, and efficient. Its strength must consist in the certainty and uniformity of its purposes, in its accord with national sentiment, in its unhesitating action, and in its honest aims. It must be steadied and approved by open administration diligently obedient to the more permanent judgments of public opinion; and its only active agency, its representative chambers, must be equipped with something besides abundant powers of legislation.

As at present constituted, the federal government lacks strength because its powers are divided, lacks promptness because its authorities are multiplied, lacks wieldiness because its processes are roundabout, lacks efficiency because its responsibility is indistinct and its action without competent direction. It is a government in which every officer may talk about every other officer's duty without having to render strict account for not doing his own, and in which the masters are held in check and offered contradiction by the servants. Mr. Lowell has called it "government by declamation." Talk is not sobered by any necessity imposed upon those who utter it to suit their actions to their words. There is no day of reckoning for words spoken. The speakers of a congressional majority may, without risk of incurring ridicule or discredit, condemn what their own Committees are doing; and the spokesmen of a minority may urge what contrary courses they please with a well-grounded assurance that what they say will be forgotten before they can be called upon to put it into practice. Nobody stands sponsor for the policy of the government. A dozen men originate it; a dozen compromises twist and alter it; a dozen offices whose names are scarcely known outside of Washington put it into execution. . . .

An intelligent observer of our politics has declared that there is in the United States "a class, including thousands and tens of thousands of the best men in the country, who think it possible to enjoy the fruits of good government without working for them." Every one who has seen beyond the outside of our American life must recognize the truth of this; to explain it is to state the sum of all the most valid criticisms of congressional government. Public opinion has no easy vehicle for its judgments, no quick channels for its action. Nothing about the system is direct and simple. Authority is perplexingly subdivided and distributed, and responsibility has to be hunted down in out-of-the-way corners. So that the sum of the whole matter is that the means of working for the fruits of good government are not readily to be found. The average citizen may be excused for esteeming government at best but a haphazard affair, upon which his vote and all of his influence can have but little effect. How is his choice of a representative in Congress to affect the policy of the country as regards the questions in which he is most interested, if the man for whom he votes has no chance of getting on the Standing Committee which has virtual charge of those questions? How is it to make any difference who is chosen President? Has the President any very great authority in matters of vital policy? It seems almost a thing of despair to get any assurance that any vote he may cast will even in an infinitesimal degree affect the essential courses of administration. There are so many cooks mixing their ingredients in the national broth that it seems hopeless, this thing of changing one cook at a time.

The charm of our constitutional ideal has now been long enough wound up to enable sober men who do not believe in political witchcraft to judge what it has accomplished, and is likely still to accomplish, without further winding. The Constitution is not honored by blind worship. The more open-eyed we become, as a nation, to its defects, and the prompter we grow in applying with the unhesitating courage of conviction all thoroughly-tested or well-considered expedients necessary to make self-government among us a straightforward thing of simple method, single, unstinted power, and clear responsibility, the nearer will we approach to the sound sense and practical genius of the great and honorable statesmen of 1787. And the first step towards emancipation from the timidity and false pride which have led us to seek to thrive despite the defects of our national system rather than seem to deny its perfection is a fearless criticism of that system. When we shall have examined all its parts without sentiment, and gauged all its functions by the standards of practical common sense, we shall have established anew our right to the claim of political sagacity; and it will remain only to act intelligently upon what our opened eyes have seen in order to prove again the justice of our claim to political genius.

22

Report of the Congressional Committees Investigating the Iran-Contra Affair with the Supplemental, Minority and Additional Views

Findings and Conclusions

THE COMMON INGREDIENTS of the Iran and Contra policies were secrecy, deception, and disdain for the law.[*] A small group of senior officials believed that they alone knew what was right. They viewed knowledge of their actions by others in the Government as a threat to their objectives. They told neither the Secretary of State, the Congress nor the American people of their

---

[*] The Iran-Contra Affair began in 1985 with the Reagan administration's secret shipment of arms to Iran in order to encourage Iran's release of American hostages. Some of the money from the arms sale was used to help the Contras, American-supported rebels who fought against the leftist Sandinista government in Nicaragua. Congressional hearings on the Iran-Contra Affair in 1987 examined the actions of government officials, from National Security Council assistant Oliver North on up to President Reagan.—EDS.

actions. When exposure was threatened, they destroyed official documents and lied to Cabinet officials, to the public, and to elected representatives in Congress. They testified that they even withheld key facts from the President.

The United States Constitution specifies the process by which laws and policy are to be made and executed. Constitutional process is the essence of our democracy and our democratic form of Government is the basis of our strength. Time and again we have learned that a flawed process leads to bad results, and that a lawless process leads to worse....

The Administration's departure from democratic processes created the conditions for policy failure, and led to contradictions which undermined the credibility of the United States....

It was stated on several occasions that the confusion, secrecy and deception surrounding the aid program for the Nicaraguan freedom fighters was produced in part by Congress' shifting positions on Contra aid.

But Congress' inconsistency mirrored the chameleon-like nature of the rationale offered for granting assistance in the first instance. Initially, Congress was told that our purpose was simply to interdict the flow of weapons from Nicaragua into El Salvador. Then Congress was told that our purpose was to harrass the Sandinistas to prevent them from consolidating their power and exporting their revolution. Eventually, Congress was told that our purpose was to eliminate all foreign forces from Nicaragua, to reduce the size of the Sandinista armed forces, and to restore the democratic reforms pledged by the Sandinistas during the overthrow of the Somoza regime.

Congress had cast a skeptical eye upon each rationale proffered by the Administration. It suspected that the Administration's true purpose was identical to that of the Contras—the overthrow of the Sandinista regime itself. Ultimately Congress yielded to domestic political pressure to discontinue assistance to the Contras, but Congress was unwilling to bear responsibility for the loss of Central America to communist military and political forces. So Congress compromised, providing in 1985 humanitarian aid to the Contras; and the NSC [National Security Council] staff provided what Congress prohibited: lethal support for the Contras.

Compromise is no excuse for violation of law and deceiving Congress. A law is no less a law because it is passed by a slender majority, or because Congress is open-minded about its reconsideration in the future. . . .

The NSC staff turned to private parties and third countries to do the Government's business. Funds denied by Congress were obtained by the Administration from third countries and private citizens. . . .

The solicitation of foreign funds by an Administration to pursue foreign policy goals rejected by Congress is dangerous and improper. . . .

Moreover, under the Constitution only Congress can provide funds for the Executive branch. The Framers intended Congress' "power of the purse" to be one of the principal checks on Executive action. It was designed, among other things, to prevent the Executive from involving this country unilaterally in a foreign conflict. The Constitutional plan does not prohibit a President from asking a foreign state, or anyone else, to contribute funds to a third party. But it does prohibit such solicitation where the United States exercises control over their receipt and expenditure. By circumventing Congress' power of the purse through third-country and private contributions to the Contras, the Administration undermined a cardinal principle of the Constitution. . . .

The Constitution of the United States gives important powers to both the President and the Congress in the making of foreign policy. The President is the principal architect of foreign policy in consultation with the Congress. The policies of the United States cannot succeed unless the President and the Congress work together.

Yet, in the Iran-Contra Affair, Administration officials holding no elected office repeatedly evidenced disrespect for Congress' efforts to perform its Constitutional oversight role in foreign policy:

• Poindexter testified, referring to his efforts to keep the covert action in support of the Contras from Congress: "I simply did not want any outside interference."

• North testified: "I didn't want to tell Congress anything" about this covert action.

• Abrams acknowledged in his testimony that, unless Members of Congressional Committees asked "exactly the right question, using exactly the right words, they weren't going to get the right answers," regarding solicitation of third-countries for Contra support.

• And numerous other officials made false statements to, and misled, the Congress.

Several witnesses at the hearings stated or implied that foreign policy should be left solely to the President to do as he chooses, arguing that shared powers have no place in a dangerous world. But the theory of our Constitution is the opposite: policies formed through consultation and the democratic process are better and wiser than those formed without it. Circumvention of Congress is self-defeating, for no foreign policy can succeed without the bipartisan support of Congress.

In a system of shared powers, decision-making requires mutual respect between the branches of government.

The Committees were reminded by Secretary Shultz during the hearings that "trust is the coin of the realm." Democratic government is not possible without trust between the branches of government and between the government and the people. Sometimes that trust is misplaced and the system falters. But for officials to work outside the system because it does not produce the results they seek is a prescription for failure....

Under our Constitution, both the Congress and the Executive are given specific foreign policy powers. The Constitution does not name one or the other branch as the exclusive actor in foreign policy. Each plays a role in our system of checks and balances to ensure that our foreign policy is effective, sustainable and in accord with our national interests.

Key participants in the Iran-Contra Affair had serious misconceptions about the roles of Congress and the President in the making of foreign policy....

The argument that Congress has but a minor role in foreign policymaking is contradicted by the language of the Constitution, and by over 200 years of history. It is also shortsighted and ultimately self-defeating. American foreign policy and our system of government cannot succeed unless the President and Congress work together.... During the public hearings, both Poindexter and North characterized Congress as meddlers in the President's arena....

North also repeatedly stated his view that "it was within the purview of the President of the United States to conduct secret activities ... to further the policy goals of the United States." North claimed that the President had the power under the Constitution to conduct "secret diplomacy" because "the President can do what he wants with his own staff." He stated that the President had a "very wide mandate to carry out activities, secretly or publicly, as he chooses."... The Constitution itself gives no support to the argument that the President has a mandate so broad. The words "foreign policy" do not appear in the Constitution, and the Constitution does not designate the President as the sole or dominant actor in foreign policy.

The only foreign policy powers expressly granted to the Executive in the Constitution are the powers to nominate Ambassadors, to negotiate treaties, and to direct the Armed Forces as Commander-in-Chief. Two of these powers are specifically conditioned on Senate approval: the Senate, through its power of advise and consent, can confirm or reject Ambassadors and ratify or reject treaties.

On the other hand, the Constitution expressly grants Congress the power to regulate foreign commerce, to raise and support armies, to provide and maintain a navy, and to declare war. Congress is given the exclusive power of the purse. The Executive may not spend funds on foreign policy projects except pursuant to an appropriation by Congress.... In testifying before these Committees, North and Poindexter indicated their view that whatever power Congress may have in foreign policy derived solely from its power of the purse. They reasoned that so long as public money was not expended, Congress had no role and the President was free to pursue his foreign policy goals using private and third-country funds....

These claims by North and Poindexter strike at the very heart of the system of checks and balances. To permit the President and his aides to carry out covert actions by using funds obtained from outside Congress undermines the Framers' belief that "the purse and the sword must never be in the same hands."... By seeking private and third-country aid for the Contras without Congressional notification—much less approval—the Administration did more than engage in an unfortunate fundraising effort that opened the door to expectations of secret return favors. This clandestine financing operation undermined the powers of Congress as a co-equal branch and subverted the Constitution.... The sharing of power over foreign policy requires consultation, trust, and coordination. As President Reagan told a joint session of Congress on April 27, 1983: "The Congress shares both the power and the responsibility for our foreign policy."... The questions before these Committees concerning the foreign policy roles of Congress and the President are not abstract issues for legal scholars. They are practical considerations essential to the making of good foreign policy and the effective functioning of government. The theory of the Constitution is that policies formed through consultation and the democratic process are better, and wiser, than those formed without it.

The Constitution divided foreign policy powers between the legislative and executive branches of government. That division of power is fundamental to this system, and acts as a check on the actions of each branch of government. Those who would take shortcuts in the constitutional process—mislead the Congress or withhold information—show their contempt for what the Framers created. Shortcuts that bypass the checks and balances of the system, and excessive secrecy by those who serve the President, do not strengthen the President. They weaken the President and the constitutional system of government.

Minority Report

We emphatically reject the idea that through these mistakes, the executive branch subverted the law, undermined the Constitution, or threatened democracy. The President is every bit as much of an elected representative of the people as is a Member of Congress. In fact, he and the Vice President are the only officials elected by the whole Nation. Nevertheless, we do believe the mistakes relate in a different way to the issue of democratic accountability. They provide a good starting point for seeing what both sides of the great legislative-executive branch divide must do to improve the way the Government makes foreign policy.... Congress has a hard time even conceiving of itself as contributing to the problem of democratic accountability. But the record of ever-changing policies toward Central America that contributed to the NSC staff's behavior is symptomatic of a frequently recurring problem. When Congress is narrowly divided over highly emotional issues, it frequently ends up passing intentionally ambiguous laws or amendments that postpone the day of decision. In foreign policy, those decisions often take the form of restrictive amendments on money bills that are open to being amended again *every year,* with new, and equally ambiguous, language replacing the old.... The Constitution created the Presidency to be a separate branch of government whose occupant would have substantial discretionary power to act. He was not given the power of an 18th century monarch, but neither was he meant to be a creature of Congress. The country needs a President who can exercise the powers the Framers intended. As long as any President has those powers, there will be mistakes. It would be disastrous to respond to the possibility of error by further restraining and limiting the powers of the office. Then, instead of seeing occasional actions turn out to be wrong, we would be increasing the probability that future Presidents would be unable to act decisively, thus guaranteeing ourselves a perpetually paralyzed, reactive, and unclear foreign policy in which mistake by inaction would be the order of the day.... Judgments about the Iran-Contra Affair ultimately must rest upon one's views about the proper roles of Congress and the President in foreign policy. There were many statements during the public hearings, for example, about the rule of law. But the fundamental law of the land is the Constitution. Unconstitutional statutes violate the rule of law every bit as much as do willful violations of constitutional statutes. It is essential, therefore, to frame any discussion of what happened with a proper analysis of the Constitutional allocation of legislative and executive power in foreign affairs.

One point stands out from the historical record: the Constitution's Framers expected the President to be much more than a minister or clerk. The President was supposed to execute the laws, but that was only the beginning. He also was given important powers, independent of the legislature's, and these substantively were focused on foreign policy....

The need for an effective foreign policy, it turned out, was one of the main reasons the country needs an "energetic government," according to Alexander Hamilton in *Federalist* Nos. 22 and 23. Madison made the same point in No. 37: "Energy in Government is essential to that security against external and internal danger, and to that prompt and salutary execution of the laws, which enter into the very definition of good Government." The relevance of these observations about the *government's* power is that the Framers saw energy as being primarily an executive branch characteristic.

Energy is the main theme of *Federalist* No. 70 ("energy in the executive is a leading character in the definition of good government.") It is said to be important primarily when "decision, activity, secrecy, and dispatch" were needed.... Presidents asserted their constitutional independence from Congress early. They engaged in secret diplomacy and intelligence activities, and refused to share the results with Congress if they saw fit. They unilaterally established U.S. military and diplomatic policy with respect to foreign belligerent states, in quarrels involving the United States, and in quarrels involving only third parties. They enforced this policy abroad, using force if necessary. They engaged U.S. troops abroad to serve American interests without congressional approval, and in a number of cases apparently against explicit directions from Congress. They also had agents engage in what would commonly be referred to as covert actions, again without Congressional approval. In short, Presidents exercised a broad range of foreign policy powers for which they neither sought nor received Congressional sanction through statute.

This history speaks volumes about the Constitution's allocation of powers between the branches. It leaves little, if any, doubt that the President was expected to have the primary role of conducting the foreign policy of the United States. Congressional actions to limit the President in this area therefore should be reviewed with a considerable degree of skepticism. If they interfere with core presidential foreign policy functions, they should be struck down. Moreover, the lesson of our constitutional history is that doubtful cases should be decided in favor of the President.... The Constitution gives important foreign policy powers both to Congress and to the President. Neither can accomplish very much over the long term by trying to go it alone. The President cannot use the country's resources to carry out policy without congressional appropriations. At the same time, Congress can prohibit some actions, and it can influence others, but it cannot act by itself, and it is not institutionally designed to accept political responsibility for specific actions. Action or implementation is a peculiarly executive branch function.

The Constitution's requirement for cooperation does not negate the separation of powers. Neither branch can be permitted to usurp functions that belong to the other. As we have argued throughout, and as the Supreme Court reaffirmed in 1983, "the powers delegated to the three branches are functionally identifiable." The executive branch's functions are the ones most closely related to the need for secrecy, efficiency, dispatch, and the acceptance by one person, the President, of political responsibility for the result. This basic framework must be preserved if the country is to have an effective foreign policy in the future.

23

NADINE COHODAS
MARK WILLEN

Reagan Vetoes *Grove City* Bill: Override Vote Set for March 22; Congress Overrides Reagan's *Grove City* Veto

---

Reagan Vetoes

PRESIDENT REAGAN March 16 vetoed a civil rights bill (S 557) that had been passed overwhelmingly by the House and Senate.

And while supporters of the bill moved quickly to override, their efforts were derailed by a handful of Senate Republicans who oppose the legislation.

Sponsors say the measure would restore the broad enforcement of four civil rights laws, but Reagan said it "would vastly and unjustifiably expand the power of the federal goverment."...

After a day of debate on the veto—most of it between chief sponsor Edward M. Kennedy, D-Mass., and chief adversary Orrin G. Hatch, R-Utah—the Senate agreed to vote on the override at noon March 22.

The House plans to take up the matter later that day.

Republicans and Democrats in both chambers say they expect Reagan's veto to be overridden. S 557 passed the Senate Jan. 28 by a vote of 75-14, with seven cosponsors absent. The House passed the bill March 2 by a vote of 315-98. After the House action, Sen. Rudy Boschwitz, R-Minn., chairman of the National Republican Senatorial Committee, wrote Reagan urging him to sign the bill, and on March 17 he went to the Senate floor to urge colleagues to override the veto....

Members of both parties see the matter as a potential campaign-year issue. Republicans up for re-election don't want to be labeled anti-civil rights, and they fear that Democrats will try to exploit the issue if the veto is sustained. Grass-roots organizations of women, blacks, the disabled and the elderly have been mobilized for months over the bill and are expected to remain active....

S 557 would overturn the Supreme Court's 1984 decision, *Grove City College v. Bell,* which limited the enforcement of the four civil rights laws. The court ruled that only the "program or activity" receiving federal aid—not the entire institution—was covered by the laws....

To overturn the *Grove City* ruling, S 557 would make clear that if one part of an entity receives federal aid, the entire entity must not discriminate....

Reagan ... said Congress had sent him a bill that would give the federal government "power over the decisions and affairs of private organizations, such as churches and synagogues, farms, businesses and state and local governments."...

"The bill presented to me would diminish substantially the freedom and independence of religious institutions in our society," Reagan added....

While debate was under way on the Senate floor March 17, there was political skirmishing in Senate and House offices over the Falwell letter.* The letter contended that S 557, "along with present court cases, will protect active homosexuals, transvestites, alcoholics and drug addicts, among others, under the government's anti-discrimination laws. These sins will be considered to be diseases or handicaps."

House Democratic Whip Tony Coelho, Calif., circulated a response March 17, accusing Falwell of a "campaign of lies and misrepresentations" and of "bearing false witness in order to defeat a civil rights bill."

Coelho asserted: "Neither Title IX nor any of the other statutes has ever been interpreted by the courts to provide protection on the basis of sexual preference.... Nothing in the bill creates any such protection."...

*The Reverend Gerald Falwell, a Baptist minister and founder of the now-defunct organization Moral Majority, was a leading spokesman for the fundamentalist wing of the New Right in the 1970s and 80s.—Eds.

Some House Republicans said privately that the letter caused concern, but Southern Democrats John Bryant, Texas, and Rick Boucher, Va., said that as soon as members started hearing the rebuttals to Falwell's letter, their concerns lessened. Both said they had not heard of any member who had voted for S 557 who was going to switch.

Congress Overrides

The House and Senate votes to override President Reagan's veto of the *Grove City* civil rights bill may prove politically costly to some Republicans and maybe a few Democrats.

Reagan's veto forced members to choose between two unpleasant alternatives: defying a still-popular president and his vocal allies in the religious right, or opposing a civil rights bill supported by a wide array of groups representing minorities, the elderly, women and the handicapped.

"People are just scared to death to vote against a civil rights bill, no matter how bad it is," said Sen. Orrin G. Hatch, R-Utah, Reagan's point man on the *Grove City* bill.

But some were also scared, or at least reluctant, to vote against Reagan. Eight senators and 32 House members who voted for the bill the first time around switched to Reagan's side on the second round. To make up for the loss, sponsors of the bill picked up the support of seven senators and ten House members who missed the first vote, and that was enough to hand Reagan a costly and embarrassing defeat on a major domestic issue.

Complicating the decision for many members was a massive lobbying campaign organized by the Moral Majority. In the week between Reagan's veto and the vote to override, Senate and House offices were besieged with thousands of phone calls and letters from constituents worried that enactment of the bill would mean government interference in church affairs....

The Senate vote to override March 22 was 73–24, eight votes more than the two-thirds necessary. All Democrats present voted for the bill, while Republicans split 21 to 24....

The House took up the bill later the same day and voted 292–133 to override. The Democratic split was 240–10; the GOP split was 52–123....

The bill (S 557—PL 100–259) would have the effect of overturning the 1984 Supreme Court decision in *Grove City College v. Bell,* which limited the enforcement of four civil rights laws. The court ruled 6–3 that when an institution receives federal aid, only the "program or activity" actually getting the aid—not the entire institution—was covered by the laws....

To overturn *Grove City,* S 557 would make it clear that if one part of an institution or entity receives federal aid, the entire institution must not discriminate....

The override vote in the House was close, 292–133, eight votes more than the two-thirds margin. Throughout the day March 22, House sponsors showed more than a little nervousness about the outcome. The original House vote on passage March 2 was 315–98....

Reluctant to have the GOP appear as the party that opposed a civil rights bill, several Republicans strongly urged Reagan to sign the bill.

Sen. Rudy Boschwitz, Minn., chairman of the National Republican Senatorial Committee, begged Reagan not to use a veto. "I implore you to sign this bill," he wrote.

GOP Chairman Frank J. Fahrenkopf Jr. warned that a veto could hurt the party in November....

Reagan also put his own political standing in jeopardy when he vetoed the bill. This was only the ninth of Reagan's 63 vetoes to be overridden, but Reagan is finding it increasingly difficult to get his way with Congress.

On the 32 votes on which the administration has taken a position in 1988, Congress has voted with Reagan 13 times, for a presidential success rate of 40.6 percent. In 1987, Reagan's success rate was 43.5 percent, and that was the lowest success rate for a president since CQ began its voting studies in 1953.

24

JAMES MADISON
Federal and State Governments

From *Federalist Papers* 39 and 46

———

No. 39: Madison

...THE FIRST QUESTION that offers itself is whether the general form and aspect of the government be strictly republican. It is evident that no other form would be reconcilable with the genius of the people of America; with the fundamental principles of the Revolution; or with that honorable determination which animates every votary of freedom to rest all our political experiments on the capacity of mankind for self-government. If the plan of the convention, therefore, be found to depart from the republican character, its advocates must abandon it as no longer defensible.

What, then, are the distinctive characters of the republican form?...

If we resort for a criterion to the different principles on which different forms of government are established, we may define a republic to be, or at least may bestow that name on, a government which derives all its powers directly or indirectly from the great body of the people, and is administered by persons holding their offices during pleasure for a limited period, or during good behavior. It is *essential* to such a government that it be derived from the great body of the society, not from an inconsiderable proportion or a favored class of it; otherwise a handful of tyrannical nobles, exercising their oppressions by a delegation of their powers, might aspire to the rank of republicans and claim for their government the honorable title of republic. It is *sufficient* for such a government that the persons administering it be appointed, either directly or indirectly, by the people; and that they hold their appointments by either of the tenures just specified; otherwise every government in the United States, as well as every other popular government that has been or can be well organized or well executed, would be degraded from the republican character. According to the constitution of every State in the Union, some or other of the officers of government are appointed indirectly only by the people. According to most of them, the chief magistrate himself is so appointed. And according to one, this mode of appointment is extended to one of the co-ordinate branches of the legislature. According to all the constitutions, also, the tenure of the highest offices is extended to a definite period, and in many instances, both within the legislative and executive departments, to a period of years. According to the provisions of most of the constitutions, again, as well as according to the most respectable and received opinions on the subject, the members of the judiciary department are to retain their offices by the firm tenure of good behavior. . . .

"But it was not sufficient," say the adversaries of the proposed Constitution, "for the convention to adhere to the republican form. They ought with equal care to have preserved the *federal* form, which regards the Union as a *Confederacy* of sovereign states; instead of which they have framed a *national* government, which regards the Union as a *consolidation* of the States." And it is asked by what authority this bold and radical innovation was undertaken? . . .

First.—In order to ascertain the real character of the government, it may be considered in relation to the foundation on which it is to be established; to the sources from which its ordinary powers are to be drawn; to the operation of those powers; to the extent of them; and to the authority by which future changes in the government are to be introduced.

On examining the first relation, it appears, on one hand, that the Constitution is to be founded on the assent and ratification of the people of America, given by deputies elected for the special purpose; but, on the other, that this assent and ratification is to be given by the people, not as individuals composing one entire nation, but as composing the distinct and independent States to which they respectively belong. It is to be the assent and ratification of the several States, derived from the supreme authority in each State—the authority of the people themselves. The act, therefore, establishing the Constitution will not be a *national* but a *federal* act.

That it will be a federal and not a national act, as these terms are understood by the objectors—the act of the people, as forming so many independent States, not as forming one aggregate nation— is obvious from this single consideration: that it is to result neither from the decision of a *majority* of the people of the Union, nor from that of a *majority* of the States. It must result from the *unanimous* assent of the several States that are parties to it, differing not otherwise from their ordinary dissent than in its being expressed, not by the legislative authority, but by that of the people themselves.... Each State, in ratifying the Constitution, is considered as a sovereign body independent of all others, and only to be bound by its own voluntary act. In this relation, then, the new Constitution will, if established, be a *federal* and not a *national* constitution.

The next relation is to the sources from which the ordinary powers of government are to be derived. The House of Representatives will derive its powers from the people of America; and the people will be represented in the same proportion and on the same principle as they are in the legislature of a particular State. So far the government is *national, not federal.* The Senate, on the other hand, will derive its powers from the States as political and coequal societies; and these will be represented on the principle of equality in the Senate, as they now are in the existing Congress. So far the government is *federal, not national.* The executive power will be derived from a very compound source. The immediate election of the President is to be made by the States in their political characters. The votes allotted to them are in a compound ratio, which considers them partly as distinct and coequal societies, partly as unequal members of the same society. ... From this aspect of the government it appears to be of a mixed character, presenting at least as many *federal* as *national* features.... The idea of a national government involves in it not only an authority over the individual citizens, but an indefinite supremacy over all persons and things, so far as they are objects of lawful government. Among a people consolidated into one nation, this supremacy is completely vested in the national legislature. Among communities united for particular purposes, it is vested partly in the general and partly in the municipal legislatures. In the former case, all local authorities are subordinate to the supreme; and may be controlled, directed, or abolished by it at pleasure. In the latter, the local or municipal authorities form distinct and independent portions of the supremacy, no more subject, within their respective spheres, to the general authority than the general authority is subject to them, within its own sphere. In this relation, then, the proposed government cannot be deemed a *national* one; since its jurisdiction extends to certain enumerated objects only, and leaves to the several States a residuary and inviolable sovereignty over all other objects....

If we try the Constitution by its last relation to the authority by which amendments are to be made, we find it neither wholly *national* nor wholly *federal*. Were it wholly national, the supreme and ultimate authority would reside in the *majority* of the people of the Union; and this authority would be competent at all times, like that of a majority of every national society to alter or abolish its established government. Were it wholly federal, on the other hand, the concurrence of each State in the Union would be essential to every alteration that would be binding on all. The mode provided by the plan of the convention is not founded on either of these principles. In requiring more than a majority, and particularly in computing the proportion by *States,* not by *citizens,* it departs from the national and advances towards the *federal* character; in rendering the concurrence of less than the whole number of States sufficient, it loses again the *federal* and partakes of the *national* character.

The proposed Constitution, therefore, even when tested by the rules laid down by its antagonists, is, in strictness, neither a national nor a federal Constitution, but a composition of both. In its foundation it is federal, not national; in the sources from which the ordinary powers of the government are drawn, it is partly federal and partly national; in the operation of these powers, it is national, not federal; in the extent of them, again, it is federal, not national; and, finally in the authoritative mode of introducing amendments, it is neither wholly federal nor wholly national.

Publius

No. 46: *Madison*

... I proceed to inquire whether the federal government or the State governments will have the advantage with regard to the predilection and support of the people. Notwithstanding the different modes in which they are appointed, we must consider both of them as substantially dependent on the great body of the citizens of the United States. I assume this position here as it respects the first, reserving the proofs for another place. The federal and State governments are in fact but different agents and trustees of the people, constituted with different powers and designed for different purposes. The adversaries of the Constitution seem to have lost sight of the people altogether in their reasonings on this subject;

and to have viewed these different establishments not only as mutual rivals and enemies, but as uncontrolled by any common superior in their efforts to usurp the authorities of each other. These gentlemen must here be reminded of their error. They must be told that the ultimate authority, wherever the derivative may be found, resides in the people alone, and that it will not depend merely on the comparative ambition or address of the different governments whether either, or which of them, will be able to enlarge its sphere of jurisdiction at the expense of the other. Truth, no less than decency, requires that the event in every case should be supposed to depend on the sentiments and sanction of their common constituents....

Many considerations, besides those suggested on a former occasion, seem to place it beyond doubt that the first and most natural attachment of the people will be to the governments of their respective States....

If ... the people should in future become more partial to the federal than to the State governments, the change can only result from such manifest and irresistible proofs of a better administration as will overcome all their antecedent propensities. And in that case, the people ought not surely to be precluded from giving most of their confidence where they may discover it to be most due; but even in that case the State governments could have little to apprehend, because it is only within a certain sphere that the federal power can, in the nature of things, be advantageously administered.   *Publius*

25

DANIEL ELAZAR

A View from the States

From *American Federalism*

———

THE SYSTEM of state-federal relations ... is not the neat system often pictured in the textbooks. If that neat system of separate governments performing separate functions in something akin to isolation is used as the model of what federalism should be to enable the states to maintain their integrity as political systems, then the states are in great difficulty indeed. If, however, the states have found ways to function as integral political systems—civil societies, if you will—within the somewhat chaotic system of intergovernmental sharing that exists, then they are, as the saying goes, in a different ball game.... We have tried to show that the states are indeed in a different ball game and as players in that game are not doing badly at all. Viewed from the perspective of that ball game, the strength and vitality of the states—and the strength and vitality of the American system as a whole—must be assessed by different standards from those commonly used.

In the first place, the states exist. This point is no less significant for its simplicity. The fact that the states survive as going concerns (as distinct from sets of historical boundaries used for the administration of centrally directed programs) after thirty-five years of depression, global war, and then cold war, which have all functioned to reduce the domestic freedom necessary to preserve noncentralized government, is in itself testimony to their vitality as political institutions.... Every day, in many ways, the states are actively contributing to the achievement of American goals and to the continuing efforts to define those goals.

Consequently, it is a mistake to think that national adoption of goals shared by an overwhelming majority of the states is simply centralization. To believe that is to deny the operation of the dynamics of history within a federal system. Any assessment of the states' position in the federal union must be made against a background of continuous social change. It is no more reasonable to assume that the states have lost power vis-à-vis the federal government since 1789 because they can no longer maintain established churches than it is to believe that white men are no longer as free as they were in that year because they can no longer own slaves. An apparent loss of freedom in one sphere may be more than made up by gains in another. Massachusetts exercises more power over its economy today than its governors ever hoped to exercise over its churches five generations ago. National values change by popular consensus and *all* governments must adapt themselves to those changes. The success of the states is that they have been able to adapt themselves well.

Part of the states' adaptation has been manifested in their efforts to improve their institutional capabilities to handle the new tasks they have assumed. In the twentieth century, there has been an extensive and continuing reorganization of state governments leading to increased executive responsibility, greater central budgetary control, and growing expertise of state personnel (whose numbers are also increasing)....

There has also been a great and continuing increase in the states' supervision of the functions carried out in their local subdivisions. The states' role in this respect has grown as fast as or faster than that of the federal government and is often exercised more stringently, a possibility enhanced by the constitutionally unitary character of the states. The states' supervision has been increased through the provision of technical aid to their localities, through financial grants, and through control of the power to raise (or authorize the raising of) revenue for all subdivisions.

In all this, though, there remains one major unsolved problem, whose importance cannot be overemphasized: that of the metropolitan areas. By and large, the states have been unwilling or unable to do enough to meet metropolitan problems, particularly governmental ones. Here, too, some states have better records than others but none have been able to deal with metropolitan problems comprehensively and thoroughly. It is becoming increasingly clear that—whatever their successes in the past—the future role of the states will be determined by their ability to come to grips with those problems.

A fourth factor that adds to the strength and vitality of the states is the manner in which state revenues and expenditures have been expanding since the end of World War II....

Still a fifth factor is the continuing role of the states as primary managers of great programs and as important innovators in the governmental realm. Both management and innovation in education, for example, continue to be primary state responsibilities in which outside aid is used to support locally initiated ideas.

Even in areas of apparent state deficiencies, many states pursue innovative policies. Much publicity has been generated in recent years that reflects upon police procedures in certain states; yet effective actions to eliminate the death penalty have been confined to the state level. The states have also been active in developing means for releasing persons accused of crimes on their own recognizance when they cannot afford to post bail, thus reducing the imprisonment of people not yet convicted of criminal activity.

Because the states are political systems able to direct the utilization of the resources sent their way, federal grants have served as a stimulus to the development of state capabilities and, hence, have helped enhance their strength and vitality. Federal grants have helped the states in a positive way by broadening the programs they can offer their citizens and strengthening state administration of those programs. Conversely, the grants have prevented centralization of those programs and have given the states the ability to maintain their position despite the centralizing tendencies of the times.

For this reason, and because the concerns of American politics are universal ones, there is relatively little basic conflict between the federal government and the states or even between their respective interests. Most of the conflicts connected with federal-state relations are of two kinds: (1) conflicts between interests that use the federal versus state argument as a means to legitimize their demands or (2) low-level conflicts over the best way to handle specific cooperative activities. There are cases, of course, when interests representing real differences are able to align themselves with different levels of government to create serious federal-state conflict. The civil rights question in its southern manifestation is today's example of that kind of situation.

Finally, the noncentralized character of American politics has served to strengthen the states. Noncentralization makes possible intergovernment cooperation without the concomitant weakening of the smaller partners by giving those partners significant ways in which to preserve their integrity. This is because a noncentralized system functions to a great extent through bargaining and negotiation. Since its components are relatively equal in their freedom to act, it can utilize only a few of the hierarchical powers available in centralized systems. In essence, its general government can only use those powers set forth in the fundamental compact between the partners as necessary to the maintenance of the system as a whole. Stated baldly, congressional authorization of new federal programs is frequently no more than a license allowing federal authorities to begin negotiations with the states and localities....

In the last analysis, the states remain viable entities in a federal system that has every tendency toward centralization present in all strong governments. They remain viable because they exist as civil societies with political systems of their own. They maintain that existence because the American political tradition and the Constitution embodying it give the states an important place in the overall fabric of American civil society. The tradition and the Constitution remain viable because neither Capitol Hill nor the fifty state houses have alone been able to serve all the variegated interests on the American scene that compete equally well without working in partnership.

The states remain vital political systems for larger reasons as well as immediate ones, reasons that are often passed over unnoticed in the public's concern with day-to-day problems of government. These larger reasons are not new; though they have changed in certain details, they remain essentially the same as in the early days of the Union.

The states remain important in a continental nation as reflectors of sectional and regional differences that are enhanced by the growing social and economic complexity of every part of the country, even as the older cultural differences may be diminished by modern communications. They remain important as experimenters and innovators over a wider range of fields than ever before, simply because government at every level in the United States has been expanding. The role of the states as recruiters of political participants and trainers of political leaders has in no way been diminished, particularly since the number of political offices of every kind seems to be increasing at least in proportion to population growth.

In at least two ways, traditional roles of the states have been enhanced by recent trends. They have become even more active promoters and administrators of public services than ever before. In part, this is simply because governments are doing more than they had in the past, but it is also because they provide ways to increase governmental activity while maintaining noncentralized government. By handling important programs at a level that can be reached by many people, the contribute to the maintenance of a traditional interest of democratic politics, namely, the maximization of local control over the political and administrative decision-makers whose actions affect the lives of every citizen in ever-increasing ways.

As the population of the nation increases, the states become increasingly able to manage major governmental activities with the competence and expertise demanded by the metropolitan–technological frontier. At the same time, the federal government becomes further removed from popular pressures simply by virtue of the increased size of the population it must serve. The states may well be on their way to becoming the most "manageable" civil societies in the nation. Their size and scale remain comprehensible to people even as they are enabled to do more things better.

In sum, the virtue of the federal system lies in its ability to develop and maintain mechanisms vital to the perpetuation of the unique combination of governmental strength, political flexibility, and individual liberty, which has been the central concern of American politics. The American people are known to appreciate their political tradition and the Constitution. Most important, they seem to appreciate the partnership, too, in some unreasoned way, and have learned to use all its elements to reasonably satisfy their claims on government.

26

DAVID WALKER
Two Hundred Years of
American Federalism

IN BROAD operational terms, the working of the American federal system from its inception to the early 1930s adhered quite closely to the dual or compartmentalized model of federalism that the framers sought to establish in this area. Moreover, even with the marked growth of national regulatory, grant-in-aid, and subsidizing roles during the New Deal and the immediate postwar years, dual federalism in most servicing and financing areas was still part of the system as late as the early sixties. Novel federal-state (and to a much lesser extent, local) relationships emerged as a consequence of the Great Depression and World War II. The various demographic, socioeconomic, and foreign-policy pressures of the Truman and Eisenhower years generated expanded federal regulatory and promotional roles and also led to a real hike in the number of federal grants-in-aid involving federal-state collaboration in certain domestic program areas, giving rise to the new concept of "cooperative federalism." Yet, the degree of national activism by 1960 or even 1963 was moderate, even reluctant, all things considered, and the operational areas left wholly to state and local discretion and control were still very significant substantively....

American federalism and the web of federal-state relationships it engenders experienced their greatest challenges and transformation during the current intergovernmental era. By 1980, there were no vestiges of "dual federalism" in any of the arenas in which federalism functioned or attempted to function. The triumph of "cooperative federalism" was brief and transitional—leading to a "cooptive federalism" in the seventies that has not receded much during this decade of Reagan and retrenchment. Contemporary federalism still is a highly centralized one whose chief federalist feature is the one found in Michael Reagan's description of "permissive federalism": "There is a sharing of power and authority between the national and state governments, but ... the state's share rests upon the permissiveness of the national government."

But enough of labels and generalizations. What actually occurred intergovernmentally during the past twenty-three years?... The dimensions of governmental transformation that occurred during the 1964–1978 period are so numerous that it would require a volume to catalogue them. In the area of *functional federalism,* its administrative, programmatic, fiscal, and regulatory dimensions experienced major shifts from Johnson through early Carter. Both in quantitative and qualitative terms, the national government's domestic role expanded exuberantly. In its breadth and depth, it far surpassed the predecessor New Deal actions and, as later analysis of the Reagan years indicates, its "heavy-duty" domestic agenda has by no means been drastically reduced by any major devolutions of national roles and functions assumed from 1964 to 1978.

Not to be overlooked here is the fact that the states and localities assumed greater—even indispensable—fiscal, administrative, and operational roles in the overall workings of functional federalism. This development resulted from the unwillingness of the national government to expand its own responsibility for directly administering and fully funding most of its domestic programs. At the same time, the new regulatory thrusts as well as other political and judicial actions of the national government were reducing the subnational governments to not much above the level of another category of pressure group....

Thus, functional federalism appeared to be a dysfunctional federalism by the late seventies, given the heavy centralization of most basic domestic policy decisions and the near exclusive reliance on subnational governments and others to implement them. The efficiencies of a territorial division of servicing responsibilities, that a federal system helps assure, were being lost.... The deference that heretofore had been accorded subnational governments, especially the states and their spokesmen, eroded to the point that by the late seventies their treatment by Congress and administrative agencies was about on par with that meted out to other interest groups. In part, this was due to the subnational government's lobbying for new aid programs and more aid dollars like various of the specific program pressure groups....

...Even as the governors moved their National Governors Association headquarters to Washington and the state legislatures merged their three previous national associations and set up a major office there and the county and municipal associations beefed up their Washington staffs all to present skillfully, separately, and sometimes in concert the views of their respective subnational governmental groups, the clout of subnational governments in the nation's capital was collapsing....

In most respects, Reagan federalism as it was revealed in 1980 campaign speeches and later administration proposals—at least in theory—constituted a reaction to and rejection of most of the intergovernmental developments of the previous sixteen years, if not more: the massive expansion of the national agenda; the highly centralized policy-making process; the resulting administrative ineffectiveness, economic inefficiencies, and lack of accountability; the cooptive approach of federal administrators and regulators; the dangers of interest group ascendancy; and the lack of clear national purposes.

[Reagan] ignored, as did most politicians of either party, the positive results of the earlier years. Between 1960 and 1980, the poverty percentage was cut in half and the gap between the economically stronger and weaker did not widen (as it might well have, given the massive influx of new "baby boom" generation job applicants). Thirty million members were added to the national work force, in part because of certain federal actions. Longer life expectancy and lower child mortality rates were achieved and a fundamental revolution was achieved in civil rights and civil liberties.

In broad-brush terms, *Reagan's federalist creed* encompassed the following: a reduction in the federal intergovernmental role, a devolution of program responsibilities, deregulation, and a reduction in the activism of all governments. How has he fared in achieving these goals thus far?

In its *drive to reduce the federal intergovernmental role*, the administration succeeded in achieving an absolute reduction of $8 billion (from the Carter figure) for grant programs for fiscal year (FY) 1982, but the projected further slashing of federal aid over the next three years did not materialize....

Turning to moves to *devolve program and other responsibilities* to the state and local levels, the administration scored its greatest successes in 1981. Some sixty-odd aid programs were scrapped by the Reconciliation Act and seventy-seven were merged into nine new block grants.... The renewal of general revenue sharing for local general governments in 1983, with White House support, marked another phase of this devolutionary drive, but its demise in 1986 was in part his doing....

In the *complicated field of intergovernmental deregulation*, the Reagan administration has curbed and softened the process, but deregulation as such has not been the focus of administration efforts. The softening strategy involved a combination of Reagan loyalists appointed to key regulatory posts; personnel cuts in their agencies; relaxed, if not permissive, agency procedures; and a highly centralized review of proposed new, or modifications of existing, regulations.

No major deregulatory legislative initiative—other than the block grant proposals—has accompanied these efforts, however. Moreover, Congress' propensity to preempt and to regulate has not slackened off and in some cases has been supported by the administration (i.e., trailer truck and teenage drinking regulations and mandated procedures for responding to reports of medical neglect of handicapped infants).

The administration's general philosophic goal of *reducing governmental activism at all levels* has met with little success. In dollar terms, there was a rise in federal spending from $983.6 billion to $1,375.9 billion; in state outlays (from own sources) from $175.6 billion to $220.4 billion; and in local expenditures (again from own sources) from $118.9 billion to $157.8 billion. When combined, these outlays rose from 33.3 percent of the GNP to 35.4 percent over this four-year period and on a per capita, constant (1972) dollar basis from $2,186 to $2,491. Since 1978, then, governmental activism, as reflected in expenditures, has been tamed somewhat but it has not been reduced in absolute dollar terms.

Any assessment of the Reagan intergovernmental record would be remiss if its *attitudinal impact* were overlooked. State and local officials no longer seek out Washington as the prime, if not the sole, solver of their respective problems as many of them did in the late 1960s and in the 1970s. This is not to say the national government is being ignored. Far from it—too many legal, regulatory, preemptive, as well as fiscal actions are taken there to permit that kind of luxury. But the image of "Uncle Sam as the problem solver" has faded from the minds of subnational governmental officials and even of many within the electorate and the interest group complexes....

27

W. JOHN MOORE
The Bridge Is Out

———

SANTA CLARA COUNTY (CALIF.) Supervisor Rod Diridon has embarked on a mission impossible. In Washington for two weeks in early March, he and other local officials from the San Francisco area prowled the corridors of Congress and buttonholed members of the California delegation and the Budget Committees in a quest for public transit dollars.

There is a sense of urgency to Diridon's task. Over the next 15 years, Santa Clara County will spend $3 billion on mass transit construction simply to keep up with the explosive growth expected for its Silicon Valley. Despite a steady increase in local taxes and the highest transit fares in the country, the county won't be able to pay the entire costs, said Diridon, who is chairman for mass transit and railroads at the National Association of Counties.

A decade or two ago, it would have been fairly routine for a local official to come to Washington and walk away with the promise of a federal check. But today, success on Capitol Hill proves elusive.

Diridon's effort to sell a hike in the federal gasoline tax was greeted by yawns. "Those candid enough to discuss it said come back next year," he said. Given the overriding concern about the federal deficit, Diridon concedes that no increases for mass transit are likely. Indeed, money that might have gone to mass transit has been diverted to pay for boosts in the Coast Guard and for additional air traffic controllers, the result being that Diridon would be satisfied if he came away with zero cuts. "We've adopted a defensive posture until hopefully we get a better President," he said.

For local officials seeking increased federal aid for public works projects, budgetary defeats are now par for the course. Though almost everyone believes more money must be spent on America's public works, nobody agrees where the dollars will be found. "Every year we have been fighting over the scraps under the table for mass transportation, and we're not getting very many," Diridon said. "Why isn't the federal government willing to recognize that they are underfunding the basic infrastructure of America?"

Other local and state officials, investment bankers and public policy experts pose a slightly different question. With the federal government reluctant to spend scarce dollars on airports, bridges, dams, highways and waterways, how else can we pay for the needed repairs and expansions of these systems?...

Although total spending on public works has increased in recent years, federal, state and local government spending on infrastructure has declined from 13.5 percent of total government spending in the late 1960s to about 6.6 percent in 1984. And during the first four years of the Reagan Administration, the composition of public works spending changed dramatically. Federal outlays for public works declined from 32 percent of total government spending in 1980 to 27 percent in 1984. But over the same period, local governments boosted their share of spending from 44 percent to 50 percent.

And regardless of who wins the White House in November, proposals for huge new spending projects will continue to be resisted in Washington, given the preoccupation with budget deficits. As Irwin T. David, national director of public-sector services at Touche Ross & Co. in Washington, cautioned: "The feds can do some things in terms of moral suasion. They can do some things in terms of coordination. And they can do some things in terms of providing technical advice and technical support. But I don't think the feds are going to provide big dollars for infrastructure."

Some states have shown a willingness to make up for the drop in federal dollars. Illinois, for instance, under Republican Gov. James R. Thompson, Jr., instituted its "Build Illinois" program, which imposed new taxes to finance its $2.3 billion effort. New Jersey and three other states have moved aggressively to establish infrastructure banks that help local governments finance public works. And Indiana has adopted a novel approach that focuses more on management and process to reduce costs.

But the lion's share of the burden will continue to fall on local governments. With the federal interstate highway program near the end of its mission, some public policy experts believe local governments should be responsible for meeting what are mostly local public works needs. Many governments coped by doing the obvious: raising local taxes. Los Angeles County, for example, has imposed a 0.5 cent sales tax, with the $320 million generated from the tax earmarked for mass transit.

One of the benefits of such a tax, noted Rick Richmond, former director of Los Angeles County's Transportation Department and now with New Jersey Transit, is that the local government keeps all the money. "We looked at future needs," he said, and found that "a local financial component had some logic to it."

Local governments, however, are squeezed by competing demands from the federal and state governments. Washington has imposed costly new mandates on local governments, such as clean water requirements that could cost $1 billion over the next decade. The 1986 Tax Reform Act limits local governments' ability to raise money for infrastructure projects. It limited the total amount of tax-exempt bonds that cities can issue. It eliminated tax breaks on depreciation as well as the investment tax credit, two crucial components in many public-private partnerships. Finally, most states restrict local governments' ability to raise taxes....

... In 1808, President Jefferson's Treasury Secretary, Albert Gallatin, argued in his *Report on Roads and Canals* that economic growth depended on new transportation facilities connecting East and West. The federal government must pay for the roads if states and private industry refused, the report argued. But Gallatin's recommendations were ignored, largely because of high costs and disputes over the federal government's financial responsibilities.

History may repeat itself. Despite calls from some quarters for a massive infusion of federal funds for public works, retrenchment is more likely. "I don't think one should predicate plans for meeting the infrastructure gap just on federal funds," said Roger D. Feldman, head of the project finance and development group at the Washington office of the Rochester (N.Y.) law firm of Nixon, Hargrave, Devans & Doyle. "What we have is the ending of the interstate highway program, the restructuring of the wastewater treatment grants program with the revolving fund, the cutback in the availability of industrial development bonds under the Tax Reform Act of 1986, the reduction of the [urban development action grant] program, so it would not seem prudent to base infrastructure needs on the federal government.". . .

As a group, the states have a lackluster record on public works spending. State spending on infrastructure accounted for only 23 percent of total government spending in 1984, down from 32 percent in 1972. Some states obviously give public works short shrift. California, for example, ranks last in per capita expenditures on streets and roads. Since 1963, it has only once increased its tax on a gallon of gasoline.

Given the federal government's fiscal paralysis, the states will be asked to boost spending. . . .

Even with financial help from states, local governments are expected to bear the burden of increased public works spending. Federal mandates require cleaner air and water. In Portland, Maine, for example, federal EPA sewer requirements costs will exceed $200 for every person in the city. Richard M. Gerwitz, managing director for public finance at the Security Pacific Merchant Banking Group in Los Angeles, notes that infrastructure costs, from jails to curbstones, are increasingly borne by local units of government. "I presume that is fair, but it is not realistic in reflecting their continued ability to pay for these large outlays," Gerwitz said. . . .

But the 1986 Tax Reform Act curtailed local governments' ability to issue bonds. So do long-standing state limitations on local government debt-raising capabilities. And some localities greeted drops in federal aid programs such as general revenue sharing by switching money from sewers to services.

Broome County (N.Y.) Commissioner Carl Young told the National Council on Public Works Improvement last June that his county shifted $1.5 million in road money to other programs after Congress eliminated revenue sharing. "So now I'm forced into the somewhat hypocritical position of being an advocate for infrastructure on the one hand and having to short-change my own infrastructure program because we just plain don't have the financial resources to absorb these other kinds of hits," he said.

A tax hike is one solution, but voter resistance remains high in many places. "What does seem to impede infrastructure financing in California and the rest of the country in varying degrees is a constant series of voter rebellions and changes," Gerwitz said.

When the expenditures would go for maintenance as opposed to new roads or bridges, citizen apathy dooms the projects. Despite the need for repairs, "it has all the sex appeal of oatmeal," conceded Pat Choate, a vice president at TRW Inc. in Washington and author of *America in Ruins* (Council of State Planning Agencies, 1981).

PART FIVE

Congress

ONGRESS is without a doubt the world's most powerful and independent legislature. Among the national legislatures of the industrial democracies there is nothing else quite like it. Most of these legislatures are parliaments—legislative institutions fused with (not separated from) an executive cabinet of ministers or "government" made up of the leaders of the majority party or, more often, a coalition of parties. Although in theory parliaments after the emasculation of monarchy possess supreme authority, they are in fact dominated by cabinets and party leaders. Such legislatures are best understood as centers of discussion between one set of party leaders who govern and another set of party leaders who function as a loyal opposition. Individual members outside the "government" have little importance. Policies hammered out behind closed doors in the cabinet are routinely supported by loyal party majorities. However furiously the opposition may question and criticize, while the government lasts, it gets the policies it wants when it wants them. The legislature has little or no independent capacity to make policy or, most often, even to wrest away information that the government does not wish to divulge. All of the above are unquestionably the case in the modern British House of Commons.

Congress is an entirely different kind of legislature. Separated from the executive by constitutional design and provided with independent powers, it cannot be dominated. Ordinary members

enjoy considerable capacity to shape legislation, oversee administration, and wrest information from the executive. Congressional
party leaders are much weaker than their parliamentary counterparts anywhere. In Congress there is never a clear line between a
group of leaders who govern and an opposition. The presidency
and one or both houses of Congress may even be controlled by
different parties. American legislators are accustomed to a level of
monetary compensation, attention from the press, staff services,
and physical amenities that are the envy of parliamentarians the
world over. In what is often rightly called an executive-dominated
age, Congress stands virtually alone as a powerful and independent
legislature.

In seeking to understand the nature of Congress we are impressed by two forces that seem to have worked in tandem since
the beginning—the Madisonian logic of the Constitution and the
social heterogeneity of the vast American republic. These forces
are brilliantly captured in the excerpt from James Young's study
of Washington as a governing community in the Jeffersonian era.
The very design of the federal district and its early residential
pattern, according to Young, reflect the separation of powers principle and the distrust of concentrated authority which underlies it.
The nation's early governing community assembled at the center
reluctantly, and formed physically and culturally distinct executive
and legislative spheres of activity. From the beginning, he observes,
members of the Washington community would consider themselves executives or legislators first and party members second.
Young's picture of the early Congress stresses the extraordinary
social diversity of members' districts and the primacy of their constituency-oriented behavior. Members from, say, New England
and the Deep South lived in different social worlds whose values
and interests they were expected to defend in Washington. The
early Congress, Young argues, was perfectly structured to articulate the great diversity of citizen interests in the extended American
republic, but at the same time, was deficient as an instrument of
governance. It is interesting to note that the same observation is
frequently made about Congress today.

Roger Davidson and Walter Oleszek, two of the best students
of the contemporary Congress, analyze the Bolling Committee's
abortive attempt to reform the committee structure in the House
of Representatives in the early 1970s in exactly these terms. The
modern Congress has evolved an extremely specialized committee

and subcommittee system to provide individual members with the ability to represent specific constituency interests effectively. From a governance perspective, however, such a fine degree of representation prevents Congress from dealing with such broad, national issues as macroeconomic policy, energy, and the environment. The Bolling Committee's efforts to create a less fragmented committee structure, Davidson and Oleszek point out, ran afoul of members' desires to "spread the action" so that as many as possible had control of policy matters of interest to their districts. As much as Congress had changed in two hundred years, the primacy of constituency-oriented behavior had remained constant.

David Mayhew, another close student of the contemporary Congress, argues that we do best to assume that the key to understanding Congress is members' desire for re-election. American legislators are in effect individual electoral entrepreneurs, and they are endlessly inventive in perfecting constituency-oriented activities that he calls "advertising," "credit claiming," and "position taking." (Be sure that you understand what he means by each of these concepts). Although many students of Congress have thought he pushes this argument too far, Mayhew argues that there is not much about Congress that "the electoral connection" will not explain.

The most striking feature of Congress when it is compared with other national legislatures is the individualism of its members. In most other systems of representation individual members are seen as party spokesmen. That is not the American practice. Richard Fenno, the ultimate anthropologist of the congressional tribe, points out that members develop highly individualized "home styles" through which they present themselves to voters. Through these activities on which they spend a great deal of time and energy, they seek to establish relationships of trust with voters in their districts. Fenno argues that these activities should not be seen as inferior to or less important than the roles that members carry out inside Congress; they should be understood as an important part of the American process of legislative representation. We remind our readers that the best historical evidence suggests that members of Congress have always been highly sensitive to the opinions of "folks back home." Despite at least a century of criticism of their district-serving behavior, members continue to maintain this orientation with no visible embarrassment.

Another interesting feature of Congress is its comparatively weak party leaders. Partisan they are, but they lack the ability to order their troops to march in rigid formation. The excerpt from former House Speaker Tip O'Neill's autobiography reveals *par excellence* the congressional leadership mentality. O'Neill understands perfectly the individualism of his Democratic rank and file. Elected largely on their own, they will not be ordered around. Like other congressional leaders he sees his role as keeping in close touch with members, helping them serve their districts and defining party policy as what the majority want to do at any given moment. Note his sense of humor, his style of story-telling. If you have to get along with members from places as diverse as Massachusetts and Mississippi, it comes in very handy.

We conclude our readings on Congress with four short journalistic pieces highlighting aspects of the "new Congress" of the post-Watergate years. The contemporary Congress is pictured here as extremely "media aware," made up of assertive, younger members who came to maturity during or after the Vietnam era, highly decentralized and impatient with still-surviving old ways. One thing, though, hasn't changed. Members continue to find imaginative ways to wrap old "pork" in new packages—to get tangible benefits for their districts into forms appropriate to the postindustrial age. "Bringing home the bacon" is a seemingly immutable feature of congressional life.

28

JAMES YOUNG

From *The Washington Community: 1800–1828*

—

DESOLATE IN SURROUNDING, derogatory in self-image, the governmental community was also distinctive for the extraordinary manner in which the personnel chose to situate themselves in Washington—the social formations into which they deployed on the terrain. The settlement pattern of a community is, in a sense, the signature that its social organization inscribes upon the landscape, defining the groups of major importance in the life of the community and suggesting the relationships among them. In the case of the early Washington community that signature is very clear.

The members did not, in their residential arrangements, disperse uniformly or at random over the wide tract of the intended city. Nor did they draw together at any single place. The governmental community rather inscribed itself upon the terrain as a series of distinct subcommunities, separated by a considerable distance, with stretches of empty land between them. Each was clustered around one of the widely separated public buildings; each was a self-contained social and economic entity. The personnel of the governmental community segregated themselves, in short, into distinct groups, and formed a society of "we's" and "they's."...

From data gathered in an 1801 survey, listing the location of houses completed and under construction in the capital, it is possible to reconstruct the settlement pattern of the early governmental community with reasonable accuracy....

Members of the different branches of government chose to situate themselves close by the respective centers of power with which they were affiliated, seeking their primary associations in extra-official life among their fellow branch members.

Despite its relative civilization, old Georgetown attracted few members of government as residents, and most of those who stayed there moved as soon as they could find quarters in Washington, nearer to their places of work....

At the opposite end of the city, about five miles from Georgetown, near the Capitol but separated from it by a dense swamp, was the village of the armed forces....

...Commercialization failing, the environs became the site of the congressional burying ground, a poorhouse, and a penitentiary with an arsenal "near, much too near" it, thus associating by coresidence the men and matériel of war with the dead, the indigent, and the incorrigible. The settlement was generally shunned by civilian members of the government as a place to live, and high-ranking military and naval officers also forsook it eventually to take up residence in the executive sector.

The chief centers of activity were the village community of the executives and the village community of the legislators, lying "one mile and a half and seventeen perches" apart as the crow flies, on the "great heath" bisected by the River Tiber.

Senators and Representatives lived in the shadow of the Capitol itself, most of them in knots of dwellings but a moment's walk from their place of meeting....

The knolltop settlement of legislators was a complete and self-contained village community from beginning to end of the Jeffersonian era. Neither work nor diversion, nor consumer needs, nor religious needs required them to set foot outside it. Eight boarding-houses, a tailor, a shoemaker, a washerwoman, a grocery store, and an oyster house served the congressional settlement in 1801. Within three years a notary, an ironmonger, a saddle maker, several more tailors and bootmakers, a liquor store, bookstores, stables, bakery, and taverns had been added. In twenty years' time the settlement had increased to more than two thousand people and the Capitol was nearly surrounded by brick houses "three stories high, and decent, without being in the least elegant," where the lawmakers lodged during the session. An itinerant barber served the community, shuttling between the scattered villages of the capital on horseback, and a nearby bathhouse catered to congressional clientele. Legislators with families could send their children to school on the Hill. The members had their own congressional library and their own post office, dispatching and receiving mail—which was distributed on the floor of the Senate and the House daily—without leaving the Hill. Page boys, doorkeepers, sergeants-at-arms, and other ancillary personnel for Congress were supplied from the permanent population of Capitol Hill—mainly the boardinghouse proprietors and their families.... The settlement pattern of early Washington clearly reveals a community structure paralleling the constitutional structure of government itself. The "separation of powers" became a separation of persons, and each of the branches of government became a self-contained, segregated social system within the larger governmental establishment. Legislators with legislators, executives with executives, judges with judges, the members gathered together in their extraofficial as well as in their official activities, and in their community associations deepened, rather than bridged, the group cleavages prescribed by the Constitution.

Why did the rulers make this highly contrived, unconventional legal structure into their community structure at Washington?... A key factor contributing to social segregation by branch affiliation is suggested by the consistency between such behavior and community attitudes about power and politicians. In the absence of any extrinsic forces compelling the rulers to segregate in community life, patterned avoidance between executives, legislators, and judges indicates that they felt a stronger sense of identification with their constitutional roles than with other more partisan roles they may have had in the community. Social segregation on the basis of branch affiliation suggests, in other words, that the rulers generally considered themselves executives, legislators, or judges first, and politicians or party members second. Such a preference for nonpartisan, constitutionally sanctioned roles fully accords with, and tends to confirm the authenticity of, the members' disparaging image of politicians. Their decided preference for associating with fellow branch members in extraofficial life is also precisely the sort of social behavior that was foreshadowed by the attitudes they held concerning power. Power-holders acculturated to anti-power values would, it was predicted, be attracted toward behaviors and associations which were sanctioned by the Constitution. By subdividing into separate societies of executives, legislators, and judges, the rulers could not have more literally translated constitutional principles of organization into social realities nor afforded themselves greater security from reproach in this aspect of their community life at Washington. When one sees, moreover, the remarkable consistency between the organizational precepts of the Constitution of 1787 and the community plan of 1791, on the one hand, and, on the other hand, the actual community structure of the governing politicians from 1800 to 1828, one must presume a consistency also in the attitudes from which these principles of organization originally derived, namely, attitudes of mistrust toward political power.

Whatever the underlying causes, here was a community of power-holders who preferred and who sanctioned, in their extraofficial life, a structural configuration that had been designed explicitly to check power. Here was a community of rulers who chose, among all the alternatives of social organization open to them, precisely the one most prejudicial to their capacity to rule.... Power made a community of cultural strangers. And power, shared, was hardly a thing to bind strangers together.

To achieve political accord among men of such disparate interests and different acculturation would not have been an easy task even under the most auspicious circumstances. For those gathered to govern on Capitol Hill in the Jeffersonian era, the circumstances were anything but auspicious.

To the political cleavages inherent in any representative assembly were added the deeper social tensions that are generated when men of widely diverging beliefs and behaviors are thrust upon each other in everyday living. Close-quarters living gave rise to personal animus even between "men whose natural interests and stand in society are in many respects similar. ... The more I know of [two New England Senators] the more I am impressed with the idea how unsuited they are ever to co-operate," commented a fellow lodger; "never were two substances more completely adapted to make each other explode." As social intimacy bared the depth of their behavioral differences, tolerance among men from different regions was strained to the breaking point. Political coexistence with the South and the frontier states was hard enough for New Englanders to accept. Social coexistence was insufferable with slaveholders "accustomed to speak in the tone of masters" and with frontiersmen having "a license of tongue incident to a wild and uncultivated state of society. With men of such states of mind and temperament," a Massachusetts delegate protested, "men educated in ... New England ... could have little pleasure in intercourse, less in controversy, and of course no sympathy." Close scrutiny of their New England neighbors in power could convince southerners, in their turn, that there was "not one [who] possesses the slightest tie of common interest or of common feeling with us," planters and gentlemen cast among men "who raised 'beef and pork, and butter and cheese, and potatoes and cabbages' " and carried on "a paltry trade in potash and codfish." Cultural antipathies, crowded barracks, poor rations, and separation from families left at home combined to make tempers wear thin as the winters wore on, leading to sporadic eruptions of violence. In a sudden affray at the table in Miss Shields's boardinghouse, Randolph, "pouring out a glass of wine, dashed it in Alston's face. Alston sent a decanter at his head in return, and these and similar missiles continued to fly to and fro, until there was much destruction of glass ware." The chambers of the Capitol themselves witnessed more than one scuffle, and, though it was not yet the custom for legislators to arm themselves when legislating, pistols at twenty paces cracked more than once in the woods outside the Capitol.

To those who would seek political agreement in an atmosphere of social tensions, the rules of proceeding in Congress offered no aid at all. On the contrary, contentiousness was encouraged by Senate and House rules which gave higher precedence to raising questions than to deciding them and which guaranteed almost total freedom from restraint to the idiosyncratic protagonist.... "Political hostilities are waged with great vigour," commented another observer, "yet both in attack and defence there is evidently an entire want both of discipline and organization. There is no concert, no division of duties, no compromise of opinion.... Any general system of effective co-operation is impossible."

The result was a scene of confusion daily on the floor of House and Senate that bore no resemblance to the deliberative processes of either the town meeting or the parliamentary assemblies of the Old World. Congress at work was Hyde Park set down in the lobby of a busy hotel—hortatory outcry in milling throngs, all wearing hats as if just arrived or on the verge of departure, variously attired in the fashions of faraway places. Comings and goings were continual—to the rostrum to see the clerk, to the anterooms to meet friends, to the Speaker's chair in a sudden surge to hear the results of a vote, to the firesides for hasty caucuses and strategy-planning sessions. Some gave audience to the speaker of the moment; some sat at their desks reading or catching up on correspondence; some stood chatting with lady friends, invited on the floor; others dozed, feet propped high. Page boys weaved through the crowd, "little Mercuries" bearing messages, pitchers of water for parched throats, bundles of documents, calling out members' names, distributing mail just arrived on the stagecoach. Quills scratched, bond crackled as knuckles rapped the sand off wet ink, countless newspapers rustled. Desk drawers banged, feet shuffled in a sea of documents strewn on the floor. Bird dogs fresh from the hunt bounded in with their masters, yapping accompaniment to contenders for attention, contenders for power. Some government!...

What emerges from a community study of Capitol Hill is, therefore, a social system which gave probably greater sanction and encouragement to constituency-oriented behavior than any institutional norms or organizational features of the modern Congress.... Constituency-oriented behavior, in other words, justified the possession of power in a context of personal and national values which seems to have demanded justification for the possession of power....

As a system for the effective representation of citizen interests the social system of Capitol Hill has probably never been surpassed in the history of republican government. But a fragmented social system of small blocs, more anarchic than cohesive, seems hardly to meet the minimal requirements for a viable system of managing social conflict, for performing "the regulation of ... various and interfering interests" which the author of *The Federalist,* No. 10 acknowledged to be "the principal task of modern legislation." Far from serving as an institution for the management of conflict, the little democracy on the Hill seems more likely to have acted as a source of conflict in the polity. An ironic and provocative judgment is thus suggested by the community record of Capitol Hill: at a time when citizen interest in national government was at its lowest point in history the power-holders on the Potomac fashioned a system of surpassing excellence for representing the people and grossly deficient in the means for governing the people.

29

ROGER DAVIDSON
WALTER OLESZEK

From *Congress Against Itself*

————

HISTORICALLY, Congress has been a traditional whipping boy of the press and the public. Several considerations help to explain the poor public image of Congress. First, Congress' decision-making process is more open to public view than that of the executive branch or judiciary. Accordingly, if a representative or senator sounds ill-informed or advances an outrageous proposal during committee or floor debate, then representatives of the media are likely to stress that newsworthy event rather than the substance of the overall debate. While inanities also exist in the other branches of government, as witness the now famous White House tapes, reporters usually lack access to the early stages of executive or judicial planning.

A second consideration is the bad press received by Congress. No doubt part of this is Congress' fault. The President has learned to utilize the media to get his message across to the American people while Congress generally has not. Equally important, many important legislative events are simply ignored by broadcasters and reporters....

Third, there appears to be general public misunderstanding about the role of Congress. Public approbation is often high when Congress appears to agree with a popular President.... In our achievement-oriented society, the legislative record looked good to the public. But if Congress approves too many of the President's proposals, it is not long before detractors call it a rubber stamp. On the other hand, if Congress works its will in a deliberative fashion, and amends or proposes alternatives to presidential suggestions, then Congress may be labeled the obstructionist body.... Congress is a consensus-building institution, which helps ensure that critical public policies will be accepted by the people. Hence, it may be unrealistic to criticize Congress for functioning as it was intended....

Fourth, Congress has often been criticized by its own members. This, too, helps to create a poor public image of the legislative branch. Legislators who attack the institution, but are unwilling to reform it, ought to be held accountable by the citizenry. In that regard, constituents might ask what their representatives are doing to improve the performance of the legislative branch, and then hold them accountable for the failures of Congress. Consequently, the performance of Congress as a whole might be strengthened.

Fifth, Congress is also criticized because it lacks sufficient modern technology to assist it in making informed policy judgments. Compared to the executive branch, Congress seems far behind in developing an independent automatic data-processing capability. If relevant and timely information is the key to informed decision making, then Congress should utilize every means possible to avail itself of the latest in computer and data-processing facilities. In this way, Congress' collective intelligence and capacity for making accurate and balanced judgments would be greatly strengthened.

Sixth, the various legislative party structures have failed to procure enough staff and other assistance to critique executive branch proposals, or to develop an independent party program. Numerous scholars have argued that disciplined political parties should formulate public policies, which could then be implemented through centralized congressional party structures. The goal of party government, so they hold, would facilitate national actions to meet national needs....

Seventh, numerous jurisdictional overlaps among standing

committees inhibit the formulation of coherent and coordinated national policies. As a *New York Times* editorial noted with regard to the 1975 energy issue, "This jurisdictional jumble undoubtedly is an important factor in the inability of the Congress to act comprehensively on one of the nation's most pressing problems."...

Eighth, with its multiplicity of voices, Congress has no single spokesman to articulate the congressional viewpoint. What, indeed, is the congressional viewpoint, and who defines it? The Speaker, the majority or minority leaders, the party caucuses, the committee chairmen, or others? As a result, a serious communications imbalance has developed between the branches. While the President can communicate quickly to the American people concerning his goals and programs, Congress lacks such capabilities. A legitimate question is, "Who speaks for Congress?"...

Ninth, Congress is often criticized because it lacks the ability to initiate policies. As the textbooks have so often stated, "The President initiates and Congress responds." However, where does the President often get many of his "innovations" before he initiates them? Often creative ideas are born and kept alive through the years and even decades within Congress by such devices as hearings and floor debate. The President, too, often tailors his proposals to meet anticipated congressional responses to them. Hence, Congress often sets the framework within which the President functions. Moreover, in numerous policy areas Congress has either taken the lead or reformulated and revised presidential proposals to make them its own.

Finally, some legislative procedures limit Congress' consideration of legislation in committee and on the floor. Some observers claim that such devices, practices, or entities as the filibuster, the House Rules Committee, or inadequate scheduling of committee and floor sessions all act to limit individual legislators' and the legislative branch's obligation to develop or enact legislation. However, numerous recent procedural changes (allowing the Speaker to nominate members to the Rules Committee, reducing the number of senators required to invoke cloture, and others) have underscored the legislative branch's willingness to reform its organization and procedures to meet new circumstances....

For a traditional and consensus-prone institution, Congress has to a surprising degree sought wide-ranging, "radical" solutions to its organizational problem. The Legislative Reorganization Act of 1946 was an omnibus measure that contemplated far-reaching structural changes in the committees, the budgetary process, and staffing. . . .

. . . The 93rd Congress (1973–1974) found the House of Representatives again groping for appropriate responses to its ever-more-complex external environment. The 1946 and 1974 reorganization efforts thus stand as major attempts at broad legislative reorganization. . . .

Members then as now believed the committee system to be the most important component of the legislative process. . . . Like members of the Select Committee on Committees of the 93rd Congress, the reformers of 1946 believed that strengthening the committee system strengthened Congress itself. This was necessary because congressmen were concerned about the growing power of the executive branch, and recognized the imperative of reestablishing Congress' role as a co-equal branch of government. . . .

Committees are the heart of the legislative process. Although early Congresses functioned mainly with ad hoc committees that ordinarily expired after their specific mission was completed, by about 1816 both chambers had developed a system of permanent standing committees. That basic structural pattern has persisted to this day, with few legislators, scholars, or journalists suggesting a return to the earlier system. Representative Bella Abzug did propose in 1973 that all House standing committees be abolished and replaced by a system of ad hoc committees. Needless to say, no one rushed to take up her suggestion.

Committees have enabled Congress to respond to the problems and complexities of the twentieth century. If they perform their tasks successfully, through a rational division of labor, the committees sustain the vitality of Congress as an equal partner in national policy making. Public policy is, of course, the outgrowth of many individuals, opinions, and influences. Often, Presidents and other individuals are given credit for policy innovations that are in fact the product of many people working over a period of months or even years. A common question is, "Where do policies originate?" To a greater extent than most observers realize, the answer lies in the committee and subcommittee rooms of Congress.

Committees serve the formation of legislative policy in a variety of ways. Most obviously, they enable a large number of measures, many of them extraordinarily complex and technical, to be developed through expert study. By dividing its membership into a number of work groups, Congress is able to consider simultaneously dozens of proposed laws. Through the committee, Congress winnows the important from the unimportant, the workable from the unworkable. The committee system is, therefore, a technique for effectively utilizing time and energy in the development of quality legislation.

Committees serve also as arenas for expressing the multitude of viewpoints that are found in our society. By serving as channels for national concerns, committees help to resolve tensions as well as to solve problems. Maintaining themselves as "listening posts" for citizens' concerns, especially by use of hearings, the committees form a vital link in the representative process.

Finally, committees perform an oversight function. They help to ensure that legislative programs are properly and efficiently administered by executive officials. This is done through such oversight techniques as investigations, field hearings, or staff studies. As a result, committees develop refinements and alternatives to existing public policies, and they assure that executive policies reflect the public interest.

On the other hand, there are several arguments against the utility of congressional committees. At times, they are dysfunctional to the national interest and to the legislative process because they can block or delay the consideration of needed programs. Moreover, committees can serve to dilute the effectiveness of our democracy by preventing most voters from knowing whom to blame for delays, if not the burial, of legislative policies.

Another weakness associated with congressional committees is their inability, as they are presently organized, to develop comprehensive and coordinated programs for the nation. Fragmentation and diffusion, rather than unity and consistency, keynote the internal decision making of Congress.... The committee reorganization of 1946 both consolidated jurisdictions and reduced the number of standing committees in the House from forty-eight to nineteen. What resulted, however, was a proliferation of subcommittees (from 91 in 1947 to more than 125 in 1973). Of equal importance, by reducing the number of standing committees and defining their jurisdictions, the 1946 Act tended to reinforce committee autonomy and inhibit the ability of the House to respond to new configurations of public problems....

This fragmented consideration of policies by numerous committees and subcommittees, with little or no consultation or cooperation among them on matters of mutual concern, has several negative consequences. First, the House rarely has the opportunity to consider comprehensive approaches to national problems. Measures that directly affect particular policy areas are usually considered on the floor in piecemeal, thus inhibiting comprehensive policy development....

There are also disadvantages associated with too much overlap, duplication, and tangled, outmoded jurisdictions. Not only is timely legislative action sometimes prevented by the fierce jurisdictional scrambles on Capitol Hill, but also the development of quality legislation is hindered when broad policy issues are fragmented into bits and pieces among rival committees who fail to talk to one another about mutual and interdependent concerns....

Although Congress has been a perennial topic of criticism, public disenchantment with it has grown in recent years....

Legislators ... are mindful that many people lack faith in Congress as a institution, and they recognize the importance of restoring public confidence in the House. A lack of faith in Congress contributes to frustration and causes the public to look to other institutions, usually the White House, for the resolution of its problems. As one congressman said, "The message is clear: either we act to reform our own procedures and [make the House] responsive and responsible, or we will no longer enjoy the privilege of representing the people.".…

Committee reform was viewed as a logical correlative of the effort to strengthen the House, but it was also the reform that many realized would be the most difficult to achieve. Any major jurisdictional realignment involves redistributing power, something most power-holding members resist. Members, too, become familiar with things as they are....

Two members were principally responsible for developing the select committee reform proposal: Speaker Albert and Richard Bolling. Minority Leader Ford also had an important role, for as leader of the Republicans his influence was considerable. In the fall of 1972, Speaker Albert began discussing the need for committee reform with Bolling, a long-time advocate of congressional reform. In Albert's judgment, the time seemed propitious for a reevaluation of the committee system. Bolling agreed. Other congressmen, including Ford and John Culver, were also talking with Albert about the need for committee reform and urged action during the 93rd Congress. They argued that while individual committees might be performing adequately, the system was not working as

an integrated unit. Committees would often spend more time fighting among themselves for jurisdictional control of measures than
working together to develop the best substantive solutions to problems....

It was now late in the evening, about 10:50, and the chamber
was crowded with over three hundred congressmen, most of
whom were anxious to go home. Every time a member rose to
propose an amendment to Hansen, the chamber echoed with a
chorus of cat-calls, hoots, and groans. Members kept shouting
"vote!" "vote!" Chairman Natcher tried to maintain order and
repeatedly pounded his gavel to silence the chamber, but the sentiment of the House was to finish debate once and for all. Finally,
after four amendments were quickly considered and rejected, no
one rose to offer another. Dingell apparently had been prevailed
upon by several Hansen members not to offer any of his pending
amendments. By then, the Hansen group had calculated that they
had the votes to win House approval of their plan.

The question, Chairman Natcher said, was now on the adoption
of the Hansen substitute. Bolling demanded a roll call vote. As
occurred on all key recorded votes, proponents and opponents
rushed to and fro talking with their colleagues; they manned the
doors leading into the chamber and grabbed members as they
entered urging them to vote this way or that; and the respective
floor managers offered advice on how to vote if asked by a colleague. As the allotted fifteen minutes for a recorded vote slipped
by, with members following the tally on the electronic scoreboards
on either side of the chamber, it became clear that the Hansen
substitute would be adopted. Apparently the Hansen forces had
won over a majority of members to their position. Bolling sat
calmly throughout the vote, remarking to an aide that at this stage
he simply wanted the democratic process to work. He refrained
from soliciting votes among his colleagues, although he did respond to questions. The Hansen substitute was adopted by a vote
of 203 to 165. The Committee of the Whole rose, and the House
voted 359 to 7 to approve H. Res. 988, now the Hansen substitute.
Martin was one of the seven who voted against final passage of
the resolution. The debate on committee reform was over....

What the House approved when it adopted the Hansen substitute was a mild dose of committee reorganization. In effect, the
House adopted the version of committee reorganization that made
the fewest jurisdictional changes. No legislator would have to relin-

quish a committee, and no committee was abolished. Responsibility for major policy areas (energy, environment, and so forth) remained scattered among several standing committees. Some committees (Ways and Means) were still overworked and others underworked (Standards of Official Conduct). The jurisdictions of several major committees—Appropriations, Armed Services, and Rules—were basically left untouched. The reshuffling represented little change from the status quo, except in a few instances....

Bolling professed not to be discouraged by the result, terming it "just the beginning." ... House committee reform was part of a complex of changes designed to deal with external and internal challenges to congressional influence. What did all this change add up to? How will it alter the way in which Congress deals with public problems?...

First, Congress has become more democratic, more responsive, more accountable, and more open to public view. The emphasis on public committee hearings and markups, including conference sessions, and open party caucuses, has increased the visibility of the decision-making process. There are also proposals to televise House and Senate floor sessions. All this should strengthen the representative character of Congress. In addition, the changes should promote more public understanding, perhaps even trust, of Congress and lead to greater legislative accountability.

Second, power in the House has been further diffused ("spreading the action") by strengthening the autonomy of subcommittees and reducing that of committee chairmen. Greater dispersion means more member participation in policy making and greater citizen access to panels where important decisions are made. It also means the probable slowing down of the decision-making process. "Spreading the action" means that more congressmen will be consulted before anything approaching a coordinated or comprehensive policy or program develops.

Third, this diffusion of power has weakened such traditional House norms as apprenticeship and specialization. (Similar trends are even further advanced in the Senate.) Junior members are no longer expected to follow Speaker Sam Rayburn's advice: "To get along, go along." Freshmen have won privileges in recent years that few of their status enjoyed in earlier Congresses.

Fourth, caucuses have evolved as major instruments of party policy making.... Members are now accountable and responsible to their caucus. Committee chairmen are elected by the caucus and may be removed if they abuse their prerogatives. No longer, then, should oligarchical chairmen forestall consideration of important legislation within their committee's jurisdiction....

Fifth, the custom of seniority has lost its rigidity, although it is still an important criterion for determining who will gain influence in the legislative process and indeed has been broadened to give regularity to subcommittee selection procedures. Ironically, seniority has become flexible regarding rank on the full committee but has become almost inviolable for subcommittees. Now seniority on the full committee is the criterion to determine which member will head what subcommittee.

Finally, and somewhat paradoxically, the Speaker gained significant new powers at a time of further diffusion....

...All in all, these new devices have the potential to strengthen significantly the Speaker's role in the legislative process, particularly his ability to coordinate the consideration of complex legislation.

30

DAVID MAYHEW

The Electoral Incentive

From *Congress: The Electoral Connection*

...I SHALL CONJURE UP a vision of United States congressmen as single-minded seekers of reelection, see what kinds of activity that goal implies, and then speculate about how congressmen so motivated are likely to go about building and sustaining legislative institutions and making policy....

I find an emphasis on the reelection goal attractive for a number of reasons. First, I think it fits political reality rather well. Second, it puts the spotlight directly on men rather than on parties and pressure groups, which in the past have often entered discussions of American politics as analytic phantoms. Third, I think politics is best studied as a struggle among men to gain and maintain power and the consequences of that struggle. Fourth—and perhaps most important—the reelection quest establishes an accountability relationship with an electorate, and any serious thinking about democratic theory has to give a central place to the question of accountability....

Whether they are safe or marginal, cautious or audacious, congressmen must constantly engage in activities related to reelection. There will be differences in emphasis, but all members share the root need to do things—indeed, to do things day in and day out during their terms. The next step here is to present a typology, a short list of the *kinds* of activities congressmen find it electorally useful to engage in....

One activity is *advertising,* defined here as any effort to disseminate one's name among constituents in such a fashion as to create a favorable image but in messages having little or no issue content. A successful congressman builds what amounts to a brand name, which may have a generalized electoral value for other politicians in the same family. The personal qualities to emphasize are experience, knowledge, responsiveness, concern, sincerity, independence, and the like. Just getting one's name across is difficult enough; only about half the electorate, if asked, can supply their House members' names. It helps a congressman to be known. "In the main, recognition carries a positive valence; to be perceived at all is to be perceived favorably." A vital advantage enjoyed by House incumbents is that they are much better known among voters than their November challengers. They are better known because they spend a great deal of time, energy, and money trying to make themselves better known. There are standard routines—frequent visits to the constituency, nonpolitical speeches to home audiences, the sending out of infant care booklets and letters of condolence and congratulation....

Some routines are less standard. Congressman George E. Shipley (D., Ill.) claims to have met personally about half his constituents (i.e. some 200,000 people). For over twenty years Congressman Charles C. Diggs, Jr. (D., Mich.) has run a radio program featuring himself as a "combination disc jockey–commentator and minister." Congressman Daniel J. Flood (D., Pa.) is "famous for appearing unannounced and often uninvited at wedding anniversaries and other events." Anniversaries and other events aside, congressional advertising is done largely at public expense. Use of the franking privilege has mushroomed in recent years; in early 1973 one estimate predicted that House and Senate members would send out about 476 million pieces of mail in the year 1974, at a

public cost of $38.1 million—or about 900,000 pieces per member
with a subsidy of $70,000 per member. By far the heaviest mail-
room traffic comes in Octobers of even-numbered years. There
are some differences between House and Senate members in the
ways they go about getting their names across. House members
are free to blanket their constituencies with mailings for all box-
holders; senators are not. But senators find it easier to appear on
national television—for example, in short reaction statements on
the nightly news shows. Advertising is a staple congressional activity, and there is no end to it. For each member there are always
new voters to be apprised of his worthiness and old voters to be
reminded of it.

A second activity may be called *credit claiming,* defined here as
acting so as to generate a belief in a relevant political actor (or
actors) that one is personally responsible for causing the government, or some unit thereof, to do something that the actor (or
actors) considers desirable. The political logic of this, from the
congressman's point of view, is that an actor who believes that a
member can make pleasing things happen will no doubt wish to
keep him in office so that he can make pleasing things happen in
the future. The emphasis here is on individual accomplishment
(rather than, say, party or governmental accomplishment) and on
the congressman as doer (rather than as, say, expounder of constituency views). Credit claiming is highly important to congressmen,
with the consequence that much of congressional life is a relentless
search for opportunities to engage in it.

Where can credit be found?... For the average congressman
the staple way of doing this is to traffic in what may be called
"particularized benefits."...

In sheer volume the bulk of particularized benefits come under
the heading of "casework"—the thousands of favors congressional
offices perform for supplicants in ways that normally do not require
legislative action. High school students ask for essay materials,
soldiers for emergency leaves, pensioners for location of missing
checks, local governments for grant information, and on and on.
Each office has skilled professionals who can play the bureaucracy
like an organ—pushing the right pedals to produce the desired
effects. But many benefits require new legislation, or at least they
require important allocative decisions on matters covered by exis-
tent legislation. Here the congressman fills the traditional role of
supplier of goods to the home district. It is a believable role; when

a member claims credit for a benefit on the order of a dam, he may well receive it. Shiny construction projects seem especially useful....

The third activity congressmen engage in may be called *position taking,* defined here as the public enunciation of a judgmental statement on anything likely to be of interest to political actors. The statement may take the form of a roll call vote. The most important classes of judgmental statements are those prescribing American governmental ends (a vote cast against the war; a statement that "the war should be ended immediately") or governmental means (a statement that "the way to end the war is to take it to the United Nations")....

The ways in which positions can be registered are numerous and often imaginative. There are floor addresses ranging from weighty orations to mass-produced "nationality day statements." There are speeches before home groups, television appearances, letters, newsletters, press releases, ghostwritten books, *Playboy* articles, even interviews with political scientists.... Outside the roll call process the congressman is usually able to tailor his positions to suit his audiences....

...On a controversial issue a Capitol Hill office normally prepares two form letters to send out to constituent letter writers— one for the pros and one (not directly contradictory) for the antis. Handling discrete audiences in person requires simple agility, a talent well demonstrated in this selection from a Nader profile:

"You may find this difficult to understand," said Democrat Edward R. Roybal, the Mexican-American representative from California's thirtieth district, "but sometimes I wind up making a patriotic speech one afternoon and later on that same day an anti-war speech. In the patriotic speech I speak of past wars but I also speak of the need to prevent more wars. My positions are not inconsistent; I just approach different people differently." Roybal went on to depict the diversity of crowds he speaks to: one afternoon he is surrounded by balding men wearing Veterans' caps and holding American flags; a few hours later he speaks to a crowd of Chicano youths, angry over American involvement in Vietnam. Such a diverse constituency, Roybal believes, calls for different methods of expressing one's convictions.

Indeed it does.

31

RICHARD FENNO

From *Home Style*

———

MOST HOUSE MEMBERS spend a substantial proportion of their working lives "at home." Even those in our low frequency category return to their districts more often than we would have guessed. Over half of that group go home more than once a month. What, then, do representatives do there? Much of what they do is captured by Erving Goffman's idea of *the presentation of self.* That is, they place themselves in "the immediate physical presence" of others and then "make a presentation of themselves to others." Goffman writes about the ordinary encounters between people "in everyday life." But, the dramaturgical analogues he uses fit the political world, too. Politicians, like actors, speak to and act before audiences from whom they must draw both support and legitimacy. Without support and legitimacy, there is no political relationship.

In all his encounters, says Goffman, the performer will seek to control the response of others to him by expressing himself in ways that leave the correct impressions of himself with others. His expressions will be of two sorts—"the expressions that he gives and the expression that he gives off." The first are mostly verbal; the second are mostly nonverbal. Goffman is particularly interested in the second kind of expression—"the more theatrical and contextual kind"—because he believes that the performer is more likely to be judged by others according to the nonverbal than the verbal elements of his presentation of self. Those who must do the judging, Goffman says, will think that the verbal expressions are more controllable and manipulable by the performer. And they will, therefore, read his nonverbal "signs" as a check on the reliability of his verbal "signs." Basic to this reasoning is the idea that, of necessity, every presentation has a largely "promissory character" to it. Those who listen to and watch the presentation cannot be sure what the relationship between themselves and the performer really is. So the relationship must be sustained, on the part of those watching, by inference. They "must accept the individual on faith." In this process of acceptance, they will rely heavily on the inferences they draw from his nonverbal expressions—the expressions "given off."

Goffman does not talk about politicians; but politicians know what Goffman is talking about. The response they seek from others is political support. And the impressions they try to foster are those that will engender political support. House member politicians believe that a great deal of their support is won by the kind of individual self they present to others, i.e., to their constituents. More than most other people, they consciously try to manipulate it. Certainly, they believe that what they say, their verbal expression, is an integral part of their "self." But, with Goffman, they place special emphasis on the nonverbal, "contextual" aspects of their presentation. At the least, the nonverbal elements must be consistent with the verbal ones. At the most, the expressions "given off" will become the basis for constituent judgment. Like Goffman, members of Congress are willing to emphasize the latter because, with him, they believe that their constituents will apply a heavier discount to what they say than to how they say it or to how they act in the context in which they say it. In the members' own language, constituents want to judge you "as a person." The comment I have heard most often during my travels is: "he's a good man" or "she's a good woman," unembossed by qualifiers of any sort. Constituents, say House members, want to "size you up" or "get the feel of you" "as a person," or "as a human being." And the largest part of what House members mean when they say "as a person" is what Goffman means by expressions "given off." Largely from expressions given off comes the judgment: "he's a good man," "she's a good woman."

So members of Congress go home to present themselves as a person and to win the accolade: "he's a good man," "she's a good woman." With Goffman, they know there is a "promissory character" to their presentation. And their object is to present themselves as a person in such a way that the inferences drawn by those watching will be supportive. The representatives' word for these supportive inferences is *trust*. It is a word they use a great deal. When a constituent trusts a House member, the constituent is saying something like this: "I am willing to put myself in your hands temporarily; I know you will have opportunities to hurt me, although I may not know when those opportunities occur; I assume—and I will continue to assume until it is proven otherwise—that you will not hurt me; for the time being, then, I'm not going to worry about your behavior." The ultimate response House members seek is political support. But the instrumental response they seek is trust. The presentation of self—that which is given in words and given off as a person—will be calculated to win trust. "If people like you and trust you as individual," members often say, "they will vote for you." So trust becomes central to the representative-constituent relationship. For their part, constituents must rely on trust. They must "accept on faith" that the congressman is what he says he is and will do what he says he will do. House members, for their part, are quite happy to emphasize trust. It helps to allay the uncertainties they feel about their relationship with their supportive constituencies. If members are uncertain as to how to work for support directly, they can always work indirectly to win a degree of personal trust that will increase the likelihood of support or decrease the likelihood of opposition.

Trust is, however, a fragile relationship. It is not an overnight or a one-time thing. It is hard to win; and it must be constantly renewed and rewon. "Trust," said one member, "is a cumulative thing, a totality thing.... You do a little here and a little there." So it takes an enormous amount of time to build and to maintain constituent trust. That is what House members believe. And that is why they spend so much of their working time at home. Much of what I have observed in my travels can be explained as a continuous and continuing effort to win (for new members) and to hold (for old members) the trust of supportive constituencies. Most of the communication I have heard and seen is not overtly political at all. It is, rather, part of a ceaseless effort to reenforce the underpinnings of trust in the congressman or the congresswoman as a person. Viewed from this perspective, the archetypical constituent question is not "What have you done for me lately?" but "How have you looked to me lately?" In sum, House members make a strategic calculation that helps us understand why they go home so much. *Presentation of self enhances trust; enhancing trust takes time; therefore, presentation of self takes time....*

Explaining Washington activity, as said at the outset, includes justifying that activity to one's constituents. The pursuit of power, for example, is sometimes justified with the argument that the representative accumulates power not for himself but for his constituents. In justifying their policy decisions, representatives some-

times claim that their policy decisions follow not what they want
but what their constituents want. Recall the member who justified
his decision not to support his own highway bill with the comment,
"I'm not here to vote my own convictions. I'm here to represent
my people." Similarly, the member who decided to yield to his
constituent's wishes on gun control said, "I rationalize it by saying
that I owe it to my constituents if they feel that strongly about it."
But this is not a justification all members use. The independent,
issue-oriented Judiciary Committee member mentioned earlier
commented (privately) with heavy sarcasm,

All some House members are interested in is "the folks." They think
"the folks" are the second coming. They would no longer do anything to
displease "the folks" than they would fly. They spend all their time trying
to find out what "the folks" want. I imagine if they get five letters on one
side and five letters on the other side, they die.

An alternative justification, of course, is that the representative's
policy decisions are based on what he thinks is good public policy,
regardless of what his constituents want. As the Judiciary Committee member told his constituents often, "If I were sitting where
you are, I think what I would want is to elect a man to Congress
who will exercise his best judgment on the facts when he has
them all." At a large community college gathering in the heart of
his district, a member who was supporting President Nixon's Vietnam policy was asked, "If a majority of your constituents signed a
petition asking you to vote for a date to end the war, would you
vote for it?" He answered,

It's hard for me to imagine a majority of my constituents agreeing on
anything. But if it did happen, then no, I would not vote for it. I would
still have to use my own judgment—especially where the security of the
country is involved. You can express opinions. I have to make the decision.
If you disagree with my decisions, you have the power every two years
to vote me out of office. I listen to you, believe me. But, in the end, I
have to use my judgment as to what is in your best interests.

He then proceeded to describe his views on the substantive question.

   To political scientists, these two kinds of policy justification
are very familiar. One is a "delegate" justification, the other a
"trustee" justification. The two persist side by side because the set
of constituent attitudes on which each depends also exist side by
side. Voters, that is, believe that members of Congress should

follow constituents' wishes; and voters also believe that members of Congress should use their own best judgment. They want their representatives, it has been said, to be "common people of uncommon judgment." Most probably, though we do not know, voters want delegate behavior on matters most precious to them and trustee behavior on all others. Nonetheless, both kinds of justification are acceptable as a general proposition. Both are legitimate, and in explaining their Washington activity members are seeking to legitimate that activity. They use delegate and trustee justifications because both are legitimating concepts.

If, when they are deciding how to vote, House members think in terms of delegates and trustees, it is because they are thinking about the terms in which they will explain (i.e., justify or legitimate) that vote back home if the need to do so arises. If members never had to legitimate any of their policy decisions back home, they would stop altogether talking in delegate or trustee language. . . .

Members elaborate the linkage between presentation and explanation this way: There are at most only a very few policy issues on which representatives are constrained in their voting by the views of their reelection constituencies. They may not *feel* constrained, if they agree with those views. But that is beside the point; they are constrained nevertheless. On the vast majority of votes, however, representatives can do as they wish—provided only that they can, when they need to, explain their votes to the satisfaction of interested constituents. The ability to get explanations accepted at home is, then, the essential underpinning of a member's voting leeway in Washington.

So the question arises: How can representatives increase the likelihood that their explanations will be accepted at home? And the answer House members give is: They can win and hold constituent trust. The more your various constituencies trust you, members reason, the less likely they are to require an explanation of your votes and the more likely they are to accept your explanation when they do ask for it. The winning of trust, we have said earlier, depends largely on the presentation of self. Presentation of self, then, not only helps win votes at election time. It also makes voting in Washington easier. So members of Congress make a strategic calculation: *Presentation of self enhances trust; trust enhances the acceptability of explanations; the acceptability of explanations enhances voting leeway; therefore, presentation of self enhances voting leeway. . . .*

The traditional focus of political scientists on the policy aspects of representation is probably related to the traditional focus on activity in the legislature. So long as concentration is on what happens in Washington, it is natural that policymaking will be thought of as the main activity of the legislature and representation will be evaluated in policy terms. To paraphrase Woodrow Wilson, it has been our view that Congress in Washington is Congress at work, while Congress at home is Congress on exhibition. The extrapolicy aspects of representational relationships have tended to be dismissed as symbolic—as somehow less substantial than the relationship embodied in a roll call vote in Washington—because what goes on at home has not been observed. For lack of observation, political scientists have tended to downgrade home activity as mere errand running or fence mending, as activity that takes the representative away from the important things—that is, making public policy in Washington. As one small example, the "Tuesday to Thursday Club" of House members who go home for long weekends—have always been criticized out of hand, on the assumption, presumably, that going home and doing things there was, ipso facto, bad. But no serious inquiry was ever undertaken into what they did there or what consequences—other than their obvious dereliction of duty—their home activity might have had. Home activity has been overlooked and denigrated and so, therefore, have those extra policy aspects of representation which can only be studied at home.

Predictably, the home activities described in this book will be regarded by some readers as further evidence that members of Congress spend too little of their time "on the job"—that is, in Washington, making policy. However, I hope readers will take from the book a different view—a view that values both Washington and home activity. Further, I hope readers will entertain the view that Washington and home activities may even be mutually supportive. Time spent at home can be time spent in developing leeway for activity undertaken in Washington. And that leeway in Washington should be more valued than the sheer number of contact hours spent there. If that should happen, we might then ask House members not to justify their time spent at home, but rather to justify their use of the leeway they have gained therefrom—during the legislative process in Washington. It may well be that a congressman's behavior in Washington is crucially influenced by the pattern of support he has developed at home, and by the allocational, presentational, and explanatory styles he displays there. To put the point most strongly, perhaps we can never understand his Washington activity without also understanding his perception of his various constituencies and the home style he uses to cultivate their support....

32

TIP O'NEILL

From *Man of the House*

—————

As SPEAKER, I continued my practice of staying in close touch with the members—to the point where I probably knew more Republicans than Sam Rayburn knew Democrats. Most of my time and energy, however, went to members of my own party. My door was always open, and not a day went by when a member didn't come to see me for advice, either in my usual spot in the front row of the House, or in my office, which was just down the hall.

Typically, one of the younger members would come by to say that although he had promised the people at home that he would vote a certain way, he had changed his mind and wanted to get out of that commitment. What should he do?

"Tell them the truth," I would reply. "Come clean about it, and do it quickly. Issue a statement saying that you were convinced by one set of arguments, but now that you've had a chance to hear the other side, you believe your earlier position was mistaken." Occasionally, I would describe my own reversal on the Vietnam War, and how I patiently explained my new position to the people in my district, some of whom were convinced I was a traitor.

It wasn't only members who came to the Speaker's office, and not all the problems I listened to had to do with legislation. Some congressmen showed up to discuss personal matters, and over the years a number of their wives came by to ask if I would speak to their husbands and help straighten out their marital problems.

One story I'll never forget came to my attention back when I was Speaker of the Massachusetts legislature. One afternoon, the wife of a member came in to complain that her husband was always running around and that he never came home. He didn't give her any money, either, so there was nothing to eat in the house. The poor woman was so broke that she actually had to hitch a ride to my office in Boston.

I was outraged by what she told me, and I ordered her husband's paycheck from the legislature to be mailed directly to his wife at home. When the fellow learned what I had done, he came to my office and wanted to fight me. But it turned out that this guy was married to two women at the same time—one in his district, and the other in Boston! Still, that didn't stop him from becoming a major power in the state.

It would be hard to imagine a situation like that today—not because people are different than they used to be, but because members of Congress have changed so dramatically. One effect of Watergate was that it brought in a whole new breed of legislators, including a huge group of 118 Democrats who were elected for the first time in 1974 and 1976, just before I became Speaker....

These so-called Watergate Babies were a highly sophisticated and talented group.[*] They were also independent, and they didn't hesitate to remind you that they were elected on their own, often without any help from the Democratic party. In some cases they had managed to tip over the regular Democrats in their districts....

These new members, then, were outsiders, even more so than Jimmy Carter, who was elected in 1976. They hadn't come up through the state legislatures. Some of them had never run for city council or county office. Close to half had never campaigned

---

[*]The Watergate scandals began with the discovery of illegal entry and installation of wiretaps at the offices of the Democratic National Committee in the Watergate apartment complex in June 1972. Although little was made of this bizarre incident in the election campaign, by the spring of 1973 it had come to threaten the foundations of the Nixon administration. It became apparent that members of the White House staff not only had directed the break-in and engaged in an elaborate cover-up, but had engaged in many other illegal activities in order to counter the supposed threat of the administration's "enemies" and win re-election for President Nixon in 1972. After months of intense coverage by the news media, investigation by a Special Prosecutor, and prolonged congressional hearings, President Nixon finally resigned in the summer of 1974 in the face of certain impeachment. Several members of the administration were subsequently convicted of criminal charges related to the incident. Among the many other consequences of the Watergate scandals were strong Democratic gains in the congressional elections of 1974. The newly elected Democrats were called "the Watergate Babies."—EDS.

for *any* elective office before running for Congress.

Many of the new members had never rung doorbells, or driven people to the polls, or stayed late stuffing envelopes at campaign headquarters. A good number were activists who had run for office because of Vietnam, or Watergate, or the environment. As I got to know these people, I was struck by how many told me they had no interest in politics until Robert Kennedy's presidential campaign in 1968. Kennedy was their hero, and he was the one who had turned them on to the possibility of running for office.

With such a large group of outspoken new members, Congress became more difficult to control than ever before. Party discipline went out the window. These people were impatient, and they wanted to be part of the action right away. New members once were seen and not heard, but now it seemed that even the lowliest freshman could be a power in the House. Almost before we knew it, there were 154 committees and subcommittees, each with its own chairman. Mo Udall used to say that if you didn't know a member's name, you were on pretty safe ground if you addressed him simply as "Mr. Chairman."...

Despite their lack of political experience, the new members were mostly well educated and well informed on the issues. And unlike my own generation, they were also media-oriented. In years past, most of us had been reluctant to appear on the national Sunday-morning talk shows like *"Meet the Press"* and *"Face the Nation."* These forums were the exclusive prerogative of the senior members, and anyone who violated this unwritten rule was seen as an upstart who needed his wings clipped.

But the new members of the mid-1970s had no such reservations. Their attitude was "I know more about what they're going to ask me than *they* know, so what is there to be afraid of?" And because they were perfectly willing to criticize their own committee chairmen, or even the President, some of them became very popular with the news media, which like nothing better than to feature politicians blasting each other.

To many of the new members, of course, Tip O'Neill was an old fogey, a symbol of the established system they were so eager to bypass. At the same time, I had their respect: they knew I had taken a strong stand against the Vietnam War, and that Tip O'Neill had been an active backstage player in the Watergate drama. Besides, I've always been able to get along with people, even when we don't agree on everything....

Within a few months of becoming Speaker, I could already see some positive changes in the House—and so did the press. I especially liked what Joseph Kraft wrote in his syndicated column–that "in O'Neill, the House has found not only a leader, but also a champion. He has arrested the demoralization of the past few years. He gives the members a feeling of pride, a little touch of class."

I certainly tried to make the House a more open and effective place, and I believe I succeeded. In my daily news conferences, I tried to give the press something real to write about, and I never had any inclination to hide my legislative priorities. I also tried to be more open in the exercise of power....

I was used to being recognized in my own district, but now, as Speaker, my face was known all over the country. I was out in Sun Valley, Idaho, a couple of years ago, and as I was leaving church after Sunday morning mass, a tourist with California license plates on his car came over to me and said, "Did anybody ever tell you that you look a lot like Tip O'Neill?"

"Oh, yes," I said, "people tell me that all the time."

"I can't get over it," he said. "You're the spitting image of Tip O'Neill."

I smiled. "Listen, pal," I said. "Suppose I tell you that I *am* Tip O'Neill?"

"If you told me that," he said, "I'd know you were a damned liar. Tip O'Neill happens to be a good friend of mine!"

As he went back to his car, I could hear him telling his friends, "See that guy over there? He tried to tell me he was Tip O'Neill. Now, I *know* Tip O'Neill, so he can't fool me."

One reason my face was so familiar was that in 1979, during my third year as Speaker, I agreed to permit live, televised coverage of the House of Representatives—which turned out to be one of the best decisions I ever made....

But even with all my appearances on C-SPAN, not to mention the network news, every now and then I would run into somebody who apparently didn't watch TV. I once promised Margaret Heckler that I'd say a few words at a Washington meeting of the National Organization for Women. I was driving Millie's Chrysler, and, as instructed, I pulled into a parking space marked "Reserved for the Speaker."

The security guard, an elderly man, came over and knocked on the window. "Get that car out of here," he hollered. "This space is reserved for the Speaker."

I got out of the car and said, "I *am* the Speaker."

"Mr. Rayburn," he said. "I didn't recognize you!"

Sam Rayburn had been dead for twenty years, but his legend lives on in Washington.

Another time, at a charity golf tournament, I was teamed up with Sam Snead, one of the greatest golfers of all time. We had a marvelous afternoon, and at the end of the day he turned to me and said, "O'Brien, you're a hell of a guy. What do you do for a living?"

I guess he could tell I wasn't a golfer.

In all fairness, though, I have no right talking about people who don't know who I am, because I'm terrible at recognizing other celebrities. Millie and my two daughters still don't believe this story, but a few years ago, when I was passing through Stapleton Airport in Denver, a good-looking fellow came up and said, "Hello, Tip, how are you?"

I didn't know the guy, so I said, "Isn't this a beautiful city. Those mountains are twenty miles away, but you can almost reach out and touch them."

"You don't know me, do you?" he said.

"Listen," I said. "You recognize me because I'm on television every day and I'm in politics. I have white hair, a big bulbous nose, and cabbage ears. Everybody knows this face. So what's your name, anyway?"

"Robert Redford," he said.

33

STEPHEN HESS

Live from Capitol Hill It's ...
Picking Committees
in the Blow-Dried Age

———

WHEN MOST of us think about why a senator chooses to serve on one committee or another, a variety of motives come to mind. Perhaps the senator wants to pursue a subject that has always interested him. Daniel Patrick Moynihan, the Democratic senator from New York, who examined the problem of poverty as a Harvard Professor, now sits on the subcommittee on Social Security and Income Maintenance Programs. Or perhaps a senator wants to be sure his state has a voice in a certain area that is vital to its economy. Thus Jesse Helms, the Republican from North Carolina, chose in 1985 to retain the chairmanship of the Agriculture Committee to better defend his state's tobacco farmers rather than become chairman of the Foreign Relations Committee. Other committee assignments guarantee the respect of campaign-contributing PACs.

But there is another important reason why senators choose the committees they do: where you sit determines how often you will be photographed. Getting on the right committees is crucial to any senator who wants to get the attention of the Washington press corps—especially the television networks. . . .

An inspection of the worksheets kept by the Senate radio and television gallery shows that between February 1979 and June 1984 the best committee for the media hound to be on was Foreign Relations, covered by 522 network cameras. Foreign Relations has traditionally been the prime Senate incubator of presidential aspirants; since 1953, its members have included Robert A. Taft, William Knowland, Hubert Humphrey, Frank Church, Stuart Symington, Eugene McCarthy, Edmund Muskie, George McGovern, Howard Baker, John Glenn, Alan Cranston, and John F. Kennedy. Some of its power has ebbed—if only because we've kept out of a full-fledged war during the past decade—but Foreign Relations still remains the locus of congressional activity in the area that Washington journalism finds most newsworthy.

The next best place for a senator to get noticed is Judiciary (252 cameras). In recent years, Judiciary repeatedly has made news because of its jurisdiction over civil rights bills, anti-crime legislation (including such questions as the death penalty and the insanity defense), proposed constitutional amendments (the equal rights amendment, school prayer, abortion), and immigration reform.

The fastest rising seat of influence in terms of media attention—with 156 cameras, now in third place—is the Budget Committee. Its importance has grown along with the federal deficit. . . .

When I asked Joseph Biden what he felt accounted for his newsworthiness, he replied without hesitation. "It's the committees, of course." In 1983 and 1984, Biden was a member of the three most

RANKING OF SENATE COMMITTEES BY NUMBER
OF TELEVISION CAMERAS COVERING THEM

COMMITTEE	NUMBER OF CAMERAS
Foreign Relations	522
Judiciary	252
Budget	156
Governmental Affairs	152
Appropriations	141
Labor and Human Resources	134
Joint Economic	133
Armed Services	131
Energy and Natural Resources	120
Finance	98
Banking, Housing, and Urban Affairs	97
Ethics	82
Commerce, Science, and Transportation	61
Environment and Public Works	60
Agriculture, Nutrition, and Forestry	43
Aging	23
Intelligence	22
Rules and Administration	20
Small Business	6
Veterans' Affairs	1
Indian Affairs	0

Source: Senate Radio, Television, and Press Gallery

televised committees—Foreign Relations, Judiciary (where he was
the ranking Democrat), and Budget—as well as the Select Committee on Intelligence.

Other familiar faces also have chosen their committees wisely.
Orrin Hatch is chairman of Labor and of the Constitution subcommittee of Judiciary and serves on Budget and the Select Committee.
Howard Metzenbaum's committees are Budget, Energy, Judiciary,
and Labor; and Charles Mathias is on Rules (chairman), Foreign
Relations, Governmental Affairs, and Judiciary. Conversely, less
familiar faces may owe their national obscurity in part to the fact
that they don't sit on the heavily televised committees. Among
those who do not belong to the networks' top eight committees

are David Boren, Wendell Ford, Chic Hecht, John Melcher, David Pryor, and Malcolm Wallop. Photographs of these senators are available on request from their office....

In the past, ambitious Senate investigations garnered enormous publicity.... Yet after the 1950s only a few hearings garnered publicity on this scale. The most prominent exception was the Watergate hearings during the summer of 1973. Viewers in more than 47 million homes became fascinated by the personalities of the senators doing the questioning—Chairman Sam Ervin, the country philosopher from Harvard Law whose eyebrows danced while he grilled the witnesses; Howard Baker, forever asking "what the president knew and when did he know it," who suddenly pulled ahead of Edward Kennedy in a Harris poll trial heat for president; Daniel Inouye, who, during one witness's testimony, made the mistake of muttering into an open mike, "What a liar"; and Joseph Montoya, whose questions, Art Buchwald observed, provided an opportunity for viewers to run to the bathroom.

Media opportunities like those provided by Watergate are rare, however. TV stardom for a senator these days means a few seconds on the network news—but that may be enough to affect a senator's choice of committee assignments.

34

JANET HOOK
Freshmen Challenge Reagan— and the Senate

———

EXACTLY ONE YEAR after they were elected to the Senate, Brock Adams of Washington and Harry Reid of Nevada found themselves exercising the institution's most jealously guarded right: leading a filibuster.

Freshman orientation, it seems, is over.

Adams, Reid and the nine other Democrats first elected in November 1986 changed the face of the Senate by putting it back under Democratic control. Now they are well-positioned to shape its future.

While these freshmen learned quickly how to take advantage of Senate powers and privileges, they still have the newcomer's knack for unsettling the status quo—both in policy and procedures.

Accounting for one-fifth of all Senate Democrats, the class of 1986 has helped shift the balance of power on key legislative issues. It arrived just as Congress hit a policy crossroads, as the end of the Reagan era came into view. Its presence already has been crucial as the Democratic-dominated Senate challenged President Reagan in areas where he once held sway, such as shaping the judiciary.

"If it hadn't been for our class, Robert Bork would be a justice of the Supreme Court," said freshman Timothy E. Wirth, D-Colo., referring to the federal appeals court judge who was Reagan's ill-fated first choice to succeed Lewis F. Powell Jr.

The freshman Democrats form the first generation of post-Reagan legislators. While most have personal memories of the pull of Reagan's personality when he overwhelmed Congress after taking office, they were elected to the Senate over his active personal campaigning. Now they feel free to defy him and they look ahead to issues that will dominate the next decade, such as offsetting the government's borrowing binge of the 1980s and restructuring the farm economy.

They see themselves as pragmatists. A few, like Wirth, attracted the label of "neo-liberalism," a kind of non-ideology that has appealed to younger Democrats. But they are uncomfortable with any labels.

"The Vietnam War, the assassinations, Watergate, the Reagan years, supply-side economics falling on its face: The lesson is that hard ideological positions carry a danger," said Kent Conrad of North Dakota. "Hiding behind rhetorical barricades doesn't get things done."

Getting things done is what the class of 1986 says it is most interested in. The current Senate, most new members find, is not very good at that. If some of these freshmen had their way, the Senate would have a Rules Committee like the House's to set the terms of floor debate and limit amendments.

"Simply to come here and work in a museum is not my idea of a modern legislative process," said Thomas A. Daschle, the freshman Democrat from South Dakota who served four terms in the House. . . .

...The new senators have gone through certain formative political experiences together and share an institutional and political outlook that has helped them to become an unusually tight-knit group in a highly individualistic institution....

In an earlier era, freshmen spent their first years in the Senate in quiet obscurity. Now, they can move quickly into the limelight....

The Democratic freshmen have supplied a significant bloc of votes in confrontations that likely would have been lost to Reagan in past years. They have been an important ingredient in Senate Democrats' party unity on key votes—in part, because their ranks include a new generation of Southern Democrats who are less inclined to part ways with the national party than their more conservative elders.

The cement that held the freshman Democrats together on the Bork nomination was set largely in the 1986 campaigns.[*] The administration lost the votes of all but two of the Southern Democrats it had counted on to help put Bork on the court—and those two were senior members.

The five Southern freshmen had a particularly vivid reason to be unresponsive to Reagan's pleas. They had been elected with considerable support from blacks, who were active in opposing Bork, and over the aggressive personal campaigning of Reagan for their Republican opponents. In campaign speeches in the South, Reagan had underscored that keeping the Senate in Republican hands would help him place his judicial nominees.

Not a single Democratic freshman helped him out.

Whatever common ground they may find on substantive issues, the freshmen have coalesced most visibly around institutional questions. Their numbers alone position them well to have a voice in future decisions about how the Senate is run and about who the next Democratic leader will be.

Already they have been a force behind recent efforts—however

[*]President Reagan nominated Robert Bork to the Supreme Court in July 1987. Bork, a brilliant legal scholar and conservative spokesman, originally gained national prominence as Solicitor General in the Nixon administration, when he executed the president's order to dismiss Special Prosecutor Archibald Cox in October 1973 after his superiors in the Justice Department refused to do so and resigned from office. Later, Bork criticized what he saw as excessive judicial policy-making to achieve civil libertarian goals such as women's rights to obtain legal abortions. The Bork nomination led to an epic confirmation struggle, and was finally defeated in the Senate in October 1987. See Bork's own explanation of his "interpretivist" jurisprudence in selection 55.—Eds.

limited in their success—to restructure and regulate how the Senate does its business.

Eager to shore up their statewide political bases, the freshmen have pressed the leadership for a schedule that accommodates frequent home-state travel. Joined by senators up for re-election in 1988 and those living in Western states, the freshmen were a factor in the leadership's decision last spring to stop holding votes on Mondays and this year to try a schedule of working three weeks and then taking one week off.

"They bring a collective need to go home a lot," said a Democratic leadership aide. "They were all elected by slim margins."

The freshmen also have been a part of a new wave of frustration with the Senate's bouts of legislative paralysis. Former House members, in particular, are chafing under Senate procedures that allow a small minority to block major bills—even though they, too, sometimes take advantage of them.

"We are legislators. Like baseball players who like to play nine innings, like farmers who like to plant all of their fields, we like to pass laws," said Daschle. "In an era of fast moving, globalized issues, the possibility that the world could pass the Senate by increases immeasurably."

The class has thrown weight behind a relatively modest package of procedural changes designed to pick up the pace of the Senate. Sponsored by David Pryor, D-Ark., the proposals include a curb on the right to filibuster procedural motions and a firm 15-minute limit on roll-call votes.

"They are rightly impatient with some of the less sensible procedures in the Senate," said George J. Mitchell, D-Maine. "If they lead us to modify some of them ... that may be their greatest contribution."...

Perhaps no factor has contributed more to the class' cohesiveness than the fact that most members came from the House. Three—Mikulski, Shelby and Wirth—even sat on the same House committee, Energy and Commerce.

That means not simply that they knew each other before coming to the Senate, but also that they had a shared set of institutional experiences forming the backdrop against which they experience the exhilaration—and the frustration—of being in the Senate.

Indeed, the impact of the freshman class on the institution is in part a story about the clash of cultures when House meets Senate. Although the differences between the chambers are not always readily apparent, many members face the political equivalent of culture shock when they move to the freewheeling, disorganized Senate of 100 members from the 435-member House, where stricter rules make floor action more predictable and disciplined.

While none would dream of returning to the House, their desire to revamp Senate procedures reflects a touch of nostalgia for the efficiency of the House, where it was routinely possible for members to have four-day weekends at home....

The sense of class cohesion doubtless will fade as its members gain seniority, pursue their own interests and find their places within the Senate. The freshmen may also lose some of their fervor for institutional change.

"A couple of them already have found out that all the sandbags and delays are pretty handy in an emergency," said a former [Democratic Majority Leader] Byrd aide. "As long as it was someone else's emergency, they didn't want to have much to do with it."

But some more-senior senators who haven't rid themselves of the desire to change the Senate are heartened by the arrival of fresh allies.

"The more people we get from the House of Representatives, the better off we'll be," said Dan Quayle, R-Ind., a former House member who headed a procedural review commission in 1984. "We'll reform this place yet."

35

JANET HOOK

A New Breed of Chairman Waits in the Wings

————

WHEN Judiciary Committee Chairman Peter W. Rodino, Jr., retires from Congress next year, it will signify the passing of an era in House politics.

The New Jersey Democrat is the only remaining chairman who won his post before the Democratic Caucus in 1975 shook the foundations of the House committee structure by ousting three autocratic chairmen—a watershed that redirected the flow of institutional power in the House.

Now, a more subtle change in committee leadership is on the horizon: The highest ranks of the hierarchy are coming within reach of a younger generation of lawmakers who were not even in Congress back when chairmen reigned supreme.

The upper echelons of the House's committees are heavily populated by chairmen in their 70s and 80s—children of another political era:

- Appropriations: Jamie L. Whitten of Mississippi, age 77.
- Education and Labor: Augustus F. Hawkins of California, 80.
- Foreign Affairs: Dante B. Fascell of Florida, 71.
- Judiciary: Rodino, 78.
- Merchant Marine and Fisheries: Walter B. Jones of North Carolina, 74.
- Public Works: Glenn M. Anderson of California, 75.
- Rules: Claude Pepper of Florida, 87.

A look at the Democrats who are likely to be the next team of long-term chairmen provides a snapshot of the House of the future—assuming Democrats continue to follow seniority in naming chairmen and Republicans do not win a majority in the House. . . .

That lineup includes several prospective committee leaders likely to be more partisan than their predecessors, more aggressive in seizing opportunities to wield legislative power, and more adept at the media-savvy, issue-oriented politics of the post-Vietnam era.

"We're looking at some major transitions," says Rep. Mike Synar, a fifth-term Democrat from Oklahoma. "Members are biting at the bit to be more active. New chairmen and old chairmen are going to realize that a lot of members want more action.". . .

It will be some time before members who came to Congress in the Vietnam and Watergate era dominate the House chairmanships. But consider the changes in style and outlook, if not of generation, that have already been made or are in the offing: . . .

The guard already has changed at Armed Services, where Les Aspin of Wisconsin has redirected the pro-Pentagon panel and teamed up with the House Democratic leadership to put the party's imprimatur on defense policy.

Rodino, a cautious legislator who has used his power more to obstruct conservative initiatives than to advance a positive agenda, will be replaced as Judiciary Committee chairman by Jack Brooks, an assertive Texas Democrat who took over the backwater Government Operations Committee in 1975 and transformed it into an aggressive machine of oversight and investigation.

At two committees that handle environmental issues, Watergate-era members with close ties to environmental activists may soon be chairmen: George Miller of California is No. 2 at Interior and Gerry E. Studds of Massachusetts is the likely heir apparent at the Merchant Marine and Fisheries Committee.

At Education and Labor, Hawkins' low-key reign may some day give way to a more-combative partisan, William D. Ford of Michigan—the kind of crafty lawmaker who once proposed shutting down 10,000 small-town post offices to comply with Reagan-era budget cuts, knowing the House would never do it.

Although it could be a few years before the powerful Appropriations Committee chairmanship is passed to another generation, its line of succession includes the most dramatic emblem of changing House politics.

It is just a matter of time before the Appropriations chair is filled by David R. Obey, the Wisconsin Democrat who is the sixth-ranking member but nearly two decades younger than anyone senior to him. An outspoken liberal with wide-ranging interests in budget issues, Obey has used his positions of power not just to shape legislation, but as platforms from which to wage high-volume arguments with the Reagan administration over foreign aid and spending priorities. . . .

As a group, these chairmen-in-waiting mirror recent changes in House leaders. Former Speaker Thomas P. O'Neill Jr. of Massachusetts wielded power inconspicuously; his strengths were backroom politics and personal relations, not legislative detail and public relations. But Speaker Jim Wright of Texas is a take-charge leader who appeals to younger members who came to Congress with more commitment to an agenda than to a party organization.

"The chairman coming down the line will probably be more idea- and issue-oriented," said one Democrat from the class of 1974. "It's just like Jim Wright was more issue-oriented than Tip was—you will see it in Dave [Obey], Les [Aspin] and others.". . .

The current committee chairmen are presiding over a transition between eras. They came to Washington at a time when committee chairmanships were independent baronies that dominated the House's power structure; but by the time they became chairmen, the job had been transformed into a gift bestowed at the pleasure of rank-and-file House Democrats.

In the 1950s and 1960s, committee chairmen could operate as if in a private preserve. They were not forced to contend with such democratic niceties as open meetings, written rules or power-sharing with subcommittees.

But by the early 1970s, the caucus had chipped away at the clout of chairmen with rules changes that dispersed their powers and underscored their responsibility to the caucus by subjecting them to secret-ballot elections.

The new era was ushered in decisively in January 1975, when House Democrats, bolstered by the large class of freshmen elected in the wake of the Watergate scandal, ousted three sitting chairmen....

Other chairmen of that generation remained in power, but all had to accommodate the new institutional realities that the revolt left in its wake. They became more responsive to the Democratic leadership and the rank-and-file members who had so dramatically flexed their muscles....

Unlike the tumult of the 1970s, the impending changing of the guard of House chairmen will be gradual.

No one knows exactly when the baton will pass in each case, or what it will mean for the House as a whole. At least three Southern chairmen are likely to be replaced by Northern members, but at the same time demographic trends will increase the number of Western and Southern members in the House as a whole.

On several committees, the next long-term chairman is likely to be more partisan than the current one. Many of today's chairmen have long-standing relationships with ranking Republican members. If the Reagan-era actions of the chairmen-in-waiting are a guide, they are willing to confront an administration they do not like.

36

PAUL STAROBIN

Pork: A Time-Honored Tradition Lives On

———

IT SEEMS House Speaker Jim Wright will get his new airport after all.

Things looked bad in May when leaders of the Public Works Committee balked at a bid by the Texas Democrat and others to tack home-district projects onto a bill reauthorizing airport programs. They argued that the Federal Aviation Administration (FAA) was better positioned to assess the merits of specific projects.

The Speaker took his airport off the list. "People on the committee thought he was following the more modern thinking that maybe pork-barreling is not such a great thing," recalls a Public Works member.

They were wrong. Wright's office simply turned to the Appropriations Committee, which obliged by citing the need for the project in a report accompanying a transportation spending measure that passed the House in July. The report pointedly directs the FAA to give "high priority consideration" to the Speaker's initiative.

"How do you respond to a request by an 800-pound gorilla?" asks William Lehman, D-Fla., chairman of Appropriations' Subcommittee on Transportation. "The answer," Lehman says with a smile, "is quickly."

Political pork. Since the first Congress convened two centuries ago, lawmakers have ladled it out to home constituencies in the form of cash for roads, bridges and sundry other civic projects. It is a safe bet that the distribution of such largess will continue for at least as long into the future.

Pork-barrel politics, in fact, is as much a part of the congressional scene as the two parties or the rules of courtesy for floor debate....

And yet pork-barrel politics always has stirred controversy.

Critics dislike seeing raw politics guiding decisions on the distribution of federal money for parochial needs. They say disinterested experts, if possible, should guide that money flow.

And fiscal conservatives wonder how Congress will ever get a handle on the federal budget with so many lawmakers grabbing so forcefully for pork-barrel funds. "Let's change the system so we don't have so much porking," says James C. Miller III, director of the White House Office of Management and Budget (OMB). Miller says he gets complaints on the order of one a day from congressional members taking issue with OMB suggestions that particular "pork" items in the budget are wasteful.

But pork has its unabashed defenders. How, these people ask, can lawmakers ignore the legitimate demands of their constituents? When a highway needs to be built or a waterway constructed, the home folks quite naturally look to their congressional representative for help. Failure to respond amounts to political suicide.

"I've really always been a defender of pork-barreling because that's what I think people elect us for," says Rep. Douglas H. Bosco, D-Calif.

Moreover, many accept pork as a staple of the legislative process, lubricating the squeaky wheels of Congress by giving members a personal stake in major bills....

Not only does the flow of pork continue pretty much unabated, it seems to be spreading to areas that traditionally haven't been subject to pork-barrel competition. Pork traditionally was identified with public-works projects such as roads, bridges, dams and harbors. But, as the economy and country have changed, lawmakers have shifted their appetites to what might be called "post-industrial" pork. Some examples:

• *Green Pork.* During the 1960s and 1970s, when dam-builders fought epic struggles with environmentalists, "pork-barrel" projects stereotypically meant bulldozers and concrete. But many of today's projects are more likely to draw praise than blame from environmentalists. The list includes sewer projects, waste-site cleanups, solar energy laboratories, pollution-control research, parks and park improvements and fish hatcheries, to name a few....

• *Academic Pork.* Almost no federal funds for construction of university research facilities are being appropriated these days, except for special projects sponsored by lawmakers for campuses back home. Many of the sponsors sit on the Appropriations committees, from which they are well positioned to channel such funds. . . .

• *The Supercollider*. The effort to build the world's most powerful atom-smasher, the "superconducting supercollider," testifies to the appeal of high-tech pork. The multibillion-dollar research facility would bring an estimated 3,000 jobs to the state where it is sited.

In April, the Department of Energy (DOE) invited states to submit bids; six months later DOE had in hand 43 proposals from 25 states. Congressmen, senators and at least three governors showed up to deliver their states' applications. "States are salivating like you wouldn't believe," says Sen. J. Bennett Johnston, D-La.

• *Defense Pork*. While the distribution of pork in the form of defense contracts and location of military installations certainly isn't new, there's no question that Reagan's military buildup has expanded opportunities for lawmakers to practice pork-barrel politics. . . .

This spread of the pork-barrel system to new areas raises a question: What exactly is pork? Reaching a definition isn't easy. Many people consider it wasteful spending that flows to a particular state or district and is sought to please the folks back home.

But what is wasteful? One man's boondoggle is another man's civic pride. Perhaps the most sensible definition is that which a member seeks for his own state or district but would not seek for anyone else's constituency.

Thus, pork goes to the heart of the age-old tension between a lawmaker's twin roles as representative of a particular area and member of a national legislative body. In the former capacity, the task is to promote the local interest; in the latter it is to weigh the national interest. . . .

Like other fraternities, the system has a code of behavior and a pecking order. It commands loyalty and serves the purpose of dividing up federal money that presumably has to go somewhere, of helping re-elect incumbents and of keeping the wheels of legislation turning. . . .

When applied with skill, pork can act as a lubricant to smooth passage of complex legislation. At the same time, when local benefits are distributed for merely "strategic" purposes, it can lead to waste. . . .

Just about everyone agrees that the budget crunch has made

the competition to get pet projects in spending legislation more intense. Demand for such items has not shrunk nearly as much as the pool of available funds.

But there is disagreement about what that means in terms of the quality of projects that now pass congressional muster.

"I don't think we get as many bad projects," says Rep. Vic Fazio, D-Calif., a member of the Appropriations panel. "People aren't trying as hard to push things that don't have a lot of support."

But others say the tougher competition has simply pushed the projects of the less well-connected off the list. "We are not seeing a tightening up of the process at all," says Robert S. Walker, R-Pa. "Those with the clout use the clout to get what they want and merit selection never enters into the thinking."

Some evidence for the importance of clout comes from the increasing value that members seem to place on a slot on the Appropriations Committee, still the pre-eminent pork-barrel panel.

As Fazio concedes, this is partly because non-committee members are having a tougher time getting colleagues on Appropriations to go to bat for their projects. Those on the committee are finding it hard enough as it is to get their own projects through the legislative cycle.

"You're not in a position to say, 'Anything I can do for you,'" says Fazio. "What you'd really like is for members to go away."

Budget reforms enacted in the early 1970s contained nothing to control the spread of pork-type spending items. While appropriators must live with the limits of the annual budget resolution, they still retain the crucial authority to determine how and where the money is spent....

Exceptions to tax law are a kind of pork that, while less tangible than dams and harbors, are nevertheless in great demand. Providing such breaks is a fact of life for congressional tax-writers.

Ironically, such provisions proved quite helpful last year in propelling a tax-overhaul measure through Congress that was intended to rid the system of special-interest loopholes....

...The bounty came in the form of "transition" rules—ostensibly, tax breaks to ease the transition from the old to the new tax law for those affected by the change. Because of the sweeping nature of the proposed bill, lawmakers were swamped with requests from business constituents and others for special rules. Lawmakers took their requests to the chairmen of the tax-writing committees, who, in accordance with tradition, controlled the award of transition rules.

As described in *Showdown at Gucci Gulch,* a book tracing the bill's enactment, at a crucial point in the deliberations of the House Ways and Means Committee, Chairman Dan Rostenkowski threatened to deny transition rules to members who did not follow his lead. The threat reportedly came before a vote on a plan, opposed by the chairman, to retain 100 percent deductions for business meals. According to the authors, it was accompanied by an emotional plea from the Illinois Democrat for the cause of tax reform; in any event, several members switched their positions to defeat the proposal.

Robert T. Matsui, D-Calif., a Ways and Means member, did not recall actually hearing any threats, but says members implicitly understood that they would be cut off from transition rules if they crossed the chairman.

"If you're going to go against the company chairman's plan of action, you shouldn't expect to use the company chairman's executive lounge," says Matsui.

Rostenkowski did not disappoint those who stuck by him, doling out scores of rules to his allies as the markup wound down. For example, New York's Raymond J. McGrath, a committee Republican whose support proved vital to Rostenkowski, received a break on bonds to build a waste-disposal plant in his district, as well as several other provisions.

The chairman also kept in mind the bill's floor prospects. Rules Committee Chairman Claude Pepper received an array of favors, including a break for a new stadium for the Miami Dolphins football team.

"There were probably sufficient votes to pass the tax bill [in the House]," says Matsui, "but the transition rules assured its passage. I don't think there's any doubt about it.". . .

Those, especially in the administration, looking to put Congress on a pork-free diet often recommend giving the president authority to veto individual items within an appropriations bill. "I don't blame people for porking if there's an opportunity to pork," says Miller of the OMB. "The problem is that you have an institutional arrangement that allows it to happen.". . .

But the administration's push for the line-item veto faces virtually insurmountable opposition from law-makers unwilling to yield power over the purse to the executive branch. . . .

Rep. E. Clay Shaw Jr., R–Fla., has another idea: limiting service on the House Appropriations Committee to three terms, mirroring a system already in use on the Budget Committee. Under a resolution (H Res 250) introduced Aug. 6 by Shaw, the committee's rotation would commence at the start of the 101st Congress and would apply only to members appointed after that time. Seniority would not be taken into account for committee selection.

"We have a very close fraternity on the Appropriations Committee, and it needs to be broken up," says Shaw. "We need some new faces."

But Shaw isn't particularly optimistic that his proposal will stir any enthusiasm. For every member of Congress who considers self-restraint a virtue and practices it, there are many more who quite unashamedly believe in the credo of Bosco: "As long as the money is going to get apportioned. I'd like to see as much of it get apportioned in my district as possible."

PART SIX

The Presidency

HOW A VAST, socially heterogeneous republic with a constitutional system consciously designed to divide and partition political authority can achieve a coherent sense of direction has always been a good question. In the eighteenth-century world of the framers, our geographical isolation from European power struggles and minimal domestic need for a national state usually imparted little urgency to finding the answer. Nevertheless, we should not forget James Young's picture (in the last section) of a Jeffersonian republic "grossly deficient" in its capacity to make and enforce national decisions. By the 1880s the end of isolation and the problems of an industrializing economy posed the question in straightforward terms. We have been struggling with it ever since. The youthful Woodrow Wilson's "parliamentary solution," as we have already seen, never found a receptive American audience. As the more mature Wilson came to realize, the only practical answer has been to seek leadership and direction through the presidency, our one truly national political institution.

Presidential government has been the American formula for achieving coherent national governance. The arguments in its favor are now so familiar that we seldom question them. If we did, we would see another aspect of our "exceptionalism"—the extraordinary individualism of our expectations about executive leadership. Whereas most other democracies look to highly organized political parties for direction, we look to individuals on the order of Lincoln,

Wilson, and the two Roosevelts. For symbolism of the American nation, ideas and programs, for legislative leadership, leadership of public opinion, and a host of other roles, we look to the White House. The expectations we focus on a single individual are simply unique. Once the modern presidential job description comes clearly into focus, we can hardly help but wonder how one so wise, inspiring, and energetic could possibly be found among us. The evidence is that more often than not the search ends in disappointment. Not many of our forty-one presidents fill the bill. Yet, we continue to look and hope. That is our way.

Our readings on the presidency appropriately begin with a selection from Clinton Rossiter's classic essay, *The American Presidency,* the first widely read treatment of the modern office that came out of the New Deal and World War II. Writing over thirty years ago, Rossiter deftly captured the demands on the office and accurately predicted that they could only grow more intense. "Emergencies will grow nastier; Congress will grow more unwieldy; politics will take on more and more the spirit of a vast town meeting." It would be hard to find better words to describe American politics from the sixties to the eighties. Rossiter's commentary on presidential government has proved to be amazingly prescient. The heady expectations playing on the presidency have run well ahead of the institutional capacity of the office to meet them; yet, there has been no way to reduce them. Rossiter clearly foresaw dangerous tendencies in "salvation by staff"—expanding the presidential bureaucracy. If future presidents were not careful, he wrote, they might well be buried under the machinery of a swollen Executive Office.

Our second author, Richard Neustadt, writing at the beginning of the Kennedy presidency, stresses the importance of the president's personal qualities. The modern office *seems* so impressive, he argues, that the public and the president may be deluded into thinking that he can simply command things done. Actually, there is little power to command. The essence of presidential power, Neustadt argues, is the ability to persuade. Presidential power invariably requires the personal performance of an artful politician who must persuade the public and the Washington community to move in the direction he prefers. No amount of Executive Office machinery will suffice if the right personal qualities are missing. Only leaders of exceptional skill and will can do this job. They must be experienced in politics and temperamentally suited to the exercise of power.

By the Vietnam era, Arthur Schlesinger's *The Imperial Presidency* depicts an office afflicted precisely by the pathologies that Rossiter and Neustadt warned against. Modern electronic communications, public relations, the swelling of the presidential establishment, the pressures of the cold war, and relentless demands for secrecy in the name of national security had combined to produce an isolated and unaccountable presidency that threatened to usurp authority which, in our coordinate system of government, properly belonged to Congress. This troubled period of the presidency motivated many other scholars to understand what had gone wrong. James David Barber in *The Presidential Character* takes another tack. Barber's analysis locates the difficulty in the personalities of Lyndon Johnson and Richard Nixon. Such "active-negative" types, he argues, are pathologically striving, yet dangerously insecure. Barber has remained convinced that the key to successful presidential performance is an "active-positive" personality—an orientation he finds in such Presidents as John Kennedy and Jimmy Carter. Barber's argument pushes the individualistic approach to presidential leadership about as far as it can go. We must learn to select the right personality types and reject those who will be misfits. Thomas Cronin develops yet another argument. The modern presidential office, he thinks, is inherently paradoxical, and thus our expectations of presidents are unavoidably contradictory. The same person is expected, for example, to be trustworthy and Machiavellian, pragmatic and ideological, both a leader and follower of public opinion. No wonder, then, that the expectations we have of presidents are seldom satisfied.

Although the presidential literature has assumed a somewhat more optimistic tone in the Reagan years, it seems fair to say that most presidential scholars continue to see the American quest for successful presidential government as inherently problematic. Looking back from this period across two centuries of experience Bert Rockman concludes that the "leadership question" is a perennial and insoluble one in the American polity. The American state is deliberately fragmented. Our political culture is suspicious of centralized authority and emphatically approving of pluralistic local interests. Yet we expect the president somehow to produce unity out of all this division. While it is not an altogether impossible task, the odds are heavily against success, barring outright national emergency. So be it, he concludes, for as a people we don't know how to have it any other way.

The themes laid out by political scientists are illustrated in some selections from recent writings by journalists and political appointees. Hedrick Smith, a journalist, discusses the slippery dynamics of power in contemporary Washington. Note that he emphasizes the elusive personal qualities that permit a Reagan to succeed where a Carter could not. Who among us fully understands this? Smith thinks that factors such as likeability, an ability to "grasp power lightly," the knack of maintaining an illusion of power, and a certain "grace" under pressure are the keys to Reagan's success. Joseph Califano, a key player in the administrations of Lyndon Johnson and Jimmy Carter, describes in gruesome detail the failure of Carter to grasp the levers of power successfully. Well into his presidency Califano shows Carter grasping at straws, without a clue. It would never get better. Michael Deaver, before his troubled days as a lobbyist, describes one of his worst episodes in the Reagan White House—the Bitburg affair, in which a seemingly unimportant visit to a German cemetery suddenly became the subject of a "media firestorm." In today's Washington things can go very bad very quickly. Finally, a light commentary on the guest lists for White House dinners highlights the very different personae of recent administrations. Here presidential wives play an undoubtedly large role. The Eisenhowers favored corporate types; the Kennedys, achievers and celebrities. The Carters alone would have included their teenage daughter, Amy. The Reagans have favored the rich and famous. Even White House dinners reflect the ultimately personal nature of the presidential performance.

37

CLINTON ROSSITER

The Future of the Presidency

From *The American Presidency*

WE NEED no special gift of prophecy to predict a long and exciting future for the American Presidency. There are those who dream of a President in the image of Calvin Coolidge; there are those who fear that the Presidency will be sapped by "the assaults of ignorance and envy." Neither the dream nor the fear is likely to find much substance in coming events. All the great political and social forces that brought the Presidency to its present state of power and glory will continue to work in the future. Our economy and society will grow more rather than less interdependent, and we will turn to the President, anxiously if not always confidently, for help in solving the problems that fall thickly upon us. Our government will become more rather than less involved in the affairs of "mankind, from China to Peru," and the peoples of the world will look to its head for bold and imaginative leadership. Emergencies will grow nastier; Congress will become more unwieldy; politics will take on more and more the spirit of a vast town meeting. And one of the few things we can say for certain about the next war is that it will convert our form of government overnight into a temporary dictatorship of the President of the United States.

Another thing we can say for certain is that we have not seen our last great man in the White House. The people of the United States are no longer interested in presidential aspirants who promise only to be meek and mild. In the foreseeable future, as in the recent past, they will expect and get a full measure of presidential leadership. Even the Republicans, who have always been distinctly less enamored of the strong Presidency than have the Democrats, are coming to realize that the scales of power have tipped drastically and probably permanently toward the White House and away from

Capitol Hill. There is a Presidency in our future, and it is the Presidency of Jackson and Lincoln rather than of Monroe and Buchanan, of Roosevelt and Truman rather than of Harding and Coolidge. . . .

A . . . major defect that men find in the Presidency is the intolerable burden laid upon him who holds it. I am not talking here about the great functions of state he discharges in our behalf, for I cannot imagine how a single one of these could be transferred safely and effectively to some other officer in the national government. It would be a constitutional disaster if the President were even to attempt to surrender his final responsibility in the areas of war, peace, politics, opinion, ceremony, and management. I am talking, rather, of the routine of these functions: of the mechanical tasks he is required to perform by law and custom; of the briefings, appointments, speeches, conferences, and appearances; of the letters he must answer and signatures he must affix. Much has been done in recent years to relieve him of his petty burdens without relieving him of his great responsibilities, and we can be grateful to Franklin Roosevelt and his successors for having taken the lead in improving their own lot. Yet much, too, remains to be done. We should expect future Presidents, Congresses, and Executive Offices to co-operate in guarding the Presidency against the paralysis of detail. . . .

In seeking to lighten the President's burden, we would do well to recall the warning of Woodrow Wilson: "Men of ordinary physique and discretion cannot be Presidents and live, if the strain be not somehow relieved. We shall be obliged always to be picking our chief magistrates from among wise and prudent athletes—a small class." At the same time, we should also recall that a long list of routine tasks, each of which appears "nonessential" when viewed by itself, may well add up to an inspired performance of a great function of state. The President cannot be a successful Chief of State if he turns all the little ceremonies and visits over to the Vice-President. He cannot lead Congress if he is unwilling to spend hours listening to Congressmen. And he cannot be a vigorous Commander in Chief unless he studies the defense budget item by item. For him as for all of us there is no final escape from hard and pedestrian labor. . . .

The real problem of the Executive Office is potential rather than actual: the danger that the President might be buried under his own machinery. The institutionalization of the Presidency could be carried so far that the man who occupies it would become a prisoner in his own house, a victim of too much and too rigid organization. I doubt very much that such a situation could last for long if it did develop. Andrew Jackson proved once and for all the capacity of a determined President to burst the bonds of restrictive custom and legislation and to beat a retreat to the plain words of Article II. Yet rather than make it necessary for another Jackson to blow across Washington like a "tropical tornado," we should be alert to steps that might weaken or smother the President's position of dominance over his own auxiliaries. Much depends, of course, on his intimate advisers. It is their unrelenting duty to protect the President against all but the most essential problems in their designated areas, to present these in such form that they can be readily mastered, and especially to preserve the President's freedom of choice among competing alternatives. Needless to say, the President himself must set the tone for the operations of the Executive Office. He must insist that he be spared routine but not thought and decision, for he is, after all, the responsible head of government. He must be careful not to rely too heavily on the briefings and opinions of his own staff, for he will soon find himself out of touch with harsh reality. Above all, he must leave channels open to the political and social pressures that excite imagination and breed sensitivity. Unfriendly visitors, hostile newspapers, and free-swinging press conferences are three such channels he must have the insight and bravery not to block off. The Presidency must not become so highly mechanized that the President himself is spared the "suffering and glory of democratic leadership."...

Since the opening day of Washington's administration the President's relations with Congress have been a target of criticism; the target is still being shot at with enthusiasm and at least passing accuracy. Much of this criticism is irrelevant, since it ignores the blunt truth that we long ago made our irrevocable choice of coordinate rather than unified government. Much is soft-headed, since it refuses to rise above the political and personal frictions that are the mark, but not the only mark, of such government. Yet much hits the target squarely, and I think we should take notice of two major areas in which the hope of improvement must never be abandoned.

In the first place, the President's leadership of Congress remains spotty and discontinuous. Although he is acknowledged widely to be the Leader of Legislation, his tools of persuasion, except his own machinery for drafting, clearing, and forwarding legislative proposals, are not one bit sharper than they were forty years ago. Here, too, as in the field of administration, there is a widening gap between what the people expect and what he can produce. He must have a program and push for its enactment, but he has no way to force a decision upon a reluctant Congress....

In the last reckoning, we will continue to make progress toward firmer and friendlier executive-legislative relations by traveling the familiar path hacked out by the successful Presidents of this century. By following this path, even when it wandered through the swamps of petty politics, we have moved to a point at which cooperation under the President's guidance is far more certain that it was before 1900. Term by term, crisis by crisis, men in and out of Congress have been educated to accept the necessity of presidential leadership, and the Presidents have gone through a cumulative learning process of their own. This process of education in statesmanship must be carried on indefinitely, for in prescriptive growth, not in clever "gimmicks," lies our best hope for the cooperation we have a right to expect.

Most political observers are now more concerned with the other side of the two-way street between President and Congress. While he is busy asserting leadership in making laws, Congress is busy asserting control over their execution, and there is evidence to support the charge that Congress has roamed farther out of bounds than the President in the past few years. It is, to be sure, an axiom of coordinate government that the independent legislature must exercise oversight of the administration. Congress, too, must be concerned with ethics, loyalty, efficiency, frugality, and responsiveness in the public service; it must judge for itself whether the laws are being faithfully executed. No one can argue that it has any less constitutional right than the President to stake its claim to the disputed territory between them. But it does not have the right, probably not constitutionally and certainly not morally, to take over effective control of any part of the executive branch. It may inquire, expose, encourage, and warn, but it may not direct; and this—straight-out direction of various agencies and officers— is what Congress has been doing too much of in recent years. The result has been disorder, dissension, indecision, and disruption of morale at key points in the public service. Needless to say, Congress as a whole is guilty only of nonfeasance. It is the members of Congress, operating as committees, subcommittees, or lone wolves, who have poked their inquiring noses beyond the limits of political decorum and constitutional practice. . . .

There is one final defect in the relations of President and Congress of which we should take careful note, especially since its correction would strengthen the President's control over the administration as well as his influence in Congress. I refer to his lack of any power to veto separate items in the overstuffed appropriations bills presented for his approval. The President often feels compelled to sign bills that are full of dubious grants and subsidies rather than risk a breakdown in the work of whole departments. While it salves his conscience and cools his anger to announce publicly that he would veto these if he could, most Congressmen have learned to pay no attention to his protests. The champions of the "item veto," who point out that forty governors have a power denied to the President, insist that nothing but great good would come from giving it to him, whether through a constitutional amendment or, failing that, a self-denying ordinance of Congress. On one hand, his leadership of Congress would be strengthened, for he would hold an efficient new weapon, one that works out in the open, for reminding Congressmen that economy in the national interest is just as important as spending in the local interest. On the other, his work as Chief Executive would run more smoothly, since he would at last have full authority to match his responsibility for the executive budget. No agency of the government would be spending new money on a project of which he had the courage to disapprove sharply.

The loudest argument that has been raised against the item veto is that it might strengthen the President's hand just a little too much in his dealings with Congress. It would open the door to presidential pressure on individual Congressmen, and thus to bargains of the hardest kind. There is much to be said for this argument, and we might well pause before amending the Constitution to grant this new power to the President. But there is no reason why Congress itself should not experiment with an occasional appropriations bill that authorizes the President to eliminate or reduce specific items subject to congressional reversal by concurrent resolution within a specified number of days. We have the assurance of several prominent constitutionalists that such a device would violate neither the letter nor the spirit of the Constitution. If Congress could once give this power outright to the governors of several territories, it can certainly give it now under wraps to the President of the United States. If we learn through these experiments that the power is one he ought to have, and is unlikely to abuse, we could then catch up with the Confederate States of America by writing it into the Constitution. We should hesitate much longer to grant him power to veto items in ordinary bills....

...Americans may take some pride in the balance they have built into the Presidency.

It provides a steady focus of leadership: of administration, Congress, and people. In a constitutional system compounded of diversity and antagonism, the Presidency looms up as the countervailing force of unity and harmony. In a society ridden by centrifugal forces, it is, as Sidney Hyman has written, the "common reference point for social effort." The relentless progress of this continental republic has made the Presidency our one truly national political institution....

It is, finally, an office of freedom. The Presidency is a standing reproach to those petty doctrinaires who insist that executive power is inherently undemocratic; for, to the exact contrary, it has been more responsive to the needs and dreams of giant democracy than any other office or institution in the whole mosaic of American life....

The American people, who are, after all, the best judges of the means by which their democracy is to be achieved, have made the Presidency their peculiar instrument. As they ready themselves for the pilgrimage ahead, they can take comfort and pride in the thought that it is also their peculiar treasure.

38

RICHARD NEUSTADT

The Power to Persuade

From *Presidential Power*

———

IN THE EARLY SUMMER of 1952, before the heat of the campaign, President Truman used to contemplate the problems of the General-become-President should Eisenhower win the forthcoming election. "He'll sit here," Truman would remark (tapping his desk for emphasis), "and he'll say, 'Do this! Do that!' *And nothing will happen.* Poor Ike—it won't be a bit like the Army. He'll find it very frustrating.".... "Do this, do that, and nothing will happen." Long before he came to talk of Eisenhower he had put his own experience in other words: "I sit here all day trying to persuade people to do the things they ought to have sense enough to do without my persuading them.... That's all the powers of the President amount to."

In these words of a President, spoken on the job, one finds the essence of the problem now before us: "powers" are no guarantee of power; clerkship is no guarantee of leadership. The President of the United States has an extraordinary range of formal powers, of authority in statute law and in the Constitution. Here is testimony that despite his "powers" he does not obtain results by giving orders—or not, at any rate, merely by giving orders. He also has extraordinary status, *ex officio,* according to the customs of our government and politics. Here is testimony that despite his status he does not get action without argument. Presidential *power* is the power to persuade....

The dismissal of MacArthur, the seizure of the steel mills, the dispatch of troops to Little Rock share a common characteristic: in terms of immediate intent the President's own order brought results as though his words were tantamount to action. He said, "Do this, do that," and *it was done.*[*] From a presidential standpoint these three orders were self-executing. To give them was to have them carried out. Literally, no orders carry themselves out; self-executed actually means executed-by-others. But self-executing does describe the practical effect as it appeared to those who gave the orders. In the order-giver's eyes command amounted to compliance....

---

[*]General Douglas MacArthur, commander of American forces in the Far East, was dismissed by President Harry Truman for insubordination in April 1951, during the Korean War. MacArthur, who barely disguised his contempt for Truman, publicly advocated war against the People's Republic of China on the Chinese mainland. Truman used what he thought was the authority of his office to seize and operate the nation's steel mills in 1951 after a protracted collective bargaining stalemate threatened to disrupt the war effort. The Supreme Court declared the seizure illegal in the same year. President Eisenhower sent the U.S. Army troops to Little Rock, Arkansas, in 1957 to enforce a U.S. Federal Court of Appeals approved integration plan for Little Rock schools, following the Supreme Court's ruling in *Brown v. Board of Education* (1954) that laws requiring racial segregation were unconstitutional. *Brown* is discussed in selection 87.—EDS.

...At least five common factors were at work. On each occasion the President's involvement was unambiguous. So were his words. His order was widely publicized. The men who received it had control of everything needed to carry it out. And they had no apparent doubt of his authority to issue it to them. It is no accident that these five factors can be found in all three instances. These are the factors that produce self-executing orders. Lacking any one of them the chances are that mere command will not produce compliance....

The first factor favoring compliance with a presidential order is assurance that the President has spoken. The three self-executing orders were given by the man himself, and not only in form but very much in fact. They were *his* orders in the double sense that they both came from him and expressed a definite decision by him personally. Recipients were left no room for doubt on either score; wording, timing, and publicity took care of that....

A second factor making for compliance with a President's request is clarity about his meaning. If it helps to have respondents know that *he* wants what he asks, it also helps to have them know precisely what he wants....

A third factor favoring compliance with a President's directive is publicity. Even when there is no need for ambiguity, no possibility of imprecision, no real discretionary leeway and nothing to misunderstand, compliance may depend not only on the respondent's awareness of what he is to do, but also on the awareness of others that he has been told to do it. In sending troops to Little Rock, in seizing the steel industry, in firing MacArthur, the whole country was taken into camp, informed of the President's commitment, invited to watch the response....

A fourth factor favoring compliance with a President's request is actual ability to carry it out. It helps to have the order-taker in possession of the necessary means....

A fifth factor making for compliance with a President's request is the sense that what he wants is his by right.... The sense of legitimate obligation, legitimately imposed, was present in MacArthur's transfer of his own commands and in the Army's response to its Little Rock directive, no less than in the union's action after seizure. Without a sense of that sort on the part of order-takers, those orders would not have been carried out so promptly....

How often is that combination likely to occur? How much,

then, can a President rely on sheer command to get him what he wants? It takes but a glance ... to suggest the answers: not very often and not very much. ...

Self-executing orders have their uses, however inconclusive or expensive they may be. In each of these three cases, even steel, the presidential order brought assurance that a policy objective would remain in reach just as its loss seemed irretrievable. This is a real accomplishment. But necessarily it is a *transitory* accomplishment. Even the last resorts turn out to share the character of all the softer measures they replace. They turn out to be incidents in a persuasive process whereby someone lacking absolute control seeks to get something done through others who have power to resist.

Truman is quite right when he declares that presidential power is the power to persuade. Command is but a method of persuasion, not a substitute, and not a method suitable for everyday employment. ...

The separateness of institutions and the sharing of authority prescribe the terms on which a President persuades. When one man shares authority with another, but does not gain or lose his job upon the other's whim, his willingness to act upon the urging of the other turns on whether he conceives the action right for him. The essence of a President's persuasive task is to convince such men that what the White House wants of them is what they ought to do for their sake and on their authority.

Persuasive power, thus defined, amounts to more than charm or reasoned argument. These have their uses for a President, but these are not the whole of his resources. For the men he would induce to do what he wants done on their own responsibility will need or fear some acts by him on his responsibility. If they share his authority, he has some share in theirs. Presidential "powers" may be inconclusive when a President commands, but always remain relevant as he persuades. The status and authority inherent in his office reinforce his logic and his charm. ...

A President's authority and status give him great advantages in dealing with the men he would persuade. Each "power" is a vantage point for him in the degree that other men have use for his authority. From the veto to appointments, from publicity to budgeting, and so down a long list, the White House now controls the most encompassing array of vantage points in the American political system. With hardly an exception, the men who share in governing this country are aware that at some time, in some degree, the doing of *their* jobs, the furthering of *their* ambitions, may depend upon the President of the United States. Their need for presidential action, or their fear of it, is bound to be recurrent if not actually continuous. Their need or fear is his advantage.

A President's advantages are greater than mere listing of his "powers" might suggest. The men with whom he deals must deal with him until the last day of his term. Because they have continuing relationships with him, his future, while it lasts, supports his present influence. Even though there is no need or fear of him today, what he could do tomorrow may supply today's advantage. continuing relationships may convert any "power," any aspect of his status, into vantage points in almost any case. When he induces other men to do what he wants done, a President can trade on their dependence now *and* later.

The President's advantages are checked by the advantages of others. Continuing relationships will pull in both directions. These are relationships of mutual dependence. A President depends upon the men he would persuade; he has to reckon with his need or fear of them. They too will possess status, or authority, or both, else they would be of little use to him. Their vantage points confront his own; their power tempers his. . . .

The power to persuade is the power to bargain. Status and authority yield bargaining advantages. But in a government of "separated institutions sharing powers," they yield them to all sides. With the array of vantage points at his disposal, a President may be far more persuasive than his logic or his charm could make him. But outcomes are not guaranteed by his advantages. There remain the counter pressures those whom he would influence can bring to bear on him from vantage points at their disposal. Command has limited utility; persuasion becomes give-and-take. It is well that the White House holds the vantage points it does. In such a business any President may need them all—and more. . . .

39

ARTHUR SCHLESINGER

From *The Imperial Presidency*

————

IN THE LAST YEARS presidential primacy, so indispensable
to the political order, has turned into presidential supremacy. The
constitutional Presidency—as events so apparently disparate as the
Indochina War and the Watergate affair showed—has become the
imperial Presidency and threatens to be the revolutionary Presidency.

This book ... deals essentially with the shift in the *constitutional*
balance—with, that is, the appropriation by the Presidency, and
particularly by the contemporary Presidency, of powers reserved
by the Constitution and by long historical practice to Congress.

This process of appropriation took place in both foreign and
domestic affairs. Especially in the twentieth century, the circumstances of an increasingly perilous world as well as of an increasingly interdependent economy and society seemed to compel a
larger concentration of authority in the Presidency. It must be said
that historians and political scientists, this writer among them,
contributed to the rise of the presidential mystique. But the imperial
Presidency received its decisive impetus, I believe, from foreign
policy; above all, from the capture by the Presidency of the most
vital of national decisions, the decision to go to war.

This book consequently devotes special attention to the history
of the war-making power. The assumption of that power by the
Presidency was gradual and usually under the demand or pretext
of emergency. It was as much a matter of congressional abdication
as of presidential usurpation. ...

The imperial Presidency was essentially the creation of foreign
policy. A combination of doctrines and emotions—belief in permanent and universal crisis, fear of communism, faith in the duty
and the right of the United States to intervene swiftly in every
part of the world—had brought about the unprecedented centralization of decisions over war and peace in the Presidency. With this
there came an unprecedented exclusion of the rest of the executive

branch, of Congress, of the press and of public opinion in general from these decisions. Prolonged war in Vietnam strengthened the tendencies toward both centralization and exclusion. So the imperial Presidency grew at the expense of the constitutional order. Like the cowbird, it hatched its own eggs and pushed the others out of the nest. And, as it overwhelmed the traditional separation of powers in foreign affairs, it began to aspire toward an equivalent centralization of power in the domestic polity.

...We saw in the case of Franklin D. Roosevelt and the New Deal that extraordinary power flowing into the Presidency to meet domestic problems by no means enlarged presidential authority in foreign affairs. But we also saw in the case of FDR and the Second World War and Harry S. Truman and the steel seizure that extraordinary power flowing into the Presidency to meet international problems could easily encourage Presidents to extend their unilateral claims at home.... Twenty years later, the spillover effect from Vietnam coincided with indigenous developments that were quite separately carrying new power to the Presidency. For domestic as well as for international reasons, the imperial Presidency was sinking roots deep into the national society itself.

One such development was the decay of the traditional party system.... For much of American history the party has been the ultimate vehicle of political expression. Voters inherited their politics as they did their religion.... By the 1970s ticket-splitting had become common. Independent voting was spreading everywhere, especially among the young. Never had party loyalties been so weak, party affiliations so fluid, party organizations so irrelevant.

Many factors contributed to the decline of parties. The old political organizations had lost many of their functions. The waning of immigration, for example, had deprived the city machine of its classical clientele. The rise of civil service had cut off the machine's patronage. The New Deal had taken over the machine's social welfare role. Above all, the electronic revolution was drastically modifying the political environment. Two electronic devices had a particularly devastating impact on the traditional structure of politics—television and the computer....

As the parties wasted away, the Presidency stood out in solitary majesty as the central focus of political emotion, the ever more potent symbol of national community....

At the same time, the economic changes of the twentieth century had conferred vast new powers not just on the national government but more particularly on the Presidency....

...The managed economy, in short, offered new forms of unilateral power to the President who was bold enough to take action on his own....

...The imperial presidency, born in the 1940s and 1950s to save the outer world from perdition, thus began in the 1960s and 1970s to find nurture at home. Foreign policy had given the President the command of peace and war. Now the decay of the parties left him in command of the political scene, and the Keynesian revelation placed him in command of the economy. At this extraordinary historical moment, when foreign and domestic lines of force converged, much depended on whether the occupant of the White House was moved to ride the new tendencies of power or to resist them.

For the American Presidency was a peculiarly personal institution. It remained, of course, an agency of government, subject to unvarying demands and duties no matter who was President. But, more than most agencies of government, it changed shape, intensity and ethos according to the man in charge.... The management of the great foreign policy crisis of the Kennedy years—the Soviet attempt to install nuclear missiles in Cuba—came as if in proof of the proposition that the nuclear age left no alternative to unilateral presidential decision....

...Time was short, because something had to be done before the bases became operational. Secrecy was imperative. Kennedy took the decision into his own hands, but it is to be noted that he did not make it in imperial solitude. The celebrated Executive Committee became a forum for exceedingly vigorous and intensive debate. Major alternatives received strong, even vehement, expression. Though there was no legislative consultation, there was most effective executive consultation.... But, even in retrospect, the missile crisis seems an emergency so acute in its nature and so peculiar in its structure that it did in fact require unilateral executive decision.

Yet this very acuteness and peculiarity disabled Kennedy's action in October 1962 as a precedent for future Presidents in situations less acute and less peculiar. For the missile crisis was unique in the postwar years in that it *really* combined all those pressures of threat, secrecy and time that the foreign policy establishment had claimed as characteristic of decisions in the nuclear age. Where the threat was less grave, the need for secrecy less urgent, the time for debate less restricted—i.e., in all other cases—the argument for independent and unilateral presidential action was notably less compelling.

Alas, Kennedy's action, which should have been celebrated as an exception, was instead enshrined as a rule. This was in great part because it so beautifully fulfilled both the romantic ideal of the strong President and the prophecy of split-second presidential decision in the nuclear age. The very brilliance of Kennedy's performance appeared to vindicate the idea that the President must take unto himself the final judgments of war and peace. The missile crisis, I believe, was superbly handled, and could not have been handled so well in any other way. But one of its legacies was the imperial conception of the Presidency that brought the republic so low in Vietnam....

...Johnson talked to, even if he too seldom listened to, an endless stream of members of Congress and the press. He unquestionably denied himself reality for a long time, especially when it came to Vietnam. But in the end reality broke through, forcing him to accept unpleasant truths he did not wish to hear. Johnson's personality was far closer than Truman's to imperial specifications. But the fit was by no means perfect....

Every President reconstructs the Presidency to meet his own psychological needs. Nixon displayed more monarchical yearnings than any of his predecessors. He plainly reveled in the ritual of the office, only regretting that it could not be more elaborate. What previous President, for example, would have dreamed of ceremonial trumpets or of putting the White House security force in costumes to rival the Guards at Buckingham Palace? Public ridicule stopped this. But Nixon saw no problem about using federal money, under the pretext of national security, to adorn his California and Florida estates with redwood fences, golf carts, heaters and wind screens for the swimming pool, beach cabanas, roof tiling, carpets, furniture, trees and shrubbery.... Nixon's fatal error was to institute within the White House itself a centralization even more total than that he contemplated for the executive branch. He rarely saw most of his so-called personal assistants. If an aide telephoned the President on a domestic matter, his call was switched to Haldeman's office.* If he sent the President a memoran-

---

* Robert Haldeman headed Richard Nixon's White House staff. He was a stern gatekeeper (the president wished it so) before his resignation in the face of the exploding Watergate scandals during the spring of 1973. He was subsequently convicted of criminal charges and imprisoned for his role in Watergate.—Eds.

dum, Haldeman decided whether or not the President would see it. "Rather than the President telling someone to do something," Haldeman explained in 1971, "I'll tell the guy. If he wants to find out something from somebody, I'll do it."

Presidents like Roosevelt and Kennedy understood that, if the man at the top confined himself to a single information system, he became the prisoner of that system. Therefore they pitted sources of their own against the information delivered to them through official channels. They understood that contention was an indispensable means of government. But Nixon, instead of exposing himself to the chastening influence of debate, organized the executive branch and the White House in order to shield himself as far as humanly possible from direct question or challenge—i.e., from reality....

As one examined the impressive range of Nixon's initiatives— from his appropriation of the war-making power to his interpretation of the appointing power, from his unilateral determination of social priorities to his unilateral abolition of statutory programs, from his attack on legislative privilege to his enlargement of executive privilege, from his theory of impoundment to his theory of the pocket veto, from his calculated disparagement of the cabinet and his calculated discrediting of the press to his carefully organized concentration of federal management in the White House—from all this a larger design ineluctably emerged. It was hard to know whether Nixon, whose style was banality, understood consciously where he was heading. He was not a man given to political philosophizing. But he was heading toward a new balance of constitutional powers, an audacious and imaginative reconstruction of the American Constitution. He did indeed contemplate, as he said in 1971 State of the Union message, a New American Revolution. But the essence of this revolution was not, as he said at the time, power to the people. The essence was power to the Presidency.... His purpose was probably more unconscious than conscious; and his revolution took direction and color not just from the external circumstances pressing new powers on the Presidency but from the needs and drives of his own agitated psyche. This was the fatal flaw in the revolutionary design. For everywhere he looked he saw around him hideous threats to the national security—threats that, even though he would not describe them to Congress or the people, kept his White House in constant uproar and warranted in his own mind a clandestine presidential response of spectacular and historic illegality. If his public actions led toward a scheme of presidential supremacy under a considerably debilitated Constitution, his private obsessions pushed him toward the view that the Presidency could set itself, at will, *above* the Constitution. It was this theory that led straight to Watergate....

Secrecy seemed to promise government three inestimable advantages: the power to withhold, the power to leak and the power to lie....

The power to withhold held out the hope of denying the public the knowledge that would make possible an independent judgment on executive policy. The mystique of inside information—"if you only knew what we know"—was a most effective way to defend the national-security monopoly and prevent democratic control of foreign policy....

The power to leak meant the power to tell the people what it served the government's purpose that they should know....

The power to withhold and the power to leak led on inexorably to the power to lie. The secrecy system instilled in the executive branch the idea that foreign policy was no one's business save its own, and uncontrolled secrecy made it easy for lying to become routine. It was in this spirit that the Eisenhower administration concealed the CIA operations it was mounting against governments around the world. It was in this spirit that the Kennedy administration stealthily sent the Cuban brigade to the Bay of Pigs and stealthily enlarged American involvement in Vietnam. It was in this spirit that the Johnson administration Americanized the Vietnam War, misrepresenting one episode after another to Congress and the people—Tonkin Gulf, the first American ground force commitment, the bombing of North Vietnam, My Lai and the rest.

The longer the secrecy system dominated government, the more government assumed the *right* to lie....

God, it has been well said, looks after drunks, children and the United States of America. However, given the number, the brazen presumption and the clownish ineptitude of the conspirators, if it had not been Watergate, it would surely have been something else. For Watergate was a symptom, not a cause. Nixon's supporters complained that his critics were blowing up a petty incident out of all proportion to its importance. No doubt a burglary at Democratic headquarters was trivial next to a mission to Peking. But Watergate's importance was not simply in itself. Its importance was in the way it brought to the surface, symbolized and made

politically accessible the great question posed by the Nixon administration in every sector—the question of presidential power. The
unwarranted and unprecedented expansion of presidential power,
because it ran through the whole Nixon system, was bound, if
repressed at one point, to break out at another. This, not Watergate,
was the central issue.... Watergate did stop the revolutionary Presidency in its tracks. It blew away the mystique of the mandate and
reinvigorated the constitutional separation of powers. If the independent judiciary, the free press, Congress and the executive agencies could not really claim too much credit as institutions for work
performed within them by brave individuals, nonetheless they all
drew new confidence as institutions from the exercise of power
they had forgotten they possessed. The result could only be to
brace and strengthen the inner balance of American democracy....

If the Nixon White House escaped the legal consequences of its
illegal behavior, why would future Presidents and their associates
not suppose themselves entitled to do what the Nixon White House
had done? Only condign punishment would restore popular faith
in the Presidency and deter future Presidents from illegal conduct—
so long, at least, as Watergate remained a vivid memory. We have
noted that corruption appears to visit the White House in fifty-
year cycles. This suggests that exposure and retribution inoculate
the Presidency against its latent criminal impulses for about half a
century. Around the year 2023 the American people would be
well advised to go on the alert and start nailing down everything
in sight.

40

JAMES DAVID BARBER

From *The Presidential Character*

———

I AM NOT about to argue that once you know a President's personality you know everything. But as the cases will demonstrate, the degree and quality of a President's emotional involvement in an issue are powerful influences on how he defines the
issue itself, how much attention he pays to it, which facts and
persons he sees as relevant to its resolution, and, finally, what

principles and purposes he associates with the issue. Every story of Presidential decision-making is really two stories: an outer one in which a rational man calculates and an inner one in which an emotional man feels. The two are forever connected. Any real President is one whole man and his deeds reflect his wholeness.

As for personality, it is a matter of tendencies. It is not that one President "has" some basic characteristics that another President does not "have." That old way of treating a trait as a possession, like a rock in a basket, ignores the universality of aggressiveness, compliancy, detachment, and other human drives. We all have all of them, but in different amounts and in different combinations.

The most visible part of the pattern is style. *Style is the President's habitual way of performing his three political roles: rhetoric, personal relations, and homework.* Not to be confused with "stylishness," charisma, or appearance, style is how the President goes about doing what the office requires him to do—to speak, directly or through media, to large audiences; to deal face to face with other politicians, individually and in small, relatively private groups; and to read, write, and calculate by himself in order to manage the endless flow of details that stream onto his desk. No President can escape doing at least some of each. But there are marked differences in stylistic emphasis from President to President. The *balance* among the three style elements varies; one President may put most of himself into rhetoric, another may stress close, informal dealing, while still another may devote his energies mainly to study and cogitation. Beyond the balance, we want to see each President's peculiar habits of style, his mode of coping with and adapting to these Presidential demands. For example, I think both Calvin Coolidge and John F. Kennedy were primarily rhetoricians, but they went about it in contrasting ways.

A President's *world view consists of his primary, politically relevant beliefs, particularly his conceptions of social causality, human nature, and the central moral conflicts of the time.* This is how he sees the world and his lasting opinions about what he sees. Style is his way of acting; world view is his way of seeing. Like the rest of us, a President develops over a lifetime certain conceptions of reality—how things work in politics, what people are like, what the main purposes are. These assumptions or conceptions help him make sense of his world, give some semblance of order to the chaos of existence. Perhaps most important: a man's world view affects what he pays attention to, and a great deal of politics is about paying attention. The name of the game for many politicians is not so much "Do this, do that" as it is "Look here!"

"Character" comes from the Greek word for engraving; in one sense it is what life has marked into a man's being. As used here, *character is the way the President orients himself toward life*—not for the moment, but enduringly. Character is the person's stance as he confronts experience. And at the core of character, a man confronts himself. The President's fundamental self-esteem is his prime personal resource; to defend and advance that, he will sacrifice much else he values. Down there in the privacy of his heart, does he find himself superb, or ordinary, or debased, or in some intermediate range? No President has been utterly paralyzed by self-doubt and none has been utterly free of midnight self-mockery. In between, the real Presidents move out on life from positions of relative strength or weakness. Equally important are the criteria by which they judge themselves. A President who rates himself by the standard of achievement, for instance, may be little affected by losses of affection....

The best way to predict a President's character, world view, and style is to see how he constructed them in the first place. Especially in the early stages, life is experimental; consciously or not, a person tries out various ways of defining and maintaining and raising self-esteem. He looks to his environment for clues as to who he is and how well he is doing. These lessons of life slowly sink in: certain self-images and evaluations, certain ways of looking at the world, certain styles of action get confirmed by his experience and he gradually adopts them as his own. If we can see that process of development, we can understand the product. The features to note are those bearing on Presidential performance.

Experimental development continues all the way to death; we will not blind ourselves to midlife changes, particularly in the full-scale prediction cases. But it is often much easier to see the basic patterns in early life histories. Later on a whole host of distractions—especially the image-making all politicians learn to practice—clouds the picture.

In general, character has its *main* development in childhood, world view in adolescence, style in early adulthood. The stance toward life I call character grows out of the child's experiments in relating to parents, brothers and sisters, and peers at play and in school, as well as to his own body and the objects around it.

Slowly the child defines an orientation toward experience; once established, that tends to last despite much subsequent contradiction. By adolescence, the child has been hearing and seeing how people make their worlds meaningful, and now he is moved to relate himself—his own meanings—to those around him. His focus of attention shifts toward the future; he senses that decisions about his fate are coming and he looks into the premises for those decisions. Thoughts about the way the world works and how one might work in it, about what people are like and how one might be like them or not, and about the values people share and how one might share in them too—these are typical concerns for the post-child, pre-adult mind of the adolescent.

These themes come together strongly in early adulthood, when the person moves from contemplation to responsible action and adopts a style. In most biographical accounts this period stands out in stark clarity—the time of emergence, the time the young man found himself. I call it his first independent political success. It was then he moved beyond the detailed guidance of his family; then his self-esteem was dramatically boosted; then he came forth as a person to be reckoned with by other people. The *way* he did that is profoundly important to him. Typically he grasps that style and hangs onto it. Much later, coming into the Presidency, something in him remembers this earlier victory and re-emphasizes the style that made it happen. . . .

The first baseline in defining Presidential types is *activity-passivity*. How much energy does the man invest in his Presidency? Lyndon Johnson went at his day like a human cyclone, coming to rest long after the sun went down. Calvin Coolidge often slept eleven hours a night and still needed a nap in the middle of the day. In between the Presidents array themselves on the high or low side of the activity line.

The second baseline is *positive-negative affect* toward one's activity—that is, how he feels about what he does. Relatively speaking, does he seem to experience his political life as happy or sad, enjoyable or discouraging, positive or negative in its main effect. The feeling I am after here is not grim satisfaction in a job well done, not some philosophical conclusion. The idea is this: is he someone who, on the surfaces we can see, gives forth the feeling that he has *fun* in political life? Franklin Roosevelt's Secretary of War, Henry L. Stimson, wrote that the Roosevelts "not only understood the *use* of power, they knew the *enjoyment* of power, too. . . . Whether a man is burdened by power or enjoys power; whether he is trapped by responsibility or made free by it; whether he is moved by other people and outer forces or moves them—that is the essence of leadership."

The positive-negative baseline, then, is a general symptom of the fit between the man and his experience, a kind of register of *felt* satisfaction.

Why might we expect these two simple dimensions to outline the main character types? Because they stand for two central features of anyone's orientation toward life. In nearly every study of personality, some form of the active-passive contrast is critical; the general tendency to act or be acted upon is evident in such concepts as dominance-submission, extraversion-introversion, aggression-timidity, attack-defense, fight-flight, engagement-withdrawal, approach-avoidance. In everyday life we sense quickly the general energy output of the people we deal with. Similarly we catch on fairly quickly to the affect dimension—whether the person seems to be optimistic or pessimistic, hopeful or skeptical, happy or sad. The two baselines are clear and they are also independent of one another: all of us know people who are very active but seem discouraged, others who are quite passive but seem happy, and so forth. The activity baseline refers to what one does, the affect baseline to how one feels about what he does.

Both are crude clues to character. They are leads into four basic character patterns long familiar in psychological research. In summary form, these are the main configurations:

Active-positive. There is a congruence, a consistency, between much activity and the enjoyment of it, indicating relatively high self-esteem and relative success in relating to the environment. The man shows an orientation toward productiveness as a value and an ability to use his styles flexibly, adaptively, suiting the dance to the music. He sees himself as developing over time toward relatively well defined personal goals—growing toward his image of himself as he might yet be. There is an emphasis on rational mastery, on using the brain to move the feet. This may get him into trouble; he may fail to take account of the irrational in politics. Not everyone he deals with sees things his way and he may find it hard to understand why.

Active-negative. The contradiction here is between relatively intense effort and relatively low emotional reward for that effort. The activity has a compulsive quality, as if the man were trying to make up for something or to escape from anxiety into hard work. He seems ambitious, striving upward, power-seeking. His stance toward the environment is aggressive and he has a persistent problem in managing his aggressive feelings. His self-image is vague and discontinuous. Life is a hard struggle to achieve and hold power, hampered by the condemnations of a perfectionistic conscience. Active-negative types pour energy into the political system, but it is an energy distorted from within.

Passive-positive. This is the receptive, compliant, other-directed character whose life is a search for affection as a reward for being agreeable and cooperative rather than personally assertive. The contradiction is between low self-esteem (on grounds of being unlovable, unattractive) and a superficial optimism. A hopeful attitude helps dispel doubt and elicits encouragement from others. Passive-positive types help soften the harsh edges of politics. But their dependence and the fragility of their hopes and enjoyments make disappointment in politics likely.

Passive-negative. The factors are consistent—but how are we to account for the man's *political* role-taking? Why is someone who does little in politics and enjoys it less there at all? The answer lies in the passive-negative's character-rooted orientation toward doing dutiful service; this compensates for low self-esteem based on a sense of uselessness. Passive-negative types are in politics because they think they ought to be. They may be well adapted to certain nonpolitical roles, but they lack the experience and flexibility to perform effectively as political leaders. Their tendency is to withdraw, to escape from the conflict and uncertainty of politics by emphasizing vague principles (especially prohibitions) and procedural arrangements. They become guardians of the right and proper way, above the sordid politicking of lesser men.

Active-positive Presidents want most to achieve results. Active-negatives aim to get and keep power. Passive-positives are after love. Passive-negatives emphasize their civic virtue. The relation of activity to enjoyment in a President thus tends to outline a cluster of characteristics, to set apart the adapted from the compulsive, compliant, and withdrawn types.

The Passive-Negative Presidents

Eisenhower did not feel a duty to save the world or to become a great hero, but simply to contribute what he could the best he was able. Throughout his life—from the family Bible readings, from the sportsmanship of a boy who wanted nothing more than to be a first-rate athlete (and risked his life to save his leg for that), from the West Point creed—Eisenhower felt amid the questions about many things that duty was a certainty.

His intimates have learned that no appeal will move him more deeply than "This is a duty you owe the American people." When he was being pressed to run for the Presidency, one aide recalls that every possible argument and pressure was employed upon him, "but the only one that made any difference was that it was his duty."

Another aide remembered that Eisenhower "never lost his view of himself as standing apart from politics generally and from his own party in particular"—he never saw himself as personally dominating political forces. "He has taken on a third-person attitude toward life," another observer wrote. " 'The President feels—' and 'It seems to the President—' have become standard marks of his speech, supplanting the widespread and overworked 'I.' The impression he gives is of standing aside, as employer, and viewing himself as employee."

Yet Eisenhower very much wanted to make a contribution. Once while laboring over a speech he said, "You know, it is *so* difficult. You come up to face these terrible issues, and you know that what is in almost everyone's heart is a wish for peace, and you want so much to do *something*. And then you wonder ... if there really *is* anything you can do ... by words and promises.... You wonder and you wonder...."

In all these respects, and also in his personal comradeliness, Eisenhower fits the character of the passive-negative type. The key orientation is toward performing duty with modesty and the political adaptation is characterized by protective retreats to principle, ritual, and personal virtue. The political strength of this character is its legitimacy. It inspires trust in the incorruptibility and the good intentions of the man. Its political weakness is its inability to produce, though it may contribute by preventing. Typically, the passive-negative character presides over drift and confusion, partially concealed by the apparent orderliness of the formalities....

John F. Kennedy and Active-Positive Commitment

As the war deepened, Jack Kennedy first tried to get into the Army but was rejected because of his back, then wangled his way into the Navy, got his father to pull strings for a sea duty assignment, and wound up as commanding officer of a patrol torpedo boat in the Pacific. One night in August 1943 a Japanese destroyer suddenly appeared and slammed into his PT-109, slicing the little ship clean in half. Two men were killed at once. The rest fell into a sea aflame with burning gasoline. Kennedy was thrown across the deck on his back. "This is how it feels to be killed," went through his mind. He pulled himself together and started rounding up the survivors. When one badly hurt man said he could not make it back to the boat, Kennedy yelled, "For a guy from Boston, you're certainly putting up a great exhibition out here." The remains of the battered crew gathered on the part of the boat still above the surface. Kennedy asked whether they wanted to fight or surrender, if the Japanese came for them. "There's nothing in the book about a situation like this," he said. "A lot of you men have families and some of you have children. What do you want to do? I have nothing to lose." They decided to swim for a small island three and a half miles away. This took four hours; Jack Kennedy, his back zinging pain through him with every stroke, pulled the most seriously hurt man through the water by gripping his life jacket strap in his teeth. They crawled ashore exhausted and vomiting.

For four days Kennedy and the ten others searched through the coral shallows, lived on cocoanut milk, and tended their severe cuts and burns. Jack was the cool commander, though his back was severely injured; when a rescuing native brought him a message headed "On His Majesty's Service," Jack laughed. "You've got to hand it to the British," he said. When a PT boat finally came, he yelled "Where the hell have you been?" "We've got some food for you," was the reply. "Thanks, I've just had a cocoanut," Kennedy said....

John Kennedy, then, brought from his childhood an orientation toward life, a combination of "vigor" and laughter, a way of approaching experience with an expectation of success. He could see how he had grown from sickliness to heroism, from second place to first, from casualness to commitment. In the family he learned love without sentimentality, acquired the capacity to act forcefully and yet with detachment. His parents did not raise him, they tended him, let him grow, fostering and stimulating such urges to excel as he had. In his relationship with his older brother, Jack developed a sustained rivalry and identification, one he was never allowed to escape by surrendering to passivity. The tension lasted, but as a critical turning point in Jack's own life, Joe was suddenly gone and Jack was in his place. That helped bring out and strengthen the gregarious, aggressive, and movie-star qualities in him—opened his character more and sharpened his thirst for action. . . .

The active-positive shows a different kind of involvement and commitment to his own experience that enables him to incorporate its meaning more directly into his behavior. Roosevelt, Truman, and Kennedy all invested themselves seriously in what they were doing at any given time, putting themselves as well as their policies on the line. Their humor and detachment also gave evidence of an inner confidence, an expectation of winning but a readiness to endure failure without defeat. As each moved from decision to decision, he accumulated not just abstractions or information but also judgment, savvy, a feel for the interplay of self and situation. A great deal of such learning is unconscious; the learner may be hard put to tell how he went about it. The active-positive person seems to treat his life as a connected series of experiments in commitment. As each experiment passes into the past, he shakes off regret and holds onto memory. But it is a memory of the whole self, not just of the mind; the experience is a trial or test of a way of being, not just of a way of acting or thinking.

For John Kennedy, experience in crisis decision-making culminated in the Cuban missile crisis of October 1962. He had some lessons in his head, such as the axiom he had learned at the Bay of Pigs: "Never trust the experts!" He knew a good bit more about his government and world problems than before. And he had begun to elaborate an approach moving out from a combination of firmness and the search for negotiations. Perhaps most important, Kennedy had experienced Khrushchev. . . .

The Construction of Richard Nixon

Nixon's early life history shows the dynamic forces underlying his political character, world view, and style. The negative cast of his character traces back to a childhood marred by trauma and insecurity. The active solution developed out of his discovery, especially in school, that hard effort could bring success. These characteristics are not temporary, not some feature of Nixon the rising politician only, but are engrained in his personality. The vagueness of Nixon's self-image and his highly moralized concentration on managing himself go back to a home situation in which young Richard was right in the middle of an extraordinarily tense, emotionally charged family constellation. Caught between Frank and Hannah, the boy had to wend his way cautiously, alertly, ever ready for whatever sudden challenge might arise. The problem of controlling aggression was not some abstract moral conflict but a continuing, personalized experience in his home. Given that primary tension, other conflicts and identifications (regarding values for instance) took second place; Nixon's attention was focused strongly on the emotional aspects of situations, and on molding to best and safest advantage his own feelings.

The meaning of power for Nixon also takes on a clearer configuration in the light of his life history. As he grew he had to develop an identity of his own which would confirm his manliness; the available model for that was Frank. The themes of loneliness, leaving, traveling, and escaping are tied together with Frank's aggressiveness and ambition for his son. That is, Richard's need to get away from the confinement of home and his need to demonstrate his fighting strength are joined in the thrust for a special kind of power: independence. To achieve he must work and fight— but always on his own, out from under the controlling influence of anyone else. He moralized his occupational identity through the image of himself as the lone lawyer against the corruptionists, and he confirmed the choice for himself by seeing a world in which most people were weak, and lazy, and uninspired—a world in which a man with the will to win and a driving dream could, if he tried very hard, make his way out. And he found the sign of success in the experience of suffering.

Nixon's style also has deep roots in his background. The stress on impression management traces to his role in a family where the flash of drama alternates with calm. Feelings, particularly "bad" feelings, were not to be aired—at least not by him—and so one had to move by watching the signs, the nuances, the facial expressions. At school he found, in speaking, debating, play-acting, and cheering-on, ways to win and at the same time unload anger. The importance of performing just right was confirmed in his first independent political success. Independence, intense preparation, and public performing became the habits of his political life.

All of these feelings come together in Nixon's "classic crisis." There he relives each time the agony of self-definition, as he decides whether or not a crisis is "his"; the confirmation of suffering, as he wearily drives himself to get ready; the freedom of aggression, as he takes clear action; and the closure of control, as he reasserts self-restriction in the aftermath. There in a short space of time Nixon acts out the drama of his life—over and over again....

These predictions panned out in Nixon's first term. The old Nixon showed through in his fight to get his Supreme Court nominees approved by the Senate—and in his fury when, for the first time in forty years, the President failed in that effort. The drama of the bombing of and military "incursion" into Cambodia laid bare, as never before, Nixon wielding power alone, in secret, with enormously destructive consequences for the Cambodians and very high political costs for him, an enterprise culminating in one of the strangest speeches ever delivered from the White House. As the 1972 election approaches, Nixon's character is still intact.

This character could lead the President on to disaster, following in the path of his heroes Wilson and Hoover and his predecessor Johnson. So far his crises have been bounded dramas, each apparently curtained with the end of the last act. The danger is that crisis will be transformed into tragedy—that Nixon will go from a dramatic experiment to a moral commitment, a commitment to follow his private star, to fly off in the face of overwhelming odds. That type of reaction is to be expected when and if Nixon is confronted with a severe threat to his power and sense of virtue.

Nixon's is a special variant of the active-negative character. With his remarkable flexibility regarding issues and ideologies, Nixon can be "defeated" any number of times of specific questions of policy without feeling personally threatened. His investment is not in values, not in standing fast for some principle—although, if he were to stand fast, his doing so would certainly be rationalized in terms of principle. His investment is in himself, and Nixon's self is taken up with its management. As Margaret Mead has noted, "The President thrives on opposition. It is a form of stimulation for him." Thus he will court the strains of political resistance, finding in them yet another confirmation of his virtue.

But let the issue reach his central concern, the concern of self-management, and the fat may go into the fire. Threats to his independence in particular—the sense that he is being controlled from without because he cannot be trusted, because he is weak or stupid or unstable—will call forth a strong inner response. For Nixon, the prime form of the active-negative command "I must,"

"I must make my own way." Only when a crisis gathers around him, one he cannot escape by moving on to some alternative crisis, and he experiences a sense of entrapment is he likely to move toward the classic form of rigidification.

The key variable here is time. "Time running out," the President wrote on his pad before Cambodia. As the clock ticks forward, Nixon confronts his future in two stages. First is 1972. As the election approaches, Nixon's Presidential fate will clarify itself. If the uncertainties fade in the light of the polls, and the probability of a defeat for Nixon rises sharply, this President will be sorely tempted to do what he feels he must do before it is too late. The loss of power to forces beyond his control would constitute a severe threat. That would be a time to go down, if go down one must, in flames.

Nixon victorious in 1972 would face a second clock. Then he would know exactly when his time would run out. Short of impeachment, he would be unremovable until 1976, and then would be removed for sure. No longer accountable to an electorate, the Nixon pragmatism would have to take a different focus, one not restrained by calculations of electoral popularity. Then the salience of Presidential virtue would rise in Nixon's mind, as power faded. Accountable then to God and history, Nixon would have before him the models of heroes....

Reagan's Rise and Rule

The Reagan Presidential *style* would be dominated by rhetoric, with "little interest in homework on the issues" and little taste for "the charms of personal negotiation ... particularly if they involve an element of disagreement or confrontation." Further, "his rhetoric is essentially ahistorical and apolitical. He is bound to contribute to the ever-widening gap in American politics between speech and meaning."

Reagan's *worldview*, despite various attributions of "ideology," would be simpler than supposed: "He is a Republican millionaire and hangs around with those folks.... As long as Reagan's business friends are happy with moderation, he will be, too. He is unlikely to go off the deep end with Milton Friedman.... His domestic economic policies may indeed turn out to be too watered down to be effective." In foreign policy, "a reasonable guess would be: distract attention by waving the fist at the Soviet Union, while quieter and more profitable arrangements are worked out 'realisti-cally' in the Third World, unhampered by 'Utopian' human rights consideration. As president, Reagan is likely to be as 'business oriented' as ever, at home and abroad."

The Reagan *character* would be "passive-positive." That meant he would be "definitely no Nixon"—not a rigidified compulsive. Rather the danger was in "his type's tendency to drift, particularly with forces in the close-up environment. The danger is confusion, delay and then impulsiveness."

That day I thought, "The best hope is that, like Gerry Ford and Jimmy Carter, Ronald Reagan will leave the Constitution about as he found it and the nation, at peace. The worst fear is that Reagan, seeking affection, will have disaster thrust upon him. . . .

Reagan the "actor" is only part—the minor part—of Reagan the political dramatist. He is miscast as a man who brings Holly-wood to Washington. Long before he became a professional actor, he had trained in pretending: that he really could see the blackboard, that his father was not really a drunk, that he really could play football, that he really did belong in the rich kids' crowd. Though the Great Depression stopped Jack Reagan in his tracks, he was for years a salesman, a man who talks people into buying things, and a wonderful Irish storyteller; Ronnie experienced that presence for a long time before he met the *Reader's Digest*. His mother put on little playlets right there in the living room. His favorite reading was Tarzan, his favorite activity talking ("an incredible talker," a writer said, meaning only that there was lots of it). And when he went off by himself to play, it was to enter "a make-believe world in which heroic deeds had the capacity to transform reality," as Cannon puts it.* Blessed with a tall, straight body, an attractive face and a winning smile, young Ronald Reagan was a natural for high school popularity and thus for student politics and drama club. . . .

Other things being equal, such dramatic calculations and con-trols are all for the best. The modern Presidency is of necessity a performance—a media performance—and the modern arts of Presi-dent-playing are to be celebrated, not disdained. They make politics interesting and thus encourage participation. They translate com-plexity into simplicity, which, in real-world politics, is a prerequi-

* Lou Cannon, *Washington Post* reporter and biographer of Ronald Reagan.—EDS.

site for action. At their best they enliven and expand the national classroom, where the lessons have to do with life and death. The bright side of Presidential dramatics is inspiration.

The dark side is the power of drama to overwhelm reason: the lure of illusion, the fracturing of logic, the collapse of political conversation. The dark side is the drift into the swamp of fantasy and on over the brink of disaster. Drama offers interest, but it risks political insanity. That process begins with contempt for the facts.

Reagan seemed to love facts. Unlike politicians who take their stand on the landscape of generality, Reagan was forever citing statistics and telling interestingly specific bits of history or biography. The trouble was that he very often said, with an air of resolute conviction, things that simply were not true. Reporters and opposing candidates collected the Errors of Ronald Reagan by the notebookful. Far from trivial, Reagan's counterfactuals bore directly on major problems of public policy. If trees cause air pollution, if oil slicks help cure tuberculosis, if welfare cheats are rampant, if the Shah of Iran was a "progressive," if the Soviet economy is about to collapse "because they've already got their people on a starvation diet of sawdust," if there is more oil under Alaska than under Saudi Arabia, if billions upon billions of federal expenditures are "fat"—then follow various highly significant directions for the relevant policies. Not that his perceptions were random; they suited his rich friends far better than his poor victims. Richard Cohen reported that Reagan, at one spring 1982 press conference, "said Social Security was not 'touched' when in fact it had been cut. He said programs for pregnant women had not been reduced, but merely merged with others. They were cut—by about $200 million. He said the overall poverty budget was increased. It wasn't. The new money went for defense." But the frequency of Reagan's "slips" or "gaffes" or "bobbles" was in itself amazing, especially given the heat Jerry Ford and Jimmy Carter had had to endure for far less significant blunders. More interesting, though, was Reagan's own apparent attitude toward his "mistakes": he did not seem to mind. Though he sometimes waxed indignant over accusations of inaccuracy, he typically acted like an actor who, having blown a line, has to forge right ahead without worrying over it. When a reporter quoted one of his strange statements back to him, he shrugged and said he did not remember saying that, but that he had "probably just read something from a piece of paper

that had been put in front of me." Or he "would just smile pleas-
antly or shake his head in disagreement with his critics, as if mastery
of provable fact were things on which gentlemen certainly could
differ in goodwill." The gaffe story had developed its plot to perfection in Presidential politics, from error to expiation—but Reagan
would not play. He was, it seemed, literally shameless when it
came to the question of factuality. As James Reston put it, "Give
Mr. Reagan a good script, a couple of invisible TV screens and a
half hour on prime time and he'll convince the people they have
nothing to fear but the facts.". . .

Adding It Up

This strange book, written in chunks over a period of twenty
years, is addressed to the future. It is both less and more than
history: less, in that it makes no claim to be the whole story of the
Presidential past; more, in that it dares to draw from what has
been a picture of what yet may be. It is meant to help the thoughtful
and sensible citizen sort out the significant particulars of the next
Presidential choice, but also to help us hear, despite the cackle of
daily events, the fundamental cultural themes that echo through
the White House time and time again. With luck and determination,
we can use what we know to build the conditions for survival—
even progress. . . .

Look to character first. At least by the time the man emerges
as an adult, he had displayed a stance toward his experience, a
proto-political orientation. The first clues are simple: by and large,
does he actively make his environment, or is he passively made by
it? And how does he feel about his experience—is his effort in life
a burden to be endured or an opportunity for personal enjoyment?
From those two starting points, we can move to a richer, more
dynamic understanding of the four types. The lives of Presidents
past and of the one still with us show, I think, how a start from
character makes possible a realistic estimate of what will endure
into a man's White House years. Character is the force, the motive
power, around which the person gathers his view of the world
and from which his style receives its impetus. The issues will
change, the character of the President will last. . . .

4I

THOMAS CRONIN
The Presidential Puzzle

From *The State of the Presidency*

—————

IT IS SAID OF the presidency that it is the most powerful political office in the world. It is said too that we have a concentration of power in the presidency that threatens our liberties and has rendered obsolete the division of powers contemplated by the Republic's founders. But presidential power is often illusive. Presidential capacity to make the country a significantly better place, from whatever point of view, is more constrained than is generally appreciated. John Steinbeck said it well when he wrote, "What is not said or even generally understood is that the power of the chief executive is hard to achieve, balky to manage, and incredibly difficult to exercise. It is not raw, corrosive power, nor can it be used willfully. Many new Presidents, attempting to exert executive power, have felt it slip from their fingers and have faced a rebellious Congress and an adamant civil service, a respectful half-obedient military, a suspicious Supreme Court, a derisive press, and a sullen electorate."

The Presidency and Its Paradoxes

Why is the presidency such a bewildering office? Why do presidents so often look powerless? Why is the general public so disapproving of recent presidential performances, so predictably less supportive the longer a president stays in office?

The search for explanations leads in several directions. Each individual president molds the office, as does the changing political environment. The Vietnam and the Watergate scandals must also be considered. The personalities of Lyndon B. Johnson and Richard M. Nixon doubtless were factors that soured some people on the office. Observers also claim that the institution is structurally defective—that it encourages isolation, palace guards, groupthink, and arrogance.

Yet something else seems at work. Our expectations of, and demands on, the office are frequently so paradoxical as to invite two-faced behavior by our presidents. We seem to want so much so fast that a president, whose powers are often simply not as great as many of us believe, gets condemned as ineffectual. Or a president often will overreach or resort to unfair play while trying to live up to our demands. Either way, presidents seem to become locked into a rather high number of no-win situations. . . .

The modern (post–Franklin Roosevelt) presidency is bounded and constrained by various expectations that are decidedly paradoxical. Presidents and presidential candidates must constantly balance themselves between conflicting demands. It has been suggested by more than one observer that it is a characteristic of the American mind to hold contradictory ideas simultaneously without bothering to resolve the potential conflicts between them. Perhaps some paradoxes are best left unresolved, especially as ours is an imperfect world and our political system is a yet to be perfected system held together by many compromises. But we should, at least, better appreciate what it is we expect of our presidents and would-be presidents. For it could well be that our paradoxical expectations and the imperatives of the job make for schizophrenic presidential performances.

We may not be able to resolve the inherent contradictions and dilemmas of these paradoxes. Still, a more rigorous understanding of these conflicts should make possible a more refined sensitivity to the limits of what a president can achieve. Exaggerated or hopelessly contradictory public expectations tend to encourage presidents to attempt more than they can accomplish and to overpromise and overextend themselves.

A more realistic appreciation of presidential paradoxes might help presidents concentrate on the practicable among their priorities. A more sophisticated and tolerant consideration of the modern presidency and its paradoxes might relieve some of the burden so a president can better lead and administer in those critical realms in which the nation has little choice but to turn to him. Whether we like it or not, the vitality of our democracy still depends in large measure on the sensitive interaction of presidential leadership with an understanding public willing to listen and willing to provide support when a president can persuade. Carefully planned innovation is nearly impossible without the kind of leadership a competent and fair-minded president can provide.

Each of the following twelve paradoxes is based on apparent logical contradictions. Each has important implications for both presidential performance and public evaluation of presidential behavior. A better understanding may lead to the removal, reconciliation, or more enlightened toleration of the contradictions to which they give rise.

Paradox: The Decent and Just but Decisive
and Guileful Leader

Opinion polls indicate that people want a just, decent "man of good faith" in the White House. Honesty and trustworthiness repeatedly top the list of qualities that the public values most highly in a president. Almost as strongly, the public also demands the qualities of toughness, forcefulness, and even a touch of ruthlessness.

Franklin Roosevelt's biographers agree that he was vain, devious, manipulative, and had a passion for secrecy. These are often the standard weaknesses of great leaders, they note. Most of the significant advances in the world have been made by people with drive, ambition, and a certain amount of irrational confidence in themselves.

We admire modesty, humility, and a sense of proportion. Yet most of our great leaders have been vain. The faults are perhaps part of being a success in politics; you don't get to be a political leader by being a wallflower.

Adlai Stevenson, George McGovern, and Gerald Ford were all criticized for being "too nice," "too decent." Being a "Mr. Nice Guy" is easily equated with being too soft. The public dislikes the idea of a weak, spineless, or sentimental person in the White House. Even Gerald Ford's own aides said he was "too nice for his own good." He seldom cracked the whip or exercised discipline over his staff and cabinet.

Would-be presidents simultaneously have to win our trust by displays of integrity, and yet to become president ordinarily requires calculation, single-mindedness, and the practical knowledge of gutter fighting. . . .

A second aspect of this paradox is that while people want a president who is somewhat religious, they are deeply wary of one who is too much so. Presidents often go out of their way to be photographed going to church or in the presence of noted religious leaders. Nixon, who was not by any definition religious ,in the usual sense, held highly publicized Sunday services in the White House itself.

John Kennedy, however, encountered considerable difficulties because of his Catholic affiliation. Jimmy Carter faced similar problems from certain Catholics and Jews as well as some Protestants as a result of his deep and open "born again" convictions....

Plainly, we demand a double-edged personality. We, in effect, demand the *sinister* as well as the *sincere,* President *Mean* and President *Nice*—tough and hard enough to stand up to Khrushchev or Brezhnev or to press the nuclear button and compassionate enough to care for the ill fed, ill clad, ill housed. The public in this case really seems to want a kindhearted son of a bitch or a clean wheeler-dealer, hard roles to cast and an even harder role to perform over eight years.

Paradox: The Programmatic but Pragmatic Leader

We want both a *programmatic* (committed on the issues and with a detailed program) and *pragmatic* (flexible and open, adjustable) person in the White House.

There is a saying that if politicians really indulged in principle, they would never have a chance for the White House. We may admire consistency in the abstract, but in politics consistency has its costs. The late Everett Dirksen, a popular Republican senator from Illinois, used to say that "I'm a man of fixed and unbending principle, but my first fixed and unbending principle is to be flexible at all times."...

A president who becomes too committed risks being called rigid; a president who becomes too pragmatic risks being called wishy-washy. The secret, of course, is to stay the course by stressing character, competence, rectitude, and experience and by avoiding strong stands that offend important segments of the population.

Jimmy Carter was especially criticized by the press and others for avoiding commitments and stressing his "flexibility" on the issues. This prompted a major discussion of what came to be called the "fuzziness issue." Jokes spread the complaint. One went as follows: "When you eat peanut butter all your life, your tongue sticks to the roof of your mouth, and you have to talk out of both sides."...

What strikes one person as fuzziness or even duplicity appeals to another person as remarkable political skill, the very capacity for compromise and negotiation that is required if a president is to maneuver through the political minefields that come with the job....

Most presidents strive to *maximize their options,* and hence leave matters up in the air or delay choices. JFK mastered this strategy, whereas on Vietnam LBJ permitted himself to be trapped in a corner that seemed to allow no escape, because his options had so swiftly dissolved. Indeed, this yearning to maximize their options may well be the core element of the pragmatism we so often see when we prefer moral leadership.

Paradox: The Innovative and Inventive Yet
Majoritarian and Responsive Leader

One of the most compelling paradoxes at the very heart of our democratic system arises from the fact we expect our presidents to provide bold, innovative leadership and at the same time respond faithfully to public-opinion majorities.

Columnist Walter Lippmann once warned against letting public opinion become the chief guide for leadership in America, but he just as forcefully warned leaders: Don't be right too soon, for public opinion will lacerate you! Hence, most presidents fear being in advance of their times. They must *lead us,* but also *listen to us.**

Put simply, we want our presidents to offer leadership, to be architects of the future and providers of visions, plans, and goals, and at the same time we want them to stay in close touch with the sentiments of the people. To *talk* about high ideals, New Deals, big deals, and the like is one thing. But the public resists being *led* too far in any one direction.

Most of our presidents have been conservatives or at best "pragmatic liberals." They have seldom ventured much beyond the crowd. They have followed public opinion rather than shaped it. John F. Kennedy, the author of the much-acclaimed *Profiles in Courage,* was often criticized for presenting more profile than courage; if political risks could be avoided, he shrewdly avoided them....

Presidents can get caught whether they are coming or going. The public wants them to be both *leaders* of the country and *repre-*

---

* See Lippmann's discussion of public opinion in selection 59.—Eds.

sentatives of the people. We want them to be decisive and rely mainly on their own judgment; yet we want them to be very responsive to public opinion, especially to the "common sense" of our own opinions. It was perhaps with this in mind that an English essayist once defined the ideal democratic leader as an "uncommon man of common opinions."

Paradox: The Inspirational but
Don't Promise More than You Can Deliver Leader

We ask our presidents to raise hopes, to educate, to inspire. But too much inspiration will invariably lead to dashed hopes, disillusionment, and cynicism. The best of leaders often suffer from one of their chief virtues—an instinctive tendency to raise aspirations, to summon us to transcend personal needs and subordinate ourselves to dreaming dreams of a bolder, more majestic America.

We enjoy the upbeat rhetoric and promises of a brighter tomorrow. We genuinely want to hear about New Nationalism, New Deals, New Frontiers, Great Societies, and New American Revolutions; we want our fears to be assuaged during a "fireside chat" or a "conversation with the President"; we want to be told that "the torch has been passed to a new generation of Americans ... and the glow from that fire can truly light the world."

We want our fearless leaders to tell us that "peace is at hand," that the "only thing we have to fear is fear itself," that "we are Number One," that a recession has "bottomed out," and that "we are a great people.". . .

Do presidents overpromise because they are congenital optimists or because they are pushed into it by the demanding public? Surely the answer is a mixture of both. But whatever the source, few presidents in recent times have been able to keep their promises and fulfill their intentions. Poverty was not ended; a Great Society was not realized. Vietnam dragged on and on. Watergate outraged a public that had been promised an open presidency. Energy independence remains an illusion just as crime in the streets continues. . . .

A president who does not raise hopes is criticized for letting events shape his presidency rather than making things happen. A president who eschewed inspiration of any kind would be rejected as un-American. For people everywhere, cherishing the dream of individual liberty and self-fulfillment, America has been the land of promises, of possibilities, of dreams. No president can stand in the way of this truth, regardless of the current dissatisfaction about the size of big government in Washington and its incapacity to deliver the services it promises. . . .

Paradox: The Open and Sharing but Courageous and Independent Leader

We unquestionably cherish our three branches of government with their checks and balances and theories of dispersed and separated powers. We want our presidents not only to be sincere but to share their powers with their cabinets, Congress, and other "responsible" national leaders. In theory, we oppose the concentration of power, we dislike secrecy, and we resent depending on any one person to provide all of our leadership. In the early 1970s repeated calls for a more open, accountable, and deroyalized presidency were heard.

Just the same, however, Americans long for dynamic, aggressive presidents even if they do cut some corners. We still celebrate the gutsy presidents who made a practice of kicking Congress around. It is still the Jeffersons, Jacksons, Lincolns, and Roosevelts who get top billing. The great presidents were those who stretched their legal authority and dominated the other branches of government. This point of view argues, Watergate notwithstanding, that the country in fact yearns for a hero in the White House, that the human heart ceaselessly reinvents royalty. . . .

Although some people would like to see a demythologized presidency, others claim we need myth, we need symbol. As a friend of mine put it, "I don't think we could live without the myth of a glorified presidency, even if we wanted to. We just aren't that rational. Happily, we're too human for that. We will either live by the myth that has served us fairly well for almost two hundred years or we will probably find a much worse one.". . .

We want our president to be not only both a lion and a fox but more than a lion, more than a fox. We want simultaneously a secular leader and a civil religious mentor; we praise our three-branched system, but we place capacious hopes upon and thus elevate the presidential branch. Only the president can give us heroic leadership, or so most people feel. Only a president can dramatize and symbolize our highest expectations of ourselves as almost a chosen people with a unique mission. Note too that only presidents are regularly honored with a musical anthem of their own: "Hail to the Chief."

Paradox: Taking the Presidency
Out of Politics

The public yearns for a statesman in the White House, for a George Washington or a second "era of good feelings"—anything that might prevent partisanship or politics as usual in the White House. In fact, however, the job of a president demands that he be a gifted political broker, ever attentive to changing political moods and coalitions.

Franklin Roosevelt illustrates this paradox well. Appearing so remarkably nonpartisan while addressing the nation, he was in practice one of the craftiest manipulators and political-coalition builders to occupy the White House. He mastered the art of politics—the art of making the difficult and desirable possible.

A president is expected to be above politics in some respects and highly political in others. A president is never supposed to act with his eye on the next election; he's not supposed to favor any particular group or party. Nor is he supposed to wheel and deal or to twist too many arms. That's politics and that's bad! No, a president is supposed to be "President of all the people," or so most people are inclined to believe. Yet he is also asked to lead his party, to help fellow party members get elected or reelected, to deal firmly with party barons and congressional political brokers. Too, he must build political coalitions around what he feels needs to be done....

In all probability, this paradox will endure. A standard diagnosis of what's gone wrong in an administration will be that the presidency has become too politicized. But it will be futile to try to take the president out of politics. A more helpful approach is to realize that certain presidents try too hard to hold themselves above politics—or at least to give that appearance—rather than engage in it deeply, openly, and creatively. A president in a democracy has to act politically in regard to controversial issues if any semblance of government by the consent of the governed is to be achieved.

Paradox: The Common Man Who Gives
an Uncommon Performance

We like to think that America is the land where the common sense of the common person reigns. We prize the common touch, the up-from-the-log-cabin "man of the people." Yet few of us settle for anything but an uncommon performance from our presidents.

This paradox is splendidly summed up by a survey conducted by the Field Research Corporation, a California public-opinion organization. Field asked a cross section of Californians in 1975 to describe in their own words the qualities a presidential candidate should have. Honesty and trustworthiness topped the list. But one of the more intriguing findings was that "while most (72%) prefer someone with plain and simple tastes, there is also a strong preference (66%) for someone who can give exciting speeches and inspire the public."

It has been said that the American people crave to be governed by a president who is greater than anyone else but not better than anyone else. We are inconsistent; we want our president to be one of the folks but also something special. If a president gets too special, however, he gets clobbered. If he tries to be too folksy, people get bored. The Lincoln and Kennedy presidencies are illustrative. We cherish the myth that anyone can grow up to be president—that there are no barriers, no elite qualifications—but we don't want a person who is too ordinary. Would-be presidents have to prove their special qualifications—their excellence, their stamina, their capacity for uncommon leadership.... The "catch 22" here, of course, is that an uncommon performance puts distance between a president and the truly common man. We persist, however, in wanting an uncommon common man as president.

Paradox: The National Unifier—
National Divider

One of the paradoxes most difficult to alleviate arises from our longing for a president who will pull us together again and yet be a forceful priority setter, budget manager, and executive leader. The two tasks are near opposites.

Our nation remains one of the few in the world that calls upon its chief executive to serve also as its symbolic ceremonial head of state. Elsewhere, these tasks are spread around. In some nations there is a monarch *and* a prime minister; in other nations there are three visible national leaders—the head of state, a premier, and a powerful party chief.

In the absence of an alternative, we demand that our presidents and our presidency act as a unifying force in our lives. Perhaps it all began with George Washington, who so artfully performed this function. At least for a while, he truly was above politics, a unique symbol of our new nation. He was a healer, a unifier, and an extraordinary man for all seasons. Today we ask no less of our presidents than that they should do as Washington did.

We have designed a presidential job description, however, that impels our contemporary presidents to act as national dividers. Presidents must necessarily divide when they act as the leaders of their political parties, when they set priorities that advantage certain goals and groups at the expense of others, when they forge and lead political coalitions, when they move out ahead of public opinion and assume the role of national educators, when they choose one set of advisers over another. A president, as a creative executive leader, cannot help but offend certain interests....

Paradox: The Longer He Is There, the Less We Like Him

Every four years we pick a president, and for the next four years we pick on him and at him, and sometimes pick him apart entirely. Because there is no adequate prepresidential job experience, much of the first term is an on-the-job learning experience. But we resent this. It is too important a job for on-the-job learning, or at least that's how most of us feel.

Too, we expect presidents to grow in office and to become better acclimated to their powers and responsibilities. But the longer they are in office, the more they find themselves involved in crises with less and less public support. An apocryphal presidential lament, "Every time I seem to grow into the job, it gets bigger," is not unfounded.

Simply stated, the more we know of a president, or the more we observe his presidency, the less we approve of him. Familiarity breeds discontent. Research on public support of presidents indicates that approval peaks soon after a president takes office and then slides downward until it bottoms out in the latter half of the four-year term. Thereafter, briefly, it rises a bit but never attains its original levels. This pattern of declining presidential support is a subject of debate among social scientists. Unrealistic early expectations are, of course, a major factor, guaranteed to ensure a period of disenchantment....

Paradox: The Reassuring the Public While Accentuating a Sense of Crisis Leader

Although a president is expected to exude hope, reassurance, and an I'm OK we're OK sense of confidence, the public nevertheless likes to see presidents visibly wrestling with crises. Presidents Ford and Carter learned, sometimes painfully, about this paradox when they found that more political support was available when the United States was at odds with the Soviet Union than when the two countries were in agreement. It is almost easier, they found, to go to the brink of war with the Soviets than to defend advances in détente or new SALT agreements. President Kennedy found that "the politics of confrontation" with Cuba as well as that with Khrushchev were politically helpful.

Presidents are simultaneously asked to build a lasting peace and at the same time maintain United States superiority as the number one superpower. Promote peace, yes. But don't yield anything to the Soviet Union! Moreover, presidents who wish to appear presidential must accentuate the nation's sense of being in a severe predicament. They perceive that a sense of heightened crisis must be created....

We expect our president, as the most visible representative of big government, to solve the entire scope of our problems by mustering all the powers and strengths to which that office entitles him—and then some—but we are unwilling to allow him to infringe upon our rights in any significant way. We don't especially like calls for sacrifice. Energy conservation is illustrative. We applauded Carter's efforts to put forth solutions to the "energy problem" but then criticized him for trying to force sacrifices in the form of higher gas prices and other individual hardships.

Stated another way, we want strong, effective presidential leadership, yet at the same time we are profoundly cautious about concentrating power in one person's hands.

Paradox: The Active in Some Areas and at Some Times
but Passive in Other Areas or at Other Times Leader

There are times when we want our president to be engaged actively in doing certain things, and there are other occasions when we would like to see him sit back and let things run their course. But different people will disagree on whether the times demand presidential passivity or activity.

If you are not directly concerned about a matter one way or another, it is easy to say the president should not take action. When the president and the executive branch are doing something you consider important, however, that's just an instance of society organizing itself to perform an urgent task. Thus a subject you are especially interested in deserves all the presidential attention it can get.

In the abstract, everyone is against the "imperial presidency," but one person's waste is another's means of survival. People want a strong presidency, but at the same time they don't want it interfering in their lives or initiating any more new taxes. There is a fair amount of disagreement on precisely how much and what kind of presidential leadership we want; this has always been the case and will continue to be so....

Paradox: What It Takes to Become President
May Not Be What Is Needed to Govern the Nation

To win a presidential election takes ambition, ambiguity, luck, and masterful public-relations strategies. To govern the nation plainly requires all of these. However, it may well be that too much ambition, too much ambiguity, and too heavy a reliance on phony public-relations tricks actually undermine the integrity and legitimacy of the presidency.

Columnist David Broder offered an apt example: "People who win primaries may become good Presidents—but 'it ain't necessarily so.' Organizing well is important in governing just as it is in winning primaries. But the Nixon years should teach us that good advance men do not necessarily make trustworthy White House aides. Establishing a government is a little more complicated than having the motorcade run on time."

Likewise, ambition (in very heavy doses) is essential for a presidential candidate, but too much hunger for the office or for success at any price is a danger to be avoided. He must be bold and energetic, but in excess these characteristics can produce a cold, frenetic candidate. To win the presidency obviously requires a single-mindedness, yet our presidents must also have a sense of proportion, be well rounded, have a sense of humor, be able to take a joke, and have hobbies and interests outside the realm of politics.

To win the presidency many of our presidents (Lincoln, Kennedy, and Carter come to mind) had to talk as more progressive or even populist than they actually felt; to be effective in the job they felt compelled to act as more conservative than they wanted to.

Another aspect of this paradox is the ambiguous or misleading positions candidates take on issues in order to increase their appeal to the large bulk of centrist and independent voters; such positions may alienate people later, after the candidate has won, when they learn that his views and policies differ. Such prepresidential pledges as LBJ's "We will not send American boys to fight the war that Asian boys should be fighting," Richard Nixon's "open presidency," and Jimmy Carter's "I will balance the budget by 1981" backfired when they were later violated....

What it takes to *become* president may differ from what it takes to *be* president. To become president takes a near megalomaniac who is also glib, dynamic, charming on television, and hazy on the issues. Yet we want our presidents to be well rounded, careful in their reasoning, clear and specific in their communications, and not excessively ambitious. It may well be that our existing primary-convention system adds up to an effective obstacle course for testing would-be presidents. Certainly they have to travel to all sections of the country, meet the people, deal with interest-group elites, and learn about the challenging issues of the day. But with the Johnson and Nixon experiences in our not-too-distant past, we have reason for asking whether our system of producing presidents is adequately reconciled with what is required to produce a president who is competent, fair-minded, and emotionally healthy.

Conclusions

Perhaps the ultimate paradox of the modern presidency is that it is always too powerful and yet it is always inadequate. Always too powerful because it is contrary to our ideals of a "government by the people" and always too powerful, as well, because it now possesses the capacity to wage nuclear war (a capacity that unfortunately doesn't permit much in the way of checks and balances and deliberative, participatory government). Yet always inadequate because it seldom achieves our highest hopes for it, not to mention its own stated intentions....

The paradoxes of the presidency do not lie in the White House but in the emotings, feelings, and expectations of us all. There exists some element in the American mind, and perhaps in the minds of people everywhere, that it is possible to find a savior-hero who will deliver us to an era of greener grass and a land of milk and honey. When this pseudomessiah fails we inflict upon him the wrath of our vengeance. It is almost a ritual destruction; we venerate the presidency, but we destroy our presidents. Perhaps this is only logical when we elect a person expecting superhuman strength, character, and restraint, and invariably get a rather fragile, overworked, fallible, and mortal human....

The reality is that all too often on the long road to the White House our sometime-to-be-presidents become the servants of what is, rather than the visionary shapers of what could be. In the long process of working their way up and learning to operate within the system they become rewarded for playing along with the dominant interests and for playing within the traditional rules of the game. "By the time they reach the top, they are very likely to be trained prisoners of the structure. This is not all bad; every vital system reaffirms itself. But no system can stay vital for long unless some of its leaders remain sufficiently independent to help it change and grow."...

Progress comes about in America not because we elect visionary presidents but because of the way our political system gradually responds to militant mobilizers and political prophets whose views take hold around the country. It is in this sense that presidents can be said to be followers as much as, or more than, they are leaders. When the country's consciousness has been raised by trailblazers, muckrakers, or out-of-office programmatic activists, it is then, and perhaps only then, that a president can provide the acceptance, approval, and spirit of renewal that can accommodate change....

Prudent efforts . . . will help us overcome our naïve preoccupation with the "storybook presidency," with the illusion that only presidents can solve our problems. We must take the initiative to assume responsibility for our problems instead of looking always to the national government to do it all. We must refine our expectations of the president and raise our expectations of ourselves.

42

BERT ROCKMAN

From *The Leadership Question*

––––––

ALTHOUGH THE PROBLEM of achieving direction is fundamentally a problem of the state, it is almost always the chief executive (and the executive's party) that becomes identified with success
or failure in attaining this direction. In the United States, especially,
the presidency has come to be considered in contemporary mythol-
ogy to be the nearest thing to a concrete embodiment of the state.
It is in the presidency that we largely have come to see (or hope
for) the principal source of policy and programmatic coherence
and direction. The successes or failures of the incumbent tend to
be identified with the prospects of governance itself. Of course,
this view of the presidency is not constitutionally given. It is instead
the product of a multitude of factors—technological, social, and
political—that place perceived responsibility for national well-being
mainly on the president.

The paradox engendered by such a situation can be expressed
as follows:

1. the American state is fragmented, splintered, and often divisive;

2. American political norms emphasize responsiveness and
maximum access (also induced by institutional characteristics),
nonelectoral participation, and thus the representation of diversity;
thus,

3. the culture and the institutions of the state make it especially
difficult (but not impossible) to arrive at programmatic expressions
of public policy;
yet,

4. in the midst of this splintering, we have focused more and
more aspirations on a single office holder.

In other words, we expect the president to be risk-taker in
chief, we weight the odds against his success, and then we excoriate
him publicly for his failures....

A ... set of cycles ..., and one that is again heavily influenced by a media saturated environment, has to do with presidential leadership ambition and temperament, and styles of managing the presidency. The table distinguishes two polar styles of leadership drive and temperament, their likely relationship to different patterns of management, and the probable stereotypes produced by such patterns of management. Ambition and temperament, on the one hand, and presidential management, on the other, need not be related but are likely to be. I apply the label "drivers" to the style of presidents with expansive agendas and expansive tastes for personal intervention. They are likely to make the White House the center of executive activity and the oval office the nucleus within that. They are likely, in other words, to seek to maximize their control of the levers of power. On the other hand, the tag "coasters" is given to those who are apt to address matters only after they first have been ingested by other officials and staff or administrative units. The premise here is that important and unresolved issues will necessarily arrive in the president's in box in due time. Inevitably, as Richard Rose rightly claims, "the way in which a President exercises his chieftainship in Washington must reflect his own vision of the kind of President that he wishes to be."

Certainly this is true, but not fully sufficient. For what presidents wish to be is, in some measure, a reflection of what they are wished to be. The ... cyclical character of demands on leadership ... suggest, in other words, a cycle of expectations about the presi-

STYLES OF PRESIDENTIAL LEADERSHIP AND MANAGEMENT

	DRIVER STYLE	COASTER STYLE
PRESIDENTIAL POLICY AMBITIONS	Expansive	Incremental or maintaining
LEADERSHIP TEMPERAMENT	Entrepreneurial, chief operating officer	Ratifying, chief executive officer
MANAGEMENT CHARACTERISTICS	Centrist, interventionist, use of informal channels and uncertain jurisdictions	Decentralized but hierarchical, delegative, use of formal channels and certain jurisdictions
NEGATIVELY STEREOTYPED AS	Ruthless, intolerant, isolated	Contradictory, inefficient, incompetent
PRESIDENTS MOST LIKELY TO FIT TYPE	Johnson, Nixon, (Kennedy, Roosevelt)	Eisenhower, Ford

dency itself. Such expectations primarily derive from the thinking of opinion leaders, particularly the tendency of political journalists to divine public moods and, thus, inevitably to help create them. What critical elites think is the reality tends to become reality, in part, through self-fulfilling behavior.

In government, as in the physical world, it takes more energy to generate direction than to sustain inertia. The energies often produce a future desire for more tranquil occasions, and, conversely, too many troubles and too little motion whet the appetite for more energetic leadership. Times during which energetic presidential leadership is most in demand are those usually associated with a preference for a "driving" leadership style and a tendency toward a White House–centric perspective. This preference usually follows upon a "coaster" style of presidency (or succession of them) which induces a sense of drift. Larger-than-life presidents, on the other hand, tend to encourage a desire for less urgency and a more delegated and consensual style of governing....

... Within the presidential term itself there are frequent recurring patterns of both constraint and opportunity. Three that I focus on here are the cycles of succession, declining support, and growing effectiveness. They are together relevant to the setting of the presidential agenda, and to its achievement.

Succession Cycles

"Let us continue," intoned Lyndon Johnson to a joint session of Congress shortly after the assassination of John F. Kennedy. But, in truth, few leaders fresh to their jobs want to continue the tasks of others. Some, like Johnson, come to office under circumstances in which deference initially must be paid to continuity. Generally, however, new leaders have an interest in distinguishing themselves from their predecessors. After all, leadership successions are often the result of changed political environments that typically cast the deposed or retired leaders in a less favorable light. Except for unusual circumstances such as when the deposed leaders leave office either as heroes or in heroic form (the latter meaning when the deposed are also departed), they are typically less well thought of and less influential than when they began. The choosing of new leaders is occasion for renewal, and for the victors to interpret generously their accession as an opportunity to proceed with promised change....

Why does succession have this effect? Several factors may be at work in helping to trigger these policy spurts. The struggle for leadership in any system is a process that encourages one or more of the following: (1) sharpened rhetoric; (2) increased partisanship; (3) the making of promises to groups important to the outcome. The process of being chosen also is occasion to converge one's aims with their apparent justification and approval by the (s)electors. Making it to the top anywhere is a heady experience; the more democratic the process of selection, the more intoxicating the experience. What one wishes to do thus quickly becomes what one has been mandated to do. Additionally, the process of changing leaders also alters an older coalition and means that a new set of expectations and pressures are to be satisfied. Diverse motives or needs, in other words, seem to beat a path to much the same outcome: Change of leaders occasions change in policy....

Declining Support

Nearly all newly chosen leaders are offered a period of relatively little criticism—in the popular parlance, a honeymoon. This honeymoon period varies in length, but ultimately in the case of American presidents, their standing plummets largely as a curvilinear function of time. Presidential popularity declines steadily and then curls upward modestly at term's end. The effects of time (in essence, the decomposition of a winning coalition) are both buffered and reinforced by particular events and circumstances, though these are too weak to disturb the main tendency. Even with the benefit of this uplift at the end of the presidential term, the recovery leaves incumbents considerably beneath where they began....

Although presidents attempt to influence the actions and alter the expectations of numerous actors within and outside their official administrations, the link between public prestige and political influence is supposedly most relevant to presidential efforts to influence Congress. One reason for this lies in the role of Congress as a representative political institution and, therefore, its presumed responsiveness to currents of opinion.... The strength of a president's electoral performance in a member's district or state, and the party affiliation of the member, are the most direct predictors of a member's support for presidentially endorsed legislative proposals. In deciphering the relationship between public prestige and legislative support for presidential proposals, this analysis concludes that "members of Congress seem to respond not to presidential prestige among the public or their district as a whole but *to presidential prestige among their own electoral supporters.* Declining presidential approval, therefore, is likely to impact most on members of the president's party who, then, will be less inclined to take risks on behalf of a president of diminished prestige, especially as that is defined by partisans within the member's district...."

Growing Effectiveness

Whereas the passage of time erodes presidential influence with forces outside the administration, Richard Neustadt contends that the key years for making the presidential record are the third, fifth, and sixth. By this, Neustadt obviously means much more than a crude measure of legislative victories can convey. The problem here is how to measure presidential effectiveness beyond the crude indicators of legislative success available to us. These indicators are simple outcomes not necessarily traceable to a president's exertions. Neustadt is obviously trying to make us look at more subtle issues, an effort that is as sensible as it is nonspecific. Clearly, what he is trying to make us see is not easy to operationalize or to subject to quantitative analysis.

Neustadt seems to be driving at the incumbent's understanding of his office, his sensitivity to his opportunities, and an ability to link these to his goals. Can the incumbent become, in other words, increasingly effective in relating objectives to opportunities and in sharpening tactics on the whetstone of power? If presidents learn successfully, they presumably become more effective in understanding the levers of the office they hold, in displaying sensitivity to the institutions and publics relevant to their success, and in perceiving the power stakes behind the decisions they make....

In recent times, one difficulty has been a notable shortage of presidents who have seen, in any normal sense, a fifth or sixth year. Neustadt could speak of Roosevelt, Truman, and Eisenhower with some assurance that these presidents were typical in the time they would have to serve. But the only subsequent president to have a sixth year, and only a portion at that, was Richard Nixon, who fled office under duress.

A more important dilemma, however, is that a president's growing effectiveness may come to naught. The tendency for presidential approval to decline principally as a function of time means a very uncertain relationship between a growing command of presidential tools and successful legislative outcomes, since the latter is mediated by the declining public prestige of the president. The irony, as Paul Light has noted, is that the cycle of decreasing influence intersects the cycle of increasing effectiveness. As presidents get to know better their office and resources, and acquire the skills and experience to manipulate them, their best opportunities will have passed them by. Over time, presidents may learn better how to play the "insider" game of Washington politics, but they will have lost the enthusiasms of novel undertakings, of shared if still distant visions, and of a fresh expression of public support.

43

HEDRICK SMITH

From *The Power Game*

———

THE FORMAL STRUCTURES of government are only the scaffolding of power. They do not account for its human chemistry. High office offers leverage, but politicians can either squander or exploit that potential. No power is absolute or guaranteed, for at its heart, our politics is a contest of persuasion. In that contest, the intangibles have always been important, but never more so than in the era of television, which plays up the politics of personality and where impressions and appearances are so crucial to a politician's power.

From recent experience, we know that one president (Ronald Reagan) appears strong and comfortable with power, while another president (Jimmy Carter) seems ill at ease with power and comes across as uncertain and strained. We have seen that a speaker of the House (Tip O'Neill) can be assertive and potent while another (his predecessor, Carl Albert) can seem almost invisible; that some committee chairmen can work their will while others flounder; that as budget director, David Stockman drove the policy process, while his successor, James Miller, was a secondary player whom congressmen kiddingly called "Miller Lite."

In short, the most vital ingredients of power are often the

intangibles. Information and knowledge are power. Visibility is
power. A sense of timing is power. Trust and integrity are power.
Personal energy is power; so is self-confidence. Showmanship is
power. Likability is power. Access to the inner sanctum is power.
Obstruction and delay are power. Winning is power. Sometimes,
the illusion of power is power.... Take credibility a step further
and we are into the politics of personality—important in ways that
the public often does not see at work in Washington. Sheer likability, or even a lively sense of humor, can be important ingredients
of power, sometimes tipping the balance on substantive issues.
Being able to entertain a banquet of several hundred political and
business bigwigs with one-liners and anecdotes, can be a more
important source of influence for Texas-born Washington lawyer
Bob Strauss than mastering budget economics.

Barney Frank, a shrewd, tough-minded liberal Democratic congressman from outside Boston, contends that success in the Washington power game parallels high school politics. Congress has to
operate informally, according to Frank, with the kinds of networks
and personality politics that work in high school, because Congress
has no clear power hierarchy. Leaders lack the corporate executive's
power to give commands or to hire and fire.

"In some ways, being in Congress is more like being in high
school than anything I've done since high school—I mean the way
the structure is," Frank asserts. "Nobody in the House of Representatives can give any other member an order. The speaker is more
influential than a new Republican from Texas, but he can't order
anybody to do anything. Nobody can fire anybody. So what that
means is that you become influential by persuading people, being
likable, and having other people respect you but not resent you.
That's why it's like high school."

Morris Udall, the popular Arizona congressman, once tested
Frank's notion; he learned the names of all new House members.
"I carried a little book of names and pictures, and kept it by my
bedside," Udall said. "You go up to a guy who's been here a year
and call him by name and say, 'I understand you represent Schenec-
tady,' or whatever, and I'd point out something interesting about
each person. It pays off. If there's a vote going on and he comes in
here and it's my bill, and otherwise the forces are equidistant,
pushing him either way, he'd give you the benefit of the doubt
because he knows you."

Of course, it takes more than that. You have to be genuinely popular, and Udall is enormously well liked, especially among younger liberals to whom he is a folk hero. Udall's personal popularity foiled an effort in 1984 by Frank and other liberals to stop subsidizing public power in some western states. Udall was sponsoring a bill that would continue the old subsidized rates; Barbara Boxer, a young California liberal working with Frank, wanted power from hydroelectric projects such as the Hoover Dam to be priced at market rates.

"Mo's a public power guy, a westerner, and it was his committee handling the bill," Frank recalled. "The environmentalists were with us; the old system was wasting water. It was bad economics. I talked to some guys on the floor. I said, 'Look, on all the merits of the bill you should be with us.' And they said, 'But how can we vote against Mo?' It was a fairly close vote but we lost. We were opposing Mo Udall, and we love Mo. We lost because of Mo—a good example of personality affecting politics."

More broadly, where Carter failed at likability, it was one secret of Reagan's success. After disclosures of the Reagan administration's secret arms deals with Iran in 1986, majorities of people registered their mistrust of Reagan. He was deeply wounded as president. Other presidents might have been destroyed, but likability helped save Reagan. Voters might mock his claims of ignorance, but they had trouble seeing him as an impeachable villain on a par with Richard Nixon at Watergate.

On lesser problems, Reagan has been rescued at times by the mass appeal of his "aw, shucks" smile, the jaunty little toss of his head, his disarming ability to laugh at himself. Bryce Harlow compared Reagan to his former boss, Dwight Eisenhower.

"Eisenhower liked people so people liked Eisenhower," Harlow reminisced. "Eisenhower trusted people; therefore, they trusted Eisenhower. Eisenhower could fall flat on his *tokhus* out in public, do something very wrong or very stupid, make a big goof, and the American people would rush forward as one and grab him and pick him up and dust him off and say, 'Don't bother at all about that. We like Ike.' And on he'd go. Reagan gets the same treatment. Because he is a man with no internal hangups whatever. He likes people. He likes a charwoman quite as much as a queen. The people react to that."

Reagan has been helped by a couple of other important intangibles; one is grasping power lightly. Bryce Harlow remarked to me that one vital secret for presidents and other top officials is to avoid appearing too hungry to wield power. Both the press and the public, he said, mistrust politicians who lust too obviously for power, as, he pointed out, was the case with Johnson and Nixon. Jimmy Carter, too, created problems by being so eager to exercise power that he became enmeshed in too many fights on too many fronts. Certainly Secretary of State Alexander Haig and White House Chief of Staff Donald Regan suffered from power hunger, as well.

"Reagan is not a power-hungry guy," suggested Lee Atwater, who helped run Reagan's 1984 campaign and later became campaign manager for Vice President Bush. "Nixon was power hungry. Johnson was power hungry. Carter was power hungry. Look at the guys who were run of town by the media—the guys who were obsessed with power. Reagan stays detached. He's got a Zen approach to power: He doesn't care about power for power's sake alone. Eisenhower is the only other person who had the same detached way of holding power."...

In short, power depends heavily on the illusion of power. Presidents—past, present, and future—have less power than the country imagines, but the successful ones convey the impression of power and get reputations as strong presidents by playing down their problems and trumpeting their few clear victories.

Fred Dutton, a White House adviser to President Kennedy and a keen student of politics ever since, made the point to me that there is far less purpose and grand design to what goes on inside the White House than most people assume. That lesson from Kennedy's time is still valid today, and will be in the future.

"Washington isn't all that thought out," Dutton remarked. "So much of it is improvisation. Too much rationality and planning can be attributed to it. Much of it is trying something, taking a pratfall, and then looking either bad or good when you do. The really shrewd players have their eyes out for the big chance. There are always a lot of cerebral people writing lots of memos to presidents or senators: *Do This, Do That*. But the constant activist cannot bring high drama to events. The constant activist loses perspective. I've got to give Reagan credit for having certain values to guide him. But like the others, he seizes opportunities. And look at the things he lets go by. You've got to do that. You've got to float above events."

The president and players in the power game are like surfers riding the waves of power. Sometimes they are careening at top speed before some giant wave; sometimes they are coasting slowly, looking for a crest. Their success depends on avoiding the thundering surf around them. From time to time, they may have to make those agile sideward shifts that enable the most skilled surfers to escape being crashed beneath the waves. Sometimes they will fall and quickly mount their boards to ride a new crest triumphantly. From the distance on shore, the best surfers appear to have uncanny balance, ever gliding and in control.

"It's a stylistic thing," Dutton said. "Both Kennedy and Reagan have ridden the thing with grace. To look at the presidency purely in terms of congressional wins and losses is a mistake. There's much more to it than that. It's a matter of grace, of looking like you're handling it. I used to think that being an actor was the worst possible background for a president, but it turns out that it's a good background. A president has to keep up appearances to protect his power."...

Politicians, bureaucrats, and lobbyists covet tokens of access and influence the way Eagle scouts collect merit badges. Senior White House officials scheme and fume over the location of their offices, their parking places, where they ride on *Air Force One,* and whether they have "POTUS phones"—direct lines to the president of the United States (POTUS). Only cabinet secretaries, the Joint Chiefs of Staff, and half a dozen other officials qualify for "porthole to porthole"—daily door-to-door chauffeur service. Other high officials on an A list and a B list, divided by rank, can order government cars for official business.

Three or four top White House officials can have lunch served in their offices by Filipino mess boys, dressed like Yale Whiffenpoofs in blue blazers and gray charcoal slacks. The others, in descending order of rank, can eat in:

1. the executive mess
2. the regular White House mess, or
3. the overflow board room.

There are only slight differences in menu; the decor and the dining compartments convey the pecking order. Only about twenty out of probably two thousand people who work in the Office of the President can use the White House gym. And Jimmy Carter himself decided who could use the tennis court on the South Lawn.

But the size and location of one's office is the main badge of status and a prime indicator of access. In any hierarchy—business, university, or military service—one's office is an important symbol of rank and eminence; in the White House power game, it has acute significance. Proximity to power is crucial for both real and symbolic reasons. Only those closest at hand can readily walk into the Oval Office or be quickly summoned.

However, as most tourists are probably amazed to discover (I was), the White House is pretty small. Only the cream of the power elite can fit into about a dozen well-appointed offices on the first and second floors of the West Wing. In that highly prized terrain, the territorial imperative is as powerful as in the jungle. Most people in the Office of the President do not have offices in the White House; they work across the street in a handsome, baroque structure that was once the State Department and is now known as the old Executive Office Building (EOB).

"People will kill to get an office in the West Wing," Mike Deaver told me while he was still Reagan's closest personal aide. "You'll see people working in closets, tucked back in a corner, rather than taking a huge office with a fireplace in the EOB. God help you if you're suddenly moved to the fourth floor of the EOB because that's death row, as they call it over there. That means you're on the way out."

Deaver and I were sitting in his office, adjoining the Oval Office. It is a room handsomely furnished with antiques, several oil paintings by Childe Hassam, a fireplace, and its own private patio. President Carter had made it his study, but Reagan had turned it over to Deaver, the trusted aide he wanted nearest to him. By Deaver's account, the president had taken him into the study after the inauguration ceremonies in 1981.

"I want you to have this office," Reagan told Deaver.

"I can't do that," Deaver demurred. "Where are you going to go if you want to get away?"

Reagan smiled and gestured toward the Oval Office, visible through the open door connecting the two rooms.

"I've been trying to get that round office in there for the last fourteen years," he said. "Why would I want to get away?". . .

When the president travels, the "access itch," the urge to be physically close to the president, becomes acute. The fewer people who can fit into a plane, a helicopter, a presidential limousine, the more competitive the inner circle becomes.

"Who rides in the limousine with the president is very important," Deaver said, shaking his head. "People sit on each other's laps. I finally had to make a rule that you couldn't put any more than three people in the president's limousine if the motorcade took more than ten minutes, because the president winds up all scrunched up.

"Jim Baker would always want to be in there as chief of staff. If [then–presidential counselor] Ed Meese was along, he would want to be in there. But if you landed in some state, you had the governor, two United States senators, the mayor, maybe you had a congressman. And you had to do it just from a protocol stand-point—and that would be the governor, who outranks everybody else in the state, and one staff member, and that was usually Baker, and if he wasn't along, it was me."

Long trips touch off a power scramble for choice seating on *Air Force One,* which carries only about twenty officials; nearly half of the plane's forty seats are assigned to Secret Service agents and a press pool. Simply traveling in high-echelon quarters of *Air Force One* is a heady experience for many politicians and visitors. Coming back from an economic summit meeting in Canada aboard *Air Force One* for an interview with Reagan, I remember being impressed by the high-backed luxury-style seats, the fancy service by Navy stewards in blazers, and by having a telephone plugged into the arm of my seat and a signal corps operator asking, "Where would you like to call, sir?" Mentally, I imagined the click of military heels coming to attention at the other end of the line. Like an overawed tourist, I scooped up souvenirs; matchboxes, napkins, swizzle sticks, any item embossed with the presidential seal.

Little tokens of status and power become enormously important to people who live in this hothouse power environment. Some officials squabble over choice seats near the president's cabin. Equally important to some high officials is being seen at the presi-dent's side as he gets off the plane. By protocol, only the president and Mrs. Reagan were to use the front exit; everyone else was to use the rear exit. But the TV cameras and welcoming parties were at the front, and the most perk-and-publicity-conscious officials—press spokesman Larry Speakes; Dick Darman, a top presidential aide; National Security Adviser Bill Clark—would violate protocol and get off the front, ahead of the president rather than exit from the rear.

"We tried to temper it by saying that the only person off the front of the plane is the president or the president and Mrs. Reagan,

or Reagan and Secretary Shultz," said Bill Sitman, a Deaver aide
whose job was to manage travel arrangements. "You'd see people
have a fit. They didn't want to get off from the back door of the
plane. After all, what's the point of being on *Air Force One* if
people don't see you get off the front of *Air Force One* with the
president?"...

Up close, just as from afar, Washington can seem a foreign
place, even though its Capitol dome, White House lawn, and
Washington Monument are familiar symbols. But to freshly minted
political victors, it is suddenly a strange universe. Near the end of
1980, on the very night that Michael Deaver arrived with his family
from California to begin work in the Reagan White House, his
five-year-old son, Blair, asked in his innocence a question that
must silently sit on many adult tongues: "Daddy, is Washington
part of this world?"

Eighteen months earlier, at the depths of his political despair in
the summer of 1979, President Carter had given his own angry,
frustrated answer to that question. Carter openly derided Washington as an island "isolated from the mainstream of our nation's
life."

In an era of Washington bashing, this is a theme that many
people voice and many politicians exploit: this theme that Washington is disconnected from the country. But it is a misleading notion....

Indeed, Washington regularly takes in newcomers, absorbs
them and makes them its own. Those who arrive to serve in Congress learn to live in two worlds—in their hometowns and states,
and in the special world of the capital. The longer they stay in
Washington, the more they become Washingtonians, buying
homes, raising children, worrying about parking places and street
crime, some even rooting for the Washington Redskins football
team against their home-state teams.

Newcomers arrive full of idealism and energy only to discover
what a tiny fragment of power they grasp. To expand that fragment, they make alliances, join groups, get appointed to com-
mittes, make contacts with the press, find friends in the administration. Before they know it, they become caught up in
Washington's internal politics, involved in the rivalries of Congress
and administration, consumed by their committee work, their
personal specialties, their Washington careers—the clout they

develop in Washington and the amount of attention they can command in the Washington power game.

In short, people who come here to serve in the executive branch or Congress catch "Potomac fever"—the incurable addiction of wielding political power or feeling at the political center. When their president leaves office or they lose their congressional seats, very few politicians go home to retire or make money. Most stay in Washington and become lawyers, lobbyists, or consultants, because they've grown accustomed to Washington's ways and to thinking of themselves as movers and shakers, and no other place has quite the same excitement and allure....

What really sets Washington apart, of course, is the heady brew of power and prominence. Washington combines the clout of the corporate boardroom and military command with the glamour of Hollywood celebrities and Super Bowl stars. That magnetism and the stakes of the battle are what draw armies of politicians, lobbyists, lawyers, experts, consultants, and journalists to Washington. It is a self-selected group, ambitious and aggressive, marked by collective immodesty. Politicians love to be noticed, and they take their notices very seriously, assuming their own importance and grasping for daily confirmation in the attention of the press and television....

That ache for applause and recognition shows in the weighty tread of senators moving onto the floor and glancing upward for some sign of recognition from the galleries. It shows in the awkward jostling for position as a group of congressmen approach the television cameras and microphones outside a hearing room, or after a White House session with the president. I have marveled at it in the purgatorial patience of politicians with endless handshakes, speeches, receptions. I have sensed it, too, in the flattered eagerness of corporate executives arriving at a White House dinner in their limousines. And I have felt it in the smug satisfaction of a select group of columnists and commentators called to a special briefing from the president in the family theater of the White House. None of us is completely immune to that siren song of being made to feel important.

"Washington is really, when you come right down to it, a city of cocker spaniels," Elliott Richardson once remarked. Richardson, a Republican Brahmin from Boston, held four cabinet positions in the Nixon and Ford administrations and after a few years out of the limelight felt the ache for attention badly enough to make an unsuccessful try for the Senate.

"It's a city of people who are more interested in being petted and admired than in rendering the exercise of power," Richardson contended. "The very tendency of the cocker spaniel to want to be petted and loved can in turn mean that to be shunned and ignored is painful, and there is a tendency in Washington to turn to the people who are in the spotlight and holding positions of visibility at a given time."

In their collective vanity, the power players are willing to endure long hours of boredom to bathe in the roar of the crowd. Talking with me in his Senate study one rainy afternoon about the vanity of the political breed, Senator Charles McC. Mathias, the Maryland Republican, recalled an incident at an American Legion dinner in Washington years ago. As Mathias arrived, he saw two fellow Republican warhorses—Leverett Saltonstall of Massachusetts with his arm in a sling and Everett Dirksen hobbling on crutches.

"It was one of those many functions which you attend but where your absence might not even be noted," Mathias observed. "Saltonstall and Dirksen had valid excuses [to stay away], but they came anyway. And I thought: Is there never surcease from this demand and this compulsion to get out to these things? But of course, they would be put at the head table and introduced, and the spotlight would fall upon them, and the people from Massachusetts and Illinois would wave their napkins in the air when their names were mentioned, and the band would play their state anthems. It is all utterly meaningless, and yet those two wanted to be part of the act, and the applauders wanted the act, too.". . .

In a very different vein, Newt Gingrich, a voluble, publicity-prone junior Republican from Georgia, admits to the exultation of making it to Washington. "There are very few games as fun as being a congressman," he gushed one evening over a Chinese dinner. "Talk to guys who spent Christmas break traveling the world. Talk to people who landed on an aircraft carrier or went to see the space shuttle launched or had dinner at the White House or got to talk to people from the *New York Times*. There's a sense of being at the center of things. This is the great game!". . .

One of the most important informal networks that has developed is among younger House members who play sports or work out together in the House gym. Located in the subbasement of the

Rayburn Office Building, the gym is a hideaway for members; they alone can use it. It is barred to their staffs, reporters, constituents, and most lobbyists (former members turned lobbyists can enter, but can do no serious lobbying on the premises). Senators have their own "baths." The House gym is not large; it has a sixty-foot pool, $28,000 in Nautilus equipment, a half-length basketball court which doubles for paddleball, as well as steam, massage, and locker rooms. Some members do little more than take a steam bath, shave, shower, and go back to work refreshed; others work out daily.

But many find that playing sports with political adversaries eases the wounds of political combat. "Ours is a very conflict-ridden profession," Frank remarked. "I vote against you. I think you're wrong. I mean, people in other professions are able to muffle that better. We are forced daily to conflict with each other. The gym promotes some stability, which is very important. But also, it's an information kind of thing. You get to know what people are like, what's important to them. You get information about what's going on with this, what's going on with that. It's that kind of chatter. And occasionally you will talk about some specific bill."

Frank, a Jewish bachelor in his late forties whose pudgy cheeks once bulged around horn-rimmed glasses, lost seventy pounds through strict dieting and weight lifting. Now, at two hundred pounds, he has shoulders like a New England Patriots tackle. He mixes with the other side: One of his weight-lifting partners is Vin Weber, a staunch Republican right-winger from Minnesota and from the far end of the ideological spectrum. That is typical of the gym. The regular pickup basketball games are bipartisan: plenty of hard-court razzing goes on, but serious partisanship is left off the court. "Republicans and Democrats play together," says Thomas Downey, a Long Island Democrat with a snappy jump shot. "It's a great way to release tension.". . .

In my years of reporting in Washington, one of the more intriguing discoveries has been the number of warm political relationships that develop across party lines and across ideological disagreements. . . . Occasionally, friendships develop from simple human chemistry. Edward Kennedy of Massachusetts and Paul Laxalt of Nevada, from the left and right ends of the Senate, sometimes play tennis together and enjoy each other as friends. In other cases, amicable relations develop from professional respect. Other politi-

cal opposites enjoy close friendships, such as conservative colum-
nist Robert Novak and liberal humorist Art Buchwald, staunch
Republican Al Haig and ardent Democrat Joseph A. Califano, con-
servative writer William Safire and left-of-center commentator
Daniel Schorr. Former House Speaker Tip O'Neill and House
Republican leader Bob Michel were longtime golfing partners....

It takes more than enthusiasm to consolidate power. In the
king of the hill game, rule number three is: *Strike quickly for a win,
during the early rush of power.* That helps establish momentum and
an aura of success. Lyndon Johnson had a colorful maxim for such
moments. "Johnson operated under the philosophy with Congress—if you're not doing it to them, they're doing it to you. And
frequently, he used a more vivid word than *doing*," recalled Doug-
lass Cater, one of Johnson's White House advisers.

Winning is power, was the gut summation given me by Jim
Baker. "I've always felt that it is extremely important in terms of
a president's power—power as opposed to popularity—that presidents succeed on the Hill with what they undertake up there,"
Baker asserted. "And I really believe that one reason that Ronald
Reagan has been so successful is that he succeeded in the high-
profile issues that he jumped on in the first term. The way presidents govern is to translate their philosophy into policy by working
with Congress. That's why Carter failed in my view. Because he
never learned that lesson."

The image of success is crucial, as Dick Darman pointed out in
a White House memo. On February 21, 1981, Darman told me
that he had urged crafting a "plan for the preservation of the appearance of the president's continuing strength and effectiveness—the
avoidance of association with 'losses,' the association with a
planned string of 'successes.' "

Political gamesmanship required quickly tapping Republican
optimism to translate electoral victory into legislative power and a
governing majority. Otherwise, momentum could slip away.

But as Carter learned, there are no automatic legislative victories
for a new president. Carter lost his first battles, on water projects,
and Reagan was nearly upset by his own troops in the very first
test—long before his celebrated victories.

In the Senate, Howard Baker faced a Republican revolt that
threatened to shatter his narrow 53–47 majority before it would
ever taste victory. That first test was critical, because Reagan had
to make the Senate his coalition cornerstone. If he could not hold

the Republican Senate majority in line, it would dash his hopes for a coalition with conservative House Democrats; if Reagan lost in the Senate, why should these House Democrats defy their own party leaders in the House to join forces with Reagan?

What forced Reagan's hand was the need to raise the legal ceiling on the national debt to $985 billion by February 6—so the government could borrow money to finance deficits and keep running. Democrats had long voted routinely to raise the debt ceiling because they believed in government programs, but conservative Republicans hated these votes. They opposed raising the debt ceiling because they opposed the government programs, and on principle they rejected deficit spending. Reagan too had felt that way, but now it was his responsibility to run the government. That meant getting conservative Republicans to bend their ideology to help him govern. In the House, Democrats and Republicans combined to pass the debt-ceiling bill.

But in the Senate, the Democrats played rougher. Initially, many voted against the bill to force the distasteful chore on the Republican majority. Very quickly, the debt-ceiling vote became a test of Reagan's and Howard Baker's ability to secure their partisan base. There was strong resistance.

Almost all thirteen Republican freshmen were opposed. Don Nickles of Oklahoma, Mack Mattingly of Georgia, Slade Gorton of Washington, Steve Symms of Idaho, and Paula Hawkins of Florida protested to Howard Baker. These Reaganites believed ardently in budget balancing. "We've told our constituents we're never going to vote to increase the debt limit," they told Baker. "We're dead set against it. It is an article of faith with us." Their rebellion left Baker shy of votes to pass the measure.

Another obstacle was posed by William Armstrong of Colorado, one of the brightest, most vigorous Senate conservatives on economic issues. In 1981, he vowed to vote against the debt bill unless it carried an amendment giving the president power to cut spending unilaterally. Armstrong saw the deadline pressure of the debt bill as a chance to restore to Reagan and future presidents power taken away by Congress in 1974. This was the power of "recision"—the power of a president to notify Congress he will not spend certain funds. As the law stood in 1981, a president's recision required congressional approval—winning majorities in both houses. But under Armstrong's amendment, the president could act and his cuts would stick—unless Congress overrode him within forty-five days. That put the burden of veto action on Congress.

The day before the debt vote, Armstrong was summoned to Baker's office to meet with Baker and Vice President Bush. Baker, fearing filibusters from Democrats, wanted a clean debt bill with no amendments to help get Reagan a quick victory.

"This is no time to rock the boat," Baker declared. "We've got a new president. We ought not to buck him."

"But this is a once-in-a-lifetime opportunity," objected Armstrong. "To dissipate it on making nickel-and-dime changes in the budget instead of going for institutional reforms would be a terrible mistake." He appealed to Bush: "The honeymoon lasts only so long. If the president asks for it, think of the leverage he has. Don't you think this is a golden opportunity?"

"It doesn't matter what I think," Bush replied. "The president wants a clean debt-ceiling bill. So please back off."

Armstrong relented, feeling it was ridiculous for a single senator to try to force on Reagan a power he did not want.

But that still left the rebellious freshmen. Baker had played high cards—senior conservatives such as Barry Goldwater of Arizona and John Tower of Texas—to try to persuade them. The president had them to the White House in ones and twos. That softened them up, but it did not change their minds.

Howard Baker's ace in the hole was Strom Thurmond, the senior Senate Republican. Thurmond epitomized tight-fisted austerity and fierce independence. He had stood against the federal establishment as the segregationist governor of South Carolina and the Dixiecrat candidate for president in 1948. He had staged a one-man filibuster for twenty-four hours and eighteen minutes against the Civil Rights Act of 1957. In twenty-seven years as a senator, first as a Democrat and then as a Republican, Thurmond had *never* voted to raise the debt ceiling.

Baker ran into Thurmond on the Senate floor, found him willing to help, and quickly rounded up the Republican freshmen.

"I sat them down around the conference table, brought in Strom, and Strom started slow and low in that measured South Carolina cadence," Baker recalled. "He started working up, and at the end of three or four minutes—it wasn't very long—he said: 'Now some of you in this room say that you have promised never to vote for a debt-limit increase, and I understand that. And you ought to understand that I've never in my whole career voted to increase the debt limit before. But I've never had Ronald Reagan as president before either. And I'm going to vote for the debt-limit increase. And so are you.' And there was a deathly silence. Strom got up and left. And there was some grumbling and grousing and leaning back in the chairs, and they got up and wandered out."

The Democrats, stung by Reagan's charges that they were big spenders, made the vote painful for the Republicans. One by one, they voted against the bill to force Republicans to swallow their ideology and their campaign promises, to show solidarity with the president. One by one, the Republicans voted aye. Henry "Scoop" Jackson, the veteran Democrat from Washington state was so tickled to see Republicans squirm that he danced a jig on the floor. Ultimately, all but three Republicans—Armstrong, Mattingly, and John East of North Carolina—supported Reagan. Baker let out a "whew" when he had fifty votes; then a score of Democrats switched sides to pass the measure, 73–18.

The public never grasped how narrowly Baker's control of the Senate had ridden in the balance. After the vote, Baker told Thurmond, "I never owed a greater debt of political gratitude to anybody than I do to you."

Because defeat that early, due to Republican defections, would have derailed the Reagan program. Had Republican ranks shattered just seventeen days after Reagan's inauguration, the initial momentum of Reagan's presidency would have been lost. Baker felt it vital to demonstrate command and to get Republicans to make sacrifices for the sake of unity behind Reagan. "Strom, more than just anybody else, maybe except me, understood how important it was that we act like a majority," Baker said.

That debt-ceiling victory, seemingly minor, did three things: It forged Republican unity, it inculcated a governing mentality, and it established a winning momentum. . . .

Success in the coalition game depends enormously on presidential influence with the individual members of Congress; a president can pull enough reluctant votes his way if he has the right political touch. It is an old maxim of politics that an effective leader, mayor, governor, and above all, president, must be both loved and feared. That is how a president marshals support from his natural followers and deters attack from his natural enemies. Issues matter, of course, but so does human chemistry. A president has to make clear there are benefits for supporting him and consequences for opposing him.

No one understood this better than Lyndon Johnson, who was masterful at ferreting out the weak points and deepest hungers of other politicians. Yet Johnson was so blatantly Machiavellian that it hampered him. He made it hard for people to go along and still retain their dignity and independence. Carter had the opposite problem. Arm-twisting and deal-making were not his forte. When he tried to act strong, he often came across as mean and willful because exaggerated forcefulness was out of character.

At bottom, Carter seemed ill at ease with power, and ill at ease hobnobbing with other politicians. He immersed himself in a substance but despised wheeling and dealing with Congress. Many a senator or House member told me that Carter was awkward or hesitant about asking directly for his or her vote. He frowned on horse-trading. Only from painful experience did he learn the value of doing little favors for other politicians. Both his intellect and his engineer's training at Annapolis made him impatient with that vital lubrication of the wheels of legislation: making other politicians feel important.

At intimate occasions—a small dinner at the White House or a personal interview at his home in Plains, Georgia—I found Carter engaging, but many members of Congress found him cool and brisk. When he had groups for breakfast, he would arrive late because he had been busy at work in his study. Then he would give a little speech on whatever policy he was pushing. Carter once complained to Jack Nelson, Washington Bureau Chief of the *Los Angeles Times,* that some members of Congress wasted his time because they were not well prepared on substance. People who meet with me, Carter told Nelson, "had better know the subject because I know it" and my time is "extremely valuable."

Carter did not sense what many members regard as the essence of such sessions. "The problem was that the congressmen didn't come to the White House to hear a logical argument from the president, which they could have gotten just as well from his aides," observed Mark Nimitz, a lawyer who served in Carter's State Department. "What Carter didn't understand was that these guys came down to the White House to swap stories and go back up to the Hill and brag to the others, 'I told the president ... and he told me...' "

"It doesn't take much in the White House to pick up the phone and say, 'Is there anything we can do for you in the next two or three months?' In the Carter White House that was regarded as treason," added Mark Siegel, a veteran Democratic party official who worked in the Carter White House. "Congress was the enemy. The Democratic party was the enemy. The Washington establishment was the enemy. Tip O'Neill wanted to help a Democratic president enact a Democratic agenda, but the Carter people didn't understand Tip O'Neill. They regarded him as a horse's ass, and if you call someone a horse's ass in the White House, do you know how fast that gets back to that someone?"

Carter and his inner circle had been ill-trained for Washington. In Georgia, a one-party state with a fairly docile legislature, Carter felt he could afford aloofness. In time, Carter came to understand how that cost him with Congress. In his third year, I heard him mock his own ineptitude at a convention of southern state legislators. He said he used to ask people how to deal with Congress. "Someone told me to treat them like the Georgia legislature," Carter recounted. He paused to let that sink in. "I tried it," he said. "And it didn't work."

As outsiders, Carter's team did not know the Washington power game or its power networks. Their lack of understanding was almost inevitable, given the type of presidential campaign Carter had waged. Carter had won the 1976 nomination by running against Washington and avoiding much contact with party leaders. After the election, Carter's Georgia political mafia arrived in Washington with a chip on their shoulders and then kept a cool distance. Initially, Jimmy and Rosalynn Carter made a point of not socializing with the Georgetown set and other Washington insiders. Carter not only disdained the trappings of the imperial presidency but the symbols of the Washington establishment. On his energy proposals, for example, Carter did not consult the Democratic legislative leaders, Tip O'Neill and Senator Robert Byrd. Hamilton Jordan was so remote that O'Neill complained months later that he had never met the president's right-hand man, whom he ridiculed as "Hannibal Jerkin."

Carter and his Georgians, having won an upstart, outsider's victory and enjoying partisan majorities in both houses, acted as if they did not need others to succeed. Carter seemed convinced that the sheer rationality of his proposals and his eminence as president would pass them. He was initially misled by enormous press attention, by his having beaten a slew of Washington politicians, and by his self-righteous self-confidence on the issues.

As Reagan roped together his first-year coalition, he profited greatly by striking contrasts with Jimmy Carter. It hardly requires much rehearsing of Reagan's Irish warmth and his love of personal banter to underscore the differences. Reagan is as comfortable shmoozing with other politicians as he is with power. He fitted the presidency easily, and that was reassuring to other politicians as well as to ordinary people.

Reagan was far from perfect. I have heard Republicans such as Bob Packwood, Pete Domenici, and Warren Rudman bridling after a session with President Reagan because he read from his cue cards or deflected serious discussion by repeating shopworn anecdotes about welfare queens supposedly defrauding taxpayers with high living. But in that first year, Reagan was in top form. He demonstrated rule number four in the coalition game: *Lavish attention on the Washington power structure.* Democrats were flattered to be courted. Republicans were tickled to walk away with a Reagan story to retell, or some Reagan cuff links, or tickets to the presidential box at the Kennedy Center.

For a man who, like Carter, had run his campaign against Washington, Reagan did a quick 180-degree turn in catering to the Washington establishment. He mounted a mellow social and political campaign that set a Dale Carnegie (*How to Win Friends and Influence People*) standard. Shelving his campaign rhetoric, Reagan played the gracious outsider eager to win acceptance inside the beltway.

That was in character: Despite his messianic rhetoric, Reagan was no dry ideologue of the right, but was ready to bend and bargain with mainstream Republicans. At the 1980 convention, Reagan had tried to enlist Gerald Ford as his vice president, shocking dyed-in-the-wool Reagan partisans, and then he picked his rival, George Bush, rather than his closest political ally, Senator Paul Laxalt. When right-wingers urged replacing Howard Baker as Senate Republican leader with Laxalt, Reagan—with Laxalt's encouragement—turned thumbs down. He reached beyond his California circle to tap former Ford and Nixon advisers for his White House staff.

On his first night in town as president-elect, Reagan wooed fifty local notables with a dinner at the F Street Club, an understated symbol of old money. Many of Washington's old names, snubbed

by the Carters, were surprised and delighted to be invited: Harold
Hughes, then Democratic governor of Maryland; Marion Barry,
the outspokenly liberal Democratic mayor of Washington who
had bashed Reagan in the campaign; James Cheek, president of
Howard University; and attorney Edward Bennett Williams, a
well-known Democrat and owner of the Baltimore Orioles. "When
you come to town, there's a tendency as an officeholder to act as if
you're a detached servant," Reagan explained to Elisabeth Bumiller
of the *Washington Post.* "Well, I decided it was time to serve notice
that we're residents."

Eight years as governor of the nation's largest state, dealing
with a Democratic majority in the California Assembly, had taught
Reagan about seducing adversaries as well as allies. The next couple
of nights, he was out first celebrating with Republican senators
and then mingling with the Washington establishment—Katharine
Graham, chairman of The *Washington Post;* Meg Greenfield, chief
of the *Post's* editorial page; and Robert Strauss, Carter's former
campaign chairman—at a small dinner given by George Will, the
unabashedly pro-Reagan columnist who had helped coach Reagan
for presidential debates. Later, Reagan met not only with friends
but with such foes as Senator Ted Kennedy and paid a courtesy
call on Speaker O'Neill, who purred afterward, "I liked him. He
was very personable." As for Reagan's staff, O'Neill added. "I get
along better with them than I did with Carter's staff."

Reagan's stroking of Washington's political egos was a brilliant
gambit. Washington was captivated. It was ready for a shift from
Georgia country to California gentry, and it was flattered by a
president who paid court to the courtiers.

In sum, Reagan's confection of charm and deference seduced
the citadels of power before the political battles began. He not
only demonstrated that the presidency was now in the hands of an
experienced politician, he also calmed the animal instincts of other
politicians that his campaign had aroused. His charm treatment
disarmed skeptics who had conjured him as a warmonger and a
rabid ideologue. . . .

That personal popularity was an incomparable advantage in
welding Reagan's coalition. It was an especially potent weapon
against wavering Republicans and southern Democrats who came
from congressional districts which Reagan had carried in 1980,
with sixty or seventy percent of the vote, and could appeal directly
to the voters. Strong, emotional public support gave Reagan the

second half of that vital amalgam of a leader's leverage—love and fear. There were two dozen House Republicans who knew they had ridden Reagan's coattails into office in 1980, and a half a dozen Republican senators for whom Reagan had added the final one or two percent for their paper-thin victories. These Republicans, indebted to Reagan, were reluctant to cross him. Southern Boll Weevil Democrats feared Reagan too—enough to extract a promise that he would not campaign against them in 1982 if they backed his program in 1981. "I couldn't look myself in the mirror in the morning if I campaigned against someone who helped me on this program," the president promised the Boll Weevils.

The fear factor helped lift Reagan to his 1981 victories.

44

JOSEPH CALIFANO

From *Governing America*

———

My first impressions of Jimmy Carter's presidential style came at Sea Island, Georgia, during his initial meetings with the Cabinet over the 1976 Christmas holidays. The Cabinet stayed at the Cloister, a luxury resort; the Carters at the nearby Musgrove Plantation of R. J. Reynolds Tobacco heir Smith Bagley on St. Simons Island ten minutes away. During those early days, I was struck by the ostentatiously nonpresidential ambience of both the new President and his associates. Carter brandished informalities and religion. He slouched in a sweater and jeans, spoke softly, constantly appearing to defer to comments by members of the new Cabinet, especially Cyrus Vance. He prayed before meals, exuded fundamentalist intensity, invoked the name of God frequently. In each of our rooms when we arrived at the Cloister was a small book of religious poems written by LaBelle Lance, the wife of his friend Bert, who had been named Director of the Office of Management and Budget. I attributed much of this to Carter's born-again Baptist beliefs, and suppressed my Northeastern Catholic discomfort at such public displays of fundamentalist religion.

Again and again he stressed "ethics" and the importance of avoiding conflicts of interest. He wanted us publicly to reveal information about our holdings and earnings, to set up blind trusts over which we had no control. Carter put his White House counsel Robert Lipshutz in charge. I proposed Stanford Ross, a friend and personal attorney, as my blind trustee. Lipshutz checked with Carter and told me that Ross was too close; I had to get someone independent. I, therefore, asked a casual acquaintance, Republican Peter Peterson, Chairman of Lehman Brothers Kuhn Loeb, who had been Secretary of Commerce in the Nixon administration, to be my blind trustee. When Carter ultimately selected his intimate friend and advisor Charles Kirbo to be his, I began to suspect that much of what was going on was for public consumption.

The odor of naïveté perfumed those two days off the coast of Georgia. The new President evidenced little sense of what Washington was like or of the complexities of governing. Except for Stuart Eizenstat, who had been a junior aide under Johnson and had worked on Hubert Humphrey's 1968 presidential campaign, and Jack Watson, who had conducted a wide-ranging transition study, Carter's staff seemed naïve to a fault and appeared to believe the anti-Washington rhetoric that had carried Carter to the White House.

In the meetings, Carter spoke sincerely of his desire to use his presidency "for good," to restore the confidence of the people in their government, to "give them an administration as good as they are," to fulfill his campaign commitments, and to "maintain a close and intimate relationship with the voters." Hamilton Jordan worked at being the country boy from Georgia, wearing work boots, affecting boredom during much of the discussions. Jody Powell was disingenuously deferential, calling each Cabinet member Mister or Madame Secretary. Watson, the only Carter staffer with whom I had discussed organizing the government, was subdued, giving some validity to news reports that he was having his wings clipped by Jordan; Eizenstat was quiet and serious. As I sat at the meetings, I thought that Watson and Eizenstat would have to provide Carter his substantive staff advice. Bert Lance, who had been Carter's Georgia Highway Commissioner and banker, was charming, but displayed neither the peronality, depth, nor motivation required to be OMB Director, and the others close to the President evidenced little interest in governing. . . .

Carter disliked the political aspects of the personnel process.

At a Cabinet meeting early in the administration, he complained about the Congress, expressing his "disgust," particularly about House members. "I try to talk to them about substantive problems, like the energy program, and all they want to talk about is whether or not they can get their buddies appointed to some regional job in HUD [Housing and Urban Development] or HEW [Health, Education and Welfare]." His attitude infuriated some key House members....

Carter's disdain of the political aspects of the appointment process sharply contrasted with the enthusiasm of Lyndon Johnson, who truly enjoyed this political give-and-take with the Congress. To him, the politics of personnel appointments were a key part of governing. He would ponder moves with the concentration of a chess master. He was interested in talent, but where he could combine that with a vote on a bill or a commitment to fund a program, he would. Indeed, Johnson would often tell a candidate he had already selected in his own mind to get some senators, congressmen, and interest groups to support his or her appointment. When the candidate did, Johnson would announce the selection, calling the supporters to say he had appointed their person. Months later, when the appointee took some action (often at Johnson's direction) that offended a group that supported him, he would say, "Hell, he's your man. You told me to appoint him."...

From the moment Edward M. Kennedy began questioning me about health policy during my confirmation hearing before the Senate Labor and Public Welfare Committee, I knew that national health insurance was going to be a major issue for him, for Carter, and for me.... I thought about Lyndon Johnson and Robert Kennedy, and about the inevitable problem any Democratic President would have with the last Kennedy brother in the Senate.

Carter's personality is very different from Johnson's. Carter is inner-directed, more like Nixon in his shyness and desire to be alone. Johnson was consumingly extroverted. He wanted company from the moment he rose in the morning until he fell asleep reading memos and talking to an aide with a masseur kneading his back. But Carter nurtured the same resentment of the liberal, Eastern establishment as Johnson, and no person could suffer the exhausting indignities of running for President without a monumental ego and enormous self-confidence, however disguised by the image-makers who told him to carry his own suitcase.

I knew how Johnson had felt about Robert Kennedy and how

some of his feelings had spilled over on Ted Kennedy near the end
of his presidency in late 1968. Carter was not immune to the same
feelings. I thought it was only a matter of time before Carter and
Edward Kennedy became a redux of Johnson and Robert Kennedy.
Only this time, I thought, national health insurance will be a crucial
issue, and Califano will be the rope for the tug of war....

The political chances for Carter and Kennedy to agree on a
national health plan were never good, given Kennedy's ambition,
his tenacious staff, and the media's great interest in reading presidential aspirations into the slightest movement of a potential challenger. Moreover, Carter was going to be as combative as Kennedy. He suspected that Kennedy might be his opponent for the
1980 nomination. Annoyed once by a Kennedy comment that he
was "indefinite and imprecise on the critical issues." during the
1976 campaign, Carter remarked privately, "I'm glad I don't have
to depend on Kennedy or people like that to put me in office. I
don't have to kiss his ass."...

That June 1 meeting lasted more than two hours. Carter opened
by noting that he found "a paradox, an anomaly" in his situation.
"I have already made a number of commitments—during my campaign and subsequently to the UAW [United Auto Workers] and
to Senator Kennedy. At the same time, there appears to be no
significant additional money for health care available in the budget
in the next few years and I will not do anything to undermine my
current effort to control inflation."

As he spoke, it struck me forcibly how Carter's face was graying
and aging. What a toll this job takes on a human being, I thought.
And meetings like this told why. He had a tough decision to
make. "I am inclined to do what I've done in the past, to tell the
American people the truth and lay out the problem." He talked
about health system problems and concluded, "I don't believe a
comprehensive program can possibly be passed this year. It is
unlikely even next year. But there are some important advantages
to be gained by discussing the problem and the issue openly."...

"It is ridiculous to think about endorsing a bill like Kennedy's.
I am not going to destroy my credibility on inflation and budgetary
matters. I intend to be honest and responsible with the American
people." Carter did "not simply view this as a matter of accommodating particular political pressure groups." It was more "a question of what we get for different expenditures." He urged me to
get on with drafting the principles and observed as he rose to

leave the Cabinet Room, "We are still in a quandary as to how to proceed."

For the first time, I felt that Carter might abandon his commitment to a comprehensive plan, and with it the chance to achieve significant reform of the health system. The larger responsibilities of the presidency—to fight inflation particularly, but also as party leader to Democratic House members running for re-election in a conservative year—were weighing heavily on him. Unlike Kennedy, the President had to be an advocate of more than a single cause, however worthy. . . .

When I was designated Secretary, I had never thought about smoking as a serious health issue, within my responsibility (although I had quit smoking on October 21, 1975). When President-elect Carter told me at St. Simons Island in December 1976 that he wanted to move forcefully in the area of preventive care, I began to read and question experts about such programs. Invariably, they suggested a major anti-smoking campaign as a critical element of any such effort. . . .

Most of Washington closed down during the Christmas holidays, but not the Tobacco Institute. Institute lobbyists made several attempts to obtain a copy of my speech announcing the anti-smoking program. . . .

Tobacco politics is a hardball game. At my invitation, Pennsylvania Democratic Congressman Fred Rooney's wife, Evie Rooney, who quit smoking during the same Smokenders session I attended, sat on the stage during my speech. When a Tobacco Institute lobbyist saw her, he told her husband that he would never get another dollar from the industry. Rooney, who had received campaign contributions of several thousand dollars from tobacco interests over many years, got no contribution for his losing 1978 campaign. Governor Jim Hunt of North Carolina said that I should travel to his state to meet with some farmers to learn what tobacco meant to the state; North Carolina Democratic Congressman Charlie Rose said, "We're going to have to educate Mr. Califano with a two-by-four, not a trip.". . .

The political fallout from the anti-smoking effort was intense. The tobacco industry financed bumper stickers announcing "Califano is Dangerous to My Health," and there were highway billboards saying, "Califano Blows Smoke." The White House staff judged the program politically too dangerous. As always when criticizing a member of the Cabinet, the White House staff spoke anonymously, charging I had mounted the campaign without getting "political clearance" or "thinking through the political details." A "high-ranking White House aide" said "With all the problems Carter has in North Carolina [a reference to the court order to desegregate its higher education system that HEW was enforcing], he doesn't need an anti-smoking campaign."...

In early August 1978, Carter made his second of three trips to North Carolina in six months. He visited a tobacco warehouse in Wilson and spoke at a Democratic Party rally. At first the President kidded the audience about me: "I had planned today to bring Joe Califano with me, but he decided not to come. He discovered that not only is North Carolina the number-one tobacco-producing state, but that you produce more bricks than anyone in the nation as well." The crowd responded with applause mixed with laughter. "Joe Califano did encourage me to come though. He said it was time for the White House staff to start smoking something regular," an allusion to rumors of pot smoking by some members of the President's staff. The crowd loved it. The President then told the audience his family had grown tobacco in North Carolina before moving to Georgia to grow peanuts. The health program the President described, however, was hardly HEW's. As he put it, we would conduct a research plan "to make the smoking of tobacco even more safe than it is today."

When the normally mild-mannered Surgeon General Julius Richmond heard that, he immediately called me. "This is terrible. The President is either terribly, ill-informed or cynically political about this." These were strong words from the most soft-spoken member of the HEW team. I told him there was nothing we could do at the moment without further embarrassing the President....

The new report of the Surgeon General on Smoking and Health was scheduled for release on Thursday, January 11, 1979. The massive, three-inch-thick book concluded that the case against cigarette smoking was "overwhelming." Indeed, the accumulation of evidence against cigarette smoking was so devastating, and the interest of government as the largest purchaser of health care so profound, that I decided to mount new and more extensive education efforts around its release....

On the eve of the report's release, Jody Powell called me from National Airport in Washington. "I'm headed for North Carolina to do a Democratic fundraiser tonight. Is there anything to bring me up to date on?"

"My God," I exclaimed, and told him about the release of the Surgeon General's report and the media blitz that was coming. "I don't know what you can do," I concluded.

"Smoke," Powell replied. "I'll just smoke like hell when I'm down there.". . .

For the President, there was one unfortunate aspect of the television coverage. After reporting the case against cigarette smoking, the three networks showed footage of Carter amidst the tobacco leaves in the Wilson, North Carolina, warehouse, talking about making smoking "even more safe." After viewing the broadcasts, Vice-President Mondale, who never lost his wry sense of humor, called me. "Jeez," he said, "those guys in the White House really have it positioned—the President's for cancer and you're for health.". . .

The anti-smoking campaign generated more political opposition than any other effort I undertook at HEW. House Speaker Tip O'Neill told me in late 1978, "You're driving the tobacco people crazy. These guys are vicious. They're out to destroy you." In April 1979, Ted Kennedy told me, "You've got to get out of the Cabinet before the election. The President can't run in North Carolina with you at HEW. He's going to have to get rid of you.". . .

The early months of the Carter administration were charged with hope and expectation, but the anticipated political honeymoon never took shape and the innocence of Carter and his closest aides about governing and Washington provided cause for misgivings. The new President did wade into some tough problems—energy, SALT II, the Panama Canal Treaties, the Middle East, the Third World, welfare and tax reform—and at first his willingness to take them on was itself enough, a refreshing change from the laid-back presidency of Gerald Ford.

Carter also seemed determined to change the ambience of the federal government: to reorganize the bureaucracy more efficiently, reduce paperwork, eliminate irritating and unnecessary regulations, make those who sign regulations read every word of them, get rid of perks such as cars and chauffeurs. He intended to honor all his campaign commitments and the White House staff compiled a book dubbed "Promises, Promises" to keep them on the front burner.

Carter was bent on mastering every detail, and as his reading load increased, he and Rosalynn took a speed reading course on

Tuesday nights at the White House and invited any interested members of the Cabinet to join them. Lyndon Johnson would have said, "Put a welfare reform program together that gives poor people some money and encourages people to work and keep their families together," and left all but the key policy and political judgments to his staff. Carter read hundreds of pages of material on welfare programs and did almost everything but draft the legislation. He displayed the same fervor for total immersion in energy, the African subcontinent, tax reform, and SALT II. In addition to being President, he was, as an HEW staffer remarked after one of my welfare reform briefings, the highest paid assistant secretary for planning that ever put a reform proposal together....

As his first year in office ended, Carter was in trouble as both executive and leader. His administration lacked cohesion. The Office of Management and Budget and its new Director, James McIntyre, floundered along a conservative course while Eizenstat and the Domestic Policy Council steered toward a liberal one. Zbigniew Brzezinski sniped at Cyrus Vance in the press, and Jordan and Powell continued to cut up several Cabinet members anonymously, Mike Blumenthal being their favorite target. Most Cabinet officers and department heads tried to read what Carter wanted and sought to serve him and his administration, each in his own way. Excepting Stu Eizenstat and Jack Watson, they had little respect for the Carter staff and no clear sense of where the President was leading them. At the same time, there was a real decline in public confidence. You could measure it not only by polls, but every time we left Washington people were anxious to tell us about it. Political leaders around the country had begun to ridicule the "governor from Georgia." "The job is too big for him," was what most business and labor leaders told us.

Things were even worse on Capitol Hill. House Speaker Tip O'Neill had been insulted by the arrogance of the Georgians in the early days. Ineptness in handling appointments and making announcements, in introducing and pushing legislation had alienated many key Democrats. The administration's initiatives were failing....

The administration's situation continued to sour, Cabinet officers began to question the value of the weekly meetings, and self-interested leaks and internecine back-biting increased. The President gave the first indication of a desire to do something at a Cabinet meeting on April 10, 1978. He wanted the Cabinet to come to Camp David the next weekend to "think long-range about problems among ourselves, to express criticism freely about the relationship between the White House and your own departments." At last, Carter seemed ready to acknowledge a serious problem in Cabinet–White House staff relations. The number of articles—based on anonymous White House sources—critical of the Cabinet had continued to accumulate. . . .

The senior White House staff arrived at Camp David early on Sunday afternoon, April 16. . . .

Carter paused before turning to internal difficulties. "The problems that we do have I attribute primarily to the White House. Some leaks from the White House are inexcusable—derogatory remarks about Mike [Blumenthal] or Pat [Harris] or Brock [Adams]. If I could find one who did it, I would kick his ass out of the White House." I was incredulous. By now I suspected he had ordered or at least condoned much of it. My God, there is some Elmer Gantry in this born-again President, I thought. Carter then turned briefly to self-criticism. "We have a lack of Washington experience. We need to learn more. . . .

Carter then turned to Hamilton Jordan, who replied, "The mood of the country is passive and nonpartisan. Americans want better government, not more government. That is why Carter was elected. The people do not want more programs." He said there was "no party loyalty, no discipline within the Congress." The administration was dealing with 535 members, and thirty or forty interest groups within the Congress itself, as well as "dozens and dozens" of other pressure groups. "We are not tough; we are not in charge; we are not managing the mechanisms of government. If this persists for three or four months, it will be irreversible. The worse thing is for [the Congress] to lose respect for us as politicians. We do not know how to use our resources politically—no rewards, no retributions. We need a system for doing better." He described himself "as basically an optimist," but said, "We must move in the next four or five months or we cannot govern. We need successes.". . .

Carter, looking suddenly tired, said he felt "like the referee between the Cabinet and the White House staff." At his meeting with the White House staff the day before, many "statements and insinuations were made that the Cabinet goes behind our back. Ninety percent of those could be resolved by thrashing issues out."

He said we did not know Jody and Ham well enough, that we should meet with them on a Saturday morning. I wondered if he knew that Jordan never returned phone calls from most of us. Carter went on in a monotone, "If Ham or Stu or Jack calls on my behalf, take their word as coming directly from me. You have been overly reluctant to respond when the White House staff calls you.". . .

But the respite was brief. On May 22, New York Senator Moynihan expressed the opinion that unless Carter acted quickly to take charge, he would soon find "that he's governing by the sufferance of" Senator Edward Kennedy. And the next day, five House Democrats started their own "Dump Carter–Draft Kennedy" movement. Kennedy refused to unequivocally take himself out of the presidential race.

During May and the first days of June, the Congress defeated Carter's proposals for Rhodesian sanctions, gasoline rationing, and decontrol of oil prices. Despite what then seemed like a bravado claim that he would "whip Kennedy's ass" in a fight for the Democratic nomination, Carter was beginning to reveal his own discouragement publicly. . . .

At 10:30 A.M., the special Cabinet meeting for "principals only" began, with Hamilton Jordan as the only non-Cabinet member present, sitting in Mondale's chair across the table from the President. Mondale was on the road, pumping for the SALT Treaty and traveling abroad, trying to get as far away as possible from what was coming.*

It was to be the most intense Cabinet meeting of the Carter administration. The Washington press corps had begun the race to discover who would go. Rumors tumbled over one another, but my name was appearing on every list. Carter entered smiling; but his smile did not soften the taut lines on his face. He took his chair with its slightly higher back. Nixon had introduced that more formal chair as a symbol of the change from Johnson, who had sat in a reclining, high-back desk chair. Ford had replaced Nixon's with a chair the same size as all the others. Carter had brought back the Nixon chair.

---

*SALT stands for Strategic Arms Limitation Treaty. The 1979 SALT treaty, the Carter Administration's major effort to achieve an understanding with the Soviet Union on nuclear weapons, was not ratified by the Senate.—EDS.

The President began softly. "I have deliberately excluded most of you from my life for the past couple of weeks." He said he had "wanted to get away from you and from Washington." He felt an obligation to reassess his presidency, to have "serious private talks about my role as President." His words were pessimistic, his voice somber. It was as close to quiet desperation as I had ever seen him. There has been "a lot of effort wasted on misdirections," he said. "My government is not leading the country. The people have lost confidence in me, in the Congress, in themselves, and in this nation." He talked of the "alarming deterioration in attitude of people toward their country." Then a tone of teeth-gritted determination came into his voice. He had held a host of meetings with all kinds of groups from all across the country. He had asked them about his Cabinet and his staff. The comments about his Cabinet were "serious and condemnatory. I was told, they are not working for you, but for themselves." He said that he had "repeatedly been told" that there was disloyalty "among some Cabinet members," that many had been the source of leaks that had hurt him. With a studied expression of hurt on his face, Carter allowed that he had given "great loyalty" to his Cabinet and had "great appreciation" for their sacrifice and service.

He paused. "I have decided to change my lifestyle, and my calendar. I have one and one-half years left as President, and I don't deserve to be re-elected if I can't do a better job. I intend to run for office and I intend to be re-elected." To get ready for this effort over the next eighteen months, personnel changes would be made in the Cabinet and the White House staff. "I will make the changes over the course of next week." He intended to change the administration's "way of doing business" as well as the "identity of key members of the administration." He complained that "some Cabinet officers do not have support among their constituents.". . .

Then the President opened the meeting. Blumenthal spoke briefly about "the difference between arguing for a point of view and disloyalty." Carter hardly listened. Pat Harris said, "We can move government forward by putting phones in the White House staff offices and the staff using them." She complained that her calls were never returned by White House aides. She said it was important to "fight fiercely for our point of view," that it was not "disloyal to disagree with the White House staff, provided one supports the administration when the decision is made."

U.N. Ambassador Andrew Young began to speak, echoing Harris's concern. The President's face reddened. He interrupted Young: "You have repeatedly embarrassed the administration. I was told this again and again at Camp David.... You have caused embarrassment to me by calling Britain the most racist country in history ... saying Cuban troops in Angola were a stabilizing influence ... saying there are hundreds of political prisoners in the United States."

Usually, Carter was uncomfortable when Cabinet members argued back to him, but now his voice and eyes were so angry that by the time he had ended his attack on Young, he had killed any other meaningful comment. He turned to Jordan.

Jordan admitted that after two and a half years "I have no relationship with many of you." He said the Cabinet had to be "more accountable, better disciplined," that we had to "resolve the little problems and not send them to the President." The redness of anger faded from Carter's face and he looked like a proud father as Jordan continued: The medium-sized problems would come to him for decision; McIntyre and Eizenstat would be involved in domestic issues, Brzezinski in foreign policy. The White House staff would "work as an organization, not as a democracy," he said. "The personnel changes will be made quickly, and the discipline will be imposed immediately, including over leaks."

Carter added an admonition to complete the personnel evaluation forms promptly, to get them back within a few days, and he left the room. Jordan distributed the personnel evaluation forms— so patently amateurish and preposterous that the expressions on several Cabinet members' faces were open-mouthed. I could think only of what a disaster Carter was headed for....

The following morning, July 18, I had a quiet breakfast with my friend and former law partner Edward Bennett Williams at the Metropolitan Club in Washington. Sitting virtually alone in the vast dining room on the fourth floor, I talked about the possibility that Carter might fire me.

"I can't believe it," Williams said. "It doesn't make any sense."

I still thought it was a possibility: "I can't believe any President would let his staff put this stuff out to the press unless he had blessed it, or at a minimum they knew that I was on the way out."

Williams then said, leaning across the table, "It would be the best damn thing that could happen to you. The guy is through and it will give you a way to get out. You ought to hope he fires you. You may not be that lucky."

At noon, I went to Woodlawn in Baltimore to celebrate the anniversary of my reorganization of Medicare and Medicaid into the Health Care Financing Administration. When I got back, Susanna McBee, who had been named to succeed Eileen Shanahan as Assistant Secretary for Public Affairs at HEW, told me that Pat Harris had been to see Carter, but that no word of what occurred had leaked. Heineman reported that OMB and Domestic Policy staff aides were suggesting me to their bosses as Secretary of Energy.

I was preparing for my testimony the next morning on the administration's Higher Education Act proposals when the President called me at 5:19 P.M. "Joe, how are you doing?" he asked softly.

"Fine, Mr. President," I responded.

"Can you come over here this afternoon?"

"Any time," I said. The President asked me to come right away.

I was prepared for whichever decision Carter reached, although I did not really think he would accept my resignation, despite all the published evidence to the contrary, because we always seemed to have gotten along well.

I walked into Nell Yates's office, between the Cabinet Room and the Oval Office. She had been Jack Valenti's secretary when I first met her on the LBJ staff. We chatted aimlessly as I watched the President in the Rose Garden through the French doors. He was looking up at the trees at some birds. As he came through the French doors, he said, "I think I may have seen one of Cec's peregrine falcons." He was referring to the birds that Interior Secretary Andrus had saved and brought to Washington.

Carter ushered me through the Oval Office into his small study. He sat behind his desk, and I sat on a couch to the right against the wall. In his desk chair, the President was perched slightly higher than me, as I sank into the soft-cushioned white couch.

"I have decided to accept your resignation," he said through a nervous smile.

45

MICHAEL DEAVER

From *Behind the Scenes*

———

WELL, we would all prefer a big finish, a graceful exit, a happy ending. But it seems safe to say that there were few generous commentaries on my final official service to the presidency of Ronald Reagan.

The trip to Bitburg started out as an afterthought, a minor footnote to the economic summit scheduled in May 1985 among the Western allies. We would be walking through a cemetery, not a minefield. The visit coincided with the fortieth anniversary of the end of the Second World War.

I was going out on a high note [as White House deputy chief of staff]. Reagan was near his peak of popularity in the polls. His reelection had resulted in a virtual shutout over Mondale, one of the two biggest landslides in history. The daily press and the weekly news magazines had hailed me as "Magic Mike," and "The Vicar of Visuals."

If I qualified as an expert on anything, it was said to be the staging of a media event; blending the gifts of Ronald Reagan with the proper pageantry. Not everyone looked on this capacity with respect. Chefs who barbecue cows for a living call it selling the sizzle.

But it was part of my job, the part I often enjoyed most. And so my final act was to help arrange the agenda and the coverage of the president's trip to Europe. The furor that came later, some suggested, was the result of my attention being divided, meaning that my mind was already at least partly on the new public-relations firm I would launch as soon as my White House resignation took effect.

Whatever mistakes were made at Bitburg were mine. Let me leave no doubt on that point and move on. But it was not the result of insensitivity, or inattention, or carelessness.

Hindsight is a wonderful tool. I know what went wrong and how the controversy could have been avoided. But when the plans were first laid, no one saw the pitfalls; or, if anyone did, they neglected to point them out.

In February 1985, having convinced the president that the time had come for me to move on, I flew to Europe to work out the details of his European trip, the highlight of which was to be the economic summit in Bonn, West Germany.

A few months earlier, in November, the president had agreed to a vague request by Helmut Kohl, the West German chancellor, to take part in a ceremony marking the friendship, the reconciliation, between our two countries. The obvious and traditional idea, the symbolic visit to a concentration camp, appealed to neither side and was quietly dropped.

There was a sense of projecting an era of hope and a closing of the book on the past. This the camps could not do; they existed as a remembrance of the ghastly deeds that occurred there. No one could or should forget them.

I had the additional factor of Ronald Reagan's nature. He was not a ease with, nor eager to confront, scenes of unrelenting depression. He was at his best when he could touch the nostalgia, the longing in each of us for a more romantic time. You put him near a flag, around uniforms, or in sight of a parade, and he could lift anyone's spirit.

Helmut Kohl suggested a joint visit to the military cemetery at Bitburg, the laying of a wreath to honor the dead of all our armies. We asked the question we always asked on such trips: Was there anything there that might embarrass our president, our country? The answer was no.

We literally could not see the pitfalls. It was February. The graves, most of the markers, were covered by blankets of snow. I added this visit to the itinerary and the wheels were put in motion.

I flew back to Washington with Bitburg fairly well down on my list of concerns. My attention was more tightly focused on assuring that Reagan would not be overscheduled and overdrawn during his weeks abroad, that he was rested and prepared for the economic policy talks. I had not forgotten—Nancy never let me forget—that I had failed to build in enough rest periods on an earlier journey, and Reagan had nodded off while talking to the pope.

The summit was planned for the second week in May. In mid-April, German newspapers carried the story that the cemetery we had selected included the graves not only of ordinary soldiers but also of forty-nine members of the Waffen SS, a branch of the dreaded Nazi guard that ran the death camps.

In Europe, the United States, and the Soviet Union, the outcry was immediate and bitter. Wounds long unhealed but ignored surfaced again. Veterans marched and mailed back their medals. Jewish groups demonstrated and begged the president to back off. No newscast, no edition of any newspaper, was complete without an interview with a person who had lost someone, or everyone, in the Holocaust.

Those reactions, those emotions, were genuine and for the most part spontaneous. The anguish we saw and heard was painful then, and I do not take it lightly now. But the judgment had been made. The only question was, at what cost would we undo it, or did we take the heat and move ahead?...

But even as the firestorm of controversy engulfed the country, there were deep divisions on the president's staff. Everyone had an opinion. But, basically, I felt it was my mess and I had to clean it up.

One of my first tasks was to keep Pat Buchanan the hell out of it. He is a tough, talented, outspoken wordsmith, a purist when it comes to the conservative faith, far enough to the right that he considers school lunches a subversive plot. Now, as the new communications director in the White House, he would be one of the people most often whispering in Ronald Reagan's ear. I will say it again: Reagan does not need anyone to the right of him.

Buchanan argued for a harder line, a bigger gesture, a clearer defense of the new Germany and virtually an amnesty for the Third Reich; whatever it took to avoid the appearance that the president was bending under pressure from Jewish or any other groups.

Once it became clear that the president was not open to suggestions that he cancel or cut back the trip, I knew that what he said there would in large measure determine how the passage to Bitburg would be judged. Ken Khachigian, a former Reagan speechwriter, was brought back to work with Josh Gilder in crafting the text of what the president would say. The theme was his own. He wanted to meet the issue squarely. He wanted to put it in the context of where we had come in forty years.

The country was still in an uproar. The memories of the Nazi atrocities, the hardships and sacrifices of the war, revived an anger that swept across the generation gap. The issue had escalated into the worst crisis of the Reagan presidency. How could anyone support us, or understand what we had meant to do? The trip to Bitburg seemed stupid, or worse, even to those who had not been born when the SS was doing its obscene work.

On April 19, Helmut Kohl called and personally asked Ronald Reagan not to give in to the critics, not to break the promise Kohl felt had been made to him. We now believed that our relationship with West Germany, and the stability of the Kohl government, depended on our ability to *not* make the situation worse.

Kohl feared we would make last-minute changes that might be taken as an insult to the West German people, and weaken his leaderhip. He was, after all, the first chancellor of the republic who had grown to manhood in the postwar era.

We inched our way toward a more favorable plan. Advice kept pouring in: Richard Nixon warned Reagan not to retreat. Henry Kissinger called, adding that if we canceled Bitburg enormous damage would be done to America's foreign policy.... The president was hurting. I felt like falling on my sword. And the disposition of neither of us was helped by the fact that the criticism had led to my first serious conflict with Nancy Reagan.

I could not recall our ever before having been on opposite sides of an issue. But now she was convinced that I had ruined her husband's presidency, and perhaps the rest of his life. We had a very painful, emotional confrontation. I let her finish and said, "Nancy, it's done. If going into a panic would help, I'd panic. But I'm trying to do my damnedest to make the best of a very difficult situation. Let me get on with it, please."

If I had injured the president, she knew I had not done so out of indifference, or any ambition of my own. I had to cut off the conversation, knowing that outside my office were five or six people waiting to help me put the pieces back together. So for me the best course was the one I had always tried to take with her: to be direct and truthful. *I made a mistake. Now I was trying to fix it.* Nancy nodded her head and, without a word, walked out.

Her attitude was that the damage had been done. Almost to the last minute, she insisted the trip should be canceled. She said so to me. She said so to her husband. I have never, not in the years I have known them, seen the Reagans engage in a no-holds-barred argument. She may push to a point where he slams a table with his hand, or throws down a fountain pen, but I doubt that they have ever exchanged the really ugly words not uncommon to most marriages. This could reflect what a very private couple they are, or it could mean that they belong in the *Guinness Book of World Records* or the Smithsonian.

In this case, it ended when the president said: "Nancy, I simply don't believe you're right and I'm not going to change my mind." She pressed him no further.

On the early part of the trip, she was almost physically ill. I felt for her deeply.

I had decided to add a side trip to a concentration camp after all, the one at Bergen-Belsen. The move exposed us to charges of flip-flopping, and reeked of politics, but our objective now was to balance Bitburg, not reject it.

The ceremony would be brief, and clean, almost sterile, and there would be no speeches. But canceling the trip never had been a serious option in the mind of Ronald Reagan (nor in mine). He was not going to abandon Helmut Kohl or embarrass the West German nation. While far from immune to public sentiment, Reagan is one of those stubborn individuals who hardens when he feels pressured....

The day dawned damp and gray and the pilgrimage began at Bergen-Belsen. The president, hand in hand with Nancy walked through the museum with row after row of horrifying photographs of pits filled with bones and piles of naked corpses and those barely living, hollow-eyed and skeletal, liberated by American troops in the spring of 1945....

We flew to Bitburg, and from the airport a motorcade carried us through the open countryside, past the demonstrators and into the cemetery. The graves, with flat markers, were arranged in thirty-two rows, with flowers placed at each stone.

The official party followed a brick walkway, taking care to avoid the area where the Waffen SS men were buried. Reagan and Kohl stopped at the main memorial, where two tall wreaths had been placed against a gray wall. With the generals standing at attention behind them, each touched a wreath and stepped back.

A lone German army bugler played an ode to lost soldiers, "Ich Hatt' Einen Kameraden" ("I Had a Comrade"). Reagan and Kohl shook hands with the honor guard, and the mayor of Bitburg, and the surviving relatives of German soldiers who had taken part in the plot to kill Hitler.

Eight minutes after it had entered the cemetery, the motorcade was on its way to the airport....

For all of the grim images and the raw, sobering, emotional scars, most of us left Germany lighter in mood than when we came. The president had endured, had in my mind *overcome* barriers that some feared, or hoped, would endanger his authority....

One thing I have learned and relearned about Ronald Reagan: When he believes he is morally right on a stand, there is hell getting him off it. Bitburg may or may not have been the right location for the symbolism we had in mind. But the trip was about reconciliation and an alliance for the future, and it was crucial that those goals not be lost in the clamor.

I want to be careful not to reduce the Bitburg episode to an exercise in public relations. But the gestures we made there did not warrant what I regarded as the overreaction of international opinion. No one in his right mind would try to play down the feelings of horror that are a legacy of World War II. There is no pairing of words any bigger or more tragic. There is no humor here, no lightness. But if we fail to seek out the hope, we are left only with the inhumanity.

I felt relief and even a touch of satisfaction as I cleaned out my desk at the White House some weeks later.

46

CHARLOTTE HAYS

Guess Who's Coming to Dinner at the White House

———

WHEN FIRST LADY Nancy Reagan read an article in "W" about Fernanda Eberstadt, a young novelist, she was intrigued. Mrs. Reagan made a note to ask her to dinner. As simply as that, Eberstadt, up and coming but hardly a major figure in American letters, joined the select company of White House state dinner invitees. It's not always so easy. "A state dinner," observed Reagan pal Nancy Reynolds, "is like going to Buckingham Palace, in the sense that the experience can never be replicated. It's the *ultimate* invitation from the head of the most powerful nation in the world."

Parties in Washington, as the axiom goes, are for business—*not* pleasure. But a state dinner breaks this rule. It's actually supposed to be fun, a pleasant evening for a foreign head of state. "They don't talk business because they've been doing that all day," said syndicated society columnist Betty Beale. But fun or not, it is also meant to convey an image. "The state dinner," said publicist Joe Canzeri, "is the only image the foreign head of state is going to have of the First Family, our leaders, and America. All they get overseas is 'Dynasty' and 'The Colbys.' "

A complete guest list for every state dinner appears the next morning in the *Washington Post's* "Style" section. An informal comparison of lists for the Carters and the Reagans suggests that some of the social stereotypes we have of both administrations are off target. The Carters, for example, catered to the rich and famous more than is often supposed, while the Reagans have wined and dined quite a few Just Plain Folks. "I've been through seven presidents," commented *Time* columnist and JFK intimate Hugh Sidey, "and they *all* have the rich and famous. They just have their *own* rich and famous."

Making the List

Compiling a guest list for a state dinner is complicated. It's part formula, part First Family preference. The first slots go, of course, to the foreign visitor and his entourage; the second batch goes to their U.S. counterparts. A list of suggested additional names trickles up to the East Wing from various governmental entities, including the State Department, the National Security Council, and the White House Office of Public Liaison. The final cut is made when the First Lady and the president add their choices. Who gets invited? "We're interested in people who're currently in the news," explained Elaine Crispen, Mrs. Reagan's press secretary. "Nobel Prize winners, sports figures who've won championships, and authors. The list is a mix taken from science, the arts, and business."

As the list emerges, it begins to reflect the social consciousness of the president and his wife. Some perennials, however, pop up from administration to administration. Advice columnist Ann Landers, for example, was a guest at Jimmy and Rosalynn Carter's dinner for Prime Minister Margaret Thatcher and again at the Reagans' dinner for Menachem Begin. Chicago oilman and banker

John Swearingen (who actually cut in on President Reagan on the dance floor!) was also a double header. Andy Warhol—apparently the guest of choice for authoritarian regimes—supped with the Shah of Iran at the Carter White House (at which Warhol told a reporter he'd seen no repression on his recent trip to Iran) and was invited back by the Reagans to meet Imelda and Ferdinand Marcos.

Frank Sinatra is another regular. "Sinatra has mystique, he's unique," explained Tish Baldridge, Jacqueline Kennedy's social secretary. Socially popular during Camelot, he was back in the limelight when the Reagans arrived in Washington. But, biographer Kitty Kelley's revelations that Sinatra was using the Reagan connection to polish his tarnished social image had a devastating effect. Now Sinatra's name is said to be high up on a clandestine White House list of people who're *not* coming to dinner any time soon.

At one time, artsy types and celebrities like Warhol and Sinatra were rare at state dinners. Dwight Eisenhower's guest lists were typical of the old style—composed almost entirely of corporation heads. Any celebrity who made it to dinner in Eisenhower's White House was probably there to sing for his supper. "Whenever you saw an entertainer," recalled Hill and Knowlton's Robert Keith Gray (Ike's cabinet secretary), "you knew he was going to get up and perform before the night was over." Eisenhower's tastes ran to Mantovani and Fred Waring.

Even a visit from the Queen of England, special as it was, didn't budge the Eisenhowers from their old habits; they trotted out the usual corporate heads. Society columnist Betty Beale was appalled. So drab! Beale wrote a column chiding the president for his dull guest list and went on to propose one of her own. It included William Faulkner, Ernest Hemingway, and Leonard Bernstein. "We don't have the English system of rewarding the people with a knighthood," Beale remarked recently, "so the least we could do was ask them to cross the threshold of the White House and show them off. Eisenhower didn't alter his lists, though he did begin to invite a few prominent U.S. scientists to the White House in the wake of the Soviet Union's *Sputnik* triumph. But real change had to wait for the Kennedys.

One of Mrs. Kennedy's first callers was New York City Ballet choreographer George Balanchine, who came to tea. With that, the modern epoch of White House entertaining dawned. The Kennedys invited a multitude of celebrities and achievers to dinner. Movie stars of the Peter Lawford–Frank Sinatra circle and other celebrities were welcome. Intellectuals like John Kenneth Galbraith and Arthur Schlesinger, Jr., sat where corporate heads had once reigned. Journalists also made their debut with the Kennedys—an indication that reporters had finally arrived as the social peers of their publishers.

One tradition the Kennedys staunchly upheld, however, was the no-escorts rule. A guest in those days was not permitted to bring along a friend. An exception was made for elderly ladies who might require an arm to lean on—they could bring a son or a nephew. According to Tish Baldrige, the reason for maintaining the stricture was that a guest was all too likely to bring "an undistinguished jerk," thereby wasting valuable space at table. Lyndon and Lady Bird Johnson lifted the ban on escorts. Socialite Barbara Howar, then a somewhat outspoken figure, who might otherwise have been invited only to less official functions, was an early date-infiltrator. Then, Gloria Vanderbilt came as a date (of entertainer Bobby Short) in the Carter years. Vanderbilt was promoted to *bona fide* invitee under Nancy Reagan's regime.

Presidents and First Ladies are aware of the image-building possibilities of the guest list. Carter self-consciously used it to paint a folksy, Jacksonian picture of the First Family. A White House description of a guest at the Carters' first state dinner—for Canadian Prime Minister Pierre Trudeau—described her simply as "a very interesting person—a numerologist and astrologer." A Mr. and Mrs. Oscar Ledford of Franklin, North Carolina at the same dinner were identified by the White House as "profession unknown—really 'just plain folks.' " Alas, Just Plain Folks don't always come for nothing: Mr. Ledford, a pig farmer, said in a telephone interview that the Carters had paid his way to Washington. He also said he'd be willing to entertain a similar offer from the Reagans.

As a matter of fact, the Reagans have had their own sprinkling of UPFs—for Unidentified Plain Folks—at their state dinners. These have included Mrs. Reagan's Los Angeles greengrocer, a White House secretary who received an invitation as a going away present, and a Catholic nun who works for an educational group on Capitol Hill. Since the Reagan's UPFs are never publicly revealed as such, they're much more difficult to spot on the lists. This may be the Reagans' overture to small "d" democracy.

Insider Trading

But the dominant flavor at a Reagan state dinner is undeniably rich and famous. "Let's face it," argued Joe Canzeri, a Reagan insider, "the president and Nancy can't help where they come from. They've lived in Beverly Hills, and that's where their friends are. If you're from Plains, Georgia, that's where your friends are, and if you're from Grand Rapids, your friends are going to be from Grand Rapids." Among the frequently invited friends are: Betsy Bloomingdale, the Armand Deutsches, designer Adolfo, Jerry Zipkin, and the Jack Wrathers. Hollywood actors have included Zsa Zsa Gabor, Kirk Douglas, Charlton Heston, Debbie Reynolds, and Mary Martin.

As might be expected, Jimmy and Rosalynn Carter's table was heavily flavored with old pals from Georgia and family members. Jesse Hill of Atlanta Life Insurance and Carter intimate Charles Kirbo joined Miz Lillian, Brother Billy, Ruth Carter Stapleton, and Mrs. J. W. Dolvin, the president's aunt from Calhoun, Georgia. A special feature of Carter state dinners was Little Amy, now making headlines as a Brown University activist, who was frequently seen—but not heard—reading Nancy Drew novels during state dinners. ("Imagine waiting all your life for a White House invitation," shuddered Robert Keith Gray, "and you end up next to a nine-year-old girl reading a book." Edmund Muskie was Amy's dinner partner for the Trudeau dinner. As a souvenir, Amy gave him her place card on which she'd printed, "Eat your spinach.")

The Carters' guest lists were more overtly political than the Reagans' have been. Political associates, not all of whom were plain people, loomed large: Pamela and Averell Harriman; the Smith Bagleys of the Reynolds Tobacco fortune; the Bruce Sundluns of Newport, Rhode Island and the Middleburg horsey set; and Washington superlawyer Lloyd Cutler. Union leaders also figured prominently, with early Carter supporter Sol Chaikin of the International Ladies' Garment Workers' Union receiving special favor: two state dinners and a small lunch upstairs with the First Family. When asked why he made it to the White House so often, Chaikin replied, "I was one of the union leaders who resisted the blandishments of Teddy Kennedy."

A category that Nancy Reagan seems to have gone out of her

way to enlarge is writers—something that hasn't been much credited in the media, perhaps because many are conservative. Tom
Wolfe, Irving Kristol, and Norman Podhoretz have been invited.
But so have Theodore White, John Updike (who went out of his
way to tell the *Post* reporter that he's a Democrat), and John Irving,
a leader in the pro-choice movement. *American Spectator* editor R.
Emmett Tyrrell has been to two state dinners. Why is he in such
demand? "I don't understand why," Tyrrell said, "except that I
have impeccable table manners and can speak Spanish to the Spanish and Australian to the Australians."

One category the Reagans have neglected is the New Right.
Mr. and Mrs. Reagan seem more at ease with the patrician Old
Right. Columnist George Will, William Rusher of *National Review,*
and James Buckley receive invitations. But the guess-who's-not-
coming-to-dinner list includes Paul Weyrich, key New Right coalition builder, and direct mail fundraiser Richard Viguerie. Patrick
Buchanan is the closest thing to a New Right invitee. He went to
a 1984 state dinner.

The Reagans also seem to have a preference for conservative
representatives from well-heeled organizations: W. Glenn Camp-
bell of the Hoover Institution and Ed Feulner of the Heritage Foundation have come to dinner. Millionaire Republicans Lew Lehrman
of New York and Richard Mellon Scaife have, too.

At least two journalists are asked to each state dinner, as a rule.
Selections are made by the press secretaries, often with an eye to
wooing a hostile member of the media. An invitation is "a high
form of bribery," Mrs. Reagan's former press secretary Sheila
Tate giggled. But when asked if the bribe works, Tate replied,
"Never!" Sam Donaldson, consistently negative toward the Reagan administration, has been to a state dinner. Steve Weisman of
the *New York Times* and *Washington Post* reporter Elisabeth Bumiller (his wife) have been on the list, as has the *New York Times's*
William Safire. (Safire may be on the guess-who's-not-coming list
after his column accusing Mrs. Reagan of masterminding Donald
Regan's ouster.)

A great deal of consideration is given—no matter what administration—to finding guests of special interest to the guest of honor.
This is probably one of the best ways to become an invitee. When,
for example, the Carters hosted a state dinner for Nigerian President Shehu Shagari, they assumed he would especially want to

meet black Americans. On the guest list that night were *Roots* author Alex Haley, Coretta Scott King, and actress Cicely Tyson. When Australian Prime Minister Malcolm Fraser came to town, the Reagans invited Olivia Newton-John, who is of Australian descent, and Evonne Goolagong Cawley.

A final miscellaneous category takes in the people whom the First Family finds interesting. Arianna Stassinopoulos Huffington, socialite C. Z. Guest, Clare Boothe Luce, Paloma Picasso—all Reagan guests—might fit in this group. A similar category for the Carters would include, judging from the lists, the mayor of Oak Ridge, Tennessee; the sheriff of Springfield, Massachusetts; and a Democratic committee-woman from Florida. European titles were rare as hen's teeth in the Carter years, but the Reagans quite like them. The Countess de Ravenel, the Vicomte and Vicomtess de Ribes, Count and Countess Rudi Crespi, not to mention Prince Sadruddin Aga Khan, have all been to state dinners.

But what can *you* do to go to a state dinner? At present, a discreet contribution of $100,000 to Blair House is said to ensure an invitation. Some people, however, have been luckier. Bob Colacello, at the time a writer at Warhol's *Interview* magazine, thinks he knows why the Reagans invited him: Doria Reagan, Ron Reagan, Jr.'s wife, was Colacello's secretary. Colacello had been to the Carter White House as a journalist and didn't like what he saw as its lack of sophistication. He had a marvelous time with the Reagans, though, who had him to the Marcos dinner. "It was quite beautiful," he recalled. "When the Marine announces your name and they play 'Hail to the Chief,' you can't help but be excited."

As a perusal of guests lists seems to imply, this may well be one of the few times in history when Republicans have more fun.

PART SEVEN

The Executive Branch

THE AMERICAN system of "separated institutions sharing powers" not only invites conflicts over public policies between the president and Congress; it places the federal bureaucracy squarely between them as a pawn of contention. Federal bureaucrats in effect work for two rival employers, both of whom have the constitutional powers and personal motivations to control their behavior. The familiar public expectation that the president is the chief executive (a kind of national CEO) and the neat, hierarchical organization charts found in government manuals obscure the messy reality of this perennial struggle for the hearts and minds of those who implement public policy.

A new president can use his appointment power to put several hundred political executives in top positions in the departments and other agencies. Most of these are subject to his power of removal. He can use a very large Executive Office staff in various ways to monitor their activities. He can also use the routines of program and regulatory review and budgeting to assert his purposes. But Congress creates the structure of the federal executive, determines who shall have specific program responsibilities, authorizes programs, appropriates money for their execution and insists on "oversight" of all this by its committees and subcommittees, which have evolved a fine division of labor for this purpose. Thus, the American executive branch is betwixt and between as is no other bureaucracy in the world's democracies—constantly pulled between the centralizing force of the modern presidency and the decentralized fiefdoms of congressional committees (and the many-splendored variety of interests represented there). In this great national tug-of-war both sides frequently experience victory and frustration. This is another legacy of the Madisonian system. It is too seldom properly understood.

Hugh Heclo, an insightful student of comparative executive behavior, points out in our first selection that America's top political executives are a "government of strangers," quickly assembled by a new president and his staff in what is usually a chaotic transition from one administration to another. In comparison with the intimately acquainted groups of party leaders who form Conservative or Labour governments in Great Britain, they usually lack familiarity with one another, shared experiences, and commitment to the task of working together to promote common, partisan goals. They come from diverse backgrounds—many from such "nonpolitical" career paths as big business, banking, and academe. They take up positions in a fragmented power structure that they do not well understand. Many of the structures they are expected to command are parts of specialized policy systems linked to interest groups and congressional subcommittees controlled by members devoted to the protection of particular interests. Such systems—variously called iron triangles, unholy alliances, or subgovernments—nearly always vigorously resist presidential efforts to assert central policy control. Presidents and top political executives come and go, but actors in these triangular structures seek policy-making autonomy in such areas as agriculture, veterans' affairs, the management of public lands, and public works. These networks are particularly shocking to political executives who lack Washington experience. Heclo argues that some presidents are more effective than others in their efforts to create coherence in the executive branch, but the causes of fragmentation are inherent in our coordinate system of government.

Harold Seidman and Robert Gilmour, in our second selection, describe what they believe is a permanent tension between the president's purposes and the fractious fiefdoms of the departments. Even the cabinet secretaries will seem to presidents and their loyal central staffs to "go off and marry the natives." This is inside-the-beltway language for being drawn into the policy networks described above. Bureaucrats, slow-moving by nature, will always seem uncreative from a presidential perspective. Washington, they believe, is permanently and unavoidably a pluralistic place. The secretary of agriculture cannot be expected to question the inherent virtue of rural life. The secretary of the treasury simply must see things from the perspective of the banking community. Even the most loyal of political appointees must do a lot of adapting to the deeply ingrained cultures of the bureaucratic organizations in which they serve.

Our third reading, by Martin Anderson, a participant in the formation of the Reagan administration and one of its staunchest academic defenders, compares the presidential transitions of presidents Nixon and Reagan. Nixon's early mistakes, Anderson argues, left him with a permanently incoherent group of political appointees. The Reagan contrast is striking. The appointments process started early and proceeded in an orderly fashion to shape an administration that would be loyal to the president and to his conservative political ideology. Even those appointed to the lowest levels of the political positions were required to pass a litmus test of personal and ideological loyalty. Still, Anderson argues, matters deteriorated with the passage of time. We agree that the Reagan presidency went about as far as possible under American conditions to produce a coherent leadership of the executive branch. In this respect it was highly unusual. Already, the Bush administration seems to point to the return of the more usual pattern of pluralism.

The American political culture is not one in which civil servants are held in high esteem. So it has always been. Often, it seems, "federal bureaucrat" is one of the nastiest epithets available in our political discourse. When this animus gets out of hand, we need to be reminded that administrative specialists are a necessary part of a good political order. They are not always wrong. Often, their professionalism, special knowledge, experience, and institutional memory provide important elements that more transient, electorally motivated actors lack. To make this point we conclude this section with a short piece to this effect from the *Washington Monthly*, a journal which, ironically, is famous for its "bureaucracy-bashing" accounts of Washington horrors. The bulk of the day-to-day work of government is done by specialists. As this article points out, they know things that generalist, political executives can never

know. They play a critical role in good administration of public
policy.

47

HUGH HECLO

From *A Government of Strangers*

EVERY NEW ADMINISTRATION gives fresh impetus to an
age-old struggle between change and continuity, between political
leadership and bureaucratic power. Bureaucrats have a legitimate
interest in maintaining the integrity of government programs and
organizations. Political executives are supposed to have a broader
responsibility: to guide rather than merely reflect the sum of special
interests at work in the executive branch.

The search for effective political leadership in a bureaucracy of
responsible career officials has become extraordinarily difficult in
Washington. In every new crop of political appointees, some will
have had government experience and a few will have worked together, but when it comes to group commitment to political leadership in the executive branch they constitute a government of strangers. And yet the fact remains that whether the President relies
mainly on his White House aides or on his cabinet officials, someone is supposed to be mastering the bureaucracy "out there." For
the President, his appointees, and high-ranking bureaucrats, the
struggle to control the bureaucracy is usually a leap into the dark.

Despite a host of management and organization studies, Washington exposés and critiques of bureaucracy, very little information
is available about the working world and everyday conduct of the
top people in government. Even less is known about the operational lessons that could be drawn from their experiences. Congress
is widely thought to have lost power to the executive branch, but
congressional rather than executive behavior remains a major preoccupation in political research. Observers acknowledge that no
president can cope with more than a tiny fraction of the decision-

making in government, yet we know far more about a president's daily social errands than about the way vital public business is conducted by hundreds of political appointees and several thousand top bureaucrats who take executive actions in the name of the United States government—which is to say, in the name of us all....

If popular impressions are any guide, few job titles are more suspect than "politician" and "bureaucrat." Periodic polls have shown that while most parents might want their offspring to become president, they dislike the notion of their becoming politicians. No pollster has dared to ask Americans what they would think of their children growing up to become Washington bureaucrats.

Yet in many ways the American form of government depends not only on a supply of able politicians and bureaucrats, but even more on a successful interaction between these two unpopular groups....

... The administrative machinery in Washington represents a number of fragmented power centers rather than a set of subordinate units under the President. As many observers have noted, the cracks of fragmentation are not random but run along a number of well-established functional specialties and program interests that link particular government bureaus, congressional committees, and interest groups. People in the White House are aware of these subgovernments but have no obvious control over them. They seem to persist regardless of government reorganizations or, perhaps more to the point, they are able to prevent the reorganizations that displease them. In coping with these Washington subgovernments, the real lines of defense and accommodation are out in the departments, with their mundane operations of personnel actions, program approval, budget requests, regulation writing, and all the rest. These are the unglamorous tools with which political leaders in the agencies either help create a broader approach to the conduct of the public's business or acquiesce to the prevailing interest in business as usual....

... Political executives who try to exercise leadership within government may encounter intense opposition that they can neither avoid nor reconcile. At such times some agency officials may try to undermine the efforts of political executives. Any number of reasons—some deplorable, some commendable—lie behind such bureaucratic opposition. Executive politics involves people, and certain individuals simply dislike each other and resort to personal vendettas. Many, however, sincerely believe in their bureau's purpose and feel they must protect its jurisdiction, programs, and budget at all costs. Others feel they have an obligation to "blow the whistle" as best they can when confronted with evidence of what they regard as improper conduct. In all these cases the result is likely to strike a political executive as bureaucratic subversion. To the officials, it is a question of higher loyalty, whether to one's self-interests, organization, or conscience.

The structure of most bureaucratic sabotage has been characterized as an "iron triangle" uniting a particular government bureau, its relevant interest group, and congressional supporters. The aims may be as narrow as individual profiteering and empire-building. Or they may be as magnanimous as "public interest" lobbies, reformist bureaucrats, and congressional crusaders all claiming somewhat incongruously to represent the unrepresented. There are alliances with fully developed shapes (e.g., the congressional sponsors of a program, the bureaucrats executing it, and its private clients or suppliers) and those made up of only a few diverse lines (e.g., a civil servant looking forward to post-retirement prospects with a particular lobby association or a congressman unconcerned about a bureaucrat's policy aims but aware that his specific favors can help win reelection). Some bureaucratic entrepreneurs initiate their own outside contacts; others have been pushed into becoming involved in outside alliances by former political appointees.

The common features of these subgovernments are enduring mutual interests across the executive and legislative branches and between the public and private sectors. However high-minded the ultimate purpose, the immediate aim of each alliance is to become "self-sustaining in control of power in its own sphere." The longer an agency's tradition of independence, the greater the political controversy surrounding its subject matter, and the more it is allied with outside groups, the more a new appointee can expect sub rosa opposition to develop to any proposed changes. If political leadership in the executive branch is to be more than the accidental sum of these alliances and if political representation is to be less arbitrary than the demands of any group that claims to speak for the unrepresented, then some conflict seems inevitable between higher political leaders and the subgovernments operating within their sphere.

Often sabotage is unrecognizable because of the virtually invisible ways civil servants can act in bad faith toward political executives. In addition to the bureaucracy's power of withholding needed information and services, there are other means. Like a long-married couple, bureaucrats and those in their networks can often communicate with a minimum of words: "If congressional staffs I trust call up and ask me, I might tell them. But I can also tell them I don't agree with the secretary by offering just technical information and not associating myself with the policy."

An official who does not want to risk direct dealings with Congress can encourage a private interest group to go to the agency's important appropriations and legislative committees, as one political executive discovered: "When we tried to downgrade the ... bureau, its head was opposed, and he had a friend in a lobby group. After they got together rumblings started from the appropriations committee. I asked [the committee chairman] if he had a problem with this reorganization, and he said, 'No, you have the problem because if you touch that bureau I'll cut your job out of the budget.'" An experienced bureaucrat may not be able to make the decision, but he can try to arrange things to create the reaction he wants. "A colleague of mine," said a supergrade, "keeps a file on field offices that can be abolished and their political sensitivity. Depending on who's pressing for cuts, he'll pull out those that are politically the worst for that particular configuration." The everyday relationships between people with specialized interests can shade effortlessly into subversion: "You know what it's like," said a bureau chief. "You've known each other and will have a drink complaining about what's happening and work up some little strategy of your own to do something about it." Or bureaucrats can work to get their way simply by not trying to know what is happening. One assistant secretary reported how his career subordinates agreed there might be mismanagement in the regional offices, "but they also said they didn't know what these offices were doing and so there wasn't enough information to justify doing what I wanted." Ignorance may not be bliss, but it can be security.

Political appointees can sometimes encounter much more vigorous forms of sabotage. These range from minor needling to massive retaliation. Since information is a prime strategic resource in Washington, the passing of unauthorized messages outside channels often approaches an art form. There are routine leaks to build credit and keep channels open for when they might be needed, positive leaks to promote something, negative leaks to discredit a person or pol-

icy, and counterleaks. There is even the daring reverse leak, an
unauthorized release of information apparently for one reason but
actually accomplishing the opposite.*

There is no lack of examples in every administration. A political
executive may discover that an agency subordinate "has gone to
Congress and actually written the rider to the legislation that nulli-
fied the changes we wanted." A saboteur confided that "no one
ever found it was [a division chief] who prepared the list showing
which lobbyist was to contact which senator with what kind of
argument." Still another official reported he had "seen appointees
kept waiting in the outer office while their subordinate bureau
officials were in private meetings with the congressional staff members." But waiting lines lack finesse. The telephone can be used
with more delicacy, particularly after office hours: "The night before the hearings [a bureaucrat] fed the questions to the committee
staff and then the agency witnesses spent the next two days having
to reveal the information or duck the questions and catch hell." A
young staff civil servant described how his superior operated:

I used to sit in [the bureau chief's] office after 6 P.M. when all the important
business got done. He'd call up a senator and say, "Tom, you know this
program that you and I got through a while back? Well, there's no crisis,
but here are some things I'd like to talk to you about." He'd hang up and
get on the phone to [a House committee chairman] and say, "I've been
talking with Tom about this issue, and I'd like to bring you in on it."
Hell, you'd find [the bureau chief] had bills almost drafted before anybody
else in the executive branch had ever heard about them.

Encountering such situations, a public executive becomes acutely aware that experience as a private manager provides scant guidance. As one corporate executive with a six-figure salary said, "The
end-runs and preselling were incredible. To find an equivalent
you'd have to imagine some of your division managers going to
the executive board or a major stockholder behind your back.''
Learning to deal with sabotage is a function of an executive's politi-

---

*One recent example involved a presidential assistant rather than a bureaucrat.
While jockeying with another staff member, the assistant leaked a disclosure of his
own impending removal from the West Wing. The opponent, who obviously
stood the most to gain from the story, was naturally asked to confirm or deny the
report. Since he was not yet strong enough to accomplish such a removal, the
opponent had to deny responsibility for the leak and its accuracy, thereby inadver-
tently strengthening the position of the presidential assistant who first leaked the
story.

cal leadership, not his private management expertise.

How do political executives try to deal with bureaucratic sabotage? ... One approach is simply to ignore bureaucratic sabotage. Since the damage that may be done can easily cripple an executive's aims, diminish his reputation, and threaten his circles of confidence, those adopting this strategy can be presumed to have abdicated any attempt at political leadership in the Washington bureaucracy.

A second approach, especially favored by forceful managers, is to try to root out the leakers and prevent any recurrence. But political executives usually discover that this straightforward approach has considerable disadvantages. For one thing, it is extremely time-consuming and difficult to actually investigate acts of subversion and pin down blame. For another thing, there are few effective sanctions to prevent recurrences. Moreover, a search for the guilty party can easily displace more positive efforts and leadership initiatives an executive needs to make in dealing with the bureaucracy. Even if it were possible, trying to censor bureaucratic contacts would probably restrict the informal help these outside relationships provide, as well as the harm they do. And in the end any serious sabotage will probably be buttressed by some mandate from Congress; punishing the saboteurs can be seen as an assault on legislative prerogatives and thus invite even sterner retribution. It is circumstances such as these that led an experienced undersecretary to conclude:

Of course you can't be a patsy, but by and large you've got to recognize that leaks and end-runs are going to happen. You can spend all your time at trying to find out who's doing it, and if you do, then what? [One of my colleagues] actually tried to stop some of his bureaucrats from accepting phone calls from the press. They did stop accepting the calls, but they sure as hell returned them quickly. In this town there are going to be people running behind your back, and there's not much you can do to stop it.

However, while academics write about the iron triangle as if it were an immutable force, prudent political executives recognize that although they cannot stop bureaucratic sabotage, neither are they helpless against it. They can use personnel sanctions where misconduct can be clearly proven. But far more important, they can work to counteract sabotage with their own efforts—strengthening their outside contacts, extending their own lines of information and competitive analysis, finding new points of countertension. In general, experienced political executives try to use all their means of self-help and working relations so as to reshape the iron triangles into more plastic polygons.

To deal with sabotage, wise political appointees try to render it more obvious:

I make it clear that all the information and papers are supposed to move through me. It increases your work load tremendously, and maybe you don't understand everything you see, but everyone knows I'm supposed to be in on things and that they are accepting risks by acting otherwise.

They try to counteract unwanted messages with their own accounts to the press and others. The more the agency's boat is leaking, "the more you go out and work the pumps. You can't plug all the leaks, but you can make sure to get your side of the story out."

Political executives also make use of timing to deal with sabotage:

I put in a one-year fudge factor for an important change. That's because I know people are going to be doing end-runs to Congress. This year lets congressmen blow off steam, and for another thing it shows me where the sensitive spots are so I can get busy trying to work out some compromises—you know, things that can serve the congressmen's interest as well as mine.

Substantial results can be achieved by bringing new forces into play, dealing not with just one alliance but creating tests of strengths among the triangles:

It's like when officials were getting together with the unions and state administrators to get at some committee chairman. I hustled out to line up governors and show the congressmen that state administrators weren't speaking for all of state government.

Washington offers more opportunities to search for allies than is suggested by any simple image of political executives on one side and bureaucratic opponents on the other. Political appointees may be "back-doored" by other appointees, higher bureaucrats by lower bureaucrats. Fights may be extended to involve some appointees and bureaucrats versus others. As the leader of one faction put it, "Often a guy preselling things on the Hill is hurting people elsewhere, making it tougher for them to get money and approval and straining their relations. I use this fact to get allies."

A political executive who works hard at outside contacts will discover what subversives may learn too late: that many groups are fickle allies of the bureaucracy. This has seemed especially true as Congress has increased its own bureaucracy of uncoordinated staffs. A veteran bureaucrat described the risks run by would-be saboteurs:

Everybody you might talk to weighs the value of the issue to them against the value of keeping you alive for the next time. I've seen [a congressman] ruin many a good civil servant by getting a relationship going with him and then dropping him to score points off the agency brass. Now, too, there are more Hill staffers running around telling appointees, "Hey, these guys from your department said this and that. How about it?" Then the appointee will go back to the agency and raise hell for the bureaucrat.

Thus the political executives' own positive efforts are the necessary—if not always a sufficient—condition for combating sabotage. Since some bureaucratic subversion is an ever-present possibility and since punishment is difficult, the government executives' real choice is to build and use their political relationships or forfeit most other strategic resources for leadership.

48

HAROLD SEIDMAN
ROBERT GILMOUR

From *Politics, Position, and Power*

———

INTELLECTUALLY, presidents recognize that their own power is not entirely separable from that of their department heads. President Reagan was echoing the words of Jimmy Carter and Richard M. Nixon when he pledged to have the Cabinet rather than the White House staff take the lead in helping him formulate policy. A plan to have Cabinet secretaries take offices in the Executive Office Building next to the White House was seriously considered but later abandoned.

But presidents operate under rigid time restraints. What they want, they want now. They are impatient with solutions that go beyond the next congressional election, and their maximum time span is four years. They say they welcome disagreement and dissent, but cannot understand why Cabinet members do not share the presidential perspective. The fiefdoms are fractious, and the machinery of government moves too slowly to suit their purposes. Their experience in the Congress has given them neither the knowledge nor the aptitude to energize the executive establishment, so as far as possible they attempt to bypass and neutralize it.

Executive departments and the bureaucracy are called on to behave in a way that is contrary to their very nature. McGeorge Bundy reflected a typical White House view when he said, "Cabinet officers are special pleaders" and "should run their part of the government for the Administration—not run to the Administration for the interests of their part of the government." One might as well repeat Professor Henry Higgins's pliant in *My Fair Lady,* "Why can't a woman be more like a man?" as ask "Why can't Cabinet members act more like presidents?" Those who accept the differences can enjoy them and put them to proper use.

The bureaucracy is damned as "uncreative" because it is unable to satisfy the White House appetite for immediate solutions to complex social and economic problems and dramatic imaginative proposals for the legislative program. "Slow moving," "unresponsive," "disloyal" are among the milder epithets used to describe the bureaucracy. Bundy is dismayed because "the contest between the President and the bureaucracy is as real today as ever, and there has been no significant weakening in the network of triangular alliances which unite all sorts of interest groups with their agents in the Congress and their agents in the bureaucracy."

As an entity, the bureaucracy is no better equipped to manufacture grand designs for government programs than carpenters, electricians, and plumbers are to be architects. But if an architect attempted to build a house, the results might well be disastrous. What the White House identifies as bureaucracy's inherent deficiencies are often its strengths. Effective functioning of the governmental machine requires a high degree of stability, uniformity, and awareness of the impact of new policies, regulations, and procedures on the affected public.

The bureaucracy all too frequently is not asked for its advice on the "how to," for which it does have the knowledge and experience to make a contribution....

Although the White House may not consider a Cabinet member's participation in the development of a legislative proposal essential, the president will hold him to account for ensuring its enactment by the Congress. As far as the president is concerned, a Cabinet member's primary responsibility is to mobilize support both within and outside the Congress for presidential measures and to act as a legislative tactician. Major questions of policy and legislative strategy are reserved, however, for decision by the White House staff.

To perform in this role, a department head must maintain the loyalty of his subordinates and strengthen his alliances with congressional committees and interest groups, which in turn raises questions about his allegiance to the president and confirms White House distrust. John Ehrlichman complained that Cabinet officers "go off and marry the natives." Senior Carter staff maintained that Cabinet secretaries were given too much leeway at the start of the administration and had to be put on notice that "we expect them to work with the President in a positive way." "Loyalty" and "ability to work with White House staff" were the primary tests employed by President Carter in determining who would be retained in his Cabinet. The net result was that more and more, those responsible for carrying out policies were excluded as "special pleaders" from the development of the policies they were to administer....

Department heads seldom start with a clean slate. Generally they must adapt to the institution rather than the institution to them. There are likely to be daily reminders that they are merely temporary custodians and spokespersons for organizations with distinct and multidimensional personalities and deeply ingrained cultures and subcultures reflecting institutional history, ideology, values, symbols, folklore, professional biases, behavior patterns, heroes, and enemies. The individual style of department heads must not do violence to the institutional mystique, and the words they speak and the positions they advocate cannot ignore the precedents recorded in the departmental archives. Most department heads are free only to be as big as the president, the bureaucracy, the Congress, and their constituencies will allow them to be.

A Cabinet member is confronted with all the problems of an actor type-cast to take over the lead role in a long-running classical drama. The audience expects the part to be played in a certain way and will react hostilely to departures from the main lines of characterization set by generations of previous actors. Responses different from those in the prepared script are highly disturbing to the bureaucracy and the principal constituencies in the Congress and the outside community on whom a department head must rely for support. It would be as unthinkable for a secretary of agriculture to question the innate goodness of the rural way of life and the inherent virtues of the family farm as it would be for an OMB director to be against economy and efficiency.

Whatever his background and individual bent, a secretary of the treasury, for example, is obliged to play the part of a "sound" money man. Given the setting in which he performs, it would be very difficult for him to do otherwise. One has only to walk into the ancient Treasury Department building adjoining the White House to sense the atmosphere of a conservative financial institution. The money cage at the main entry way, the gilt pilasters, the gold-framed portraits on the walls all reinforce the Treasury "image." As the leader of a rugged "outdoors-type" department, a secretary of the interior is not out of character when he climbs mountains, shoots the Colorado River rapids, and organizes well-publicized hiking and jogging expeditions. Identical conduct by the secretary of the treasury would shake the financial community to its core....

Cabinet secretaries rarely bring to their jobs the unique combination of political insight, administrative skill, leadership, intelligence, and creativity required for the successful management of heterogeneous institutions with multiple and sometimes conflicting purposes. Most are content to be a "mediator-initiator" or a reactor to initiatives coming from the White House, the Congress, the bureaucracy, and the several constituencies represented by the department....

49

MARTIN ANDERSON

Getting Ready

From *Revolution*

———

IN EARLY November 1968, a few days after Richard Nixon was elected president, the deputy campaign manager, Peter Flanigan, eagerly opened about seven or eight big cardboard boxes, each stuffed with lists and résumés of people suggested for appointment to high government office. They were very important files. Some of these people would become the heart and soul of the new administration, the Republican troops who would take over the U.S. government and implement the policies that Nixon had campaigned and won on.

But when Flanigan and a few others from the campaign began reading through the neatly typed lists of suggested names and examined some of the accompanying résumés, the joy of winning and the anticipated pleasure of staffing the government with people who shared the political values we all worked so hard for over the years turned quickly to shocked despair. We could hardly believe what we were seeing. Most of the people on the lists were already in their jobs, or were Democrats or Independents. Many of them would have been excellent appointments if Hubert Humphrey, Nixon's liberal Democratic opponent, had won.

The staffing work was a disaster. The day after the boxes were opened there were hurried, secretive consultations among the top officials of the campaign and with Nixon. Then all the personnel recommendations, painstakingly and expensively accumulated during the campaign, were thrown out. Temporarily, the boxes were stashed in a bathtub in one of the rooms in the hotel we were using for transition headquarters; later they just disappeared. A week after the election, with just ten weeks before the inauguration of the new administration, the staff started over, from nothing, to find thousands of qualified people and match them up with the proper jobs.

The roots of the personnel disaster reached far back to the beginning of the campaign. Nixon rejected numerous recommendations, including a memo from me, to start preliminary planning on the long and difficult task of identifying several thousand highly qualified, willing men and women to fill the key policy-making positions if he should win the election. Nixon's reasoning was simple. His energies and efforts were focused totally on gaining the nomination. He was very skeptical of anything that would divert the resources of the campaign from that primary goal, whether it was staff or money or his time.

In fact, none of the top campaign staff had thought very much about what to do if he won the nomination, let alone the presidency....

Creating a massive personnel operation from nothing in a few weeks was an impossible administrative task. As one indication of how bad it got, I remember visiting Flemming's headquarters and noticing dozens of large cardboard boxes scattered all over the floors. On each box someone had written a date with a heavy black marking pen. When I asked what was in the boxes the reply was, "That's our filing system. All the letters that came in on, say, November 24, went into this box." When I asked how they would go about finding a person's application I got no answer.

There were over two thousand positions to be filled. And there simply were not enough hours remaining before Nixon's inauguration to analyze the positions, identify candidates for those positions, interview the candidates, make selections, offer the jobs and then, as occurred in many cases, be turned down and have to start all over again.

Toward the end of December we realized it was hopeless. Without an immense amount of prior planning and staff work it was going to be impossible to retain control of appointments. So it was decided that the remainder of the personnel selections would be delegated to the cabinet and subcabinet who were already selected. Nixon had no choice, but he did realize that a blunder was made. Immediately after agreeing to give his cabinet the authority to make appointments he remarked to an aide, "I just made a big mistake."

The consequences of the Nixon personnel disaster were serious and long-lasting. The U.S. Government is so large and so complex that it takes thousands of dedicated, competent, loyal people to turn campaign promises into national policy. The Nixon administration never recovered from the personnel blunder. The departments were staffed primarily with people with an agenda different from that of the White House, and once Nixon missed that initial opportunity to put his own people in key positions it was too late. . . .

Nixon lost his opportunity to govern before he started.

The people around Reagan in 1980 were determined not to repeat Nixon's mistake. As far back as 1976, when Reagan made his first serious try for the presidency, I discussed this problem with Ed Meese and recounted to him what happened to Nixon. Meese had already thought about planning and, after hearing about the Nixon transition fiasco, was even more convinced that it was foolhardy not to do some extensive, prior work. By the time the 1980 campaign was under way, Reagan and all of his top campaign aides were committed to diverting some campaign resources to planning effective takeover of the government, with special attention paid to staffing.

Those planning efforts paid tremendous dividends after Reagan won the election in November 1980. Because then came the hard part. Throughout the campaign Reagan laid out a comprehensive program that seemed to make sense on paper. The difficult process of translating ideas into policy and law now lay ahead....

For a newly elected president the transition is a time of delicious chaos. The victor and his campaign staff and supporters can scarcely believe they have really won, and will rub their eyes in wonderment the morning after election day. Then the eleven-week span that lies ahead of them will be seen for what it is—a brief flash of time that is far, far too short for them to do what must be done before assuming the awesome responsibility of governing the most powerful, largest, most complex, most important institution on earth. Even if you work twelve to fourteen hours a day, including Saturdays and Sundays, less perhaps a day for Christmas, you only have approximately 1,000 working hours to prepare....

One major task of the Reagan transition effort was the briefing of incoming cabinet officers. As so often happens when a new administration takes power, the cabinet members are usually chosen from outside the immediate campaign staff because these positions require people with extensive experience, people who by seniority and stature are less likely to be involved in the hurly-burly, revolutionary world of a presidential campaign.

On the other hand, it is the candidate and his campaign aides who fashion the policy agenda. The problem every winning campaign faces is how to ensure that those with more distinguished public reputations who will be chosen for the cabinet posts do not betray the policies the campaign was fought on. In Reagan's situation, it was easily the most thorough and comprehensive effort undertaken in the history of American transitions. The president-elect placed Ed Meese in charge of all transition activities, and Meese came up with an approach that proved very successful.

Meese's plan for briefing new cabinet officers was a major reason why presidential scholars concluded that "the Reagan transition was the most carefully planned and effective in American political history." Rather than have one general orientation briefing, providing the new secretary-designate with a few suggestions for personnel, and then leaving him or her to determine policy and hire people for the key policy-making positions, Meese established *three* separate briefing procedures.

Nobody ever said so, but basically it was an indoctrination course for cabinet members, especially those who were not closely connected with the campaign or fully familiar with Ronald Reagan's positions on major policy issues. There were two primary things we wanted to indoctrinate the new cabinet on: ideas and people....

The first briefing group was headed by William Timmons, an old political pro, with long experience in the campaigns and administrations of Nixon and Ford. Separate teams were established for each major government department and agency. Most of the people on the teams, besides being smart and tough-minded, had a lot of government experience. They knew how Washington worked. They fanned out across the city to compile reports covering just about anything a new cabinet officer might want to know about the government responsibility he or she was about to assume— where the office was located, how many people worked there, what government programs were involved, what congressmen and senators had special responsibilities for those programs, a detailed list of major decisions to make within a few weeks (in some cases days) after taking office in January, and any pending legal problems. The Timmons' reports were the sort of detailed dossier that might be put together on a large company being considered for purchase.

The second briefing group was directed by Pen James. A tall, intense Californian who ran a Los Angeles executive recruiting firm, James was an experienced hand at this, having worked for several years in Nixon's White House personnel office. He also worked easily with Reagan. Later, he would himself be appointed to the White House staff, in charge of all personnel selection for the early years of the Reagan administration.

The selection of political appointments was governed by three basic assumptions. First, the appointments were absolutely critical to the success of the administration. Second, the number and quality of appointments could only be achieved if we had a careful, thorough personnel organization. And third, control of appointments had to be centralized and controlled tightly by President Reagan and a few others on the White House staff.

The James group did not select subcabinet staff without consulting cabinet officers, but it was made clear to the incoming cabinet that they could not freely choose the people who would work for them. All key subcabinet appointments were cleared by Reagan and/or his top personal aides. They were treated as presidential appointments even when they were not. It was also made clear that, with very few exceptions, all incumbent political appointments should be fired. As Ed Meese put it, "We made sure that we cleaned out all the appointees of the past administration. We felt an empty office was better than to have a holdover.". . .

The last of the three briefing groups Ed Meese set up was something new to transition politics, something that had never been done in a systematic, organized way. It was called the Office of Policy Coordination, headed by my campaign deputy, Darrell Trent. On paper Trent was responsible for coordinating the issue reports of forty-eight policy task forces we established earlier in the campaign, and the efforts of the thirty people who reported to him, into a systematic program to forge the policy directions of the new administration. What was not written down was the real purpose of the Trent group—to educate the incoming cabinet and other key members of the administration on exactly what Ronald Reagan's policies were.

Over the years, Reagan and his people developed these ideas into a comprehensive, consistent, integrated policy that had been hardened, tempered, and confirmed during the presidential campaigns of 1976 and 1980. Now we wanted to make very, very sure that anyone who accepted a cabinet post would have no doubts about what was expected. We did not assume that everyone knew Reagan's policies. The elaborate briefing procedure on policy was to ensure that no one could ever say later, "I didn't know.". . .

If anyone was going to try to obstruct or change Reagan's program they were not going to be able to claim ignorance. Every key player in the decision-making process was carefully chosen and fully indoctrinated. It worked. There were a lot of arguments and discussions about how the policy should be implemented, but none about whether or not it should be done. By the time Reagan was sworn in on that cold January day, a powerful, smart, tough and very, very loyal team of economic policy decision-makers was in place and ready to run.

The stunning success of Reagan's economic policy and many of his other successes during the early years of his administration were largely due to the efforts of the transition team. They assembled a large, talented group of people, and briefed them thoroughly on what Reagan wanted done and how to do it. When Reagan took the field to begin his brilliant political quarterbacking, his team was ready.

Unfortunately, the kind of systematic and thorough staffing that took place during the transition was not sustained. Slowly, gradually, one by one, people less talented and less completely committed to Reagan's policy agenda began to fill the ranks of the administration. The results were disastrous. One consequence, for example, was the Iran-Contra fiasco, something that almost certainly never would have happened if Jim Baker, Ed Meese, Michael Deaver, and Dick Allen had remained close by the president, advising him in the White House.

50

CHARLES PETERS

From Ouagadougou to Cape Canaveral: Why the Bad News Doesn't Travel Up

EVERYONE IS ASKING why the top NASA officials who decided to launch the fatal *Challenger* flight had not been told of the concerns of people down below, like Allan McDonald and the other worried engineers at Morton Thiokol.*

In the first issue of the *Washington Monthly*, Russell Baker and I wrote, "In any reasonably large government organization, there exists an elaborate system of information cutoffs, comparable to that by which city water systems shut off large water-main breaks, closing down, first small feeder pipes, then larger and larger valves. The object is to prevent information, particularly of an unpleasant character, from rising to the top of the agency, where it may produce results unpleasant to the lower ranks.

*In January 1986, the space shuttle *Challenger* exploded a few minutes after its launch. Seven astronauts were killed. The space shuttle program went through many technical and administrative changes before the next shuttle was launched in September 1988.—EDS.

"Thus, the executive at or near the top lives in constant danger of not knowing, until he reads it on Page One some morning, that his department is hip-deep in disaster."

This seemed to us to be a serious problem for government, not only because the people at the top didn't know but because the same system of cut-offs operated to keep Congress, the press, and the public in the dark. (Often it also would operate to keep in the dark people within the organization but outside the immediate chain of command—this happened with the astronauts, who were not told about the concern with the O-rings.) ... Deke Slayton, the former astronaut, when he was asked about the failure of middle-level managers to tell top NASA officials about the problems they were encountering [said]:

"You depend on managers to make a decision based on the information they have. If they had to transmit all the fine detail to the top people, it wouldn't get launched but once every ten years."

The point is not without merit. It is easy for large organizations to fall into "once every ten years" habits. Leaders who want to avoid that danger learn to set goals and communicate a sense of urgency about meeting them. But what many of them never learn is that once you set those goals you have to guard against the tendency of those down below to spare you not only "all the fine detail" but essential facts about significant problems....

In NASA's case chances have been taken with the shuttle from the beginning—the insulating thermal tiles had not gone through a reentry test before the first shuttle crew risked their lives to try them out—but in recent years the pressure to cut corners has increased markedly. Competition with the European Ariane rocket and the Reagan administration's desire to see agencies like NASA run as if they were private businesses have led to a speedup in the launch schedule, with a goal of 14 this year and 24 by 1988.

"The game NASA is playing is the maximum tonnage per year at the minimum costs possible," says Paul Cloutier, a professor of space physics. "Some high officials don't want to hear about problems," reports Newsweek, "especially if fixing them will cost money."...

Under pressures like these, the NASA launch team watched Columbia, after seven delays, fall about a month behind schedule and then saw Challenger delayed, first by bad weather, then by damaged door handles, and then by bad weather again. Little wonder that Lawrence Mulloy, when he heard the warnings from the

Thiokol engineers, burst out: "My God, Thiokol, when do you want me to launch? Next April?"...

... With NASA's senior officials, the conviction that everything was A-OK was fortified by skillful public relations....

At NASA, Julian Scheer began a tradition of inspired PR that endured until *Challenger*. These were men who could sell air conditioning in Murmansk. The trouble is they also sold their bosses the same air conditioning. Every organization has a tendency to believe its own PR—NASA's walls are lined with glamorizing posters and photographs of the shuttle and other space machines—and usually the top man is the most thoroughly seduced because, after all, it reflects the most glory on him....

One of the hottest rumors around Washington is that the White House had put pressure on NASA to launch so that the president could point with pride to the teacher in space during his State of the Union speech. The White House denies this story, and my sources tell me the denial is true. But NASA had—and this is fact, not rumor—put pressure on *itself* by asking the president to mention Christa McAuliffe. In a memorandum dated January 8, NASA proposed that the president say:

"Tonight while I am speaking to you, a young elementary school teacher from Concord, New Hampshire, is taking us all on the ultimate field trip as she orbits the earth as the first citizen passenger on the space shuttle. Christa McAuliffe's journey is a prelude to the journeys of other Americans living and working together in a permanently manned space station in the mid-1990s. Mrs. McAuliffe's week in space is just one of the achievements in space we have planned for the coming year."

The flight was scheduled for January 23. It was postponed and postponed again. Now it was January 28, the morning of the day the speech was to be delivered, the last chance for the launch to take place in time to have it mentioned by the president. NASA officials must have feared they were about to lose a PR opportunity of stunning magnitude, an opportunity to impress not only the media and the public but the agency's two most important constituencies, the White House and the Congress. Wouldn't you feel pressure to get that launch off this morning so that the president could talk about it tonight?

NASA's sensitivity to the media in regard to the launch schedule was nothing short of unreal. Here is what Richard G. Smith, the director of the Kennedy Space Center, had to say about it after the disaster:

"Every time there was a delay, the press would say, 'Look, there's another delay. ... here's a bunch of idiots who can't even handle a launch schedule.' You think that doesn't have an impact? If you think it doesn't, you're stupid.". . .

I suspect what happened is that the top NASA administrators, who were pushing employees down below to dramatically increase the number of launches, either consciously or unconsciously did not want to be confronted with the dangers they were thereby risking.

This is what distinguishes the bad leaders from the good. The good leader, realizing that there is a natural human tendency to avoid bad news, traps himself into having to face it. He encourages whistleblowers instead of firing them. He visits the field himself and talks to the privates and lieutenants as well as the generals to find out the real problems. He ... must have some independent knowledge of what's going on down below in order to have a feel for whether the chain of command is giving him the straight dope.

What most often happens, of course, is that the boss, if he goes to the field at all, talks only to the colonels and generals. Sometimes he doesn't want to know what the privates know. He may be hoping that the lid can be kept on whatever problems are developing, at least until his watch is over, so that he won't be blamed when they finally surface. Or he may have a very good idea that bad things are being done and simply wants to retain "deniability," meaning that the deed cannot be traced to him. The story of Watergate is filled with "Don't tell me" and "I don't want to know."

When NASA's George Hardy told Thiokol engineers that he was appalled by their verbal recommendation that the launch be postponed and asked Thiokol to reconsider and make another rec-ommendation, Thiokol, which Hardy well knew was worried about losing its shuttle contract, was in effect being told, "Don't tell me" or "Don't tell me officially so I won't have to pass bad news along and my bosses will have deniability."

In addition to the leader himself, others must be concerned with making him face the bad news. This includes subordinates. Their having the courage to speak out about what is wrong is crucial, and people like Bruce Cook of NASA and Allan McDonald of Thiokol deserve great credit for having done so. But it is a fact that none of the subordinates who knew the danger to the shuttle took the next step and resigned in protest so that the public could find out what was going on in time to prevent disaster. The almost universal tendency to place one's own career above one's moral responsibility to take a stand on matters like these has to be one of the most depressing facts about bureaucratic culture today. ... If the press studies the *Challenger* case, I do not see how it can avoid perceiving the critical role bureaucratic pressure played in bringing about the disaster. What the press must then realize is that similar pressures vitally influence almost everything this government does, and that we will never understand why government fails until we understand those pressures and how human beings in public office react to them.

PART EIGHT

The Judiciary

WE HAVE SEEN that the Madisonian formula leaves considerable room for disagreement over the constitutional powers of Congress and the president. The proper role of the national judiciary is even less clear. After two centuries it remains one of the least-settled basic questions of American political life. Little about the courts' towering role in American politics can be gleaned from the bare language of Article III of the Constitution. Yet, there is no great issue of American public policy throughout our history in which the courts have not contributed mightily in one way or another to its resolution. The list is long: the national government's ability to regulate commerce; the many issues surrounding slavery and its aftermath; the national government's powers to legislate for public welfare, civil rights, civil liberties, to name but a few. In all of these, the courts have made important, sometimes critical, decisions. How does it happen that judges have come to play such a role?

Simply speaking, the federal courts influence public policy in two ways. Both must be understood. First, they interpret the Constitution. Since *Marbury v. Madison* (1803), the national judiciary has exercised what is called the power of judicial review to examine acts of the legislative and executive branches to determine their constitutionality. If they are found in violation of the Constitution's provisions, they may be declared invalid—null and void. The exercise of such an awesome power (to define the basic rules under which our politics is conducted) by officials not subject to electoral accountability raises many difficult questions. Did the framers of the Constitution intend it? Is it democratic? What, if anything, prevents judges from reading into the general language of the Constitution's most important provisions their own values, even where legislative majorities disagree? Courts influence public policy in a second way by interpreting statute law. Statutory interpretation raises the same questions as judicial review. No statute is ever entirely clear, and most leave substantial room for interpretation. How inhibited should judges be in deciding what the legislature meant to reach or require when it passed a particular law? Courts in the United States can and do exercise power through their ability to interpret the Constitution and the laws passed by Congress and the state legislatures. That is what arguments over the proper role of the judiciary are all about.

We begin our readings on the judiciary with Alexander Hamilton's classic discussion of the constitutional provisions establishing the new federal court system in *Federalist Paper* 78. Hamilton, a strong advocate of a vigorous, independent national judiciary, here musters his impressive powers of persuasion to convince his readers that the judiciary is not to be feared; it will be "the least dangerous branch." The legislature will control the purse; the executive, the sword. The courts' only weapon will be judgment. Hamilton openly makes the case for judicial review by appointed judges with permanent tenure. There can be no unlimited legislative power in a limited government, he argues. The Constitution is a fundamental law. "No legislative act ... contrary to the Constitution can be valid." An independent judiciary must be able to negate ill-considered "innovations" and "oppressions of the minor party" that might gain popular support.

David O'Brien, writing some two hundred years later about the landmark school desegregation case *Brown v. Board of Education* (1954), cites Hamilton's argument that the judiciary's power depends on the persuasiveness of its rulings. Ultimately, they must gain acceptance of the other branches and the public. When, as in *Brown,* the Supreme Court attempts to play a major role in settling a great issue of public policy, it must pay careful attention to strategies for getting its decisions accepted. In such cases, as Hamilton foresaw, the Court may be at odds with public opinion. If it tries to push things too far too fast, its legitimacy will be threatened.

Is judicial review democratic? That remains a matter of considerable dispute. Eugene Rostow's selection makes a strong case for its democratic character. Such fundamental questions of the individual's relationship to the state as life, liberty, property, freedom to worship, to express ideas and to assemble, he argues, are not ones that Americans have ever wished to make dependent on electoral outcomes. It is not undemocratic to see them as fundamental constitutional matters, better decided at some distance from day-to-day popular sentiment. Judicial review, he thinks, is "a tool of proven use" in our system of limited and balanced powers.

By the 1970s, however, many observers had begun to think that the courts had intruded too far into matters that ought to be settled by elected officials. Nathan Glazer's article is a seminal one in this tradition of criticizing "the imperial judiciary." Without arguing that courts should never make policy, he reasons that they have clearly exceeded their proper role. In such areas as public education, health care, housing, welfare policy, and prison administration they have seemed intent on taking over the functions of legislators and administrators—in some cases mandating levels of expenditure and deciding administrative details, things courts have no business doing in a democracy. If elected officials don't act, he argues, either they don't know what to do, there isn't enough money, or "the people simply don't want it."

More than a decade after Glazer's warning, a conservative Republican president provoked another of our historic confrontations over the proper role of the judiciary by naming the brilliant legal scholar, Robert Bork, to the Supreme Court. The Bork nomination, of course, failed to receive Senate confirmation, but it provided for several days a fascinating televised legal seminar as the Senate Judiciary Committee heard testimony for and against Bork and debated the issues the nomination raised. The essence of these issues is presented here in Bork's discussion of his "interpretivist" judicial philosophy and Laurence Tribe's attack on it in his testimony before the Judiciary Committee. It will be apparent that their ideas on the proper role of the judiciary are worlds apart. Bork argues that people like Tribe ("noninterpretivists"), however much they talk about constitutional rights, really want the courts to legislate what amounts to "the values ... of the university-educated upper middle class." Tribe holds that Bork's jurisprudence of "original intent" is a radical departure from "the entire 200-year-old tradition of thought about rights that underlies the American Constitution." You should read closely here, for the assumptions underlying these arguments are far more important to the outcomes of hard judicial cases on such matters as abortion than "the facts." The argument is about whether elected officials or judges should make law.

Ultimately, as the fictional Mr. Dooley said long ago, "th' Supreme Court follows th' iliction returns." Presidents generally try to appoint judges who agree with them. Both presidential pragmatism and a sense of the public's ambivalent attitudes on majority rule and minority rights generally favor the appointment of judges with less clear-cut philosophies than Bork or Tribe. Yet, their personal mind-sets have great influence. Our final selection, from Bob Woodward and Scott Armstrong's *The Brethren,* presents an unusual journalistic account of the human beings beneath the judicial robes and how they interact in the unique environment of the Supreme Court.

51

ALEXANDER HAMILTON

Judicial Review

From *Federalist Paper* 78

———

No. 78: Hamilton

WE PROCEED now to an examination of the judiciary department of the proposed government. . . .

Whoever attentively considers the different departments of power must perceive that, in a government in which they are separated from each other, the judiciary, from the nature of its functions, will always be the least dangerous to the political rights of the Constitution; because it will be least in a capacity to annoy or injure them. The executive not only dispenses the honors but holds the sword of the community. The legislature not only commands the purse but prescribes the rules by which the duties and rights of every citizen are to be regulated. The judiciary, on the contrary, has no influence over either the sword or the purse; no direction either of the strength or of the wealth of the society, and can take no active resolution whatever. It may truly be said to have neither FORCE nor WILL but merely judgment; and must ultimately depend upon the aid of the executive arm even for the efficacy of its judgments.

This simple view of the matter suggests several important consequences. It proves incontestably that the judiciary is beyond comparison the weakest of the three departments of power;[*] that it can never attack with success either of the other two; and that all possible care is requisite to enable it to defend itself against their attacks. It equally proves that though individual oppression may now and then proceed from the courts of justice, the general liberty of the people can never be endangered from that quarter; I mean so long as the judiciary remains truly distinct from both the legislature and the executive. For I agree that "there is no liberty if the power of judging be not separated from the legislative and executive powers."[†] And it proves, in the last place, that as liberty can have nothing to fear from the judiciary alone, but would have everything to fear from its union with either of the other departments; that as all the effects of such a union must ensue from a dependence of the former on the latter, notwithstanding a nominal and apparent separation; that as, from the natural feebleness of the judiciary, it is in continual jeopardy of being overpowered, awed, or influenced by its co-ordinate branches; and that as nothing can contribute so much to its firmness and independence as permanency in office, this quality may therefore be justly regarded as an indispensable ingredient in its constitution, and, in a great measure, as the citadel of the public justice and the public security.

The complete independence of the courts of justice is peculiarly essential in a limited Constitution. By a limited Constitution, I understand one which contains certain specified exceptions to the legislative authority; such, for instance, as that it shall pass no bills of attainder, no *ex post facto* laws, and the like. Limitations of this kind can be preserved in practice no other way than through the medium of courts of justice, whose duty it must be to declare all

---

[*]The celebrated Montesquieu, speaking of them, says: "Of the three powers above mentioned, the JUDICIARY is next to nothing."—*Spirit of Laws*, Vol. I, page 186.

[†]*Idem*, page 181.

acts contrary to the manifest tenor of the Constitution void. Without this, all the reservations of particular rights or privileges would amount to nothing.

Some perplexity respecting the rights of the courts to pronounce legislative acts void, because contrary to the Constitution, has arisen from an imagination that the doctrine would imply a superiority of the judiciary to the legislative power. It is urged that the authority which can declare the acts of another void must necessarily be superior to the one whose acts may be declared void. As this doctrine is of great importance in all the American consitutions, a brief discussion of the grounds on which it rests cannot be unacceptable.

There is no position which depends on clearer principles than that every act of a delegated authority, contrary to the tenor of the commission under which it is exercised, is void. No legislative act, therefore, contrary to the Constitution, can be valid. To deny this would be to affirm that the deputy is greater than his principal; that the servant is above his master; that the representatives of the people are superior to the people themselves; that men acting by virtue of powers may do not only what their powers do not authorize, but what they forbid.

If it be said that the legislative body are themselves the constitutional judges of their own powers and that the construction they put upon them is conclusive upon the other departments it may be answered that this cannot be the natural presumption where it is not to be collected from any particular provisions in the Constitution. It is not otherwise to be supposed that the Constitution could intend to enable the representatives of the people to substitute their *will* to that of their constituents. It is far more rational to suppose that the courts were designed to be an intermediate body between the people and the legislature in order, among other things, to keep the latter within the limits assigned to their authority. The interpretation of the laws is the proper and peculiar province of the courts. A constitution is, in fact, and must be regarded by the judges as, a fundamental law. It therefore belongs to them to ascertain its meaning as well as the meaning of any particular act proceeding from the legislative body. If there should happen to be an irreconcilable variance between the two, that which has the superior obligation and validity ought, of course, to be preferred; or, in other words, the Constitution ought to be preferred to

the statute, the intention of the people to the intention of their
agents.

Nor does this conclusion by any means suppose a superiority
of the judicial to the legislative power. It only supposes that the
power of the people is superior to both, and that where the will of
the legislature, declared in its statutes, stands in opposition to that
of the people, declared in the Constitution, the judges ought to be
governed by the latter rather than the former. They ought to regulate their decisions by the fundamental laws rather than by those
which are not fundamental....

If, then, the courts of justice are to be considered as the bulwarks
of a limited Constitution against legislative encroachments, this
consideration will afford a strong argument for the permanent
tenure of judicial offices, since nothing will contribute so much as
this to that independent spirit in the judges which must be essential
to the faithful performance of so arduous a duty.

This independence of the judges is equally requisite to guard
the Constitution and the rights of individuals from the effects of
those ill humors which the arts of designing men, or the influence
of particular conjunctures, sometimes disseminate among the people themselves, and which, though they speedily give place to
better information, and more deliberate reflection, have a tendency,
in the meantime, to occasion dangerous innovations in the government, and serious oppressions of the minor party in the community. Though I trust the friends of the proposed Constitution will
never concur with its enemies in questioning that fundamental
principle of republican government which admits the right of the
people to alter or abolish the established Constitution whenever
they find it inconsistent with their happiness; yet it is not to be
inferred from this principle that the representatives of the people,
whenever a momentary inclination happens to lay hold of a majority of their constituents incompatible with the provisions in the
existing Constitution would, on that account, be justifiable in a
violation of those provisions; or that the courts would be under a
greater obligation to connive at infractions in this shape than when
they had proceeded wholly from the cabals of the representative
body. Until the people have, by some solemn and authoritative
act, annulled or changed the established form, it is binding upon
themselves collectively, as well as individually; and no presumption, or even knowledge of their sentiments, can warrant their

representatives in a departure from it prior to such an act. But it is easy to see that it would require an uncommon portion of fortitude in the judges to do their duty as faithful guardians of the Constitution, where legislative invasions of it had been instigated by the major voice of the community.

But it is not with a view to infractions of the Constitution only that the independence of the judges may be an essential safeguard against the effects of occasional ill humors in the society. These sometimes extend no farther than to the injury of the private rights of particular classes of citizens, by unjust and partial laws. Here also the firmness of the judicial magistracy is of vast importance in mitigating the severity and confining the operation of such laws. It not only serves to moderate the immediate mischiefs of those which may have been passed but it operates as a check upon the legislative body in passing them; who, perceiving that obstacles to the success of an iniquitous intention are to be expected from the scruples of the courts, are in a manner compelled, by the very motives of the injustice they meditate, to qualify their attempts. This is a circumstance calculated to have more influence upon the character of our governments than but few may be aware of. The benefits of the integrity and moderation of the judiciary have already been felt in more States than one; and though they may have displeased those whose sinister expectations they may have disappointed, they must have commanded the esteem and applause of all the virtuous and disinterested. Considerate men of every description ought to prize whatever will tend to beget or fortify that temper in the courts; as no man can be sure that he may not be tomorrow the victim of a spirit of injustice, by which he may be a gainer today. And every man must now feel that the inevitable tendency of such a spirit is to sap the foundations of public and private confidence and to introduce in its stead universal distrust and distress....   *Publius*

52

DAVID O'BRIEN
The Court and American Life

From *Storm Center*

———

"WHY DOES the Supreme Court pass the school desegregation case?" asked one of Chief Justice Vinson's law clerks in 1952. *Brown v. Board of Education of Topeka, Kansas* had arrived on the Court's docket in 1951, but it was carried over for oral argument the next term and then consolidated with four other cases and reargued in December 1953. The landmark ruling did not come down until May 17, 1954. "Well," Justice Frankfurter explained, "we're holding it for the election"—1952 was a presidential election year. "You're holding it for the election?" The clerk persisted in disbelief. "I thought the Supreme Court was supposed to decide cases without regard to elections." "When you have a major social political issue of this magnitude," timing and public reactions are important considerations, and, Frankfurter continued, "we do not think this is the time to decide it." Similarly, Tom Clark has recalled that the Court awaited, over Douglas's dissent, additional cases from the District of Columbia and other regions, so as "to get a national coverage, rather than a sectional one." Such political considerations are by no means unique. "We often delay adjudication. It's not a question of evading at all," Clark concluded. "It's just the practicalities of life—common sense."

Denied the power of the sword or the purse, the Court must cultivate its institutional prestige. The power of the Court lies in the pervasiveness of its rulings and ultimately rests with other political institutions and public opinion. As an independent force, the Court has no chance to resolve great issues of public policy. *Dred Scott v. Sandford* (1857) and *Brown v. Board of Education* (1954) illustrate the limitations of Supreme Court policy-making. The "great folly," as Senator Henry Cabot Lodge characterized *Dred Scott,* was not the Court's interpretation of the Constitution or the unpersuasive moral position that blacks were not persons under the Constitution. Rather, "the attempt of the Court to settle the slavery question by judicial decision was simple madness." ... A hundred years later, political struggles within the country and, notably, presidential and congressional leadership in enforcing the Court's school desegregation ruling saved the moral appeal of *Brown* from becoming another "great folly."

Because the Court's decisions are not self-executing, public reactions inevitably weigh on the minds of the justices....

... Opposition to the school desegregation ruling in *Brown* led to bitter, sometimes violent confrontations. In Little Rock, Arkansas, Governor Orval Faubus encouraged disobedience by southern segregationists. The federal National Guard had to be called out to maintain order. The school board in Little Rock unsuccessfully pleaded, in *Cooper v. Aaron* (1958), for the Court's postponement of the implementation of *Brown's* mandate. In the midst of the controversy, Frankfurter worried that Chief Justice Warren's attitude had become "more like that of a fighting politician than that of a judicial statesman." In such confrontations between the Court and the country, "the transcending issue," Frankfurter reminded the brethren, remains that of preserving "the Supreme Court as the authoritative organ of what the Constitution requires." When the justices move too far or too fast in their interpretation of the Constitution, they threaten public acceptance of the Court's legitimacy.

The political struggles of the Court (and among the justices) continue after the writing of opinions and final votes. Announcements of decisions trigger diverse reactions from the media, interest groups, lower courts, Congress, the President, and the general public. Their reactions may enhance or thwart compliance and reinforce or undermine the Court's prestige. Opinion days thus may reveal something of the political struggles that might otherwise remain hidden within the marble temple. They may also mark the beginning of larger political struggles for influence in the country....

When deciding major issues of public law and policy, justices must consider strategies for getting public acceptance of their rulings. When striking down the doctrine of "separate but equal" facilities in 1954 in *Brown v. Board of Education (Brown I)*, for instance, the Warren Court waited a year before issuing, in *Brown II*, its mandate for "all deliberate speed" in ending racial segregation in public education.

Resistance to the social policy announced in *Brown I* was expected. A rigid timetable for desegregation would only intensify opposition. During oral arguments on *Brown II,* devoted to the question of what kind of decree the Court should issue to enforce *Brown,* Warren confronted the hard fact of southern resistance. The attorney for South Carolina, S. Emory Rogers, pressed for an open-ended decree—one that would not specify when and how desegregation should take place. He boldly proclaimed

Mr. Chief Justice, to say we will conform depends on the decree handed down. I am frank to tell you, right now [in] our district I do not think that we will send—[that] the white people of the district will send their children to the Negro schools. It would be unfair to tell the Court that we are going to do that. I do not think it is. But I do think that something can be worked out. We hope so.

"It is not a question of attitude," Warren shot back, "it is a question of conforming to the decree." Their heated exchange continued as follows:

CHIEF JUSTICE WARREN: But you are not willing to say here that there would be an honest attempt to conform to this decree, if we did leave it to the district court [to implement]?
MR. ROGERS: No, I am not. Let us get the word "honest" out of there.
CHIEF JUSTICE WARREN: No, leave it in.
MR. ROGERS: No, because I would have to tell you that right now we would not conform—we would not send our white children to the Negro schools....

Agreement emerged that the Court should issue a short opinion-decree. In a memorandum, Warren summarized the main points of agreement. The opinion should simply state that *Brown I* held radically segregated public schools to be unconstitutional. *Brown II* should acknowledge that the ruling creates various administrative problems, but emphasize that "local school authorities have the primary responsibility for assessing and solving these problems; [and] the courts will have to consider these problems in determining whether the efforts of local school authorities" are in good-faith compliance....

Enforcement and implementation required the cooperation and coordination of all three branches. Little progress could be made, as Assistant Attorney General Pollack has explained, "where historically there had been slavery and a long tradition of discrimination [until] all three branches of the federal government [could] be lined up in support of a movement forward or a requirement for change." The election of Nixon in 1968 then brought changes both in the policies of the executive branch and in the composition of the Court. The simplicity and flexibility of *Brown,* moreover, invited evasion. It produced a continuing struggle over measures, such as gerrymandering school district lines and busing in the 1970s and 1980s, because the mandate itself had evolved from one of ending segregation to one of securing integration in public schools....

"By itself," the political scientist Robert Dahl observed, "the Court is almost powerless to affect the course of national policy." *Brown* dramatically altered the course of American life, but it also reflected the justices' awareness that their decisions are not self-executing. The rulings [in] *Brown* ... were unanimous but ambiguous. The ambiguity in the desegregation rulings ... was the price of achieving unanimity. Unanimity appeared necessary if the Court was to preserve its institutional prestige while pursuing revolutionary change in social policy. Justices sacrificed their own policy preferences for more precise guidelines, while the Court tolerated lengthy delays in recognition of the costs of open defiance and the pressures of public opinion....

Public opinion serves to curb the Court when it threatens to go too far or too fast in its rulings. The Court has usually been in step with major political movements, except during transitional periods or critical elections. It would nevertheless be wrong to conclude, along with Peter Finley Dunne's fictional Mr. Dooley, that "th' supreme court follows th' iliction returns." To be sure, the battle over FDR's "Court-packing" plan and the Court's "switch-in-time-that-saved-nine" in 1937 gives that impression. Public opinion supported the New Deal, but turned against FDR after his landslide reelection in 1936 when he proposed to "pack the Court" by increasing its size from nine to fifteen. In a series of five-to-four and six-to-three decisions in 1935–1936, the Court had struck down virtually every important measure of FDR's New Deal program. But in the spring of 1937, while the Senate Judiciary Committee considered FDR's proposal, the Court abruptly handed down three five-to-four rulings upholding major pieces of New Deal legislation. Shortly afterward, FDR's close personal friend and soon-to-be nominee for the Court, Felix Frankfurter, wrote

Justice Stone confessing that he was "not wholly happy in thinking that Mr. Dooley should, in the course of history turn out to have been one of the most distinguished legal philosophers." Frankfurter, of course, knew that justices do not simply follow the election returns. The influence of public opinion is more subtle and complex.

Life in the marble temple is not immune from shifts in public opinion. ... The justices, however, deny being directly influenced by public opinion. The Court's prestige rests on preserving the public's view that justices base their decisions on interpretations of the law, rather than on their personal policy preferences. Yet, complete indifference to public opinion would be the height of judicial arrogance....

"The powers exercised by this Court are inherently oligarchic," Frankfurter once observed when pointing out that "[t]he Court is not saved from being oligarchic because it professes to act in the service of humane ends." Judicial review is antidemocratic. But the Court's power stems from its duty to give authoritative meaning to the Constitution, and rests with the persuasive forces of reason, institutional prestige, the cooperation of other political institutions, and, ultimately, public opinion. The country, in a sense, saves the justices from being an oligarchy by curbing the Court when it goes too far or too fast with its policy-making. Violent opposition and resistance, however, threaten not merely the Court's prestige but the very idea of a government under law.

Some Court watchers, and occasionally even the justices, warn of "an imperial judiciary" and a "government by the judiciary." For much of the Court's history, though, the work of the justices has not involved major issues of public policy. In most areas of public law and policy, the fact that the Court decides an issue is more important than what it decides. Relatively few of the many issues of domestic and foreign policy that arise in government reach the Court. When the Court does decide major questions of public policy, it does so by bringing political controversies within the language, structure, and spirit of the Constitution. By deciding only immediate cases, the Court infuses constitutional meaning into the resolution of the larger surrounding political controversies. But by itself the Court cannot lay those controversies to rest.

The Court can profoundly influence American life. As a guardian of the Constitution, the Court sometimes invites controversy by challenging majoritarian sentiments to respect the rights of mi-

norities and the principles of a representative democracy. The
Court's influence is usually more subtle and indirect, varying over
time and from one policy issue to another. In the end, the Court's
influence on American life cannot be measured precisely, because
its policy-making is inextricably bound up with that of other political institutions. Major confrontations in constitutional politics, like
those over school desegregation, school prayer, and abortion, are
determined as much by what is possible in a system of free government and in a pluralistic society as by what the Court says about
the meaning of the Constitution. At its best, the Court appeals to
the country to respect the substantive value choices of human dignity and self-governance embedded in our written Constitution.

53

EUGENE ROSTOW

The Democratic Character of Judicial Review

THE IDEA that judicial review is undemocratic is not an
academic issue of political philosophy. Like most abstractions, it
has far-reaching practical consequences. I suspect that for some
judges it is the mainspring of decision, inducing them in many
cases to uphold legislative and executive action which would otherwise have been condemned. Particularly in the multiple opinions
of recent years, the Supreme Court's self-searching often boils
down to a debate within the bosoms of the Justices over the appropriateness of judicial review itself.

The attack on judicial review as undemocratic rests on the premise that the Constitution should be allowed to grow without a
judicial check. The proponents of this view would have the Constitution mean what the President, the Congress, and the state legislatures say it means....

It is a grave oversimplification to contend that no society can
be democratic unless its legislature has sovereign powers. The social
quality of democracy cannot be defined by so rigid a formula.

Government and politics are after all the arms, not the end, of social life. The purpose of the Constitution is to assure the people a free and democratic society. The final aim of that society is as much freedom as possible for the individual human being. The Constitution provides society with a mechanism of government fully competent to its task, but by no means universal in its powers. The power to govern is parcelled out between the states and the nation and is further divided among the three main branches of all governmental units. By custom as well as constitutional practice, many vital aspects of community life are beyond the direct reach of government—for example, religion, the press, and, until recently at any rate, many phases of educational and cultural activity. The separation of powers under the Constitution serves the end of democracy in society by limiting the roles of the several branches of government and protecting the citizen, and the various parts of the state itself, against encroachments from any source. The root idea of the Constitution is that man can be free because the state is not.

The power of constitutional review, to be exercised by some part of the government, is implicit in the conception of a written constitution delegating limited powers. A written constitution would promote discord rather than order in society if there were no accepted authority to construe it, at the least in cases of conflicting action by different branches of government or of constitutionally unauthorized governmental action against individuals. The limitation and separation of powers, if they are to survive, require a procedure for independent mediation and construction to reconcile the inevitable disputes over the boundaries of constitutional power which arise in the process of government....

So far as the American Constitution is concerned, there can be little real doubt that the courts were intended from the beginning to have the power they have exercised. The Federalist Papers are unequivocal; the Debates as clear as debates normally are. The power of judicial review was commonly exercised by the courts of the states, and the people were accustomed to judicial construction of the authority derived from colonial charters. Constitutional interpretation by the courts, Hamilton said, does not

by any means suppose a superiority of the judicial to the legislative power. It only supposes that the power of the people is superior to both; and that where the will of the legislature, declared in its statutes, stands in opposition to that of the people, declared in the Constitution, the judges ought to be governed by the latter rather than the former. They ought to regulate their decisions by the fundamental laws, rather than by those which are not fundamental.

Hamilton's statement is sometimes criticized as a verbal legalism. But it has an advantage too. For much of the discussion has complicated the problem without clarifying it. Both judges and their critics have wrapped themselves so successfully in the difficulties of particular cases that they have been able to evade the ultimate issue posed in the Federalist Papers.

Whether another method of enforcing the Constitution could have been devised, the short answer is that no such method has developed. The argument over the constitutionality of judicial review has long since been settled by history. The power and duty of the Supreme Court to declare statutes or executive action unconstitutional in appropriate cases is part of the living Constitution. "The course of constitutional history," Mr. Justice Frankfurter recently remarked, has cast responsibilities upon the Supreme Court which it would be "stultification" for it to evade. The Court's power has been exercised differently at different times: sometimes with reckless and doctrinaire enthusiasm; sometimes with great deference to the status and responsibilities of other branches of the government; sometimes with a degree of weakness and timidity that comes close to the betrayal of trust. But the power exits, as an integral part of the process of American government. The Court has the duty of interpreting the Constitution in many of its most important aspects, and especially in those which concern the relations of the individual and the state. The political proposition underlying the survival of the power is that there are some phases of American life which should be beyond the reach of any majority, save by constitutional amendment. In Mr. Justice Jackson's phrase, "One's right to life, liberty, and property, to free speech, a free press, freedom of worship and assembly, and other fundamental rights may not be submitted to vote; they depend on the outcome of no elections." Whether or not this was the intention of the Founding Fathers, the unwritten Constitution is unmistakable.

If one may use a personal definition of the crucial word, this way of policing the Constitution is not undemocratic. True, it employs appointed officials, to whom large powers are irrevocably delegated. But democracies need not elect all the officers who exercise crucial authority in the name of the voters. Admirals and generals can win or lose wars in the exercise of their discretion. The independence of judges in the administration of justice has been the pride of communities which aspire to be free. Members of the Federal Reserve Board have the lawful power to plunge the country into depression or inflation. The list could readily be extended. Government by referendum or town meeting is not the only possible form of democracy. The task of democracy is not to have the people vote directly on every issue, but to assure their ultimate responsibility for the acts of their representatives, elected or appointed. For judges deciding ordinary litigation, the ultimate responsibility of the electorate has a special meaning. It is a responsibility for the quality of the judges and for the substance of their instructions, never a responsibility for their decisions in particular cases. It is hardly characteristic of law in democratic society to encourage bills of attainder, or to allow appeals from the courts in particular cases to legislatures or to mobs. Where the judges are carrying out the function of constitutional review, the final responsibility of the people is appropriately guaranteed by the provisions for amending the Constitution itself, and by the benign influence of time, which changes the personnel of courts. Given the possibility of constitutional amendment, there is nothing undemocratic in having responsible and independent judges act as important constitutional mediators. Within the narrow limits of their capacity to act, their great task is to help maintain a pluralist equilibrium in society. They can do much to keep it from being dominated by the states or the Federal Government, by Congress or the President, by the purse or the sword.

In the execution of this crucial but delicate function, constitutional review by the judiciary has an advantage thoroughly recognized in both theory and practice. The power of the courts, however final, can only be asserted in the course of litigation. Advisory opinions are forbidden, and reefs of self-limitation have grown up around the doctrine that the courts will determine constitutional questions only in cases of actual controversy, when no lesser ground of decision is available, and when the complaining party would be directly and personally injured by the assertion of the power deemed unconstitutional. Thus the check of judicial review upon the elected branches of government must be a mild one, limited not only by the detachment, integrity, and good sense of the Justices, but by the structural boundaries implicit in the fact that the power is entrusted to the courts. Judicial review is inherently adapted to preserving broad and flexible lines of constitutional growth, not to operating as a continuously active factor in legislative or executive decisions. . . .

Democracy is a slippery term. I shall make no effort at a formal definition here. . . . But it would be scholastic pedantry to define democracy in such a way as to deny the title of "democrat" to Jefferson, Madison, Lincoln, Brandeis, and others who have found the American constitutional system, including its tradition of judicial review, well adapted to the needs of a free society. As Mr. Justice Brandeis said,

the doctrine of the separation of powers was adopted by the Convention of 1787, not to promote efficiency but to preclude the exercise of arbitrary power. The purpose was, not to avoid friction, but, by means of the inevitable friction incident to the distribution of governmental powers among three departments, to save the people from autocracy.

It is error to insist that no society is democratic unless it has a government of unlimited powers, and that no government is democratic unless its legislature had unlimited powers. Constitutional review by an independent judiciary is a tool of proven use in the American quest for an open society of widely dispersed powers. In a vast country, of mixed population, with widely different regional problems, such an organization of society is the surest base for the hopes of democracy.

54

NATHAN GLAZER
Towards an Imperial Judiciary?

—————

. . .THE COURTS truly have changed their role in American life. American courts, the most powerful in the world—they were that already when Tocqueville wrote and when Bryce wrote—are now far more powerful than ever before; public opinion—which Tocqueville, Bryce, and other analysts thought would control the courts as well as so much else in American life—is weaker. The legislatures and the executive now moderate their outbursts, for apparently outbursts will do no good. And courts, through interpretation of the Constitution and the laws, now reach into the lives of the people, against the will of the people, deeper than they ever have in American history....

... In the past the role of activist courts was to *restrict* the executive and legislature in what they could do. The distinctive characteristic of more recent activist courts has been to *extend* the role of what the government could do, even when the government did not want to do it. The *Swann* and *Keyes* decisions meant that government *must* move children around to distant schools against the will of their parents. The *Griggs* decision meant that government *must* monitor the race and ethnicity of job applicants and test-takers. The cases concerning the rights of mental patients and prisoners, which are for the most part still in the lower courts, say that government *must* provide treatment and rehabilitation whether it knows how or not. Federal Judge Weinstein's ruling in a New York school desegregation case seems to say that government *must* racially balance communities. And so on.

An interesting example of this unwilled extension of governmental action is that of the Environmental Protection Agency (EPA). It did not wish to issue rules preserving pure air in areas without pollution or imposing drastic transportation controls. To the EPA, this did not seem to be what Congress intended; but under court order, it was required to do both. Similarly, the Department of Health, Education, and Welfare (HEW) apparently did not want to move against the Negro colleges of the South, now no longer segregated under law but still with predominantly black enrollments, nor was this in the interests of those colleges, or their students, or indeed anyone else—but Federal judges required HEW to do so.

In these, as in other cases, government is required to do what the Congress did not order it to do and may well oppose, what the executive does not feel it wise to do, and most important what it does not know how to do. How *does* one create that permanently racially balanced community that Judge Weinstein wants so that the schools may be permanently racially balanced? How does one create that good community in Boston public housing that Judge Garrity wants so that vandalism repair costs may be brought down to what the authority can afford? How does one rehabilitate prisoners? Or treat mental patients? Like Canute, the Judges decree the sea must not advance, and weary administrators—hectored by enthusiastic, if ignorant, lawyers for public advocacy centers—must go through the motions to show the courts they are trying.... The Court's actions now seem to arouse fewer angry reactions from the people and the legislatures. The power of the Court has been exercised so often and so successfully over the last 20 years, and the ability to restrict or control it by either new legislation, constitutional amendment, or new appointments has met with such uniform failure, that the Court, and the subordinate courts, are now seen as forces of nature, difficult to predict and impossible to control....

This is, of course, not necessarily witness to the strength of the Court as such: What it reflects, in addition, is the agreement of large sectors of opinion—even if it is still minority opinion—with the Court's actions. But this opinion in favor of the Court is shaped by the reserves of strength the Court possesses: the positive opinion of the Court in the dominant mass media—the national television news shows, the national news magazines, and the most influential newspapers; and the bias in its favor among the informed electorate generally, and among significant groups of opinion-leaders....

... [A] factor that sustains the permanent activism of the court is the enormous increase in the reach of government itself. When government expands, it could seem reasonable that the Court must extend its reach also. It must consider issues of equity and due process and equal protection in all the varied areas of education, health care, housing, and access to government services of all types. It must consider the varied impact of new subsidies, and controls and restrictions based on safety or environmental considerations. It is true that as government expands it sets up quasi-judicial bodies to adjudicate difficult decisions, but there is one major route of appeal in our system from these multifarious quasi-judicial bodies, and that is to the federal courts, and only one final appeal, to the Supreme Court....

The expanded reach of government not only explains a more activist Court; in the minds of many analysts, it also justifies it. Perhaps it does. But one reason it does is that courts are dissatisfied with how legislatures and executives run their respective spheres, and while they do not egregiously reach out to express their dissatisfaction—courts, after all, must wait for cases to come to them—when the cases do come to them, they stretch their hands out very far indeed to make corrections. Consider issues raised in some recent cases: inadequate medical treatment for prisoners; welfare to applicants delayed beyond some reasonable time; public housing poorly maintained and in poor repair; mental patients not receiving treatment. The courts and their defenders say that if the legislature and executive are incapable of action in these and similar cases, then the courts must act....

... Increasingly, however, the courts have gone beyond the wrong presented to them to sweepingly reorganize a complex service of government so that the wrong can be dealt with—in the Court's mind, at least—at its root. Thus, a judge might decree, "Let this prisoner receive adequate medical care"—or, as he did instead, go to experts to provide a complete program of medical services for prisons on the basis of what professionals asserted was necessary, a program which the state insisted it could not afford. A court could require that welfare recipients receive more rapid treatment, but what a federal judge in Massachusetts did was to suspend all federal government welfare reimbursements to the state until the state hired 255 more social workers. If public housing was demonstrated to be in poor repair, the judge could have said, "Fix it." But in this case, he enjoined the expenditure of other state funds for new housing, requiring that they be used for massive rehabilitation of old housing, appointed a master to determine the best way to repair and keep the house in repair, and suggested that the Boston Housing Authority didn't know how to create the kind of good community in which vandalism would not take place. Similarly, judges are now determining with the aid of psychiatric experts what a proper system of psychiatric care in a mental hospital should be.

The justification in these and many other cases is that the legislature and executive won't act. This justification will not hold water. The legislature and executive have far more resources than the courts to determine how best to act. If they don't, it is because no one knows how to, or there is not enough money to cover everything, or because the people simply don't want it. These strike me as valid considerations in a democracy, but they are not considered valid considerations when issues of social policy come up as court cases for judgment. For example, no desegregation decision that I know of has been stayed by the fact that there is not enough money or that other school and educational services will suffer, perfectly valid considerations for legislatures, executives, and administrators—but the kind of consideration that no judge considers worthy of notice.

Having decided that the other two branches won't act, judges decide to act on their own, and increasingly are intrigued by the opportunity to go to the root of the problem. Unfortunately in many of these areas of social policy there is no clear knowledge of what the root of the problems is, though an expert can always be found who will oblige a judge with an appropriate program. A public health specialist will oblige the judge with a program for medical care that follows the standards of his professional association, standards that hardly any public body may be able to afford to meet or is interested to meet. And so with a psychiatrist, social work specialist, or school specialist. Clearly, if the judge has decided that the services in question are inadequate, or that they violate the constitution, or the laws, or the health code, or equal treatment, or whatever, he will find some expert who agrees with him.

Thus, the reach of government, already grossly expanded beyond its capacity to perform, is further expanded by the courts. Many elected officials now believe that government cannot deliver what has been promised in certain areas, either because of limited resources or knowledge; but it will be an interesting question whether the courts will now allow government to withdraw from these areas. Efforts to restrict welfare expenditure in those states where it has become a huge burden have been fought tooth and nail in the courts, and one may be sure that every other effort to withdraw from the provision of service will also be fought, by the professional groups providing the services, by the publicly-funded legal advocacy centers now established to protect the rights of various groups of citizens and recipients of government benefits, and by the beneficiaries themselves. Much will depend on the temper of the courts, and on the guidance the Supreme Court gives.

55

ROBERT BORK

Interpretivism

————

WHATEVER ONE THINKS about the performance of courts today, a subject upon which I shall have nothing to say here, it is quite clear that there have been times in our history when courts have gone well beyond their proper constitutional sphere. When that occurs, democratic government is displaced and the question is how to restore a proper allocation of powers. Absent a constitutional amendment, a general means to ensure that courts stay within the limits the Constitution provides for them can only be intellectual and moral.

That may seem a weak control. It does not seem so to me. Intellectual criticism in the short run may be quite ineffective. In the long run, ideas will be decisive. That is particularly true with respect to courts, more so perhaps than with any other branch of government.

Courts are part of a more general legal-constitutional culture and ultimately are heavily influenced by ideas that develop elsewhere in that culture. It is not too much to say, for example, that the Warren Court was, in a real sense, the culmination of a version of the legal-realist movement that dominated the Yale Law School years before. Similarly, the outcome of a present debate taking place in the law schools will surely affect the courts of today and the future.

A new struggle for intellectual dominance in constitutional theory is under way at this moment. The struggle is about the duty of judges with respect to the Constitution. It is taking place out of public sight, in a sense, because it is carried on almost entirely in the law schools and in the law reviews. But that doesn't mean it won't affect our entire polity in the years ahead. The ideas that win hegemony there will govern the profession, including judges, for at least a generation and perhaps more.

Let me sketch the nature of the debate. The contending schools of thought are called, somewhat unhappily, "interpretivism" and "noninterpretivism." In popular usage, "interpretivism" is often called strict construction. And "noninterpretivism" is what we loosely refer to as activism or imperialism.

John Hart Ely, then of Harvard Law School, described them this way: Interpretivism is the tenet "that judges deciding constitutional issues should confine themselves to enforcing norms that are stated or are clearly implicit in the written Constitution.... What distinguishes interpretivism"—or, if you will, strict construction—"from its opposite is its insistence that the work of the political branches is to be invalidated only in accord with an inference whose starting point, whose underlying premise, is fairly discoverable in the Constitution." Noninterpretivism—or activism, if you will—advances "the contrary view, that courts should go beyond that set of references and enforce norms that cannot be discovered within the four corners of the document."

The noninterpretivists, in a word, think that in litigation which is nominally constitutional the courts may—indeed should—remake the Constitution. These theorists are usually careful to say that a judge should not simply enforce his own values. And they variously prescribe as the source of this new law, which is to control the judge, such things as natural law, conventional morality, the understanding of an ideal democracy, or what have you.

There is a curious consistency about these theories. No matter from which base they start, the professors aways end up at the same place, prescribing a constitutional law which is considerably more egalitarian and socially permisive than either the written Constitution or the state of legislative opinion in the American public today. That may be the point of the exercise.

My own philosophy is interpretivist. But I must say that this puts me in a distinct minority among law professors. Just how much of a minority may be seen by the fact that a visitor to Yale who expressed interest in debating my position was told by one of my colleagues that the position was so passé that it would be intellectually stultifying to debate it.

By my count, there were in recent years perhaps five interpretivists on the faculties of the ten best-known law schools. And now the President has put four of them on courts of appeals. That is why faculty members who don't like much else about Ronald Reagan regard him as a great reformer of legal education.

If the theory of noninterpretivism—that judges can draw their constitutional rulings from outside the document—achieves entire intellectual hegemony in the law schools, as it is on the brink of doing, the results will be disastrous for the constitutional law of this nation. Judges will feel justified in continually creating new individual rights, and those influential groups which form what might be called the Constitution-making apparatus of the nation— that is, the law professors, the courts, the press, the leaders of the bar—will support the courts in doing this. It will be very hard to rally public opinion against groups so articulate and in control of most of the means of communication. It will be particularly hard since much opposition will be disarmed by being told that this is what the Constitution commands. We are a people with a great and justified veneration for the Constitution.

The hard fact is, however, that there are no guidelines outside the Constitution that can control a judge once he abandons the lawyer's task of interpretation. There may be a natural law, but we are not agreed upon what it is, and there is no such law that gives definite answers to a judge trying to decide a case.

There may be a conventional morality in our society, but on most issues there are likely to be several moralities. They are often regionally defined, which is one reason for federalism. The judge has no way of choosing among differing moralities or competing moralities except in accordance with his own morality.

There may be immanent and unrealized ideals of democracy, but the Constitution does not prescribe a wholly democratic government. It is difficult to see what warrant a judge has for demanding more democracy than either the Constitution requires or the people want.

The truth is that the judge who looks outside the Constitution always looks inside himself and nowhere else.

Noninterpretivism, should it prevail, will have several entirely predictable results. In the first place, the area of judicial power will continually grow and the area of democratic choice will continually contract. We will have a great deal more constitutional law than the Constitution itself contains.

Rights will be created, and they will often conflict with one another, so the courts will find that they must balance them in a process which is indistinguishable from legislation.

There is a good example of this. Recently, a federal court of appeals had occasion to consider a state statute which required a wife to consult her husband before having an abortion. The husband was given no control over the decision, merely a sort of due-process right to be heard. Naturally, someone claimed that even that violated the Constitution. The court of appeals said that it had to balance the wife's right to privacy against the husband's right to procreation.

Neither of those rights is to be found anywhere in the Constitution. The court upheld the statute, but the point is that a court, without any guidance from the Constitution, or any source other than its own views, had to make an accommodation of values and interests of a sort that used to be entirely the business of the legislature. That will become the general situation if noninterpretivism becomes dominant.

Another result of this theory, which, as I say, is the dominant theory of the law schools—at least it appears to be winning the debate at the moment—will be the nationalization of moral values as state legislative choices are steadily displaced by federal judicial choices. This is directly contrary to the theory of the Constitution, which is that certain moral choices specified in the document are national, but that unless Congress defines a new national consensus, all other moral choices are to be made democratically by the people in their states and in their cities.

Finally, there will occur what I have called the gentrification of the Constitution. The constitutional culture—those who are most intimately involved with constitutional adjudication and how it is perceived by the public at large: federal judges, law professors, members of the media—is not composed of a cross-section of America, either politically, socially, or morally. If, as I have suggested, noninterpretivism leads a judge to find constitutional values within himself, or in the values of those with whom he is most intimately associated, then the values which might loosely be described as characteristic of the university-educated upper middle class will be those that are imposed.

There is nothing wrong with that class, but there is also no reason why its values should be imposed upon everybody else. If that happens, then the Constitution will have been gentrified.

Perhaps I've said enough to show why I think this dominant philosophy in the major law schools must not be allowed to go unchallenged intellectually. But I want to make two last points about the rhetoric of its adherents.

Noninterpretivism—activism—is said to be the means by which courts add to constitutional freedom and never subtract from it. That is wrong. Among our constitutional freedoms or rights,

clearly given in the text, is the power to govern ourselves democratically.

Every time a court creates a new constitutional right against
government or expands, without warrant, an old one, the constitutional freedom of citizens to control their lives is diminished. Freedom cannot be created by this method; it is merely shifted from a
larger group to a smaller group.

G. K. Chesterton might have been addressing this very controversy when he wrote: "What is the good of telling a community it
has every liberty except the liberty to make laws? The liberty to
make laws is what constitutes a free people."

The claim of noninterpretivists, then, that they will expand
rights and freedom is false. They will merely redistribute them.

What is perhaps even more troubling is the lack of candor—
and I think it can only be called that—which so often characterizes
the public rhetoric of constitutional scholars who subscribe to this
theory.

Professor Paul Bator of Harvard put the point very well at the
Federalist Society meeting at Yale. He explained that there are
two different kinds of arguments that the constitutional in-group
uses, depending on its purposes at the moment.

On Monday, while we are arguing for a result in court that
would be hard to justify in terms of the written Constitution, we
say things like: "Oh well, any sophisticated lawyer understands
that the text of the Constitution is really not very clear, its history
is often extremely ambiguous, and in many areas simply unknown.
That being so, why shouldn't the court just do good as we define
the good?"

But on Tuesday, after the decision has been made, we find
ourselves talking to a different and much larger group, people
who are not constitutional theorists and who may be enraged at
what the court has done. These tend to be regarded by the constitutional cognoscenti as the great unwashed. To them, we do not
mention the ambiguities, the uncertainties that underlie the decision. We certainly don't mention the political basis for the decision.
Instead, we say to them, "Why, you are attacking the Constitution." That, of course, is not what the critics are doing.

If noninterpretivism is to be respectable, its scholars must stop
talking this way. When they address the public, they should say,
frankly, "No, that decision does not come out of the written or
historical Constitution. It is based upon a moral choice the judges

made, and here is why it is a good choice, and here is why judges are entitled to make it for you."

That last is going to be a little sticky, but that is what honesty requires. Until the public understands the basis by which constitutional argument moves, there will be little chance for the public to decide what kind of courts it really wants.

These concerns are not new. There is a great deal of dissatisfaction with courts today. It is important, in some sense, to recognize that those concerns, that kind of anger is as old as our Republic. Americans have never been entirely at ease with the concept of judicial supremacy, and they have also never wanted to try democracy without any judicial safeguards.

Thomas Jefferson spoke feelingly of the dangers of judicial power: "The Constitution, on this hypothesis [of judicial supremacy], is a mere thing of wax in the hands of the judiciary, which they may twist, and shape into any form they please. It should be remembered, as an axiom of eternal truth in politics, that whatever power in any government is independent is absolute also. . . . Independence can be trusted nowhere but with the people in mass."

But Alexander Hamilton spoke with equal feeling on the necessity for safeguards enforced by independent judges when he said: "there is no liberty if the power of judging be not separated from the legislative and executive powers. . . . The complete independence of the courts of justice is peculiarly essential in a limited Constitution."

Both Jefferson and Hamilton had powerful points. It seems to me that only a strictly interpretivist approach to the Constitution, only an approach which says the judge must get from the Constitution what is in that document and in its history and nothing else, can preserve for us the benefits that Hamilton saw, while avoiding the dangers that Jefferson prophesied.

56

LAURENCE TRIBE
On the Nomination of Robert Bork

———

JUDGE BORK'S position seems to have changed least of all with respect to the Supreme Court's long line of cases protecting personal liberties, rights and freedoms, many centering on family privacy, that are not specifically mentioned in the Constitution— the so-called "unenumerated rights."*

Although Judge Bork recognized, in a discussion with Senator [Arlen] Specter on September 19, that these cases reflect "a very powerful argument from a very strong tradition," and although Judge Bork has suggested in his testimony that there might be alternative ways of reaching the same *results* in a few of these cases, Judge Bork emphatically repeated to this Committee his fundamental belief that he cannot properly read the Constitution as recognizing an individual right unless he can find that right specifically pointed out in a particular provision of the document. Judge Bork has often said, in public speeches and in writings both predating his appointment as a judge and while he has been on the bench, that the Supreme Court's entire line of cases establishing the contrary conclusion is therefore "indefensible," "intellectually empty," and even "unconstitutional," because in his view they do not flow clearly and directly enough from specific provisions of the Constitution....

In his testimony, Judge Bork has repeatedly refused to treat these decisions as establishing a body of settled law—in sharp contrast to what he testified about the law of the Commerce Clause and the law of the First Amendment, as I indicate below. He has thus reaffirmed here his firmly held view that there exists no constitutionally permissible way to distinguish a private sphere of liberty concerning intimate family and sexual matters from such matters as the decision of a company to pollute the environment, or the

———

*In October 1987 the Senate Judiciary Committee and then the full Senate rejected Judge Robert Bork, President Reagan's nominee for the Supreme Court.—EDS.

conduct of businessmen who engage in price-fixing in a private
hotel room. To Judge Bork, the idea of a right of personal privacy
is "undefined" and "free-floating." Thus, he said in a speech at
Catholic University on March 31, 1982, that in "not one" of the
privacy cases "could the result have been reached by interpretation
of the Constitution." ...

[Yet] as revealed by *Turner v. Safley,* 107 S.Ct. 2254 (1987), a
case handed down this June, in which the Court unanimously
struck down a ban on marriage by prison inmates, *no current Justice*
disputes that the protection of substantive "liberty" in the Constitution encompasses at least *some* fundamental personal matters.
There, Justice O'Connor, in an opinion joined by every Justice
(including Chief Justice Rehnquist and Justice Scalia), noted "that
the decision to marry is a fundamental right" even for prisoners.
107 S.Ct. at 2265.

Whatever the proper results of specific cases testing the limits
of personal freedom, Judge Bork's is a uniquely narrow and con-
stricted view of "liberty" and of the Supreme Court's place in
protecting it. It sets Judge Bork apart from the entire 200-year-old
tradition of thought about rights that underlies the American Constitution. And it suggests an incapacity to address in any meaningful
way a whole spectrum of cases that we can expect will be vital in
our national life during the next quarter century.

The problem with Judge Bork's extraordinary philosophy of
liberty goes far beyond his refusal to respect the long line of Supreme Court decisions protecting personal privacy. This refusal is
only part of a radical view of the meaning of the Constitution
itself. As Judge Bork understands the Constitution, the Framers
and the People of the United States who ratified that document
two hundred years ago surrendered to government all of the fundamental, natural rights they regarded themselves as possessing—the
rights that the Revolutionary War had been fought to preserve—
with the sole exception of whatever specific rights were to be
mentioned in a Bill of Rights which had been promised but had
not yet been written. Judge Bork suggests that one provision of
the Bill of Rights, the Ninth Amendment, might have preserved
certain other rights that were specifically mentioned in the constitutions of the thirteen states, although he testified that he is unsure
of even that much, and he suggested, as recently as 1984 in a
speech at the University of Southern California, that uncertainty
about the meaning of the Ninth Amendment may require that a

judge simply "ignore the provision" and "treat it as non-existent," as though it were "nothing more than a water blot on the document."

Despite Judge Bork's espousal of a theory of "original intent," no understanding of the Constitution could be further from the clear purpose of those who wrote and ratified the Constitution and its first ten amendments. The principal aim of the original Constitution—and the impetus for the insistence, as a condition of ratification, upon a Bill of Rights to preserve natural rights that had been recognized for centuries—was to create a national government that, although sufficiently powerful to bind together states of great diversity, would not threaten the individual liberty that the people retained and did not cedè to any level of government. The broad purposes of this plan are clear from the wording of the Fifth Amendment's protection of "liberty" and the Ninth Amendment's explicit mandate that "[t]he enumeration in the Constitution, of certain rights, shall not be construed to deny or disparage others retained by the people." So too, the major purpose of the Fourteenth Amendment—again with its specific protection of "liberty"—was to impose similar restraints, in the aftermath of the Civil War, on the power of the states to infringe on the fundamental rights of any person.

From the very beginning of our Republic, the Supreme Court has consistently and unanimously recognized that, in adopting the Constitution, the people of the United States did not place the bulk of their hard-won liberty in the hands of government, save only for those rights specifically mentioned in the Bill of Rights or elsewhere in the document....

Justices in the modern era as well have had no trouble understanding that the rights of the people are not, and cannot properly be, limited to those specifically mentioned in the Constitution or directly inferable from those expressly listed. In his 1980 opinion upholding the right of the public to attend criminal trials, Chief Justice Burger refuted the argument that such a right could not exist because it was "nowhere spell[ed] out"—in part by pointing to the Ninth Amendment, which he recognized had been included by draftsmen who "were concerned that some important rights might be thought disparaged because not specifically guaranteed." *Richmond Newspapers v. Virginia,* 448 U.S. 555, 579 & n.15 (1980) (plurality opinion of Burger, C.J.). The Chief Justice noted that rights such as "the rights of association and of privacy, ... as well as the right to travel, appear nowhere in the Constitution," but that "these important but unarticulated rights have nonetheless been found to share constitutional protection in common with explicit guarantees." ... Indeed, a careful review of the Supreme Court's precedents reveals that *not one of the 105 past and present Justices of the Supreme Court* has ever taken a view as consistently radical as Judge Bork's on the concept of "liberty"—or the lack of it—underlying the Constitution. ...

... Judge Bork's rejection of the Supreme Court's historic role in articulating *an evolving concept of "liberty"* protected by the Constitution—not simply protecting a *fixed* set of "liberties" from an evolving set of threats—has great practical significance in an era when government bureaucracies may be tempted to dictate the deployment of medical technology so as to control choices about the very young and the very old, the infirm and the disabled— threatening to usurp the most intimate family decisions in these areas and to control who may have children, which children may be brought into the world, and which must be discarded before they come to term. Without the last line of defense defined by the established tradition that the protection of the Constitution extends beyond those rights specifically mentioned in the text, the chilling spectre presented by these and other issues in our increasingly complex world must be of abiding concern.

57

BOB WOODWARD
SCOTT ARMSTRONG

From *The Brethren*

———

IN LATE AUGUST 1971, the Chief invited his new clerks to join him for lunch. It was a last-minute invitation. Several arrived at the ground-floor Ladies Dining Room carrying their cafeteria lunches on trays. Since they had come to the Court at various times over the summer, Burger's clerks had had only fleeting contact with their boss.

Alvin Wright, the Chief's messenger and valet, stood in the doorway wearing a white waiter's jacket. The sight of the familiar messenger dressed as a waiter was startling enough, but suddenly Wright pivoted and snapped to attention. "The Chief Justice of the United States of America," he called out.

By reflex, the clerks rose.

"You've got to be shitting me," one mumbled in the face of a hostile stare from Burger's senior clerk.

Burger strolled into the room, greeted each clerk graciously, and took his place at the head of the table. The antique table was covered with a linen cloth and set with the Court Historical Society's china and silver. Here in this dining room with pale-yellow walls covered with portraits of the wives of the former Chief Justices, Burger felt comfortable. He had taken a great interest in the proper refurbishing of this room. Newly acquired antiques, financed through the Society with donations from prominent Washingtonians and members of the bar, were selected by the Chief with great care. The room itself was a vestige of an age when the Court's oral arguments were among Washington's premier social events attended by the Justices' wives and their guests.

Burger enjoyed entertaining in the midst of this elegant collection of period pieces. The guests that he invited to dinners here were as carefully selected as the décor, drawn for the most part from admirers he encountered as he moved through social Washington. But the esteem of outsiders was not enough. Burger genuinely sought understanding and respect from the young men who came each year to work as his clerks. He missed the relaxed days of the Court of Appeals, when he often took his clerks to his house in Arlington and cooked them a gourmet meal. Now, with the press of Court and administrative duties, he was lucky to manage lunch with his clerks once a month.

Burger began this gathering with an introduction to the approaching term. Lamenting the fact that both John Harlan and Hugo Black had recently been hospitalized, he told some anecdotes about the warm affection that existed between these ideological opponents. He emphasized his respect and admiration for the two legal giants.

The Chief also expressed concern about Marshall's recent emergency appendectomy. Marshall had not allowed the news media to know about complications that had arisen from a stomach ulcer. And though Douglas was healthy, he had had his heart "pacemaker" batteries replaced three months before.

The message was clear. Reluctantly but inevitably, the Chief was having to assume additional burdens of leadership. One of the most pressing problems of the approaching term was the evident confusion of the lower federal courts in the wake of the Charlotte desegregation and busing decision. Many district judges had ordered massive busing in an apparent attempt to achieve racial balance in each school, the Chief explained. This had provoked a massive public outcry. It was all unnecessary, the Chief said. The Charlotte decision did not require racial balance. He told the clerks how he had struggled to overcome Black's adamant opposition to any busing. Only his personal effort had allowed the Court to come down with a unanimous decision.

One of the clerks, familiar with the case from a year's clerking at the Fourth Circuit Court of Appeals, politely challenged Burger. In the Charlotte case, the Supreme Court had approved Judge McMillan's order and McMillan had used racial balance in devising the busing remedy.

No, the Chief explained patiently, as the author of the opinion he knew what the Court was trying to achieve. Since the original school desegregation decisions in 1954 and 1955, the lower courts had been confused about whether the Supreme Court was calling for desegregation or for integration. Clearly, the Court was calling only for desegregation. Forced racial mixing, racial balance, or total integration had not been demanded.

Federal district judges in about twenty desegregation cases in large Southern metropolitan regions had misread the Charlotte opinion, Burger told them, and the result had been orders for massive busing. As it happened, he had an emergency request on his desk from the Winston-Salem, North Carolina, school district to stay a busing plan ordered by a district court judge. The judge had mistakenly ordered busing to achieve racial balance. Burger said he would end the unnecessary confusion over busing by writing a single-justice opinion to accompany his order. This would be no *"post hoc"* repair job, Burger said, but simply a clarification.

The clerks had heard the rumors of the rancorous debates over the Charlotte case. Varying scenarios placed Stewart, Brennan, Harlan, Douglas and even Marshall in key roles resolving a conflict brought to a head by the obstinacy of both Black and the Chief. Now, they were bewildered to find that Burger expected them to believe that he had been the single author of the final opinion.

Several wondered whether the Chief even understood what he had "authored" in the Charlotte case. He was espousing the position he had been forced to surrender last term. . . .

Nixon had certain concerns about nominating Rehnquist. It would look like an "in-house" appointment, and Rehnquist was relatively unknown in establishment legal circles. A former clerk to Justice Robert Jackson in 1952, Rehnquist had practiced law for sixteen years in Phoenix where he was part of the Goldwater wing of the Republican party. He had joined the Justice Department to head the Office of Legal Counsel as an assistant attorney general in 1969. He had been, in effect, Attorney General Mitchell's lawyer.

Nixon had some trouble remembering Rehnquist's name; he once called him "Renchburg." He was also somewhat taken aback by the easygoing lawyer's appearance, once referring to him as "that clown" because of his long sideburns and pink shirts. But Rehnquist was very bright and extremely conservative. And at forty-seven, he could be expected to serve many years. . . .

Rehnquist received a rougher grilling. His most serious problem arose when a memo surfaced that he had written in the Brown case, when he was clerking for Justice Jackson nineteen years earlier. The memo recommended that the Court not order school desegregation. "Separate but equal" facilities were all that was constitutionally required, Rehnquist had stated.

Rehnquist testified that he had written the memorandum, but he denied that it had reflected his views. He was merely summarizing Jackson's views for the conference.

Rehnquist's account was disputed by a lawyer who had clerked with him on the Court, and by Jackson's secretary. Press reports played up the discrepancies in testimony.[*] But the Committee dropped the matter. In two full days of hearings, the liberals could do no more than establish that Rehnquist was every bit as conservative as he appeared to be when defending administration policies. On December 10, the Senate voted to confirm him 68 to 26. . . .

Douglas had long wanted the Court to face the abortion issue head on. The laws in effect in most states, prohibiting or severely restricting the availability of abortions, were infringements of a

---

[*]Douglas, the only remaining member of the Court that had decided the Brown case, examined a copy of Rehnquist's testimony. Rehnquist was correct, he told clerks. The views were, in fact, Jackson's. But see also Richard Kluger, *Simple Justice*.

woman's personal liberty. The broad constitutional guarantee of "liberty," he felt, included the right of a woman to control her body.

Douglas realized, however, that a majority of his colleagues were not likely to give such a sweeping reading to the Constitution on this increasingly volatile issue. . . .

Douglas ascribed to Burger the most blatant political motives. Nixon favored restrictive abortion laws. Faced with the possibility that the Court might strike abortion laws down in a presidential-election year, the Chief wanted to stall the opinion, Douglas concluded.

Blackmun was by far the slowest writer on the Court. The year was nearly half over and he had yet to produce a first circulation in a simple business case that had been argued the first week (*Port of Portland v. U.S.*). It was the kind of case in which Douglas produced drafts within one week of conference. But in the abortion cases, Douglas had a deeper worry. The Chief was trying to manipulate the outcome.

Blackmun might circulate a draft striking portions of the restrictive abortion laws. But as a judicial craftsman, his work was crude. A poor draft would be likely to scare off Stewart, who was already queasy, and leave only four votes. Or if Blackmun himself were to desert the position—a distinct possibility—precious time would be lost. Either defection would leave only a four-man majority. It would be difficult to argue that such a major decision should be handed down on a 4-to-3 vote. There would be increasing pressure to put the cases over for rehearing with the two new Nixon Justices. This was no doubt exactly the sort of case that Nixon had in mind when he chose Powell and Rehnquist.

Blackmun was both pleased and frightened by the assignment. It was a no-win proposition. No matter what he wrote, the opinion would be controversial. Abortion was too emotional, the split in society too great. Either way, he would be hated and vilified.

But from Blackmun's point of view, the Chief had had little choice but to select him. Burger could not afford to take on such a controversial case himself, particularly from the minority. Douglas was the Court's mischievous liberal, the rebel, and couldn't be the author. Any abortion opinion Douglas wrote would be widely questioned outside the Court, and his extreme views might split rather than unify the existing majority. Lastly, Blackmun had noticed a deterioration in the quality of Douglas's opinions; they had become increasingly superficial. . . .

Blackmun had long thought Burger an uncontrollable, blustery braggart. Now, once again in close contact with him, he was at once put off and amused by the Chief's exaggerated pomposity, his callous disregard for the feelings of his colleagues, his self-aggrandizing style. "He's been doing that since he was four," he once told Stewart.

Blackmun was just as aware as Douglas was of the Chief's attempts to use his position to manipulate the Court. Douglas was correct to despise that sort of thing. But this time, Blackmun felt, Douglas was wrong. When he arrived at the Court, Blackmun had assumed the Chief's job as scrivener for the conference. Burger had finally given up trying to keep track of all the votes and positions taken in conference, and had asked Blackmun to keep notes and stay behind to brief the Clerk of the Court. Even then the Chief sometimes misstated the results. Blackmun would deftly field the Chief's hesitations, filling in when he faltered. When Burger misinformed the Clerk of the Court, Blackmun's cough would cue him.

"Do you recall what happened there, Harry?" the Chief would then say. "My notes seem to be a bit sporadic."

Blackmun would fill in the correct information as if Burger had initiated the request.

Part of the problem was that the Chief spread himself too thin. He accepted too many social, speaking and ceremonial engagements, and exhibited too little affection for the monastic, scholarly side of the Court's life. As a result, Burger was often unprepared for orals or conference. Too often, he had to wait and listen in order to figure out which issues were crucial to the outcome. His grasp of the cases came from the summaries, usually a page or less, of the cert memos his clerks prepared. The Chief rarely read the briefs or the record before oral argument.

The problem was compounded by Burger's willingness to change his position in conference, or his unwillingness to commit himself before he had figured out which side had a majority. Then, joining the majority, he could control the assignment. Burger had strained his relationship with everyone at the table to the breaking point. It was as offensive to Blackmun as it was to the others. But one had to understand the Chief. For all his faults, here was a self-made man who had come up the ladder rung by rung. Blackmun did not begrudge him his attempts at leadership. . . .

Blackmun began each day by breakfasting with his clerks in the Court's public cafeteria, and clerks from the other chambers had a standing invitation to join them. Blackmun would often spot a clerk from another chamber eating alone and invite him over. He seemed, at first, the most open, unassuming and gracious of the Justices.

Breakfast-table conversation generally began with sports, usually baseball, and then moved on to the morning's headlines. There was an unspoken rule that any discussion of cases was off limits. Where other Justices might openly debate cases with the clerks, Blackmun awkwardly side-stepped each attempt. The law in general was similarly out of bounds. Blackmun turned the most philosophical of discussions about law around to his own experience, or to the clerk's family, or the performance of a younger sibling in school.

The clerks in his own chambers saw a different side of Blackmun which betrayed more of the pressure that he felt. The stories were petty. An office window left open all night might set him off on a tirade. It was not the security that worried Blackmun, but the broken social contract—all clerks were supposed to close all windows each night. Number-two pencils, needle-sharp, neatly displayed in the pencil holder, need include only one number three or a cracked point to elicit a harsh word. If Blackmun wanted a document photocopied, and somehow the wrong one came back, he might simply fling it aside. An interruption, even for some important question, might be repulsed testily.

The mystery of the Blackmun personality deepened. His outbursts varied in intensity and usually passed quickly. "Impatient moods," his secretary called them. But they made life more difficult; they added an extra tension.

Yet none of his Court family—clerks, secretaries, or his messenger—judged Blackmun harshly. They all knew well enough the extraordinary pressures, real and imagined, that he worked under.

From his first day at the Court, Blackmun had felt unworthy, unqualified, unable to perform up to standard. He felt he could equal the Chief and Marshall, but not the others. He became increasingly withdrawn and professorial. He did not enjoy charting new paths for the law. He was still learning. The issues were too grave, the information too sparse. Each new question was barely answered, even tentatively, when two more questions appeared on the horizon. Blackmun knew that his colleagues were concerned about what they perceived as his indecisiveness. But what others saw as an inability to make decisions, he felt to be a deliberate withholding of final judgment until all the facts were in, all the arguments marshaled, analyzed, documented.

It was a horribly lonely task. Blackmun worked by himself, beginning with a long memo from one of his clerks, reading each of the major briefs, carefully digesting each of the major opinions that circulated, laboriously drafting his own opinions, checking each citation himself, refining his work through a dozen drafts to take into account each Justice's observations. He was unwilling, moreover, to debate the basic issues in a case, even in chambers with his own clerks. He preferred that they write him memos.

Wearing a gray or blue cardigan sweater, Blackmun hid away in the recesses of the Justices' library, and his office had instructions not to disturb him there. The phone did not ring there, and not even the Chief violated his solitude. Working at a long mahogany table lined on the opposite edge with a double row of books, Blackmun took meticulous notes. He spent most of his time sorting facts and fitting them to the law in a desperate attempt to discover inevitable conclusions. He tried to reduce his risks by mastering every detail, as if the case were some huge math problem. Blackmun felt that if all the steps were taken, there could be only one answer....

For White the term had its ups and downs like any other year at the Court. He had been a fierce competitor all his life. He loved to take control of a case, pick out the weaknesses in the other Justices' positions, and then watch them react to his own twists and turns as he pushed his own point of view. When he could not, which was often, he took his frustrations to the third-floor gym to play in the clerks' regular full-court basketball game.

Muscling out men thirty years his junior under the boards, White delighted in playing a more competitive game than they did. He dominated the games by alternating savage and effective drives to the basket with accurate two-hand push shots from twenty feet. White consistently pushed off the clerk trying to cover him, calling every conceivable foul against the hapless clerk, while bitching about every foul called against himself. He regularly took the impermissible third step before shooting. The game was serious business for White. Each man was on his own. Teamwork was valuable in order to win, not for its own sake.

One Friday afternoon White was out of position for a rebound, but he went up throwing a hip. A clerk pulled in the ball and White came crashing down off balance and injured his ankle.

The Justice came to the office on crutches the next Monday: he would be off the basketball court for the rest of the season. He asked the clerks to keep the reason for his injury secret. The clerks bought him a Fussball game, a modern version of the ancient game of skittles. It was competition, so White enjoyed it, but it lacked for him the thrill of a contact sport like basketball—or law.

On Friday, May 26, Byron White read a draft dissent to Blackmun's abortion decision that one of his clerks had prepared. He then remolded it to his liking. The structure of Blackmun's opinion was juvenile; striking the Texas law for vagueness was simply stupid. The law might have several defects, but vagueness was not among them. The law could not be more specific in delineating the circumstance when abortion was available—it was only to protect the life of the mother.

Blackmun was disturbed by White's attack....

Two weeks into the term, the Court heard the first of the obscenity cases. These were three cases that Brennan wanted considered first. They posed the question of whether states could ban consenting adults from walking into a theater or store and buying or seeing what they wanted and expected to see. There was no exposure of books or movies to unwilling viewers or children....

Burger's position was hardening. He hated pornography and smut peddlers. Something had to be done to suppress them. Care had to be taken, of course, to preserve legitimate First Amendment rights, but Douglas's concerns were overstated. For Burger, the issue was more than anything else a question of taste. Obscenity was vulgar; citizens had a right to be protected from it....

Rehnquist usually voted with Burger; they agreed on many things. But Rehnquist didn't share Burger's concern with appearances and formality. He was very casual. During the nice weather, he and his clerks sometimes ate lunch in one of the two enclosed courtyards. They brought their food in paper bags and simply enjoyed the sun and the outdoors. As they were picnicking in shirtsleeves one day, Burger's messenger, Alvin Wright, set up a small table with silver service and a white linen tablecloth. Moments later, Burger came out with his clerks. Burger, his jacket on, poured the wine.

Rehnquist and his clerks chuckled a bit. But as they gazed on the solemnity at the Burger table, Rehnquist's laughter grew almost uncontrollable. He and his clerks had to dash inside.

During his first term, Rehnquist worried some about what influence his clerks might have on his opinions. He had clerked at the Court after law school and had written a magazine article in 1957 alleging that most law clerks were generally "to the 'left' of either the nation or the Court." He described the bias as "extreme solicitude for the claims of Communists and other criminal defendants, expansion of federal power at the expense of State power, great sympathy toward any government regulation of business."

He mentioned the possibility of "unconscious slanting of material by clerks" when reviewing cert petitions. And though he had written that he didn't think clerks exercised too much influence in the actual drafting of opinions, he was careful when he got to the Court to write all the first drafts himself. Midway through his first full term, he realized that he had been wrong. The legal and moral interchanges that liberal clerks thrived on were good for the Justices and for the Court. Rehnquist grew to trust his clerks; they would not be so foolish as to try putting something over on him. And there was the question of efficiency. The clerks were helpful with first drafts. It saved him time, and helped focus his own thinking.

Rehnquist was known around the Court for his friendliness toward clerks. He learned their names, and found some of them as interesting as the Justices. He suggested letting the clerks into the Justices' dining room or setting up a lounge for both clerks and Justices. Those ideas got nowhere, but he did get a Ping-Pong table for the Court.

Rehnquist's clerks occasionally took a moment out to play basketball on the court in the upstairs gym, and since there was very little time, they often overlooked the rule against playing in street shoes. One day, at oral argument, Rehnquist's clerks noticed their boss whispering with some of the other Justices. He scribbled a note and summoned a messenger who carried it to where the clerks were sitting in the audience. They felt very important.

"We have just talked it over and from now on the rule against street shoes will be strictly enforced," the note read.

As the junior Justice, Rehnquist was in charge of the annual Christmas Party. It was a noisy party, and Rehnquist found it hard to get all personnel together for the carolling. Finally, he stood on a piano bench. "Achtung!" he shouted.

One clerk thought it was too good to be true. Rehnquist, the fascist. But most thought that it showed that Rehnquist had a sense of humor....

Rehnquist slipped into the conference room one day and took his seat.

He pulled a magazine from his stack of papers. The *National Lampoon,* a humor magazine, had just released its February issue. The centerfold was entitled "Amicae Curiae"—Friends of the Court—and it depicted, in a color cartoon, all nine of the Justices engaged in a variety of sexual activity.

The Chief, naked except for holster and pistol, was on the floor licking the boot of an otherwise naked young woman.

Brennan was standing in front of two very young girls holding his robe open....

Stewart was measuring the throat of a young woman with a ruler, apparently in preparation for oral sex.

Rehnquist, clad in a woman's bra and red garter belt, was parading before the others cracking a black whip.

White, a blindfold partially covering his glasses, was apparently engaged in some taxing sexual activity, though the cartoon did not make it clear what that activity was.

Powell was kneeling naked, his hands bound together, while a black woman in underwear marked "Exhibit A" flogged him.

Marshall stood by the side of the bench doing nothing but looking up at Douglas, who sat alone on the bench with a naked young boy at his side.

Blackmun was sodomizing a kangaroo.

Chuckling, Rehnquist passed the issue around the table. Most of them laughed. The Chief was angered both by the cartoon and the fact that it had been brought into conference.

Afterward, Marshall sent a clerk to buy extra copies for his college-age children.

Brennan proudly told his clerks that while every other Justice was portrayed engaging in some sexual activity, *he* was pictured protecting several young children by blocking their view with his robe.

His clerks decided that they owed it to him to explain "flashing."

Blackmun told his clerks how funny the centerfold was, especially the portion depicting Rehnquist "in drag." The only problem, Blackmun said, was that he couldn't figure out what he was supposed to be doing with the kangaroo.

The clerks drew straws to see who would tell him....

Rehnquist was remarkably unstuffy. He thought it funny that there was a Rehnquist Club at Harvard Law School in which the leader was called the "Grand Rehnquisitor," and a weekly discussion called the "Rehnquisition." ...

Stewart appreciated Rehnquist's sense of humor. At one particularly dull moment at conference, after Burger and Blackmun had performed predictably, Stewart passed a note to Rehnquist on which he had drawn two tombstones. On Burger's tombstone, Stewart had inscribed: "I'll Pass for The Moment." On Blackmun's he had written: "I Hope The Opinion Can Be Narrowly Written." Rehnquist laughed out loud.

Ignoring tradition, Rehnquist attended one conference in a Court softball team T-shirt. He also did little to dispel the impression that he was drinking straight Scotch or bourbon at his desk, even though the amber liquid in the glass was really his favorite beverage, apple juice.

Rehnquist's affability did not stop with his colleagues. He paid attention to all the Court personnel, addressing even the humblest by name. When the police at the Court had their chairs taken away from their duty stations as punishment for letting a tourist wander into a restricted area, a delegation came to Rehnquist for help. The chairs were soon returned to the posts.

He had an equally easy relationship with his clerks. By the end of the term, Rehnquist's clerks felt comfortable speaking openly about Burger's faults. Rehnquist listened and occasionally defended the Chief. He called the bad mouthing a "sport for law clerks," but it was clear that the subject was not off limits. He once asked a group of clerks what surprised them the most about the Court.

"The Chief's asinine memos," one clerk answered.

Rehnquist laughed heartily.

PART NINE

Public
Opinion

PUBLIC OPINION seems so straightforwardly essential to democracy that we might suppose that the subject had long ago been fully understood. What is there to say other than "the people shall rule"? It would seem that we ought to know what public opinion is, agree on its proper role, know how to measure it scientifically and be able to stipulate exactly its contribution to the formation of public policy. Would that it were so. Two hundred years after theorists of democracy won the battle over the right of the people to rule, scholars still argue over what public opinion *is*, dispute its worth as a basis for making public policy, disagree on what "scientifically" conducted polls really mean, and most of all, differ greatly in their understanding of how much public opinion counts in the actual decisions that government officials make. The beginning student of this subject will do well to realize that it is much more complex than it seems.

Some of the most troublesome questions about public opinion are really questions about democratic theory. Our first two selections illustrate this point. Lord Bryce's commentary on public opinion and its role in American government dates from the 1880s—long before the advent of modern polling. Bryce, who had travelled from his native Britain to observe American politics firsthand, was clearly struck by the lofty expectations Americans held of public opinion. Here "all classes in the community" have "a clearer and stronger consciousness of being the rulers of their country than European peoples have." In more modern terms, he found American political culture much more populistic than its European counterparts. American political thought, at least in its more exuberant expressions, really expects the people to govern. Some fifty years earlier Tocqueville had made the same observation. While Bryce admired the sentiment of this view, he was clearly somewhat taken aback by it. In an interesting nautical metaphor he wondered if the people are not like able seamen, who know how to work spars and ropes, but are "ignorant of geography and navigation." How much we expect public opinion to determine is largely a function of what we think of the capability of ordinary people. How knowledgeable, interested, and virtuous should we expect them to be? Bryce seems to think Americans err on the side of optimism, yet he concludes that our faith in the public has produced a "patient, tolerable and reasonable" politics.

Walter Lippmann's *The Phantom Public,* from which our next reading is drawn, presents a theory of public opinion in the modern democratic state. It remains one of the most cogent discussions of the subject after some sixty years. A mass public, he argues, can never govern. Theories that require the public to know about everything and to have well-formed opinions about everything are hopelessly unrealistic. The idea of "the omnicompetent, sovereign citizen is . . . a false ideal." None of us, however well educated, however attentive to public affairs, can have worthy opinions on the broad range of questions with which modern governments must deal. Note well that Lippmann includes himself and professors of political science in this generalization. His purpose is not to demean the public, but to argue that it should not be expected to govern. It is for elites to govern and for the public to approve or disapprove of broad policy alternatives. That is Lippmann's argument. We think Lippmann makes a strong point here—one that modern pollsters still run afoul of when they ask questions which expect people to perform like Quiz Kids or policy experts.

Our next three selections deal with the interpretation of modern survey (polling) data. The advent of scientific sampling some fifty years ago allowed pollsters to study the entire American public by addressing questions to small samples that were highly representative of the whole population. At once commercial polling became feasible as newspapers and other clients saw that it was possible to measure accurately such things as presidential popularity, voting intentions, and opinions on the issues of the day. We now have a wealth of survey data bearing on all aspects of American political life, but as these readings show, we continue to differ vigorously about their interpretation. Leo Bogart's piece argues that public opinion should be differentiated from mores (deep-lying values or norms of the sort we called attention to in our section on American ideology). Public opinion is much more subject to change. Our opinions about such things as a president's performance or the war in Vietnam are the products of our individual thought in a social context. We may well change our minds on such matters as we think and test our thoughts against those of others. He argues that we should not overlook evidence indicating the coexistence of contradictory opinions in the minds of the same people. Most of us, even "the highly political" minority, are ambivalent about many things. Pollsters should take this into consideration in designing questionnaires, and we should remember it as we interpret responses.

Tom Smith's article on the Attorney General's Commission on Pornography's interpretation of survey data draws attention to the importance of question wording and response categories—seemingly technical aspects of polling that in fact make all the difference in the world in deciding what responses to questions really mean. Much that polls "find" is really the artifact of how questions are asked. Smith points out that several of the Commission's conclusions are highly suspect on methodological grounds. The moral here is that consumers of reports based on polling data should always be aware that they may not be what they seem. Let the buyer beware.

Karlyn Keene and Everett Ladd's discussion of polls on Americans' opinions about government in recent years provides a striking example of ambivalent opinions. Pollsters largely ask questions to find out if we are for or against government. The answer, it seems, is both. Americans are profoundly ambivalent on this subject. Government is seen as too meddlesome, intrusive, wasteful, and so on; at the same time it is expected to perform extensive welfare and regulatory functions. This is the messy reality of current opinion on government. There is no law that says public opinion has to be internally consistent.

Our last selection returns to public opinion and democratic
theory. V. O. Key wrote these words at the end of a monumental
book in which he had analyzed a mountain of survey data in his
usual big-minded way to understand the role of public opinion in
American democracy. He concluded that his best effort had left a
good deal of mystery to the subject. The missing link, he thought,
was the interplay of opinion and the ruling elites of our democratic
order. Public opinion counts for a great deal in the end because
democratic elites take it seriously. They really believe it ought to
prevail. They seem to accept norms that inhibit the use of many
possible means by which opinion might be manipulated. Although
our elections manifest a good deal of humbug, American politicians
by and large refrain from wholesale lying and demagoguery. Activists are linked to interests and opinion blocs in society, and, although they are disproportionately from the higher social and occupational strata, they come from all parts of society. The interplay
of opinion and these activists is unfortunately "so complex as to
defy simple description." His last word on the subject is in the
form of a metaphor—a sure sign that there is no possibility of
scientific exactitude. Opinion is not a public will capable of governing, but a system of dikes which channel public action and limit
the range of what government can do. Thirty years later, with a
good twenty years of survey research at his disposal, he was reaching a conclusion not very different from the one Walter Lippmann
reached in *The Phantom Public*.

58

JAMES BRYCE

Public Opinion

From *The American Commonwealth*

———

OF ALL the experiments which America has made, this
is that which best deserves study, for her solution of the problem
differs from all previous solutions, and she has shown more bold

ness in trusting public opinion, in recognizing and giving effect to it, than has yet been shown elsewhere. Towering over Presidents and State governors, over Congress and State legislatures, over conventions and the vast machinery of party, public opinion stands out, in the United States, as the great source of power, the master of servants who tremble before it. . . .

In the United States public opinion is the opinion of the whole nation, with little distinction of social classes. The politicians, including the members of Congress and of State legislatures, are, perhaps not (as Americans sometimes insinuate) below, yet certainly not above the average level of their constituents. They find no difficulty in keeping touch with outside opinion. Washington or Albany may corrupt them, but not in the way of modifying their political ideas. They do not aspire to the function of forming opinion. They are like the Eastern slave who says "I hear and obey." Nor is there any one class or set of men, or any one "social layer," which more than another originates ideas and builds up political doctrine for the mass. The opinion of the nation is the resultant of the views, not of a number of classes, but of a multitude of individuals, diverse, no doubt, from one another, but, for the purposes of politics far less diverse than if they were members of groups defined by social rank or by property.

The consequences are noteworthy. One is, that statesmen cannot, as in Europe, declare any sentiment which they find telling on their friends or their opponents in politics to be confined to the rich, or to those occupied with government, and to be opposed to the general sentiment of the people. In America you cannot appeal from the classes to the masses. What the employer thinks, his workmen think. What the wholesale merchant feels, the retail storekeeper feels, and the poorer customers feel. Divisions of opinion are vertical and not horizontal. Obviously this makes opinion more easily ascertained, while increasing its force as a governing power, and gives the people, that is to say, all classes in the community, a clearer and stronger consciousness of being the rulers of their country than European peoples have. Every man knows that he is himself a part of the government, bound by duty as well as by self-interest to devote part of his time and thoughts to it. He may neglect this duty, but he admits it to be a duty. . . .

. . . The government is his own, and he individually responsible for its conduct. . . . The Americans are an educated people. . . . They know the constitution of their own country, they follow public affairs, they join in local government and learn from it how government must be carried on, and in particular how discussion must be conducted in meetings, and its results tested at elections....

That the education of the masses is nevertheless a superficial education goes without saying. It is sufficient to enable them to think they know something about the great problems of politics: insufficient to show them how little they know. The public elementary school gives everybody the key to knowledge in making reading and writing familiar, but it has not time to teach him how to use the key.... This observation, however, is not so much a reproach to the schools, ... as a tribute to the height of the ideal which the American conception of popular rule sets up.... For the functions of the citizen are not ... confined to the choosing of legislators, who are then left to settle issues of policy and select executive rulers. The American citizen is virtually one of the governors of the republic. Issues are decided and rulers selected by the direct popular vote. Elections are so frequent that to do his duty at them a citizen ought to be constantly watching public affairs with a full comprehension of the principles involved in them, and a judgment of the candidates derived from a criticism of their arguments as well as a recollection of their past careers. As has been said, the instruction received in the common schools and from the newspapers, and supposed to be developed by the practice of primaries and conventions, while it makes the voter deem himself capable of governing, does not completely fit him to weigh the real merits of statesmen, to discern the true grounds on which questions ought to be decided, to note the drift of events and discover the direction in which parties are being carried. He is like a sailor who knows the spars and ropes of the ship and is expert in working her, but is ignorant of geography and navigation; who can perceive that some of the officers are smart and others dull, but cannot judge which of them is qualified to use the sextant or will best keep his head during a hurricane....

The frame of the American government has assumed and trusted to the activity of public opinion, not only as the power which must correct and remove the difficulties due to the restrictions imposed on each department, and to possible collisions between them, but as the influence which must supply the defects incidental to a system which works entirely by the machinery of popular elections. Under a system of elections one man's vote is as good as another, the vicious and ignorant have as much weight as the wise and good. A system of elections might be imagined which would provide no security for due deliberation or full discussion, a system which, while democratic in name, recognizing no privilege, and referring everything to the vote of the majority, would in practice be hasty, violent, tyrannical. It is with such a possible democracy that one has to contrast the rule of public opinion as it exists in the United States. Opinion declares itself legally through elections. But opinion is at work at other times also, and has other methods of declaring itself. It secures full discussion of issues of policy and of the characters of men. It suffers nothing to be concealed. It listens patiently to all the arguments that are addressed to it. Eloquence, education, wisdom, the authority derived from experience and high character, tell upon it in the long run, and have, perhaps not always their due influence, but yet a great and growing influence. Thus a democracy governing itself through a constantly active public opinion, and not solely by its intermittent mechanism of elections, tends to become patient, tolerant, reasonable, and is more likely to be unembittered and unvexed by class divisions.

It is the existence of such a public opinion as this, the practice of freely and constantly reading, talking, and judging of public affairs with a view to voting thereon, rather than the mere possession of political rights, that gives to popular government that educative and stimulative power which is so frequently claimed as its highest merit.

59

WALTER LIPPMANN

From *The Phantom Public*

————

THE PRIVATE CITIZEN today has come to feel rather like a deaf spectator in the back row, who ought to keep his mind on the mystery off there, but cannot quite manage to keep awake. He knows he is somehow affected by what is going on. Rules and regulations continually, taxes annually and wars occasionally re-

mind him that he is being swept along by great drifts of circumstance.

Yet these public affairs are in no convincing way his affairs.
They are for the most part invisible. They are managed, if they
are managed at all, at distant centers, from behind the scenes, by
unnamed powers. As a private person he does not know for certain
what is going on, or who is doing it, or where he is being carried.
No newspaper reports his environment so that he can grasp it; no
school has taught him how to imagine it; his ideals, often, do not
fit with it; listening to speeches, uttering opinions and voting do
not, he finds, enable him to govern it. He lives in a world which
he cannot see, does not understand and is unable to direct.

In the cold light of experience he knows that his sovereignty is
a fiction. He reigns in theory, but in fact he does not govern. . . .

There is then nothing particularly new in the disenchantment
which the private citizen expresses by not voting at all, by voting
only for the head of the ticket, by staying away from the primaries,
by not reading speeches and documents, by the whole list of sins
of omission for which he is denounced. I shall not denounce him
further. My sympathies are with him, for I believe that he has
been saddled with an impossible task and that he is asked to practice
an unattainable ideal. I find it so myself for, although public business is my main interest and I give most of my time to watching
it, I cannot find time to do what is expected of me in the theory of
democracy; that is, to know what is going on and to have an
opinion worth expressing on every question which confronts a
self-governing community. And I have not happened to meet anybody, from a President of the United States to a professor of
political science, who came anywhere near to embodying the accepted ideal of the sovereign and omnicompetent citizen. . . .

[Today's theories] assume that either the voters are inherently
competent to direct the course of affairs or that they are making
progress toward such an ideal. I think it is a false ideal. I do not
mean an undesirable ideal. I mean an unattainable ideal, bad only
in the sense that it is bad for a fat man to try to be a ballet dancer.
An ideal should express the true possibilities of its subject. When
it does not it perverts the true possibilities. The ideal of the omnicompetent, sovereign citizen is, in my opinion, such a false ideal.
It is unattainable. The pursuit of it is misleading. The failure to
achieve it has produced the current disenchantment.

The individual man does not have opinions on all public affairs.

He does not know how to direct public affairs. He does not know what is happening, why it is happening, what ought to happen. I cannot imagine how he could know, and there is not the least reason for thinking, as mystical democrats have thought, that the compounding of individual ignorances in masses of people can produce a continuous directing force in public affairs....

The need in the Great Society not only for publicity but for uninterrupted publicity is indisputable. But we shall misunderstand the need seriously if we imagine that the purpose of the publication can possibly be the informing of every voter. We live at the mere beginnings of public accounting. Yet the facts far exceed our curiosity.... A few executives here and there ... read them. The rest of us ignore them for the good and sufficient reason that we have other things to do....

Specific opinions give rise to immediate executive acts; to take a job, to do a particular piece of work, to hire or fire, to buy or sell, to stay here or go there, to accept or refuse, to command or obey. General opinions give rise to delegated, indirect, symbolic, intangible results: to a vote, to a resolution, to applause, to criticism, to praise or dispraise, to audiences, circulations, followings, contentment or discontent. The specific opinion may lead to a decision to act within the area where a man has personal jurisdiction; that is, within the limits set by law and custom, his personal power and his personal desire. But general opinions lead only to some sort of expression, such as voting, and do not result in executive acts except in coöperation with the general opinions of large numbers of other persons.

Since the general opinions of large numbers of persons are almost certain to be a vague and confusing medley, action cannot be taken until these opinions have been factored down, canalized, compressed and made uniform.... The making of one general will out of a multitude of general wishes ... consists essentially in the use of symbols which assemble emotions after they have been detached from their ideas. Because feelings are much less specific than ideas, and yet more poignant, the leader is able to make a homogeneous will out of a heterogeneous mass of desires. The process, therefore, by which general opinions are brought to cooperation consists of an intensification of feeling and a degradation of significance. Before a mass of general opinions can eventuate in executive action, the choice is narrowed down to a few alternatives.

The victorious alternative is executed not by the mass but by individuals in control of its energy....

...We must assume, then, that the members of a public will not possess an insider's knowledge of events or share his point of view. They cannot, therefore, construe intent, or appraise the exact circumstances, enter intimately into the minds of the actors or into the details of the argument. They can watch only for coarse signs indicating where their sympathies ought to turn.

We must assume that the members of a public will not anticipate a problem much before its crisis has become obvious, nor stay with the problem long after its crisis is past. They will not know the antecedent events, will not have seen the issue as it developed, will not have thought out or willed a program, and will not be able to predict the consequences of acting on that program. We must assume as a theoretically fixed premise of popular government that normally men as members of a public will not be well informed, continuously interested, nonpartisan, creative or executive. We must assume that a public is inexpert in its curiosity, intermittent, that it discerns only gross distinctions, is slow to be aroused and quickly diverted; that, since it acts by aligning itself, it personalizes whatever it considers, and is interested only when events have been melodramatized as a conflict.

The public will arrive in the middle of the third act and will leave before the last curtain, having stayed just long enough perhaps to decide who is the hero and who the villain of the piece. Yet usually that judgment will necessarily be made apart from the intrinsic merits, on the basis of a sample of behavior, an aspect of a situation, by very rough external evidence....

...The ideal of public opinion is to align men during the crisis of a problem in such a way as to favor the action of those individuals who may be able to compose the crisis. The power to discern those individuals is the end of the effort to educate public opinion....

Public opinion, in this theory, is a reserve of force brought into action during a crisis in public affairs. Though it is itself an irrational force, under favorable institutions, sound leadership and decent training the power of public opinion might be placed at the disposal of those who stood for workable law as against brute assertion. In this theory, public opinion does not make the law. But by canceling lawless power it may establish the condition under which law can be made. It does not reason, investigate, invent, persuade, bargain or settle. But, by holding the aggressive party in check, it may liberate intelligence. Public opinion in its highest ideal will defend those who are prepared to act on their reason against the interrupting force of those who merely assert their will.

That, I think, is the utmost that public opinion can effectively do. With the substance of the problem it can do nothing usually but meddle ignorantly or tyrannically....

For when public opinion attempts to govern directly it is either a failure or a tyranny. It is not able to master the problem intellectually, nor to deal with it except by wholesale impact. The theory of democracy has not recognized this truth because it has identified the functioning of government with the will of the people. This is a fiction. The intricate business of framing laws and of administering them through several hundred thousand public officials is in no sense the act of the voters nor a translation of their will....

Therefore, instead of describing government as an expression of the people's will, it would seem better to say that government consists of a body of officials, some elected, some appointed, who handle professionally, and in the first instance, problems which come to public opinion spasmodically and on appeal. Where the parties directly responsible do not work out an adjustment, public officials intervene. When the officials fail, public opinion is brought to bear on the issue....

This, then, is the ideal of public action which our inquiry suggests. Those who happen in any question to constitute the public should attempt only to create an equilibrium in which settlements can be reached directly and by consent. The burden of carrying on the work of the world, of inventing, creating, executing, of attempting justice, formulating laws and moral codes, of dealing with the technic and the substance, lies not upon public opinion and not upon government but on those who are responsibly concerned as agents in the affair. Where problems arise, the ideal is a settlement by the particular interests involved. They alone know what the trouble really is. No decision by public officials or by commuters reading headlines in the train can usually and in the long run be so good as settlement by consent among the parties at interest. No moral code, no political theory can usually and in the long run be imposed from the heights of public opinion, which will fit a case so well as direct agreement reached where arbitrary power has been disarmed.

It is the function of public opinion to check the use of force in a crisis, so that men, driven to make terms, may live and let live.

60

LEO BOGART
How Opinions Change

From *Silent Politics*

———

TODAY, opinion surveys, professional and amateur, are an integral part of the decision-making in politics as well as business. Presidents John F. Kennedy and Lyndon B. Johnson both took particularly strong interest in the polls. Johnson once told a Gridiron Dinner that Patrick Henry had conducted a poll before he made his "Give Me Liberty or Give Me Death" speech. (The results: 46 percent for liberty, 29 percent for death, and the rest "didn't know.") This show of cynicism masked an extraordinary sensitivity to surveys. Johnson kept in his pocket a chart of his Gallup Poll popularity standing and drew it forth often to impress visitors.

"Why did Johnson retire, do you think?" asks political analyst Walter Lippmann. "He knew that he was beaten. And where did he get that? He got it from polls, a little bit, but mostly he just knew, as a public man very well trained in public affairs—he assumed it. I don't think you can measure everything."

"I don't need any poll," says Franz Xaver Unertl, a German politician. "When I want to know what people are thinking, I go to the toilet during the intermission at a meeting and listen to what they say.". . .

[Yet] few political figures in contemporary America would publicly contest the findings of opinion polls by insisting on the superiority of their own insights. . . .

A ... congressman remarked, "Polling your people with questionnaires is a greater gimmick than mailing out free flower seeds. ... Everyone is flattered to be asked his opinion on great issues. You get credit for putting 'democracy' into action; you advertise yourself. By releasing the compiled results to newspapers you can live off the publicity for weeks. You can use your poll to justify questionable votes later, or even to beg off a dangerous commitment when the House leadership is twisting your arm. And the beautiful thing is you can mail your poll out free!"

A voter poll made by New Jersey Congressman Peter H. B. Frelinghuysen yielded a questionnaire returned by his mother. She wrote, "I can't answer these questions. Why do you think we sent *you* to Washington?" Mothers aside, an official who says or does something that is disapproved by a plurality of respondents in a survey risks the pragmatic political hazard of defending a minority position. He also faces the accusation that he has "defied" public opinion, even though the very exercise of his leadership can shift opinion toward the course of action he supports....

We are rarely aware of opinion which is static and universally held. There is little reason to question the general habit of rising in the morning and retiring at night, though there are many alternative ways for people to cycle their time. We take it for granted that things should be this way, yet if we took a poll on the subject we could no doubt find a minority who prefer other arrangements. (By asking a question we would no longer be taking the matter for granted, and we would be bound to find a substantial number of "night people" who might never previously have thought of themselves as such.)

What distinguishes opinions from faith or from mores is their propensity for change. Views which are fixed and held by everyone cannot be called opinions at all; they are simply part of the social fabric. Heterogeneity and dynamism within a society, challenge from nature or human adversaries, contact and conflict with other cultures—all these produce and reflect differences of outlook, judgment, and individual courses of action. Changes in the forms of social organization, in cultural expression, in the balance of political power, in the generation and distribution of wealth, all express themselves in changes of opinion, just as changes of opinion lead to actions which transform human institutions.

People change their opinions because the world changes around them, because their own place in that world changes, because the people around them change; because they are swept up by social movements....

As an individual seeks continually to reduce the inconsistencies in his own opinions, to align his views with those of the people with whom he identifies, to check his nonconformist instincts against the prevailing sentiments of his group—so his own expressions are constantly subject to change.

Studies of switches in voting preferences in the course of United States electoral campaigns demonstrate that individuals caught in "cross-pressures," who at first lean toward a candidate other than the one who might be predicted from knowledge of their social background, often tend to revert to the predictable choice when they finally enter the voting booth....

...In an increasingly mobile society, cross-pressures inevitably increase, and it is harder for people to remain totally consistent in their political choices....

At any given moment in time, all of us hold tentative, inchoate, half-formed views on a variety of subjects about which we may have never had a conversation and on which we have never had to take a public position. The extent to which we become publicly committed to the opinions we hold varies not only according to the length, vigor, and frequency with which we have expressed them, but also with the informality or formality of the occasion and the number, familiarity, and importance of those present....

One's change of mind on a topic of discussion may follow simply from a change of perception about an individual who advocates a particular position, or from a change in one's relationship to him. Just as our opinions can be swayed by the authority, prestige, esteem, or affection we feel toward people who have established positions on the matter, so our altered view of a significant person may lead us to alter our own opinions on the subjects with which we identify him. We go through such changes in perception constantly in our associations with other human beings.

Getting to know someone better may lead us to value more or less than before the opinions he holds on particular subjects. Knowing a person in a social context when one formerly knew him at work, or vice versa, changes our assessment of his aptitudes and charms. Knowing a former equal as a superior or as a subordinate brings out new dimensions of character which influence our views of the things we think he stands for.

Such changes also work in reverse; our opinions and feelings about people reflect the congruity of their opinions with our own, as well as the stimulation we get from their opinions and the style with which they are expressed. Studies of interpersonal influence show that people tend to be selective in the way they accept or reject the opinions of others; they recognize areas of special knowledge or competence and distinguish the garage attendant's authority on carburetors from his evaluation of school board candidates. But while they tend to accept leadership in many areas from those above them on the social and educational scale, their peers are the primary source of their principal opinions.

Everyone stands in the midst of cross-pressures from the many people with whom we come into personal contact, toward whom we have varying allegiances and hostilities, for whose views we have different degrees of respect. The formulation, hardening, and shattering of our own opinions is inseparable from the daily joys and strains that accompany our relations to others. But just because people's opinions are often rationalizations of their loyalties and loves, this hardly means that change in opinion is outside the domain of reason. We may change our minds because of a change in the situation, but we may also change our minds on an unchanged situation as we learn more about it.

A group of social scientists on the staff of the Rand Corporation, employed on Vietnam studies by the United States military, issued a public statement in the fall of 1969 calling for American withdrawal. They had arrived at this conclusion, in obvious contradiction to their immediate personal and professional self-interest, by their exposure to mounting evidence of the war's toll in Vietnam and its consequences in the United States. Their underlying political beliefs and premises had not changed; but their changed appraisal of the facts led them to what appeared to be an about-face in policy conclusions. One of these scholars, incidentally, was Daniel Ellsberg, whose transformation from militant Hawk to passionate Dove led him two years later to turn a top-secret Pentagon war history over to the press.

In a television interview, Ellsberg reported that the turning point in his opinions came when he read an account of Army Secretary Stanley Resor's decision to quash the trial of Green Berets involved in the killing of a Vietnamese double agent. This made him vividly aware, he said, that members of the administration had been trapped in a web of rationalizations by their need to justify policy, and he suddenly felt an impelling need to break out of this trap himself.

The Rand scholars' 1969 statement was cited at the time by a friend of mine who had been a strong supporter of the Johnson policy on the war and had similarly undergone a change of heart. Now an advocate of an immediate and unconditional withdrawal, he said that the Rand document "really shook me up, because those fellows were working for the government, they were close to the thing, and they changed their minds." He had recently changed jobs, moving to an organization where he led a youthful staff, many of whom held radical views. Queried further about his conversion, he acknowledged, "I couldn't survive a day in my place if I were known as a Hawk." He went on to argue that the Johnson administration had mishandled the war, and cited its failure to bomb the port of Haiphong. "They could have interdicted the flow of Russian supplies and won the war. They were just afraid of hitting a Russian ship. They should have taken the risk."

There seems to be at least a good probability that my friend's susceptibility to persuasion by the Rand statement was enhanced by the intimate social pressures of his new work environment. Yet his associates in the demand for immediate withdrawal inevitably must have started from totally different premises than his very pragmatic ones: he would hardly have shared the conviction that a Communist regime in South Vietnam would be preferable to the rightist military one in power! One may, in short, arrive at the same position by different paths, and with different supporting arguments. Parents whose sons arrive at draft age are apt to undergo striking transformations as well as crystallizations of opinion. Are their more passionate and articulate views less valid than those they held when personal involvement and self-interest were not at stake?

To "change one's mind" may mean painfully reworking an entire system of belief. More often, it means starting with an emotional judgment from which a ready-made structure of rationalizations follows automatically....

In a democratic society that exercises no sanctions against a changed belief, the first acknowledgment of a shift, in the case of the average private citizen, may come in a discussion with intimates; then as the discussion is repeated the expression of the changed opinion loses its tentative character. As it hardens it may acquire the full set of supporting arguments which are readily available through the media or through the spokesmen for those institutions, political parties, sects or other groupings which have an established point of view, or even a vested interest in the matter. The man who has publicly changed his mind inevitably seeks out the evidence which confirms that he had done so wisely, and the very fact that he has changed must become an example to others. . . .

The forces that impel a man to change his tune in public are not always forces that he can keep under control. Greed, power lust, and other forms of base self-interest may lead an individual to dissemble his real thoughts, and reiteration of the statements eventually leads to acceptance and belief. There is often a thin line between opportunism and the urge to survive, or the altruistic wish to have others survive. . . .

On the day in 1939 when Franco's Fascist armies marched into Madrid, the streets were alive with cheering crowds. When these same streets had been full of crowds applauding the troops of the Republic, were the people in the crowds different or were some of them the same? And did either ovation echo the mass sentiments of the moment? Throughout this century this phenomenon has been seen over and over again. . . .

Does this kind of sharp reversal of sides reflect a change of opinion? Does not the phenomenon of sudden political change rather reflect the coexistence of antagonistic systems of thought, alignment, loyalty, and opinion in the minds of the same people? These coexisting systems can reverse their dominance when this seems to be called for by the objective realities of the situation or by immediate short-run personal self-interest.

For the highly political man who recognizes the inconsistencies, weaknesses, gaps, and fallacies in his own intellectual value system, there already exists in embryo the contradictory argument, the antithesis to his thesis.

61

TOM SMITH

The Use of Public Opinion Data by the Attorney General's Commission on Pornography

———

AS PART of its general analysis of social and behavior science research on pornography, the Attorney General's Commission on Pornography examined [1985] public attitudes toward pornography and how they have changed since the report of the earlier Commission on Obscenity and Pornography in 1970....

The Commission's analysis of public opinion on pornography is marred by several factors.... As a general rule for comparing similar, but not identical questions, the Commission (1986:912) formulated the following rule:

[W]here questions were examining similar issues but were not worded the same, only the questions which were more narrowly defined for the 1985 survey were included and any resulting error would be on the side of conservativism.

By this the Commission means that if the 1985 measure would measure lower levels of a behavior or less affect toward an object because of its phrasing compared to the 1970 question *and* the 1985 levels still exceeded the 1970 levels, then the observed difference between 1970 and 1985 would indicate that change had occurred and would underestimate the magnitude of the change. The Commission applies their subset comparison rule to the following questions from the 1970 and 1985 surveys:

1970: During the past year, have you seen or read a magazine which you regarded as pornographic?

1985: Have you *ever* read *Playboy* magazine or *Penthouse* magazine? Please tell me if the following apply to you or not?
Sometimes buy or read magazines like *Playboy*.
Sometimes buy or read magazines like *Hustler*.

The Commission notes that 20% reported reading a "pornographic magazine" in 1970, while "In contrast, two thirds of the
1985 respondents had read *Playboy* or *Penthouse* at some time"
(p. 913). The Commission applies its subset comparison rule and
draws the conclusion that exposure to sexually explicit magazines
increased from 1970 to 1985. They note, "this is a loose comparison, only afforded by the fact that the 1985 question is more specific
in nature and, therefore, a more conservative estimate" (p. 913).

But the Commission is wrong on this point. First, the 1970
question refers to the "past year" while the 1985 question refers to
"ever." The 1985 question clearly covers a longer time span than
the 1970 question and therefore is not a subset of the former and
the subset comparison rule cannot apply. Nor do the separate questions about *Playboy* and *Hustler* provide an appropriate base of
comparison. They refer to a vague "sometimes" rather than the
past year.

Even if the time frames were the same, it is unlikely that the
1985 questions would refer to a subset of the 1970 question. Many
people may not consider "*Playboy* magazine or *Penthouse* magazine"
or even "magazines like *Hustler*" to be pornographic. For example,
in 1970 readers of "magazines like *Playboy*" may well have responded in the negative to the 1970 "pornographic" question.

Also, we cannot be at all sure of the differential impact on
reporting of mentioning specific magazines (*Playboy, Penthouse,
Hustler*) as compared to an abstract categorization such as "a magazine which you regarded as pornographic." It is likely that these
two forms of questioning would trigger different cognitive processing and therefore result in differences in the response distributions.

Overall, for the above reasons, it is impossible to draw any
conclusions on trends in reading sexually explicit magazines from
the above two surveys. . . .

The Commission (1986:932–933) compared questions asked in
1970 and in 1985 regarding perceptions of the effects of sexually
explicit material:

1970: On this card are some opinions about the effects of looking at or reading sexual materials. As I read the letter of each one
please tell me if you think sexual materials *do* or *do not* have these
effects. Let's start with letter a.
a. Sexual materials provide entertainment
b. Sexual materials make people bored with sexual materials

c. Sexual materials provide an outlet for bottled up impulses
d. Sexual materials make people sex crazy
e. Sexual materials give relief to people who have sex problems
f. Sexual materials lead to a breakdown of morals
g. Sexual materials improve sexual relations of some married couples
h. Sexual materials provide information about sex
i. Sexual materials excite people sexually
j. Sexual materials lead people to commit rape
k. Sexual materials lead people to lose respect for women
l. Sexual materials make men want to do new things with their wives

1985: Thinking of sexually explicit magazines, movies, video cassettes, and books, tell me if you believe the following are true or not true:
a. They provide information about sex
b. They lead some people to commit rape or sexual violence
c. They provide a safe outlet for people with sexual problems
d. They lead some people to lose respect for women
e. They can help improve the sex lives of some couples
f. They provide entertainment
g. They lead to a breakdown of morals

In comparing these two questions the Commission felt it was on solid ground, noting that the "1970 and 1985 data in this case were directly comparable since the same categories of effects were used" (p. 932) and the "item choices provided the 1970 respondents were worded in the same way or were reasonably similar" (p. 933). They conclude that several notable changes occurred in the public perceptions of the effects of sexually explicit materials and stress the increases in the percent believing that these materials lead to less respect for women (43% in 1970 to 76% in 1985) and more sexually motivated violence toward women (49% in 1970 to 73% in 1985) (Commission, 1986:933, 937).

But once again the Commission is off the track. First, the 1970 question refers only to "looking at or reading sexual materials" while the 1985 question mentions sexually explicit magazines, movies, video cassettes, and books." It is unclear whether the 1970 question covers both written and audio-video presentations. The inclusion of movies depends on whether respondents interpreted "seeing" as including films. Also, the 1970 question refers to "sexual" materials while the 1985 question uses the term "sexually explicit." In both cases, the 1970 question offers a weaker stimulus, probably not including movies in the minds of many respondents and perhaps also making respondents think of a less provocative range of materials. Second, several of the compared categories differ in notable and biasing ways between surveys. The item on respect for women (k in 1970, and d in 1985) is significantly qualified by the insertion of the word "some." It is obviously much easier to agree to the 1985 wording with this qualification than the 1970 wording that implies "most" or "in general." The item on rape or sexual violence is compromised in a similar fashion. Moreover, the addition of the phrase "or sexual violence" probably makes it easier to agree with the 1985 wording. Since in both cases the question is easier to answer in the affirmative in its 1985 version, it is not possible to interpret the increase in percentages as representing true change for these highlighted questions. Notable changes also occurred in the items about relief from sexual problems (1970e and 1985c) and improved sex relations for couples (1970g and 1985e).

In sum, virtually every over-time comparison that the Commission carried out is extremely suspect, suffering from serious incompatibility of questions and other measurement variations.... The Commission concluded on the basis of its comparison of the 1970 and 1985 surveys that public permissiveness toward pornography had increased over the last decade and a half. The table presents three time series that question that conclusion. From 1973 to 1986 there was no change in the percentages favoring "laws against the distribution of pornography whatever the age," but there was a significant linear decline in the percentages favoring "no laws forbidding the distribution of pornography" (0.5 percentage points per annum). For the period of 1975 to 1982, the question on a government crackdown also shows a complex pattern. Overall, the trend is nonconstant and nonlinear. Support for a crackdown rises rapidly from 1975 to 1977 and then falls between 1977 and 1982. If we look only at the two end points (1975 and 1982), we find a significant decline in disagreement with a government crackdown. This trend is butressed by the significant ($p = .002$) shift between 1976 and 1982 in approval of banning pornographic bookstores from residential shopping areas. In brief, there are at least three time series with identically worded questions on various aspects of government regulation of pornography that the Commis-

TRENDS ON GOVERNMENT REGULATION
OF PORNOGRAPHY

A[1]. Which of these statements comes closest to your feeling about pornography laws?

There should be laws against the distribution of pornography whatever the age.
There should be laws against the distribution of pornography to persons under 18.
There should be no laws forbidding the distribution of pornography.

	1973	1975	1976	1978	1980	1983	1984	1986
Laws whatever the age	41.8%	40.4%	40.0%	43.2%	40.3%	41.1%	40.6%	42.6%
Laws for under 18	47.1	47.6	49.8	48.5	51.4	53.1	54.0	52.8
No laws	9.2	10.7	8.1	7.3	6.1	4.5	4.2	3.6
Don't know	1.9	1.2	2.1	1.0	2.2	1.3	1.2	1.0
(N)	(1498)	(1489)	(1496)	(1531)	(1468)	(1595)	(1464)	(1469)

B[2]. A number of controversial proposals are being discussed these days. I'd like you to tell me for each one whether you strongly agree with it, partially agree with it, or disagree with it.

The government should crack down more on pornography in movies, books, and nightclubs.

	5/1975	1/1976	7/1977	6/1982
Strongly agree	45%	47%	56%	50%
Partially agree	19	22	20	22
Disagree	36	32	24	28
(N)	(1014)	(951)	(1044)	(1010)

C[3]. Here is a list of laws that have been proposed. Would you read down that list and for each tell me whether you would be for or against such a law?

A law banning pornographic book stores in residential shopping areas.

	12/1976	7/1982
For	70%	75%
Against	25	23
Don't know	5	3
(N)	(2000)	(2000)

[1] Source: GSS, NORC. For full details see Davis and Smith (1986).
[2] Source: Data from Yankelovich, Skelly, and White for *Time*. "Don't knows" or "no answers" excluded from the base. Surveys conducted by telephone. For details contact the Roper Center, University of Connecticut.
[3] Source: Data from the Roper Organization. Surveys were conducted in person. For details contact the Roper Center, University of Connecticut.

sion could have drawn upon. If they had done so, they would probably have come to the conclusion that support for government regulation of pornography rose from the mid-seventies to the mid-eighties....

The Commission's analysis of public opinion toward pornography is seriously flawed. It rested on a series of comparisons between variant wordings that provide little useful insight, since true change and measurement variations are completely confounded. While the Commission expressed wariness about the use of variant questions, they repeatedly proceeded to make inappropriate comparisons. Second, their analysis ignored statistical tests for significance. This makes both their subgroup and time-trend analysis problematic. Third, they either were unaware of or ignored relevant time series that employed consistent wordings and would have provided a solid empirical base for their analysis of recent trends. For these and related reasons, the Commission's analysis of public opinion is methodologically unsound and therefore substantively suspect.

62

KARLYN KEENE
EVERETT LADD

Ambivalence

———

...IT's VERY MUCH a love-hate affair. Government is both problem and solution. Civil servants, as individuals, are appreciated, but as a class of people they are held in low esteem. Just as partners in a marriage have ups and downs, the public's mood about government swings. Recently, the positive view of government has been gaining some ground.

But ambivalence remains strong, as it has ever since the public opinion polls began measuring such things. The dichotomy in views was given powerful voice in an October 1986 survey taken by the Roper Organization. Eighty percent of those polled said that cuts in the government's social programs threatened the future of the American Dream. At the same time, 88 percent said that government interference in people's lives posed exactly the same threat.

Modern polls reflect centuries-old traditions in American politics. Our intellectual and philosophical experience differs dramatically from that of most, if not all, industrial democracies. We have no strong, coherent pro-state tradition. Nor do we have a philosophical tradition that can be accurately described as strongly anti-government.

Leaders in both political parties, of course, have often chosen to emphasize one tendency to the exclusion of the other. Polling questions too often require that Americans choose between pro- and anti-government positions—when, in fact, they do not perceive the choice that way.... Where is the public today on "the role of government" questions?

First and foremost, Americans remain intensely ambivalent. Solid majorities told Gallup interviewers this past spring they think the federal government controls too much of our lives. In the same survey for Times Mirror Co., three-quarters said that the federal government should run only those things that cannot be run at the local level. Sixty-three percent agreed that "when something is run by government, it is usually inefficient and wasteful." (See Figure 1 on the next page.)

In another survey, this one commissioned by the Advisory Committee on Intergovernmental Relations (ACIR) in June 1987, two-thirds maintained that the national government wastes the most tax money, while only 14 percent cited state, and 8 percent local, government. This harsh view of the federal government was strongest among professionals, those with some college or a college degree, and those earning over $40,000—groups that are the most knowledgeable about government and the most likely to vote.

At the same time, two-thirds of those polled by Yankelovich Clancy Shulman said they wanted the federal government to be very involved in helping people receive an affordable education (67 percent). Seventy-four percent said the federal government should be very involved in helping people meet their health needs, and 69 percent felt that way about helping the poor. The public appetite for government services and assistance remains robust. (See Figure 1.)

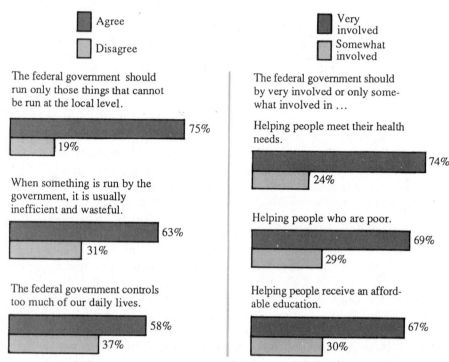

Figure 1 · GOVERNMENT IS TOO BIG ...
BUT SHOULD BE BIGGER

Agree

Disagree

Very involved

Somewhat involved

The federal government should run only those things that cannot be run at the local level.

75%

19%

When something is run by the government, it is usually inefficient and wasteful.

63%

31%

The federal government controls too much of our daily lives.

58%

37%

The federal government should by very involved or only somewhat involved in ...

Helping people meet their health needs.

74%

24%

Helping people who are poor.

69%

29%

Helping people receive an affordable education.

67%

30%

Source: Survey by the Gallup Organization for Times Mirror Company, April 25–May 10, 1987, Survey by *Time*/Yankelovich Clancy Shulman, February 17–18, 1987.

The same tensions are evident surrounding the question of government regulation. In an NBC News/*Wall Street Journal* survey last October, 37 percent said there is too much government regulation of the economy. Only 21 percent said government was not doing enough, while 31 percent put regulation at about the right level. The April survey conducted by Gallup for Times Mirror showed considerable skepticism about governmental regulation, with 55 percent agreeing that "government regulation of business usually does more harm than good."

And yet, another NBC News/*Wall Street Journal* poll in March found majorities favoring more regulation with regard to job health and safety (50 percent) and the environment (61 percent). (See Figure 2.)

Government should be involved in these areas, the public says, because it is needed to check the activities of another big institution, business. Americans simply don't believe that business will do the job.

Mixes of answers like those cited above become a lot less confusing if one keeps in mind that most Americans approach questions of government's role and performance on a case-by-case basis, without any overall organizing notion of the state as inherently helpful or harmful.

A good sense of this emerges from a survey done last spring by the University of Chicago's National Opinion Research Center. Respondents were asked to locate themselves on a scale: choosing one end affirmed that the national government should do everything possible to improve the living standards of all poor Ameri-

Figure 2 · REGULATION IS OFTEN HARMFUL ...
AND WE NEED MORE OF IT

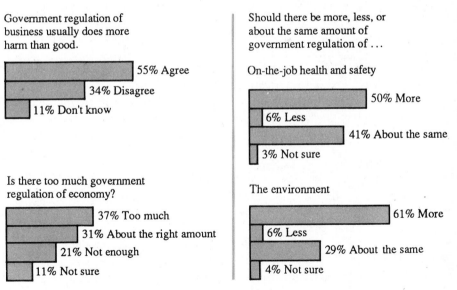

Government regulation of business usually does more harm than good.

55% Agree
34% Disagree
11% Don't know

Is there too much government regulation of economy?

37% Too much
31% About the right amount
21% Not enough
11% Not sure

Should there be more, less, or about the same amount of government regulation of ...

On-the-job health and safety

50% More
6% Less
41% About the same
3% Not sure

The environment

61% More
6% Less
29% About the same
4% Not sure

Source: First question: survey of the Gallup Organization for Times Mirror Company, April 25–May 10, 1987. Other questions: Surveys by NBC News/*Wall Street Journal,* March 15–17; October 25–27, 1987.

cans; selecting the other end was to insist that this is not government's responsibility and that each individual should take care of himself. Twenty-nine percent put themselves in the first camp, 24 percent in the latter. Forty-four percent, however, put themselves at a mid-point on this scale which was labeled, "agree with both positions."

Other surveys show the same thing. Pollsters—and politicians—keep trying to get the public to declare itself as pro- or anti-government. Americans keep responding that they are neither, or both—or, more precisely, that they just don't see why the issue must be cast in such terms.... A presidential candidate who convinces the electorate that he will really cut government back substantially will have convinced them to vote against him. So will a candidate who manages to be perceived as pushing for a significant expansion of government.

Recently, Americans have seemed a bit more concerned about the dangers of expansion than about cuts in government. When NBC News and the *Wall Street Journal* asked likely voters last May whether "electing someone who goes too far in cutting back on the role of government and domestic programs" would worry them more than "electing someone who goes too far in increasing the role of government and domestic spending," 53 percent were more worried about growth of government, while 38 percent worried about contraction of government....

In the 1930s, the Democrats scored political gains by championing new governmental initiatives, such as Social Security, that quickly won widespread approval. Republicans profited in the 1970s when the sense of the problems of big government became as vivid as the view of government as the provider of needed services.

In the 1980s, Americans have not resolved the dichotomy. With the public's backing for government-provided services and its concern about the size of government both firmly ingrained, it is difficult to see how or when any major change might come. Ambivalence has a tenacious grip on the public's mind. The budgeteers on Capitol Hill and in the White House can't hope for guidance from the polls as they attack the government's budget deficits.

Through opinion surveys, the best the public can do is to tell policy-makers when it thinks that Washington has tilted too far toward one of the extremes of its opinion about government. The present balance may seem messy, but it accords with what Americans want—and thus is likely to prove durable. The United States seems to be in for a prolonged period—certainly through the 1988 election—in which the public will refuse to endorse any departure from the governmental status quo.

63

V. O. KEY

Public Opinion and Democratic Politics

From *Public Opinion and American Democracy*

———

THE EXPLORATION of public attitudes is a pursuit of endless fascination—and frustration. Depiction of the distribution of opinions within the public, identification of the qualities of opinion, isolation of the odd and of the obvious correlates of opinion, and ascertainment of the modes of opinion formation are pursuits that excite human curiosity. Yet these endeavors are bootless unless the findings about the preferences, aspirations, and prejudices of the public can be connected with the workings of the governmental system. The nature of that connection has been suggested by the examination of the channels by which governments become aware of public sentiment and the institutions through which opinion finds more or less formal expression.

When all these linkages are treated, the place of public opinion in government has still not been adequately portrayed. The problem of opinion and government needs to be viewed in an even broader context. Consideration of the role of public opinion drives the observer to the more fundamental question of how it is that democratic governments manage to operate at all. Despite endless speculation on that problem, perplexities still exist about what critical circumstances, beliefs, outlooks, faiths, and conditions are conducive to the maintenance of regimes under which public opinion is controlling, at least in principle, and is, in fact, highly influential. . . . Though the preceding analyses did not uncover the secret of the conditions precedent to the practice of democratic politics, they pointed to a major piece of the puzzle that was missing as we sought to assemble the elements that go into the construction of a democratic regime. The significance of that missing piece may be made apparent in an indirect manner. In an earlier day public opinion seemed to be pictured as a mysterious vapor that emanated from the undifferentiated citizenry and in some way or another enveloped the apparatus of government to bring it into conformity with the public will. These weird conceptions, some of which were mentioned in our introductory chapter, passed out of style as the technique of the sample survey permitted the determination, with some accuracy, of the distribution of opinions within the population. Vast areas of ignorance remain in our information about people's opinions and aspirations; nevertheless, a far more revealing map of the gross topography of public opinion can now be drawn than could have been a quarter of a century ago.

Despite their power as instruments for the observation of mass opinion, sampling procedures do not bring within their range elements of the political system basic for the understanding of the role of mass opinion within the system. Repeatedly, as we have sought to explain particular distributions, movements, and qualities of mass opinion, we have had to go beyond the survey data and make assumptions and estimates about the role and behavior of that thin stratum of persons referred to variously as the political elite, the political activists, the leadership echelons, or the influentials. In the normal operation of surveys designed to obtain tests of mass sentiment, so few persons from this activist stratum fall into the sample that they cannot well be differentiated, even in a static description, from those persons less involved politically. The data tell us almost nothing about the dynamic relations between the upper layer of activists and mass opinion. The missing piece of our puzzle is this elite element of the opinion system. . . .

While the ruling classes of a democratic order are in a way invisible because of the vagueness of the lines defining the influentials and the relative ease of entry to their ranks, it is plain that the modal norms and standards of a democratic elite have their peculiarities. Not all persons in leadership echelons have precisely the same basic beliefs; some may even regard the people as a beast. Yet a fairly high concentration prevails around the modal beliefs, even though the definition of those beliefs must be imprecise. Fundamental is a regard for public opinion, a belief that in some way or another it should prevail. Even those who cynically humbug the people make a great show of deference to the populace. The basic doctrine goes further to include a sense of trusteeship for the people generally and an adherence to the basic doctrine that collective efforts should be dedicated to the promotion of mass gains rather than of narrow class advantage; elite elements tethered to narrow group interest have no slack for maneuver to accommodate themselves to mass aspirations. Ultimate expression of these faiths comes in the willingness to abide by the outcome of popular elections. The growth of leadership structures with beliefs including these broad articles of faith is probably accomplished only over a considerable period of time, and then only under auspicious circumstances.

If an elite is not to monopolize power and thereby to bring an end to democratic practices, its rules of the game must include restraints in the exploitation of public opinion. Dimly perceptible are rules of etiquette that limit the kinds of appeals to public opinion that may be properly made. If it is assumed that the public is manipulable at the hands of unscrupulous leadership (as it is under some conditions), the maintenance of a democratic order requires the inculcation in leadership elements of a taboo against appeals that would endanger the existence of democratic practices. Inflammation of the sentiments of a sector of the public disposed to exert the tyranny of an intolerant majority (or minority) would be a means of destruction of a democratic order. Or by the exploitation of latent differences and conflicts within the citizenry it may at times be possible to paralyze a regime as intense hatreds among classes of people come to dominate public affairs. Or by encouraging unrealistic expectations among the people a clique of politicians may rise to power, a position to be kept by repression as disillusionment sets in. In an experienced democracy such tactics may be "unfair" competition among members of the politically active class. In short, certain restraints on political competition help keep competition within tolerable limits. The observation of a few American political campaigns might lead one to the conclusion that there are no restraints on politicians as they attempt to humbug the people. Even so, admonitions ever recur against arousing class against class, against stirring the animosities of religious groups, and against demagoguery in its more extreme forms. American politicians manifest considerable restraint in this regard when they are tested against the standards of behavior of politicians of most of those regimes that have failed in the attempt to establish or maintain democratic practices....

...Certain broad structural or organizational characteristics may need to be maintained among the activists of a democratic order if they are to perform their functions in the system. Fundamental is the absence of sufficient cohesion among the activists to unite them into a single group dedicated to the management of public affairs and public opinion. Solidification of the elite by definition forecloses opportunity for public choice among alternative governing groups and also destroys the mechanism for the unfettered expression of public opinion or of the opinions of the many subpublics....

...Competitive segments of the leadership echelons normally have their roots in interests or opinion blocs within society. A degree of social diversity thus may be, if not a prerequisite, at least helpful in the construction of a leadership appropriate for a democratic regime. A series of independent social bases provide the foundations for a political elite difficult to bring to the state of unification that either prevents the rise of democratic processes or converts them into sham rituals....

Another characteristic may be mentioned as one that, if not a prerequisite to government by public opinion, may profoundly affect the nature of a democratic order. This is the distribution through the social structure of those persons highly active in politics. By various analyses, none founded on completely satisfactory data, we have shown that in the United States the political activists—if we define the term broadly—are scattered through the socio-economic hierarchy. The upper-income and occupational groups, to be sure, contribute disproportionately; nevertheless, individuals of high political participation are sprinkled throughout the lesser occupational strata. Contrast the circumstances when the highly active political stratum coincides with the high socio-economic stratum. Conceivably the winning of consent and the creation of a sense of political participation and of sharing in public affairs may be far simpler when political activists of some degree are spread through all social strata....

Allied with these questions is the matter of access to the wider circles of political leadership and of the recruitment and indoctrination of these political activists. Relative ease of access to the arena of active politics may be a preventive of the rise of intransigent blocs of opinion managed by those denied participation in the regularized processes of politics. In a sense, ease of access is a necessary consequence of the existence of a somewhat fragmented stratum of political activists....

This discussion in terms of leadership echelons, political activists, or elites falls painfully on the ears of democratic romantics. The mystique of democracy has in it no place for ruling classes. As perhaps with all powerful systems of faith, it is vague on the operating details. Yet by their nature governing systems, be they democratic or not, involve a division of social labor. Once that axiom is accepted, the comprehension of democratic practices requires a search for the peculiar characteristics of the political influentials in such an order, for the special conditions under which they work, and for the means by which the people keep them in check. The vagueness of the mystique of democracy is matched by the intricacy of its operating practices. If it is true that those who rule tend sooner or later to prove themselves enemies of the rights of man—and there is something to be said for the validity of this proposition—then any system that restrains that tendency however slightly can excite only awe....

Analytically it is useful to conceive of the structure of a democratic order as consisting of the political activists and the mass of people. Yet this differentiation becomes deceptive unless it is kept in mind that the democratic activists consist of people arranged along a spectrum of political participation and involvement, ranging from those in the highest posts of official leadership to the amateurs who become sufficiently interested to try to round up a few votes for their favorite in the presidential campaign.... It is in the dynamics of the system, the interactions between these strata, that the import of public opinion in democratic orders becomes manifest. Between the activists and the mass there exists a system of communication and interplay so complex as to defy simple description; yet identification of a few major features of that system may aid in our construction of a general conception of democratic processes.

Opinion Dikes

In the interactions between democratic leadership echelons and the mass of people some insight comes from the conception of public opinion as a system of dikes which channel public action or which fix a range of discretion within which government may act or within which debate at official levels may proceed. This conception avoids the error of personifying "public opinion" as an entity that exercises initiative and in some way functions as an operating organism to translate its purposes into governmental action.

In one of their aspects the dikes of opinion have a substantive nature in that they define areas within which day-to-day debate about the course of specific action may occur. Some types of legislative proposals, given the content of general opinion, can scarcely expect to attract serious attention. They depart too far from the general understandings of what is proper. A scheme for public ownership of the automobile industry, for example, would probably be regarded as so far outside the area of legitimate public action that not even the industry would become greatly concerned. On the other hand, other types of questions arise within areas of what we have called permissive consensus. A widespread, if not a unanimous, sentiment prevails that supports action toward some general objective, such as the care of the ill or the mitigation of the economic hazards of the individual. Probably quite commonly mass opinion of a permissive character tends to develop in advance of governmental action in many areas of domestic policy. That opinion grows out of public discussion against the background of the modal aspirations and values of people generally. As it takes shape, the time becomes ripe for action that will be generally acceptable or may even arouse popular acclaim for its authors....

The idea of public opinion as forming a system of dikes which channel action yields a different conception of the place of public opinion than does the notion of a government by public opinion as one in which by some mysterious means a referendum occurs on very major issue. In the former conception the articulation between government and opinion is relatively loose. Parallelism between action and opinion tends not to be precise in matters of detail; it prevails rather with respect to broad purpose. And in the correlation of purpose and action time lags may occur between the crystallization of a sense of mass purpose and its fulfillment in public action. Yet in the long run majority purpose and public action tend to be brought into harmony....

The argument amounts essentially to the position that the masses do not corrupt themselves; if they are corrupt, they have been corrupted. If this hypothesis has a substantial strain of validity, the critical element for the health of a democratic order consists in the beliefs, standards, and competence of those who constitute the influentials, the opinion-leaders, the political activists in the order.

That group, as has been made plain, refuses to define itself with great clarity in the American system; yet analysis after analysis points to its existence. If a democracy tends toward indecision, decay, and disaster, the responsibility rests here, not in the mass of the people.

PART TEN

Interest Groups

YOU WILL REMEMBER that James Madison in *Federalist Paper* 10 saw conflicts rising out of differing social interests as the most persistent problem facing republican government. He argued that complex societies, if they permitted freedom of expression and association, would inevitably generate many constellations of interest or "factions" based on degrees of wealth, the economic division of labor (farming, manufacturing, commerce, and so on), religion, and many other social differences. Although Madison did not go on to discuss how such interests might become actual organizations with permanent membership, staffs, buildings, and budgets, he surely understood the underlying dynamic that would create the modern "Gucci Gulch" of organized groups along Washington's K Street and many other parts of the city. From the beginning, the United States, founded as a liberal society in which individuals were free to define and promote their private interests, was destined to develop a politics particularly hospitable to interest groups. Interest groups have in fact been so prominent in American politics that some political scientists have literally taken them to be the basic stuff of all politics, and have attempted to create a "group theory" of politics. That, we think, was an unfortunate mistake. Interest groups are a legitimate *part* of modern politics, but only a part. To understand the role of groups we need to see them in relation to other parts of the polity.

Our readings in this section emphasize what we think is the most important part of the study of interest groups: group theory, an enterprise that has carried Madison's original concerns right up to the present day. The big question about interest groups is always how they fit into the theory and practice of American democracy. That is what we want to encourage you to think about here. In what respects are interest groups positive contributors to a healthy democratic politics? In what respects do they pose problems? As usual, these are not questions on which theorists easily agree. Madison's perspective, you will remember, is that groups are a necessary part of the process of popular government, but they are also problematic. Even in a relatively simple agrarian, commercial republic one interest or a combination of interests might attempt to oppress others, or enact policies for their own benefit rather than the good of all. Madison hoped that civic virtue and institutional arrangements—mainly the separation of powers and federalism in an extended republic—would prevent this from happening, but many others have doubted that his solution has passed the test of time.

With the coming of industrialization, national corporations and trade associations formed lobbies in Washington and state capitals to advocate their views on public policy. Other groups were quick to follow. With vast economic resources at their disposal, could they not dominate the political process? How could the views of ordinary citizens possibly compete on an equal basis with those of Standard Oil or the Union Pacific Railroad, or with those of many other narrow interests that enjoyed the benefits of organization? These questions have been at the center of interest group theories ever since, and they have continued to generate sharp disagreement among political scientists. Some theorists (generally called "pluralists") have argued that groups compete with one another and create a kind of balance in the system as a whole. Others have countered that interest group politics is inherently biased in favor of the more privileged elements of society. The latter group has generally argued that many real social interests are poorly organized or not organized at all. Unless they are mobilized by political parties in the context of democratic elections, they will not be able to compete effectively with the interests articulated by organized groups.

Our readings begin with Alexis de Tocqueville's prescient account of "the principle of association" in *Democracy in America.* The liberal individualism of American society, he observes, disposes citizens to a new kind of activism. In this new kind of society all manner of associations are formed to promote a multitude of ideas, causes, and interests. The formation of an actual group gives an interest an "exact and explicit form," energizes it, and creates "a separate nation in the midst of the nation, a government within the government.".... Tocqueville, as usual, sees both sides of what he clearly finds a fascinating phenomenon. The principle of association is essential to democracy, but it is a force a people have to learn how to use with some restraint if it is not to weaken government to the point of anarchy.

Our next selection, by E. E. Schattschneider, is taken from *The Semisovereign People,* a modern classic of interest group theory. Against those who took the activity of organized interest groups to be the very heart of democratic politics Schattschneider waged a long scholarly battle. Groups, he argues, are only part of the political process. We need to locate their activity in the larger context of political parties, elections, and formal institutions. Note carefully Schattschneider's distinctions between public and special interests and organized and unorganized interests. Essentially, he is arguing that *organized special-interest groups* can never produce a balanced representation of all groups in society. They are inherently unbalanced in favor of the more privileged social strata, and especially toward the representation of various kinds of business interests. In perhaps his most notable phrase he says that theories of pluralist group balance fail to note that the pluralist "heavenly chorus sings with a strong upper-class accent." A pure pressure group politics will produce policy outcomes skewed toward privilege. Ordinary citizens, many of whom are represented by no organized groups, must look to the wider process of partisan elections for a voice in the political process. Interest group politics and party politics are two different things. Depending on how the "size and scope of conflict" are determined by one or the other, policy outcomes can be very different.

Theodore Lowi, the author of our next reading, has done more than any other writer in recent years to cast doubt on theories of pluralist balance. In *The End of Liberalism,* from which this selection is drawn, he coins the term "interest group liberalism" to conceptualize what he sees as a wrongheaded ideology that makes government little more than a referee of organized group interests. Since this is one of the most difficult readings we present, you will want to study it with special care. Somehow, Lowi argues, we have traded the Madisonian way of looking at interest groups as a necessary evil requiring regulation for one that sees them as tools of democratic government, needing only accommodation. This new view holds that organized groups are representative of all real social interests, in competition with one another, and at the macro level in a kind of balance or equilibrium that amounts to the public interest. Lowi argues that "interest group liberalism" seems to make government benign, but it actually uses the inevitable coercive powers of the state in favor of those who are most effectively organized. The public is shut out of participation, and democratic accountability is lost as organized interests build themselves into privileged relationships with government. The result is not macro-level balance, but systematic advantage for the interests that are most easily organized. Like Schattschneider, Lowi argues that a politics of organized groups alone is a poor substitute for the pursuit of good public policies through the formal institutions of American democracy.

In our final selection Andrew McFarland suggests that elections, public-interest groups and social movements help to check what would otherwise be a strong tendency for narrow, particularistic groups to dominate the political landscape. While he concludes that narrow interests constitute the bulk of organized groups because they are easier to organize, broader interests can be mobilized and are in fact more in evidence in recent years than many "minority faction" theorists predict. Whatever we call them, the black civil rights movement; the consumer, environmental and women's movements; and the Christian fundamentalist movement, have had considerable effect on American politics in the last two decades. It is by no means inevitable that narrow economic interests must dominate. McFarland's point is a good one, but we would remind our readers of Schattschneider's argument that wider social interests must look to the electoral process to expand the size and scope of political conflicts. All of these "public" or wide social interests have taken hold because they engaged the interest of partisan electoral politicians, who saw that they could win votes. Schattschneider's main argument was always that electoral politics was superior to interest group politics as a means of achieving democracy. With that judgment we agree.

64

ALEXIS DE TOCQUEVILLE
Political Associations

From *Democracy in America*

———

IN NO COUNTRY IN the world has the principle of association been more successfully used, or applied to a greater multitude of objects, than in America. Besides the permanent associations, which are established by law, under the names of townships, cities, and counties, a vast number of others are formed and maintained by the agency of private individuals.

The citizen of the United States is taught from infancy to rely upon his own exertions, in order to resist the evils and the difficulties of life; he looks upon the social authority with an eye of mistrust and anxiety, and he claims its assistance only when he is unable to do without it. This habit may be traced even in the schools, where the children in their games are wont to submit to rules which they have themselves established, and to punish misdemeanors which they have themselves defined. The same spirit pervades every act of social life. If a stoppage occurs in a thoroughfare, and the circulation of vehicles is hindered, the neighbors immediately form themselves into a deliberative body; and this extemporaneous assembly gives rise to an executive power, which remedies the inconvenience before anybody has thought of recurring to a pre-existing authority superior to that of the persons immediately concerned. If some public pleasure is concerned, an association is formed to give more splendor and regularity to the entertainment. Societies are formed to resist evils which are exclusively of a moral nature, as to diminish the vice of intemperance. In the United States, associations are established to promote the public safety, commerce, industry, morality, and religion. There is no end which the human will despairs of attaining through the combined power of individuals united into a society....

An association consists simply in the public assent which a number of individuals give to certain doctrines; and in the engagement which they contract to promote in a certain manner the spread of those doctrines. The right of associating with such views is very analogous to the liberty of unlicensed printing; but societies thus formed possess more authority than the press. When an opinion is represented by a society, it necessarily assumes a more exact and explicit form. It numbers its partisans, and compromises them in its cause: they, on the other hand, become acquainted with each other, and their zeal is increased by their number. An association unites into one channel the efforts of diverging minds, and urges them vigorously towards the one end which it clearly points out.

The second degree in the exercise of the right of association is the power of meeting. When an association is allowed to establish centres of action at certain important points in the country, its activity is increased, and its influence extended. Men have the opportunity of seeing each other; means of execution are combined; and opinions are maintained with a warmth and energy which written language can never attain. Lastly, in the exercise of the right of political association, there is a third degree: the partisans of an opinion may unite in electoral bodies, and choose delegates to represent them in a central assembly. This is, properly speaking, the application of the representative system to a party.

Thus, in the first instance, a society is formed between individuals professing the same opinion, and the tie which keeps it together is of a purely intellectual nature. In the second case, small assemblies are formed, which represent only a fraction of the party. Lastly, in the third case, they constitute, as it were, a separate nation in the midst of the nation, a government within the government. . . .

It cannot be denied that the unrestrained liberty of association for political purposes is the privilege which a people is longest in learning how to exercise. If it does not throw the nation into anarchy, it perpetually augments the chances of that calamity. On one point, however, this perilous liberty offers a security against dangers of another kind; in countries where associations are free, secret societies are unknown. In America, there are factions, but no conspiracies.

The most natural privilege of man, next to the right of acting for himself, is that of combining his exertions with those of his fellow-creatures, and of acting in common with them. The right of association therefore appears to me almost as inalienable in its nature as the right of personal liberty.

65

E. E. SCHATTSCHNEIDER
The Scope and Bias of the Pressure System

From *The Semisovereign People*

———

More than any other system American politics provides the raw materials for testing the organizational assumptions of two contrasting kinds of politics, *pressure politics* and *party politics*. The concepts that underlie these forms of politics constitute the raw stuff of a general theory of political action. The basic issue between the two patterns of organization is one of size and scope of conflict; pressure groups are small-scale organizations while political parties are very large-scale organizations. One need not be surprised, therefore, that the partisans of large-scale and small-scale organizations differ passionately, because the outcome of the political game depends on the scale on which it is played.

To understand the controversy about the scale of political organization it is necessary first to take a look at some theories about interest-group politics. Pressure groups have played a remarkable role in American politics, but they have played an even more remarkable role in American political theory. Considering the political condition of the country in the first third of the twentieth century, it was probably inevitable that the discussion of special interest pressure groups should lead to development of "group" theories of politics in which an attempt is made to explain everything in terms of group activity, i.e., an attempt to formulate a universal group theory. Since one of the best ways to test an idea is to ride it into the ground, political theory has unquestionably been improved by the heroic attempt to create a political universe revolving about the group. Now that we have a number of drastic statements of the group theory of politics pushed to a great extreme, we ought to be able to see what the limitations of the idea are....

One difficulty running through the literature of the subject results from the attempt to explain *everything* in terms of the group theory. On general grounds it would be remarkable indeed if a single hypothesis explained everything about so complex a subject as American politics. Other difficulties have grown out of the fact that group concepts have been stated in terms so universal that the subject seems to have no shape or form.

The question is: Are pressure groups the universal basic ingredient of all political situations, and do they explain everything? To answer this question it is necessary to review a bit of rudimentary political theory.

Two modest reservations might be made merely to test the group dogma. We might clarify our ideas if (1) we explore more fully the possibility of making a distinction between public interest groups and special-interest groups and (2) if we distinguished between organized and unorganized groups....

As a matter of fact, the distinction between *public* and *private* interests is a thoroughly respectable one; it is one of the oldest known to political theory. In the literature of the subject the public interest refers to general or common interests shared by all or by substantially all members of the community. Presumably no community exists unless there is some kind of community of interests, just as there is no nation without some notion of national interests. If it is really impossible to distinguish between private and public interests the group theorists have produced a revolution in political thought so great that it is impossible to foresee its consequences. For this reason the distinction ought to be explored with great care.

At a time when nationalism is described as one of the most dynamic forces in the world, it should not be difficult to understand that national interests actually do exist. It is necessary only to consider the proportion of the American budget devoted to national defense to realize that the common interest in national survival is a great one. Measured in dollars this interest is one of the biggest things in the world. Moreover, it is difficult to describe this interest as special. The diet on which the American leviathan feeds is something more than a jungle of disparate special interests. In the literature of democratic theory the body of common agreement found in the community is known as the "consensus" without which it is believed that no democratic system can survive.

The reality of the common interest is suggested by demonstrated capacity of the community to survive. There must be something that holds people together.

In contrast with the common interests are the special interests. The implication of this term is that these are interests shared by only a few people or a fraction of the community; they *exclude* others and may be *adverse* to them. A special interest is exclusive in about the same way as private property is exclusive. In a complex society it is not surprising that there are some interests that are shared by all or substantially all members of the community and some interests that are not shared so widely. The distinction is useful precisely because conflicting claims are made by people about the nature of their interests in controversial matters....

Is it possible to distinguish between the "interests" of the members of the National Association of Manufacturers and the members of the American League to Abolish Capital Punishment? The facts in the two cases are not identical. First, *the members of the A.L.A.C.P. obviously do not expect to be hanged.* The membership of the A.L.A.C.P. is not restricted to persons under indictment for murder or in jeopardy of the extreme penalty. *Anybody* can join A.L.A.C.P. Its members oppose capital punishment although they are not personally likely to benefit by the policy they advocate. The inference is therefore that the interest of the A.L.A.C.P. is not adverse, exclusive or special. It is not like the interest of the Petroleum Institute in depletion allowances....

We can now examine the second distinction, the distinction between organized and unorganized groups. The question here is not whether the distinction can be made but whether or not it is worth making. Organization has been described as "merely a stage or degree of interaction" in the development of a group.

The proposition is a good one, but what conclusions do we draw from it? We do not dispose of the matter by calling the distinction between organized and unorganized groups a "mere" difference of degree because some of the greatest differences in the world are differences of degree. As far as special-interest politics is concerned the implication to be avoided is that a few workmen who habitually stop at a corner saloon for a glass of beer are essentially the same as the United States Army because the difference between them is merely one of degree. At this point we have a distinction that makes a difference....

If we are able, therefore, to distinguish between public and private interests and between organized and unorganized groups we have marked out the major boundaries of the subject; *we have given the subject shape and scope.* We are now in a position to attempt to define the area we want to explore. Having cut the pie into four pieces, we can now appropriate the piece we want and leave the rest to someone else. For a multitude of reasons *the most likely field of study is that of the organized, special-interest groups.* The advantage of concentrating on organized groups is that they are known, identifiable and recognizable. The advantage of concentrating on special-interest groups is that they have one important characteristic in common: they are all exclusive. This piece of the pie (the organized special-interest groups) we shall call the *pressure system.* The pressure system has boundaries we can define; we can fix its scope and make an attempt to estimate its bias....

The organized groups listed in the various directories (such as *National Associations of the United States,* published at intervals by the United States Department of Commerce) and specialty yearbooks, registers, etc., and the *Lobby Index,* published by the United States House of Representatives, probably include the bulk of the organizations in the pressure system. All compilations are incomplete, but these are extensive enough to provide us with some basis for estimating the scope of the system....

When lists of these organizations are examined, the fact that strikes the student most forcibly is that *the system is very small.* The range of organized, identifiable, known groups is amazingly narrow; there is nothing remotely universal about it. There is a tendency on the part of the publishers of directories of associations to place an undue emphasis on business organizations, an emphasis that is almost inevitable because the business community is by a wide margin the most highly organized segment of society. Publishers doubtless tend also to reflect public demand for information. Nevertheless, the dominance of business groups in the pressure system is so marked that it probably cannot be explained away as an accident of the publishing industry....

The business or upper-class bias of the pressure system shows up everywhere. Businessmen are four or five times as likely to write to their congressmen as manual laborers are. College graduates are far more apt to write to their congressmen than people in the lowest educational category are....

Broadly, the pressure system has an upper-class bias. There is overwhelming evidence that participation in voluntary organizations is related to upper social and economic status; the rate of participation is much higher in the upper strata than it is elsewhere....

The bias of the system is shown by the fact that *even nonbusiness organizations reflect an upper-class tendency....*

The class bias of associational activity gives meaning to the limited scope of the pressure system, because *scope and bias are aspects of the same tendency.* The data raise a serious question about the validity of the proposition that special-interest groups are a universal form of political organization reflecting *all* interests. As a matter of fact, to suppose that everyone participates in pressure-group activity and that all interests get themselves organized in the pressure system is to destroy the meaning of this form of politics. The pressure system makes sense only as the political instrument of a segment of the community. It gets results by being selective and biased; *if everybody got into the act the unique advantages of this form of organization would be destroyed, for it is possible that if all interests could be mobilized the result would be a stalemate.*

Special-interest organizations are most easily formed when they deal with small numbers of individuals who are acutely aware of their exclusive interests. To describe the conditions of pressure-group organization in this way is, however, to say that it is primarily a business phenomenon. Aside from a few very large organizations (the churches, organized labor, farm organizations, and veterans' organizations) the residue is a small segment of the population. *Pressure politics is essentially the politics of small groups.*

The vice of the groupist theory is that it conceals the most significant aspects of the system. The flaw in the pluralist heaven is that the heavenly chorus sings with a strong upper-class accent. Probably about 90 percent of the people cannot get into the pressure system.

The notion that the pressure system is automatically representative of the whole community is a myth fostered by the universalizing tendency of modern group theories. *Pressure politics is a selective process* ill designed to serve diffuse interests. The system is skewed, loaded and unbalanced in favor of a fraction of a minority....

The competing claims of pressure groups and political parties for the loyalty of the American public revolve about the difference between the results likely to be achieved by small-scale and large-scale political organization. Inevitably, the outcome of pressure politics and party politics will be vastly different.

66

THEODORE LOWI

Interest-Group Liberalism

From *The End of Liberalism*

———

THE MOST clinically accurate term to capture the American variant ... is *interest-group liberalism*. It is liberalism because it is optimistic about government, expects to use government in a positive and expansive role, is motivated by the highest sentiments, and possesses a strong faith that what is good for government is good for the society. It is interest-group liberalism because it sees as both necessary and good a policy agenda that is accessible to all organized interests and makes no independent judgment of their claims. It is interest-group liberalism because it defines the public interest as a result of the amalgamation of various claims. A brief sketch of the working model of interest-group liberalism turns out to be a vulgarized version of the pluralist model of modern political science: (1) Organized interests are homogeneous and easy to define. Any duly elected representative of any interest is taken as an accurate representative of each and every member. (2) Organized interests emerge in every sector of our lives and adequately represent most of those sectors, so that one organized group can be found effectively answering and checking some other organized group as it seeks to prosecute its claims against society. And (3) the role of government is one of insuring access to the most effectively organized, and of ratifying the agreements and adjustments worked out among the competing leaders.

This last assumption is supposed to be a statement of how a democracy works and how it ought to work. Taken together, these assumptions amount to little more than the appropriation of the Adam Smith "hidden hand" model for politics, where the group is the entrepreneur and the equilibrium is not lowest price but the public interest....

...Interest-group liberalism...had the approval of political scientists because it could deal with so many of the realities of power. It was further appealing because large interest groups and large memberships could be taken virtually as popular rule in modern dress.... And it fit the needs of corporate leaders, union leaders, and government officials desperately searching for support as they were losing communal attachments to their constituencies....

A[n].... increasingly important positive appeal of interest-group liberalism is that it helps create the sense that power need not be power at all, control need not be control, and government need not be coercive. If sovereignty is parceled out among groups, then who is out anything? As a major *Fortune* editor enthusiastically put it, government power, group power, and individual power may go up simultaneously. If the groups to be controlled control the controls, then "to administer does not always mean to rule." The inequality of power and the awesome coerciveness of government are always gnawing problems in a democratic culture....

In sum, leaders in modern, consensual democracies are ambivalent about government. Government is obviously the most efficacious way of achieving good purposes, but alas, it is efficacious because it is coercive. To live with that ambivalence, modern policy-makers have fallen prey to the belief that public policy involves merely the identification of the problems toward which government ought to be aimed. It pretends that through "pluralism," "countervailing power," "creative federalism," "partnership," and "participatory democracy" the unsentimental business of coercion need not be involved and that unsentimental decisions about how to employ coercion need not really be made at all. Stated in the extreme, the policies of interest-group liberalism are end-oriented but ultimately self-defeating. Few standards of implementation, if any, accompany delegations of power. The requirement of standards has been replaced by the requirement of participation. The requirement of law has been replaced by the requirement of contingency. As a result, the ends of interest-group liberalism are nothing more than sentiments and therefore not really ends at all....

...Interest-group liberals have the pluralist paradigm in common and its influence on the policies of the modern state has been very large and very consistent. Practices of government are likely to change only if there is a serious reexamination of the theoretical components of the public philosophy and if that reexamination reveals basic flaws in the theory. Because they guide so much of the analysis of succeeding chapters, contentions about the fundamental flaws in the theory underlying interest-group liberals ought to be made explicit here at the outset. Among the many charges to be made against pluralism, the following three probably best anticipate the analysis to come.

1. The pluralist component has badly served liberalism by propagating the faith that a system built primarily upon groups and bargaining is self-corrective. Some parts of this faith are false, some have never been tested one way or the other, and others can be confirmed only under very special conditions. For example, there is the faulty assumption that groups have other groups to confront in some kind of competition. Another very weak assumption is that people have more than one salient group, that their multiple or overlapping memberships will insure competition, and at the same time will keep competition from becoming too intense. This concept of overlapping membership is also supposed to prove the voluntary character of groups, since it reassures us that even though one group may be highly undemocratic, people can vote with their feet by moving over to some other group to represent their interests. Another assumption that has become an important liberal myth is that when competition between or among groups takes place the results yield a public interest or some other ideal result. As has already been observed, this assumption was borrowed from laissez-faire economists and has even less probability of being borne out in the political system. One of the major Keynesian criticisms of market theory is that even if pure competition among factors of supply and demand did yield an equilibrium, the equilibrium could be at something far less than the ideal of full employment at reasonable prices. Pure pluralist competition, similarly, might produce political equilibrium, but the experience of recent years shows that it occurs at something far below an acceptable level of legitimacy, or access, or equality, or innovation, or any other valued political commodity.

2. Pluralist theory is also comparable to laissez-faire economics in the extent to which it is unable to come to terms with the problem of imperfect competition. When a program is set up in a specialized agency, the number of organized interest groups surrounding it tends to be reduced, reduced precisely to those groups and factions to whom the specialization is most salient. That almost

immediately transforms the situation from one of potential competition to one of potential oligopoly. As in the economic marketplace, political groups surrounding an agency ultimately learn that
direct confrontation leads to net loss for all the competitors. Rather
than countervailing power there is more likely to be accommodating power. Most observers and practitioners continue to hold on
to the notion of group competition despite their own recognition
that it is far from a natural state. Galbraith was early to recognize
this but is by no means alone is his position that "the support of
countervailing power has become in modern times perhaps the
major peace-time function of the Federal government." Group
competition in Congress and around agencies is not much of a
theory if it requires constant central government support.

3. The pluralist paradigm depends upon an idealized conception
of the group. Laissez-faire economics may have idealized the enterprise and the entrepreneur but never more than the degree to which
the pluralist sentimentalizes the group, the group member, and
the interests. We have already noted the contrast between the traditional American or Madisonian definition of the group as adverse
to the aggregate interests of the community with the modern view
that groups are basically good things unless they break the law or
the rules of the game. To the Madisonian, groups were a necessary
evil much in need of regulation. To the modern pluralist, groups
are good, requiring only accommodation. Madison went beyond
his definition of the group to a position that "the regulation of
these various interfering interests forms the principal task of modern legislation." This is a far cry from the sentimentality behind
such notions as "supportive countervailing power," "group representation in the interior processes of...," and "maximum feasible
participation."...

The problems of pluralist theory are of more than academic
interest. They are directly and indirectly responsible for some of
the most costly attributes of modern government: (1) the atrophy
of institutions of popular control; (2) the maintenance of old and
the creation of new structures of privilege; and (3) conservatism in
several senses of the word. These three hypotheses do not exhaust
the possibilities but are best suited to introduce the analysis of
policies and programs in the next six chapters.

1. In *The Public Philosophy*, Walter Lippmann was rightfully
concerned over the "derangement of power" whereby modern
democracies tend first toward unchecked elective leadership and
then toward drainage of public authority from elective leaders

down into the constituencies. However, Lippmann erred if he thought of constituents as only voting constituencies. Drainage has tended toward "support-group constituencies," and with special consequences. Parceling out policy-making power to the most interested parties tends strongly to destroy political responsibility. A program split off with a special imperium to govern itself is not merely an administrative unit. It is a structure of power with impressive capacities to resist central political control.

When conflict of interest is made a principle of government rather than a criminal act, programs based upon such a principle cut out all of that part of the mass of people who are not specifically organized around values salient to the goals of that program. The people are shut out at the most creative phase of policy-making— where the problem is first defined. The public is shut out also at the phase of accountability because in theory there is enough accountability to the immediate surrounding interests. In fact, presidents and congressional committees are most likely to investigate an agency when a complaint is brought to them by one of the most interested organizations. As a further consequence, the accountability we do get is functional rather than substantive; and this involves questions of equity, balance, and equilibrium, to the exclusion of questions of the overall social policy and whether or not the program should be maintained at all. It also means accountability to experts first and amateurs last; and an expert is a person trained and skilled in the mysteries and technologies of that particular program.

Finally, in addition to the natural tendencies, there tends also to be a self-conscious conspiracy to shut out the public. One meaningful illustration, precisely because it is such an absurd extreme, is found in the French system of interest representation in the Fourth Republic. As the Communist-controlled union, the Confédération Générale du Travail (CGT), intensified its participation in postwar French government, it was able to influence representatives of interests other than employees. In a desperate effort to insure that the interests represented on the various boards were separated and competitive, the government issued a decree that "each member of the board must be *independent of the interests he is not representing.*"

2. Programs following the principles of interest-group liberalism tend to create and maintain privilege; and it is a type of privilege particularly hard to bear or combat because it is touched with a symbolism of the state. Interest-group liberalism is not merely

pluralism but is *sponsored* pluralism. Pluralists ease our consciences about the privileges of organized groups by characterizing them as representative and by responding to their "iron law of oligarchy" by arguing that oligarchy is simply a negative name for organization. Our consciences were already supposed to be partly reassured by the notion of "overlapping memberships." But however true it may be that overlapping memberships exist and that oligarchy is simply a way of leading people efficiently toward their interests, the value of these characteristics changes entirely when they are taken from the context of politics and put into the context of pluralistic government. The American Farm Bureau Federation is no "voluntary association" if it is a legitimate functionary within the extension system. Such tightly knit corporate groups as the National Association of Home Builders (NAHB), the National Association of Real Estate Boards (NAREB), the National Association for the Advancement of Colored People (NAACP), or the National Association of Manufacturers (NAM) or American Federation of Labor-Congress of Industrial Organizations (AFL-CIO) are no ordinary lobbies after they become part of the "interior processes" of policy formation. Even in the War on Poverty, one can only appreciate the effort to organize the poor by going back and pondering the story and characters in *The Three Penny Opera*. The "Peachum factor" in public affairs may be best personified in Sargent Shriver and his strenuous efforts to get the poor housed in some kind of group before their representation was to begin....

The more clear and legitimized the representation of a group or its leaders in policy formation, the less voluntary its membership in that group and the more necessary is loyalty to its leadership for people who share the interests in question. And, the more widespread the policies of recognizing and sponsoring organized interest, the more hierarchy is introduced into our society. It is a well-recognized and widely appreciated function of formal groups in modern society to provide much of the necessary everyday social control. However, when the very thought processes behind public policy are geared toward these groups they are bound to take on the involuntary character of *public* control.

3. The conservative tendencies of interest-group liberalism can already be seen in the two foregoing objections: weakening of popular control and support of privilege. A third dimension of conservatism, stressed here separately, is the simple conservatism of resistance to change. David Truman, who has certainly not been a strong critic of self-government by interest groups, has, all the

same, provided about the best statement of the general tendency of established agency-group relationships to be "highly resistant to disturbance":

> New and expanded functions are easily accommodated, provided they develop and operate through existing channels of influence and do not tend to alter the relative importance of those influences. Disturbing changes are those that modify either the content or the relative strength of the component forces operating through an administrative agency. In the face of such changes, or the threat of them, the "old line" agency is highly inflexible.

If this already is a tendency in a pluralistic system, then agency-group relationships must be all the more inflexible to the extent that the relationship is official and legitimate.

Innumerable illustrations will crop up throughout the book. They will be found in new areas of so-called social policy, such as the practice early in the War on Poverty to co-opt neighborhood leaders, thereby creating more privilege than alleviating poverty.... Old and established groups doing good works naturally look fearfully upon the emergence of competing, perhaps hostile, new groups. That is an acceptable and healthy part of the political game—until the competition between them is a question of "who shall be the government?" At that point conservatism becomes a matter of survival for each group, and a direct threat to the public interest. Ultimately this threat will be recognized.

67

ANDREW McFARLAND

Public Interest Lobbies vs. Minority Faction

———

IN THE CLASSIC Federalist Number 10, James Madison directed the attention of Americans to the need to control the evils of "majority faction."* In Madison's words: "By a faction I under-

---

* Madison's *Federalist Paper* 10 is presented as selection 11.—EDS.

stand a number of citizens, whether amounting to a majority or minority of the whole, who are united and actuated by some common impulse of passion, or of interest, adverse to the rights of other citizens, or to the permanent and aggregate interests of the community." He noted that a majority faction was the greater problem for a republic because a minority faction could be defeated in voting....

At a time when almost everyone lived in a rural or a small-town environment, and most political issues were local issues, it made sense to say that minority factions could be controlled by "regular vote" of town meetings, state legislatures, town selectmen, or boards of burgesses. Modern government, however, is organized on a much larger scale. Most important governmental decision making involves activity by the national government....

What, then, is to prevent minority factions from seizing control of single pieces of this vast network of policy making and administration? Certainly most observers would doubt that "regular vote" remains a sufficient remedy to factional control of particular public policies....

From the perspective of the twentieth century, it is evident that Madison's observations about minority faction need to be supplemented by additional theory. In 1965, Mancur Olson published an especially important volume, *The Logic of Collective Action,* which argued that minorities are more easily organized into interest groups than majorities, and hence that minorities may frequently prevail in government....

One of Olson's arguments focuses upon the "organization costs" of assembling a large number of constituent units (one hundred or more people, businesses, local governments, etc.) into a cohesive, long-lasting interest group. Olson presumes that individuals, either acting for their own benefit or as decision makers for a business or other group, will act rationally, meaning that persons will make a cost-benefit calculation as to whether to organize or to contribute to an interest group. Given this circumstance, why would anyone spend the time and money to organize a large number of units into an interest group? The existence of an environmentalist or a consumer lobby might save an individual money, but not if that individual must suspend his economic activity and devote full time to organizing it....

Assuming such a "logic of collective action," it seems safe to predict that a higher percentage of small interest groups will be organized than will groups comprising a large number of units. In the case of industries having only a small number of corporations, for example, it is often in the economic interest of one corporation to organize a lobby. In the automobile manufacturing sector, General Motors could easily profit from an investment of one or two million dollars a year to support a lobby in Washington. Furthermore, General Motors would have little trouble persuading the other American auto manufacturers—Ford, Chrysler, American Motors, and Volkswagen of America—to contribute to the interest group....

A corollary to Olson's theory on organizational costs is known as "the free-rider problem." Even assuming that a political entrepreneur has established an interest group with a large membership, Olson maintains that ordinarily such a group will collapse if individual members engage in economic, cost-benefit reasoning in deciding whether to contribute to the group. Interest groups, when they successfully lobby governments, produce collective benefits for the members of the group. In other words, a governmental policy favorable to the group—such as a tax break or a subsidy for the group's product—usually will benefit all its members, whether or not they are actually contributors....

Olson maintains that a rational individual in such situations ordinarily will *not* contribute to the group and instead will become a "free rider," climbing on board the train without paying for a ticket. And, sooner or later, everyone will neglect to pay, the train will "run out of steam," and the group will get nowhere.

In Olson's view, large groups are particularly prone to the organizational problem posed by free riders. Everyone thinks that others contribute to maintain the group; no one knows who contributes and who does not. The logic of small groups is a different one, according to Olson. If, for instance, there are 25 or fewer individuals or businesses in a group, it is possible to know who are contributors and who are free riders. The contributors then are in a position to put social pressure on the free riders to pull their own weight and on each other to continue contributing. Consequently, Olson argues, large-group organizations will tend to decay, while small-group organizations will maintain themselves. Small groups will therefore defeat large ones in conflicts over legislation and administration of laws, because the small groups will be better organized. In Madison's terminology, Olson's work is a theory of the predominance of minority faction in government. Such a theory has been elaborated by the thought of other political scientists who emphasize the significance of minority factions in American politics....

The late E. E. Schattschneider was a minority faction theorist with great influence over other political scientists, particularly in the 1950s and 1960s....

Another important minority faction theorist was Grant McConnell, whose views were similar to Schattschneider's....

A third minority faction theorist is Theodore Lowi, Jr., one of the most influential political scientists during the 1970s....

Olson provides a convincing set of reasons why we may expect small groups and particularistic interests to be better organized than majorities in some areas of political action. The three other writers describe specific mechanisms through which minority factions gain and maintain control over particular public policies: Schattschneider, narrowing of the scope of conflict; McConnell, decentralizing to the advantage of local power groups; and Lowi, the passage of ambiguous statutes....

Taken together, the works of Olson, Schattschneider, McConnell, and Lowi also provide a good start for building a coherent theory stating that American government is splintered into hundreds of separable arenas of politics and policy making....

The minority faction theorists tend to see American government as a collection of such coalitions, each controlling its own "turf," public policy making in a particular area of economic interest. This situation might be called "a confederation of oligarchies," hundreds of specific minority coalitions in uneasy coexistence, striving to prevent the intrusion of strong, central authority into their discrete jurisdictions....

The idea of American government as a confederation of oligarchies is persuasive but does not go unchallenged. While minority faction theorists tend to ignore their impact, elections do seem to make some difference in public administration. Most persons would agree that the policies followed by the Departments of the Interior, Justice, Energy, and Education under President Ronald Reagan were considerably different from those followed by Jimmy Carter's administration. If there has been rule by special interest coalitions in these areas, at the very least one must admit that the agency heads, interest groups, and congressmen in the coalitions can be changed by the outcome of a presidential election. One might also assume that the most powerful minority coalitions are those protecting the interests of the largest corporations. Yet such corporations do not always get their way. Since 1965, for instance, the American automobile industry has been forced to accept standards for fuel usage, air pollution, and safety; the financially hard pressed steel industry and the coal-burning electric utilities have been forced to spend billions of dollars for air pollution equipment; and the airlines have been forced into a new "deregulated" system of pricing and routing. Other challenges to minority faction include public interest lobbies that exist to promote the causes of environmental preservation, consumer rights, and good government. Union lobbyists sometimes are able to thwart corporate-government coalitions in areas such as National Labor Relations Board regulations on the organization and conduct of unions.

Such examples indicate that there are limitations to the confederation of oligarchies idea, and that these limitations might be codified in another category of theories about interest groups....

...Middle-class based public interest groups are an important factor in the most neglected of these theories—the significance of social movements in American politics....

In the 1950s, political scientist David Truman and other "group theorists" argued that the panoply of organized interests was a roughly accurate measure of the interests held by individuals. Group theorists believed that (1) people know their own interests; (2) they are able without inordinate difficulty to organize these interests into political groups; (3) American political institutions provide numerous opportunities for organized interest groups to influence the political process; (4) the resulting public policy is usually representative, because it reflects the balance of power among organized interests, whose relative strength in turn is a measure of the relative incidence of interests among individual citizens.

These assumptions constitute a large part of the "interest-group liberalism" so roundly denounced by Professor Lowi. Moreover, these group theory propositions are now in disrepute, largely because of their refutation in Olson's *The Logic of Collective Action*. But group theory cannot be totally invalidated. Political groups have been organized to represent diffuse but widely shared interests such as protecting the consumer, maintaining a clean environment, and combatting corruption in government. Such groups include the "public interest groups," supported by a middle-class constituency.

Social Movements

Social movements are another phenomenon inconsistent with the minority faction argument. By "social movement," one might denote recent political developments such as the black civil rights movement, the women's movement, environmentalism, consumerism, the peace movement of the 1960s, or the conservative activism of Christian fundamentalism and the tax revolt of 1977–1980. While the term "social movement" is widely used, it is difficult to define. . . .

For our purposes, a social movement is characterized by activity directed toward changing institutions and behaviors of importance to a society, as opposed to peripheral institutions or routine behaviors. Another defining feature of a social movement is its mode of political expression, often consisting of unconventional tactics and behavior, such as civil disobedience, organizing demonstrations, breaking up into small groups for the purpose of "consciousness raising," and even the threat or actual use of violence.

Writers such as McConnell, Schattschneider, and Olson published their works before the impact of the black civil rights movement and the other movements of the 1960s. Writing later, Lowi ascribed some political importance to social movements, but stressed their imminent bureaucratization, increasing control by organizational oligarchies, and acceptance of the status quo. Nonetheless, social movements are sometimes an important part of American politics and have been associated with major public policy changes such as federal initiation of civil rights laws and federal regulation of pollution. . . .

Intuitively, it seems that the impact of the black civil rights movement, the women's movement, and the various public interest movements (environmentalism, consumerism, government reform) have been quite significant in changing American society and politics since the 1950s. Moreover, social movements have an additional analytical significance—they are a source of countervailing power to "special interest" groups.

Recent social movements in America can be categorized in Madisonian terms. One type of movement is that of some minority—

such as blacks, Native Americans, or homosexuals—that protests what is seen to be a majority faction, a majority "united and actuated by some common impulse of passion, or of interest, adverse to the rights of other citizens...." A second type of social movement protests what are considered to be instances of minority faction, in which a minority "actuated by some common ... interest, adverse to the rights of other citizens" acts adversely "to the permanent and aggregate interests of the community." Often, protestors against minority tyranny have claimed to be speaking for a majority, as opposed to being just one minority protesting the actions of another....

Few would deny that the public interest advocates achieved great success in the early and middle 1970s. Environmentalist lobbies helped push through federal extensions of clean water and clean air legislation that amounted to the redistribution of scores of billions of dollars. Environmental impact statements were mandated and proved to be a great boon to public interest litigation strategy. Numerous other measures were passed to commit the federal government to preserve wilderness areas, to regulate strip mining, to protect endangered species, to regulate the dumping of toxic wastes, and so forth. Even in defeat, environmentalist lobbies showed considerable strength. They delayed the Alaskan oil pipeline project for five years through litigation, even though the pipeline was backed by the federal government, the state government of Alaska, and the corporate giants of the oil industry.

In response to the growing popularity of consumerism, members of Congress passed legislation in the late 1960s and early 1970s to institute safety standards for automobiles, to establish a Consumer Product Safety Commission to investigate the safety of various products, and to strengthen the federal inspection of the meat packing industry. President Richard Nixon took the lead in revitalizing the Federal Trade Commission (FTC), which subsequently became active in regulating business on behalf of the consumer. The public interest movement was largely responsible for transforming an unregulated automobile industry in 1965 into a heavily regulated industry by 1975 (subject to safety requirements, fleet standards for gasoline consumption, and emissions standards).

Thus, middle-class social movements, through their lobbying capability and indirect impact on politicians seeking to increase their popularity, may be formidable opponents of minority faction.

In the Public Interest?

The environmentalists, consumerists, and government reform-ers believe that they are representing public interests—the unrepre-sented, widely shared interests discussed by Olson in *The Logic of Collective Action*. But a claim to represent "the public interest" can be accepted or rejected according to a wide range of political and social values....

Because of the diversity of middle-class protest movements in American politics, most persons support some movements and oppose others, rather than advocating social movement politics as an end in itself. Accordingly, while social movements frequently act to limit the power of minority factions, that does not necessarily mean that their existence is always in the public interest....

On balance, theories of the political impact of social movements suggest many limitations to the idea of American government as a confederation of oligarchies. Yet the idea of oligarchical control remains valid with some considerable qualifications. The pattern of American government may be envisioned as a "checkerboard of oligarchy." There are hundreds of different areas of public policy and some of these are controlled by minority factions or iron trian-gles, which might be represented by the dark squares on the board. Other areas of public policy seem to have broader public participa-tion, and might be represented by lighter shades on the board. Extending the metaphor, one might view various areas of public policy as growing darker or lighter at a particular time. Public participation in a given area usually varies considerably.

Social movements constitute one type of public participation in politics. They affect decision making by drawing attention to areas of policy that might otherwise attract little interest. Demon-strations, consciousness-raising groups, and various forms of pro-test may condition public opinion to look favorably upon a move-ment's goals. Interest groups organize as the movement develops and lobby legislatures for changes in the law or initiate litigation to achieve the same end. Public participation in one or more areas of policy increases and oligarchy or special interest rule decreases. In some cases, skeptics will argue that the new form of policy making is no more democratic than the former practices: Do envi-ronmentalists always represent the interests of the majority? Does bargaining with school prayer advocates make school politics more democratic? Nevertheless, social movements involve more people in policy making, and thus have important effects on public policy. While theories of minority faction cannot be discounted, it is likely that the future will bring new social movements to challenge the power of special interests.

PART ELEVEN

Voting and Elections

THE TECHNICAL literature of American elections has told us since the first careful election studies based on survey data were done some thirty years ago that all elections, like Caesar's Gaul, can be divided into three parts. One part has to do with party, another with issues, and the third with candidates as people. True enough. American elections, however, have always mixed these three elements differently than elections in most other of the world's democracies. At no time in our history have American political parties been strongly centralized national organizations. At their strongest stage of organization around the beginning of this century they were mainly state and local entities, and the party label by no means meant that candidates from different parts of the country stood for the same policies. As European observers of American elections have been telling us for more than a hundred years, our elections are more candidate-centered. The personality of the American electoral politician has always been relatively important. And, as we have noted in our readings on American ideology, all of our political conflict has taken place in the liberal part of the political spectrum. Aristocratic conservatism and socialism have simply not been viable forces in American elections. In the liberal center, candidates of both parties have often taken different stands on "the issues," but always in a manner that has seemed to Europeans confusingly "nonideological."

The American electoral process, always "different," has become decidedly more so in the last twenty or so years. More than ever, candidates and personalities have been at the forefront in the context of a new politics in which professional campaign consultants have largely displaced the state and local party "bosses" so much in evidence from the Civil War to the years just after World War II. Candidates now put together their own personal organizations, raise their own money, hire their own pollsters, campaign managers, "idea people," and media consultants. In this new electoral world campaigns are long, expensive, and individualistic. Candidates are "packaged" by public relations professionals who share the faith of Edward L. Bernays, the founder of their craft, that consent can in large part be "engineered." If they are mistaken, a great deal of money is being wasted. If they are not, a good deal of democratic theory is in deep trouble. At any rate, it is increasingly clear that we are in a new era of American electoral politics. Not much that was written before the late 1960s can tell us much about it. Thus, we present here no classics. In this realm of activity we are all struggling to keep up with the evening news.

Our first reading, from Larry Sabato's *The Rise of Political Consultants,* argues that the main force behind the recent transformation of American electoral politics is television. The medium, he argues, lends itself extraordinarily well to packaging candidates as "images." On the principle that "ugly folks get less votes," diets, wardrobes, and hairstyles become the subject of minute attention. As Bob Newhart put it in his 1960s comedy routine, "Abe, baby, ahhh, better get rid of the stovepipe hat." Candidates must be associated with "symbols" that are carefully tested to elicit public approval. Opponents are not so much argued with as associated with negative "symbols." Negative ads are used so often because the professionals are convinced that they work. It is hard to prove it, but we strongly suspect Sabato is right that "no single medium has ever transformed American politics to the extent that television has."

Joe McGinniss next describes the heavy influence of public relations and advertising techniques in Richard Nixon's successful presidential campaign of 1968. Nixon, by his own admission, had done poorly on television in 1960. In 1968 his handlers would try to "package" him much more carefully as "a person larger than life, the stuff of legend." Note well the *ideas* underlying the new campaign professionals' approach as they are expressed by one of the main Nixon packagers, William Gavin. Voters are basically lazy. They don't want to make the effort to understand candidates' policy positions. Reasoning is hard work—too much to demand. The good campaign, therefore, doesn't make any intellectual demands. Feelings and impressions are the key to selling the candidate. Gavin is nothing if not frank, and there can be little doubt that he is honestly putting forth the principles of his craft. That they are much more Machiavellian than Jeffersonian is of no concern to him.

Few political scientists have had much that is good to say about this way of looking at elections. Moreover, most do not believe that efforts to manipulate images and symbols, however extensive, are the major determinants of election outcomes. Stuart Rothenberg, a close observer of American elections, argues in our next selection that voters' perceptions about the economy were much more important than such symbolic "issues" as the pledge to the flag, Willie Horton, and the American Civil Liberties Union in presidential voting in 1988. Rothenberg, like most political scientists who study elections closely, holds that voters' partisanship and their approval or disapproval of the incumbent administration's record are the most important factors in election outcomes. In 1988, he thinks, the main concern was with the economy, not foreign policy. While he does not deny the role of personality or symbolic appeals in presidential and senatorial elections, he argues that the election process of the near future will continue to be an exercise in which voters register approval or disapproval of economic conditions.

Our next three readings deal with money in elections. There is wide agreement that American elections are the most expensive in the world, but there agreement ends. Elizabeth Drew argues that candidates ever in need of more money become beholden to the Political Action Committees that contribute to their campaigns. The PACs are not altruistic. They are investing in influencing public policy, and the result is a politics skewed in favor of those who can pay. The excessive role of campaign money has, she thinks "delivered us into the special-interest state." Michael Malbin maintains that PAC money has only replaced money contributed in a more shabby manner before the election reform laws of the

1970s. In general, he argues, PACs have much less influence on election outcomes and policy-making in Washington than most observers think. While PAC money is often supposed to have made incumbents in the House of Representatives less vulnerable to challenge, Malbin argues that other factors such as modern communications techniques and the decline of partisanship are more important causes of incumbents' advantage. Amy Dockser's article points out that congressmen are hardly innocents at the mercy of big-spending PACs. Rather, they have become expert at shaking down the PAC system for all it is worth. Members now pursue contributions and honoraria with amazing energy and imagination. In such a system the PACs are virtually forced into making contributions as the price of "access." The clear implication is that a great deal of their money is wasted.

Peter Bragdon's article on political consultants helps to explain why money is so important in contemporary campaigns. These highflyers of the new politics charge a great deal for what they do. Trading on campaigns won, like professional baseball players on their batting averages, they are in great demand. So prominent have they become that media coverage of elections now is as likely to focus on consultants and their strategies as on the candidates themselves. Indeed the consultants are the stars of recent media like the *Elections Hot Line* and other insider newsletters that have grown up to cover the growth industry of the new electoral politics.

Kirk Victor's piece, "The Braintrusters," discusses another class of actors in the new politics, the "idea people." Heaven help the candidate who has to fall back on his own mind. In a world in which candidates "recognize that ideas are important in giving them identity with the public," the thinking has to be done by policy experts. In case anyone is listening, there must be positions on this, that and the other, and if something new comes up—like "a sudden crisis in the international money markets"—impressive-sounding answers can be hastily concocted.

Even humor, Mark Shields argues in our concluding reading, has now been professionalized. Most candidates don't possess a sense of it, yet none can be without it. Presto, the rise of professional campaign humorists. Shields, himself, is one of the few political humorists to make a living in his own right off the stuff of this grim new political world. Most days he has his job cut out for him. As we would have said in the old days, " 'taint funny, McGee."

68

LARRY SABATO

From *The Rise of Political Consultants*

———

FOR YEARS political observers have wondered aloud why more and more successful politicians resembled television game-show hosts. Television itself is the answer, of course. No single medium has even transformed American politics to the extent that television has, and the development of a group of political media experts was an inevitable consequence. Mixing style with substance and imagery with reality, media consultants have developed a wide range of formats, strategies, techniques, and gimmicks both to inform and to deceive a television-addicted electorate. The candidate advertisements they produce are perhaps the most precisely and carefully crafted part of a modern campaign. Nothing has been left to chance; every aspect has been included for some purpose—from the colors to the background scenery to the inflections in the announcer's voice. In the hands of a media master, a political commercial can become a work of art—impressive, effective, enthralling, and, in afterthought, disturbing.

The strongest case *for* any candidate (and *against* his opponent) is crystallized in the advertisement package, and the approach and often the themes are the product of a consultant's political instincts. If the instincts are good, and the capacity to convert instinct into effective communication is present, the media consultant *can* have an influence of the results of an election. What is more important, the consultant is normally *thought* to have had an impact by the candidates he supports. . . .

In the relatively nonparty and nonideological American political system, it is the individual *candidate* who is the center of the electoral process, and the audience responds accordingly. The electorate has a better recall of the content of "image" commercials compared with issue-oriented advertisements, for example, and recall is vital considering the intense competition for the attention of the voter not just among candidates but by commercial advertisers. In 1976

Ford and Carter together were outspent on television during the general election by just two product advertisers, General Motors and Proctor & Gamble. And, sadly, media consultants do not package candidates so much as they package voters' prejudices. Professionals attempt to make their candidates physically handsomer and more attractive, for instance, because (as one consultant put it) "ugly folks get less votes." Focus-group experiments have shown that respondents select the most attractive candidate of the available alternatives and impute worse motives and capabilities to less attractive ones. It was with good reason, then, that political consultants interviewed for a national Republican party study unanimously agreed that "candidates should be pictured in a television spot only when they are physically attractive." (What would the GOP's rather ugly Abe Lincoln have done in the television age?)

Little wonder, too, that candidates all over the country have been forcefully and painfully reshaped by consultant-ordered diets, new coiffures, refurbished wardrobes, and voice lessons. Richard Nixon, after the lesson of his 1960 presidential debates, did not have to be coaxed in 1968 to lose weight so as to reduce his facial jowls, to keep a constant suntan for color television, and to shave several times a day to alter his "shadowy" look. U.S. Senator Henry Jackson of Washington, in preparation for his 1976 bid for the Democratic presidential nomination, hired speech instructors to speed his delivery and improve his pronunciation, slimmed down twenty pounds, had plastic surgery to correct sagging eyelids, let his hair grow longer, and purchased a number of "made-for-TV" suits. Candidates are also "improved" by association with symbols of desired qualities or favored groups. Put a candidate on a surfer's beach or in a tackle football game or a discussion with a group of young people and he is more youthful, and the generation gap is bridged. To emphasize warmth and sincerity, the roaring fire is a perfect accompaniment, and a study with bookcases crammed full will signify wisdom and competence. To stress a candidate's power or patriotism, the emotion-laden symbols of democracy (the White House, Capitol Hill, monuments of various descriptions, the seals of office, and the ubiquitous flag) are made to order.

The brevity of most political commercials puts a premium on image making symbols, which permit a consultant to communicate far more than time would allow in words. For the same reason, sloganeering and shorthand language are also highly prized skills in the media arts. A candidate does not discuss inflation as an economist does; his purposes are better served by quipping "Prices are so high that bologna is a gourmet food."...

As image-dominated as presidential campaigns may be, image making is much more prevalent at the state and congressional district levels, where, unlike most presidential contenders, candidates are often unknowns, with no sharply defined public images. Unknowns, if sufficiently pliant, present ripe opportunities for creative consultants. There is no better example than Bob Goodman's media work for Malcolm Wallop, Republican nominee for the U.S. Senate from Wyoming in 1976 who up-ended three-term incumbent Democrat Gale McGee in a major upset (for which Goodman's ad campaign was given a good part of the credit.) As the selected spots in table 1 suggest, few real issues existed in the campaign, and a generalized enemy (big, inefficient government) was made Wallop's target in an orgy of gimmickry. Scenery and extras reminiscent of the old West (seventy-five horses and riders, filmed by a helicopter) were combined with the accent, tone, and dramatic music of a Marlboro commercial. The stirring, patriotic presentations focus all the emotion and virtue on the candidate in the ten-gallon hat, who is transformed into a cowpoke even though he is a Yale graduate, born in New York, and a polo-playing cousin of Queen Elizabeth II. Yet any viewer of these extraordinarily moving spots would not be surprised to learn they were highly rated by voters in a national focus-group test....

While comedies consistently rank among the most popular television shows—and most any political campaign would make a grand situation comedy—a good portion of the electorate looks askance at candidates who take their politics too lightly, or so consultants fear. A joke also becomes old quickly, and when aired repeatedly it can be stale and irritating. Occasionally, though, humor is used with great effect. The Michigan Republican party delighted the state's voters in 1978 with the clever and witty Bailey, Deardourff spots presented in table 2, which compared the Democratic legislature to the "Lansing Zoo" in an attempt to increase GOP representation in the state capitol....

Even when television is used to communicate political truth (at least from one candidate's perspective), the truth can be negatively packaged—attacking the opponent's character and record rather

Table 1 · SELECTED ADVERTISEMENTS BY ROBERT GOODMAN FROM THE MALCOLM WALLOP FOR U.S. SENATE CAMPAIGN (WYOMING, 1976)

1. The Wallop Senate Drive (30 seconds)

ANNOUNCER Malcolm Wallop.

WALLOP Time used to be on our side, but now we know better.

MUSIC Come join the Wallop Senate Drive, the Wallop Senate Drive/It's alert, it's alive/It's Wyoming to the spurs/The Wallop Senate Drive.

WALLOP [While music plays in background] The ideas that served the sixties no longer serve today. Let's put the past to rest and dedicate ourselves to a new and better tomorrow. Come on Wyoming, this is our day!

POSTER Malcolm Wallop for United States Senate.

2. Ride with us, Wyoming (60 seconds)

MUSIC ["The Wallop Senate Drive," as three cowboys saddle up their horses out on the range.]

ANNOUNCER The Wallop Senate Drive starts here. Three riders with a proclamation.

VISUALS [Men are mounting horses as the music builds. Wallop is pictured in a close-up shot pulling the brim of his cowboy hat down over his eyes, á la Marlboro advertisement—except for the dark-blue business suit he is wearing. As the theme song is sung, the camera shows Wallop in slow motion, swinging a saddlebag through the air; then the three riders come over the crest of a hill. The focus now shifts to Wallop riding his horse.]

ANNOUNCER Go forth for Wyoming, Malcolm Wallop. Tell them in the United States Senate that the people of Wyoming are proud of their land and life, and a Wyoming senator will fight every intrusion upon it. That you, Malcolm Wallop, will serve the nation best by serving Wyoming first—the very special needs of this great state. And in so doing share its blessing with America.

VISUALS [Wallop is now leading a horde of cowboys on horseback, resembling a cavalry scene. They parade through town, as crowds cheer and Wallop waves.]

ANNOUNCER Malcolm Wallop for U.S. Senate. Ride with us, Wyoming!

3. Post Office (30 seconds)

VISUALS [Camera shows a letter to Mrs. John Smith with four one-cent stamps in the corner.]

ANNOUNCER We paid exactly four cents to mail a first-class letter in 1959.

Table 1 (CONTINUED)

That's about the time Senator Gale McGee came to the United States Senate. Since then a lot has happened. [One-cent stamps of various sizes begin to appear across the top of the letter, down the left-hand side, then across the bottom of the letter. Camera begins to move to the right of the letter, hesitates.] Oh, yes [camera moves back to the letter], McGee is chairman of the Senate Post Office Committee. [Camera begins to move to the right of the letter again, and hesitates.] And, oh, yes [as camera moves back to the letter], Mrs. Smith is still waiting for the letter.

POSTER Join the Wallop Senate Drive.

---

4. *Porta-Potty* (30 *seconds*)

VISUAL [Wallop, dressed as a cowboy, is saddling and mounting a horse.]

ANNOUNCER Everywhere you look these days, the federal government is there, telling you what they think, telling you what they think you ought to think. Telling you how to do things, setting up rules you can't follow. I think the federal government is going too far. Now they say if you don't take the portable facility along with you on a roundup, you can't go!

VISUALS [Wallop appears angry and disgusted, matching the announcer's sarcastic tone, as the camera pans a porta-potty strapped to a donkey tied to Wallop's horse.]

ANNOUNCER We need someone to tell 'em about Wyoming. Malcolm Wallop will.

POSTER: Malcolm Wallop for U.S. Senate.

---

than supporting one's own. If there is a single trend obvious to most American media consultants, it is the increasing proportion of negative political advertising. Going on the offensive, "attack politics," is becoming more popular because, while vicious, it has gained a reputation for effectiveness among professionals. At least a third of all spot commercials in recent campaigns have been negative, and in a minority of campaigns half or more of the spots are negative in tone or substance. Interestingly, product advertising appears to have moved in the same direction; while previously the cardinal rule of product (as political) advertising was never to mention the name of one's competitor, commercial marketers have rushed to pounce on competing brands by name.

In politics, negative advertising is believed to be more attention

Table 2 · Humorous Advertisements by Bailey, Deardourff &
Associates for the Republican Party of Michigan
(State Legislative Elections, 1978)

---

1. *The Lansing Zoo: A Friendly Place* (30 *seconds*)

VISUALS [Groups of animals in captivity or in the wild, with a steady background of animal noises; same for all commercials.]

ANNOUNCER The Lansing Zoo. Otherwise known as the Democratic State Legislature. It's a friendly place. [Monkeys applauding.] They take care of each other in fine style. [Monkeys cleaning each other.] They've fitted their nest with a $3.5 million office building just for Democrats and their staff. [Birds and rabbits in droves.] And they increased their staff an average of 166 percent per legislature, all in just the last seven years. [Hundreds of donkeys.] Maybe it's time we picked them clean for a change. [Preening animals.] After all, when we want something, like property tax reduced, they're not so friendly. [An ostrich attacks the cameraman's lens.]

---

2. *The Lansing Zoo: A Shy Place* (30 *seconds*)

ANNOUNCER When you visit the Lansing Zoo, otherwise known as the Democratic State Legislature, do you wonder why they're so shy? [Animals run away from camera.] Where were they when they could have increased our state personal tax exemption by $100? [Flock of birds flies away.] Where were they when they could have allowed installment payments on the property tax? [Ostriches run away.] Where was the Democratic legislature when the elderly wanted property tax relief? [Herd of zebras running.] Just because they're shy, is no reason for us to be shy. [Ground hog goes into burrow.] Maybe we should help them disappear. [A hippo goes underwater.]

---

3. *The Lansing Zoo: A Sleepy Place* (30 *seconds*)

AUDIO [Lullaby on sound track.]

ANNOUNCER Have you noticed how the Lansing Zoo, otherwise known as the Democratic State Legislature, is such a sleepy place? [Lion yawns and rolls over.] Maybe that's why it took them thirteen months to lower the tolerance levels on PPB and four years to pass plant rehabilitation to save Michigan jobs. [Lions and tigers sleeping, some with limbs dangling from trees.] On the energy crisis the DEMOCRATIC state LEGISLATURE just couldn't quite summon the energy to do anything. Maybe they need a good long rest; looks like it. [A hippo's massive yawn.]

Table 2 (CONTINUED)

---

4. *The Lansing Zoo: A Painful Place* (30 *seconds*)*

VISUAL: [Two gargantuan rhinos, mating.]

ANNOUNCER Do you know what is being done to us by the Democratically controlled legislature in this state? Do you have any idea how it hurts taxpayers to have the Democrats behind things in Lansing? Why would anyone want to be in this position for ten years? Isn't it about time we get the Democrats off our back?

---

* The fourth spot, which quite obviously would not meet television's antiobscenity standards, was not actually broadcast. Rather it was designed and used as a fund-raising device at dinners—the video equivalent of a dirty joke, which, if properly enjoyed by participants, traditionally opens checkbooks at such affairs.

grabbing and exciting, and to be particularly effective against incumbents. The most common circumstances under which negative ads are produced, however, are when a candidate is far behind and not gaining in the polls or when a leading candidate falls precipitously in the trial heats. . . .

Despite its perceived advantages, negative advertising is approached with caution and handled with care by consultants, who are well aware of its backlash-generating potential. A Republican-sponsored study of media termed the negative approach "high-risk" advertising, because "it must walk the fine line between making its point and turning off the voter." Research has indicated that, in general, voters prefer positive, informational ads and, above all, a spot must appear to be fair. . . . Standing negative devices, such as the "weathervane," are repeatedly used. The weathervane ads highlight an opponent's flip-flops, and the technique has been employed by Johnson in 1964, Humphrey in 1968, and Nixon in 1972. The Ford campaign designed but did not use an ad of that variety against Carter in 1976 as well, and his staff director of advertising, Malcolm MacDougall, described the standard operating procedures in its design:

The principle behind it is simple. To make your own weathervane ad, you research your opponent's speeches over a period of about ten years. You study every newspaper article written about him during that period. You then look for the slightest indication that he may have changed his position on an issue. You make a list of all the times that your opponent's position has changed, and you are in business.

The cleverest weathervane ad was produced as an anti-Nixon spot in 1968. It showed Nixon's left hand pointing eastward, his right hand westward, and his nose shifting from north to south. Nixon was so outraged when he saw the commercial that he called Hubert Humphrey personally to demand that it be withdrawn, and a rather shaken Humphrey complied. Four years later Nixon's concern (as expressed to Humphrey) that weathervane ads were demeaning to the political system was apparently forgotten, as the Committee to Re-Elect the President broadcast a remarkably similar spot that had Democratic nominee George McGovern revolving in the shifting winds of his alleged positions....

69

JOE McGINNISS

From *The Selling of the President 1968*

POLITICS, in a sense, has always been a con game.

The American voter, insisting upon his belief in a higher order, clings to his religion, which promises another, better life; and defends passionately the illusion that the men he chooses to lead him are of finer nature than he.

It has been traditional that the successful politician honor this illusion. To succeed today, he must embellish it. Particularly if he wants to be President.

"Potential presidents are measured against an ideal that's a combination of leading man, God, father, hero, pope, king, with maybe just a touch of the avenging Furies thrown in," an adviser to Richard Nixon wrote in a memorandum late in 1967. Then, perhaps aware that Nixon qualified only as father, he discussed improvements that would have to be made—not upon Nixon himself, but upon the image of him which was received by the voter.

That there is a difference between the individual and his image is human nature. Or American nature, at least. That the difference is exaggerated and exploited electronically is the reason for this book.

Advertising, in many ways, is a con game, too. Human beings

do not need new automobiles every third year; a color television set brings little enrichment of the human experience; a higher or lower hemline no expansion of consciousness, no increase in the capacity to love.

It is not surprising then, that politicians and advertising men should have discovered one another. And, once they recognized that the citizen did not so much vote for a candidate as make a psychological purchase of him, not surprising that they began to work together.

The voter, as reluctant to face political reality as any other kind, was hardly an unwilling victim. "The deeper problems connected with advertising," Daniel Boorstin has written in *The Image,* "come less from the unscrupulousness of our 'deceivers' than from our pleasure in being deceived, less from the desire to seduce than from the desire to be seduced. . . .

"In the last half-century we have misled ourselves. . .about men. . .and how much greatness can be found among them. . . . We have become so accustomed to our illusions that we mistake them for reality. We demand them. And we demand that there be always more of them, bigger and better and more vivid."

The Presidency seems the ultimate extension of our error. . . .

The television celebrity is a vessel. An inoffensive container in which someone else's knowledge, insight, compassion, or wit can be presented. And we respond like the child on Christmas morning who ignores the gift to play with the wrapping paper.

Television seems particularly useful to the politician who can be charming but lacks ideas. Print is for ideas. Newspapermen write not about people but policies; the paragraphs can be slid around like blocks. Everyone is colored gray. Columnists—and commentators in the more polysyllabic magazines—concentrate on ideology. They do not care what a man sounds like; only how he thinks. For the candidate who does not, such exposure can be embarrassing. He needs another way to reach the people.

On television it matters less that he does not have ideas. His personality is what the viewers want to share. He need be neither statesman nor crusader; he must only show up on time. Success and failure are easily measured: how often is he invited back? Often enough and he reaches his goal—to advance from "politician" to "celebrity," a status jump bestowed by grateful viewers who feel that finally they have been given the basis for making a choice.

The TV candidate, then, is measured not against his predecessors—not against a standard of performance established by two centuries of democracy—but against [talk-show host] Mike Douglas. How well does he handle himself? Does he mumble, does he twitch, does he make me laugh? Do I feel warm inside?

Style becomes substance. The medium is the massage and the masseur gets the votes.

In office, too, the ability to project electronically is essential. We were willing to forgive John Kennedy his Bay of Pigs; we followed without question the perilous course on which he led us when missiles were found in Cuba; we even tolerated his calling of reserves for the sake of a bluff about Berlin.

We forgave, followed, and accepted because we liked the way he looked. And he had a pretty wife. Camelot was fun, even for the peasants, as long as it was televised to their huts.

Then came Lyndon Johnson, heavy and gross, and he was forgiven nothing. He might have survived the sniping of the displaced intellectuals had he only been able to charm. But no one taught him how. Johnson was syrupy. He stuck to the lens. There was no place for him in our culture.

"The success of any TV performer depends on his achieving a low-pressure style of presentation," McLuhan has written. The harder a man tries, the better he must hide it. Television demands gentle wit, irony, understatement: the qualities of Eugene McCarthy. The TV politician cannot make a speech; he must engage in intimate conversation. He must never press. He should suggest, not state; request, not demand. Nonchalance is the key word. Carefully studied nonchalance.

Warmth and sincerity are desirable but must be handled with care. Unfiltered, they can be fatal. Television did great harm to Hubert Humphrey. His excesses—talking too long and too fervently, which were merely annoying in an auditorium—became lethal in a television studio. The performer must talk to one person at a time. He is brought into the living room. He is a guest. It is improper for him to shout. Humphrey vomited on the rug.

It would be extremely unwise for the TV politician to admit such knowledge of his medium. The necessary nonchalance should carry beyond his appearance while *on* the show; it should rule his attitude *toward* it. He should express distaste for television; suspicion that there is something "phony" about it. This guarantees him good press, because newspaper reporters, bitter over their loss of prestige to the television men, are certain to stress anti-television remarks. Thus, the sophisticated candidate, while analyzing his own on-the-air technique as carefully as a golf pro studies his swing, will state frequently that there is no place for "public relations gimmicks" or "those show business guys" in his campaign. Most of the television men working for him will be unbothered by such remarks. They are willing to accept anonymity, even scorn, as long as the pay is good.

Into this milieu came Richard Nixon: grumpy, cold, and aloof. He would claim privately that he lost elections because the American voter was an adolescent whom he tried to treat as an adult. Perhaps. But if he treated the voter as an adult, it was as an adult he did not want for a neighbor.

This might have been excused had he been a man of genuine vision. An explorer of the spirit. Martin Luther King, for instance, got by without being one of the boys. But Richard Nixon did not strike people that way. He had, in Richard Rovere's words, "an advertising man's approach to his work," acting as if he believed "policies [were] products to be sold the public—this one today, that one tomorrow, depending on the discounts and the state of the market.". . .

He nearly became President in 1960, and that year it would not have been by default. He failed because he was too few of the things a President had to be—and, because he had no press to lie for him and did not know how to use television to lie about himself.

It was just Nixon and John Kennedy and they sat down together in a television studio and a little red light began to glow and Richard Nixon was finished. Television would be blamed but for all the wrong reasons.

They would say it was makeup and lighting, but Nixon's problem went deeper than that. His problem was himself. Not what he said but the man he was. The camera portrayed him clearly. America took its Richard Nixon straight and did not like the taste.

The content of the programs made little difference. Except for startling lapses, content seldom does. What mattered was the image the viewers received, though few observers at the time caught the point. . . .

What the camera showed was Richard Nixon's hunger. He lost, and bitter, confused, he blamed it on his beard. . . .

America still saw him as the 1960 Nixon. If he were to come at the people again, as candidate, it would have to be as something new; not this scarred, discarded figure from their past.

He spoke to men who thought him mellowed. They detected growth, a new stability, a sense of direction that had been lacking. He would return with fresh perspective, a more unselfish urgency.

His problem was how to let the nation know. He could not do it through the press. He knew what to expect from them, which was the same as he had always gotten. He would have to circumvent them. Distract them with coffee and doughnuts and smiles from his staff and tell his story another way.

Television was the only answer, despite its sins against him in the past. But not just any kind of television. An uncommitted camera could do irreparable harm. His television would have to be controlled. He would need experts. They would have to find the proper settings for him, or if they could not be found, manufacture them. These would have to be men of keen judgment and flawless taste. He was, after all, Richard Nixon, and there were certain things he could not do. Wearing love beads was one. He would need men of dignity. Who believed in him and shared his vision. But more importantly, men who knew television as a weapon: from broadest concept to most technical detail. This would be Richard Nixon, the leader, returning from exile. Perhaps not beloved, but respected. Firm but not harsh; just but compassionate. With flashes of warmth spaced evenly throughout....

"Voters are basically lazy, basically uninterested in making an *effort* to understand what we're talking about...," [William] Gavin [former high school English teacher and later speechwriter for President Nixon] wrote. "Reason requires a high degree of discipline, of concentration; impression is easier. Reason pushes the viewer back, it assaults him, it demands that he agree or disagree; impression can envelop him, invite him in, without making an intellectual demand.... When we argue with him we demand that he make the effort of replying. We seek to engage his intellect, and for most people this is the most difficult work of all. The emotions are more easily roused, closer to the surface, more malleable...."

So, for the New Hampshire primary, Gavin recommended "saturation with a film, in which the candidate can be shown better than he can be shown in person because it can be edited, so only the best moments are shown; then a quick parading of the candidate in the flesh so that the guy they've gotten intimately acquainted with on the screen takes on a living presence—not saying anything, just being seen...."

"[Nixon] has to come across as a person larger than life, the stuff of legend. People are stirred by the legend, including the living legend, not by the man himself. It's the aura that surrounds the charismatic figure more than it is the figure itself, that draws the followers. Our task is to build that aura. . . .

"So let's not be afraid of television gimmicks . . . get the voters to like the guy and the battle's two-thirds won."

William Gavin was brought to the White House as a speech writer in January of 1969. . . .

Some of the most effective ideas belonged to Raymond K. Price, a former editorial writer for the *New York Herald Tribune,* who became Nixon's best and most prominent speech writer in the campaign. . . .

Price suggested attacking the "personal factors" rather than the "historical factors" which were the basis of the low opinion so many people had of Richard Nixon.

"These tend to be more a gut reaction," Price wrote, "unarticulated, non-analytical, a product of the particular chemistry between the voter and the *image* of the candidate. *We have to be very clear on this point: that the response is to the image, not to the man.* . . . It's not what's *there* that counts, it's what's projected—and carrying it one step further, it's not what *he* projects but rather what the voter receives. It's not the man we have to change, but rather the *received impression.* And this impression often depends more on the medium and its use than it does on the candidate himself."

So there would not have to be a "new Nixon." Simply a new approach to television. . . .

So this was how they went into it. Trying, with one hand, to build the illusion that Richard Nixon, in addition to his attributes of mind and heart, considered, in the words of Patrick J. Buchanan, a speech writer, "communicating with the people. . . one of the great joys of seeking the Presidency"; while with the other they shielded him, controlled him, and controlled the atmosphere around him. It was as if they were building not a President but an Astrodome, where the wind would never blow, the temperature never rise or fall, and the ball never bounce erratically on the artificial grass.

They could do this, and succeed, because of the special nature of the man. There was, apparently, something in Richard Nixon's character which sought this shelter. Something which craved regulation, which flourished best in the darkness, behind clichés, behind phalanxes of antiseptic advisers. Some part of him that could breathe freely only inside a hotel suite that cost a hundred dollars a day.

And it worked. As he moved serenely through his primary campaign, there was new cadence to Richard Nixon's speech and motion; new confidence in his heart. And, a new image of him on the television screen.

TV both reflected and contributed to his strength. Because he was winning he looked like a winner on the screen. Because he was suddenly projecting well on the medium he had feared, he went about his other tasks with assurance. The one fed upon the other, building to an astonishing peak in August as the Republican convention began and he emerged from his regal isolation, traveling to Miami not so much to be nominated as coronated. On live, but controlled, TV....

Meanwhile, the new advertising men who worked for Hubert Humphrey had produced a half-hour film called *The Mind Changer*. It was awful in many ways. It showed Hubert Humphrey and Edmund Muskie crawling down a bowling alley in their shirt sleeves. It showed Humphrey wearing a stupid fisherman's hat and getting his lines snarled on a lake near his home and it took shameless advantage of the fact he has a mentally retarded grand daughter. It was contrived and tasteless. But it was the most effective single piece of adverting of the campaign.

It showed Hubert Humphrey as a person. It began with the assumption that of course he had faults as a politician and of course he had made a lot of mistakes, but it said again and again that Hubert Humphrey, at least, is a person. Here he is sweating, laughing, crying, out in the open air. The contrast with Nixon was obvious. Nixon, who depended on a television studio the way a polio victim relied on an iron lung.

That one Humphrey film made a mockery of Richard Nixon's year-long quest for warmth. You can't create humanity, it said. You either have it or you don't. Hubert Humphrey has it. Guess who does not....

By eight o'clock we were out of the hotel, moving toward the airport in the heavy morning traffic. A man on the car radio said that the first signs of concern had begun to show up among the Nixon staff, which, he said, until a day or two before, had been almost infuriating with its smugness. Harry Treleaven laughed.

The plane took off at nine o'clock. The stewardess passed out plastic glasses of champagne that was sweet and warm. Treleaven drank his and then mine. He was trying to relax. It was hard, after a year of eighteen-hour days, to suddenly have nothing to do. There would be no calls to make when the plane landed, no meetings to rush to in a cab. It was done. Now there was only the wait.

"There was a lot we didn't do because we didn't think we had to," Treleaven said. "The big lead influenced our whole approach."

"Then we had the basic problem of Nixon's personality. There were certain things people just would not buy about the guy. For instance, he loves to walk on the beach, but we couldn't send a camera out to film him picking up seashells. That would not have been credible."

He was already looking for reasons why things had gone wrong. There was no question anymore about whether they had or not. The perfect campaign, the computer campaign, the technicians' campaign, the television campaign, the one that would make them rewrite the textbooks had collapsed beneath the weight of Nixon's grayness.

"That total split between the advertising and political people was very bad," Treleaven said. "It left us much less effective than we could have been."

And then, Harry Treleaven said, there had been Spiro Agnew. "More than any other single thing," he said, "I think that damaged the image we were trying to build."

He shook his head in bewilderment. One thing about advertising cigarettes or airplanes: they don't resist.

70

STUART ROTHENBERG

Pocketbook Issues Still Matter the Most

———

IT REMAINS much in vogue to believe that the 1988 election demonstrated that politics has entered a new era—an era where cultural issues have replaced economic ones as the prime force in determining election outcomes. But dismissing economic issues both misreads the 1988 results and establishes flawed expectations for the 1990 elections, particularly if inflation becomes a serious national problem or the economy falls into recession next year.

The Bush campaign's mileage from the Pledge of Allegiance, Willie Horton and the ACLU allegedly offer hard evidence that non-economic issues drove the electorate in 1988. It would be silly to dismiss those campaign themes, but it is important to look beyond them and recognize that the state of the near-term economy once again proved to be a necessary, if not sufficient, ingredient of the GOP victory.

The "Reagan Boom"

George Bush maintained leads in early hypothetical ballot tests against various opponents primarily because voters knew little about the Democratic contenders. Once Michael Dukakis emerged as the all-but-certain Democratic nominee, Mr. Bush's stock plummeted. A May CBS News/*New York Times* poll showed Mr. Bush trailing Mr. Dukakis by 10 points, while a *Los Angeles Times* survey had the Massachusetts governor ahead by 17 points. The voters were telling pollsters that it was time for a change and that they doubted the vice president's leadership abilities.

All major polls showed Mr. Dukakis clearly ahead during June and July, with an early June NBC/*Wall Street Journal* poll pegging the race at 49% to 36% among likely voters. The same survey also found that by 46% to 40%, voters believed that Mr. Dukakis was better able to handle "the nation's economic problems."

But by mid-1988, with less talk about a near-term recession or inflation (and the 1987 stock market collapse fading into more distant memory), Mr. Bush was able to take credit for the "Reagan boom" and suddenly was regarded as being better able than Mr. Dukakis to handle the economy. With that development came a surge by Mr. Bush in head-to-head polls against Mr. Dukakis.

Mr. Dukakis held a lead of three to six points on the economic question ("Which candidate do you think would be better able to handle the nation's economic problems?") at the same time he was ahead of Mr. Bush on the ballot question. By mid-September, however, Mr. Bush had pulled ahead on both the economics question and the ballot test. By mid-October and after the second televised debate, Mr. Bush had opened a wide lead on both.

Mr. Bush's turnaround in the polls cannot be explained by an issue like defense policy, even though much has been made of the Dukakis photo opportunity featuring the governor, in battle gear, riding around in a tank. Historically, defense policy has been a secondary factor in presidential elections held when the U.S. was not involved in a war or international crisis, though there are exceptions such as the "missile gap" in 1960. The NBC News/ *Wall Street Journal* June poll showed Mr. Dukakis ahead 49% to 36% even while Mr. Bush maintained a 20-point lead as the candidate "better able to maintain a strong defense." In other words, Mr. Bush was winning on defense even while he was trailing Mr. Dukakis.

The public's mood swing on Mr. Bush's ability to deal with the economy and handle future economic matters resulted from a change in the public's *perception* of the economy.

UCLA political scientist John Petrocik and GOP pollster Fred Steeper argue in the winter issue of *Election Politics* that by continually telling voters he was responsible for the economic good times, the vice president both educated them about the economy and highlighted it as an issue. "By increasing the proportion who thought the economy was prosperous, and increasing by about twelve points his share of the vote among those who perceived a strong economy, [Mr. Bush] helped to drive his support from 44 percent in July to 53 percent in November," they write.

Further evidence of the importance of the economy comes from political scientists Richard Brody of Stanford and Greg Markus of the University of Michigan, both of whom came extremely close to predicting the final presidential election percentages using models that relied on political measures (such as partisanship and presidential popularity) and economic ones (such as changes in income and personal financial well-being). Cultural issues were ignored.

Interestingly, an NBC News/*Wall Street Journal* survey conducted just days before the general election found that 57% of likely voters said Mr. Dukakis represented "traditional American values," compared with 60% who said the same for Mr. Bush. And Mr. Dukakis scored a lopsided victory when the same respondents were asked whether Mr. Bush or the Massachusetts governor "really cares about people like you." If cultural issues were decisive, those numbers don't show it.

But it is not necessary to dismiss the role cultural issues played in the election to argue the crucial point: Mr. Bush would never have been able to dominate the campaign debate with his themes if the economy had been staggering or if the public had been worried about the vice president's ability to maintain prosperity.

And if cultural issues were of some concern to voters last year, that hardly makes 1988 unique. Similar issues were important in 1968 and 1972, and they will be significant in future presidential elections. But they were only part of the 1988 package, and they are likely to be far less important during the 1990 midterm elections....

In fact, off-year elections invariably are referendums on the president's performance, with the state of the economy being the most visible factor. Without the president on the ballot, the only way voters can show the extent of their disappointment and displeasure with the chief executive is by voting against his party's candidates for lower office....

Since gubernatorial and Senate candidates run high-profile campaigns, they are more able to establish independent identities, allowing them to buck any national trend, economic or otherwise. The uneven partisan makeup of Senate classes every two years and the wide disparity in quality of candidates can also produce Senate results with no national message. That is not to say that the national economy is of no consequence to Senate candidates—the 1958 results proved otherwise—but only that Senate candidates have a greater ability to overcome the economic environment.

Not Purely Coincidental

Congressional and state legislative candidates running in non-presidential years are particularly vulnerable to economic downturns because, despite their increased use of incumbency, they run much less visible races than do Senate candidates. It is not purely coincidental that in 1982 the Republicans lost more than two dozen House seats in the midst of a serious recession. Nor is it an accident that four years later, when the economy was strong, the GOP lost only a handful of seats, an excellent off-year showing for the party controlling the White House.

Next year, of course, could be different, depending on a number of Supreme Court decisions (e.g., abortion) and how Congress handles issues during the next 18 months. But even if other issues come into play (and the Republicans surely wish they would), the economy will determine the playing field on which the 1990 elections will take place. That is no small consideration.

71

ELIZABETH DREW
The Chase for Money

From *Politics and Money*

———

IT IS OFTEN SAID that what is driving the chase for money
on the part of candidates for Congress is the ever-increasing cost
of campaigning, but that gets it backward. What is driving the
chase for money is its own momentum. It is the domestic equivalent of the arms race. A candidate feels compelled to spend so
much money because his opponent is spending so much, or might
spend so much, or groups intent on his defeat might spend so
much. Of course, the costs of the components of campaigns—
polling, consultants, direct mail, and, most of all, television time—
have risen; but the sum total of what is spent on campaigns has
risen because the political system as it now functions has allowed,
even encouraged, it to. A candidate for office doesn't set out to
spend a half million or a million dollars for the sheer joy of it; he
does it because he fears the consequences of not doing it. And
unless he is independently wealthy he has to raise that money—or
be more vulnerable to defeat. It is not accidental that the number
of independently wealthy people entering politics is rising. And
the quest for money has distended and distorted the political system
to the point where it bears little resemblance to what it was supposed to be.

A candidate entering politics now must systematically make
the rounds of the interest groups and win their approval, and their
money, by declaring himself, usually in very specific terms, in
favor of the legislative goals they seek. He is therefore imprisoned
before he ever reaches Congress. Once there, he must worry about
maintaining the groups' support or about finding other groups to
support him or about casting some vote that might cause monetary
retaliation. He must measure every action in terms of what the
financial consequences to himself might be. The difference between
that and corruption is unclear. . . .

An argument is sometimes made that since everyone is in the game—since all the interests are raising and distributing money—it all evens out in the end. But, for one thing, the premise is not true. As Robert Dole says, "There aren't any Poor PACs or Food Stamp PACs or Nutrition PACs or Medicare PACs." Moreover, comparisons between spending by business and by labor are misleading, because often business is fighting business, and sometimes, as in the case of a weapons system or construction project (the B-1 bomber, the Clinch River Breeder Reactor), business and labor are on the same side. Senator Dale Bumpers, Democrat of Arkansas, says, "You can't have a sensible debate about how much is enough for defense when those PACs are contributing so much. The decisions aren't based on what the likely mission of the Pentagon is going to be." And, even if the premise were true, the logical conclusion of the argument that there is no problem because everyone is in on the game is that the political system should go to the highest bidder.

The point about everyone being in the game also lacks relevance because, irrespective of who is winning or losing, the real problem is what the system does to the politicians. We now have a system in which even the best-intentioned politicians get caught up in either actual or apparent conflicts of interest, in which it is difficult to avoid in effect selling votes for campaign contributions. We have a system in which even the best people do these things, not because they want to but because they are trapped. After every election, we get analyses showing that not everyone who spends more money wins. Of course not; there are numerous factors in a campaign, ranging from the state of the economy to what might be termed the "jerk factor"—having to do with the quality of the candidates. But money can make the difference in what would otherwise be a close race.

Politicians on Capitol Hill have a little joke that goes, "I'm a man of principle. Once I'm bought, I stay bought." It is a fact that special-interest money as a percentage of campaign funds has grown. Increasingly, the shape and nature of our politics is being determined by the interests that have the money to contribute and the technicians who instruct the candidates in how to raise it and use it. Increasingly, the question of who gets funds is a decision made within Washington, by people who have an eye on some piece of the national agenda. The young lawyer-lobbyist says, "The interests run this city; everyone knows it." A member of

Congress says, "The lobbyists set the national agenda." Some of the interest groups talk about how their political decisions are made at the "grass roots," but of course that, for the most part, is nonsense. Their Washington representatives are paid to monitor, and try to influence, the behavior of the politicians in Washington. Politicians are forced to respond less and less to their constituents and more and more to the interests with the money. The money flows into a district or a state at the direction of interests that have little or nothing to do with the area. Campaigns are increasingly centralized in Washington by the technicians and the money men. The more money that is involved in the political process, the more important the technological decisions become, and, in a circular way, the more important money becomes. One lobbyist says that the role of money is what has led to so many "plastic politicians"—politicians groomed for the television age (sometimes known as the "blow-dried politicians"), whose beliefs are malleable. The Democratic pollster Patrick Caddell says, "What worries me is what technology—the pollsters and the technicians—has done to the system. We pick the candidates, and we say what works on television. We're the arbitrators. We say what fits the mold, and we reject the mavericks."

It is the role of money that has given us, increasingly, politicians who are exhausted, who can't think clearly, who don't think about broad questions—don't have the time, even if they have the inclination, to do so. Who don't lead. The Burkean ideal—the ideal of the politician leading his constituents, rather than simply reacting to "the convenience of the hour"—is not just diminishing as a factor in our politics; it has almost disappeared. The role of money has delivered us into the special-interest state. As Jim Leach, the Republican congressman from Iowa, says, we have "a breakdown of constitutional democracy, which is supposed to be based upon citizen access and constituency access." Dale Bumpers says, "Money is the number-one political problem our country is facing. I know that money distorts the democratic process." There are things that can be done to help restore the process to its original purpose, and they will be gone into later. First, we have to decide whether we want to try to restore the political process to its original purpose.

72

MICHAEL MALBIN

Looking Back at the Future of Campaign Finance Reform

From *Money and Politics in the United States*

———

ANYONE inclined to romanticize the world before PACs should be required to spend some time thinking about 1972, the last presidential election in what campaign finance buffs may think of as the *ancien régime*. In the three years after that election, 21 different corporations were found guilty of having illegally contributed $958,540 in corporate funds to the 1972 presidential candidates, $842,500 to President Richard M. Nixon. We have no way of knowing how many in-kind or cash contributions escaped prosecution in 1972 or previous years, but we do know they existed and were substantial. In addition, in the noncorporate business world, the investigations of the Senate Watergate Committee chaired by Sam S. Ervin (Democrat of North Carolina) uncovered a milk producer pledge of $2 million and actual contributions of $632,500 made to the President's reelection effort, allegedly in exchange for favorable treatment on dairy price supports.

On the legal side of the table, the Finance Committee to Reelect the President (FCRP) also engaged in what the Ervin committee described as a "systematic solicitation of contributions from corporate executive, and middle management salaried employees" to bypass pre-1975 legal prohibitions on government contractors' corporate or PAC contributions....

[But] some of those solicited have made the requests sound closer to extortion. Two tracks were followed for corporate solicitations. One was a "corporate conduit program" in which FCRP officials would persuade officers from the top 1000 Fortune industrials and about 900 other companies to "stimulate" their employees to contribute directly to the President's reelection. The other, which overlapped the first, was arranged by industry and concentrated on 60 major industry groups.

The contributions produced by these and other solicitations were substantial. Even if one limits the analysis to large ($10,000 +) contributions raised after April 7, 1972 (the date disclosure was required by the 1971 law), the large contributors accounted for 46 percent of the $23.7 million in postdisclosure money raised by Nixon, 43 percent of $11.7 million raised by Democratic nominee George S. McGovern, and 60 percent of the $1.7 million raised by Hubert H. Humphrey, McGovern's main challenger in the late primaries.

As impressive as these numbers may seem, they do not begin to tell the story of the role played by large givers in 1972. According to the Ervin committee, the systematic effort to solicit large contributions was run unofficially in the early stages by Herbert W. Kalmbach, Nixon's long-time associate and personal attorney. Kalmbach did not hold a government position, but his fund raising was conducted "under the supervision of" White House chief of staff H. R. Haldeman. The following lengthy passage from the report of the Ervin committee describes the importance of Kalmbach's efforts.

In November 1970, Kalmbach was requested by Haldeman to involve himself in early fund raising. According to Kalmbach, on a number of occasions, before as well as after the November meeting, Haldeman told him to obtain cash contributions wherever he could. Thereafter, Kalmbach sought out friends in an effort to obtain what amounted to commitments for campaign contributions. Kalmbach states that he never asked for a commitment in so many words, but rather approached people, suggested an amount to them and asked if they would accept that as a "goal figure."

Kalmbach acknowledged that he told contributors that there were different classes of contributors, and he had different "cut-off points," for example, at $25,000, $50,000 and $100,000. Kalmbach said that on occasions he referred to a "100 Club"—meaning contributors who gave $100,000. He indicated that he told contributors that there were a lot of people in the $25,000 class, and if one wanted to be known as a major contributor, he should give more....

In all, Kalmbach solicited pledges of over $13.4 million. [Of these, three were for less than $25,000, five were for $25,000 to $49,999, fifteen were for $50,000 to $99,999, 32 were for $100,000 to $199,999, nine were for $200,000 to $300,000, one was for $1 million and two were for $3 million.] In fact, a total of $10,658,000 was given.... Of this total, over $8.8 million was contributed prior to April 7, with over $1.8 million coming after April 7, 1972. Kalmbach emphasized the importance to his solicitation efforts of being able to assure potential contributors that their contributions would remain confidential if made before April 7. Kalmbach was also concerned about having his own solicitation role disclosed. In fact, Kalmbach resigned his position with FCRP when the new disclosure law went into effect on that date....

Kalmbach's efforts thus amounted to a commitment for one-third of the total campaign budget, virtually all of which was committed prior to April 7, 1972. Most significant was the proportion of contributions in the highest ranges listed by Kalmbach. Of anticipated contributions of $100,000, or more, which constituted $22.5 million of the $40 million budget, Kalmbach solicited pledges of $12.725 million, or over 57 percent of the budgeted amount.... In terms of actual contributions, Kalmbach was responsible for about $9.69 million of the total of $22.5 million required from contributors of $100,000 and over, or 43 percent of the amount sought.

What emerges from the sordid record of the 1972 campaign is a picture of semicoercive fund raising, under-the-table cash contributions, and financial dominance by a handful of large givers most of whom had an interested ax to grind. It seems almost ludicrous, therefore, to suggest that the growth of PACs has somehow reduced the dignity of the process. The 1974 law was a direct reaction to the practices of 1972 and has in fact achieved many of its original purposes. Interested money still is contributed, but the amount any one person may give is limited, and all contributions are disclosed. PACs have increased their proportionate share, but to do so they have had to disclose their activities and involve more people, most of whom contribute relatively small amounts. Some might think the country would be better off if there were no interested money in politics or smaller amounts of it. Whatever one may think, it takes a large set of blinders to miss the fact that the emergence of PACs represents an improvement over what went on before.

...In what precise ways have elections, and the political–governmental environment, been affected by the professionalization of interest-group electoral participation stimulated by the campaign laws of the 1970s?...

I stated earlier that even if the existence and role of interested money is not new to elections, the proliferation of formally organized, professionally staffed groups is. What difference does it make if money is channeled through PACs instead of being given directly to candidates by interested individuals? The differences are significant, affecting actual contribution patterns, other political and lobbying activities of a PAC's parent organization, and perhaps the behavior of members of Congress. Each of those effects contributes to a concluding evaluation of the role of PACs.

PACs and Challengers

It is vitally important for a representative government to preserve a serious threat of competition in legislative elections. Since 1950, however, approximately 90 percent of all incumbent members of the House who have sought reelection have won. Since 1968, more than 70 percent have won with at least 60 percent of the two-party vote. Competition in House races was at a low level before the PAC phenomenon, in other words, and has stayed that way. Nevertheless, if it can be shown that the role of PACs significantly adds to the advantage of incumbency in this uncompetitive climate, that would be a strong argument on the side of those who see PACs as harmful.

It is well known that PACs contribute more, on the whole, to incumbents than nonincumbents. But when the distribution of PAC contributions ... is measured against the distribution of candidates by party and candidate status..., it becomes clear that what is called a pro-incumbent bias in fact covers several phenomena. Labor's money is almost entirely Democratic; it tilts toward Democratic incumbents, but a fair share also goes to Democratic challengers. Very little labor money goes to Republican incumbents or challengers. Corporate PACs, in contrast, give Democratic incumbents about as much as one would expect from a random distribution of funds, but give almost as much on these terms to Republican challengers and more to Republican incumbents. Reversing labor's partisanship, corporations tend not to give to Democratic challengers. Thus, ...it would not be accurate to treat PAC contributions merely as if they favor incumbents. The pro-incumbent bias of the aggregate numbers results from trade associations, and from the fact that labor's partisanship exceeds that of corporate PACs.

PACs are more cautious in their contribution patterns than individuals, however, even if they are not simply pro-incumbent....

At first glance, the figures seem to support the common assertion that economic PACs, seeking access for lobbying, reinforce the political advantages of incumbency. Some other considerations point in the opposite direction, however. First, while PACs may not provide seed money to new people, they do seem to weigh in with significant amounts of money for nonincumbents later in the race. Second, we know that when we separate candidates by the competitiveness of their race, most nonincumbent PAC money is concentrated in close races while incumbent money is spread more broadly....

...On balance, therefore, we suspect that the effects of PAC giving may vary with the calendar. Early in the election cycle, when the bulk of organized giving goes to incumbents, the effect may be to help incumbents scare off good challengers or otherwise solidify their position. Later, when strong challengers have been identified, the overall effort may be the opposite. By concentrating their resources on close races, PACs may help to increase the net number of incumbent defeats in a campaign's closing weeks—but only after they have helped reduce the number of potentially vulnerable incumbents in earlier months.

PACs and Lobbying

If PACs are not simply seeking to improve their lobbying position by reinforcing incumbents, perhaps having a PAC helps lobbying in other ways. I argued earlier that it is difficult, when talking about legislative influence, to separate direct campaign contributions from the other electoral and lobbying activities in which interest groups engage. In fact, the activities tend to reinforce each other within the group. When a group organizes itself to solicit employees or members, it is better able to stimulate its employees or members to engage in other activities, and the contributing employees or members are more likely to respond. Two business PAC representatives made this point in 1982 hearings before the House Administration Committee's Task Force on Elections. The first was Gregg Ward, director of governmental affairs for the Sheet Metal and Air Conditioning Contractors National Association:

Simply writing a check doesn't constitute, in and of itself, much in the way of participation in the process. What we have found is that only begins their interest in the process, and to a neophytic group, an unsophisticated one largely like the one I am with, they now see that they can be involved.

They want to know what has happened with their money. We try to keep them informed as to what we are doing with it, but beyond that, it stimulates and generates an interest factor. That interest factor generally then translates into them doing something about it in other manifest ways.

Don V. Cogman, vice-president of MAPCO Inc. for governmental affairs, and president of the National Association of Business Political Action Committees, expanded upon Ward's point by describing some of the specific programs his company uses:

> I can tell you that coming from the political side of this game, and now being on the corporate side, that in my opinion the individual involvement, the people involvement, the volunteer involvement, is more important than money and I think you are finding in the corporate community particularly a new awareness of that. Our counterparts in the labor movement have understood that for decades. The business community has not. I think you are finding that they are beginning to understand it.
>
> In my company specifically we have a program called the citizenship involvement program, which tries to educate, promote, motivate and get involved our employees in all phases of the political system. The PAC is just part of it. I think there is a growing awareness in the corporate community of that fact.

In short, forming a PAC helps a corporation or association get its members or employees active in other aspects of politics and it helps them get members or employees to respond when it is time for grass-roots lobbying. . . . The campaign laws. . .may well have stimulated or facilitated other forms of electoral and lobbying activity when they legitimized direct campaign contributions through PACs, but PAC contributions are not necessary for those activities to continue. Thus, even though a change in the law historically may have been responsible for something, it does not follow that changing the law back will reverse what has happened. The new techniques, once learned, will not be so readily forgotten.

PACs and Members of Congress

The indirect connection between PACs and lobbying is an easy one to understand. Far more complicated is how the growth of PACs may have affected the direct relationships between interest groups and members of Congress. Here we must be even more speculative than we have been so far. I suspect that members of Congress and lobbyists both tend to look at the issue from the wrong end. Both speak of contributors directly pressuring members, using scorecards and other similar devices to get members to behave or vote *against* their inclinations. I frankly do not believe this happens very often. Direct conversion of an opponent is the most difficult of lobbying techniques, tried only in desperation and with rare success. Even when it is successful, or when it results in a slight tempering of a legislator's attitude, we would still have to separate the effect of contributions from lobbying.

...PAC money is and will remain the easiest money for most incumbents to raise. Tens of thousands of dollars typically change hands in any of the hundreds of Washington fund raisers held every year. Far from being events at which lobbyists hold the whip hand and buy favors from members, these fund raisers normally are attended by people who either want to reward their friends for past behavior or are afraid of turning down "invitations" from members whose committees have jurisdictions over their organizations' futures. The members, clearly on top of the situation, use the events to raise $250 or so in quasi-tribute fees from people who might not otherwise support them, in modest latter-day versions of the reverse pressure techniques perfected by Herbert Kalmbach in the 1972 Nixon campaign....

...We can begin to see that the problems of campaign finance in the modern communications age do not lend themselves to easy solutions, for at least two reasons. First, there was always an inherent, and healthy, tension between the desire for accountability and the desire to preserve freedom for members of Congress to think about the national interest. The tension has been exacerbated in recent years. The complexity of government makes it all but impossible for voters to follow individual issues. In addition, a legislator who wants to serve the national interest cannot possibly learn about the potential effects of proposed legislation without the reaction of organized groups. In this situation, the wishes of groups should not be seen merely as nuisances. They also help confer and sustain support for people in government, and they help facilitate the process of both government and opposition by keeping the governors and governed informed.

If interest groups are not merely nuisances, neither has their proliferation been just a blessing. It may be important for people to organize on a national level, especially as the role of government expands. The proliferation of a multiplicity of interests also has some important benefits, as James Madison argued in *Federalist Paper 10.** But I am not one of those twentieth-century pluralist

*See selection 11.—Eds.

misinterpreters of Madison who believes the public good is simply the sum of, or a compromise among, interest-group claims. Group conflict does sometimes produce legislative stalemate, and groups do sometimes win special benefits, at the expense of the general public, when the public is not looking.

It would be misleading, however, to treat campaign finance, or even lobbying, as if they were the fundamental causes of legislative outcomes. They do make a difference, but only at the margins. Lobbyists can win when their activities generally go along with what the public wants, when public opinion is divided, or when the public has no particular opinion. Lobbyists can also help lighten the burden of defeat when the public is against them. Campaign finance may modestly help reinforce the effects of lobbying. But to address the contemporary role of interest groups fully, in its most basic aspects, would force one ultimately to look broadly at the reasons institutional power has been decentralized and at the public philosophy elected members tend to believe or, at least, act upon. These considerations go well beyond the scope of this chapter. Suffice it for now to say that the problem *exists* because most people, in part of their souls, want the government to look after their special, intensely felt desires and needs. It is *perceived* as a problem by most of these same people because, in another part of their souls, they want the government to listen to their more general, less intensely felt, needs and desires when they conflict with the special desires of others. Politically, there is no easy solution because, as Aaron Wildavsky has noted, the Pogo Principle applies: "We have seen the enemy and they are us." All of us react strongly to our own particular concerns, and a fair number of us are likely to let those special concerns determine our vote. As long as that is true, organized interests will continue to play an important role in electoral politics, whatever the rules of campaign finance.

The second reason there are no easy solutions has to do with another byproduct of modern government and communication: the advantages of incumbency, especially for members of the House. The communication resources available to incumbent members, the fractionalization of the congressional policy process, and the long-term weakening of the importance of party to voters all make it hard to defeat incumbents without spending a great deal of money. But a system within which a lot of private money is available almost assuredly is a system in which special interests will participate on an individual or group basis. Interest-group participation may not be all that bad, therefore, if it is a necessary condition for assuring there will be enough money in the system to make the threat of subsequent accountability real.

73

AMY DOCKSER

Nice PAC You've Got Here ...
A Pity if Anything Should Happen to It

———

Senator Rudy Boschwitz prides himself on being accessible to all his constituents, often pointing out that his home telephone number is listed in the Minneapolis phone book. But during much of 1986 some constituents had more access than others. Those who had given at least $1,000 to Boschwitz's campaign during the previous five years became members of his "Washington Club" and were given a booklet of blue "special access stamps." Boschwitz's staff was told to respond to mail with special access stamps faster than the rest of the letters. This summer, after press reports revealed the practice, it stopped.

Of course it should come as no surprise that large contributors enjoy greater access to legislators than those who confine themselves to the more pedestrian forms of support like voting. John Q. Public has always suspected that his call might be returned more slowly than John D. Rockefeller's. But Boschwitz's access stamps illustrate a new brazenness among politicians.

The days of innocent congressmen being corrupted by nefarious PACs and wealthy constituents are gone. It is now the politicians who aggressively pursue the special interests.

The Fish Go Fishing

The phenomenal growth of political action committees has been well documented, their perniciousness well noted. What has been less noted is that candidates now shake down the PACs. "I would guess that 99 percent of PAC contributions are in response to candidates' requests," says Elaine Mullican, election counsel to the Senate Rules Committee.

The strategies for hitting up PACs have grown increasingly imaginative and bold. Seven months ago, then-Senator James Abdnor was involved in a tough primary race. President Reagan had agreed to host a reception for him, but PAC responses to the $1,000-a-plate function were lukewarm. So Abdnor hired couriers to go to 40 PAC offices and present a card soliciting their contributions. The couriers were instructed not to leave an office until they had a response. One PAC representative crumpled the card up and threw it in the courier's face in disgust. That one rebuff notwithstanding, the strategy succeeded: the fund raiser raised $225,000.

After the 1982 elections, successful Democratic senators gave a workshop for those up for reelection in 1984 on how to influence PACs. One strategy they discussed was playing one PAC against another. "They told us how to go to a bank PAC, for example, and tell them that the savings and loan and insurance PACs were already on board, and that they should contribute too or they would miss out," says Senator David Boren, author of legislation to limit PAC contributions. PACs might not believe their contribution will put a legislator in their pockets, but they want to make sure that he or she is not swayed by an economic competitor. "It's a blackmail situation and even the lobbyists and PACs realize it's out of control," says Boren.

A variation on this theme is to play the jealous younger sibling, asking the PAC: if you gave to Congressman Blowhard, why can't you give to me? This ploy requires some homework. Typically, a staff member goes to the Federal Election Commission, copies the quarterly PAC contribution reports, and makes note of the congressmen on the same committees as the boss. "If they know Shell is going to one member of the committee, they call up Shell and tell them that their guy's vote is just as important as other committee members'," recalls a former administrative assistant to a Republican congressman. "If your senator is the fourth ranking member on the Appropriations Committee, for example, you get the chairman's list of contributors and then gauge your senator's worth accordingly, proportionate to the chairman's. If a PAC or lobbyist comes into your office or wants an appointment, you tell them 'you gave $500 to that senator and only $250 to me.'"

It used to be that PACs gave money in order to assure access; now the candidates demand money as the price for access. Boschwitz and Senator Charles Grassley both keep lists of the PACs that have contributed to them on their desks for easy reference. The *Wall Street Journal* recently showed how New York Senator Alfonse D'Amato, former chairman of the securities subcommittee, used his ability to block legislation on regulating junk bonds to elicit $33,000 from employees of Drexel Burnham Lambert, one of the leading promoters of such bonds. The *Journal* quoted one Wall Street lobbyist as saying, "Nothing is enough. It's continuous pressure. If you don't contribute, they don't return your calls."

The fund-raising pitch can be pretty blunt. "If you say you can't come to an event because you'll be out of town, they say, 'We'll tell the senator you don't want to contribute to his campaign.' " says one political consultant who used to manage a PAC. "So then you contribute to his campaign because you don't want to be on a shit list. To raise money you have to ask for it, and if you ask more, you get more."

The bigger the fish, the more bait he or she can demand. Many PACs complained that Senate Finance Committee chairman Robert Packwood used his position and the impending tax reform bill to raise campaign funds. Packwood, for example, asked real estate brokers to hold "real estate industry nights" to raise money for him. The real estate industry was among the industries most petrified in 1985 and 1986 by the prospect of tax reform.

One California legislator told a California commission investigating electoral reforms that during one of the panel's hearings, instead of listening to the testimony, he had been making lists of who might contribute $1,000 to his next fund raiser. "If you're a legislator it has got to cross your mind: a rent control bill is coming up, and it's important to the real estate brokers, landowners, and developers," says Roger Carrick, an aide to former California Governor Jerry Brown. "So you call ten PACs the day before the vote and invite them all to a fund raiser. A friendly phone call.... The potential for corruption is enormous and more people are driven over the edge."

The same tactics apply toward honoraria, the gifts organizations give legislators as "speaking fees." One executive at an electric company says, "Many times candidates call us up and say, 'I'd like to come by and see your plant.' That means 'invite us to give a talk and pay us an honorarium,' and we usually do." Representative Andrew Jacobs, Jr., tells a similar tale. "I know staffers for congressmen that call ahead when their boss is coming into a town and tell PACs and corporations: 'he needs honoraria while he's there, and he expects to get them.' The only reason that's not called bribery is because the congressmen are the ones that decide what constitutes bribery."

The rise of candidate-sponsored PACs have added yet another new twist. Candidates now set up their own PACs, raise money, and distribute it among their colleagues, winning friends along the way. "When members start raising money for other people, saying, 'I want you to give money to my friend,' it makes everyone uncomfortable," says Boren. "You're placed in a position of not just turning down one senator, but any others he's raising money for."

Legislators now hound PACs with such intensity and persistence that one can almost feel sorry for the PACs.

Charles Frazier, Washington director of the National Farmer's Organization, a small PAC, says he gets as many as 100 invitations a week, ten times the number he used to. "What bothers me most, though, is that some congressmen have my home address and they solicit me there. It's annoying to come home after work and find a whole mailbox full of them," Frazier says.

The PAC solicitation process has become routinized and mechanized. Congressional staff members keep close tabs on organizations that write or call the legislator, storing any names in the potential contributors file of their computer. The National Asphalt Pavement Association disbanded its PAC four years ago, in part, they say, because they were tired of being swamped with requests. "We still get ten invitations a day," says the organization's president, John Gray. Senator Bob Graham's campaign corresponded regularly with more than 1,000 PACs, sending them the latest polls, FEC reports, and press clips.

In general, PACs are likely to be kept informed of the date of the next fund raiser—even if the PAC doesn't share the concerns or positions of the legislator. The Consumer Federation of America, for example, this year received several mailings from Representative Joe Skeen. The Federation gave Skeen a lifetime rating of 14 percent on consumer issues, yet his letters always begin, "Because your organization and I share the same concerns and we have worked together on issues affecting my constituents and your members, I thought you'd be interested in the enclosed material."

Bucking Opponents

The principal reason for this aggressiveness is obvious and has been well-covered by the media: the cost of campaigns has skyrocketed. The total amount spent on U.S. Senate races in 1986 was $140 million, twice the amount in 1980. House candidates spent $146 million in 1986, compared to $117 million in 1980.

But most incumbents aggressively raise their money not to finance tough elections, but to avoid them. A hefty war chest can help them avoid contested elections altogether by scaring off potential opponents. That's one reason more than 95 percent of the incumbents won their last election. Not coincidentally, 83 percent of all PAC contributions to House races went to incumbents. Incumbents seeking job security now farm the increasingly fertile PAC fields; there were roughly 4,400 PACs at last count.

In addition, candidates with extra money can gain themselves power in Congress by using their campaign committees or personal PACs to funnel contributions, the 1980s equivalent of Lyndon Johnson greasing his path to congressional power by funneling campaign contributions to colleagues.

A final reason for high-pressure fund-raising is the need to maintain a certain lifestyle. "You can live a fancy life in D.C. or not," says Jacobs. "It's your choice to have nice dinners, hire caterers, and be served by guys in jackets, but that's a heck of an expense. Politicians need money to keep up with lifestyles that aren't really necessary. But it's like taking drugs. Accepting money leads to an addiction."

More than ever before, legislators focus on raising money, now spending as much time fund-raising as legislating. Keith Abbott, finance director of the Democratic Senatorial Campaign Committee, advises Democratic candidates for the Senate to spend at least 50 percent of their time raising money.

The late Representative Phillip Burton warned against the current situation during the debates about the 1974 electoral reforms. "We are the ones who are going to be corrupted," Burton said. "The enemy is going to be us."

When politicians start to see a dollar sign behind every vote, every phone call, every solicitation, those other factors sometimes weighed during governance, like the public good and equal access to government, become less and less important.

74

PETER BRAGDON
What's in a Name?
For Consultants, Much Cash

Advertising's a fashion business. There are five stages. 'Who is this guy, John Fortune?' The second stage: 'Gee, it would be great if we could get that guy, what's his name? John Fortune.' The third stage: 'If we could only get John Fortune.' The fourth stage: 'I'd like to get a young John Fortune.' The fifth stage: 'Who's John Fortune?'

—STUDS TERKEL, *Working*

———

THE MATCHING of media consultants and candidates—what one consultant calls "a mating dance of peacocks"—has become one of the most closely watched facets of American politics.

In the eyes of reporters and contributors, a candidate who manages to land a well-known, well-connected media consultant gains instant credibility. So naturally, candidates get quite anxious about lining up a consultant with a first-rate reputation.

But to a significant and unappreciated degree, the tension is a two-way street. Consultants, knowing that their reputations depend on the success of their candidates, also devote considerable effort to finding the perfect match. Their task is complicated by the fact that the ideal mate is not always the wealthiest candidate, or the one who is favored to win.

The Impossible Dream

As a classic case in reputation-building, consider media consultant Frank Greer's 1986 accomplishments. When the year began, the question might have been "Who is Frank Greer?" Though he had been working as a Democratic media consultant for some time, Greer was not among the most prominent in his field.

But by the end of Election Day that November, he had vaulted into the top tier of Democratic media consultants, propelled by his firm's work for three successful Senate candidates who started their campaigns as long shots—North Dakota's Kent Conrad, Georgia's Wyche Fowler, Jr., and Washington's Brock Adams.

"Greer hit the quinella," says another Democratic consultant.

That feat—helping topple three GOP senators in a year when all eyes were focused on control of the Senate—is the stuff of consultants' fantasies. And like winning the quinella bet at the race track, it is rare.

"The way people establish credibility in this business is very simple," says Bob Squier, who is widely viewed as the top Democratic media consultant. "You take on races that are considered to be impossible or very, very difficult, and you win them. Usually you take on the outsiders and you beat the insiders, and then the insiders want you to work for them."

As in any business venture, credibility lures cash. But even some consultants marvel at how much cash changes hands in their line of work. "In some ways it is outrageous what you can make off of a statewide race," says Democratic consultant Karl Struble.

On top of charging a straight fee, which may range from $25,000 to $75,000, the average consultant also picks up a 15 percent cut of the money spent to buy media advertising time. In a large state such as California, where both 1986 Senate candidates spent more than $11 million, the payoff is significant.

"It's clearly possible for some people in this business to be making a quarter- to a half-million dollars off of each race," says Struble. "The economics are incredible."

Acceptable Risks

One who has shared in that wealth is Greer, who set up his firm, Greer and Associates, in 1983. In 1986, his clients included several candidates whose names were not at the top of anyone's "likely winners" list.

Adams, a former Seattle-area House member and transportation secretary in the Carter administration, had an impressive résumé, but Washingtonians did not seem particularly dissatisfied with GOP Senator Slade Gordon until just a few weeks before the election. In North Dakota, Republican Senator Mark Andrews was rated a likely winner when Democratic Representative Byron L. Dorgan decided against the race, leaving the nomination to Tax Commissioner Conrad. And in Georgia, Fowler, who represented Atlanta in the House, was widely regarded as too urbane and urban to defeat Republican Senator Mack Mattingly.

That Greer has gotten so much attention for those three campaigns illustrates a fundamental tenet of media consulting: While all victories are important, some wins are more equal than others.

By his count, Greer has won 30 of 32 campaigns in his career. His firm handled 14 races in 1986, including Democratic Senator Christopher J. Dodd's in Connecticut. But Dodd's victory did not enhance Greer's reputation as a media magician, for there was no suspense about the outcome.

Many consultants say that helping a challenger usually offers more "psychic rewards" than working to reelect an incumbent.

"An election is an interruption into an incumbent's year," says GOP media consultant Robert Goodman. "He's been working his tail off for five years, he's done a lot of important things...wrestled with a lot of tough votes. Having to go and say, 'Hey, do you like me?' is not enjoyed."

But quite often, bottom-line business concerns discourage a consultant from risking a long-shot client. A consultant is constantly under pressure to keep his overall winning percentage high, and incumbents are more likely to help him do that.

"I enjoy doing underdogs," says Struble. "When you are an underdog you are often on the offensive. I think you get the opportunity to be more creative. The down side is, you can run the best goddam campaign in the world and lose by one point and you've done absolutely nothing to help yourself get new clients the next cycle."

"Incumbents tend to meet the business qualifications more," says GOP media consultant Don Sipple, a partner at Bailey, Deardourff and Sipple. They offer "a better chance of winning, more certainty of funding, and potential repeat business."

No Place to Hide

The down side of working for an incumbent is the embarrassment a consultant can suffer if the incumbent loses. Losing with a long shot is not a black mark on a consultant's ledger, but losing with an incumbent may be. Rumors of how a campaign was botched travel swiftly in Washington, particularly in the clubby Senate. "A reputation can be dashed in an afternoon," says Democratic consultant Raymond Strother.

But once a consultant achieves a certain stature in the profession, he can withstand even a dreadful drubbing on Election Day. While Greer had every reason to pop the champagne cork in 1986, his fellow consultant Goodman had every reason to mourn. Goodman, who says "I die on election night," must have come close last year.

Goodman's agency, based in Baltimore, handled four losing Republican Senate incumbents—Paula Hawkins of Florida, Jeremiah Denton of Alabama, James T. Broyhill of North Carolina and Mark Andrews of North Dakota—an unsuccessful candidate for Louisiana's open Senate seat—GOP Representative Henson Moore—and an unsuccessful House challenger in Tennessee's 3rd District—Jim Golden.

"I have learned great humility on the idea that we can take a man off the street, put him in a pinstripe suit and elect him to the Senate," says Goodman, whose campaign work dates to 1966, when he helped elect Spiro Agnew governor of Maryland.

Goodman says that a year like 1986 does not help his business, but his success in lining up accounts for 1988 suggests that when big-name consultants trip, they don't fall far.

Goodman already is working for three GOP Senate candidates—incumbents Pete Wilson of California and David Karnes of Nebraska and Cleveland Mayor George Voinovich, who is challenging Ohio Democratic Senator Howard M. Metzenbaum. Despite his 1986 defeats, Goodman still is regarded as one of the most talented people in political media.

"I can't believe the season he had hurt him, because those were all very tough, very tight races," says Squier, whose clients defeated Goodman's clients in Alabama, Florida and North Carolina. "A swing of a few thousand votes either way and he would have had a great season and we would have had a mediocre season."

The Big Picture

Squier's generosity toward Goodman points up a sentiment among many consultants that their reputations should not be pegged strictly to their won-lost record, but instead to the entire circumstances of the campaigns in which they work.

"It is probably much better to look at [a consulting firm's] relationship with candidates, and to consider the other factors in a race that they may have no control over" that might have caused the loss, says Greer.

Instead of considering those "other factors" when shopping for a consultant, candidates may be tempted to look simply at a consultant's won–lost record, the only statistical measure of success.

But as the media consulting field has boomed, candidates, faced with an array of choices, have become more adept at sorting out the market.

"[Candidates] are very sophisticated consumers now," says Greer. "Not only do they have a pretty good understanding of what kind of expertise they are going to need, they are very sophisticated buyers of services. They know what questions to ask."

One matter that media consultants are more likely to be judged on these days is their reputation for managing their workload. Some in the business are more careful than others about getting overcommitted, and a campaign that expects a strong helping hand in the weeks just before the November election wants to know how many and what kind of other candidates a consultant is going to have.

"I think that Democratic politics is a small town of about ten thousand people nationally," says Democratic consultant Gary Nordlinger. "The best way to get a bad reputation is to get overextended. Word of that gets all over the country really fast."

Promising the Moon

Nonetheless overpromising does occur. "I think there are some people in this business that will do anything to get a client," says one media consultant. "They lie to them about how much time they are going to get. They deceive them about what the services are going to cost. And then they are not there when the time comes to produce the goods."

Now that media consultants have the technological capacity to produce television advertisements overnight in response to the opposition's ads, consultants may run an even greater risk of getting overextended in the campaign's hectic final weeks.

"The last six weeks is, they throw a grenade, we catch it, throw one back, they catch it," says Goodman. "It's a war. It's not the sweet old days where by August 20 we were all finished [taping ads] and would say to a candidate, 'Well, call us in November and see how you made out.' "

The parties' campaign committees are taking more of a role in educating candidates about media consultants. When a consultant gets involved in Senate, gubernatorial and House campaigns, "sometimes the House becomes a lower priority," says Peggy Connolly of the Democratic Congressional Campaign Committee.

The National Republican Congressional Committee's Steve Lotterer concurs: "Just because you get the prestigious name of a consulting company doesn't mean that you're ever going to see that consultant."

To avoid an overbooked October filled with calls from irate clients, media consultants usually try not to load up on competitive contests, and a number of them shun presidential candidates altogether. A White House campaign can be an all-consuming endeavor that prevents a consultant from paying attention to much else.

And if the presidential candidate drops out amid the primary season, the consultant may be left scrambling for other business at a time when the best non-presidential candidates have already hired their consultants.

A defeated candidate will never enjoy losing, but consultants who manage their workload well say it is possible for a candidate to lose and still be satisfied with his media adviser.

Greer says he tries to keep in mind what clients will say about his performance after the election. When asked about their experience with Greer and Associates, he wants them to be able to say that the agency was not only creative, but also dependable.

Turn on the Spotlight

In addition to a robust winning percentage and a good reputation for delivering promised services, many consultants cite a third factor as crucial to their success—attention.

"One thing people in this business are forced to do is get publicity," says Strother.

It is not surprising that those in the business of selling candidates understand the benefits that can come from drawing attention to themselves.

One way they do so is by choosing their clients according to which contests offer the most exposure. "If there is a mayor's race in Los Angeles or a statewide in Rhode Island," says Republican media consultant Jim Innocenzi, "which one would you rather have? The mayor's race in Los Angeles," a city with three times

Rhode Island's population. The question, Innocenzi says, is this: "Where is there a crucial race, where is a race that you can get some press on?"

A desire for attention is one reason Innocenzi is working for GOP Representative Hal Daub's 1988 Senate campaign in Nebraska. "You have an incumbent Republican congressman challenging an incumbent Republican senator [David Karnes] in a state where the incumbent Republican governor [Kay Orr] appointed the senator," Innocenzi says. "There's a lot of controversy, so you go there."

Who's in Charge Here?

A sure sign of media consultants' growing influence is the increasing propensity of media coverage to focus as much on the advisers' role in a race as on the candidates' activities. There were numerous examples of this in 1986, partly because the media paid a lot of attention to negative television advertising, and thus to the consultants who created those ads.

But even beyond stories on negative ads, consultants got attention in 1986. During the Georgia Senate contest between Fowler and Mattingly, an Atlanta TV station set up a debate between Greer and Mattingly's consultant, Mike Murphy, having failed to arrange a debate between the candidates.

Added proof that consultants can become media stars came when *Life* magazine profiled Goodman shortly before the 1986 election.

Though the spotlight is tempting and helpful to attracting business, there are pitfalls to being a high-profile consultant. "When you're quoted all the time, that makes you very visible in the field, and it gives you credibility," says Sipple. "On the other hand, candidates tire quickly of the press' confusion on who is important in the race."

Many candidates hire consultants precisely because they are well-known, have good press contacts and can get stories on the campaign into the media.

"We're a good source of information on campaigns," says Greer. "We're in touch with them on a day-to-day basis, and [reporters] can reach us sometimes when they can't reach the candidate."

But even some consultants express concern that there are those in the business more worried about covering their flank than about helping their clients. "There are consultants in this town who leak things that are bad for their clients all the time," complains one consultant.

Such leaks often occur when a consultant fears his client is losing: The consultant then tries to portray the race in a way that exempts himself from blame for the defeat.

During an interview with *Congressional Quarterly*, one consultant took a phone call from a client and told him he was likely to lose, without informing him that a reporter was present. Once off the phone, the consultant explained the campaign's weaknesses, exempting his own work on advertising from fault.

Everyone Loves a Winner

While media consulting is a growth industry, the field still is dominated by a handful of firms, and breaking into the top tier is no small feat. That is why Greer's 1986 accomplishment is so envied by the lesser-known practitioners in the business.

The challenge for Greer is to stay on top, but that may turn out to be much less of a feat than getting to the top. In media consulting as in many other fields, the rich get richer.

"If you can get to the point where you have been successful enough so that your winning record looks good," says Squier, "then you are in a position to attract the very best candidates. It is like jockeys. If you get better horses you're going to win more races, and the more races you win, the better horses you get."

75

KIRK VICTOR

The Braintrusters

———

MARTIN ANDERSON thought the idea was great—a defense shield that would eliminate the need to rely on nuclear weapons. The timing was perfect, too, or so thought Anderson, who headed the policy research operation for Ronald Reagan's presidential campaign in 1980.

But the "political people" in the Reagan campaign believed that introducing such an issue at that time would leave the candidate open to attack on his nuclear policy, Anderson recalled.

"Everyone liked the idea of a missile defense system, but we all put it on the back burner for political reasons," recalled Anderson, who is now a senior fellow at the Hoover Institution on War, Revolution and Peace at Stanford University. At the time, Anderson said, he thought the political advisers were wrong, but in retrospect, he believes the decision was correct. (In 1983, Reagan finally proposed his Strategic Defense Initiative.)

In the 1984 campaign, Walter F. Mondale, as he accepted the Democratic Party's presidential nomination, decided to advance an idea that posed similar political risks. "Mr. Reagan will raise taxes, and so will I," Mondale said in his acceptance speech. "He won't tell you. I just did."

Robert G. Beckel, Mondale's national campaign manager in 1984, recalled that the issues experts advising the candidate had advocated the idea as a way to attack the budget deficit but that he and some of the other political people were opposed to it, and "we lost out."

Both episodes illuminate the tension between the immediate demands of the political situation and the opportunity to advance new ideas promoted by experts to whom the candidate looks for imaginative approaches to address the country's problems.

Policy experts advocate ideas they have researched, nurtured and championed but that in the course of a presidential campaign are examined in a political environment that has a far different standard of review than that used by their peers in think tanks or academe. Their proposals must not simply meet exacting peer review standards but must also pass the test of political marketability....

The lack of political acumen that sometimes handicaps "braintrusters" not only in campaigns but also in government service was captured by journalist David Halberstam in *The Best and the Brightest* (Random House, 1972) as he profiled the impressively credentialed people whom President Kennedy looked to for counsel as the country became involved in the war in Vietnam.

In a telling anecdote, Halberstam described how an excited Vice President Lyndon B. Johnson, after attending his first Cabinet meeting, raced to tell his friend and mentor, House Speaker Sam Rayburn, how impressed he had been with the great minds of those in the Cabinet. Rayburn responded, "Well, Lyndon, you may be right and they may be every bit as intelligent as you say, but I'd feel a whole lot better about them if just one of them had run for sheriff once."

Because of their vulnerability to the accusation that they lack political savvy, the policy experts frequently find their ideas challenged by a campaign's political advisers even though the political operatives often lack the expertise to evaluate the idea except in the sense of how they believe it will play to constituents. The experts are also at a disadvantage because they are not on the campaign payroll and often do not have the routine access to the candidate that someone on the staff has.

If, indeed, the political adviser has a disproportionate influence on the campaign, that can lead to unfortunate results. "Regrettably, too many political people are without substance," said Ted Van Dyk of Van Dyk Associates Inc., who has advised Democratic candidates in six presidential campaigns and began this political season advising Hart until Hart dropped out of the race in May. "They want to please constituents ... and tell them what they want to hear."

On the other hand, he said, "the programmatic issues people are often devoid of political reality," and their substantive proposals have frequently been developed in a vacuum....

But even when a policy adviser persuades the issues director and ultimately the candidate to adopt his approach to a problem, he still faces another problem inherent in political campaigns, according to John D. Holum of the Washington office of the Los Angeles law firm of O'Melveny & Myers, who directed Hart's issues operation in 1984 and again last year until Hart dropped out.

All candidates "recognize that issues are important in giving them identity with the public," Holum said. But the problem is "how to convey relatively complex issues through the filter of political journalism and television sound bites.... The institutions don't mesh well in terms of getting through to the public at large what the candidates would do as President in any depth. That is part of the reason the candidates avoid complex issues: There's no payoff; they can't get it across to the public."

As candidates shy away from advancing complex new ideas,

the experts they might rely on may become relegated to the sidelines or, perhaps, listed among a large number of people whose ideas may be secondary to the public relations benefits a candidate may be seeking by publishing lists of luminaries. . . .

"The candidates this time around are more conservative in terms of their relative unwillingness to stick their necks out with bold visions or come out with specific programmatic options," said Robert B. Reich, a professor of political economy and management at Harvard University's John F. Kennedy School of Government.

Reich said that the "macroeconomic straitjacket" the country is in makes it more difficult to discuss new federal programs and that character has become such a "palpable issue" that many of the candidates are "willing to run on policy generalities while putting character and personality into the fore."

This means that "issues people are not as central to these campaigns as they have been in certain elections," said Reich, who has provided advice to several of this year's Democratic candidates. "Neither programmatic solutions nor specific policy themes or policies are going to be at the center of the debate."...

Another kind of counsel needed...comes in the context of "rapid reaction events," such as the U.S. military encampment in Lebanon or the invasion of Grenada. William A. Glaston, who directed the issues staff for Mondale's campaign and is now director of economic and social programs at the Roosevelt Center for American Policy Studies, said "If you're a presidential candidate, you'll be asked [about such events] within 24 hours or sooner. Usually [the candidate] will believe there's a need to weigh options and hear the opinions of those who have spent careers in an area."

Anderson recalled that in 1980, he carried "a little black book on the campaign plane" in which the names of several dozen key advisers were listed. One day while on the plane, he said, news was developing about a sudden crisis in the international money markets, and Reagan advisers knew the press would be asking about it when the plane landed. So calls were made from the plane to economist Milton Friedman and former Federal Reserve Board chairman Arthur F. Burns. By the time the plane touched down, a press release had been issued and the candidate was prepared for press inquiries.

Madeleine K. Albright, professor of international relations at the Georgetown University School of Foreign Service and the senior foreign policy adviser to Michael S. Dukakis, stresses that the candidate does not rely on a small coterie of advisers. Dukakis "would like to get as many varied opinions as possible" and is not "a hostage to anyone in particular" for advice, she said.

"We haven't structured [the campaign] in such a way as to produce lists of advisers that would persuade opinion shapers that we're elaborately tied into the Establishment," said Christopher Edley, Dukakis's issues director.

As if to rebut the notion that a governor might lack foreign policy expertise, Albright said "a lot of foreign policy is a process" that requires the skills of someone who is able to arrive at decisions after hearing from a wide range of people with differing views, a skill that, not surprisingly, she calls one of Dukakis's strengths.

Even as the candidates decide which policy proposals to pursue, there is the issue of why university scholars and experts, who are secure in their professional fields, should subject their work to the vicissitudes of a political campaign where well-researched ideas may be rejected as a result of political exigencies that have nothing to do with the proposal's merits.

Janne E. Nolan, a guest scholar at the Brookings Institution who was Gary Hart's foreign policy and defense adviser in the Senate and in his 1984 presidential campaign identified three schools of thought about what attracts policy experts to presidential campaigns. Some, she said, feel strong commitments to the issues. Some are flattered to participate and to share their expertise in an arena they are generally not a part of. And others tend to be attached to a particular candidate and "really believe that working on a campaign advances their career and have great hopes and plans for a Cabinet or sub-Cabinet position."

As for those hoping for a job as a reward for providing expertise to a campaign, Reich believes that there has been a dramatic change in attitudes about government service since President Kennedy.

"Unlike the 1960s and the lure of Camelot, there are few hard-headed individuals plotting, scheming and clawing their way to a position of power inside the beltway," he said. For anyone who has been in government service before, as he has, Reich said, "there's little luster and almost no lust left."

76

MARK SHIELDS

Political Humor:
Who Are All These Jokers?

———

DURING THE 1960 campaign, when Richard Nixon attempted to make Harry Truman's profanity into a campaign issue, John Kennedy, aware that his Catholicism was on voters' minds, handled the matter this way: "I would not want to give the impression that I am taking President Truman's use of language lightly. I have sent him the following wire: 'Dear Mr. President: I have noted with interest your suggestion as to where those who vote for my opponent can go. While I understand and sympathize with your deep motivation, I think it is important that our side try to refrain from raising the religious issue.' "

Political humor is a very serious business. It's so serious that every 1988 presidential campaign will spend considerable effort, energy, and time proving that its candidate possesses a well-rounded sense of humor. At a minimum, a national campaign must be able to disprove any malicious rumor that its candidate is *without* a sense of humor, a condition regarded as probably un-American and certainly a character defect.

Good American character is usually understood to include a good sense of humor. In a president or presidential candidate, that sense of humor can be reassuring to the voter whose vote for president is the most personal one he casts. The presidential choice is much more personal than a congressional vote, for example, which is far more likely to be based on a candidate's party affiliation or his stands on issues such as AIDS or acid rain. In a president, we look for—and are confident we'll be able to detect—those special qualities of character, personality, and intellect we most value in our national leader.

Humor, especially the self-deprecatory variety with which a politician publicly and voluntarily kids his own perceived weaknesses and mistakes, can communicate an emphatically positive message about that politician's emotional security to the voters. Nobody in American politics understood this reality better than Dick Drayne, whose untimely death this year at age 49 followed a career at CBS News and earlier tours as press secretary to both Senators Robert and Edward Kennedy. After Ted Kennedy lost the Whip's position in a secret ballot of the Senate Democratic Caucus, Kennedy used the following Drayne line: "I want to take this opportunity to thank the twenty-eight senators who promised to vote for me. I especially want to thank the twenty-four who actually did."

While Dick Drayne wrote for only a few, he undoubtedly spoke for many Americans when he once observed, "Presidents without a sense of humor make me nervous." Bob Orben, who wrote jokes for Red Skelton and speeches for President Ford and now publishes *Orben's Current Comedy,* put the same thought just a little differently: "I'm afraid of people who don't laugh."

Circumstantial evidence that a presidential candidate lacks a sense of humor can turn that unlucky fellow into a laughingstock. Regardless how bright he may be, that candidate will be branded dull. That was the unhappy fate of Senator Henry M. "Scoop" Jackson when he ran for president in 1976. The joke circulated then that Scoop Jackson was so boring, he gave a fireside chat and the fire went out.

To rebut the charge of humorlessness, Senator Jackson memorized a story about Richard Nixon's first visit to the White House following President Ford's pardon of him. As Nixon and Ford walked into the Oval Office, Nixon bumped into Ford. Quickly Mr. Nixon apologized by saying, "Pardon me," to which President Ford immediately replied, "I already did." Not exactly a sidesplitter, most would agree, but good for a smile from a partisan Democratic crowd. That is, until Scoop Jackson told it. When Jackson reached the point where Nixon bumped into Ford, he changed Nixon's line to "Excuse me," which made Ford's "I already did" an unfunny *non sequitur* that left Jackson's audience befuddled.

Jackson might still have had a chance in 1976, a year when candidate humor was obviously not a top priority with presidential voters. How else to explain the election of President Jimmy Carter, whose own White House speechwriter responsible for humor, Jerry Doolittle, later observed, "Making Jimmy Carter funny was like

being FDR's tap dance coach." Another White House aide added
that "Carter's idea of self-deprecatory humor is to insult his staff."

Wooing with One-Liners

Humor can humanize a politician, and really good humor can
help him professionally. Witness the 1985 election of Wyoming's
Alan Simpson as Senate Republican Whip. Much earlier, his masterful managing of the controversial immigration bill had shown
that Senator Simpson knew the fundamental rules for putting together a majority: viz. politics is a matter of addition, not subtrac-
tion, and it's always easier for anyone to vote with, or for, somebody he or she likes.

Smiling is a bipartisan activity, and not even Grumpy could
suppress a smile when hearing Simpson's favorite response to flow-
ery and fulsome introductions. Simpson would just thank the intro-
ducer and add that today's introduction had been "a lot nicer than
the one I received the other day in Cheyenne, where the master of
ceremonies said, 'Now for the latest dope from Washington—Alan
Simpson.' "

The political genius of that line lies in what it immediately
conveys to any audience. He's implicitly stating, "I am really not
pompous or self-important or even impressed by public praise.
Although I'm up here on the platform, I don't consider myself
any better than any of you down in the crowd." All those expressions are political pluses in democratic America.

As good as it is, the self-deprecating "latest dope" line finishes
a distant second to the classic irreverence of Simpson's comeback
to an inquiry about his "church preference." He answered, "Red
brick."

A working sense of humor can help a presidential candidate to
woo the public, and it can practically guarantee favorable press for
him or her. On the campaign trail, where the candidate and the
reporter are both sentenced—one to give the same speech, the
other to listen to it—a little humor can go a long way.

It can pierce the boredom and provide the reporter with a fresh
angle. Political reporters, a proudly disrespectful lot, are mostly
suckers for the candidate who can naturally laugh at himself and
make them laugh, too. A poll of the campaign press bus would
show overwhelming agreement with the late Adlai Stevenson's
analysis that "Humor helps to distinguish the really bright and

thoughtful, and also the humble, from the self-conscious and the self-righteous presumptuous type."

That respected political philosopher, Mae West, probably did not have campaign humor in mind when she observed "Too much of a good thing can be wonderful." For a national candidate, humor can be risky; the wisecrack that earns voter chuckles may do so at the price of voter reassurance. Recall candidate Barry Goldwater's throwaway line about lobbing "a grenade into the men's room of the Kremlin." At the Legion post on a Friday night where some of the guys were having a shot and a beer, that one would have undoubtedly played to favorable reviews. But in a would-be president, such confrontational cockiness was unnerving and unacceptable.

For Senate Republican leader and 1988 presidential candidate Bob Dole, an authentically witty man, humor has been an occasional problem with certain grim party activists (that humorless variety now found in both parties in depressingly increasing numbers). Some Republican primary voters have yet to forgive Dole for the following classic, which Independents and a few Democrats cite as proof of the Kansan's admirable appreciation of the absurd: Seated at the head table of a black-tie dinner honoring Admiral Hyman Rickover were former presidents Jimmy Carter, Gerald Ford, and Richard Nixon, or as Dole described the trio, "See No Evil, Hear No Evil, and ... Evil."

FUNNY GIRLS

Women in politics had to struggle to be taken seriously, so women politicians were reluctant to use humor. Happily, their growing confidence is overcoming that reluctance.

No political woman is funnier than former Johnson White House aide and Texas feminist Liz Carpenter, a Democrat. In 1972, when polls showed Richard Nixon crushing George McGovern by 35 percentage points, former Texas Governor John Connally agreed to become chairman of the Democrats for Nixon. This prompted Carpenter to state, "If John Connally had been at the Alamo, he would have organized Texans for Santa Ana."

Then there was Secretary of Transportation Elizabeth Dole, a native of North Carolina, at the Gridiron

dinner. Declaring that she, like the president, had been
born a Democrat, Secretary Dole went on, "I was ten
years old before I discovered there was a Republican
party. Of course, when the president was ten years
old, there was no Republican party."

In New York this year, prominent feminists held
the third annual roast of a prominent feminist. The
evening's most memorable line was Gloria Steinem's.
Asked what Geraldine Ferraro had taught women about
running for office, she said: "Never get married." That's
funny.

Laughing It Off

Humor may be helpful or even crucial to winning the White
House, but it's probably indispensable to presidential success. The
United States has had in the last twenty-five years only two popular
presidents, Democrat John Kennedy and Republican Ronald
Reagan.

Besides a way with words and an Irish heritage, what did these
decidedly different leaders have in common? Both politicians have
possessed a comfortable sense of self and an engaging sense of
humor of the kind that could consolidate their political allies, convert the unaligned, and confound their adversaries. Each man successfully employed humor to neutralize his political negatives and
to enhance his public persona.

Kennedy's use of wit during the 1960 campaign was especially
daring. In spite of memorable passages such as, "Nixon is the
kind of politician who would cut down a redwood tree, then mount
the stump for a speech on conservation," Adlai Stevenson had lost
the two previous elections. Stevenson's cerebral wit, most party
leaders agreed, had not helped him in those campaigns. If Stevenson
had been clever and lost, the reasoning went, then JFK ought to
be sober and solemn.

But Kennedy's approach was unconventional. In the face of
repeated charges that he was too young and too rich, with a ruthless
millionaire father determined to buy the White House, the Massachusetts Democrat neutralized his negatives with humor. He told
the 1958 Washington Gridiron dinner, "I have just received the
following telegram from my generous daddy. It says, 'Dear Jack:
Don't buy a single vote more than is necessary. I'll be damned if

I'm going to pay for a landslide.' "

Self-deprecatory humor enabled Kennedy and others to laugh at the rich kid criticism and to defuse a potentially bothersome issue. To the suggestion that, at just forty-three, he was too young to be president, Kennedy answered, "It has recently been observed that whether I serve one or two terms in the presidency, I will find myself at the end of that period at what might be called the awkward age—too old to begin a new career and too young to write my memoirs." By focusing attention on an inconsequential hypothetical dilemma he might possibly confront some eight years in the future, Kennedy made the age issue as well as his opponents who raised it look a little silly.

Once in office, Kennedy provoked loud and furious opposition by nominating his thirty-five-year-old brother—who had a limited legal background—to be U.S. Attorney General. The new president used an old twist to take the edge off the controversy, "I don't see what's wrong with giving Bobby a little experience before he goes out to practice law." But the JFK needle that has been most frequently repackaged by subsequent speakers was delivered the night he hosted all the living Nobel Prize winners in the western hemisphere. "I think," said the president, "this is the most extraordinary collection of talent, of human knowledge, that has ever been collected together at the White House—with the possible exception of when Thomas Jefferson dined alone." Certain glory awaits the 1988 candidate who, before a Washington press dinner, observes: "This is the most extraordinary collection of journalistic talent, with the possible exception of when Evans and Novak have breakfast together."

At the use of humor to deflect criticism of his presidential performance, John Kennedy was good, but Ronald Reagan has been better. It could be because Reagan—having received more criticism—has had a lot more practice. Typical of Ronald Reagan's self-tweaking on the potentially sensitive subject of his own age was the president's 1983 line at the Washington Press Club. After mentioning that the Club had been founded in 1919, Mr. Reagan added: "It seems like only yesterday." But truly effective self-deprecatory humor by a politician doesn't come any better than President Reagan at the 1987 Gridiron dinner.

That was a time when confidence in the president's job performance had plummeted, when doubt was spreading about whether a seventy-six-year-old Ronald Reagan was up to the job, and when the First Lady's hostility for the White House chief of staff was an open secret.

Here's how Ronald Reagan dealt with his political problems that night:

• "With the Iran thing occupying everyone's attention, I was thinking. Do you remember the flap when I said, 'We begin bombing in five minutes?' Remember when I fell asleep during my audience with the Pope? Remember Bitburg?...Boy, those were the good old days."

• "Nineteen eighty-six was the year of hostile takeover attempts, inside maneuverings, high-stakes intrigue—and that was just at the White House."

• "Nancy and Don (Regan) at one point tried to patch things up. They met privately over lunch. Just the two of them and their food tasters."

• "It's true hard work never killed anybody, but I figure why take the chance?"

In the midst of personal adversity, Reagan showed a robust sense of self-confidence that confounded his political adversaries. Earlier, when Reagan's tax cuts had failed to produce enough new revenues to balance the federal budget and instead had led to giant deficits, Reagan said: "I'm not going to worry about the deficit. It's big enough to take care of itself."

Just a minute, argues the Reagan critic, the president doesn't produce these lines; he just delivers them like a pro. Other professionals write them. That may be true, but there were no 3×5 cards or Hollywood gag writers in the George Washington University Hospital emergency room that day in 1981 when Ronald Reagan barely avoided death. And the nation held its breath. The president lifted the national spirits when, borrowing a line from former heavyweight champ Jack Dempsey, he explained to Mrs. Reagan, "Honey, I forgot to duck."

Of course, the quality of the humor of the 1988 candidates is still largely unknown. But early returns are not encouraging, as indicated by this gem from Illinois Senator Paul Simon at a Washington roast of New Jersey Senator Bill Bradley: Simon announced that his first cabinet appointment would be Bradley as Secretary of Transportation, because "he was a Rhodes Scholar." We can only hope that, for once, the brilliant Mark Russell was wrong when he said, "George Bush versus Michael Dukakis. There isn't enough caffeine in the world to keep us awake for that."

PART TWELVE

Political Parties

NOWHERE is there more convincing evidence of what we have called the exceptionalism of American politics than in the unique dynamic of our party system. Operating entirely in the liberal center of the usual European political spectrum, organizationally weak and decentralized, often so indifferent to ideology as to seem unprincipled, and comparatively undisciplined as they go about the work of governing, American political parties have always puzzled students of comparative politics who have sought to place them convincingly in any kind of cross-national conceptual or theoretical scheme. Try as one might, they just do not seem to fit. American political parties, like so many other aspects of the American polity, simply do not fit the European mold; they have followed a different developmental dynamic. There is nothing quite like them anywhere else.

Most American political scientists have been content to study American parties "on native grounds," more or less unconcerned with how they might be understood on the larger world stage. Some twenty-five years ago it seemed that our efforts had begun to yield a fairly impressive body of knowledge. At the center of this work was what we called, (following its pioneering theorist,

V. O. Key) the concept of "critical elections" or "critical realignments." According to the theory, these events occurred with something like generational regularity in American history, facilitating
adjustments to socio-economic change and permitting big issues
to be settled in a decisive manner through the electoral process.
Particularly at these critical junctures, it was argued, the parties
became significantly different in issue-orientation, permitting voters to choose between relatively clear options on the big public
policy questions of the time. Although there was considerable disagreement on how well they did their job, political parties were
seen as centrally important agents in American politics. It was
widely agreed that they pulled together a system of separated powers, providing the leadership and direction that modern government required. So things were understood in the early 1960s. Subsequent developments have rendered all of this much less clear.
The expectation established by realignment theory that decisive
political change would come in the form of something like the
electoral events that ushered in the New Deal in the 1930s has
been unfulfilled. Clearly, no such "big bang" realignment has happened. Meanwhile, the parties themselves have undergone largely
unanticipated changes that have weakened their old structural base,
the state and local organizations, and their hold on the minds of
voters. Television, campaign consultants, electronic data processing, legal reforms, and a host of other factors have radically altered
the American electoral landscape. Today it seems very doubtful
that parties are the central agents in our politics that we once
supposed them to be. Perhaps the clearest thing about the contemporary party system is that it does not accord well with what we
thought we understood only a few years ago. The events of the
last twenty-five or so years have outrun our ability to put them in
conceptual and theoretical order.

Our readings on the party system begin with a selection from
Walter Dean Burnham's *Critical Elections and the Mainsprings of
American Politics,* a classic statement of realignment theory written
in 1970. The elements of the theory are all here. According to
Burnham, at least five critical elections have occurred during the
course of American history. Coming roughly once a generation
between 1800 and 1932, these elections stand in sharp contrast to
others in that they mark abrupt alterations in usual electoral behavior. Burnham sees critical elections as moments of intense feelings,
high participation, and ideological polarization, which bring about

a new partisan majority and new directions in public policy. Critical elections, he argues, are the mechanisms whereby our unique party system (which he sees as organizationally "archaic" and "rudimentary" compared with European systems) permitted the management of tensions created by socioeconomic change.

In the same year that Burnham produced his account of historical realignments in the party system, the journalist David Broder voiced his concern in *The Party's Over,* from which our next reading is drawn, that American political parties had entered a period of decline which seriously threatened their ability to perform their traditional functions. Lower rates of electoral participation, weakened party identification, and ticket splitting indicated a significant erosion of political parties' ability to mobilize voters, clarify policy alternatives, reconcile conflict, and impart coherence to the activity of government. Broder was particularly alarmed at the new enthusiasm of voters for ticket splitting and its tendency to produce divided party control of the presidency and Congress—a condition that would become virtually institutionalized in the next twenty years. Broder implored voters to think about what they were doing when they cast ballots, so as to give neither party full responsibility for the performance of government. His logic, the traditional logic of party government, is that we should give responsibility to one party at a time. To do otherwise would be to invite deadlock and irresponsibility.

Xandra Kayden and Eddie Mahe, two observers close to the new politics of the Democratic and Republican parties respectively, take up Broder's subject in a different way in their 1985 book *The Party Goes On.* Kayden and Mahe stress that the American party system is anything but moribund. The parties go on, adapting to a new setting. While the old state and local organizations are less important, new cadres of "professionals" have grown up at the center, allowing both parties to operate more efficiently in a new socioeconomic environment. As the old parties thrived in earlier social settings, the new ones will continue to adapt. They argue that new communications technologies and new life-styles require the parties to operate in new ways. We should not confuse transformation of the party system with party decline.

Our final reading, by Everett Ladd, was written just after the elections of 1988. Ladd argues that the 1988 elections are best seen as a continuation of a process of realignment that began in the late 1960s that has made the Republicans the majority party in presidential elections and the carrier of the ascendant public philosophy. Implicit in Ladd's analysis is the argument that realignments take place in different ways; there is no reason to suppose that they all fit a single model. Looked at in sufficient detail, each one looks different from the other. The post–New Deal alignment with its split partisan majorities (the Republicans' in the presidency, the Democrats' in Congress) is now a fact. What has happened since the late 1960s is not like what happened in the 1930s, but it is a realignment nevertheless because it has significantly altered partisan behavior and the course of public policy. The present system, he argues, has a structure so vastly different from that of the New Deal system that there can be no doubt that we are now in an entirely different political world.

Do all of these perspectives add up neatly? Clearly, they do not. That is because the contemporary literature of the party system is in considerable disarray. Our readings are intended to convey the disagreements and conceptual confusion that are actually there in the classroom and the professional journals. As we said at the beginning, that is the current state of affairs.

77

WALTER DEAN BURNHAM
Critical Realignments

From *Critical Elections and the Mainsprings of American Politics*

———

FOR MANY DECADES it has been generally recognized that American electoral politics is not quite "all of a piece" despite its apparent diverse uniformity. Some elections have more important long-range consequences for the political system as a whole than others, and seem to "decide" substantive issues in a more clear-cut way. There has long been agreement among historians that the elections of those of 1800, 1828, 1860, 1896, and 1932, for example, were fundamental turning points in the course of American electoral politics.

Since the appearance in 1955 of V. O. Key's seminal article, "A Theory of Critical Elections," political scientists have moved to give this concept quantitative depth and meaning. . . .

It now seems time to attempt at least an interim assessment of the structure, function, and implications of critical realignments for the American political process. Such an effort is motivated in particular by the author's view that critical realignments are of fundamental importance not only to the system of political action called "the American political process" but also to the clarifications of some aspects of its operation. It seems particularly important in a period of obvious political upheaval not only to identify these phenomena and place them in time, but to integrate them into a larger (if still very modest) theory of movement in American politics.

Such a theory must inevitably emphasize the elements of stress and abrupt transformation in our political life at the expense of the consensual, gradualist perspectives which have until recently dominated the scholar's vision of American political processes and behavior. For the realignment phenomenon focuses our attention on "the dark side of the moon." It reminds us that politics as usual in the United States is not politics as always; that there are discrete types of voting behavior and quite different levels of voter response to political stimuli, depending on what those stimuli are and at what point in time they occur; and that American political institutions and leadership, once defined (or redefined) in a "normal phase" of our politics, seem to become part of the very conditions that threaten to overthrow them. . . .

In its "ideal-typical" form, the critical realignment differs from stable alignments eras, secular [gradual] realignments, and deviating elections in the following basic ways.

1. The critical realignment is characteristically associated with short-lived but very intense disruptions of traditional patterns of voting behavior. Majority parties become minorities; politics which was once competitive becomes noncompetitive or, alternatively, hitherto one-party areas now become arenas of intense partisan competition; and large blocks of the active electorate—minorities, to be sure, but perhaps involving as much as a fifth to a third of the voters—shift their partisan allegiance.

2. Critical elections are characterized by abnormally high intensity as well.

  a. This intensity typically spills over into the party nominating and platform-writing machinery during the upheaval and results in major shifts in convention behavior from the integrative "norm" as well as in transformations in the internal loci of power in the major party most heavily affected by the pressures of realignment. Ordinarily accepted "rules of the game" are flouted; the party's processes, instead of performing their usual integrative functions, themselves contribute to polarization.

b. The rise in intensity is associated with a considerable increase in ideological polarizations, at first within one or more of the major parties and then between them. Issue distances between the parties are markedly increased, and elections tend to involve highly salient issue-clusters, often with strongly emotional and symbolic overtones, far more than is customary in American electoral politics. One curious property of established leadership as it drifts into the stress of realignment seems to be a tendency to become more rigid and dogmatic, which itself contributes greatly to the explosive "bursting stress" of realignment....

c. The rise in intensity is also normally to be found in abnormally heavy voter participation for the time....

3. Historically speaking, at least, national critical realignments have not occurred at random. Instead, there has been a remarkably uniform periodicity in their appearance....

4. It has been argued, with much truth, that American political parties are essentially constituent parties. That is to say, the political-party subsystem is sited in a socioeconomic system of very great heterogeneity and diversity....

Critical realignments emerge directly from the dynamics of this constituent-function supremacy in American politics. ... In other words, realignments are themselves constituent acts: they arise from emergent tensions in society which, not adequately controlled by the organization or outputs of party politics as usual, escalate to a flash point; they are issue-oriented phenomena, centrally associated with these tensions and more or less leading to resolution adjustments; they result in significant transformations in the general shape of policy; and they have relatively profound aftereffects on the roles played by institutional elites. They are involved with redefinitions of the universe of voters, political parties, and the broad boundaries of the politically possible.

To recapitulate, then, eras of critical realignment are marked by short, sharp reorganizations of the mass coalitional bases of the major parties which occur at periodic intervals on the national are often preceded by major third-party revolts which reveal the incapacity of "politics as usual" to integrate, much less aggregate, emergent political demand; are closely associated with abnormal stress in the socioeconomic system; are marked by ideological polarizations and issue-distances between the major parties which are exceptionally large by normal standards; and have durable consequences as constituent acts which determine the outer boundaries of policy in general, though not necessarily of policies in detail.... There is much evidence ... that realignments do recur with rather remarkable regularity approximately once a generation, or every thirty to thirty-eight years.

The precise timing of the conditions which conduce to realignment is conditioned heavily by circumstance, of course: the intrusion of major crises in society and economy with which "politics as usual" in the United States cannot adequately cope, and the precise quality and bias of leadership decisions in a period of high political tension, cannot be predicted in specific time with any accuracy. Yet a broadly repetitive pattern of oscillation between the normal inertia of mass electoral politics and the ruptures of the normal which realignments bring about is clearly evident from the data. So evident is this pattern that one is led to suspect that the truly "normal" structure of American electoral politics at the mass base is precisely this dynamic, even dialectic polarization between long-term inertia and concentrated bursts of change in this open system of action. It may well be that American political institutions, including the major political parties, are so organized that they have a chronic, cumulative tendency toward underproduction of other than currently "normal" policy outputs. They may tend persistently to ignore, and hence not to aggregate, emergent political demand of a mass character until a boiling point of some kind is reached.

In this context, the rise of third-party protests as what might be called protorealignment phenomena would be associated with the repeated emergence of a rising gap between perceived expectations of the political process and its perceived realities over time, diffused among a constantly increasing portion of the active electorate and perhaps mobilizing many hitherto inactive voters....

The periodic rhythm of American electoral politics, the cycle of oscillation between the normal and the disruptive, corresponds precisely to the existence of largely unfettered developmental change in the socioeconomic system and its absence in the country's political institutions. Indeed, it is a prime quantitative measure of the interaction between the two. The socioeconomic system develops but the institutions of electoral politics and policy formation remain essentially unchanged. Moreover, they do not have much capacity to adjust incrementally to demand arising from socioeconomic dislocations. Dysfunctions centrally related to this process become more and more visible, until finally entire classes, regions, or other major sectors of the population are directly injured or come to see themselves as threatened by imminent danger. Then the triggering event occurs, critical realignments follow, and the universe of policy and of electoral coalitions is broadly redefined. It is at such moments that the constitution-making role of the American voter becomes most visible, and his behavior, one suspects, least resembles the normal pattern....

In this context, then, critical realignment emerges as decisively important in the study of the dynamics of American politics. It is as symptomatic of political nonevolution in this country as are the archaic and increasingly rudimentary structures of the political parties themselves. But even more importantly, critical realignment may well be defined as the chief tension-management device available to so peculiar a political system. Historically it has been the chief means through which an underdeveloped political system can be recurrently brought once again into some balanced relationship with the changing socioeconomic system, permitting a restabilization of our politics.... Granted the relative inability of our political institutions to make gradual adjustments along vectors of *emergent* political demand, critical realignments have been as inevitable as they have been necessary to the normal workings of American politics. Thus once again there is a paradox: the conditions which decree that coalitional negotiation, bargaining, and incremental, unplanned, and gradual policy change become the dominant characteristic of American politics in its normal state also decree that it give way to abrupt, disruptive change with considerable potential for violence....

Such a dynamically oriented frame of reference presupposes a holistic view of American politics which is radically different from that which until very recently has tended to dominate the professional literature. The models of American political life and political processes with which we are most familiar emphasize the well-known attributes of pluralist democracy. There are not stable policy majorities. Intense and focused minorities with well-defined interests exert influence on legislation and administrative rule making out of all proportion to their size. The process involves gradual, incremental change secured after bargaining has been completed among a wide array of interested groups who are prepared to accept the conditions of bargaining. It is true that such descriptions apply to a "politics as usual" which is an important fragment of political reality in the United States, but to describe this fragment as the whole of that reality is to assume an essentially ideological posture whose credibility can be maintained only by ignoring the complementary dynamics of American politics as a whole. . . .

The reality of this process taken as a whole seems quite different from the pluralist vision. It is one shot through with escalating tensions, periodic electoral upheavals, and repeated redefinitions of the rules and outcomes-in-general of the political game, as well as redefinitions—by no means always broadening ones—of those who are in fact permitted to play it. One very basic characteristic of American party politics which emerges from a contemplation of critical realignments is a profound incapacity of established political leadership to adapt itself sequentially—or even incrementally?—to emergent political demand generated by the losers in our stormy socioeconomic transformations. American political parties are not action instrumentalities of definable and broad social collectivities; as organizations they are, consequently, interested in control of offices but not of government in the broader sense of which we have been speaking. It follows from this that once successful routines are established or reestablished for winning office, there is no motivation among party leaders to disturb the routines of the game. These routines are disturbed not by adaptive change within the party-policy system, but by the application of overwhelming external force.

78

DAVID BRODER

Partakers in the Government

From *The Party's Over*

MY VIEW is that American politics is at an impasse, that we have been spinning our wheels for a long, long time; and that we are going to dig ourselves ever deeper into trouble, unless we find a way to develop some political traction and move again. I believe we can get that traction, we can make government responsible and responsive again, only when we begin to use the political parties as they are meant to be used. And that is the thesis of this book.

It is called *The Party's Over,* not in prophecy, but in alarm. I am not predicting the demise of the Republicans or the Democrats. Party loyalties have been seriously eroded, the Democratic and Republican organizations weakened by years of neglect. But our parties are not yet dead. What happens to them is up to us to decide. If we allow them to wither, we will pay a high price in the continued frustration of government. But, even if we seek their renewal, the cost of repairing the effects of decades of governmental inaction will be heavy. The process will be painful and expensive. Whatever the fate of our political parties, for America the party *is* over....

...The reason we have suffered governmental stalemate is that we have not used the one instrument available to us for disciplining government to meet our needs. That instrument is the political party.

Political parties in America have a peculiar status and history. They are not part of our written Constitution. The Founding Fathers, in fact, were determined to do all they could to see they did not arise. Washington devoted much of his Farewell Address to warning his countrymen against "the dangers of party in the state." And yet parties arose in the first generation of the nation, and have persisted ever since. Their very durability argues that they fill a need. That need is for some institution that will sort out, weigh, and, to the extent possible, reconcile the myriad conflicting needs and demands of individuals, groups, interests, communities and regions in this diverse continental Republic; organize them for the contest for public office; and then serve as a link between the constituencies and the men chosen to govern. When the parties fill their mission well, they tend to serve both a unifying and a clarifying function for the country. Competitive forces draw them to the center, and force them to seek agreement on issues too intense to be settled satisfactorily by simple majority referendum. On the other hand, as grand coalitions, they are capable of taking a need felt strongly by some minority of the population and making it part of a program endorsed by a majority.

When they do not function well, things go badly for America. The coming of the Civil War was marked by a failure of the reconciling function of the existing parties. Long periods of stagnation, too, can be caused by the failure of the parties to bring emerging public questions to the point of electoral decision. When the parties fail, individual citizens feel they have lost control of what is happening in politics and in government. They find themselves powerless to influence the course of events. Voting seems futile and politics a pointless charade....

The governmental system is not working because the political parties are not working. The parties have been weakened by their failure to adapt to some of the social and technological changes taking place in America. But, even more, they are suffering from simple neglect: neglect by Presidents and public officials, but, particularly, neglect by the voters. It is to remind us that the parties can be used for positive purposes that this book is written.

Some students of government who share this view of the importance of political parties in American government nonetheless think it futile to exhort readers on their behalf. Such political scientists as James L. Sundquist and Walter Dean Burnham, whose knowledge of American political history is far deeper than my own, believe we are simply in the wrong stage of the political cycle to expect anything but confused signals and weak responses from the parties.

The last major party realignment, it is generally agreed, took place in 1932, and set the stage for the New Deal policies of government intervention in the economy and the development of the welfare state. We are, these scholars argue, perhaps overdue for another realignment, but until an issue emerges which will produce one, an issue as powerful as the Great Depression, it is futile to complain that party lines are muddled and governmental action is all but paralyzed. Their judgment may be correct, but I do not find it comforting. The cyclical theory of party realignment is an easy rationalization for throwing up our hands and doing nothing. But we do not know when the realignment will take place. Some scholars have thought there was a thirty-six-year cycle, with 1896 and 1932 as the last "critical elections." But 1968, the scheduled date, on this theory, for another "critical election," has come and gone, and our drift continues....

...Basically, I believe that our guarantee of self-government is no stronger than our exercise of self-government; and today the central instruments of self-government, the political parties, are being neglected or abused. We must somehow rescue them if we are to rescue ourselves....

...Popular dissatisfaction with the two-party system is manifested in many ways: by the decline in voting; by the rise in the number of voters who refuse to identify themselves with either party; by the increase in ticket splitting, a device for denying either party responsibility for government; and by the increased use of third parties or ad hoc political coalitions to pressure for change.... Is there not a better way to resolve our differences, to move ahead on our common problems? I believe there is.... The instrument that is available to us ... is the instrument of responsible party government. The alternative to making policy in the streets is to make it in the voting booth....

But, if that is to be more than a cliché answer, there must be real choices presented at election time—choices involving more than a selection between two sincere-sounding, photogenic graduates of some campaign consultant's academy of political and dramatic arts. The candidates must come to the voters with programs that are comprehensible and relevant to our problems; and they must have the kind of backing that makes it possible for them to act on their pledges once in office.

The instrument, the only instrument I know of, that can nominate such candidates, commit them to a program and give them the leverage and alliances in government that can enable them to keep their promises, is the political party....

...Where do we turn? To ourselves. Obviously, that must be the answer. There is no solution for America except what we

Americans devise. I believe that we have the instrument at hand, in the party system, that can break the long and costly impasse in our government. But it is up to us to decide whether to use it.

What would it entail on our part if we determined to attempt responsible party government? First, it would mean giving strong public support to those reform efforts which in the recent past have been carried on entirely by a small group of concerned political insiders, aimed at strengthening the machinery of political parties and government.

We should seek to strengthen the liaison between the presidency and Congress, on a mutual basis, and between the presidency and the heads of state and local government. We should elect the President in the same way we elect all other officials, by direct vote of his constituents, with high man winning.

We should expand the role and responsibilities of the party caucuses and the party leaders in Congress. The caucus should choose the floor leaders and policy committee members, the legislative committee chairmen and committee members, not on the basis of seniority but on the basis of ability and commitment to the party program. That leadership ought to be held accountable for bringing legislation to which the party is committed to a floor vote in orderly and timely fashion, with adequate opportunity for debate and particularly for consideration of opposition party alternatives. But procedures for due consideration should not justify devices like the filibuster, which prevent the majority party from bringing its measures to a final vote. . . .

We need to take every possible measure to strengthen the presidential nominating convention as the key device for making the parties responsible. The current effort to open the Democratic delegate-selection process to wider public participation is a promising start, and its emphasis on the congressional-district nominating convention offers corollary benefits for integrating congressional and presidential constituencies. Both parties should experiment with devices for putting heavier emphasis on the platform-writing phase of the convention's work, including the possibility of a separate convention, following the nomination, where the party's officeholders and candidates debate the program on which they pledge themselves to run and to act if elected.

Most important of all the structural reforms, we need to follow through the effort to discipline the use of money in politics, not only by setting realistic limits on campaign spending and by publicizing individual and organizational gifts, but also by channeling much more of the money (including, in my view, all general election spending) through the respective party committees, rather than through individual candidates' treasuries.

We need to strengthen the party organizations and their staffs, and recapture for them the campaign management functions that have been parceled out to independent firms which tend to operate with a fine disdain for the role of party and policy in government. We need to devise ways to make television—the prime medium of political communication—somewhat more sensitive to the claims of the parties to be a regular part of the political dialogue, and to protect the vital institution of the nominating convention from being distorted by the demands of the television cameras.

All these reforms would help, I believe, but they would not accomplish the invigoration of responsible party government unless they were accompanied by a genuine increase in the participation by the public in party affairs. The cure for the ills of democracy truly is more democracy; our parties are weak principally because we do not use them. To be strong and responsible, our parties must be representative; and they can be no more representative than our participation allows. Millions more of us need to get into partisan political activity.

We need also to become somewhat more reflective about what we do with our votes. We need to ask ourselves what it is that we want government to accomplish, and which candidate, which party comes closest to espousing that set of goals. That may sound so rationalistic as to be unrealistic. But this nation has more education, more communication, more leisure available to it than ever before. In the nineteenth century, James Bryce wrote of us, "The ordinary citizens are interested in politics, and watch them with intelligence, the same kind of intelligence (though a smaller quantity of it) as they apply to their own business. . . . They think their own competence equal to that of their representatives and office-bearers; and they are not far wrong." Are we to think less of ourselves today?

Finally, we need to examine some of our habits. It seems to me we should ask, before splitting a ticket, what it is we hope to accomplish by dividing between the parties the responsibility for government of our country, our state or our community. Do we think there is no difference between the parties? Do we distrust them both so thoroughly that we wish to set them against each other? Do we think one man so superior in virtue and wisdom that he must be put in office, no matter who accompanies him there? Why are we splitting our tickets? My guess is that, if we asked those questions, we would more often be inclined to give a temporary grant of power to one party at a time, rather than dividing responsibility so skillfully between the parties that neither can govern. If we were willing to risk this strategy, knowing that we would be able to throw the rascals out if they failed, we might even discover to our amazement that they are not always rascals.

79

XANDRA KAYDEN
EDDIE MAHE

The New Party System

From *The Party Goes On*

———

IN MANY RESPECTS, the party of the future is here; it is the gap in perception of this fact that binds us to the past. If a new animal is lurking in the guise of a dead system, it will emerge sooner or later, and there may not be anything to be done about it at all. We think it is important to know what has happened and to consider the possibilities for the future, partly because it is our system of government and something we must responsibly cherish, and partly because we still seem intent on "ironing out the wrinkles" in the political system. The spirit of reform has not entirely died. The potential for leadership to improve upon or undermine growth always exists. . . .

The political elite—the tiny percentage of the population that actively participates in electoral politics—used to organize campaigns, and fill the posts of party office from election district captains to party chairpersons. Committee membership led from precinct, to ward, to city, county, state, and national levels. There were other committees as well on rules, issues, and so on. There were honorary groups within the parties for large donors who could gain access to high elected officials and special perks at party conventions in return for their contributions. The honorary groups did not necessarily give anything more than money to the party, but they did make their power felt as they sought to influence public policy....

The political hacks, whether paid or unpaid, still hang about, but their role is severely curtailed. There used to be what might be referred to as "The Savior of the Week" syndrome, wherein every campaign could rely on someone dropping by the headquarters, willing to tell the staff just what was required to turn the campaign around because he or she was "in touch with The People" (having talked to a cab driver on the way over). If the Savior was sufficiently esteemed by the staff and willing to take a hand in trying out the new tactic, it might be added to the repertoire. More typically, the staff would try to ignore the interruption and continue the battle of sorting out the power structure within the campaign organization. Polling has helped to eliminate much of the uncertainty about what people are thinking and what is likely to motivate them to vote.

Today, campaigns are run by professionals (and even volunteers) who are trained in their tasks and who rely on advice and assistance from the national and state parties and the private consulting firms they employ to do their advertising, fund raising, and general campaigning. There is less room for ad hoc campaign strategy and there are definite restraints on unplanned expenditures. Storefronts may still exist, but they are not the seat of campaign decision making. In fact, they tend to do very little at all but pass out literature or house phone banks. And even the phone banks tend to be run by professional callers who can be trained and relied upon to complete their assigned tasks.

Case work was another function of local parties in the days of yore. When people needed help in coping with the public (or even private) authorities, they could turn to the party to mediate on their behalf. As local parties become less visible, that function has fallen more and more to elected officials who typically hire a staff of one or two to provide that service. Little city halls and local congressional offices are recent phenomena and represent the shift of functions.

What then is left for the new volunteer, and how will the party continue to perform that integrating function of linking private citizens with public roles and responsibilities? ...

Finding volunteers for voter registration, canvassing, and getting out the vote remain a vehicle for participation, although it is not as essential as it once was. Campaigns used to be far more labor-intensive operations, but that is no longer the case. Bodies can still be used to stand on busy intersections holding signs during rush hour, but many of the traditional tasks have been taken over by machines or by professionals in today's more centralized campaign organizations.

One critical question the parties and their campaign organizations must resolve is how to motivate support, and once motivated, how to apply it in a meaningful way for both the participant and the organization. It goes back to the question of incentives and rewards, which is the basis of all organizations. It goes back to the constant theme of would-be party leaders that they want to "rebuild the grassroots."

It is our contention that the part of motivation dependent upon communication—upon reaching the minds (and maybe hearts) of party supporters—is very much within the sphere of party control. If anything, it has improved in quality and in quantity. Some of that communication has been in the form of direct mail solicitations which provide the recipient the opportunity to act on it, and as many fund raisers know, commitment tends to follow money: once you invest money in a cause, you come to believe in it more strongly. In that regard, then, it is likely that millions of Americans have a more firmly rooted commitment to their party.

But what of those who want to come out and contribute their spare time and energy? One reality everyone must face (including those who would like to contribute their time) is that there is less of it around these days. Seventy percent of the women under thirty-five work. Both women and men want to spend more time with their families and more time in health-related activities. The question is What can an organization do with individuals who want to make a contribution but have limited time and, usually, little to offer beyond their enthusiasm?

There will undoubtedly be many efforts made by both parties to find satisfying useful tasks. The probability remains, however, that the only elections to rely entirely on that sort of grassroots efforts will be local elections. Even state legislative races have become more expensive and more dependent on the sophisticated campaign technologies available, as PAC money moves increasingly in that direction.

Politics appears to be becoming a more passive activity, but it should be borne in mind that the percentage of the population who used to be active was always small and not always representative of the population as a whole. The legitimacy and acceptance of the entire system depended and continues to depend not on this small elite but on the proportion of the population who vote. They are being reached; they are better informed; they may be more committed in the future. More of them are contributing money to the parties, and they may feel that their participation is anything but passive, given that it was more than they did before, and they are engaged in more communication with the party as a result of their donation. . . .

By the end of the 1980s, both parties will probably have their own cable networks reaching out to the party faithful, educating them to the party's principles and the skills required for running campaigns. The lists of registered voters maintained by the parties and their affiliates will be more extensive, and the communication between the party and the voters will increase accordingly in the mails, by telephone, probably even by computer. More people will have access to more information than ever before and that, we believe, will lead to an increase in partisan intensity. The capacity to communicate so much so easily will make our politics much less labor-intensive, not unlike many of the activities in the rest of our lives.

The increased communication may mean that politics becomes more passive because so much of the former activity had to do with reaching out to voters. Certainly many of the old tasks are no longer relevant, and the campaign finance law has added to the passivity by requiring a centralization of the process in order to keep track of the income and expenditures. The general election of the president makes that point most dramatically because it is the one most likely to generate the greatest amount of enthusiasm. But the public financing prohibits contributions directly to the campaigns, and the spending limitations (combined with the uncertain relations between the presidential campaign staff and state and local parties) encourage even more centralization. It is a time when many people want to do more and find that there is less to do. The fact that there is less for the volunteer to do and the fact that, presidential elections aside, there are fewer volunteers is both cause and effect of the new circumstances. . . .

The professionalization of politics has its strengths and its weaknesses. It is part and parcel of the new system, however, and it brings us back to the focus of this book. We have been writing principally about the people who actively participate: the party structure and the individuals who make it work. It has been our view that the parties lost ground with the voters because they did not mean very much. One reason they lost control of their destiny was because most of the reforms in this century effectively weakened the structure—the ability of party leaders to make their organizations do very much at all. The strength of the new party system rests on the capability of these new professionals to make decisions about candidates and issues, and to reach out to the citizenry and make those decisions known. . . .

In some respects the parties seem like giant amoeba covering the political environment. Everything falls under them, but they are formless. Political observers talk about party decline, or even party resurgence, but the parties seem to shift only slightly, shuddering perhaps in the South as realignment takes place. They are hard to grasp intellectually; they are certainly not easy to grasp in the day-to-day practice of politics by political leaders. If parties are about power, then those who participate in them want power and they are loath to give it away to someone else. What is required of party leadership is a reshifting of the power structure to emphasize some things and move away from others. It is one reason the parties move slowly: it is not an organization with easy measures for success or failure. Elections can be won and lost for so many reasons, most of them having to do with the personalities of the candidates and the specific choices voters make between candidates.

Many people working together—sometimes working at odds with each other—have brought about dramatic changes in both major parties in the last few years. The effort seems herculean when viewed in retrospect, but it inched along with many seeming backward steps at the time. Even with all of that effort, to most observers and to most voters, the parties seem to be not very different. They still appear to be as inefficient and amoebalike as ever. Part of leadership is bringing about change, and part of it is raising our expectations. We would argue that things have changed; we are only awaiting someone to point that out and lift our spirits about what can be.

This is not to say that we have not had political leadership during this time, but rather to suggest that the leaders we have had brought new generations into the parties and that it is to those new participants we must look for evidence of the style and substance of the changes that are taking place....

There are similarities between the new activists in both parties: They are more professional; they think of themselves as being more pragmatic; they tend to be more inclusive in their decision-making style than exclusive or elitist. They are concerned about the organizational structure of the parties and they have paid attention to rebuilding. David Broder ... described the new participants in *The Changing of the Guard,* published in 1980. Both he and Xandra Kayden, writing in 1974, characterized the new people as "organizers." Broder said of them "The next ones who will take power—the babies born between 1930 and 1955—were shaped in a very different time. Theirs has been a time of affluence and inflation, of extraordinary educational advance, and of wrenching social change and domestic discord." Their objective is to change the system, not to destroy it. Their style is cool, in keeping with a television age. They contrast themselves with earlier generations who were either less educated or more elitist, and with the radicals of their own years who lost faith with the society.

This new generation, which itself will be replaced someday, has a quiet technocratic quality to it. If it were not that the individuals involved were forged out of the turmoil of the 1960s and 70s, they might seem rather boring. They can and have transformed the party structure, but they have yet to transform the public mind. It might be that we need to await another kind of personality with the capacity to mold the imagination as well as the organization....

It is our view that the voters will not become strong partisans until imaginative leadership binds their hopes to the structure. The intensity of today's politics of morality and frustration may be part of that process, but we would hope for something more positive in the long run. We would hope that tolerance and a generosity of spirit enter the equation lest the partisanship become not a vehicle for structuring political thought but the front lines of battle.

The parties go on partly because the political system depends on them, even if the citizenry feels their inadequacy from time to time. They go on despite our rather feckless attitude toward them. It is our view that the parties have responded to the caring attention that those who love them have bestowed and have emerged in the 1980s as strong institutions capable of recapturing their innate functions, capable of having meaning to the voters. We expect that

partisanship will increase in the 1990s if nothing cataclysmic inter-
feres to alter our political structure.

The parties have changed because the old structures no longer
worked and a new generation fought for and won the mantle of
leadership. The new organization reflects the values of those leaders
and the circumstances of today's society: incredibly rapid and intense communication; varied, private lifestyles; a certain cynicism
or caution about all our institutions and the people who lead them.

80

EVERETT LADD
Election '88: The National Election

———

THE MOST STRIKING thing about the 1988 election was
how predictable it was. Just about everything happened as it
"should have," based on what we knew when the election year
began.

A major reason for this predictability is that the balloting took
place well into the latest of our country's great partisan realignments—this one having begun in the late 1960s. When a realignment is new, its central features—changes in group ties to the
political parties, issues cutting in novel directions, and so on—
often startle us. But after we have seen them over a series of
elections, we take them as givens. That's what happened in 1988.
The election told us little we didn't already know. Instead, it was
a confirming, or reaffirming, election. The New Deal era now
seems as remote as the Age of McKinley.

Our present-day electoral alignment, the product of a quarter-
century of change, has five principal components.

• A variety of groups vote differently now than they did in the
New Deal years. The most notable group is white southerners,
long the strongest of Democratic supporters, who are now the
strongest of presidential Republicans. The oldest voters, long the
Republicans' best age cohort, are now their worst. Men and
women, who until a decade ago voted almost identically, today

differ signficantly; women are relatively more Democratic, men more Republican.

• The present mix of issues differs from that of the New Deal period, and the Democrats' public philosophy has lost favor.

• The Republicans are the majority party in presidential elections—precisely because their public philosophy is ascendant.

• Dealignment—the weakening of voters' ties to the parties—is a key factor distinguishing the current partisan competition from all previous ones.

• For well over a decade now the new alignment has displayed a split personality: one face evident in presidential voting, another in state and local contests.

Group Voting

Michael Dukakis won the black vote in 1988 by the kind of margin that has been familiar since the civil rights revolution of the 1960s—by 86 to 12 percent, according to the CBS News/*New York Times* Election Day survey of 11,645 voters. Whites, in contrast, strongly backed George Bush. The most striking feature of their vote on November 8 was the extent to which the Republicans' share among whites in the South exceeded that in the rest of the country. According to the Election Day polls of NBC News and the *Wall Street Journal,* for example, Bush received 57 percent of the white vote nationally—but his margins in the South ranged from a low of 63 percent in Florida to a high of 80 percent in Mississippi. According to the ABC News exit poll, an extraordinary 72 percent of southern white Protestants voted for Bush, just 27 percent for Dukakis. In the New Deal era white southerners' overwhelming support for the national Democratic party had two main sources: racial tensions and memories reaching back to the Civil War; and in fact they were then the most liberal—that is, New Deal policy supporting—regional group in the country. In the contemporary alignment, things have been almost exactly reversed. White southerners have become the most Republican regional group in presidential voting because of the racial division that finds blacks overwhelmingly Democratic, and because they are now the most conservative regional group. . . .

Election Day poll data show that the pattern of voting among Hispanics evident in recent past elections persisted almost entirely unchanged in 1988. Nationally, the GOP is the minority party among the nation's Hispanic voters, but it gets a healthy minority share. And one group of Hispanics, those of Cuban background concentrated in Florida, is heavily Republican.

For a decade now the Republicans have been beating the Democrats in their competition for the support of new voters. This is highly important because realignments involve not so much shifts in the loyalties of older voters, who have long political memories and experience, as they do movement of those just beginning to form partisan attachments in a new political era. Today, voters in their late teens and twenties identify with the GOP in greater proportions than do any other age group.

Pre-election polls in 1988 showed Bush getting his biggest margins over Dukakis among the young, but the Election Day surveys did not find this. Age-related differences in voting were not significant. The reason for this discrepancy between pre-election poll findings and actual results was made clear by a survey that CBS News and the *New York Times* conducted November 10–16. It found that young people, always the group least likely to vote, had an especially low turnout this year. Indeed, two-fifths of all nonvoters in the country were under thirty years of age. The CBS News/*New York Times* study showed that the young nonvoters would have picked Bush by a bigger margin than the rest of the populace and that they were more pro-Bush than the young who voted.

The gender gap is of interest here as an example of group divisions not evident in previous eras. Realignments occur, of course, when old divisions fade while new ones appear, reflecting changing social needs and circumstances. In the wake of big gender-related demographic shifts, which included a surge of women into the labor force, polls in the 1970s began showing differences of opinion between men and women on a range of policy questions. A gender gap first appeared in presidential voting in 1980.

This year, according to the CBS News/*New York Times* exit poll, the gender gap was fifteen percentage points: men favored Bush over Dukakis by a sixteen-percentage-point margin, women by just one percentage point. The NBC News/*Wall Street Journal* poll put the gap at fourteen points.

Class differences in voting have declined markedly from what they were in the New Deal era. This year differences in Bush/Dukakis support by economic position were modest indeed once one controls race. Low-income blacks were only marginally more

Democratic than those in higher income categories, according to the ABC News exit poll. Whites with family incomes under $20,000 were just twelve points more Democratic than those with incomes over $30,000....

The Republican Majority

Democrats are again debating the "lessons" of the presidential balloting. "Did we just run a bad campaign, or is our problem deeper?" One lesson should by now be clear: they are the minority party in contemporary presidential politics.

Does this mean Michael Dukakis could not have won? Of course not—no more than one could say that Democrat Woodrow Wilson could not win in 1912 and 1916, when the Republicans were the majority party. Minority parties win presidential elections as a result of any one of a number of circumstances—when they nominate more attractive candidates, for instance, when the majority party fractures, or when people think "it's time for a change." Minority status simply means that the party begins each contest with an underlying disadvantage: the *regular* alignment of groups and cut of issues favor its opponents.

When an out-of-power minority must contend for the presidency in a period of peace and relative prosperity, it is likely to lose. That was the Democrats' problem in 1988. The election results were not inevitable, but they were both likely and predictable....

Dealignment

The New Deal realignment was accompanied by an unambiguous strengthening of Democratic party loyalties across the electorate. In contrast the present one finds more and more people splitting their tickets and deciding their votes on grounds related to the candidates and issues in specific elections, rather than going down the line for their party. Party ties count for less today than at any point since a mature party system took shape in the United States in the 1830s.

In the case of less visible offices, such as members of Congress, where most voters know little about the candidates' records and officeholders enjoy prodigious advantages over their challengers in resources for painting their image in a vaguely rosy glow, the precipitous decline of party voting has resulted in an extraordinarily uncompetitive set of results. Incumbents now routinely win these contests by overwhelming margins.

When candidates take policy stands that to some degree encourage the desertion of their partisans, the extent of ticket splitting can be quite extraordinary. In this year's Connecticut Senate contest, 38 percent of Republicans crossed over to vote for Lieberman, and 34 percent of Democrats backed Weicker.

Split-Level Results

The New Deal realignment was as complete and decisive as it was rapid. By 1936 the Democrats were unquestionably the majority party at all levels: they "owned" the presidency, dominated Congress, held sway in the state houses, and had a substantial lead in party identification. Today's realignment is anything but complete, as data from the November 8 balloting again reminded us. Bush won strongly, carrying forty states and 426 electoral votes; but the Democrats retained their ample majorities in Congress and the state houses.

Divided results are a fact. They mean that the Republicans have a power base in the presidency, the Democrats a base in Congress. But they do not have anything much to say about the silliest of all our election-related debates—"Who has the mandate?"

As we have seen, congressional voting simply is not about issues. It revolves around incumbency advantages. With a seemingly permanent lock on the House of Representatives, Democratic congressional incumbents now enjoy enormous advantage in special-interest money. This year, confounding the story of Republicans as plutocrats, political action committees backed Democratic House candidates over Republicans by a margin of two to one....

The Republicans, running as a conservative party, have won the presidency five of the last six times, by a cumulative margin of eleven percentage points over their Democratic opposition. That may not be "mandate," but it is certainly not the chance product of various short-term forces, such as how individual campaigns are run. Rather, it represents an expression of opinion on the parties' stands on national issues as decisive as was that of the New Deal years.

PART THIRTEEN

The Media

IN THE COURSE of a few decades Americans have been brought into a much closer relationship with events in Washington and throughout the world than ever before. It is commonplace now to speak of a communications revolution, but it is still hard to grasp just how much that revolution has changed our lives. A citizen living in a rural area anywhere in the United States as recently as the 1920s might go for weeks on end hearing *nothing at all* about what transpired beyond the local community. Washington was a remote place—out of sight and out of mind—and the rest of the world was no more than blurry images constructed over the course of a lifetime from snatches of schooling, picture books, and word of mouth. Even major events like the outcome of national elections and the coming of war still reached most people slowly as conversation spread the word which someone had read in a newspaper.

All of this changed with electronic communication. Radio by the 1930s had brought everyone into the reach of President Roosevelt's "fireside chats" and the evening news reports of major events in Washington and throughout the world. By the late 1960s the powerful new picture medium of television flashed into our homes a daily account of the war in Vietnam, the president's activities (by this time themselves heavily influenced by the new medium's needs), stories about environmental threats from the remotest areas of the planet, instant accounts of our astronauts walking on the moon, and much else. For all practical purposes these pictures put people into a closer relationship with things thousands of miles away than with their local town halls.

The effects of these changes on American politics have been profoundly revolutionary. Upwards of fifty million of us now see in some fashion whatever is on the evening news. We see many things daily that our citizen of the 1920s would never have thought about, for example, an oil spill in Prince William Sound, homeless people in New York City, sailors frantically trying to interpret electronic images on their state-of-the-art equipment in the Persian Gulf, a gay rights demonstration in Washington. National and international political events are insistently present in our daily lives. The personalities of national political actors (at least some of them) become better known to us than those of our next-door neighbors. National elections are conducted in a manner that would have been unrecognizable to anyone before the 1950s. Even the least attentive citizen is now constantly besieged with communications that bring national political events into the home. For the first time in history we are brought, by electronic communications, face to face with things that were heretofore remote, and, indeed for most of us, of little or no concern.

Making sense of the political role of the communications media in American politics is now a matter of urgent importance, but it is much too difficult a task for the beginning student. We can only scratch the surface of the subject here. And we would do you little service to suggest that this is an area in which social scientists have achieved impressive understanding. There is in fact probably no important subject on which greater disagreement persists. Our purpose here is to focus your attention on some basic issues and get you to think about them in light of your own experience. Technical and methodological questions are better left for other, more specialized courses.

Our first reading, by Paul Weaver, raises the question of what the media do when they report the news. What is their proper role in a democratic political process? Can they be and should they be neutral conduits through which information flows back and forth between government and the public? Or should they be something else? And, if so, what? Weaver's piece, which created quite a stir when it appeared in 1974, maintains that the turbulent years of

Vietnam, student rebellion, and Watergate gave rise to a new "adversary journalism" in which the press came to assume that its proper role was to be a kind of opposition to government and institutionalized critic of established institutions. The American press, Weaver argues, moved in these years from an understanding of itself that entailed a certain sympathy with the work of government and politicians to one based on distrust and suspicion of political activity in general. To Weaver, the effects of a press so committed seemed clear and problematic. If journalists continued to see themselves as adversaries of the political order, we could only move in the direction of weakened and less-open government, public distrust, and "Europeanized" politics characterized by hostile, ideological groupings in the public.

Many reacted to Weaver's article at the time with the observation that he had gotten things backwards, that it was the penchant of government for secrecy, deception, and manipulation of the press during the Johnson and Nixon administrations that created journalistic distrust in the first place. Certainly, government officials came in these years to see the press as "the enemy." The opening section of our selection from Larry Speakes's account of his years as Ronald Reagan's press secretary makes clear that this attitude has not changed. The Reagan administration, Speakes says, always saw the press operation as "us against them." This is especially interesting in light of the frequent observations of press watchers during the Reagan years that the press had become "patsies" of the administration. Speakes's candid account describes the assumptions underlying relations between the press and the presidency in the television era. Presidential news coverage, he makes clear, must be carefully managed by White House operatives and heavily television-oriented. In effect, he says, "we had to think like a television producer." The main part of the effort, he explains, is to get a picture and a "good solid soundbite" on the evening news. Weaver's fears were seemingly not without basis. Speakes describes a system of presidential press coverage that is loveless on both sides. The president thinks the press is "out to get him," and the press constantly resents what it takes (accurately enough) to be a well-organized effort to deceive and manipulate the news.

Our remaining readings stress the importance of personalities in the press. All of the major American media—newspapers, radio, and television—have produced in their own time their own "stars."

We should never forget the highly individualistic and competitive nature of the journalistic enterprise and the commercial motivations which largely drive it. These are prominent people in our public life by any standard. There can be little doubt that they are important actors in modern American politics in their own right. And they are aware of it. Their own perceptions of their role make very clear that they do not see themselves as neutral conduits through which information simply flows as they file their stories. In his memoirs, Harrison Salisbury, a great reporter on many beats for the *New York Times,* is clearly aware of his own importance in the high drama of the events he describes. Note well his account of how he became personally involved in the coverage of the confrontation between the student left and Richard Daley's Chicago police at the Democratic National Convention in 1968. Sam Donaldson, an authentic superstar of the television age, tells in our selection from his book, *Hold On, Mr. President!* (what better title to make Paul Weaver's day?) how he came to national prominence through his coverage of the Watergate scandal. One would be hard pressed to invent a more convincing practitioner of "adversary journalism." "I concluded," he writes, "that a reporter's role ought to be one of continuing, unrelenting skepticism about government's actions." His style, now familiar to millions, is "to speak early and aggressively." He clearly has something about contemporary communications figured out. By such feats of assertion as forcing his way onto the podium with Jimmy Carter at the 1976 Democratic National Convention he has earned fame and fortune. In the meantime both political parties have so contrived their conventions to televise well (so far a futile attempt) that delegates in the convention halls complain they cannot tell what is going on unless they go back to their hotel rooms to watch what the networks are reporting. Got to go now. It's time for the evening news. *Quid nunc?*

81

PAUL WEAVER
Adversary Journalism

————

THE "FOURTH ESTATE" of the realm—that was Burke's
way of summing up the role of the press in his time, and when
one has discounted the medieval terminology, his phrase is no less
apt today. It reminds us that the press, as the coequal of other
"estates," is a political institution in its own right, intimately bound
up with all the institutions of government. It affects them and is
affected by them in turn, and together they determine the nature
of the regime and the quality of public life. Governmental institutions have political effects through their exercise of legislative,
executive, or judicial powers; the press achieves its impact through
the way it influences the entry of ideas and information into the
"public space" in which political life takes place. So the basic question to be asked about the press is: What is its relation to other
political institutions, and how does it consequently manage the
"public space"?

The aftermath of Watergate provides a suitable occasion for
rethinking this question—though not because the press was in any
way at fault in this episode. The Watergate scandals emerge solely
from the Nixon Administration's abuse of its Presidential powers
in matters ranging from campaign finance and civil liberties to
national security. By covering the emerging scandals as it did, the
press was acting in accord with a venerable journalistic tradition
that dates back to the *New York Times'* exposé of the corrupt
Tweed Ring in 1871.

Yet Watergate was more than a series of criminal and corrupt
actions; it also has raised basic Constitutional questions concerning
the interrelationship among all our political institutions, including
of course the press. One of these issues was the freedom of the
press. Many of the abuses symbolized by Watergate—the plumb

ers, unjustified investigations and wiretaps, and so forth—were in fact directed at the press as part of the Administration's campaign to make the news media less critical.* If these efforts had been successful, they would have reduced press freedom and altered the balance between government and the press in favor of the former. For the time being at least, that danger has been averted.

So the press emerges from Watergate as free, self-confident, and enterprising as at any other time in its history. But it also emerges a bit different from what it was before. For the press today is an institution in limbo—an institution in that distinctive kind of trouble which derives from not having a settled idea of its role and purpose. It is in limbo because it now occupies an ambiguous middle ground between its longstanding tradition of "objective" journalism and a new movement for an "adversary" journalism—no longer massively committed to the one but not yet certain, let alone unanimous, about the other. To the extent that it is committed to the new movement, it is committed to a journalistic idea that is not easily compatible with American institutions in their current form, nor easily reconciled with some of its most valuable traditions. And to the extent that the press embraces this movement, its political role will remain in flux until some new practical adaptation to adversary journalism is worked out by government, public opinion, and the press itself. Watergate did not create this problem—it has been growing for a decade now—but it did intensify it. And this is the problem which confronts American journalism after Watergate. . . .

To put the matter briefly: Traditionally, American journalism has been very close to, dependent upon, and cooperative with, official sources. This has been one of its problems, but it has also been its greatest strength and virtue. For in various ways this arrangement has maximized both the openness and flexibility of American government and the amount of information available to the citizenry. Over the past ten years, however, a small but significant and still-growing segment of the journalistic community has begun to revise this relationship by assuming a posture of greater

---

*The Watergate Plumbers (so-called because of their location in the basement of the Nixon White House) specialized in illegal entry and wiretapping, supposedly to counter risks to national security. The Plumbers' ineptitude in the June 1972 break-in at Democratic National Headquarters brought the Watergate scandals to light.—EDS.

independence and less cooperativeness. They see this change as a modest reform which will render American journalism purer, better, and truer to its traditional aspirations. In fact, it represents a radical change. In the long run it could make the press "freer" but also less informative and possibly more partisan; and this in turn could make the political system more closed, less flexible, and less competent.

To appreciate the meaning of what has happened, we may begin with the simple fact that journalism is the enterprise of publishing a current account of current events. As such, it cannot proceed until three prior questions have been settled. First, there is the question of how, where, and on what basis to find and validate information. Second, there is the question of the point of view from which events are to be surveyed and characterized. And third, there is the question of the audience to be addressed and the basis on which it is to be aggregated. Abstractly, one can imagine any number of possible resolutions of these issues, but in practice things work out more simply. For wherever one looks in the modern world, daily journalism seems to assume one of two general forms: the partisan and the liberal.

Partisan journalism, which prevails in many European countries, and which has traditionally been represented in the United States by the "journal of opinion" rather than the newspaper, begins with an explicitly political point of view. It is ideological journalism. It aims at assembling an audience that shares its point of view; its object is to interpret public affairs from within that point of view; and it gathers information for the purpose of illuminating and particularizing such interpretation. Such a journalism is less concerned with information as such than with the maintenance and elaboration of its point of view. To it, events are more interesting for the light they cast on its "position" than for what they are, or seem, on their face.

Liberal journalism, by contrast, which prevails in the English-speaking world, is characterized by a preoccupation with facts and events as such, and by an indifference to—indeed, a systematic effort to avoid—an explicitly ideological point of view. It aims instead at appealing to a universal audience on the basis of its non-political, "objective" point of view and its commitment to finding and reporting only "facts" as distinct from "opinion." Liberal journalism strives to be a kind of *tabula rasa* upon which unfolding events and emerging information inscribe themselves. Its principal concern is to find as many events and as much information as it can, and it does this by going to "sources"—persons and organizations directly involved in the events, upon whom it relies both for information and for the validation of this information.

Throughout the 20th century, American journalism has been solidly in the liberal camp. It has sought a universal audience rather than a factional one; its central objective has been to find and publish as much information about as many events as quickly as possible; and it has striven to do this on the basis of a non-partisan, non-political, "facts-only" point of view. . . .

In the liberal tradition, then, the relationship between newsman and source, between press and government, is one of structured interdependence and bartering within an atmosphere of amiable suspiciousness. Each side knows its role. The job of government is to give access and information—*and to do so to a far greater extent than would or could be required by law*. This last point is worth emphasizing, since in this respect American government differs markedly from European (even British) governments. All European journalists are immediately struck by this difference. The American reporter not only has access to official announcements and press releases; he also has the opportunity of becoming the confidant of the official and of enjoying limited but regular access to his personal thoughts, official secrets, internal departmental gossip, and the like.

Of course, there is a price tag on such extraordinary access. The reporter is expected to be generally sympathetic to the public official and his government and to cooperate with them as far as his sense of professionalism permits. Beyond that, the press is expected to have no strong and comprehensive ideas about the general shape of public affairs; it is officialdom which is collectively entitled to define the topography and limits of public discussion and the news—and each individual official is to have the further opportunity of attempting to shape the content of news to suit his own preferences or purposes.

But the press also has its role and rights. Its main job is to exploit its access and, one way or another, to get as much information as it can into public circulation. It has the right to select freely among the often widely divergent ideas and information circulating within officialdom and to expose corruption and foulups. In exchange, it is expected to see to it that the impression being made on the public is not radically at odds with the reality of affairs as newsmen and officials, from their "inside" perspective, know it to be.

At the level of day-to-day individual interaction, of course, the relationship between press and government in the "objective" tradition is ill-defined and highly variable. There are a few rules of thumb that all parties are expected to observe. Officials are not supposed to lie—at least, hardly ever, and then only for some good public reason. They are also supposed to keep their efforts to deceive newsmen and the public to modest proportions. And they are not ever to use the powers of government to harrass or coerce newsmen. Newsmen, for their part, are expected not to "editorialize" in their news stories and are supposed to give persons accused or disputed in a story an opportunity to tell their own side of the matter. And newsmen are also expected not to publish certain kinds of information without permission: official secrets, information about the seamy side of officials' private lives, and "inside dope" of no particular relevance to public policy. But within these limits, more or less anything goes. There is much uncertainty and much room for maneuver, manipulation, and enterprise on both sides—and for all their mutuality and cooperation, there is also endless conflict between government and press. But in this general scramble there are limits that both of the parties respect.

What I have just described is the operational reality of the liberal tradition of American journalism. The image which that journalism has of itself is not exactly congruent with the reality. Some elements of this image, to be sure, are accurate enough. For instance, newsmen correctly believe that they perform three quite different public functions: For the most part, they act as neutral finders and conveyors of information; to some extent they are the "watchdogs" of government; and on rare occasions they advocate the reform of observable inequities. But in other respects, and especially as it depicts the relationship between press and government, the image is a romantic fiction. To listen to traditional newsmen, one would think that the press is completely independent of government in its quest for news, that it routinely searches out vast amounts of hidden, jealously guarded information, that it is constantly defying persons in high office, and that it is the day-in, day-out adversary of "the Establishment" and the equally faithful defender of "the People."

Now this myth of the autonomous, investigative, adversary press does serve a useful purpose. One of the greatest problems of traditional journalism is its proneness to cooptation by its sources. To the extent that newsmen believe and act on their romantic notion of who they are and what they do, the likelihood of their becoming mere uncritical puppets in the hands of their sources is diminished. Moreover, their morale would be lower, their energy smaller, and their self-respect weaker if they subscribed to a truly realistic conception of daily journalism. The romantic image of the "adversary press," then, is a myth: "functional" for certain purposes, but wholly inaccurate as a model of what newsmen actually do or can hope to achieve.

The movement for a new, genuinely adversary journalism which has gained such ground over the past decade arises out of this romantic myth. . . .

Although this movement for a newly purified journalism did not attain real strength until the late 1960s, its origins lay somewhat farther in the past. Within the journalistic community, three events were critical in fomenting dissatisfaction with the existing press–government relationship: McCarthyism, the U-2 incident, and the Bay of Pigs. Each cast discredit upon the Cold War itself or the spirit in which government conducted it, and together they caused newsmen to revise their opinion of American institutions and their own relationship to them. . . . [In each case] a member . . . of government had abused the power that the objective tradition gave him over the press. The answer, it was generally agreed, was that the press should become more vigilant and critical, and should exercise much more discretion about what it printed in connection with known demagogues, even those in high public office. . . .

. . . It was not merely that government had lied and suppressed news, and been caught at it. Nor was it only that the press had been used, used easily and with cavalier disrespect, and used wrongly. It was rather that two *Presidents* had publicly admitted lying and suppressing news, and that one of them said the press shouldn't have listened to him. Clearly the problem which the press had identified in the aftermath of McCarthyism was not confined to an occasional demagogue in Congress; it extended to the highest and most respected officials in the land. If one couldn't trust them, evidently one couldn't trust anyone.

These events marked the beginning of both the "credibility gap" theme in public affairs reporting and a growing truculence among newsmen. . . . [In addition,] the spirit of the. . . [1960s involving a dramatic expansion and intensification of political conflict and the emergence of countercultural, anti-establishment, and other oppositional movements] had its impact on the journalistic community, especially on its younger, newly-recruited members. The psychological distance between press and government and the frequency of stories critical of established policy grew....

The upshot of these developments was that the liberal press particularly—and to an increasing extent other parts of the journalistic community as well—found itself ever more committed to a stance of truculent independence from government and officialdom. Increasingly it felt that its proper role was not to cooperate with government but to be independent of it, or even opposed to it. Increasingly newsmen began to say that their job was to be an autonomous, investigative adversary of government and to constitute a countervailing force against the great authority of all established institutions. And increasingly they began to see as illegitimate, the few traditional formal constraints upon the press: libel law, "fair trial" restrictions on news coverage, testimonial obligations upon all citizens to give their evidence under subpoena, and the laws defining and protecting government secrets. These sentiments, and the actions which in modest but growing number gave concrete expression to them, define the movement for a "new journalism" which exists today and which poses the central question which the press will have to cope with after Watergate....

[The] problem with this movement for a new journalism, ... is that it represents an incipient retreat, not merely from an intelligible idea of the public interest and of the responsibility of the press to serve it, but also from the entire liberal tradition of American journalism and the system of liberal democracy which it has fostered and served. The problem of the press publishing a few government secrets or withholding the names of an occasional criminal may be serious in principle but it is usually negligible in practice. But there is a larger practical question raised by "adversary" journalism that is not at all negligible: the question of the persistence of the open, fragmented, liberal system of American democracy as we have known it and benefited from it for the past many decades.

Our instinct is to assume that this system is virtually indestructible, rooted as it is in the pragmatic temper of the American people, the Constitutional system of division of powers, and other such factors apparently beyond the influence of what we do or think. This is a reasonable assumption within limits, but it isn't entirely true. The system also depends on many institutions and attitudes which are indeed changeable, and one of the most important—if least acknowledged—of these is the kind of press we have. Its capacity to find and publish vast amounts of information about politics and government, and its success in reaching universal audiences without regard to ideology or political affiliations, have contributed in an important way to the openness and flexibility of American government and to the ability of public opinion to influence the conduct of public affairs and to attain consensus. As the press has become wealthier in recent decades, its ability to gather and print information has increased; as political party organizations have declined, the need and willingness of officials to give newsmen access have also grown; so even while the complexity of government and the amount of "classified" information have increased, the capacity of the press to help the American system realize its ideals has at least kept pace.

The new movement abroad in the journalistic community threatens all this. For the press can make its contribution to the system only by maintaining close access—a closer access, as I have said, than can ever be provided by law. The price of such access is some degree of cooperation and sympathy for government—*not* a slavish adulation, as is sometimes said, but a decent respect for authority, a willingness to see government and persons in government given the opportunity to do their job, and at least a slight sense of responsibility for and commitment to the goals inherent in those jobs. When these are not present, access diminishes. And when newsmen begin to assert they are positively the adversaries of government, access diminishes drastically, and with it not only the contribution journalism can make but also the openness and flexibility of government itself. Politicians and officials are no more than human; they have their needs and interests; above all they intend to survive. If they feel themselves to be threatened or harmed, they will eventually take steps to insulate themselves as best they can from the danger.

The history of the Nixon Administration shows some of the ways in which this can occur. At one extreme there is Watergate itself—that is, the Plumbers, wiretaps and investigations of newsmen, harrassment of news organizations, and the like. This is an irrational and pathological response which is as unnecessary as it is intolerable, and we are not likely to see a recurrence in the discernible future. But the Nixon Administration used other methods as well, and these we can expect to see more of, regardless of who is

in the White House, if the movement continues to gain ground.
There is "jawboning": making speeches criticizing press coverage
in hopes of reducing the press' credibility and increasing its cooperativeness. More important, there is the technique of organizing
and formalizing all press-government contacts through the instrument of the Public Affairs/Public Information office and the centralized public relations operation. . . . And most powerful of all, there
is the simple device of self-isolation, on the theory that it is better
to have less of a bad press than more of a good press, especially in
light of the fact that the effort to seek the latter can so easily end
up earning one more of the former. Such a "low-profile" strategy—
with infrequent and irregular press conferences, sharply limited
informal contact between officials and reporters, even reliance on
a praetorian staff lacking extensive ties outside the official family—
is one of Richard Nixon's original contributions to the American
political tradition. It is clearly an undesirable contribution, especially in its Nixonesque form, and yet it represents a logical adaptation to the perceived existence of an adversary press; the chances
are we will see more of it insofar as the new movement gains
ground. . . . Journalism will change—and the logical direction of
change is toward the partisan form of journalism, with its ideological basis, politically based relationship to the government in power,
and fractionated audiences. It is possible, of course, that an adversary journalism could persist indefinitely, but this seems unlikely.
A stance of "pure" opposition—opposition as an end in itself,
rather than as an expression of some larger, positive political commitment—is self-contradictory in theory and likely to be short-
lived in practice. The probability is that an adversary press would
eventually ally itself with a political faction and so become partisan—an ideologically divisive factor rather than a politically unifying force. The consequences could be enormous.

Now the partisan mode of journalism has its virtues. It does
not evade the problem of "point of view" as liberal journalism
does, and in this sense it has an appealing honesty. It also has the
capacity to create and sustain coherent bodies of political opinion;
at a time when political opinion in this country is so often contradictory and inchoate, that is a very important trait. This is why "journals of opinion," existing on the margins of American journalism,
have been so important and desirable.

But if, over the long run, American journalism were ever to
turn massively to the partisan mode, the consequences of this devel-

opment would extend to nearly every aspect of our political system. Partisan journalism would not increase the openness of the system, it would sharply decrease it. It would not reduce the scope of political conflict, but enlarge it. It would not increase the capacity of American government to act effectively and flexibly in meeting emergent needs, but would tend to paralyze it. It would not empower public opinion as a whole, but would transform it into a congeries of rigid ideological factions eternally at war with one another and subject to the leadership of small coteries of ideologues and manipulators. Indeed, it would tend to transform the entire nature of American politics: From having been a popular government based on a flexible consensus, it would become Europeanized into a popular government based on an equilibrium of hostile parties and unchanging ideologies.

The alternative to such a "Europeanization" of journalism and politics, it should be emphasized, does not have to be a massive and uncritical reversion to the way things were during the 1950s and early 1960s. Even if this were possible—which it isn't—it would clearly be undesirable. Both officialdom and the press were then busily abusing the "objective" tradition, officialdom by treating the media as an institution to be deliberately "managed" for its own expediential purposes, and the press by encouraging and acquiescing in these efforts out of inertia and a generalized avidity to print "big news" as often and as easily as possible.

There are ways to curb these abuses while still preserving the benefits of the liberal tradition of our press which the "adversary" approach would squander. Government can increase the amount of information which is formally made available on the public record. It can scale down its "public relations" operations to the point where they cannot easily operate as instruments of press management and are content instead merely to disseminate information. As Joseph Lee Auspitz and Clifford W. Brown, Jr., have suggested, the "strategic" cast of mind giving rise to, among other things, the habit of "managing" the press for purposes of personal power can be discouraged by strengthening the political party, which embeds individual actors in an institutional context, channels and restrains their ambition, and promotes a "representative" as against a "strategic" ethos. And the press, for its own part, can help to recover the objective tradition by abandoning its flirtation with the "oppositional" posture and by ceasing to exploit public affairs for their sensation value (since the desire to exploit public affairs in this way is the main incentive leading the press to acquiesce in the manipulations of "strategically"-minded officials). The result, I believe, will be a journalism that provides more, and more useful, information to the citizenry, and a political system that, in consequence, comes a bit closer than in the past to realizing its historic ideals.

82

LARRY SPEAKES

From *Speaking Out*

———

FOR MY SIX YEARS as White House spokesman, it was Us Against Them. Us was a handful of relatively underpaid but dedicated public servants in the White House press office. Them was the entire White House press corps, dozens strong, many of them Rich and Famous and Powerful. My job was like that of anyone in the public relations business, to tell the press only what my client, in this case the President of the United States, and his top aides wanted me to, while the job of the press was to try to find out everything, and I do mean everything, including the most intimate details about President Reagan's health. We had our innings and they had theirs.

To give credit to the reporters who covered the White House, they were a talented group who ferreted out stories so efficiently that almost everything leaked out before we were ready for it to, and we had very few scoops that hadn't already broken in the press. The press, however, did miss out on the biggest story of the Reagan administration, the diversion to the Nicaraguan Contras of money from our sales of weapons to Iran, which didn't become public until Attorney General Edwin Meese announced it to a shocked group of reporters in the White House briefing room on November 25, 1986. Of course, that story also caught most of us within the Reagan Administration by surprise. Among the other major stories that had not become public in advance of our announcing them were the appointment in 1981 of Sandra Day

O'Connor as Associate Justice of the Supreme Court; the 1982 resignation of Alexander Haig as secretary of state; the Don Regan–Jim Baker job swap in 1985, which saw Regan move from secretary of the treasury to White House chief of staff and Baker go the opposite way; and the resignation of Chief Justice Warren Burger in June 1986, with William Rehnquist replacing him and Antonin Scalia taking Rehnquist's seat on the Supreme Court.

President Reagan sometimes became frustrated because most of his major announcements had already been reported in the newspapers that morning or on television the evening before. He would often say, "It's a total mystery to me how I can say something here in the Oval Office, and before I turn around it's out in the press." Occasionally, he would facetiously address the chandelier as if there were a microphone there. He would look up and say, "Get that, *Washington Post,* and be sure you get it right!"

One round that went to us was on September 24, 1986, when the President traveled to Omaha for a campaign rally. It was during the height of the Daniloff crisis, when *U.S. News & World Report* correspondent Nicholas Daniloff was under arrest on espionage charges in Moscow. President Reagan wanted to avoid having to discuss the Daniloff arrest, and he boarded *Air Force One* so fast for the flights to Omaha and back that the press people could only report how they were unable to get answers to the questions they always shouted at him. I told the assembled multitudes from the media that we had invented a new game. It was called "Beat the Press," and definitely not "Meet the Press."

Once in frustration, I gave a memorable retort to the press that became known as "Speake's Law." ABC Television's art department even had it made into a sign that I put on my desk: "You don't tell us how to stage the news and we don't tell you how to cover it.".... Underlying our whole theory of disseminating information in the White House was our knowledge that the American people get their news and form their judgments based largely on what they see on television. We knew that television had to have pictures to present its story. We learned very quickly that when we were presenting a story or trying to get our viewpoint across, we had to think like a television producer. And that is a minute and thirty seconds of pictures to tell the story, and a good solid soundbite with some news. So when Reagan was pushing education, the visual was of him sitting at a little desk and talking to a group of students, or with the football team and some cheerleaders, or in a science lab. Then we would have an educator's forum where the President would make a newsworthy statement. We knew very quickly that the rule was no pictures, no television piece, no matter how important our news was. If we saw nothing on the President's schedule that would make the evening news that night, we would say, "No coverage." And if the press didn't like it, the press didn't like it. There was no need to have cameras in there and reporters trying to ask questions that would embarrass the President unless we could get our story on TV.

Before we entered the White House we had decided that the sole focus of the first year was to be the President's economic program. Part of it was the strike-while-the-iron-is-hot theory: Everybody is interested in whatever the President does during his first year in office. And we were changing the parameters of the debate. Under Reagan, the operative question would be, not how much are we going to spend, but how little are we going to spend? Almost no news item, no speech, no trip, no photo-op whatsoever was put on the President's schedule during 1981 unless it contributed to the President's economic program. The day Reagan was sworn in, he went to a private office in the Capitol and signed an order directing a reduction in force throughout the federal government, which was carried on live television. Ordering a cutback in the number of federal employees on the first day was a dramatic, although probably hollow action, but it looked good.

Throughout the Reagan years, we not only played to television, we based all of our television judgments strictly on audience size. If ABC's "Good Morning, America" was the leading morning show, which it was during most of Reagan's term, they got our number-one person on a given subject, like George Shultz on foreign policy. On the evening shows, when Dan Rather was the leader, we'd put our number-one guy on there. So we played entirely to the ratings, and made no bones about it. Sunday shows were the same way. If you wanted to make an impact, you would go with ABC's David Brinkley show on Sundays. No doubt mistakenly, we kept "The MacNeil-Lehrer NewsHour" on PBS about third or fourth in our priorities, because the viewership wasn't that much. I say mistakenly, because more movers and shakers watched "MacNeil-Lehrer" than any other news show. We hardly ever made the President available for that show, and the same with the Shultzes and the Caspar Weinbergers. "MacNeil-Lehrer" generally got the second tier, the assistant secretaries, and that was not wise on our part....

Picture the White House at Christmastime: beautiful decorations, a festive atmosphere, and, at the annual Christmas party for the press, an open bar; a lavish buffet featuring shrimp, roast beef, and ham; an open bar; individual photographs of each member of the press and his/her additional guest posing with the President and Mrs. Reagan; an open bar; gifts like Christmas ornaments or ski caps with a White House emblem on them; and an open bar.

Judging by some of the imaginative requests we got for invitations, not being invited to the Christmas party was akin to not being asked to the senior prom.

The annual White House Christmas party actually became the annual White House Christmas parties on my watch; the guest list grew so large that we had to hold the party on two nights. By the time of my last Christmas party in 1986, we had to invite five hundred journalists and their guests each night. Posing for 250 pictures a night with some of their harshest critics was about all the Reagans could handle.

The transition from a one-night Christmas affair to two nights, like almost every other logistical question involving the press, was not without controversy. No matter which night they were invited, some people were unhappy, and rumors began circulating that we had an A list and a B list. That just wasn't true. After the White House social office said the size of the press corps had grown too large for us to hold our Christmas party on one night, the Reagans agreed to have it on two nights, and we simply went down the list at random, assigning one person to the first night and the next to the second night. The White House reporters made such a big deal about A lists and B lists that I finally started having some fun at their expense. When a reporter would ask me, "Which night is for the A list?" I'd say, "Which night are you coming?" They'd innocently reply, "Tuesday," and I'd catch them with "Oh, I'm so sorry, but Wednesday night is for the A list."

Planning the Christmas party for the press was always a nightmare. My secretary, Connie Gerrard, would start in August, reviewing the press list to see who should be invited. The goal was to limit it to people who actually covered the White House regularly. Each network would have four correspondents, which was okay, but then they would rotate camera crews once a month so that over the course of a year you would have six or eight cameramen from each network. Moreover, the networks obtained White House press credentials for virtually everyone in their Washington bureaus—150 to 200 per network. And, naturally, everyone from the bureau chief to the file clerks would want to come to our Christmas party....

Members of the Fourth Estate would come to the Christmas party looking their best, wearing suits and ties and nice dresses and high heels, which for many was their annual exception to their own dress code. You would expect those who had won the prestigious assignment of covering the President of the United States to dress and conduct themselves accordingly. You would be wrong.

I had a running battle with the press corps over their attire, which had deteriorated tremendously during the four years between the time I left the White House in January 1977 and returned in January 1981. At a White House event there would be a roomful of people in business suits or black tie, and the press would come in grimy T-shirts and jeans, unshaved, and with their hair uncombed. There were really some scruffy types among the regulars.

One of the first things I did was to require the reporters to wear business suits for White House dinners, in or out of the White House, and black tie when there was a black-tie event. But that didn't apply to informal, everyday occasions. The windows in the Reagans' living room overlooked that lawn on the north side of the White House, just outside the West Wing, where the press would gather to see who was going in and out. The reporters would lounge around out there in the sun, sometimes take their shirts off, sometimes have their lunch out there, and just make a mess. Eventually, we built a fence to keep them off the lawn, and we insisted that when they were on the White House grounds, they wear shirts.

A lot of the news media's harshest criticism of Ronald Reagan has been directed at his perceived lack of contact with the press. During the approximately 2,000 days I worked for Reagan, he had "only" 535 sessions with the press—more than one every four days. His press contacts consisted of 257 interviews; 216 question-

and-answer periods in the Rose Garden, on his way to or from various other meetings, or going to an airplane or helicopter; thirty-nine full-fledged press conferences, and twenty-three other news conferences, which usually took place in the White House briefing room.

But reporters apparently believed he should have spent approximately one hundred percent of his presidency in consultation with them. What upset them the most was his relatively small number of press conferences, at least by their definition; they gave him credit for only the thirty-nine full-scale conferences in the East Room of the White House, refusing to count the other twenty-three. I constantly pushed for Reagan to hold more press conferences and conduct interviews on a regular basis, but other advisers always found excuses to scratch them from the President's schedule.

Reagan did hold far fewer full-fledged press conferences than most of his predecessors, and there's a good reason for it: Press conferences no longer serve the presidency or the press, and are in danger of becoming obsolete unless reporters decide to use them as information-gathering sessions, which is what they're intended to be. More and more, the reporters present in the East Room are second-stringers, while the first-stringers are back in the office watching on television, particularly those that are facing A.M. deadlines or wire deadlines.

In the wake of Watergate and Vietnam, press conferences have deteriorated into a game of "How can I trip him up?" and "I gotcha." Instead of asking legitimate questions on matters of importance, most of the reporters who attend press conferences are there only to try to trap the President. They are trying to make news, not report it. The incredibly arrogant television networks even go one step further—when they show excerpts from the news conference afterwards, they generally try to use only the questions that come from their own correspondents and ignore the rest. It's a case of "It wasn't important unless we asked it."

One thing to remember about press conferences is that they are strictly theater. The press is asking questions that they've written down beforehand, and the President is giving answers he has developed during a rehearsal. There's no spontaneity.

As a result, press conferences are in danger of becoming a waste of time. They no longer serve the President, the press, or, more important, the public.

Despite news media claims to the contrary, Reagan himself did not object at all to press conferences. The preparation for press conferences was always tedious, but he didn't mind standing there and answering questions. He would kid a lot about going out in front of "my friends in the press corps," or say, "Here we go again for my favorite pasttime," but he always said at the end of press conferences, "I wish we could figure out a way that we didn't have to leave so many hands uplifted when I leave the room. It just kills me to have to leave the room with everybody wanting to ask another question." But there were time constraints, both on him and on the networks, who didn't want to devote an entire evening of prime-time to something that didn't bring in revenue, like a press conference.... Reagan's briefing material for press conference preparation was usually presented in a Q-and-A format: "Mr. President, what about the shipment of Soviet helicopters to Nicaragua?" He would be given an answer of three or four sentences, sometimes along with information—only items, like the helicopters are capable of doing this or that. He didn't have the luxury as I did of reading from a piece of paper—he had to really know the material.

It makes me angry whenever I hear people say that Reagan was not adequately prepared for his press conferences. If he did do badly, I would fault myself, and ask myself how I could have prepared him better. Usually there weren't many things you could have done: You would tell the President what to say, and if he said it, he said it, and if he didn't, he didn't. I don't say that as a disinterested observer; I was in charge of preparing him.

We would set a tentative date for a press conference, ten days to two weeks in advance, and we would send word out through my office to the departments and agencies that we would appreciate questions and answers on the subjects that they thought might come up. Then we would put together a briefing book by the Friday before a press conference, for the President to take with him to Camp David and study over the weekend. It would have several dozen domestic and foreign topics, with questions and answers on each topic.

If the press conference was scheduled for Tuesday night, we would have our first rehearsal Monday afternoon at two in the family theater in the upstairs part of the White House. There would be a presidential podium, television-type lighting, a microphone, a public address system, and three or four of us at a table, acting as reporters and posing questions. Others, like Stockman, Meese, Deaver, and Baker, would sit in to observe and evaluate the President's performance. We would fire questions, we would follow up, and we would try to trap him; we would try to play the exact role of the press. We would spend forty-five or fifty minutes on domestic questions and then break for ten minutes to critique: "Mr. President, on Aid to Dependent Children, you could have mentioned that in 1982 we did increase the budget in this area by ten percent." Or, "the budget figure you quoted was $900,000 and it should have been $9 million." The President took criticism very much in stride. Occasionally he would debate an answer with you or say, "That's a good idea." Then we would do the same thing on the foreign policy side. And we would have a repeat rehearsal for two hours Tuesday afternoon before the President went upstairs to rest for the press conference.

That may seem like a lot of preparation, and in truth it was, but you have to remember that Nixon would shut down totally for forty-eight hours in advance to prepare himself for a press conference. Press conferences, after all, are—or, at least should be—one of the primary ways in which a President communicates directly with the American people, and there's nothing wrong with trying to make sure you're properly prepared for one.

In press conferences, out of thirty questions and follow-ups the press would ask, we might fail to anticipate one. And often we could even predict which reporters were going to ask which questions. In spite of all our groundwork, we never could tell how Reagan would do. Many times the dress rehearsal bore no resemblance to the actual event. Sometimes the rehearsal would be bad and you would be living in fear that the President was going to make a series of major mistakes in a press conference and he'd be absolutely brilliant, or you might feel entirely comfortable after the briefing sessions and the final act would be riddled with mistakes....

When Jim Baker or Don Regan and I would go up to the White House living quarters to get the President a few minutes before a press conference began, there would be as much tension as there would be if he were getting ready to enter the ring for a prize fight. Mrs. Reagan would be there in a bathrobe—she would watch it on live TV—and there would be this long farewell between the two of them. Sometimes their good-byes would last so long that I would be afraid we'd be late for the news conference. She would hold his hand, wish him luck, tell him to do well, and remind him, "Now when Helen [Thomas] says, 'Thank you,' you leave," and he would say, "I will, honey." Then they would kiss and he would be off to his fate, waving to her as he got on the elevator.

As we walked over to the press conference, I would always repeat the First Lady's admonition, urging Reagan to zip out of the East Room as soon as Helen said her "Thank you." "It's always the last question that gets you," I would tell him. "If we could figure out when it was coming and quit just before it was asked, you'd bat 1,000." But, nice guy that he is, the President would linger as reporters surged up around him for another shot at making news. Often, they'd begin with a softball question, like, "When are you going to hold another press conference?" Then the gut punch: "What about the Israeli invasion of Lebanon?"...

Some of... [Reagan's] strengths were also weaknesses. His ability to cut through the political clutter down to the *Reader's Digest* item often backfired, especially with that collection of three-by-five cards he kept containing facts or quotes. A lot of those "facts," although they had been reported in the press, were incorrect, but when he saw something he thought was a good idea he would file it away and use it. His statement that trees cause as much pollution as automobiles was something he had read somewhere. A lot of those facts would get locked in and then would come out at inopportune times.

Mike Deaver used to say that you had to be very cautious with the President right before a press conference because the last thing you put in was the first thing that would come out. Reagan had an actor's ability to memorize. He had a propensity to deal in figures and percentages in order to illustrate his stories. But if you confronted him with a blizzard of numbers at the very last minute, he might get confused and screw up. So we had a rule that you just didn't clutter him up with a heavy dose of minutiae at the last second. Generally we would quit about three o'clock on the afternoon of a press conference, to give him time to rest and absorb all he had learned during the preparations.

One person I watched very closely at the beginning of Reagan's term was Jim Baker, who, like me, had not worked with Reagan before. Baker had a real ability to communciate with the President. Baker spoke in short sentences, used anecdotes to illustrate his points, and repeated what he said, and I tried to do the same myself whenever possible, in order to get my views across to the President. . . .

Throughout my six years with Reagan, I pleaded with him and his inner circle for more openness in government—more openness to their own press office and more openness to the press and the American people. If the President and Poindexter had not been so obsessed with secrecy on the initiative to Iran and it had been more widely discussed, it might never have happened at all. Had there been no arms shipments, there would have been no profits from them to funnel to the Contras.

On the other side of the equation, however, just as the White House has to change its ways of dealing with the press, the news media needs to treat the presidency differently. I recall the time back in January 1983 when the press all but went into a feeding frenzy over the President's proposal that the corporate income tax be abolished. I finally accused the White House reporters of "licking your chops and clapping your hands and doing back flips" over the story. When President Reagan heard what I had said, he shook my hand.

First and foremost, let's restore what is potentially one of the most important institutions of democracy in the television era, the presidential press conference, to what it should be: an information-gathering device, not a tool for establishing journalistic reputations. The time has come when each and every reporter who covers the President must stop thinking of himself or herself as Bob Woodward, and must stop asking variation after variation of the old question, "When did you stop beating your wife?" Many reporters come to *create* news, not to *cover* it.

Politicians and the press corps have an adversary relationship, as they must in a democracy, but it doesn't have to be an "I gotcha!" relationship. Let the reporters ask questions about subjects they truly need information on, instead of approaching press conferences as a vehicle for making headlines themselves. It's time to abolish the cult of personality in the press corps itself. If reporters think they can do a better job of running the country than those who are in power, let them run for office themselves.

83

HARRISON SALISBURY

From *A Time of Change*

I HAVE SPENT most of my life on the front lines of reporting, and it has often been a stormy passage. I was thrown out of
the University of Minnesota as editor of the college daily for my
uppity campaigns against the administration. I nearly lost my first
journeyman's job for my reports on the Great Depression in my
hometown of Minneapolis. Stalin and Molotov threatened to expel
me from Russia in World War II. Some editors of the *New York
Times* wanted to fire me for my reports from Moscow; Moscow
banned me from Russia for the same reports. Birmingham entered
millions of dollars in libel suits because I warned that the city was
going to blow up in race violence—which it did. Lyndon Johnson
and the Pentagon exploded when I went behind the enemy lines
to Hanoi during Vietnam.

So it has been, and that is the way it should be. If a reporter is
not a "disturber of the peace," he should go into cost accounting.
I said at the time of Hanoi that, if I was getting nothing but
bouquets, I must be missing part of the story—the vital part....

I got to know Jack Kennedy in the Presidential campaign of
1960. I covered both Kennedy and Nixon in that year, and I was
not wild about either. I often spoke of Kennedy as a "lace curtain
Nixon," by which I meant I did not think there was much difference, if any, in their ideology. That was not true, but there was, I
think, a nubbin of truth in my remark. Nixon was shabby in
character but had a better grasp of the world. He had seen more of
it and thought more. Kennedy had style; there were not many
reporters he didn't charm, but he was lazy. I think that had he not
been martyred, his Presidential rating would be much lower.

Most newsmen thought Kennedy loved them. That was not
true. I have observed every President since Calvin Coolidge. None
of them loved the press. FDR, Kennedy, and Reagan were the
best at conning the reporters, Hoover and Carter the worst. One
of Harry Truman's most amiable traits was his honest dislike of

reporters. He put up with the marriage of his beloved Margaret to Clifton Daniel, but it was a bitter pill that Clifton was a newspaper-man.

Jack Kennedy gave me a lift one evening from West Virginia, where he was campaigning against Hubert Humphrey. He was on his way to Washington. The plane was a puddle-jumper, and only the two of us were aboard. He spent the brief ride cursing "those sons-a-bitches," the newspaper men. He had a big envelope of clips which he pawed through and tossed away. Most of them seemed to be pieces about his father Joseph, and most of them, Jack felt, went out of their way to dig up the old Joe Kennedy scandals—his borderline bank manipulations, his speculative deals in Wall Street, the maneuvers that got him the Scotch whiskey franchises and the great Chicago Merchandise Mart (where in pro-hibition days, the building almost empty, a huge speakeasy with a 100-foot bar was the liveliest activity under its roof—I often ate my lunch there), and his role as spokesman for America First* and appeasement before FDR yanked him out of London as the U.S. ambassador. "Bastards," gritted Kennedy as he leafed through the reports. "Just a bunch of lies. They never tell the truth. Bunch of bastards." I didn't talk up the case for newspapering. It was his father, and he was a true member of the clan—the Kennedys against the world and, in this case, against the newsmen. But I had been given an insight into the true Kennedy feeling about the press. One thing was certain about the Kennedys. You were with them or against them. Totally. The press was on the other side.

I don't want to suggest that Nixon had any more love for the press. I think the feeling of the two men was mutual in this regard. But Kennedy could put on a bravado act, make a half dozen impor-tant Washington correspondents believe they were real friends (in-side the clan). Nixon was a poor actor. His lies stuck out like cold sores. He was forever wrapping his anger at the press in a sleazy tangle of "I know what your problems are," or "Of course you have your job to do," "I don't mean to include you personally," and then out would come the hurt and anger. I guess you could say that, in his way, Nixon was the more honest man. Jack rarely let his distaste show in public. . . .

By the time Jack Kennedy was shot to death in Dallas at 12:30

*America First was a prominent "isolationist" organization in the 1930s. The group opposed American involvement in European affairs, especially our taking sides against Hitler's Germany and its expansionist policies.—EDS.

P.M. of November 22, 1963, a lot had changed for me. Reluctantly
I had bowed to Turner Catledge's insistence and taken on the post
of national editor of the *New York Times*. (Catledge coined the
title "Director of National Correspondence" so as not to hurt the
feelings of Ray O'Neill, who held the title "National Editor.")

Catledge's proposal had reached me in Kabul, Afghanistan,
where I was trying to persuade the authorities to let me go through
the Khyber Pass. A small war was in progress. I never did get to
the Khyber, going to Tashkent, Bokhara, and Mongolia instead. I
had to accept Catledge's proposal—much as I preferred reporting.
He had twice tried to make me an editor, and I knew I couldn't
say no a third time. But I did get his pledge that once or twice a
year I could abandon my desk and go off on a reporting trip. The
promise was meticulously kept by Catledge and Punch Sulzberger,
even after I set up the Op-Ed page and became an associate editor
of the *Times*.

I had concluded before going to work for the *Times* in 1949
that the essence of journalism was reporting and writing. I wanted
to find things out—particularly things which no one else had managed to dig out—and let people have the best possible evidence on
which to make up their minds about policy. It was essentially a
gloss on the old Scripps slogan: "Give Light and the People Will
Find Their Way." I have never ceased to believe in it.

One day in November 1963 I was sitting at the long table in
the third floor dining room of the Century Club, waiting for my
lunch.

At that moment, just on one o'clock, the waiter having brought
my purée mongole, Alfred De Liagre, the theatrical producer,
elegant as always in English tweeds, rounded into the room, raised
his voice over the cheerful hum of Century conversation, and
said, a bit theatrically: "Gentlemen, I am sorry to interrupt, but
the President has just been shot in the head . . . in Dallas." I dropped
my napkin, leaped down the stairs, and ran the two and a half
blocks west on 43rd Street to 229, up on the elevator, and to my
national news desk just south of my old spot, the Hagerty desk
which I had occupied for nine years. There I would remain almost
continuously for the next several days.

I was used to violence in the South, violence in the country as
a whole. It seemed to me that I had inhabited a violent world
since I had come back from the deceptive quiet of the Moscow
streets—violence in the slums of Brooklyn and Manhattan, a na-

tionwide uprooting of populations, technological revolution in the farm belt, the bondage of the great cities in straitjackets of steel and concrete freeways, and now rising terror in the South.

Dallas ... Kennedy ... violence ... it seemed an almost inevitable pattern, and my mind leaped instantly to the passion in Dallas that had raged since before Kennedy's election. Dallas had seemed like another country, ranting against *everything*. I knew of the threats and the hate ads that spewed out before the Kennedy visit. I had hardly gotten on the telephone to order staff to Dallas— everyone I could reach who could fly in by nightfall—than my mind spun with thoughts of a conspiracy by the radical right or even—I hardly dared formulate the thought—by some in the die-hard LBJ camp who so hated the Kennedys. What it might be I did not know. But plots, conspiracy, coups raced through my head. From the vicious anti-Kennedy propaganda, there seemed to me but one short step to a conspiracy to assassinate the President....

... On November 27, 1963, five days after Kennedy was killed, the first moment I had time and strength to put down what I felt, I wrote a memorandum to myself. I said that in the year 2000 the Kennedy assassination would still be a matter of debate, new theories being evolved how and why it happened. The lone, crazed killer would not then—or ever—be accepted. It offended nature. For the Sun King to be struck down by a vagrant with bulging eyes—no, the concept was repugnant to our very being. For a man so noble the cause of death must lie in high conspiracy, the most powerful courtiers, the great barons, the captains of the earth....

It was no surprise to me that the Warren Commission report did not halt the "revelations," the rumors, the legend making of the conspiracy theorists, now grown to a kind of carrion industry.

I did not think the Warren Commission had dug out any essential fact that the *Times* had not found in its intense coverage in the days and weeks after the assassination. The coverage had begun with classic reportage—Tom Wicker's on-the-scenes eyewitness. It could not be beat. Tom was the only *Times* man in Dallas that day. I made one contribution to Tom's beautiful story. At 5 P.M. I ordered him—no, *command* is the word—to halt reporting and start writing. No interruptions. Any new details we could put into the piece, if necessary, after it went into type about 8:30 P.M. that night. Just write every single thing you have seen and heard. Period. He did. No more magnificent piece of journalistic writing has been published in the *Times*. Through Tom's eye we lived through each minute of that fatal Friday, the terror, the pain, the horror, the mindless tragedy, elegant, blood–chilling prose.

To this day not one material fact has been added to the *New York Times* account of the assassination and the events that followed it. . . .

Ever since I arrived at the Union Station from Minneapolis on a frozen January 13, 1931, I have thought of Chicago as *my* city. . . .

Nothing that happens in Chicago really surprises me. But the 1968 Democratic National Convention was an exception. I expected trouble. I expected violence. I expected the nomination of Lyndon Baines Johnson. I was right about trouble and violence. I was wrong—but perhaps not that wrong—about Lyndon.

On the night of August 28, 1968, a Wednesday, I was sitting at my command post in the press section of the convention hall at the Chicago Stockyards. I *knew* there would be violence. It had been building up.

Robert Kennedy had been assassinated in June in Los Angeles. Martin Luther King had been killed in Memphis in May. The country was going up in smoke. One afternoon I was running to board an airplane in Newark when I heard a young woman ask the man she was with: "What's all that smoke?" He (and I) looked back. "Oh," he said, "It's just Newark burning down. Let's hurry." From the takeoff I could see Newark's black ghetto burning in the rage of King's murder.

That was my America in the summer of 1968. No way that Chicago, Hog Butcher Chicago, Daley's Chicago, wouldn't explode.

I had arrived on the watch for a Draft Johnson movement. I hadn't believed LBJ was sincere in his March 31 speech.

Mayor Daley didn't seem to take LBJ's "withdrawal" any more seriously than I did. Daley had backed Robert Kennedy until Robert was killed, then switched to LBJ. He prepared a monster birthday party for Lyndon at Soldier Field. It sounded like a campaign kickoff to me. By this time the White House was leaking to every visitor nasty stories about Humphrey. He was a loser. "He cries too much." There was no doubt what the White House was up to. I was not amazed when on an inspection of the Chicago Amphitheater, I stumbled into a storeroom where LBJ placards, banners, and posters were stacked to the ceiling. Everything was set for the convention to rise and sweep LBJ into the nomination.

But nothing in Chicago went according to plan. The antiwar forces—David Dellinger, Tom Hayden, and the Yippies led by Abbie Hoffman—had mustered their supporters by the thousand. Daley mobilized his forces—8,000 police, 5,000 Illinois guardsmen (some 5,000 U.S. regulars were alerted and held in reserve). The convention hall looked like Hitler's last bunker, barbed wire coils everywhere, barricades, checkpoints outside and inside the hall. American politics had never seen such security.

Confrontation quickly became the order of the day. The decibel count went up and up. The higher it rose, the faster prospects for a Johnson coup de theatre faded. The Secret Service would not guarantee his safety. He was confined to his Texas ranch, on the telephone to Daley, but the Blue Helmets washed LBJ out with their street brawls. Daley had to cancel the Soldier Field birthday party. Those tons of LBJ banners never left the stadium bins....

Behind cordons of police and barbed wire the convention hall was an island of quiet. Not so the central convention hotel, the Conrad Hilton, which spanned a long block on Michigan Avenue. The police beat and hounded young people from Lincoln Park down to Grant Park opposite the Hilton.

Tony Lukas, just back from the Congo wars, was handling the street story. He knew the protesters, the gentle pacifists, the wild radicals, the eccentric Yippies. He knew them all.

On Tuesday evening Wallace Turner, the best of the *Times's* investigative reporters, was walking back to his hotel. He spotted three or four squad cars blocking a street. In a courtyard he saw a huddle of police and heard a patrolman say: "Sergeant, can I have me a hippie to beat the shit out of?"

The next evening it started.

Tom Wicker was standing at the big window of the *Times* news room on the twenty-first story of the Conrad Hilton, looking down on Michigan Avenue, when he saw the police charge past the National Guardsmen into Grant Park. Several hundred youngsters sat there singing: "God Bless America." The Daley men burst among them, beating, kicking, and dragging them by the feet to paddy wagons. "These are our children!" Wicker exclaimed. Next day he wrote a column headed: "These were our children, and the police were beating them." His colleague Ned Kenworthy rushed for the elevator, down to the street, two blocks up Michigan and over into the park. "Get out! Get Out!" he shouted to the young people. "The police are coming. You're doing no good to your cause." (They were mostly Gene McCarthy supporters.)

Times reporter John Kifner was with the young people marching down Michigan. He watched the police charge, clubs and blackjacks swinging. He watched them drive young and old back against the Hilton and through the plate-glass window, shards splintering, police tumbling into the dark, air-conditioned, panel-lined bar, beating and slugging everyone in their path.

Kifner raced to a telephone. He got Charlotte Curtis on the line. She was filling in for Sylvan Fox, a deskman who had suffered a heart attack and been sent to the hospital by ambulance. Charlotte Curtis listened a moment to Kif and then handed the telephone to Lukas. "You better take this yourself."

At the stockyards I was going crazy. A *Times* photographer had been beaten and dragged off—no one knew where—by the police. I was on the phone to the hospital, to the police, to Lukas' post at Tribune Tower, to our main news room in the Hilton and, most of all, to New York, trying to convey to the editors that the story had shifted away from the convention hall, where the slow nominating process was underway, onto the Chicago streets. It wasn't politics this night; it was a riot. The editors found it hard to grasp.

Kifner was trying to get Lukas to understand. "I've just witnessed something unbelievable," Kifner told him. "The police have charged on a lot of innocent people and driven them through the glass window in the Hilton cocktail lounge, following them in and are beating them."

"Come on, John," said Tony. "Don't get carried away. Don't give me that stuff. I don't believe it."

"I saw it with my own eyes," Kifner insisted.

"You saw them inside, beating people up?"

"I did."

So Lukas wrote it. He knew Kifner was an experienced reporter. If Kifner saw it, it happened.

Kenworthy was writing what he saw, too, the young people singing, police charges, bystanders' reactions, 1,500 or 2,000 words. But trouble arose in New York. I got on the phone again and again, telling the responsible editors, Abe Rosenthal and night editor Ted Bernstein, that Chicago had gone into orbit. They didn't believe me. They thought the reporters had gone out of control. I told the editors to look at TV. The TV cameras were beginning to focus on the streets. Finally most of Lukas' story was published, but only a couple of paragraphs of Kenworthy. "We don't want to influence the convention balloting" was the excuse.

I knew it was hard for anyone to get the feel of Chicago that night, anyone who did not smell the teargas and vomit in the Hilton halls, who did not hear the crack of walnut sticks on skulls, who did not see the blood-stained carpets, who did not witness the police frog-walking people out of the hotel and into patrol wagons, flailing unfortunate youngsters, male or female, who appeared on the scene; you had to see the face of Mayor Daley, sitting in the front row of the Convention, mouthing "you son of a bitch" as Senator Abraham Ribicoff of Connecticut tried to remonstrate from the podium against the hatred loosed on Chicago that night by Daley and his men.

The gap between hot reality in Chicago and the cool of the air-conditioned offices in New York was wide as an ocean. A news analysis that Lukas wrote of the "blundering" of Daley and the "brutality of his blue-helmeted police" said Daley and his police had turned certain defeat for the young radicals into a startling victory. This language was too blunt for New York. "Blundering" became "miscalculation" and "Brutality" became "over-reaction."

Nowhere in the *Times* the next morning was the true tragedy of Chicago delineated, the hideous blow to American democracy inflicted by Daley's truculence and the abandon of the young; the tawdry tainting of the nomination so grudgingly released by LBJ to hapless Hubert Horatio Humphrey. Nor did we catch the melodrama of LBJ's last hurrah, setting the stage for the triumph of Richard Nixon. I left Chicago convinced that LBJ was a "mean man." And I felt that I and my *New York Times* had fallen far short of our capability to present to the country a sharp-edge, unshadowed picture of Chicago. . . .

. . . I had been editing the Op-Ed page of the *Times,* since the day it was launched, September 26, 1970, three months after I had abandoned the unquiet realm of the third floor and gone up to the tenth to create a new world. It had been a long time coming, debated for years but thwarted by bureaucracy. Three powerful editors—John Oakes of the editorial page, Lester Markel of the *Sunday Times,* and Turner Catledge (and later Abe Rosenthal) of the *Daily* had fought for jurisdiction. In 1970 Punch Sulzberger decided to start the page and put it in my hands. I packed my things and moved off the fine old warehouse third floor, now raddled with hutches and cubicles, and up to that gothic relic of Mr. Ochs' enchantment with the *Times* of London, the editorial boardroom. In Mr. Ochs' day the editors (beards and frock coats) each morning sat and decided upon the policies of the day. I inherited the mullioned windows, oak cabinets, and, for a while, the great oaken table where the fate of nations had been pondered. I don't think Mr. Ochs or his editors would have liked the work to which I put my hand.

I created Op-Ed at a moment when the country had entered an uncharted, unproclaimed, and largely unrecognized revolution. Each day conflict engulfed another institution—the Pentagon, the CIA, the White House, the State Department, Congress, the Supreme Court, the legal system, the Catholic Church, most other faiths, universities, the educational system, social and racial relationships, banks, corporate America, the great foundations, Rockefeller and Ford, the moral system—marriage, the family, sex, lifestyle—the arts, the way we dressed (jeans) and the way we cut or didn't cut our hair. Nothing shattered nerves as did hair. Establishment America was under siege. From the watch post of Op-Ed, we brought the latest bulletins to the readers of the *Times*.

That was not exactly what I or anyone intended when the long debate (it lasted seven years) over the Op-Ed page was going on. My idea (and that of Punch Sulzberger) was that it would present an alternate opinion to those expressed by *Times* editorials and columnists. It was to be opposite in the true sense. If the *Times* was liberal, the Op-Ed articles would be reactionary or conservative or radical or eccentric. The page would offer a window on the world, particularly that scene which for one reason or another (usually the parochialism and timidity of editors) the *Times* was not presenting in its news pages and editorial comment.

I am sorry to say that, with the passage of time, Op-Ed has lost most of its Op quality. It has become a wallow of predictability. Not so the page of the early days. Op the page was from its start, and the revolutionary nature of the epoch put it on the crust, the breaking edge of the issues that spewed like volcanic lava from the depths of America. The page was a hit, quickly becoming (next to page 1) the most read section of the *Times*. Within a year every paper of consequence in the country had adopted Op-Ed.

Even TV and radio and the news weeklies were trying to create imitations. The *Washington Post* was so eager to get into the game (on hearing the *Times* was launching Op-Ed) that it threw out a haberdasher's ad which had run for forty years across from its editorial page and started its own Op-Ed a few days before the *Times*. . . .

The world as seen from Op-Ed was far from commonplace. It was the world of C. D. Darlington and Patrick Buchanan, of B. F. Skinner and Milovan Djilas, of Anaïs Nin and Charles Reich (*The Greening of America*), of LBJ and Hannah Arendt, of Walt Rostow (who shared all-time tops in frequency of appearance on Op-Ed with Mary Mebane, the black North Carolina writer), of Bernadette Devlin and Yukeo Mishima, of Robert Bly and Yevgeny Yevtushenko, of Buckminster Fuller and Aleksandr Solzhenitsyn, of Loren Eiseley and William C. Westmoreland, of Andrei Sakharov and Bernadine Dohrn, of Roger Wilkins and Spiro T. Agnew, of Fred Hampton (the slain Black Panther), and Halldor Laxness (Nobel writer of Iceland).

The world of Op-Ed expanded at the rate of almost 100 names a month, and a great many were not names anyone would recognize, had ever before heard, or ever would hear again: a Mississippi doctor's letter to his freshman son at Tulane, promising that if the boy was shot in a demonstration, he would grieve, but he would buy a dinner for the National Guardsman who pulled that trigger; from an Ohio father whose daughter, Sandy, was shot and killed at Kent State; from a man fighting to save a Connecticut mountain from despoliation by a power company; from a drug addict, writing of a fourteen-year-old girl addict and prostitute; from a professor fed up with the slobism of his students, male and female; from prisoners in jails and camps from Siberia to Central America; from a man aroused at the destruction of the Newark he grew up in and a woman lamenting the loss of the prairies of her Midwestern childhood.

There was not much that did not get said on Op-Ed. I had feared we might run out of materials and piled up an inventory of 150 articles. I was stupid. We got 100 to 200 submissions a week. Everyone in the country wanted to speak out, and we let their voices be heard. . . .

I sit at this Remington portable which I have used for forty-five years. I have spent hundreds of dollars to keep it going. I hate to think how many words I have pounded out, how many ribbons

I have worn to rags, how many quires of paper I've used. It has been faithful to me, has responded when I battered at it in deep Siberian forests, on a plane I thought for sure was going down over New Guinea, in an air raid shelter in Hanoi, in a pigsty on Roswell Garst's farm in Coon Rapids, Iowa.

It has been faithful to my use. Have I been faithful to it? I am not so sure. It seems to me that a lot of mile-wide, inch-deep conclusions have sailed off these keys. How often have I got down to bedrock? Not as often as I would like to remember....

The rottenness in our government, the growing deceit, blundering, and hypocrisy since World War II has made me a First Amendment absolutist—that is, I oppose any government restrictions on the press except for what is called the "troopship exception." No one, I hold, has a right to publish the date of a troopship sailing in wartime or war crisis.... I would prohibit the government from concealing its blunders and embarrassing mistakes. I believe ... that democracy and secrecy are incompatible, that people will not in the long run permit the kind of government cover-ups which have become so common....

The *New York Times* electrified the nation in 1871 when it exposed the financial crimes of Tammany and the Tweed ring. It dozed through the Koch years, even sending its outraged and brutally honest columnist, Sydney Schanberg, to the showers. The press drowsed along with the government and its opulent contractors until *Challenger* blew up. Nearly twenty years ago Emma Rothschild in *The New Yorker* forecast the demise of Detroit. It took David Halberstam's book to detail the sordid story not of Japanese skill but of American sloth. The press slept.

I could go on and on. The world of electronic journalism, once sparkling with men like Edward R. Murrow and Walter Cronkite, slipped into the gray wasteland, with bottom-line barons taking it over, men whose testicles seemed to have been replaced by puffballs.... The press yawns. Candidate after candidate rolls out of the electronic image processors. Nobody hires Sy Hersh to see what skeletons lurk behind their gussified hairdos. I mean real scandals, not Gary Hart trifles.

And no one complains of all this. Not the public, not Congress, not the White House—heavens, no, not the White House. Not opposition parties. Not the princes of the press—with a few honorable exceptions: the *New York Times,* the *Washington Post,* the *Boston Globe,* the *Los Angeles Times*. The others are too busy with their accountants and tax laywers. We sleep. Oh, a few eccentrics raise a paranoid cry of Conspiracy. But nothing breaks the somnolence. We are, it seems, as Lincoln Steffens found Philadelphia, corrupt and content. . . .

There is no story—literally none—which the great electronic news media and the billion-dollar press aggregates cannot extract, be it from the Kremlin or the Pentagon, and bring to the public of America. Instead, they tinker with sitcoms and fourcolor ad pages. Priorities? Forget it.

84

SAM DONALDSON

From *Hold On, Mr. President!*

WATERGATE was the most intense story I've covered. And Watergate proved to be the most difficult story I've covered when it came to keeping my own emotions and feelings from coloring my reporting.* As the facts of Watergate accumulated, I became convinced that Richard Nixon was participating in a criminal conspiracy to obstruct justice and ought to be punished for it through the constitutional and legal process. I tried to keep this personal view out of my reporting, but in retrospect, I didn't always succeed.

Professionally, the story helped me reach a wider audience and flex my wings, thanks to the fact that the networks rotated live coverage of the Senate Watergate hearings in the summer of 1973, and every third day, if you wanted to watch, you had to watch me.

Frank Reynolds anchored from our Connecticut Avenue stu-

---

*One of the biggest news stories in recent times was Watergate, which began with the 1972 break-in at Democratic National headquarters by several men associated with President Nixon's re-election committee. Watergate ended two years later with the resignation of President Nixon. Nixon and his closest aides were implicated in the cover-up of the Watergate burglary. Tapes made by President Nixon of his Oval Office conversations revealed lying and obstruction of justice at the highest levels of government.—EDS.

dios, and I reported from the hall outside the old Senate Caucus
Room, where Senator Sam Ervin presided over the hearings. Frequently, the bells would ring on the Senate floor for a vote and
the committee would recess for twenty minutes or so while its
members went over to vote. During that time, Frank and I would
talk back and forth about the testimony and the story, and I would
grab whomever I could to interview.

On the day the Nixon enemies list was revealed in committee
testimony, I grabbed Mary McGrory, the *Washington Post* columnist, who was then with the now defunct *Washington Star.*

"It says here that you write daily 'hate Nixon' articles," I told
her, reading from the enemies list, which Nixon speechwriter Patrick J. Buchanan had helped compile—the same man who later
returned to the White House to serve for two years as Reagan's
communications director.

"That's not true," replied McGrory in that-ever-so-gentle,
sweet manner of hers that masks the instincts of a barracuda. "I
only write three days a week.". . .

The Saturday Night Massacre when Nixon ordered special
prosecutor Cox fired and Attorney General Elliot Richardson and
his deputy, William Ruckelshaus, refused to do it and resigned
made the impeachment investigation inevitable. And I moved on
to cover it. Which meant covering Peter Rodino, chairman of the
House Judiciary Committee. Most of us didn't know much about
Rodino but suspected he might not be up to the job of organizing
the first serious impeachment investigation of a president since
Andrew Johnson. Rodino proved us wrong. Of course, he had
help. John Doar, who had been an official in JFK's Justice Department, did an excellent job directing the staff. And Francis O'Brien,
who took over as Rodino's administrative assistant, handled the
press expertly.

In the beginning, Rodino was sort of overwhelmed and intimi-
dated by the media. But O'Brien had the sure touch. He knew
that if reporters realize you think they are serious about their work
and their coverage and if you do not resent the adversary relationship that exists between them and you, then things will usually
work out to your advantage. Moreover, O'Brien further understood what reporters needed for their stories, whether print or
TV, and tried to make sure they had it whenever he could. Finally,
he resisted the temptation to try to punish reporters or news organizations that didn't tell it the way he would have liked.

One noontime, Jack Nelson and Paul Houston of the *Los Angeles Times* and I were in O'Brien's office talking over the events of the morning when Chairman Rodino opened the door from his own office and came in. We started talking to him about the upcoming impeachment vote on Richard Nixon in the committee. Nelson asked him how he thought the vote was shaping up on Article One. Without hesitating, Rodino said he was confident all twenty-one committee Democrats would vote for impeachment, and while less confident about the Republicans, thought five or six of them would vote aye also.

It was certainly injudicious for Rodino to make such a prediction, since the committee had not yet reached the point of deliberation. But the ground rules for such informal sessions, whether in Rodino's office or the White House press office, are always "guidance" or "background," meaning in the first instance, no direct disclosure of the information, in the second instance, the information may be reported but not attributed to the source by name. The ground rules that day were not clear because no one had set them in so many words.

The next morning, Nelson had the story on the front page of the *Times*. Nelson wrote that "Rodino was quoted as saying that all twenty-one Democrats on the House Judiciary Committee are prepared to vote to impeach President Nixon ..." Nelson did not attribute the information directly to Rodino, but said that visitors to Rodino's office had relayed his views. I hadn't done the story at all. I should have.

All hell broke loose. The White House attack team, led by Kenneth Clawson, insisted that this proved Rodino was biased against Nixon, had no intention of judging the evidence fairly, and was simply leading a partisan Democratic lynch mob.

Speaker Carl Albert called Rodino and told him he had to deny the story before the House or the consequences would be incalculable. Rodino took to the House floor and denied flatly that he had ever said the Democrats "are prepared" to vote for impeachment. He said he didn't know how committee members would vote, and he had never made the prediction ascribed to him.

Reporters everywhere that day were doing the story. They could say that the *Los Angeles Times* reported Rodino was predicting all the Democrats would vote for impeachment but that Rodino said he had never made such a prediction. Reporters everywhere could say that except for one: me. I had been there. I *knew* Rodino had said it. And Francis O'Brien knew I knew it.

As the afternoon wore on, O'Brien kept trying to get me to agree to do the story in the same way all the other reporters would have to do it. He said it was clear Rodino was not reporting a Democratic plot to prejudge the evidence, but giving an estimate based on what committee members were freely saying about their feelings and intentions in the privacy of the cloakroom. To let this candid observation by the chairman jeopardize the entire investigation would be wrong, argued O'Brien.

I thought about it. O'Brien was right. Rodino had told us that he *thought* the Democrats would vote that way, not that he knew it for a certainty. Furthermore, by this time I was personally convinced that Richard Nixon was guilty as hell and that he should be removed from office. I was tempted. But having done the wrong thing by not reporting the story in the first instance, I was not about to make things worse by fudging the truth. If you can't say to your audience you're telling them the truth the best you know it, you aren't saying anything that matters to them.

So that night I reported what the *Times* said. I quoted Rodino as telling the House that he wanted to state "... unequivocally and categorically that this statement is not true ..." After which, I concluded, "This reporter was present when Rodino made his remarks yesterday.... It is true as he says, he did not state that he had specific individual knowledge that all the Democrats would vote for impeachment. But he did say it was his sense of the mood and of the way members were reacting to the evidence that he thought all twenty-one Democrats would most likely reach that conclusion."

O'Brien never said another word about it.

When Committee Clerk Garner "Jim" Cline began calling the role on Article One of the Bill of Impeachment at 7:03 P.M., July 27, 1974, Frank Reynolds and I were both there. I can still call the roll from memory: Mr. Donohue, "Aye"; Mr. Kastenmeier, "Aye"; Mr. Edwards, "Aye"... When it was over, chairman Rodino had gotten his twenty-one Democrats plus six Republicans. Article One was adopted, twenty-seven to eleven.

It was a thrilling moment and the most unique experience any political reporter can imagine. What Judge John J. Sirica started, with his pressure on the Watergate burglars, and the Supreme Court expedited, with its unanimous decision forcing Nixon to turn over his tapes, culminated in that committee room as thirty-eight men and women wrestled with the evidence and their consciences over whether to vote to recommend impeachment of a president. With one or two exceptions, I respect every one of them.

A lot of people say Richard Nixon has been rehabilitated. Not for me. Richard Nixon disgraced himself and the presidency, and that stain can't be wiped away. I've spent some time talking about the Vietnam War and Watergate because these two events left a lasting impression on reporters in my generation and convinced many of us that we should adopt a new way of looking at our responsibilities.

When I first came to town in February 1961, many reporters saw themselves as an extension of the government, accepting, with very little skepticism, what government officials told them. Everyone in Washington seemed to be in the club. Reporters loved to brag about their social connections with presidents and members of his cabinet, they loved being consulted and made to feel that while the secretary of state might eventually have stumbled on the right policy, he certainly wouldn't have done it as quickly without their help. But then along came Vietnam and Watergate. In both those two great events, the highest officials in our government pursued policies harmful to this country; in the course of which they persistently lied and attempted to cover up the truth. And to some extent they were able to do it initially, because the press wasn't skeptical enough.

Along with many others, I concluded that a reporter's role ought to be one of continuing, unrelenting skepticism about government's actions. Not hostility, but a continuing eyes-open look at what the establishment is doing.

This skepticism I'm advocating should also be extended to the *conventional wisdom* about things. If everyone says we'll bring North Vietnam to its knees in ninety days of bombing, be skeptical. If it's clear that Edmund Muskie has the 1972 Democratic nomination locked up or that Ronald Reagan is too far to the right ever to be elected president, take it with several grains of salt. If world oil prices can do nothing but go up and up, watch out. The conventional wisdom isn't *always* wrong, but wrong just often enough to make it dangerous for reporters to accept it and stop doing their job. The time to really question something strongly is when everyone says it's true. Today, some members of the press still instinctively rally to the side of the establishment no matter who's in power or what the issue.

But I think in order to do their job, reporters should keep their distance from the powerful people they cover. I think we should consider ourselves outsiders. I'm not saying you can't ever have a drink with a politician or occasionally go to dinner with members of the cabinet. But I don't think a reporter's goal ought to be to get in *The Green Book,* the Washington social register. The goal ought to be to keep tabs on those who are.... The payoff in presidential political campaigns may be election day, but the real election year olympics for television has always been the nominating conventions. At the networks, gold medals are awarded for scoops. I've covered every major party convention beginning with 1964, and I've always enjoyed the competition on the convention floor for scoops....

I sharpened my live interview technique on both local and national figures during my time at WTOP-TV. I noticed one thing over and over about beating the competition to an up-for-grabs interview. You had to speak early and aggressively. If you waited until you were called on or until someone came forward voluntarily, you always waited too long.

In 1972, I put that lesson to work at the Democratic National Convention in Miami Beach. George McGovern was nominated, and on the last night, he came to the podium, on which dignitaries of the party were seated, to deliver his acceptance speech. I was waiting with other reporters behind those seats. We all wanted to get the first interview with McGovern when he was finished but were being held back by a lone security guard, whose instructions were clearly to allow none of us on the podium to talk to McGovern.

At the end of McGovern's speech, I asked the guard if he would let me go on the podium to talk to Senator Edward Kennedy. "Sure," he said. "Go ahead."

I alerted our floor control room to the situation, and Howard K. Smith threw it to me live as I stepped onto the podium and walked up to Senator Kennedy, who was in the back row.

"What did you think of the speech, Senator?" I asked.

"A very good speech," he said.

"Thank you, Senator," I said, moving past him toward the front, still on the air.

Halfway up, I asked Senator Hubert Humphrey what he thought of the speech, never pausing in my forward motion. I think he said it was fine, but his exact words trailed behind as I burst through the front row and fell on McGovern, who was still waving and nodding to the applauding audience. The other networks went wild trying to find camera shots other than the podium as I proceeded to interview McGovern exclusively on ABC.

It was a scoop. It was also 3:30 A.M. and very few people saw it.

But as luck would have it, I got another, even better, chance to beat the competition a few weeks later at the Republican National Convention, which was also held in Miami Beach. Richard Nixon had been renominated, had delivered his acceptance speech, and had stepped onto a specially constructed ramp in order to shake hands with every single delegate in the hall. They lined up and started up the ramp to partake of this singular honor. I, too, started up the ramp until I was stopped by the staff aide guarding the approach.

"Where are you going?" he asked. I was wearing my press credentials and all the bulky gear that floor reporters used to wear. I had a battery pack around my waist, earphones on my head with an antenna sticking out, and a microphone in my hand. That guard knew exactly who and what I was.

"I'm going up to shake the president's hand," I told him.

"Okay, go ahead," he said with a smile, motioning me on.

My God. What a scoop was in the works! It was late, about 12:30 A.M., but not as late as with McGovern. I started trying frantically to raise Av Westin, who was the producer in charge of the control room that handled floor correspondents. As I inched forward, I grew more frantic, yelling into the microphone. At a convention, floor control must listen for signals from four, maybe six, maybe more correspondents, who have radio gear on. With the noise from all those correspondents coming through the speaker monitors at once, it's often hard to pick out the one person who really has something that must go on the air.

Finally, Westin heard me and wanted to know where I was. I told him I was in the line going up the ramp and within a moment or two I would be in a position to interview the president. He immediately started pitching this to the senior producers and news department executives, who make the final decision on what to program.

I got to the top of the ramp, thrilled about the scoop that was going to be mine, when suddenly I heard Howard K. Smith, our anchorman say, "And so, that wraps up our coverage of the 1972 Republican National Convention ..."

"No," I screamed in Mrs. Nixon's face as she stood in line next to her husband. The dear lady shrugged back in alarm.

"... this is Howard K. Smith, thanking you for being with us and saying good night from Miami Beach," said the voice in my ear.

I lurched forward into the imperial presence. Nixon extended his hand, and sixteen years after I had first shaken it back in El Paso, I shook it again. He looked at me, at my headphones and antenna, at my microphone. He did not look pleased and was clearly bracing for the misfortune he suspected was about to befall him. He had nothing to fear. I was so frustrated, so desperately angry, that I was no threat to anyone. I cannot now remember what one or two pro-forma questions I asked Nixon, but they weren't important.

I ran down the other side of the ramp intending to find the executive responsible for taking us off the air at my moment of triumph and throttle him. I never found out who was responsible. But I'm still looking.

Things finally worked out in 1976.

There stood Jimmy Carter in New York's Madison Square Garden, his acceptance speech to the Democratic National Convention as its presidential nominee just completed. Robert Strauss, chairman of the Democratic Party and the greatest political showman since P. T. Barnum, was dragging to the podium every Democratic official ever elected anywhere to share a moment in television's spotlight. The county tax assessor of Bernalillo County, New Mexico, could easily have been up there waving to the crowd.

I was standing on the press area of the podium platform with other reporters watching all this. Through my radio gear, I told floor control what I was going to do. Harry Reasoner called me in and put me on the air and I simply walked through the throng of governors, senators, and county assessors, stuck a microphone in Jimmy Carter's face, and asked him how he felt. It was shortly after 11:00 P.M., near enough to prime time to count. The other neworks began trying to find some shot that didn't include me. They failed. Of course, they didn't have any audio from my microphone, which had one of those ABC plates on it, just to rub it in.

Within a couple of minutes, Ed Bradley of CBS and John Hart of NBC came rushing up, but they might as well have been hours late for all the good it did them.

I will not insult your intelligence by trying to make you think that scoop was a landmark event in television journalism. It was not. The ABC promotion department put it in my network biography for a while, and I'm still trying to get all copies of the version destroyed so well-meaning people introducing me to speak don't continue to say, "And he obtained the first interview with candidate Jimmy Carter after Carter was nominated in 1976." But at that moment, for me and for ABC—which wasn't yet noted for getting there first—it felt great.

My last effort at this kind of thing came in 1980, at the Republican National Convention in Detroit. Ronald Reagan finished his acceptance speech, retired to the back of the podium, and fled down a stairway on one side of the platform. I came charging down the stairway on the other side of the platform, playing out cable behind me from a technician on top, who was pointing the electronic gear in the right direction to put me on the air. I was live and yelled something inane like "What are your thoughts now?" as Reagan swept by. He answered briefly in the same spirit of fervent nonsense: "I feel good, great," and was gone. Some scoop! ...

Political reporters love to sit around and retell these "war stories" of campaigns and politicians gone by. But what we spend most of our time doing is trying to figure out who will be the winners of tomorrow. More often than not, of course, we're just as wrong as everybody else.

Before the 1984 election, when people asked me who would be elected president, I would sometimes dodge the questions by spinning out a humorous description of my own checkered history of covering only losers.

I would point out that I covered Goldwater in '64, McCarthy in '68, and Humphrey in '72. The audience would begin to get the idea.

"True," I would continue, "I covered Carter in '76, but he started that campaign fourteen points ahead and only won by half a point. If I'd had another week, I would have gotten him. You see what happened when I covered him again in 1980."

By this time, everyone listening knew I was making a joke of the whole thing and would laugh uproariously when I delivered the punch line: "You ask me who's going to win in '84," I'd conclude. "I'll be covering Reagan; he doesn't have a chance."

Ha! Ha! Until one day someone sent me one of those right-wing magazines. Exhaling fire and brimstone from every pore, the magazine predicted that the despicable left-wing press would do everything it could to defeat Reagan. "Why," said the magazine, "Sam Donaldson of ABC openly boasts, 'You ask me who's going to win in '84? I'll be covering Reagan; he doesn't have a chance.' "

I've always said right-wingers can't take a joke.

PART FOURTEEN

Civil Liberties and Civil Rights

THE AMERICAN CREED, as we have seen, is a powerful assertion of individual freedom and the duty of government to protect that freedom. We need only to recall the words of the Declaration of Independence to understand that this doctrine, derived from Locke and other European liberal constitutionalists of the seventeenth and eighteenth centuries, was the ideological foundation on which the American nation was built. "We hold these truths to be self-evident, that all men are created equal, that they are endowed by their Creator with certain unalienable rights, that among these are Life, Liberty, and the pursuit of Happiness." The Declaration goes on to say that the protection of rights is the very purpose of government, and that no government "destructive of these ends" can be a legitimate one.

Clearly, we have not always lived up to our ideals. That government should never be used to discriminate against a category of people on the basis of race would seem to be beyond dispute on American ideological grounds; yet we know that both state and federal statutes and administrative rules have been used extensively for this purpose for the better part of our history. Equal citizenship for black Americans is a very recent accomplishment. Free expression of ideas, free exercise of religious belief, fair treatment of persons accused of crimes, and many other rights are guaranteed by our national and state constitutions, but they have often been very imperfectly realized. During World War I, members of pitifully small socialist and anarchist minorities were jailed and deported for advocating resistance to the draft. As late as the 1940s the children of Jehovah's Witnesses were compelled to salute the flag in schoolrooms, in violation of their religious convictions. And, before the 1960s confessions obtained by "third-degree" tactics were routinely used to convict persons accused of crimes.

More often than not, such failures to realize our highest creedal ideals have followed from a persistent problem of democratic government: the tension between majority rule and individual rights. Again and again throughout our history the two have been at odds, as James Madison foresaw in *Federalist Paper* 10. In some cases, such as de jure segregation, there cannot be much doubt whose position is the more just. Even so, remedies have come hard. In other cases, such as the exact requirements of a fair trial or the question of abortion, majoritarian claims in favor of community interests run up against individuals' claims to fair procedure or privacy in such a manner that something like Solomonic wisdom is required to identify the just party. Oftentimes in these cases there just does not seem to be a "right" answer. Where we are seriously committed both to majority rule and minority or individual rights, who is to decide what justice requires?

In the American polity, such questions of civil rights and liberties are to an extraordinary degree the province of the judiciary. Through cases adjudicated mainly in the federal courts, individuals assert claims of constitutional rights against state or federal actions which are deemed to violate them. The courts are then required, in essence, to decide what statutes and provisions of the Constitution mean. Our readings in this section consist of three landmark cases that illustrate this process.

Our selection from Anthony Lewis's book *Gideon's Trumpet* tells the fascinating story of the Supreme Court's ruling that failure of a state to provide counsel for indigent persons in criminal trials constitutes denial of "fundamental fairness" guaranteed by the Fourteenth Amendment. Clarence Earl Gideon, a broken-down petty larcenist, is hardly the sort of person for whom society has much sympathy. Yet, his handwritten pauper's petition was accepted by the Court and became the vehicle for a major constitutional decision. Gideon, who through his many years behind bars had become something of a "jail-house lawyer," felt that his rights had been violated. The Court agreed, even though in order to do so it had to overrule an earlier decision that had stood for many years. Henceforth, it would be the law of the land that the due-process clause of the Fourteenth Amendment required representation by counsel in all state criminal trials.

Our next case, *Miranda v. Arizona* (1966), deals with the admissibility of a confession obtained from a suspected kidnapper and rapist, Ernesto Miranda, that had served to convict him in an Arizona court. The state admitted that Miranda had not been advised of his right to have an attorney present during his interrogation. Did this taint his confession? The Arizona Supreme Court said that it did not. The United States Supreme Court reversed that decision, establishing the "Miranda rule" that confessions obtained in custodial interrogation are inadmissible unless there is clear evidence that accused persons are advised of their right to remain silent and to be represented by counsel (appointed, if necessary). The Court was again interpreting the due-process clause of the Fourteenth Amendment so as to protect an individual who could expect little social sympathy. Clearly, no popular vote would have saved Miranda. This case was one of several that provoked public outrage against the Warren Court. The Court, quite aware of what it was doing, was saying that the right of *all* Americans to be free of self-incrimination is so fundamental to our system of criminal justice that it must be rigorously enforced by the federal judiciary, even if the occasional conviction is lost in the process.

Our third case example is without a doubt one of the most important decisions in the entire body of American constitutional law. In *Brown v. Board of Education* (1954) the United States Supreme Court overturned the separate-but-equal doctrine that had stood for more than half a century to hold that de jure segregation of public schools by race violates the equal protection clause of the Fourteenth Amendment. Our selection from Richard Kluger's book *Simple Justice* takes us behind the scenes at this critical moment. Chief Justice Earl Warren understood, Kluger argues, that this case would have wide repercussions throughout much of the country. Schools had been segregated by race for many years precisely because local majorities had insisted that they be. Yet, he was determined to end this greatest of all contradictions of the promise of American life. Warren personally coaxed his colleagues

into a unified stance, delivered the opinion himself so as to emphasize its importance, and skillfully devised a strategy to delay the
implementation of the desegregation ruling for some time while
tempers cooled. Even so, the process would take many years. The
Court was well ahead of public opinion on this issue; yet who can
doubt, in retrospect, what justice required? No case better illustrates the role of the judiciary in defending our highest ideals against
our own unwillingness to realize them. Would that the cause of
rectitude were always so clear.

85

ANTHONY LEWIS

From *Gideon's Trumpet*

IN THE MORNING MAIL of January 8, 1962, the Supreme
Court of the United States received a large envelope from Clarence
Earl Gideon, prisoner No. 003826, Florida State Prison, P.O. Box
221, Raiford, Florida. Like all correspondence addressed to the
Court generally rather than to any particular justice or Court employee, it went to a room at the top of the great marble steps so
familiar to Washington tourists. There a secretary opened the envelope. As the return address had indicated, it was another petition
by a prisoner without funds asking the Supreme Court to get him
out of jail—another, in the secretary's eyes, because pleas from
prisoners were so familiar a part of her work....

...A federal statute permits persons to proceed in any federal
court *in forma pauperis,* in the manner of a pauper, without following the usual forms or paying the regular costs. The only requirement in the statute is that the litigant "make affidavit that he is
unable to pay such costs or give security therefor."

The Supreme Court's own rules show special concern for *in
forma pauperis* cases. Rule 53 allows an impoverished person to file
just one copy of a petition, instead of the forty ordinarily required,
and states that the Court will make "due allowance" for technical

errors so long as there is substantial compliance. In practice, the men in the Clerk's Office—a half dozen career employees, who effectively handle the Court's relations with the outside world—stretch even the rule of substantial compliance. Rule 53 also waives the general requirement that documents submitted to the Supreme Court be printed. It says that *in forma pauperis* applications should be typewritten "whenever possible," but in fact handwritten papers are accepted.

Gideon's were written in pencil. They were done in carefully formed printing, like a schoolboy's, on lined sheets evidently provided by the Florida prison. Printed at the top of each sheet, under the heading Correspondence Regulations, was a set of rules ("Only 2 letters each week ... written on one side only ... letters must be written in English ...") and the warning: MAIL WILL NOT BE DELIVERED WHICH DOES NOT CONFORM TO THESE RULES. Gideon's punctuation and spelling were full of surprises, but there was also a good deal of practiced, if archaic, legal jargon, such as "Comes now the petitioner ...".

Gideon was a fifty-one-year-old white man who had been in and out of prisons much of his life. He had served time for four previous felonies, and he bore the physical marks of a destitute life: a wrinkled, prematurely aged face, a voice and hands that trembled, a frail body, white hair. He had never been a professional criminal or a man of violence; he just could not seem to settle down to work, and so he had made his way by gambling and occasional thefts. Those who had known him, even the men who had arrested him and those who were now his jailers, considered Gideon a perfectly harmless human being, rather likeable, but one tossed aside by life. Anyone meeting him for the first time would be likely to regard him as the most wretched of men.

And yet a flame still burned in Clarence Earl Gideon. He had not given up caring about life or freedom; he had not lost his sense of injustice. Right now he had a passionate—some thought almost irrational—feeling of having been wronged by the State of Florida, and he had the determination to try to do something about it. Although the Clerk's Office could not be expected to remember him, this was in fact his second petition to the Supreme Court. The first had been returned for failure to include a pauper's affidavit, and the Clerk's Office had enclosed a copy of the rules and a sample affidavit to help him do better next time. Gideon persevered. . . .

Gideon's main submission was a five-page document entitled "Petition for a Writ of Certiorari Directed to the Supreme Court State of Florida." A writ of certiorari is a formal device to bring a case up to the Supreme Court from a lower court. In plain terms Gideon was asking the Supreme Court to hear his case.

What was his case? Gideon said he was serving a five-year term for "the crime of breaking and entering with the intent to commit a misdemeanor, to wit, petty larceny." He had been convicted of breaking into the Bay Harbor Poolroom in Panama City, Florida. Gideon said his conviction violated the due-process clause of the Fourteenth Amendment to the Constitution, which provides that "No state shall ... deprive any person of life, liberty, or property, without due process of law." In what way had Gideon's trial or conviction assertedly lacked "due process of law"? For two of the petition's five pages it was impossible to tell. Then came this pregnant statement:

"When at the time of the petitioners trial he ask the lower court for the aid of counsel, the court refused this aid. Petitioner told the court that this Court made decision to the effect that all citizens tried for a felony crime should have aid of counsel. The lower court ignored this plea."

Five more times in the succeeding pages of his penciled petition Gideon spoke of the right to counsel. To try a poor man for a felony without giving him a lawyer, he said, was to deprive him of due process of law. There was only one trouble with the argument, and it was a problem Gideon did not mention. Just twenty years before, in the case of *Betts v. Brady,* the Supreme Court had rejected the contention that the due-process clause of the Fourteenth Amendment provided a flat guarantee of counsel in state criminal trials.

Betts v. Brady was a decision that surprised many persons when made and that had been a subject of dispute ever since. For a majority of six to three, Justice Owen J. Roberts said the Fourteenth Amendment provided no universal assurance of a lawyer's help in a state criminal trial. A lawyer was constitutionally required only if to be tried without one amounted to "a denial of fundamental fairness."...

Later cases had refined the rule of *Betts v. Brady.* To prove that he was denied "fundamental fairness" because he had no counsel, the poor man had to show that he was the victim of what the

Court called "special circumstances." Those might be his own illiteracy, ignorance, youth, or mental illness, the complexity of the charge against him or the conduct of the prosecutor or judge at the trial....

But Gideon did not claim any "special circumstances." His petition made not the slightest attempt to come within the sophisticated rule of *Betts v. Brady*. Indeed, there was nothing to indicate he had ever heard of the case or its principle. From the day he was tried Gideon had had one idea: That under the Constitution of the United States he, a poor man, was flatly entitled to have a lawyer provided to help in his defense....

Gideon was wrong, of course. The United States Supreme Court had not said he was entitled to counsel; in *Betts v. Brady* and succeeding cases it had said quite the opposite. But that did not necessarily make Gideon's petition futile, for the Supreme Court never speaks with absolute finality when it interprets the Constitution. From time to time—with due solemnity, and after much searching of conscience—the Court has overruled its own decisions. Although he did not know it, Clarence Earl Gideon was calling for one of those great occasions in legal history. He was asking the Supreme Court to change its mind....

Clarence Earl Gideon's petition for certiorari inevitably involved, for all the members of the Court, the most delicate factors of timing and strategy. The issue he presented—the right to counsel—was undeniably of first-rank importance, and it was an issue with which all of the justices were thoroughly familiar....

...Professional comment on the Betts case, in the law reviews, had always been critical and was growing stronger, and within the Supreme Court several justices had urged its overruling. On the other hand, a majority might well draw back from so large a step.... At the conference of June 1, 1962, the Court had before it two jurisdictional statements asking the Court to hear appeals, twenty-six petitions for certiorari on the Appellate Docket, ten paupers' applications on the Miscellaneous Docket and three petitions for rehearing....

The results of the deliberations at this conference were made known to the world shortly after ten A.M. the following Monday, June 4th, when a clerk posted on a bulletin board the mimeographed list of the Supreme Court's orders for that day. One order read:

890 Misc. GIDEON v. COCHRAN

The motion for leave to proceed *in forma pauperis* and the petition for writ of certiorari are granted. The case is transferred to the appellate docket. In addition to other questions presented by this case, counsel are requested to discuss the following in their briefs and oral argument:

"Should this Court's holding in *Betts v. Brady, 316 U.S. 455,* be reconsidered?"...

In the Circuit Court of Bay County, Florida, Clarence Earl Gideon had been unable to obtain counsel, but there was no doubt that he could have a lawyer in the Supreme Court of the United States now that it had agreed to hear his case. It is the unvarying practice of the Court to appoint a lawyer for any impoverished prisoner whose petition for review has been granted and who requests counsel.

Appointment by the Supreme Court to represent a poor man is a great honor. For the eminent practitioner who would never, otherwise, dip his fingers into the criminal law it can be an enriching experience, making him think again of the human dimensions of liberty. It may provide the first, sometimes the only, opportunity for a lawyer in some distant corner of the country to appear before the Supreme Court. It may also require great personal sacrifice. There is no monetary compensation of any kind—only the satisfaction of service. The Court pays the cost of the lawyer's transportation to Washington and home, and it prints the briefs, but there is no other provision for expenses, not even secretarial help or a hotel room. The lawyer donates that most valuable commodity, his own time....

The next Monday the Court entered this order in the case of *Gideon v. Cochran:*

"The motion for appointment of counsel is granted and it is ordered that Abe Fortas, Esquire, of Washington, D.C., a member of the Bar of this Court be, and he is hereby, appointed to serve as counsel for petitioner in this case."

Abe Fortas is a high-powered example of that high-powered species, the Washington lawyer. He is the driving force in the firm of Arnold, Fortas and Porter.... A lawyer who has worked with him says: "Of all the men I have met he most knows why he is doing what he does. I don't like the s.o.b., but if I were in trouble I'd want him on my side. He's the most resourceful, the boldest, the most thorough lawyer I know."...

..."The real question," Fortas said, "was whether I should

urge upon the Court the special-circumstances doctrine. As the record then stood, there was nothing to show that he had suffered from any special circumstances....

When that transcript was read at Arnold, Fortas and Porter, there was no longer any question about the appropriateness of this case as the vehicle to challenge *Betts v. Brady*. Plainly Gideon was not mentally defective. The charge against him, and the proof, were not particularly complicated. The judge had tried to be fair; at least there was no overt bias in the courtroom. In short, Gideon had not suffered from any of the special circumstances that would have entitled him to a lawyer under the limited rule of *Betts v. Brady*. And yet it was altogether clear that a lawyer would have helped. The trial had been a rudimentary one, with a prosecution case that was fragmentary at best. Gideon had not made a single objection or pressed any of the favorable lines of defense. An Arnold, Fortas and Porter associate said later: "We knew as soon as we read that transcript that here was a perfect case to challenge the assumption of *Betts* that a man could have a fair trial without a lawyer. He did very well for a layman, he acted like a lawyer. But it was a pitiful effort really. He may have committed this crime, but it was never proved by the prosecution. A lawyer—not a great lawyer, just an ordinary, competent lawyer—could have made ashes of the case."...

As Abe Fortas began to think about the case in the summer of 1962, before Justice Frankfurter's retirement, it was clear to him that overruling *Betts v. Brady* would not come easily to Justice Frankfurter or others of his view. This was true not only because of their judicial philosophy in general, but because of the way they had applied it on specific matters. One of these was the question of precedent.

"In most matters it is more important that the applicable rule of law be settled than that it be settled right." Justice Brandeis thus succinctly stated the basic reason for *stare decisis,* the judicial doctrine of following precedents....

Another issue ... cut even deeper than *stare decisis,* and closer to Gideon's case. This was their attitude toward federalism—the independence of the states in our federal system of government....

The Bill of Rights is the name collectively given to the first ten amendments to the Constitution, all proposed by the First Congress of the United States in 1789 and ratified in 1791. The first eight contain the guarantees of individual liberty with which we are so familiar: freedom of speech, press, religion and assembly; protection for the privacy of the home; assurance against double jeopardy and compulsory self-incrimination; the right to counsel and to trial by jury; freedom from cruel and unusual punishments. At the time of their adoption it was universally agreed that these eight amendments limited only the Federal Government and its processes....

There matters stood until the Fourteenth Amendment became part of the Constitution in 1868. A product of the Civil War, it was specifically designed to prevent abuse of individuals by state governments. Section 1 provided: "No State shall make or enforce any law which shall abridge the privileges or immunities of citizens of the United States; nor shall any State deprive any person of life, liberty, or property, without due process of law; nor deny to any person within its jurisdiction the equal protection of the laws." Soon the claim was advanced that this section had been designed by its framers to *incorporate,* and apply to the states, all the provisions of the first eight amendments.

This theory of wholesale incorporation of the Bill of Rights has been adopted by one or more Supreme Court justices from time to time, but never a majority....

But if wholesale incorporation has been rejected, the Supreme Court has used the Fourteenth Amendment to apply provisions of the Bill of Rights to the states *selectively.* The vehicle has been the clause assuring individuals due process of law. The Court has said that state denial of any right deemed "fundamental" by society amounts to a denial of due process and hence violates the Fourteenth Amendment....

The difficult question has been which provisions of the first eight amendments to absorb....

Grandiose is the word for the physical setting. The W.P.A. Guide to Washington called the Supreme Court building a "great marble temple" which "by its august scale and mighty splendor seems to bear little relation to the functional purposes of government." Shortly before the justices moved into the building in 1935 from their old chamber across the street in the Capitol, Justice Stone wrote his sons: "The place is almost bombastically pretentious, and thus it seems to me wholly inappropriate for a quiet group of old boys such as the Supreme Court." He told his friends that the justices would be "nine black beetles in the Temple of Karnak."

The visitor who climbs the marble steps and passes through the marble columns of the huge pseudo-classical façade finds himself in a cold, lofty hall, again all marble. Great bronze gates exclude him from the area of the building where the justices work in private—their offices, library and conference room. In the courtroom, which is always open to the public, the atmosphere of austere pomp is continued: there are more columns, an enormously high ceiling, red velvet hangings, friezes carved high on the walls. The ritual opening of each day's session adds to the feeling of awe. The Court Crier to the right of the bench smashes his gavel down sharply on a wooden block, everyone rises and the justices file in through the red draperies behind the bench and stand at their places as the Crier intones the traditional opening: "The honorable, the Chief Justice and the Associate Justices of the Supreme Court of the United States. Oyez, oyez, oyez. All persons having business before the honorable, the Supreme Court of the United States, are admonished to draw near and give their attention, for the Court is now sitting. God save the United States and this honorable Court."

But then, when an argument begins, all the trappings and ceremony seem to fade, and the scene takes on an extraordinary intimacy. In the most informal way, altogether without pomp, Court and counsel converse. It is conversation—as direct, unpretentious and focused discussion as can be found anywhere in Washington....

Chief Justice Warren, as is the custom, called the next case by reading aloud its full title: Number 155, Clarence Earl Gideon, petitioner, versus H. G. Cochran, Jr., director, Division of Corrections, State of Florida....

The lawyer arguing a case stands at a small rostrum between the two counsel tables, facing the Chief Justice. The party that lost in the lower court goes first, and so the argument in *Gideon v. Cochran* was begun by Abe Fortas. As he stood, the Chief Justice gave him the customary greeting, "Mr. Fortas," and he made the customary opening: "Mr. Chief Justice, may it please the Court...."

This case presents "a narrow question," Fortas said—the right to counsel—unencumbered by extraneous issues....

"This record does not indicate that Clarence Earl Gideon was a person of low intelligence," Fortas said, "or that the judge was unfair to him. But to me this case shows the basic difficulty with Betts versus Brady. It shows that no man, however intelligent, can conduct his own defense adequately."...

"I believe we can confidently say that overruling Betts versus Brady at this time would be in accord with the opinion of those entitled to an opinion. That is not always true of great constitutional questions.... We may be comforted in this constitutional moment by the fact that what we are doing is a deliberate change after twenty years of experience—a change that has the overwhelming support of the bench, the bar and even of the states.''...

It was only a few days later, as it happened, that *Gideon v. Wainwright* was decided. There was no prior notice; there never is. The Court gives out no advance press releases and tells no one what cases will be decided on a particular Monday, much less how they will be decided. Opinion days have a special quality. The Supreme Court is one of the last American appellate courts where decisions are announced orally. The justices, who divide on so many issues, disagree about this practice, too. Some regard it as a waste of time; others value it as an occasion for descending from the ivory tower, however briefly, and communicating with the live audience in the courtroom....

Then, in the ascending order of seniority, it was Justice Black's turn. He looked at his wife, who was sitting in the box reserved for the justices' friends and families, and said: "I have for announcement the opinion and judgment of the Court in Number One fifty-five, Gideon against Wainwright."

Justice Black leaned forward and gave his words the emphasis and the drama of a great occasion. Speaking very directly to the audience in the courtroom, in an almost folksy way, he told about Clarence Earl Gideon's case and how it had reached the Supreme Court of the United States.

"It raised a fundamental question," Justice Black said, "the rightness of a case we decided twenty-one years ago, Betts against Brady. When we granted certiorari in this case, we asked the lawyers on both sides to argue to us whether we should reconsider that case. We do reconsider Betts and Brady, and we reach an opposite conclusion."

By now the page boys were passing out the opinions. There were four—by Justices Douglas, Clark and Harlan, in addition to the opinion of the Court. But none of the other three was a dissent. A quick look at the end of each showed that it concurred in the overruling of *Betts v. Brady*. On that central result, then, the Court was unanimous....

That was the end of the Clarence Earl Gideon's case in the Supreme Court of the United States. The opinions delivered that Monday were quickly circulated around the country by special legal services, then issued in pamphlets by the Government Printing Office. Eventually they appeared in the bound volumes of Supreme Court decisions, the United States Reports, to be cited as *Gideon v. Wainwright,* 372 U.S. 335—meaning that the case could be found beginning on page 335 of the 372nd volume of the reports.

Justice Black, talking to a friend a few weeks after the decision, said quietly: "When *Betts v. Brady* was decided, I never thought I'd live to see it overruled."...

The reaction of the states to *Gideon v. Wainwright* was swift and constructive. The most dramatic response came from Florida, whose rural-dominated legislature had so long refused to relieve the problem of the unrepresented indigent such as Gideon. Shortly after the decision Governor Farris Bryant called on the legislature to enact a public-defender law....

Resolution of the great constitutional question in *Gideon v. Wainwright* did not decide the fate of Clarence Earl Gideon. He was now entitled to a new trial, with a lawyer. Was he guilty of breaking into the Bay Harbor Poolroom? The verdict would not set any legal precedents, but there is significance in the human beings who make constitutional-law cases as well as in the law. And in this case there was the interesting question whether the legal assistance for which Gideon had fought so hard would make any difference to him....

...After ascertaining that Gideon had no money to hire a lawyer of his own choice, Judge McCrary asked whether there was a local lawyer whom Gideon would like to represent him. There was: W. Fred Turner.

"For the record," Judge McCrary said quickly, "I am going to appoint Mr. Fred Turner to represent this defendant, Clarence Earl Gideon."...

The jury went out at four-twenty P.M., after a colorless charge by the judge including the instruction—requested by Turner—that the jury must believe Gideon guilty "beyond a reasonable doubt" in order to convict him. When a half-hour had passed with no verdict, the prosecutors were less confident. At five twenty-five there was a knock on the door between the courtroom and the jury room. The jurors filed in, and the court clerk read their verdict, written on a form. It was *Not Guilty*.

"So say you all?" asked Judge McCrary, without a flicker of emotion. The jurors nodded....

After nearly two years in the state penitentiary Gideon was a free man.... That night he would pay a last, triumphant visit to the Bay Harbor Poolroom. Could someone let him have a few dollars? Someone did.

"Do you feel like you accomplished something?" a newspaper reporter asked.

"Well I did."

86

Miranda v. Arizona

MR. CHIEF JUSTICE WARREN delivered the opinion of the Court.

The cases before us raise questions which go to the roots of our concepts of American criminal jurisprudence: the restraints society must observe consistent with the Federal Constitution in prosecuting individuals for crime. More specifically, we deal with the admissibility of statements obtained from an individual who is subjected to custodial police interrogation and the necessity for procedures which assure that the individual is accorded his privilege under the Fifth Amendment to the Constitution not to be compelled to incriminate himself.

We dealt with certain phases of this problem recently in *Escobedo v. Illinois,* 378 U.S. 478 (1964). There, as in the four cases before us, law enforcement officials took the defendant into custody and interrogated him in a police station for the purpose of obtaining a confession. The police did not effectively advise him of his right to remain silent or of his right to consult with his attorney. Rather, they confronted him with an alleged accomplice who accused him of having perpetrated a murder. When the defendant denied the accusation and said "I didn't shoot Manuel, you did it," they hand-cuffed him and took him to an interrogation room. There, while handcuffed and standing, he was questioned for four hours until he confessed. During this interrogation, the police denied his request to speak to his attorney, and they prevented his retained attorney, who had come to the police station, from consulting with him. At his trial, the State, over his objection, introduced the confession against him. We held that the statements thus made were constitutionally inadmissible.... We adhere to the principles of *Escobedo* today.

Our holding will be spelled out with some specificity in the pages which follow but briefly stated it is this: the prosecution may not use statements, whether exculpatory or inculpatory, stemming from custodial interrogation of the defendant unless it demonstrates the use of procedural safeguards effective to secure the privilege against self-incrimination. By custodial interrogation, we mean questioning initiated by law enforcement officers after a person has been taken into custody or otherwise deprived of his freedom of action in any significant way. As for the procedural safeguards to be employed, unless other fully effective means are devised to inform accused persons of their right of silence and to assure a continuous opportunity to exercise it, the following measures are required. Prior to any questioning, the person must be warned that he has a right to remain silent, that any statement he does make may be used as evidence against him, and that he has a right to the presence of an attorney, either retained or appointed. The defendant may waive effectuation of these rights, provided the waiver is made voluntarily, knowingly and intelligently. If, however, he indicates in any manner and at any stage of the process that he wishes to consult with an attorney before speaking there can be no questioning. Likewise, if the individual is alone and indicates in any manner that he does not wish to be interrogated, the police may not question him. The mere fact that he may have answered some questions or volunteered some statements on his own does not deprive him of the right to refrain from answering any further inquiries until he has consulted with an attorney and thereafter consents to be questioned....

The constitutional issue we decide in each of these cases [being decided today] is the admissibility of statements obtained from a defendant questioned while in custody or otherwise deprived of his freedom of action in any significant way. In each, the defendant was questioned by police officers, detectives, or a prosecuting attorney in a room in which he was cut off from the outside world. In none of these cases was the defendant given a full and effective warning of his rights at the outset of the interrogation process. In all the cases, the questioning elicited oral admissions, and in three of them, signed statements as well which were admitted at their trials. They all thus share salient features—incommunicado interrogation of individuals in a police-dominated atmosphere, resulting in self-incriminating statements without full warnings of constitutional rights.... We stress that the modern practice of in-custody interrogation is psychologically rather than physically oriented.... Interrogation still takes place in privacy. Privacy results in secrecy and this in turn results in a gap in our knowledge as to what in fact goes on in the interrogation rooms. A valuable source of information about present police practices, however, may be found in various police manuals and texts which document procedures employed with success in the past, and which recommend various other effective tactics....

The officers are told by the manuals that the "principal psychological factor contributing to a successful interrogation is *privacy*—being alone with the person under interrogation." The efficacy of this tactic has been explained as follows:

"If at all practicable, the interrogation should take place in the investigator's office or at least in a room of his own choice. The subject should be deprived of every psychological advantage."...

After this psychological conditioning, however, the officer is told to point out the incriminating significance of the suspect's refusal to talk:

"Joe, you have a right to remain silent. That's your privilege and I'm the last person in the world who'll try to take it away from you. If that's the way you want to leave this, O.K. But let me ask you this. Suppose you were in my shoes and I were in yours and you called me in to ask me about this and I told you, 'I don't want to answer any of your questions.' You'd think I had something to hide, and you'd probably be right in thinking that. That's exactly what I'll have to think about you, and so will everybody else. So let's sit here and talk this whole thing over."

Few will persist in their initial refusal to talk, it is said, if this monologue is employed correctly.

In the event that the subject wishes to speak to a relative or an attorney, the following advice is tendered:

"[T]he interrogator should respond by suggesting that the subject first tell the truth to the interrogator himself rather than get anyone else involved in the matter. If the request is for an attorney, the interrogator may suggest that the subject save himself or his family the expense of any such professional service, particularly if he is innocent of the offense under investigation. The interrogator may also add, 'Joe, I'm only looking for the truth, and if you're telling the truth, that's it. You can handle this by yourself.' "...

Even without employing brutality, the "third degree" or the specific stratagems described above, the very fact of custodial interrogation exacts a heavy toll on individual liberty and trades on the weakness of individuals....

...In each of the cases [heard by the court], the defendant was thrust into an unfamiliar atmosphere and run through menacing police interrogation procedures. The potentiality for compulsion is forcefully apparent, for example, in *Miranda,* where the indigent Mexican defendant was a seriously disturbed individual with pronounced sexual fantasies, and in *Stewart,* in which the defendant was an indigent Los Angeles Negro who had dropped out of school in the sixth grade. To be sure, the records do not evince overt physical coercion or patent psychological ploys. The fact remains that in none of these cases did the officers undertake to afford appropriate safeguards at the outset of the interrogation to insure that the statements were truly the product of free choice.

It is obvious that such an interrogation environment is created for no purpose other than to subjugate the individual to the will of his examiner. This atmosphere carries its own badge of intimidation. To be sure, this is not physical intimidation, but it is equally destructive of human dignity. The current practice of incommunicado interrogation is at odds with one of our Nation's most cherished principles—that the individual may not be compelled to incriminate himself. Unless adequate protective devices are employed to dispel the compulsion inherent in custodial surroundings, no statement obtained from the defendant can truly be the product of his free choice....

To summarize, we hold that when an individual is taken into custody or otherwise deprived of his freedom by the authorities in any significant way and is subjected to questioning, the privilege against self-incrimination is jeopardized. Procedural safeguards must be employed to protect the privilege, and unless other fully effective means are adopted to notify the person of his right of silence and to assure that the exercise of the right will be scrupulously honored, the following measures are required. He must be warned prior to any questioning that he has the right to remain silent, that anything he says can be used against him in a court of law, that he has the right to the presence of an attorney, and that if he cannot afford an attorney one will be appointed for him prior to any questioning if he so desires. Opportunity to exercise these rights must be afforded to him throughout the interrogation. After such warnings have been given, and such opportunity afforded him, the individual may knowingly and intelligently waive these rights and agree to answer questions or make a statement. But unless and until such warnings and waiver are demonstrated by the prosecution at trial, no evidence obtained as a result of interrogation can be used against him.... We turn now to these facts to consider the application to these cases of the constitutional principles discussed above....

On March 13, 1963, petitioner, Ernesto Miranda, was arrested at his home and taken in custody to a Phoenix police station. He was there identified by the complaining witness. The police then took him to "Interrogation Room No. 2" of the detective bureau. There he was questioned by two police officers. The officers admitted at trial that Miranda was not advised that he had a right to have an attorney present. Two hours later, the officers emerged from the interrogation room with a written confession signed by Miranda. At the top of the statement was a typed paragraph stating that the confession was made voluntarily, without threats or promises of immunity and "with full knowledge of my legal rights, understanding any statement I make may be used against me."

At his trial before a jury, the written confession was admitted into evidence over the objection of defense counsel, and the officers testified to the prior oral confession made by Miranda during the interrogation. Miranda was found guilty of kidnapping and rape. He was sentenced to 20 to 30 years' imprisonment on each count, the sentences to run concurrently. On appeal, the Supreme Court of Arizona held that Miranda's constitutional rights were not violated in obtaining the confession and affirmed the conviction. 98 Ariz. 18, 401 P. 2d 721. In reaching its decision, the court emphasized heavily the fact that Miranda did not specifically request counsel.

We reverse. From the testimony of the officers and by the admission of respondent, it is clear that Miranda was not in any way apprised of his right to consult with an attorney and to have one present during the interrogation, nor was his right not to be compelled to incriminate himself effectively protected in any other manner. Without these warnings the statements were inadmissible.

87

RICHARD KLUGER

From *Simple Justice*:
***A History of* Brown v. Board of Education**
and Black America's Struggle for Equality

———

IN THE two and a half years since they had last sat down to decide a major racial case, the Justices of the Supreme Court had not grown closer. Indeed, the philosophical and personal fissures in their ranks had widened since they had agreed—unanimously—to side with the Negro appellants in *Sweatt, McLaurin,* and *Henderson* in the spring of 1950. That had been a rare show of unanimity. By the 1952 Term, the Court was failing to reach a unanimous decision 81 percent of the time, nearly twice as high a percentage of disagreement as it had recorded a decade earlier....

It was perhaps the most severely fractured Court in history—testament, on the face of it, to Vinson's failure as Chief Justice. Selected to lead the Court because of his skills as a conciliator, the low-key, mournful-visaged Kentuckian found that the issues before him were far different from, and far less readily negotiable than, the hard-edged problems he had faced as Franklin Roosevelt's ace economic troubleshooter and Harry Truman's Secretary of the Treasury and back-room confederate.

Fred Vinson's lot as Chief Justice ... had not proven a happy one....

What, then, could be expected of the deeply divided Vinson Court as it convened on the morning of December 13, 1952, to deliberate on the transcendent case of *Brown v. Board of Education*? The earlier racial cases—*Sweatt* and *McLaurin*—they had managed to cope with by chipping away at the edges of Jim Crow but avoiding the real question of *Plessy*'s continued validity.* The Court could no longer dodge that question, though it might continue to stall in resolving it. Hovering over the Justices were all the repressive bugaboos of the Cold War era. The civil rights of Negroes and the civil liberties of political dissenters and criminal defendants were prone to be scrambled together in the public mind, and every malcontent was a sitting target for the red tar of anti-Americanism. No sector of the nation was less hospitable to both civil-liberties and civil-rights claimants than the segregating states of the South, and it was the South with which the Justices had primarily to deal in confronting *Brown....*

And so they were divided. But given the gravity of the issue, they were willing to take their time to try to reconcile their differences. They clamped a precautionary lid on all their discussions of *Brown* as the year turned and Fred Vinson swore in Dwight David Eisenhower as the thirty-fourth President of the United States. The Justices seemed to make little headway toward resolving the problem, but they all knew that a close vote would likely be a disaster for Court and country alike. The problem of welding the disparate views into a single one was obviously complicated by the ambivalence afflicting the Court's presiding Justice. As spring came and the end of the Court's 1952 Term neared, Fred Vinson seemed to be in increasingly disagreeable and edgy spirits. Says one of the people at the Court closest to him then: "I got the distinct impression that he was distressed over the Court's inability to find a strong, unified position on such an important case."

What evidence there is suggests that those on or close to the Court thought it was about as severely divided as it could be at this stage of its deliberations....

During the last week of the term in June, the law clerks of all the Justices met in an informal luncheon session and took a two-part poll. Each clerk was asked how he would vote in the school-segregation cases and how he thought his Justice would vote. According to one of their number, a man who later became a professor

---

*The Supreme Court in *Plessy v. Ferguson* (1896) interpreted the equal protection clause of the Fourteenth Amendment to mean that the states could require separation of the races in public institutions if these institutions were equal (the "separate but equal doctrine"). From 1937 until 1954 the Court subjected "separate but equal" to increasingly rigorous scrutiny. In *Sweatt v. Painter* (1950) and *McLaurin v. Oklahoma State Regents* (1950), for example, the Court invalidated specific state racial segregationist practices in higher education on grounds that they did not permit truly equal access to black students. Yet, the Court had not overturned *Plessy.*—EDS.

of law: "The clerks were almost unanimous for overruling *Plessy*
and ordering desegregation, but, according to their impressions,
the Court would have been closely divided if it had announced its
decision at that time. Many of the clerks were only guessing at the
positions of their respective Justices, but it appeared that a majority
of the Justices would not have overruled *Plessy* but would have
given some relief in some of the cases on the ground that the
separate facilities were not in fact equal.". . .

All such bets on the alignment of the Court ended abruptly a
few days later when the single most fateful judicial event of that
long summer occurred. In his Washington hotel apartment, Fred
M. Vinson died of a heart attack at 3:15 in the morning of September 8 [1953]. He was sixty-three.

All the members of the Court attended Vinson's burial in
Louisa, Kentucky, his ancestral home. But not all the members of
the Court grieved equally at his passing. And one at least did not
grieve at all. Felix Frankfurter had not much admired Fred Vinson
as judge or man. And he was certain that the Chief Justice had
been the chief obstacle to the Court's prospects of reaching a humanitarian and judicially defensible settlement of the monumental
segregation cases. In view of Vinson's passing just before the *Brown*
reargument, Frankfurter remarked to a former clerk, "This is the
first indication I have ever had that there is a God.". . . Fred Vinson
was not yet cold in his grave when speculation rose well above a
whisper as to whom President Eisenhower would pick to heal and
lead the Supreme Court as it faced one of its most momentous
decisions in the segregation cases. . . .

Dwight Eisenhower's principal contribution to the civil rights
of Americans would prove to be his selection of Earl Warren as
Chief Justice—a decision Eisenhower would later say had been a
mistake. The President was on hand, at any rate, on Monday,
October 5, when just after noon the clerk of the Supreme Court
read aloud the commission of the President that began, "Know
ye: That reposing special trust and confidence in the wisdom, up-
rightness and learning of Earl Warren of California, I do appoint
him Chief Justice of the United States. . . ." Warren stood up at the
clerk's desk to the side of the bench and read aloud his oath of
office. At the end, Clerk Harold Willey said to him, "So help you
God." Warren said, "So help me God." Then he stepped quickly
behind the velour curtains and re-emerged a moment later through

the opening in the center to take the presiding seat. His entire worthy career to that moment would be dwarfed by what fol-lowed.... At the reargument, Earl Warren had said very little. The Chief Justice had put no substantive questions to any of the attorneys. Nor is it likely that he had given any indication of his views to the other Justices before they convened at the Saturday-morning conference on December 12. But then, speaking first, he made his views unmistakable.

Nearly twenty years later, he would recall, "I don't remember having any great doubts about which way it should go. It seemed to me a comparatively simple case. Just look at the various decisions that had been eroding *Plessy* for so many years. They kept chipping away at it rather than ever really facing it head-on. If you looked back—to *Gaines,* to *Sweatt,* to some of the interstate-commerce cases—you saw that the doctrine of separate-but-equal had been so eroded that only the *fact* of segregation itself remained unconsid-ered. On the merits, the natural, the logical, and practically the only way the case could be decided was clear. The question was *how* the decision was to be reached."

At least two sets of notes survive from the Justices' 1953 confer-ence discussion of the segregation cases—extensive ones by Justice Burton and exceedingly scratchy and cryptic ones by Justice Frank-furter. They agree on the Chief Justice's remarks. The cases had been well argued, in his judgment, Earl Warren told the conference, and the government had been very frank in both its written and its oral presentations. He said he had of course been giving much thought to the entire question since coming to the Court, and after studying the briefs and relevant history and hearing the argu-ments, he could not escape the feeling that the Court had "finally arrived" at the moment when it now had to determine whether segregation was allowable in the public schools. Without saying it in so many words, the new Chief Justice was declaring that the Court's policy of delay, favored by his predecessor, could no longer be permitted.

The more he had pondered the question, Warren said, the more he had come to the conclusion that the doctrine of separate-but-equal rested upon the concept of the inferiority of the colored race. He did not see how *Plessy* and its progeny could be sustained on any other theory—and if the Court were to choose to sustain them, "we must do it on that basis," he was recorded by Burton as saying. He was concerned, to be sure, about the necessity of

overruling earlier decisions and lines of reasoning, but he had concluded that segregation of Negro schoolchildren had to be ended.
The law, he said in words noted by Frankfurter, "cannot in 'this
day and age' set them apart." The law could not say, Burton
recorded the Chief as asserting, that Negroes were "not entitled to
exactly same treatment of all others." To do so would go against
the intentions of the three Civil War amendments.

Unless any of the other four Justices who had indicated a year
earlier their readiness to overturn segregation—Black, Douglas,
Burton, and Minton—had since changed his mind, Warren's opening remarks meant that a majority of the Court now stood ready
to strike down the practice.

But to gain a narrow majority was no cause for exultation. A
sharply divided Court, no matter which way it leaned, was an
indecisive one, and for Warren to force a split decision out of it
would have amounted to hardly more constructive leadership on
this transcendent question than Fred Vinson had managed. The
new Chief Justice wanted to unite the Court in *Brown*. . . .

He recognized that a number of Court precedents of long standing would be shattered in the process of overturning *Plessy,* and
he regretted that necessity. It was the sort of reassuring medicine
most welcomed by Burton and Minton, the least judicially and
intellectually adventurous members of the Court.

He recognized that the Court's decision would have wide repercussions, varying in intensity from state to state, and that they
would all therefore have to approach the matter in as tolerant and
understanding a way as possible. Implicit in this was a call for
flexibility in how the Court might frame its decree.

But overarching all these cushioning comments and a tribute
to both his compassion as a man and his persuasive skills as a
politician was the moral stance Earl Warren took at the outset of
his remarks. Segregation, he had told his new colleagues, could be
justified only by belief in the inferiority of the Negro; any of them
who wished to perpetuate the practice, he implied, ought in candor
to be willing to acknowledge as much. These were plain words,
and they did not have to be hollered. They cut across all the legal
theories that had been so endlessly aired and went straight to the
human tissue at the core of the controversy. . . .

The Warren opinion was "finally approved" at the May 15
conference, Burton noted in his diary. The man from California
had won the support of every member of the Court.

...Not long before the Court's decision in *Brown* was announced, Warren told *Ebony* magazine twenty years later, he had
decided to spend a few days visiting Civil War monuments in
Virginia. He went by automobile with a black chauffeur.

At the end of the first day, the Chief Justice's car pulled up at a
hotel, where he had made arrangements to spend the night. Warren
simply assumed that his chauffeur would stay somewhere else,
presumably at a less expensive place. When the Chief Justice came
out of his hotel the next morning to resume his tour, he soon
figured out that the chauffeur had spent the night in the car. He
asked the black man why.

"Well, Mr. Chief Justice," the chauffeur began, "I just couldn't
find a place—couldn't find a place to..."

Warren was stricken by his own thoughtlessness in bringing
an employee of his to a town where lodgings were not available to
the man solely because of his color. "I was embarrassed, I was
ashamed," Warren recalled. "We turned back immediately...."

...In the press room on the ground floor, reporters filing in at
the tail end of the morning were advised that May 17, 1954, looked
like a quiet day at the Supreme Court of the United States.

All of the opinions of the Court were announced on Mondays
in that era. The ritual was simple and unvarying. The Justices
convened at noon. Lawyers seeking admission to the Supreme
Court bar were presented to the Court by their sponsors, greeted
briefly by the Chief Justice, and sworn in by the clerk of the
Court. Then, in ascending order of seniority, the Justices with
opinions to deliver read them aloud, every word usually, without
much effort at dramaturgy. Concurrences and dissents were read
after the majority opinion. And then the next case, and then the
next. There was no applause; there were no catcalls. There were
no television or newsreel cameras. There were no questions from
the newsmen in the audience. There was no briefing session in the
press room or the Justices' chambers after Court adjourned. There
were no weekly press conferences. There were no appearances on
Meet the Press the following Sunday. There were no press releases
elaborating on what the Court had said or meant or done. The
opinions themselves were all there was....

Down in the press room, as the first three routine opinions
were distributed, it looked, as predicted, like a very quiet day at
the Court. But then, as Douglas finished up, Clerk of the Court

Harold Willey dispatched a pneumatic message to Banning E. Whittington, the Court's dour press officer. Whittington slipped on his suit jacket, advised the press-room contingent, "Reading of the segregation decisions is about to begin in the courtroom," added as he headed out the door that the text of the opinion would be distributed in the press room afterward, and then led the scrambling reporters in a dash up the marble stairs.

"I have for announcement," said Earl Warren, "the judgment and opinion of the Court in No. 1—*Oliver Brown et al. v. Board of Education of Topeka.*" It was 12:52 P.M. In the press room, the Associated Press wire carried the first word to the country: "Chief Justice Warren today began reading the Supreme Court's decision in the public school segregation cases. The court's ruling could not be determined immediately." The bells went off in every news room in America. The nation was listening.

It was Warren's first major opinion as Chief Justice. He read it, by all accounts, in a firm, clear. unemotional voice. If he had delivered no other opinion but this one, he would have won his place in American history.

Considering its magnitude, it was a short opinion. During its first part, no one hearing it could tell where it would come out....

Without in any way becoming technical and rhetorical, Warren then proceeded to demonstrate the dynamic nature and adaptive genius of American constitutional law.... Having declared its essential value to the nation's civic health and vitality, he then argued for the central importance of education in the private life and aspirations of every individual.... That led finally to the critical question: "Does segregation of children in public schools solely on the basis of race ... deprive the children of the minority group of equal educational opportunities?"

To this point, nearly two-thirds through the opinion, Warren had not tipped his hand. Now, in the next sentence, he showed it by answering that critical question: "We believe that it does.".. .

This finding flew directly in the face of *Plessy*. And here, finally, Warren collided with the 1896 decision....

The balance of the Chief Justice's opinion consisted of just two paragraphs. The first began: "We conclude"—and here Warren departed from the printed text before him to insert the word "unanimously," which sent a sound of muffled astonishment eddying around the courtroom—"that in the field of public education the doctrine of 'separate but equal' has no place. Separate educational facilities are inherently unequal." The plaintiffs and others similarly situated—technically meaning Negro children within the segregated school districts under challenge—were therefore being deprived of the equal protection of the laws guaranteed by the Fourteenth Amendment.

The concluding paragraph of the opinion revealed Earl Warren's political adroitness both at compromise and at the ready use of the power of his office for ends he thought worthy. "Because these are class actions, because of the wide applicability of this decision, and because of the great variety of local conditions," he declared, "these cases present problems of considerable complexity.... In order that we may have the full assistance of the parties in formulating decrees," the Court was scheduling further argument for the term beginning the following fall. The attorneys general of the United States and all the states requiring or permitting segregation in public education were invited to participate. In a few strokes, Warren thus managed to (1) proclaim "the wide applicability" of the decision and make it plain that the Court had no intention of limiting its benefits to a handful of plaintiffs in a few outlying districts; (2) reassure the South that the Court understood the emotional wrench desegregation would cause and was therefore granting the region some time to get accustomed to the idea; and (3) invite the South to participate in the entombing of Jim Crow by joining the Court's efforts to fashion a temperate implementation decree—or to forfeit that chance by petulantly abstaining from the Court's further deliberations and thereby run the risk of having a harsh decree imposed upon it. It was such dexterous use of the power available to him and of the circumstances in which to exploit it that had established John Marshall as a judicial statesman and political tactician of the most formidable sort. The Court had not seen his like since. Earl Warren, in his first major opinion, moved now with that same sure purposefulness....

It was 1:20 P.M. The wire services proclaimed the news to the nation. Within the hour, the Voice of America would begin beaming word to the world in thirty-four languages: In the United States, schoolchildren could no longer be segregated by race. The law of the land no longer recognized a separate equality. No Americans were more equal than any other Americans.

PART FIFTEEN

The Political Economy

POLITICAL ECONOMY, a nineteenth-century term that has largely gone out of fashion, conveys a useful meaning that many modern economists prefer to de-emphasize or ignore entirely: that the polity always sets the rules within which economic activity takes place. This is no less true in capitalist than in socialist systems. Classical liberals of the eighteenth century (among them the American founders) understood this quite well. Although they aimed to abolish many kinds of state regulations surviving from prior feudal and mercantile economies, they clearly saw the importance of laws protecting private property, providing for the enforcement of contracts, ensuring a sound currency and a stable money supply, defending frontier areas where various developmental activities were underway, maintaining a navy to protect maritime commerce, and so on. Even the strongest advocates of free-market capitalism have recognized the critical role of the state in maintaining an environment of law and policy that would permit capitalism to work. As we have said, economies are always political.

Economic development and optimal economic performance have always been primary concerns of American politics. By com-

parative standards there has been extraordinary agreement on how
to proceed. With no feudal regime to attack, and the feeblest articulation of the socialist vision of a propertyless utopia in the Western
world, American economic discussion has been largely concerned
with how best to make democratic capitalism work. *Everyone* has
wanted economic development and a prosperous economy in
which more and more people could enjoy a better and better standard of living. Put another way, America has always been a middle-
class or "bourgeois" society. Whereas in Europe the businessman
has frequently been the object of scorn from both the aristocracy
and a militant socialist movement, his American cousin has for all
practical purposes gone unchallenged. Even in the worst moments
of panic and depression the American businessman has been more
criticized for poor performance than castigated as an exploiter who
must be expropriated. The Democratic Party, for example, has
long supported a more active role for government in economic
management than has its Republican rival, but it has never behaved
like a European party of the left. As Franklin Roosevelt put it in
the 1930s, we needed a new deal, not a new game.

Our readings in this section are meant to convey a sense of the
main streams of discussion about government's proper role in promoting optimal economic performance over the last thirty or so
years. Our first selection is from John Kenneth Galbraith's *The
Affluent Society,* published in 1958. In this widely read and influential book, Galbraith, an economist and advisor to then presidential
candidate John F. Kennedy, argued the most persuasive case in
many years for a larger public sector to remedy what he saw as a
striking imbalance between our affluence in private goods and our
poverty in public services. From this point of view Americans
need fewer shiny new cars and electronic gadgets, but better public
transportation, public housing, sanitation facilities, parks, schools,
and other public goods. Galbraith thought then (and has continued
to think) that we need a tax system that "makes a pro rata share of
increasing income available to public authority for public purposes." Galbraith, who would be called in Europe a social democrat, is a bit too far to the left by American standards to be seriously
considered for the key economic positions in Democratic administrations. Nevertheless, there is much evidence that the public services he advocated enjoy wide public support. A vast expansion of
the public sector did in fact take place during the Kennedy–Johnson
years and continued even during Republican administrations until

the election of Ronald Reagan in 1980. Oddly enough, something like the "automatic" financing system that Galbraith called for was created accidentally as inflation and higher tax brackets produced windfall federal revenues in the 1970s. Then came Reagan. (More on that below.)

Our next reading, by Milton Friedman, was published in 1979. Just as his title argues, the tide was turning then toward a point of view that he had persistently advocated for many years, and it would soon be the ideological basis for much of what is now called the Reagan Revolution. Friedman's argument is as far from Galbraith's as we can get in America; it is at the other end of our centrist political spectrum. The American economy (or for that matter any other), he asserts, works best when government limits itself to the minimal functions approved by classical liberals. Quoting Adam Smith, the founder of modern economic theory, he argues that the public good is best served when economic transactions are undertaken in free markets and all individuals are left free to pursue their own values. Big government is a threat both to prosperity and freedom, in this way of looking at things. Friedman is especially outraged at the activities of what he sees as a "new class" of public servants who specialize in spending other people's money, although he is confident that the American public will soon turn them out.

In our next reading, Lester Thurow, an economist who like Galbraith has been influential on the Democratic side of partisan discussions of economic policy, holds that our real problem in managing the American economy is political. Our system, he argues, is simply too fragmented to make hard decisions. An almost infinite pluralism allows virtually every interest to prevent the adoption of policies that threaten the group with economic losses. There is only one real question in political economy, he asserts: Whose income do you want to cut? Thurow, like Galbraith, advocates a larger public sector. Only the public sector, he thinks, will allow us to provide good jobs for all who want them.

If, as we have argued, America is a middle-class society in which everyone has wanted economic development and social mobility, there would be a serious problem indeed if the American economy in the 1980s were no longer able to create new jobs with good wages. On just this question a sharp, partisan argument has occurred in the last few years. In our next two selections this "shrinking middle class" argument is joined. Barry Bluestone and

Bennett Harrison see the economy's recent record of job creation as unimpressive, consisting mainly of low-wage, relatively dead-end positions. Marvin Kosters and Murray Ross reject this argument. Although they agree that real wages have flattened over the last fifteen years, they think the problem lies not in the effect of new, low-wage jobs, but in a decline of productivity across the whole job distribution. If this is so, the only corrective is increasing productivity. Here you have a major disagreement on economic policy between the two parties that cannot be settled in these pages.

Our last two selections take us back to Ronald Reagan. David Stockman's *The Triumph of Politics* provides Reagan's first budget director's perspective of how the administration made "a massive fiscal policy error" in 1981. If the president's program of lower taxes, fewer federal domestic programs, and military expansion were to work, Stockman argues, significant losses would have to be imposed on virtually every sector of American society. Taxes were cut, but Congress simply would not make the necessary program cuts. Our Madisonian system would not permit such a radical alteration of policy in the face of such strong opposition. Stockman concludes that, in the final analysis, the public wants both low taxes and an extensive welfare state. Our system allows them to have both at the cost of an enormous federal budget deficit.

Whether Ronald Reagan ever intended it or not, the result of the 1981 tax cuts was to create a "deficit culture" in Washington, the end of which is not yet in sight. If that result *were* intended, the cuts would have to be seen as extraordinarily clever since they deprived government of the funds to do all manner of things that advocates of a larger public sector want done. Our last reading describes accurately the new Washington community in which everything is driven by budgetary concerns. However short of David Stockman's goals the Reagan Revolution fell, it has in fact significantly constrained the public sector. This new Washington is a far cry from the city we remember in the late seventies. Members of both parties now talk much the same game, realizing that there is just no money to do anything new. So it promises to be for many years to come.

88

JOHN KENNETH GALBRAITH
The Redress of Balance

From _The Affluent Society_

...WE MUST find a way to remedy the poverty which afflicts us in public services and which is in such increasingly bizarre contrast with our affluence in private goods. This is necessary to temper and, more hopefully, to eliminate the social disorders which are the counterpart of the present imbalance. It is necessary in the long run for promoting the growth of private output itself. Such balance is a matter of elementary common sense in a country in which need is becoming so exiguous that it must be cherished where it exists and nurtured where it does not. To create the demand for new automobiles, we must contrive elaborate and functionless changes each year and then subject the consumer to ruthless psychological pressures to persuade him of their importance. Were this process to falter or break down, the consequences would be disturbing. In the meantime, there are large ready-made needs for schools, hospitals, slum clearance and urban redevelopment, sanitation, parks, playgrounds, police and a thousand other things. Of these needs, almost no one must be persuaded. They exist because, as public officials of all kinds and ranks explain each day with practiced skill, the money to provide for them is unavailable. So it has come about that we get growth and increased employment along the dimension of private goods only at the price of increasingly frantic persuasion. We exploit but poorly the opportunity along the dimension of public services. The economy is geared to the least urgent set of human values. It would be far more secure if it were based on the whole range of need....

...For a very large part of our public activity, revenues are relatively static. Although aggregate income increases, many tax systems return a comparatively fixed dollar amount. Hence new public needs, or even the increase in the requirements for old ones incident on increasing population, require affirmative steps to transfer resources to public use. There must first be a finding of need. The burden of proof lies with those who propose the expenditure. Resources do not automatically accrue to public authority for a decision as to how they may best be distributed to schools, roads, police, public housing and other claimant ends. We are startled by the thought. It would lead to waste.

But with increasing income, resources do so accrue to the private individual. Nor when he buys a new automobile out of increased income is he required to prove need. We may assume that many fewer automobiles would be purchased than at present were it necessary to make a positive case for their purchase. [Yet] such a case must be made for schools.... The solution is a system of taxation which automatically makes a pro rata share of increasing income available to public authority for public purposes. The task of public authority, like that of private individuals, will be to distribute this increase in accordance with relative need. Schools and roads will then no longer be at a disadvantage as compared with automobiles and television sets in having to prove absolute justification.

The practical solution would be much eased were the revenues of the federal government available for the service of social balance. These, to the extent of about four-fifths of the total, come from personal and corporation income taxes. Subject to some variations, these taxes rise rather more than proportionately with increases in private income. Unhappily they are presently preempted in large measure by the requirements (actual or claimed) of national defense and the competition of arms....

Hopefully the time will come when federal revenues and the normal annual increase will not be preempted so extensively for military purposes. Conventional attitudes hold otherwise; on all prospects of mankind, there is hope for betterment save those having to do with an eventual end, without war, to the arms race. Here the hard cold voice of realism warns there is no chance. Perhaps things are not so utterly hopeless....

However, even though the higher urgency of federal expenditures for social balance is conceded, there is still the problem of providing the revenue. And since it is income taxes that must here be used, the question of social balance can easily be lost sight of in the reopened argument over equality. The truce will be broken and liberals and conservatives will join battle on this issue and forget about the poverty in the public services that awaits correction and, as we shall see presently, the poverty of people which can only be corrected at increased public cost. All this—schools, hospitals, even the scientific research on which increased production depends—must wait while we debate the ancient and unresolvable question of whether the rich are too rich.

The only hope—and in the nature of things it rests primarily with liberals—is to separate the issue of equality from that of social balance. The second is by far the more important question. The fact that a tacit truce exists on the issue of inequality is proof of its comparative lack of social urgency. In the past, the liberal politician has countered the conservative proposal for reduction in top bracket income taxes with the proposal that relief be confined to the lower brackets. And he has insisted that any necessary tax increase be carried more than proportionately by the higher income brackets. The result has been to make him a co-conspirator with the conservative in reducing taxes, whatever the cost in social balance; and his insistence on making taxes an instrument of greater equality has made it difficult or impossible to increase them. Meanwhile the individuals with whom he sympathizes and whom he seeks to favor are no longer the tax-ridden poor of Bengal or the First Empire but people who, by all historical standards, are themselves comparatively opulent citizens. In any case, they would be among the first beneficiaries of the better education, health, housing and other services which would be the fruits of improved social balance, and they would be the long-run beneficiaries of more nearly adequate investment in people.

The rational liberal, in the future, will resist tax reduction, even that which ostensibly favors the poor, if it is at the price of social balance. And, for the same reason, he will not hesitate to accept increases that are neutral as regards the distribution of income. His classical commitment to greater equality can far better be kept by attacking as a separate issue the more egregious of the loopholes in the present tax law. These loopholes ... are strongly in conflict with traditional liberal attitudes, for this is inequality sanctioned by the state. There is work enough here for any egalitarian crusader....

...One final observation may be made. There will be question as to what is the test of balance—at what point may we conclude that balance has been achieved in the satisfaction of private and public needs. The answer is that no test can be applied, for none exists. The traditional formulation is that the satisfaction returned to the community from a marginal increment of resources devoted to public purposes should be equal to the satisfaction of the same increment in private employment. These are incommensurate, partly because different people are involved, and partly because it makes the cardinal error of comparing satisfaction of wants that are systematically synthesized as part of an organic process with those that are not.

But a precise equilibrium is not very important. For another mark of an affluent society is the existence of a considerable margin for error on such matters. The present imbalance is clear, as are the forces and ideas which give the priority to private as compared with public goods. This being so, the direction in which we move to correct matters is utterly plain. We can also assume, given the power of the forces that have operated to accord a priority to private goods, that the distance to be traversed is considerable. When we arrive, the opulence of our private consumption will no longer be in contrast with the poverty of our schools, the unloveliness and congestion of our cities, our inability to get to work without struggle and the social disorder that is associated with imbalance. But the precise point of balance will never be defined. This will be of comfort only to those who believe that any failure of definition can be made to score decisively against a larger idea.

89

MILTON FRIEDMAN
The Tide Is Turning

From *Free to Choose*

———

THE STORY of the United States is the story of an economic miracle and a political miracle that was made possible by the translation into practice of two sets of ideas—both, by a curious coincidence, formulated in documents published in the same year, 1776.

One set of ideas was embodied in *The Wealth of Nations,* the masterpiece that established the Scotsman Adam Smith as the father of modern economics. It analyzed the way in which a market system could combine the freedom of individuals to pursue their own objectives with the extensive cooperation and collaboration needed in the economic field to produce our food, our clothing, our housing. Adam Smith's key insight was that both parties to an exchange can benefit and that, *so long as cooperation is strictly voluntary,* no exchange will take place unless both parties do benefit. No external force, no coercion, no violation of freedom is necessary to produce cooperation among individuals all of whom can benefit. That is why, as Adam Smith put it, an individual who "intends only his own gain" is "led by an invisible hand to promote an end which was no part of his intention. Nor is it always the worse for the society that it was no part of it. By pursuing his own interest he frequently promotes that of the society more effectually than when he really intends to promote it. I have never known much good done by those who affected to trade for the public good."

The second set of ideas was embodied in the Declaration of Independence, drafted by Thomas Jefferson to express the general sense of his fellow countrymen. It proclaimed a new nation, the first in history established on the principle that every person is entitled to pursue his own values: "We hold these truths to be self-evident, that all men are created equal, that they are endowed by their Creator with certain unalienable Rights; that among these are Life, Liberty, and the pursuit of Happiness.". . .

Economic freedom is an essential requisite for political freedom. By enabling people to cooperate with one another without coercion or central direction, it reduces the area over which political power is exercised. In addition, by dispersing power, the free market provides an offset to whatever concentration of political power may arise. The combination of economic and political *power* in the same hands is a sure recipe for tyranny. . . .

Ironically, the very success of economic and political freedom reduced its appeal to later thinkers. The narrowly limited government of the late nineteenth century possessed little concentrated power that endangered the ordinary man. The other side of that coin was that it possessed little power that would enable good people to do good. And in an imperfect world there were still many evils. Indeed, the very progress of society made the residual evils seem all the more objectionable. As always, people took the favorable developments for granted. They forgot the danger to freedom from a strong government. Instead, they were attracted by the good that a stronger government could achieve—if only government power were in the "right" hands....

These views have dominated developments in the United States during the past half-century. They have led to a growth in government at all levels, as well as to a transfer of power from local government and local control to central government and central control. The government has increasingly undertaken the task of taking from some to give to others in the name of security and equality....

These developments have been produced by good intentions with a major assist from self-interest. [Yet] even the strongest supporters of the welfare and paternal state agree that the results have been disappointing....

The experience of recent years—slowing growth and declining productivity—raises a doubt whether private ingenuity can continue to overcome the deadening effects of government control if we continue to grant ever more power to government, to authorize a "new class" of civil servants to spend ever larger fractions of our income supposedly on our behalf. Sooner or later—and perhaps sooner than many of us expect—an ever bigger government would destroy both the prosperity that we owe to the free market and the human freedom proclaimed so eloquently in the Declaration of Independence.

We have not yet reached the point of no return. We are still free as a people to choose whether we shall continue speeding down the "road to serfdom," as Friedrich Hayek entitled his profound and influential book, or whether we shall set tighter limits on government and rely more heavily on voluntary cooperation among free individuals to achieve our several objectives. Will our golden age come to an end in a relapse into the tyranny and misery that has always been, and remains today, the state of most of mankind? Or shall we have the wisdom, the foresight, and the courage to change our course, to learn from experience, and to benefit from a "rebirth of freedom"?... If the cresting of the tide ... is to be followed by a move toward a freer society and a more limited government rather than toward a totalitarian society, the public must not only recognize the defects of the present situation but also how it has come about and what we can do about it. Why are the results of policies so often the opposite of their ostensible

objectives? Why do special interests prevail over the general interest? What devices can we use to stop and reverse the process?...

...Whenever we visit Washington, D.C., we are impressed all
over again with how much power is concentrated in that city.
Walk the halls of Congress, and the 435 members of the House
plus the 100 senators are hard to find among their 18,000 employees—about 65 for each senator and 27 for each member of the
House. In addition, the more than 15,000 registered lobbyists—
often accompanied by secretaries, typists, researchers, or representatives of the special interest they represent—walk the same halls
seeking to exercise influence.

And this is but the tip of the iceberg. The federal government
employs close to 3 million civilians (excluding the uniformed military forces). Over 350,000 are in Washington and the surrounding metropolitan area. Countless others are indirectly employed
through government contracts with nominally private organizations, or are employed by labor or business organizations or
other special interest groups that maintain their headquarters, or
at least an office, in Washington because it is the seat of government....

...Both the fragmentation of power and the conflicting government policies are rooted in the political realities of a democratic
system that operates by enacting detailed and specific legislation.
Such a system tends to give undue political power to small groups
that have highly concentrated interests, to give greater weight to
obvious, direct, and immediate effects of government action than
to possibly more important but concealed, indirect, and delayed
effects, to set in motion a process that sacrifices the general interest
to serve special interests, rather than the other way around. There
is, as it were, an invisible hand in politics that operates in precisely
the opposite direction to Adam Smith's invisible hand. Individuals
who intend only to promote the *general interest* are led by the
invisible political hand to promote a *special interest* that they had
no intention to promote....

The benefit an individual gets from any one program that he
has a special interest in may be more than canceled by the costs to
him of many programs that affect him lightly. Yet it pays him to
favor the one program, and not oppose the others. He can readily
recognize that he and the small group with the same special interest
can afford to spend enough money and time to make a difference
in respect of the one program. Not promoting that program will

not prevent the others, which do him harm, from being adopted. To achieve that, he would have to be willing and able to devote as much effort to opposing each of them as he does to favoring his own. That is clearly a losing proposition....

Currently in the United States, anything like effective detailed control of government by the public is limited to villages, towns, smaller cities, and suburban areas—and even there only to those matters not mandated by the state or federal government. In large cities, states, Washington, we have government of the people not by the people but by a largely faceless group of bureaucrats.

No federal legislator could conceivably even read, let alone analyze and study, all the laws on which he must vote. He must depend on his numerous aides and assistants, or outside lobbyists, or fellow legislators, or some other source for most of his decisions on how to vote. The unelected congressional bureaucracy almost surely has far more influence today in shaping the detailed laws that are passed than do our elected representatives.

The situation is even more extreme in the administration of government programs. The vast federal bureaucracy spread through the many government departments and independent agencies is literally out of control of the elected representatives of the public. Elected Presidents and senators and representatives come and go but the civil service remains. Higher-level bureaucrats are past masters at the art of using red tape to delay and defeat proposals they do not favor; of issuing rules and regulations as "interpretations" of laws that in fact subtly, or sometimes crudely, alter their thrust; of dragging their feet in administering those parts of laws of which they disapprove, while pressing on with those they favor....

Bureaucrats have not usurped power. They have not deliberately engaged in any kind of conspiracy to subvert the democratic process. Power has been thrust on them....

The growth of the bureaucracy in size and power affects every detail of the relation between a citizen and his government.... Needless to say, those of us who want to halt and reverse the recent trend should oppose additional specific measures to expand further the power and scope of government, urge repeal and reform of existing measures, and try to elect legislators and executives who share that view. But that is not an effective way to reverse the growth of government. It is doomed to failure. Each of us would defend our own special privileges and try to limit government at someone else's expense. We would be fighting a many-headed hydra that would grow new heads faster than we could cut old ones off.

Our founding fathers have shown us a more promising way to proceed: by package deals, as it were. We should adopt self-denying ordinances that limit the objectives we try to pursue through political channels. We should not consider each case on its merits, but lay down broad rules limiting what government may do....

We need, in our opinion, the equivalent of the First Amendment to limit government power in the economic and social area—an economic Bill of Rights to complement and reinforce the original Bill of Rights....

The proposed amendments would alter the conditions under which legislators—state or federal, as the case may be—operate by limiting the total amount they are authorized to appropriate. The amendments would give the government a limited budget, specified in advance, the way each of us has a limited budget. Much special interest legislation is undesirable, but it is never clearly and unmistakably bad. On the contrary, every measure will be represented as serving a good cause. The problem is that there are an infinite number of good causes. Currently, a legislator is in a weak position to oppose a "good" cause. If he objects that it will raise taxes, he will be labeled a reactionary who is willing to sacrifice human need for base mercenary reasons—after all, this good cause will only require raising taxes by a few cents or dollars per person. The legislator is in a far better position if he can say, "Yes, yours is a good cause, but we have a fixed budget. More money for your cause means less for others. Which of these others should be cut?" The effect would be to require the special interests to compete with one another for a bigger share of a fixed pie, instead of their being able to collude with one another to make the pie bigger at the expense of the taxpayer....

...The two ideas of human freedom and economic freedom working together came to their greatest fruition in the United States. Those ideas are still very much with us. We are all of us imbued with them. They are part of the very fabric of our being. But we have been straying from them. We have been forgetting the basic truth that the greatest threat to human freedom is the concentration of power, whether in the hands of government or anyone else. We have persuaded ourselves that it is safe to grant power, provided it is for good purposes.

Fortunately, we are waking up....

Fortunately, also, we are as a people still free to choose which way we should go—whether to continue along the road we have been following to ever bigger government, or to call a halt and change direction.

90

LESTER THUROW

Solving the Economic Problems
of the 1980s

From *The Zero-Sum Society*

OUR ECONOMIC problems are solvable. For most of our problems there are several solutions. But all these solutions have the characteristic that someone must suffer large economic losses. No one wants to volunteer for this role, and we have a political process that is incapable of forcing anyone to shoulder this burden. Everyone wants someone else to suffer the necessary economic losses, and as a consequence none of the possible solutions can be adopted.

Basically we have created the world described in Robert Ardrey's *The Territorial Imperative*. To beat an animal of the same species on his home turf, the invader must be twice as strong as the defender. But no majority is twice as strong as the minority opposing it. Therefore we each veto the other's initiatives, but none of us has the ability to create successful initiatives ourselves.

Our political and economic structure simply isn't able to cope with an economy that has a substantial zero-sum element. A zero-sum game is any game where the losses exactly equal the winnings. All sporting events are zero-sum games. For every winner there is a loser, and winners can only exist if losers exist. What the winning gambler wins, the losing gambler must lose.

When there are large losses to be allocated, any economic decision has a large zero-sum element. The economic gains may exceed the economic losses, but the losses are so large as to negate a very substantial fraction of the gains. What is more important, the gains and losses are not allocated to the same individuals or groups. On average, society may be better off, but this average hides a large number of people who are much better off and large numbers of people who are much worse off. If you are among those who are worse off, the fact that someone else's income has risen by more than your income has fallen is of little comfort. . . .

The problem with zero-sum games is that the essence of problem solving is loss allocation. But this is precisely what our political process is least capable of doing. When there are economic gains to be allocated, our political process can allocate them. When there are large economic losses to be allocated, our political process is paralyzed. And with political paralysis comes economic paralysis.

The importance of economic losers has also been magnified by a change in the political structure. In the past, political and economic power was distributed in such a way that substantial economic losses could be imposed on parts of the population if the establishment decided that it was in the general interest. Economic losses were allocated to particular powerless groups rather than spread across the population. These groups are no longer willing to accept losses and are able to raise substantially the costs for those who wish to impose losses upon them.

There are a number of reasons for this change. Vietnam and the subsequent political scandals clearly lessened the population's willingness to accept their nominal leader's judgments that some project was in their general interest. With the civil rights, poverty, black power, and women's liberation movements, many of the groups that have in the past absorbed economic losses have become militant. They are no longer willing to accept losses without a political fight. The success of their militancy and civil disobedience sets an example that spreads to other groups representing the environment, neighborhoods, and regions. . . . Given the problem of loss allocation, it is not surprising that government stands in the middle of an adversary relationship. Each group wants government to use its power to protect it and to force others to do what is in the general interest. . . .

To be workable, a democracy assumes that public decisions are made in a framework where there is a substantial majority of concerned but disinterested citizens who will prevent policies from being shaped by those with direct economic self-interests. Decisions in the interests of the general welfare are supposed to be produced by those concerned but disinterested citizens. They are to arbitrate and judge the disputes of the interested parties. As government grows, however, the number of such citizens shrinks. Almost everyone now has a direct economic stake in what government does.... With everyone's economic self-interest at stake, we all form perfectly proper lobbying groups to bend decisions in our favor. But with the disinterested citizen in a minority, how are decisions to reflect the general welfare? Who is to arbitrate? Our natural inclination is to rely on the adversary process, where different self-interested groups present their case. But somewhere there has to be a disinterested judge with the power to decide or tip a political decision in the right way. The general welfare is not always on the side of those who can mobilize the most economic and political power in their own behalf. If we really were to enforce the rule that no one could vote on an issue if his or her income would go up or down as a result of the action, we would end up with few or no voters on most issues. The problem is to establish a modicum of speedy, disinterested decision-making capacity in a political process where everyone has a direct self-interest....

Since government must alter the distribution of income if it is to solve our economic problems, we have to have a government that is capable of making equity decisions. Whose income ought to go up and whose income ought to go down? To do this, however, we need to know what is equitable. What is a fair or just distribution of economic resources? What is a fair or just procedure for distributing income? Unless we can specify what is equitable, we cannot say whose income ought to go down. Unless we can say whose income ought to go down, we cannot solve our economic problems.

The difficulties of specifying economic equity neither obviate the need for equity decisions nor stop such decisions from being made. Every time a tax is levied or repealed, every time public expenditures are expanded or contracted, every time regulations are extended or abolished, an equity decision has to be made. Since economic gains are relatively easy to allocate, the basic problem comes down to one of allocating economic losses. Whose income "ought" to go down?...

...Our society has reached a point where it must start to make

explicit equity decisions if it is to advance. The implicit, unde-
fended, unanalyzed equity decisions that have been built into our
tax, expenditures, and regulatory policies of the past simply won't
carry us into the future. To implement public policies in the future
we are going to have to be able to decide when losers should
suffer income losses and when losers should be compensated. We
have to be be able to decide when society should take actions to
raise the income of some group and when it should not take such
actions. If we cannot learn to make, impose, and defend equity
decisions, we are not going to solve any of our economic problems. . . .

The problem is identical to that of designing the rules of a
football game. To design a fair football game, several decisions
need to be made. First, what is the initial starting score? Is it zero–
zero or something else? Second, how does one advance the ball
and score? Third, how often does the game start over? The answer
to none of these questions is axiomatic in either the sporting world
or the economic world. At Oxford there is, for example, a rowing
race that started only once. Every year boats begin where they left
off the year before. The race is never over. Would we define the
equivalent game as "equal opportunity" in the economic world?
History decides the unequal starting point of each individual economic runner and each economic runner is now allowed to hand
in his or her baton to whomever he wishes and at whatever point
he wishes. The race never starts over. Once a duke always a
duke.

But leaving aside the starting score and the problem of how
often do you start over, how would you decide whether the rules
of advancing the ball are fair or unfair? Presumably, it has something to do with a determination that players of equal ability have
an equal probability of scoring, if not winning. How do you determine this in an economic game as complicated as that of the real
economy? If women, for example, who work full-time, full-year
earn less than 60 percent of what males earn, and that has been
true for the entire forty years that we have kept track of such
statistics, does that prove that the rules of advancing the ball are
unfair? It is either unfair or you have to be willing to defend the
position that women are inferior to men.

As a result, it is not possible to retreat to the position that we
should specify the rules of a fair economic game and then let this

game determine the fair distribution of purchasing power—an initial score. This requires an equity decision. Many fair games that produce many different distributions of prizes could be constructed. To pick which fair game we wish to play we must decide which distribution of prizes we want. There is no escape from having to make explicit equity decisions....

Let me start by suggesting a possible specification of economic equity. In the United States there is a strong allegiance to the principle that people should fairly compete for a distribution of market prizes. At the same time, there is the recognition that the market has not given everyone an equal chance to win. The group that comes closest to our ideal vision of the natural lottery is composed of fully employed white males. They do not suffer from the handicaps of discrimination, lack of skills, or unemployment. If we look at their earnings rather than their income, inherited wealth plays a relatively small role in their current position.

Let me suggest that our general equity goal should be to establish a distribution of earnings for everyone that is no more unequal than that which *now* exists for fully employed white males.... Since this distribution of earnings is the current incentive structure for white males, there are no problems with work incentives. With more than half of the labor force (measured in hours of work) now participating in this natural lottery, it is hardly a distribution of economic resources that anyone could consider un-American....

How can we go about organizing a society where everyone gets to play the same economic game as that of fully employed white males?... The principal way to narrow income gaps between groups is to restructure the economy so that it will, in fact, provide jobs for everyone. Since we regard the United States as a *work ethic* society, this restructuring should be a moral duty as well as an economic goal. We consistently preach that work is the only "ethical" way to receive income. We cast aspersions on the "welfare" society. Therefore we have a moral responsibility to guarantee full employment. Not to do so is like locking the church doors and then saying that people are not virtuous if they do not go to church.

Since private enterprise is incapable of guaranteeing jobs for everyone who wants to work, then government, and in particular the federal government, must institute the necessary programs. No one should attempt to deny that a real, open-ended, guaranteed job program would constitute a major restructuring of our economy. Patterns of labor market behavior and the outputs of our economy would be fundamentally altered.

It should be pointed out, however, that real economic competition would almost certainly increase. If the guaranteed jobs are to be real jobs, then any guaranteed job program must produce some economic outputs. These outputs might consist of street cleaning in competition with public sanitation departments, or the rebuilding of railway roadbeds in competition with private industry. The problem is not finding worthwhile things to do. Anyone with even a little imagination can think of many things that could be done to make this society a better one. If the option is between idleness and work, the choice is simple. As long as any useful output is produced, a work project takes precedence over involuntary unemployment.

A guaranteed job program must have several characteristics in order to achieve the objectives for which it is intended. First, it cannot be a program of employment at minimum wage rates. The objective is to open to everyone a structure of economic work opportunities equivalent to those open to fully employed white males. Thus, the program would have to structure earnings and promotion opportunities in the same way as they are structured for fully employed white males. There would be some low-wage jobs and some high-wage jobs, but most jobs would be in the middle. Some or all of the workers might be unionized. Second, the program must be open-ended, providing jobs to everyone who is able and willing to work regardless of age, race, sex, or education. Abilities and talents will play a role within the distribution of job opportunities, but no one who desires full- or part-time work will be denied it. Third, the program should not be viewed as a temporary anti-recessionary measure. The lack of employment opportunities is not a temporary, short-run aspect of the U.S. economy. It is permanent and endemic. . . .

What would such a program cost? Payments for labor, materials, and capital might be high, but as with all economic projects, the costs would depend upon the difference between the value of output produced and the payments made to factors of production. If care is shown in project selection, there is no reason why the projects could not generate substantial net benefits. If you are employing idle economic resources (workers without jobs), the real economic costs (opportunity costs) would be substantially less than the monetary costs....

Politically, we are reluctant to give jobs, because to do so would require a major restructuring of the economy. A new source of competition would arise for both public agencies and private firms. To the extent that we were unable or unwilling to hold the private economy at the full-employment level, we would have a socialized economy.

The time has come, however, to admit that the pursuit of equity and equal economic opportunity demands a fundamental restructuring of the economy. Everyone who wants to work should have a chance to work. But there is no way to achieve that situation by tinkering marginally with current economic policies. The only solution is to create a socialized sector of the economy designed to give work opportunities to everyone who wants them but cannot find them elsewhere.

I am not naïve enough to think that such a plan is about to be adopted, but the basic problem is already of long standing. Can you really imagine continuing for another thirty years with black unemployment twice that of whites? Full-time, full-year female workers have earned less than 60 percent of men ever since record keeping began more than forty years ago. Can it continue for another forty years? Perhaps, but I doubt it. Should it continue? I have no problem answering in the negative. Will it continue if we don't do something to change the structure of the economy fundamentally? I have no problem answering in the positive. Will we fail as a society to address this fundamental problem and let it drag us down with it? Perhaps....

...It is well to remember that there is really only one important question in political economy. If elected, whose income do you and your party plan to cut in the process of solving the economic problems facing us? Our economy and the solutions to its problems have a substantial zero-sum element. Our economic life would be easier if this were not true, but we are going to have to learn to play a zero-sum economic game. If we cannot learn, or prefer to pretend that the zero-sum problem does not exist, we are simply going to fail.

91

BARRY BLUESTONE
BENNETT HARRISON

The Great American Job Machine: The Proliferation of Low-Wage Employment in the U.S. Economy

FOR MORE THAN a decade the United States has been in the enviable position of producing more new jobs than most of the rest of the industrialized nations combined. Indeed, Europe had virtually zero employment growth between 1973 and 1984, while the U.S. added nearly twenty million new jobs during the same period.

As a result, America has been justifiably termed "The Great Jobs Machine." While unemployment rates are clearly much higher than in previous decades, the economy has generated employment opportunity for millions in the "baby boom" generation and for an unprecedented number of women who have entered and remained in the labor force....

Those charged with responsibility for current economic policy have been particularly pleased with recent employment gains. Since 1981, the total number of jobs in the U.S. has expanded by nearly 10 million, despite the severe 1981–1982 recession, and the grand total has grown nearly every month since the end of 1982. The tax cuts initiated under the Reagan Administration and the expansion in the nation's money supply beginning in 1983 have indeed brought about a substantial economic recovery.

Yet for all of the jubilation surrounding this accomplishment, the recent employment record is not quite as good as the raw numbers seem to suggest. For one thing, the civilian labor force—the number of Americans who are working or who *want* to work—grew at an even faster pace than the rate of job growth....

What is most important, however, is that none of the aggregate numbers reveal anything about the types of jobs created during this period, or how much they pay. As for the first question, the record reveals a continuation into the 1980s of a strong trend toward employment growth in the service sector, with literally *no* expansion whatsoever in employment in goods production. In fact, since 1981, the number of people employed in construction and manufacturing has *declined* by more than 500,000, while private sector service employment (including transportation and public utilities; wholesale and retail trade; finance, insurance, and real estate; and business and personal services) has been responsible for *all* of the total net growth in the number of civilian jobs. Clearly, the radical sectoral restructuring of the American economy continues apace....

...In 1973, as the table indicates, there were 93.2 million persons who were employed sometime during the year. Nearly 30 million of them (29.6 million) earned $7,000 or less for their effort, while 15.4 million earned $28,000 or more (in 1984 dollar terms). By our definition, then, 31.8 percent of the workforce was low-wage while 16.6 percent were located at the high end of the distribution. By 1979, the total workforce had increased by 12.1 million to 105.3 million. Of this increase, only 2.4 million or 19.9 percent of the net new persons employed received annual wages and salaries that placed them within the lowest stratum. This was sufficient to reduce the overall proportion of low-wage workers to 30.4 percent. Almost two-thirds (64.2%) of the net new employment was found in jobs that paid between $7,000 and $28,000.

By 1984 total employment had increased to more than 113

EMPLOYMENT LEVELS AND EMPLOYMENT SHARES
ALL U.S. WORKERS (000's)

	NUMBER OF EMPLOYEES			EARNINGS SHARES			SHARES OF NET NEW EMPLOYMENT	
	1973	1979	1984	1973	1979	1984	1973–1979	1979–1984
Low stratum	29648	32063	36750	31.8%	30.4%	32.4%	19.9%	58.0%
Middle stratum	48107	55908	59745	51.6	53.1	52.7	64.2	47.5
High stratum	15441	17374	16932	16.6	16.5	14.9	15.9	−5.5
Total	93196	105345	113427	100%	100%	100%	100%	100%

Source: Calculations from Uniform CPS (Mare-Winship) Data Files.

million or 8 million more than in 1979. But of these 8 million net new employees, 58 percent earned no more than $7,012—the nominal dollar value that kept them in the low-wage stratum. Hence, *nearly three-fifths of the net new employment generated between 1979 and 1984 was low wage, compared with less than one-fifth during the preceding period.*

During the same period, the number of high stratum positions actually declined by 5.5 percent—a loss of more than 440,000 high-wage employees. Comparing the wage stratum shares in 1984 and 1979 suggests that the entire real earnings structure slid downward during this five year period. The middle and high stratum shares declined, while the low-wage share grew significantly. The figure graphically depicts this trend.

The continuing decline in high-wage manufacturing, combined with the expansion in the low-wage retail trade and service sectors,

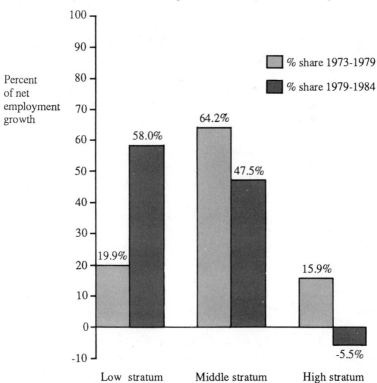

PERCENT SHARES OF NEW JOB GROWTH (ALL WORKERS)

have led to the popular perception that America may be on the
verge of losing its middle class. Writers often equate "middle class"
with "recipients of middle-level incomes." In those terms, our
results confirm an unmistakable trend in this direction for individual working people.

At the margin, the net additions to employment being generated
in the U.S. since the late 1970s have been disproportionately and
increasingly concentrated at the low-wage end of the spectrum.
That 58 percent of all net new employment between 1979 and
1984 paid annual wages of less than $7,000 clearly supports this
conclusion. Indeed, if the ratio of net new low-wage employment
to net new total employment for the earlier period (1973–1979)
had prevailed for the period after 1979, the total number of new
low-wage positions would have been only 1.6 million, rather than
the 4.7 million that we actually experienced. Hence, the strong
and apparently enviable record of job creation since 1979 masked
the fact that more than 3.1 million of the 8 million net new jobs
represented additional low-wage employment over and above the
number of low-wage jobs that would have been created under
earlier conditions. That there was an absolute decline of more than
450,000 jobs paying high wages confirms the recent shift toward
low-wage work.

Of all the demographic groups in the U.S., younger white
men have been the biggest losers in the sense that *all* of the net
new jobs held by this group after 1979 paid very low wages. In
contrast, the share of all new jobs held by white women which
pay high wages grew between 1973–1979 and 1979–1984, while
the incidence of very low-paying work increased only slightly.
The earnings of workers of color of both genders have not continued to improve as in the earlier period. Notable in this regard is
the apparent halt in the previous trend toward a growing high
wage share for non-white men. In the period 1973–1979, 42 percent
of the net employment growth among minority men was in the
high-wage end of the distribution. In the years since 1979, that
proportion has dropped to 6.4 percent.

The tendency toward the expansion of the low-wage end of
the earnings distribution appears to be concentrated especially in
the Midwest, but no region of the country is completely immune
from it. Finally, the tendency toward low wages is particularly
pronounced within the manufacturing sector (which started the
period with the smallest low-wage stratum), but it appears even in

high tech and in the broadly defined service sector.

A growing volume of research ... all points in the same general direction—a tendency toward low wages in particular and growing income inequality in general in the United States. It would seem that a serious political debate over how this unsettling development might be reversed should be on the agenda of the next Congress.

92

MARVIN KOSTERS
MURRAY ROSS
A Shrinking Middle Class?

THE U.S. ECONOMY has generated employment growth during the 1980s—indeed, during the past two decades—that is the envy of Western Europe. This impressive record of job creation, however, has been called into question by critics who fear that the quality of jobs has been deteriorating. Workers are said to be getting mainly low-paying jobs with little opportunity for advancement; "good jobs" that pay middle-class wages are said to be disappearing.

This new view of what has been happening to jobs and earnings in America has been nurtured by articles with provocative titles like "The Shrinking Middle Class," "An Ominous Trend to Greater Inequality," "The Disappearing Middle Class," "A Low-Wage Explosion," "The Grim Truth about the Job Miracle," "A Surge in Inequality," and "American Job Machine has Begun to Sputter." Although this view of labor-market trends has been so widely popularized in the media that it is rapidly approaching the status of conventional wisdom, it is based on very limited research. Moreover, a re-examination of the data shows that the analysis on which this new view rests is seriously flawed. Consequently, it paints a grossly distorted view of what is happening to work and jobs.

To understand why this view of jobs and wages has gained such wide popular acceptance, we will first consider the economic setting that has given it superficial plausibility. Then we will examine the evidence on wage, employment, and earnings trends to place in perspective what has been happening to the quality of jobs for the workforce as a whole. . . .

Several trends that were readily apparent in the early 1980s lent credence to the view that something fundamentally disturbing was happening to industry and jobs. Recession, deregulation, introduction of new technology, and appreciation of the dollar forced many large firms to make dramatic labor adjustments. The average size of wage increases came down sharply, wage increases previously negotiated by unions were cut back, and in some cases wages were significantly reduced. In addition, indefinite layoffs of large numbers of workers and permanent job losses resulting from plant closures focused attention on "displaced workers," many of whom were unable to find jobs that paid wages comparable to those of their previous jobs.

These temporary and cyclical developments reinforced a long-term trend toward a larger share of employment in services, compared with "goods-producing" industries such as manufacturing. The perception that the U.S. economy was "deindustrializing" was augmented by the concern that "good jobs" were disappearing and being replaced by low-wage service jobs. These trends were portrayed as producing (1) stagnating or declining real wages; (2) disproportionate growth in low-wage jobs; and (3) a decline in jobs that pay middle-class wages.

This interpretation of events in the labor market is superficially appealing in view of broad trends in the economy. Both the lower average wages in services and the large shift in the industry-employment mix toward services lend credence to this explanation. Wages *are* considerably lower in the service sector. Wages for service workers (as measured by average hourly earnings for production workers) are about 83 percent of manufacturing wages. Thus, replacement of an average job in manufacturing with an average job in services would tend to reduce overall average wages.

The growth in services employment has also been dramatic when compared with manufacturing employment. During the past two decades, manufacturing has usually employed between eighteen and twenty million workers. During that same twenty-year period, however, total civilian employment went up from 74 to 112 million workers—an increase of more than 50 percent. This produced a pronounced decline in the manufacturing employment share, a decline that is particularly remarkable in view of the roughly constant share of total output of the economy accounted for by real output in manufacturing.

The well-known shift to services has not only been presumed to have had adverse effects on the average wage level; it has also been portrayed as the source of increased wage inequality. Service jobs have frequently been described as sharply divided between those paying very low wages and those held by highly-paid professionals. Janitors or fast-food employees "flipping hamburgers" are usually mentioned as examples of typical low-wage employees while accountants, brokers, doctors, and lawyers exemplify those who hold high-wage service jobs. The implication is that as service employment comes to account for a larger fraction of jobs, the middle class is disappearing or at least suffering erosion. . . .

The claim that the middle class is disappearing is usually accompanied by the proposition that most who are displaced from the middle end up among the poor rather than the rich. The subtitle of the widely-publicized study prepared for the Joint Economic Committee by Barry Bluestone and Bennett Harrison is "The Proliferation of Low-Wage Employment in the U.S. Economy."* After making reference to the "popular perception that America may be on the verge of losing its middle class," they conclude that "our results confirm an unmistakable trend in this direction for individual working people.". . .

Bad news about the economy remains a more potent attention-getter than headlines describing a stable or slightly improved employment situation. Puncturing the "myth" of the "American job machine," a matter affecting the livelihood of America's workers, also possesses substantial political appeal. A hint that this did not go unnoticed by the authors of the JEC study is contained in the concluding sentence of their report: "It would seem that a serious political debate over how this unsettling development might be reversed should be on the agenda of the next Congress.". . .

The new view—namely, that the quality of jobs has been deteriorating markedly—has not been based mainly on analysis of trends in average hourly pay or of the consequences of the continuing shift toward employment in services. The primary support for this view has come from data on changes in the distribution of employment among broad earnings categories. The study written

*See selection 91.—EDS.

for the Joint Economic Committee (JEC) by Barry Bluestone and Bennett Harrison (to which we have already referred), which was released on December 9, 1986, has provided the basis for much of the subsequent popular discussion.

This JEC study, entitled *The Great American Job Machine: The Proliferation of Low-Wage Employment in the U.S. Economy,* is based on earnings of wage and salary workers—*not* hourly rates of pay. The importance of this distinction is discussed below in a section on workers with low earnings. In view of the wide publicity it has received and the journalistic commentary it has generated, we think it would be useful to reexamine the data employed in the JEC study in order to facilitate comparison of our results with the results reported there.

The main elements of the approach used in the JEC study and its central conclusions can be described quite simply. The median wage and salary income of all wage and salary workers in 1973 was calculated, and three earnings categories were defined based on cutoffs at 50 percent and 200 percent of the median. These cutoffs were adjusted using the CPI to permit comparison with earnings data for 1979 and 1984....

...The central conclusion of the study is that the share of employment in the low-wage and -salary earnings stratum increased disproportionately between 1979 and 1984, compared with its change between 1973 and 1979. According to the authors, *"nearly three fifths of the net new employment generated between 1979 and 1984 was low wage, compared with less than one fifth during the preceding period"* (italics in the original).

In addition to data for all workers, comparisons using a similar framework were presented for components of the work force by age, race, sex, work experience, years of schooling, industry, and region. The results for most of these categories were qualitatively similar, leading the authors to conclude that there has been a pronounced rise in the share of workers in the low stratum, as it is defined in the JEC study....

Our reexamination of the underlying data points to conclusions that are radically different from those of the JEC study....

In contrast to the central conclusion of the JEC study, our analysis shows no increase in the share of "new jobs" with low earnings. Indeed, the share of net additions to employment for each subperiod (about 24 percent) is well below the share of overall employment in the low-earnings category (about 30 percent), confirming a continuing trend toward a *smaller* share of employment in the lower part of the earnings distribution.

Results for subperiods are clearly sensitive to the particular years chosen for comparison. It is instructive, therefore, to look at trends shown by annual data on employment shares as well. Employment shares from 1967 through 1985 for low-, middle-, and high-earnings categories are shown in the Figure....

...According to these data the share of employment in the low-earnings category has declined over time, that in the high-earnings category has increased, and it is difficult to see any trend up or down in the middle earnings category....

In contrast to the JEC study, our analysis shows neither a disproportionate nor a growing share of new jobs in the low-earnings category. The relatively low share of net additional employment in the low-earnings category means that the overall share of workers with low earnings has declined gradually over the years. The share of employment at the high end of the distribution has increased by an amount roughly equal to the decline in the share at the low end. Although the share of employment in the middle-earnings range has varied from year to year, and has indeed declined

EMPLOYMENT SHARES BY EARNINGS CATEGORY,
BASED ON CURRENT-YEAR MEDIANS, 1967–1985
(IN PERCENTAGE)

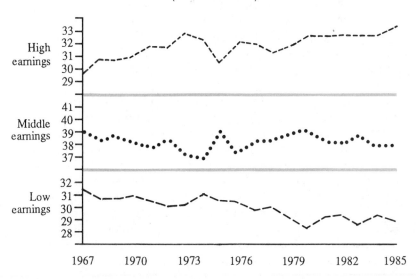

since 1980, there is no evidence that the long-term trend is down. It is particularly hard to argue that the small decline in the share of employment accounted for by workers in the middle-earnings category since 1980 portends a decline in economic well-being, with workers slipping below middle-class status, because the small decline in the middle is more than offset by the increase in the share at the top. . . .

The broad implication of these results is that although real wages have flattened out during the past fifteen years, this is not because of a disproportionate growth in jobs that pay low wages. The focus of attention should accordingly be shifted away from the supposed deterioration in the quality of new jobs. That is, the deterioration in real wage and earnings growth is a phenomenon applicable to the entire distribution; it does not reflect an abnormal expansion in jobs with low earnings.

For this reason the primary focus of attention should be shifted toward the earnings distribution as a whole. If the problem of the slowdown in real pay growth is seen as one that extends across the entire spectrum of jobs, it becomes clear that policies intended to discourage the creation of particular kinds of jobs, and to protect or maintain others, are unlikely to succeed. Discouraging the creation of new jobs that actually do pay low wages—by increasing the minimum wage, for example—means lower overall current earnings and poorer earnings in the future, to the extent that there are fewer jobs and that less valuable on-the-job training is provided. Protecting high-wage jobs—by blunting competition from imports, for example—tends to reduce real wages across the distribution because of higher prices. As strategies to improve real wage and income growth, these policies are self-defeating.

Improved real earnings across the distribution as a whole can be achieved only through changes and adjustments that lead to improved productivity. Strategies to raise real incomes must accordingly be evaluated in terms of their potential for recovering the growth in productivity that has faded since the late 1960s and early 1970s. A favorable climate for investment in human and material capital is certainly one essential element of policies to improve productivity growth. To realize higher productivity growth, it will be necessary to continue to make adjustments, in order to reflect changing market conditions and to accommodate the introduction of new technologies. Policies that facilitate the requisite adjustments—instead of inhibiting them by protecting particular jobs—are another essential element. A realistic diagnosis of the problem—recognizing that it involves productivity growth for the work force as a whole—is in any event the first step in appraising the promise of potential policies to ameliorate it. . . .

In view of the dramatic difference between the results of our study and those reported in the JEC study (both using the same basic data),. . . we believe that a strong case can be made for using our approach and procedures, which result in a more realistic appraisal of jobs and earnings trends.

93

DAVID STOCKMAN

From *The Triumph of Politics*

BY MIDSUMMER [1981] I had become somewhat disillusioned. . . . But my worry was not about the President's basic program. The problem was just the opposite. The congressional politicians were threatening to split his program at the seams by intransigently blocking the deep spending reductions that had to matched up with the big tax cut. This resistance was now incubating a deficit that could soar out of control and hobble the economy.

I had feared that from the beginning. But I hadn't reckoned that there would be so much opposition on our side of the aisle. I was shocked to find that the Democrats were getting so much Republican help in their efforts to keep the pork barrel flowing and the welfare state intact. I had been worried because the votes didn't add up, not the economic plan.

I had also come to realize that in my haste to get the Reagan Revolution launched in February, we have moved too fast. There were numerous loose ends. The spending reductions needed to pay for the tax cuts had turned out to be even bigger and tougher than I had originally thought. . . . Even then, the massive fiscal policy error that had been unleashed on the national and world economy was beyond recall. It should have been evident to me in the circumstances of those bitter hours. But it wasn't because I did not yet know that I was as much the problem as were my would-be executioners.

The fact was, metaphor and reality had been at odds from the very beginning. . . .

Revolutions have to do with drastic, wrenching changes in an established regime. Causing such changes to happen was not Ronald Reagan's real agenda in the first place. It was mine, and that of a small cadre of supply-side intellectuals.

The Reagan Revolution, as I had defined it, required a frontal assault on the American welfare state. That was the only way to pay for the massive Kemp-Roth tax cut.

Accordingly, forty years' worth of promises, subventions, entitlements, and safety nets issued by the federal government to every component and stratum of American society would have to be scrapped or drastically modified. A true economic policy revolution meant risky and mortal political combat with all the mass constituencies of Washington's largess—Social Security recipients, veterans, farmers, educators, state and local officials, the housing industry, and many more.

Behind the hoopla of the Kemp-Roth tax cut and my thick black books of budget cuts was the central idea of the Reagan Revolution. It was minimalist government—a spare and stingy creature, which offered even-handed public justice, but no more. Its vision of the good society rested on the strength and productive potential of free men in free markets. It sought to encourage the unfettered production of capitalist wealth and the expansion of private welfare that automatically attends it. It envisioned a land the opposite of the coast-to-coast patchwork of dependencies, shelters, protections, and redistributions that the nation's politicians had brokered over the decades.

The true Reagan Revolution never had a chance. It defied all of the overwhelming forces, interests, and impulses of American democracy. Our Madisonian government of checks and balances, three branches, two legislative houses, and infinitely splintered power is conservative, not radical. It hugs powerfully to the history behind it. It shuffles into the future one step at a time. It cannot leap into revolutions without falling flat on its face. . . .

My blueprint for sweeping, wrenching change in national economic governance would have hurt millions of people in the short run. It required abruptly severing the umbilical cords of dependency that ran from Washington to every nook and cranny of the nation. It required the ruthless dispensation of short-run pain in the name of long-run gain.

To make a revolution required defining fairness in terms of exacting, abstract principles—not human hard-luck stories. It meant complete elimination of subsidies to farmers and businesses. It required an immediate end to welfare for the ablebodied poor. It meant no right to draw more from the Social Security fund than retirees had actually contributed, which was a lot less than most were currently getting.

These principles everywhere clashed with the political reality. Over the decades, the politicians had lured tens of millions of citizens into milking ... cows, food stamps, Social Security, the Veterans Hospitals, and much more. They were getting more than they deserved, needed, or were owed. For the Reagan Revolution to add up, they had to be cut off. The blueprint was thus riddled with the hardship and unfairness of unexpected change. Only an iron chancellor would have tried to make it stick. Ronald Reagan wasn't that by a long shot. . . .

. . . Ronald Reagan proved to be too kind, gentle, and sentimental for that. He always went for hard-luck stories. He sees the plight of real people before anything else. Despite his right-wing image, his ideology and philosophy always take a back seat when he learns that some individual human being might be hurt.

That's also why he couldn't lead a real revolution in American economic policy. . . .

In the final analysis, there has been no Reagan Revolution in national economic governance. All the umbilical cords of dependency still exist because the public elects politicians who want to preserve them. So they have to be paid for. That is the unyielding bottom line. Economic and financial disaster is the only alternative.

I joined the Reagan Revolution as a radical ideologue. I learned the traumatic lesson that no such revolution was possible. I end up giving two cheers for the politicians. But only that.

The fact is, politicians can be a menace. They never stop inventing illicit enterprises of government that bleed the national economy. Their social uplift and pork barrel is wasteful; it reduces our collective welfare and wealth. The politicians rarely look ahead or around. Two years and one Congressional District is the scope of their horizon.

There is only one thing worse, and that is ideological hubris. It is the assumption that the world can be made better by being remade overnight. It is the false belief that in a capitalist democracy we can peer deep into the veil of the future and chain the ship of state to an exacting blueprint. It can't be done. It shouldn't have been tried.

This is the story of the lessons which taught me why....

The feverish work of January and early February 1981 was not policymaking, at least in the normal sense. No basic policy options were appraised, discussed, or debated.

There was no final compromise, reflecting an ultimate balance between the policymaker's claims as to what should be done and the politician's sense of what *can* be done. Yet this is the very equation which ordinarily keeps the system hitched. It is what bends every aspiration to make things better toward the powerful inertia which keeps everything the same.

The fundamentals of the Reagan fiscal program—the big tax cut, the defense buildup, an anti-inflation monetary policy, and a balanced budget—had been given *a priori*. The tumultuous work prior to February 18 was purely ministerial. It amounted to the translation of doctrine into the customary details, numbers, and formats of workaday policy.

The broad policy architecture of the plan was riddled with potential contradictions. It cried out for a good afternoon and evening's debate.

The main reason there was no debate was that the remaining variable in the policy equation was domestic spending cuts, and in the mind of the plan's architect—me—that remained almost infinitely elastic. The domestic spending cut could be sized modestly or massively, depending upon what was required to make everything else add up.

There was only one heavy task to perform prior to the February 18 launching of the revolution. In forty days, the budget-cutting assembly line would have to be geared up to run at breakneck speed.

Ordinarily, the White House politicians would have had their eyes glued on this aspect of the operation especially. The size of the spending-cut number was where ideological doctrine and political possibility should have had their showdown.

But the showdown never happened. The pace was so hectic that the White House never really knew what the domestic spending-cut number was. The linchpin of the plan was shrouded in a haze of rapidly changing figures.

There was another problem, too. None of the key White House advisers—Meese, Deaver, Baker—knew enough about American fiscal politics to assess the number, even if they had had it. The President had no idea of its political implications at all. . . .

I wanted the President and his advisers to know from the start that we would be working toward a huge spending cut total, at least by all prior standards. Raging political controversies and allegations that millions of people would be impacted or "hurt" had to be expected.

The Reagan economic policy revolution would not be a simple matter of "limiting the rate of increase in federal spending," as Meese kept phrasing it. It would involve drastic reductions in dozens of programs. It amounted to a substantial retraction of welfare state benefits that people had come to feel "entitled" to receive. . . .

Reagan's body of knowledge is primarily impressionistic: he registers anecdotes rather than concepts. I soon learned that it made less sense to tell him that you were eligible for a 35-cents-a-meal lunch subsidy if your income was above 190 percent of the poverty line than to tell him, "The kids of cabinet officers qualify." He was not surprised by these revelations; they conformed to his *a priori* understanding of what outrages the federal government was capable of perpetrating.

Still, these simplifications undoubtedly had a cost that I didn't recognize at the time. They made the impending bruising political battle to shrink welfare state spending sound too much like nostrums about fraud, waste, and abuse. It wasn't the same thing at all. . . .

Only later would I appreciate the vast web of confusion and self-delusion I was creating. I instilled so much confidence by appearing to know all the answers, but I was just beginning to understand the true complexities and mysteries of the federal budget. . . .

. . .No one raised any questions about what *wasn't* being reviewed and what *wasn't* being learned. The fiscal and economic illiteracy among the core White House group was simply too great to have elicited any doubts. We thus recklessly charged ahead. . . .

As I started work in my new office, I began fully to comprehend how ill-prepared I was for the job ahead. The realization came late, but these realizations always do: the new ship's captain, biographer, or architect seldom, I suppose, feels truly inadequate to his task until it is too late. What lay ahead for me had nothing to do with the elegant theories of my Grand Doctrine; it was all planning, processing, negotiating, deciding, and leading. And I had no experience in any of it....

...Defense, which was going to cost hundreds of billions more, had to be assigned huge, arbitrary out-year numbers without any debate or review. This permitted us to prove on paper that the tax cut, which would yield hundreds of billions less, was fiscally affordable and prudent.

Still, the Secretary of Defense was "Cap the Knife" Weinberger. He would find ways to rebuild the nation's flagging defenses at less cost than the arbitrary "plug" numbers we would temporarily insert in the out-year budget.

I was sure that Cap still had some of the Knife left in him from his own OMB days.... So I suggested we split the difference down the middle and go with an interim 7 percent real growth increase. A fully developed Reagan defense budget could be worked out later in the spring and then we'd get the real answer.

Weinberger thought about it a moment.

"In light of the disgraceful mess we're inheriting," he said, "seven percent will be a pretty lean ration." But he agreed to go along....

When we had finished, Weinberger looked at his watch, yawned, and noted it was not yet eight o'clock.

"I'd call this a good night's work," he said.

My day had begun at 4:30 A.M. and wouldn't end until after midnight, so to me a half hour was a nanosecond, but I had to agree with him. We'd accomplished a lot in a short time.

Or so I thought, until the constant dollar figures we'd come up with were translated into current dollar values. When I finally took a hard look at them several weeks later, I nearly had a heart attack. We'd laid out a plan for a five-year defense budget of *1.46 trillion dollars!*

As my eyes traced along the computer printout, seeing the "plug" balloon with each progressive out-year, I could hardly believe what I saw. The number started at $142 billion in 1980, and rose to $368 billion by 1986—an increase of 160 percent over the current dollar defense budget in just six years.

"How can this *be?*" I sputtered to Schneider. Patiently, he walked me back through the numbers, step by step. Gradually, I realized what haste can do.

The GOP campaign proposals for a defense hike of 5, 7, or

even 9 percent real growth had been predicated on Carter's 1980 defense budget of $142 billion. But in response to Desert One, Congress had raised Carter's request for defense funds and enacted a 1981 budget with 9 percent real growth built into it. The Reagan "get well" package had further raised that to 12 percent real growth. Then, the second Reagan "get well" installment for 1982 had added another 15 percent real growth increase on top of the big 1981 numbers.

What it boiled down to was a gigantic fiscal syllogism: We had taken an already-raised defense budget and raised that by 7 percent. Instead of starting from a defense budget of $142 billion, we'd started with one of $222 billion. And by raising that by 7 percent— and compounding it over five years—we had ended up increasing the real growth rate of the United States defense budget by *10 percent* per year between 1980 and 1986. That was double what candidate Ronald Reagan had promised in his campaign budget plan.

I stormed about the office fuming over my mistake. But by then the February 18 budget was out and they were squealing with delight throughout the military-industrial complex. . . .

I had already casually moved the target date for a balanced budget from 1983, which Reagan had promised during the campaign, to 1984. There hadn't been so much as a "What's *that* again?" from anyone in the White House. But then everyone's nose was so deep in paper they simply hadn't noticed.

But that was merely a straw in the wind compared to what would come next. I soon became a veritable incubator of shortcuts, schemes, and devices to overcome the truth now upon us—that the budget gap couldn't be closed except by a dictator. . . .

. . . No one squinted hard at the scoresheet or maybe even looked at all. No one said, "Now just where are you going to get the $58 billion savings in the last three categories? Name names. Kick some tail! Gore some oxen! Slay some sacred cows right here on the cabinet table!"

To be sure, I went over the numbers and tried to convey the meaning.

"We can make it add up, but what remains to be cut," I told them, "is nearly as big as what we've already cut. The additional cuts will be far tougher than anything we've already agreed upon."

There was no dissent. The cabinet apparently figured there was room in the Reagan Revolution for the Russell Long caveat:

"Don't cut you, don't cut me, cut the guy behind the tree."

The President nodded. "We're here to do whatever it takes," he said. He would make this statement over and over in the future. It was his mantra.

In effect, the President was letting his fiscal architect develop his economic policy revolution for him. He was taking my plan on faith alone, having no reason to suspect that the numbers wouldn't add up.

If there were no questions or dissent at the cabinet meeting, however, there was something much worse: confusion....

Had I been a standard policymaker and not an ideologue with a Grand Doctrine for changing the whole complexion of American government, I would have panicked at this point and said, "This won't work." To close a $44 billion budget gap *after* already cutting the budget by $64 billion would have involved nothing less than trench-style political warfare. But I had my own agenda. Four weeks of nonstop budget cutting, congressional briefings, press interviews, and Washington show stopping had given me an exaggerated sense of power.

I knew that the remaining $44 billion gap was huge. I remembered it was probably going to end up even larger, due to our cockeyed economic forecast. But I saw in this only the potential leverage it provided to further my Grand Doctrine, not its danger to the nation's finances.... This wasn't arrogance of the normal sort; it was grandiosity of the historical variety....

The luncheon should have been a victory celebration. But I was worried to death about where my numbers were going. If the President and Cabinet had been paying attention, I would have already scared the hell out of them with my numerous warnings, especially the most recent one on July 13 [1981].

It was then that I had reminded everyone of the "growing budget squeeze" and a dramatically "worsening out-year problem." To balance our 1984 budget, I repeated, we would have to make draconian, bone-wrenching additional cuts in the domestic budget—25 percent cuts in everything from the FBI to food stamps, farm subsidies, education aid, the National Park Service, and the Washington Monument. *One fourth.*

My July 13 numbers and warnings, however, had floated out the Cabinet Room windows and into the Rose Garden. They had been accompanied by a tabulation of all that we were on the verge of accomplishing in the pending tax and reconciliation bills. As a consequence, the good news had blacked out the bad.

So today I had come with the whole can of worms, deliberately prepared to ruin everyone's lunch. I was going to shock them into recognizing that the budget picture was bad going on awful.

At the end of the dessert, I passed out a stack of thick black binders, each one forty-two pages long. Groans around the table— another Stockman paper flood.

I didn't usually prepare opening lines for these occasions, but I had given careful thought to these. What I had settled on was not Churchillian, perhaps, but it was designed to get their attention.

"The scent of victory is still in the air," I began, "but I'm not going to mince words. We're heading for a crash landing on the budget. We're facing potential deficit numbers so big that they could *wreck* the President's entire economic program."

The chatter suddenly stopped. Even Mike Deaver, as I recall, stuck his spoon back in his sherbet and started listening.

"It's going to be harder than hell to get to a balanced budget even by 1986," I continued. "On the margin, every single important number in the budget is going in the wrong direction.

"So I want to beg your indulgence for about thirty minutes. We have to systematically walk through this step by step so everyone understands it.

"Then we're going to have to take a hard look at the options. We've reached the point where we have to make strategic choices, fundamental choices.". . . .

The failed September Offensive had been aimed at reducing the 1984 deficit by $75 billion. Now the deficit estimate had increased by an order of magnitude—to $150 billion. We were suddenly faced with the stark reality of what had been hidden from the beginning. Our sweeping fiscal plan had led straight into the jaws of triple-digit deficits.

In early November, I briefed the President and senior White House staff on this radical transformation of the budget outlook. I now projected nearly $400 billion in red ink for 1982 to 1984. . . .

The dilemma at the moment was awful. Now that we saw the real magnitude of the problem, we were out of political muscle to cut domestic spending and the President was unwilling to change the tax and defense programs. . . .

The bitter truth was that Ronald Reagan faced an excruciating test of presidential decision-making. After an exhausting and prolonged political struggle, he had emerged in July triumphant. Only three months later, he had to admit that the triumph had been an illusion.

Even worse, it had not been his fault. He had been misled by a crew of overzealous—and ultimately incompetent—advisers. The original budget plan I had devised for him had been fatally flawed. It is even harder to eat crow when you haven't cooked it yourself.

The situation was now a pathetic parody of the warning he had issued to the politicians in his September Offensive speech. The President could run, but he couldn't hide. Who would help him? Not the Democrats, who were sullen and revengeful; not the Republicans, who were hunkered down in their separate camps, frantic and confused. The only real option open to him was retreat. Economic reality and democratic fact had conspired to make it so. The American welfare state had found its permanent boundaries and the politicians had drawn their defensive perimeters. The laws of sound public finance and economics ruled out a free lunch— permanent continuation of the half-revolution embodied in the giant tax cut.

He had no choice but to repeal, or substantially dilute, the tax cut. That would have gone far toward restoring the stability of the strongest capitalist economy in the world. It would have been a great act of statesmanship to have admitted the error back then, but in the end it proved too mean a test. In November 1981, Ronald Reagan chose to be not a leader but a politician, and in so doing he showed why passion and imperfection, not reason and doctrine, rule the world. His obstinacy was destined to keep America's economy hostage to the errors of his advisers for a long, long time....

What came out of the OMB budget models when this new forecast was applied was horrifying. For 1982, the deficit figures *started* at $97 billion—more than double the $42 billion we had been straining for all year. The deficit for 1984, the year of our balanced budget, rose to $146 billion. After that the numbers just kept rising, until they reached $170 billion by 1986, the final year of our five-year fiscal plan.

Thus the new consensus economic forecast resulted in a budget which showed cumulative red ink over five years of more than *$700 billion*. That was nearly as much national debt as it had taken America two hundred years to accumulate. It just took your breath away. No government official had ever seen such a thing....

...I told Jim Baker that I was going to resign. I couldn't defend a planned trillion-dollar deficit; I couldn't defend no taxes; I couldn't defend a policy of fiscal know-nothingism.

"I can't make a fool of myself any longer, Jim," I told him. "This budget is so bad, it's beyond the pale."

Baker came back at me with a voice I hadn't heard since November 12, 1981. It was ice-cold.

"You do that and you'll stab the President right in the back," he said. "The Democrats will have a field day in the 1984 campaign.

"Let me remind you of something, my friend. He stuck by you. Now you stick by him. You've made as many mistakes as the rest of us around here. So stick that unwarranted pride of yours right up your ass, and get back in the trenches with the rest of us."

So I did, because I knew Jim was right. As I shuffled back to my office on that brisk January day in 1984, it seemed ironic that in only four years my Grand Doctrine for remaking the world had turned, finally, into a dutiful loyalty to nonsense. That was the worst lesson of all....

The fundamental reality of 1984 was not the advent of a new day, but a lapse into fiscal indiscipline on a scale never before experienced in peacetime. There is no basis in economic history or theory for believing that from this wobbly foundation a lasting era of prosperity can actually emerge.

Indeed, just beneath the surface the American economy was already being twisted and weakened by Washington's free lunch joy ride. Thanks to the half-revolution adopted in July 1981, more than a trillion dollars has already been needlessly added to our national debt—a burden that will plague us indefinitely. Our national savings has been squandered to pay for a tax cut we could not afford. We have consequently borrowed enormous amounts of foreign capital to make up for the shortfall between our national production and our national spending. Now, the U.S. economy will almost surely grow much more slowly than its potential in the decade ahead. By turning ourselves into a debtor nation for the first time since World War I, we have sacrificed future living standards in order to service the debts we have already incurred.

Borrowing these hundreds of billions of dollars has also distorted the whole warp and woof of the U.S. economy. The high dollar exchange rate that has been required to attract so much foreign capital has devastated our industries of agriculture, mining, and manufacturing. Jobs, capital, and production have been permanently lost.

All of this was evident in 1984, and so was its implication for the future. We had prosperity of a sort—but it rested on easy money and borrowed time. To lift the economy out of the recession against the weight of massive deficits and unprecedented real interest rates, the Fed has had to throw open the money spigots as never before. This in turn has stimulated an orgy of debt creation on the balance sheets of American consumers and corporations that is still gathering momentum today. Its magnitude is numbing. When the government sector's own massive debt is included, the nation will shortly owe $10 trillion—three times more than just a dozen years ago....

Some will be tempted to read into the failure of the Reagan Revolution more than is warranted. It represents the triumph of politics over a particular doctrine of economic governance and that is all. It does not mean American democracy is fatally flawed: special interest groups do wield great power, but their influence is deeply rooted in local popular support. Certainly, it does not mechanically guarantee the inevitability of permanent massive budget deficits or economic doom.

Its implications are deeply pessimistic only for the small and politically insignificant set of anti-statist conservatives who inhabit niches in the world of government, academia, business, and journalism. For us, there is no room for equivocation. The Reagan Revolution amounted to the clearest test of doctrine ever likely to occur in a heterogeneous democracy like our own. And the anti-statist position was utterly repudiated by the combined forces of the politicians—Republican and Democrat, those in the executive branch as well as the legislative.

This verdict has implications, however, which go well beyond the invalidation of anti-statist doctrine. The triumphant welfare state principle means that economic governance must consist of a fundamental trade-off between capitalist prosperity and social security. As a nation we have chosen to have less of the former in order to have more of the latter....

...Our budget is now drastically out of balance not because this condition is endemic to our politics. Rather, it is the consequence of an accident of governance which occurred in 1981. That it persists is due to the untenable anti-tax position of the White

House. After five years of presidential intransigence, all of the normal mechanisms of economic governance have become ensnared in a web of folly.... Extricating ourselves from the fiscal folly now upon the nation by means of an alternative legislative solution will test our institutions of governance and our political leaders as rarely before. Folly has begotten folly, and the web has become hopelessly entangled in a five-year history of action and reaction. But the politicians of both parties still have a sound and valid reason for disengaging from the Reagan Revolution's destructive aftermath. A radical change in national economic policy was not their idea; economic utopia was not their conception of what was possible in 1981 when the policies of the past collapsed. Republican and Democratic politicians together can tell the American people that a few ideologues made a giant mistake, and that the government the public wants will require greater sacrifices in the future in the form of the new taxes which must be levied.

The politicians can tell the American people that a dangerous experiment has been tried and an old lesson has been demonstrated once again. Economic governance of the world's greatest democracy has been shown to be a deadly serious business. There is no room in its equation for scribblers, dreamers, ideologues, and passionate young men bent upon remaking the world according to their own grand prescriptions. The truth to be remembered is that history in a democracy does not live to be rewritten and rerouted; it just lives for another day, finding its way into the future along the trajectory of its well-worn and palpable past....

In a way, the big tax increase we need will confirm the triumph of politics. But in a democracy the politicians must have the last word once it is clear that their course is consistent with the preferences of the electorate. The abortive Reagan Revolution proved that the American electorate wants a moderate social democracy to shield it from capitalism's rougher edges. Recognition of this in the Oval Office is all that stands between a tolerable economic future and one fraught with unprecedented perils.

94

LAWRENCE HAAS
The Deficit Culture

EVEN THE OLD-TIMERS couldn't remember when it happened before. Facing a tight budget next year and probably more down the road, the House Appropriations Committee on May 11 approved a fiscal 1989 energy and water bill that included no money to begin constructing dams and other projects. The House passed it a week later.

But it's not just new hometown projects that are scarcer for lawmakers these days. Money for old ones is also harder to protect. Two years after the Air Force, citing budget pressures, moved to cancel a $1.5 billion contract with Fairchild Republic Co. for 650 planes, Fairchild in early 1987 said that it would close shop in Farmingdale, N.Y. The plant, which had employed 3,000, now has 200 employees tying up loose ends.

Military bases, perhaps the most sacred of all hometown cows, could be next on the chopping block. For the first time in a decade, Congress may be ready to let a new commission, with members chosen by Defense Secretary Frank C. Carlucci III, decide which bases to close. The money saved would presumably be used to beef up the Pentagon's readiness accounts, which face severe fiscal constraints.

As the deficit alters policy making, so does it change the lives of those who make and influence policy in Washington. "Every Member likes to go to a testimonial dinner and get a plaque from some group that just got more funding," said Norman F. Lent, an 18-year House Republican from Long Island, who watched Fairchild's debacle helplessly. "I can't document it, but the occasions when you could announce a new program or a grant or deliver a check to a school district have dropped off."

In a sense, cultures are defined by the problems they face. For Washington, the deficit has become an all-consuming problem of perhaps unprecedented proportions. It establishes limits, if not straitjackets, for policy makers in the White House, Congress and the private sector. It shapes the day-to-day lives of lawmakers. It sets the strategies of lobbyists, and it limits their aspirations.

The deficit culture that has grown up around this problem has a distinct, undeniable tone: tentative, defensive, penurious, frustrated, gloomy. Issues that were once tackled with gusto are sidestepped, put off for another day or handed off to others. Supporters of existing programs withhold ideas for improving them for fear that negotiations could lead to cuts. Time is spent protecting the status quo.

With entrenched interests keeping programs in place, policy makers scrimp and save around the edges, slicing wherever they can. "Shared sacrifice," heard in any serious discussions about deficit reduction, means more mechanical, formulaic approaches, such as fixed-percentage, across-the-board cutting. New programs, if approved at all, get modest, sometimes barely adequate sums. Fiscal change comes only at the margins.

"There have been many issues that come on the horizon," said Stuart E. Eizenstat, President Carter's chief domestic policy adviser, citing energy as an example. "They have their time, and they're dealt with. I can't think of another issue [besides the budget deficit] that's been so pervasive and had such a dramatic effect on so many other issues." As a result, he said, "Washington has become a town where everyone is circling the wagons. You don't have the leeway to be creative."

Wendell Belew, who used to be the House Budget Committee's chief counsel, said: "What I've seen in the late '70s and '80s is a period of time really defined by a single consideration, a kind of brooding omnipresence over a whole array of issues.... I think there were periods before where broad issues did tend to dominate political discourse. Civil rights—that was an issue that pervaded Washington. The Vietnam war did, as well. It's hard, however, to find a period of time that is so dominated by a single issue."

A culture's origins are never easy to pinpoint. For the deficit culture, everybody has a watershed, a turning point in the past decade at which the deficit began affecting the business of official Washington as never before, when the city seemed like a different place because of it and when the lives of its participants had changed....

Whenever it arrived, the deficit is now a mainstream issue. Lawmakers who once boasted of pushing through new spending now brag as much about their cost-cutting prowess. A bipartisan

House group led by Timothy J. Penny (Democrat of Minnesota) and Thomas J. Tauke (Republican of Iowa) has made budget cutting a day-to-day challenge by targeting appropriations bills on the floor. Senator Phil Gramm (Republican of Texas) has done likewise by largely writing, and then using, the complex rules in the 1985 Balanced Budget Act.

Where the parties used to debate deficit spending as a policy issue, with Republicans clearly expressing more concern than Democrats, their messages, now hardly differ. As a House aide put it, you can't tell Democratic floor speeches from Republican ones. Nor can you on the presidential stump. All candidates at least pay lip service to deficit reduction. And even the most liberal candidates, such as Democrat Jesse Jackson, ponder such nonfederal financing sources as public pension funds.

The change is profound. People come to Washington to do things, to create, to innovate. As the Reagan years have demonstrated, liberals and conservatives now differ not on whether government spending is a legitimate policy tool but only on what it's a tool for: domestic or military spending. Either way, programs cost money. If, as Tauke said, Congress basically has three ways to make policy—spend, allocate tax breaks and regulate—the first two have been drastically curtailed, tying policy makers' hands.

At the same time, countervailing pressures on lawmakers have risen. Not only do they serve on about the same number of committees and subcommittees as they did when money flowed freely, but their staffs of young, policy-hungry aides are also larger than ever. Lawmakers also hear from more interest groups; the number of groups with Washington offices continues to rise, as does that of well-heeled political action committees. At least, say those who are looking for a silver lining, the deficit has provided an easy excuse for lawmakers to say no to many demands.

"You don't get the innovation, the excitement of creating a new, what you hope will be a great, solution to a national problem," said Senator Brock Adams (Democrat of Washington), who served in the House from 1965 to 1977. "I think it's shared among a number of people. I see around me people who say, 'You just can't do anything.' "...

The wrenching process of deficit reduction has concentrated budgeting into fewer hands, leading to more frustration among rank-and-file Members.

While the budget occupies more time of Congress as a whole,

the most important decisions are left for omnibus appropriations and deficit-cutting "reconciliation" measures, for which key party and committee leaders choose what to include.

With some exceptions, the policy-making authorizing committees have been relegated to second fiddle, their chairmen forced to lobby party leaders to include their panels' bills in the year-end omnibus measures. Though their actions violate congressional rules, appropriators are more inclined than ever to make policy themselves in spending bills; last year's changes in energy and highway policy and the airplane smoking ban are good examples. Other Members have caught on; the competition for seats on the Budget, Appropriations and taxwriting committees has risen as interest in some once-major authorizing panels, such as House Education and Labor, has waned.

Frustration with the budget process is bubbling over, particularly in the Senate, where long debates over annual budget resolution have left little floor time for policy making. Nearly half of all Members responding to a survey last year by the Center on Responsive Politics said the process had weakened policy making in their committees. Two-thirds of Senators held that view. Many Members have declared their intention to oppose omnibus measures.

Governors, who once used their offices as stepping-stones to the Senate, now show less interest in moving to Washington. "I could tell you there is a reluctance by governors, I think, to go to the Senate," said Raymond C. Sheppach, executive director of the National Governors' Association. "And part of the reason is, what can you get done?... Governors are generally in and out of Washington. They spend time on the Hill. They see the frustration. They talk about it."

Deficit cutting has made Washington a defensive city, on and off Capitol Hill. Advocates spend more time protecting their largesse than seeking more. They check out "hit lists" prepared by federal agencies, such as the Congressional Budget Office (CBO), and by think tanks and private groups and marshal their forces against proposed cuts. Instead of considering proposals for policy changes, staff members of authorizing committees spend more time monitoring the budget resolution, trying to stave off proposed cuts in their committees' programs.

As advocates hunker down for the annual spending battles, deficit cutting takes either two paths: First, there are formulaic approaches, where programs "on the table" take across-the-board spending cuts, perhaps exemplified by the 1985 Balanced Budget Act, which mandates such reductions if deficit targets aren't reached. Second, while few federal programs are eliminated outright (the $4.6 billion-a-year general revenue sharing program, terminated in 1986, is a notable exception), they are slashed, squeezed or nibbled at year after year....

Even if their programs end up with tiny amounts of money, saving them is vital to advocates in the current environment. Once eliminated, they'd be nearly impossible to restart, as the advocates of a refurbished revenue sharing program have found. But, if they're still alive, there's always a remote chance that in a prosperous future, funds can be restored.

"The Congress, outside of social security, medicare and a few other big programs, has cut the budget fairly successfully, but by penny-pinching everywhere, not so much by eliminating programs," said Charles L. Schultze, chairman of Carter's Council of Economic Advisers and President Johnson's budget director....

What's largely missing from all this are decisions about bold, new directions. The nation keeps the programs it has. But as the domestic discretionary (or nonentitlement) share of the budget shrinks in inflation-adjusted terms, there's hardly room for new ones.

So, rather than creating anew, the challenge is on managing what's here. "What we have to do is say, 'How can we effectively use the money that we have in a better way?'" said Representative Ralph Regula (Republican of Ohio), an Appropriations Committee member. "I think we are challenged at this point to deliver better government, and not necessarily more government."...

The chairmen of the tax-writing House Ways and Means and Senate Finance Committees have played key roles. Facing the prospect of bruising battles over budget busters, particularly on the Senate floor, where points of order can be invoked, they've demanded that bills approved by their committees be "revenue-neutral."

Revenue neutrality, institutionalized by Reagan's dictum against using tax reform (eventually enacted in the 1986 Tax Reform Act) to raise taxes, helped then-Finance Committee chairman Bob Packwood (Republican of Oregon), guide his version of tax reform through his committee and the full Senate. With each sponsor of a proposed tax break required to offer ways to pay for it, the fervor for such breaks was severely constrained by the difficulty of finding politically acceptable offsets.

Today, revenue neutrality is perhaps even more inhibiting to tax policy. With much of the debris of the tax code cleaned out by the 1986 law, and with the remaining deductions popular enough to survive that process, it's harder than ever for lawmakers to curtail some existing tax breaks in the interest of expanding or instituting others....

On the spending side, the search for ways to finance new programs can be just as vexing. Proposals that result in any net losses to the Treasury are brushed off by many as unrealistic....

New programs today? On the domestic side, if enacted at all, they tend to start at only $10 million, $100 million, perhaps $500 million, when the need is considered huge. After enactment, even the more pressing items aren't safe from budget-cutting efforts....

With annual deficit targets as constraints, investments are harder to push through. A proposal that might save money down the road, such as child care, is nevertheless problematic if it includes a first-year investment of "seed" money. Although Washington pays attention to future-year costs and savings, it budgets annually. Multiyear budgeting, often endorsed as a way to unclog Congress's jammed schedule, could open up policymaking opportunities if deficit targets didn't have to be met every year....

For lobbyists, effective advocacy now entails providing proof of ... long-term savings. It also calls for slimmed-down requests for spending increases in a few, well-targeted programs. Sweeping wish lists, often fulfilled when 1970s-era inflation was generating more and more federal receipts, aren't taken seriously today....

"When you go in and talk to Members, it's important that you're able to talk about priorities in a realistic way," said Ellen Nissenbaum, the legislative director for the Center on Budget and Policy Priorities. "You don't go in with 25 programs.... So what we've been able to do is talk about targeted, effective and preventive programs that we think ought to be their priorities when they look at this."

Even the fiercest spending advocates see a bright side in this. With so much scrutiny of programs, waste becomes harder to justify. The demise of general revenue sharing was linked to its allocation formula, in which even the wealthiest localities—Beverly Hills, for example, or Montgomery County, Maryland—received aid....

With spending and tax options severely limited, regulation has

become a more appealing policy tool. Washington is shifting burdens and responsibilities to business or to state and local governments, either by mandating certain actions or simply leaving business or states and localities as the obvious places for advocates to
turn. . . .

With the government's money problems likely to continue,
federal efforts at burden-shifting seem likely to intensify. Whether
businesses, states and local governments can convince Washington
otherwise is open to question. "There's going to be a lot of friction
over the next few years," Eizenstat predicted. "Somebody is going
to pay."

PART SIXTEEN

Public Welfare

THE WELFARE STATE came later to America
than to any other Western industrial democracy; for all practical
purposes there was nothing there before the passage of the Social
Security Act in 1935. Yet, over the last half century it has grown
steadily to become an enterprise of monumental proportions.
Americans, like modern democratic citizens the world over, have
come to expect the state to assume extensive responsibility for
education, unemployment compensation, health care, retirement
income, insurance against many kinds of loss (e.g., farm crops or
bank savings), and, of course, the needs of the poor, who continue
to be with us despite our general affluence. Here again, however,
we must note an American "differentness" that is more apparent
to foreigners than to ourselves. Even Canadians looking to the
south perceive it immediately. Our welfare state *is* comparatively
less extensive than that of other Western democracies. The United
States is, for example, the only industrial democracy yet to install
a comprehensive system of national health insurance. But more
important, the very idea of an American welfare state rests on a
shaky ideological foundation. It exists, but it is only marginally
legitimate. To understand why this is so, we have to return to our

first subject in these readings—American ideology.

The American ideology, as we have seen, is strongly individualist. It places very strong emphasis on individual freedom, and it holds that opportunity is available for all who will take it. If social mobility is available through individual effort, why should there be need for government to redistribute wealth or income? It is especially difficult in American ideological terms to explain why any worthy individual should remain poor. Oddly enough, both aristocratic conservatism with its ethic of noblesse oblige and the socialist ideology of workers in industrial societies with sharp class distinctions provide an *ideational* support for the welfare state that is lacking in American liberalism. Two centuries after its founding, the United States retains a strong element of its classical liberal heritage. Operationally, Americans want the welfare state, but in theory they are often unable to justify it—especially when it is attacked in the pure language of classical liberalism. This is no doubt why Democrats prefer to talk in practical language about "government helping people" while Republicans prefer to talk in more abstract terms about individualism, opportunity, and the evils of big government. The American people agree with both, and they can go either way depending on their mood at the time. Polls illustrate this ambivalent state of mind in a fascinating way. Ask about "welfare" in abstract terms and you get one answer; ask about "helping the needy" and you get another.

Anyone seriously trying to understand the "differentness" of the American welfare state and its politics must also come to grips with the subject of race. For whatever reasons black Americans remain disproportionately poor, and not surprisingly, since the 1930s they have been consistently much more approving than white Americans of policies designed to benefit the less fortunate. In the United States ethnic and racial divisions have been much more important than social class divisions, and they have seldom been more apparent than in discussions of welfare politics. There is no way to know how different the politics of social welfare would be without the element of race, but we must suppose that the difference would be substantial. At times (particularly since the late 1960s) such key programs of the American welfare state as Aid to Families with Dependent Children (AFDC) and the Food Stamp Program have been discussed as if the vast majority of their beneficiaries were black. This is very far from the truth of the matter, but in democratic politics perception is reality. There is every reason to believe that the politics of race and the politics of social welfare will continue to be closely related in years to come. In no other Western democracy do racial considerations influence discussions of social welfare to this extent.

Our readings on welfare policy begin with a selection from Michael Harrington's *The Other America,* a book that almost single-handedly put the subject of "poverty" on the national political agenda in the early 1960s. Harrington's analysis provided much of the intellectual thrust behind the Johnson administration's famous War on Poverty. The poor in our affluent society, Harrington argues, are politically invisible. For the first time in history they are a small minority, out of sight and out of mind. Without organizations to articulate their interests, they are without a voice in pluralist politics. The federal government, then, must act largely on the basis of public "vision" and "sensitivity" to plan a nation-wide program to eradicate poverty. The program should not be centrally controlled, but rather implemented through "myriad institutions" as close as possible to local problems. The Johnson administration would follow this recommendation exactly in designing its War on Poverty.

In our second selection Harrington returns to his subject some twenty years later. In the middle of the Reagan years Harrington sees "a structural economic crisis, the most severe that we have known in almost a century." Now, the nonpoor as well as the poor are threatened by economic decline and what he sees as benighted governmental policies. As more and more people perceive that they can become "them," Harrington hopes that a broad coalition of the middle class and the poor will see the need for a social democratic politics at last. If they do not, he foresees a grim future in which the middle class will shrink, the rich will have to rely on electronic security, and the increasingly demoralized lower orders will engage in sporadic violence.

George Gilder's perspective on these matters in our next reading is so at odds with Harrington's (although it also was written in the Reagan years) that we may wonder how it is possible for two intelligent people to perceive the same world so differently. The short, but mainly correct, answer to this question is that they have utterly different ideological orientations. Harrington is one of the few prominent American social commentators to proudly identify himself as a democratic socialist. Gilder, just as proudly, identifies with the "new capitalism" of the Reagan era. Gilder does not deny that there are many poor people in American society, but he argues that redistributionist policies are not the answer to their problems. The *only* route up from poverty, he argues, is "always work, family, and faith." In Gilder's perspective people work for income and enjoy leisure. If they can get these things for nothing, they will opt to do so. The poor need to marry, lead conventional lives, accept responsibilities, and work hard. The cure for poverty in America and elsewhere is a belief in a "spirit of work and enterprise" shared by European classical liberals and the founders of American society. There must be "faith in man, faith in the future, faith in the rising returns of giving, faith in the mutual benefits of trade, [and] faith in the providence of God ...".

Our final two readings deal specifically with the problems of the black poor in America. Thomas Sowell, a black economist, believes that while black Americans have had a historically unique experience of discrimination in this society, the answer to the current problems of the black poor is not to be found in what he calls the "civil rights vision." While it is clearly the case that the average income of blacks is far lower than that of whites, Sowell sees the cause of this disparity in cultural differences that must be addressed if poor blacks are to overcome poverty. Today, he maintains, young black husband–wife families outside the South have incomes virtually identical to those of their white counterparts. The answer lies, then, in achieving family stability and middle–class morality in the black community. Sowell's position, you will see, has a good deal in common with Gilder's. Not only does he believe that government programs are not the answer to the problem of black poverty, he suggests that the policies advocated by civil rights leaders have actually contributed to a "decline in community and personal standards ... and in family responsibility" in the black community.

Our last selection, by the Joint Center for Political Studies, an organization that has done as much as any other to promote systematic analysis of the black community in America, argues that the worsening problems of the black urban "underclass"—poverty, crime, poor schooling, drug abuse, illegitimacy, female–headed households, etc.—cannot be successfully met without federal programs. Black Americans, the Center argues, have always embraced the central values of this society. While black self–help is important, this perspective sees continuing need for government policies to create jobs, better schools, affordable housing, social services, and so on. From this perspective the "present posture of passivity and abdication" of the federal government must be abandoned in favor of a much more active federal effort to achieve social welfare.

These readings make no attempt to paper over the real disagreements that characterize discussions of welfare policy in the 1980s. This is a subject on which intelligent people can and do greatly differ. If these points of view do not provoke spirited discussion, it would be hard to know what would.

95

MICHAEL HARRINGTON
The Invisible Land: Poverty in America

From *The Other America*

———

THERE IS a familiar America. It is celebrated in speeches and advertised on television and in the magazines. It has the highest mass standard of living the world has ever known.

In the 1950s this America worried about itself, yet even its anxieties were products of abundance. The title of a brilliant book was widely misinterpreted, and the familiar America began to call itself "the affluent society." There was introspection about Madison Avenue and tail fins; there was discussion of the emotional suffering taking place in the suburbs. In all this, there was an implicit assumption that the basic grinding economic problems had been solved in the United States. In this theory the nation's problems were no longer a matter of basic human needs, of food, shelter, and clothing. Now they were seen as qualitative, a question of learning to live decently amid luxury.

While this discussion was carried on, there existed another America. In it dwelt somewhere between 40,000,000 and 50,-000,000 citizens of this land. They were poor. They still are.

To be sure, the other America is not impoverished in the same sense as those poor nations where millions cling to hunger as a defense against starvation. This country has escaped such extremes. That does not change the fact that tens of millions of Americans are, at this very moment, maimed in body and spirit, existing at levels beneath those necessary for human decency. If these people are not starving, they are hungry, and sometimes fat with hunger, for that is what cheap foods do. They are without adequate housing and education and medical care.

The Government has documented what this means to the bodies of the poor, and the figures will be cited throughout this book. But even more basic, this poverty twists and deforms the spirit. The American poor are pessimistic and defeated, and they are victimized by mental suffering to a degree unknown in Suburbia.

This book is a description of the world in which these people live; it is about the other America. Here are the unskilled workers, the migrant farm workers, the aged, the minorities, and all the others who live in the economic underworld of American life....

The millions who are poor in the United States tend to become increasingly invisible. Here is a great mass of people, yet it takes an effort of the intellect and will even to see them....

...The other America, the America of poverty, is hidden today in a way that it never was before. Its millions are socially invisible to the rest of us. No wonder that so many misinterpreted Galbraith's title and assumed that "the affluent society" meant that everyone had a decent standard of life. The misinterpretation was true as far as the actual day-to-day lives of two-thirds of the nation were concerned. Thus, one must begin a description of the other America by understanding why we do not see it.

There are perennial reasons that make the other America an invisible land.

Poverty is often off the beaten track. It always has been....

...The American city has been transformed. The poor still inhabit the miserable housing in the central area, but they are increasingly isolated from contact with, or sight of, anybody else. Middle-class women coming in from Suburbia on a rare trip may catch the merest glimpse of the other America on the way to an evening at the theater, but their children are segregated in suburban schools. The business or professional man may drive along the fringes of slums in a car or bus, but it is not an important experience to him. The failures, the unskilled, the disabled, the aged, and the minorities are right there, across the tracks, where they have always been. But hardly anyone else is.

In short, the very development of the American city has removed poverty from the living, emotional experience of millions upon millions of middle-class Americans. Living out in the suburbs, it is easy to assume that ours is, indeed, an affluent society.

This new segregation of poverty is compounded by a well-meaning ignorance. A good many concerned and sympathetic Americans are aware that there is much discussion of urban renewal. Suddenly, driving through the city, they notice that a familiar slum has been torn down and that there are towering, modern buildings where once there had been tenements or hovels. There is a warm feeling of satisfaction, of pride in the way things are working out: the poor, it is obvious, are being taken care of....

And finally, the poor are politically invisible. It is one of the cruelest ironies of social life in advanced countries that the dispossessed at the bottom of society are unable to speak for themselves. The people of the other America do not, by far and large, belong to unions, to fraternal organizations, or to political parties. They are without lobbies of their own; they put forward no legislative program. As a group, they are atomized. They have no face; they have no voice.

Thus, there is not even a cynical political motive for caring about the poor, as in the old days. Because the slums are no longer centers of powerful political organizations, the politicians need not really care about their inhabitants. The slums are no longer visible to the middle class, so much of the idealistic urge to fight for those who need help is gone. Only the social agencies have a really direct involvement with the other America, and they are without any great political power....

Indeed, the paradox that the welfare state benefits those least who need help most is but a single instance of a persistent irony in the other America. Even when the money finally trickles down, even when a school is built in a poor neighborhood, for instance, the poor are still deprived. Their entire environment, their life, their values, do not prepare them to take advantage of the new opportunity. The parents are anxious for the children to go to work; the pupils are pent up, waiting for the moment when their education has complied with the law.

Today's poor, in short, missed the political and social gains of the thirties. They are, as Galbraith rightly points out, the first minority poor in history, the first poor not to be seen, the first poor whom the politicans could leave alone....

What shall we tell the Amercian poor, once we have seen them? Shall we say to them that they are better off than the Indian poor, the Italian poor, the Russian poor? That is one answer, but it is heartless. I should put it another way. I want to tell every well-fed and optimistic American that it is intolerable that so many millions should be maimed in body and in spirit when it is not necessary that they should be. My standard of comparison is not how much worse things used to be. It is how much better they could be if only we were stirred....

First and foremost, any attempt to abolish poverty in the United States must seek to destroy the pessimism and fatalism that flourish in the other America. In part, this can be done by offering real opportunities to these people, by changing the social reality that gives rise to their sense of hopelessness. But beyond that (these fears of the poor have a life of their own and are not simply rooted in analyses of employment chances), there should be a spirit, an élan, that communicates itself to the entire society.

If the nation comes into the other America grudgingly, with the mentality of an administrator, and says, "All right, we'll help you people," then there will be gains, but they will be kept to the minimum; a dollar spent will return a dollar. But if there is an attitude that society is gaining by eradicating poverty, if there is a positive attempt to bring these millions of the poor to the point where they can make their contribution to the United States, that will make a huge difference. The spirit of a campaign against poverty does not cost a single cent. It is a matter of vision, of sensitivity....

Second, this book is based upon the proposition that poverty forms a culture, an interdependent system. In case after case, it has been documented that one cannot deal with the various components of poverty in isolation, changing this or that condition but leaving the basic structure intact. Consequently, a campaign against the misery of the poor should be comprehensive. It should think, not in terms of this or that aspect of poverty, but along the lines of establishing new communities, of substituting a human environment for the inhuman one that now exists....

There is only one institution in the society capable of acting to abolish poverty. That is the Federal Government. In saying this, I do not rejoice, for centralization can lead to an impersonal and bureaucratic program, one that will be lacking in the very human quality so essential in an approach to the poor. In saying this, I am only recording the facts of political and social life in the United States. . . .

[However] it is not necessary to advocate complete central control of such a campaign. Far from it. Washington is essential in a double sense: as a source of the considerable funds needed to mount a campaign against the other America, and as a place for coordination, for planning, and the establishment of national standards. The actual implementation of a program to abolish poverty can be carried out through myriad institutions, and the closer they are to the specific local area, the better the results. There are, as has been pointed out already, housing administrators, welfare workers, and city planners with dedication and vision. They are working on the local level, and their main frustration is the lack of funds. They could be trusted actually to carry through on a national program. What they lack now is money and the support of the American people. . . .

There is no point in attempting to blueprint or detail the mechanisms and institutions of a war on poverty in the United States. There is information enough for action. All that is lacking is political will. . . .

These, then, are the strangest poor in the history of mankind.

They exist within the most powerful and rich society the world has ever known. Their misery has continued while the majority of the nation talked of itself as being "affluent" and worried about neuroses in the suburbs. In this way tens of millions of human beings became invisible. They dropped out of sight and out of mind; they were without their own political voice.

Yet this need not be. The means are at hand to fulfill the age-old dream: poverty can now be abolished. How long shall we ignore this underdeveloped nation in our midst? How long shall we look the other way while our fellow human beings suffer? How long?

96

MICHAEL HARRINGTON

From *The New American Poverty*

———

THE POOR are still there.

Two decades after the President of the United States declared an "unconditional" war on poverty, poverty does not simply continue to exist; worse, we must deal with structures of misery, with a new poverty much more tenacious than the old....

The great, impersonal forces have indeed created a context in which poverty is much more difficult to abolish than it was twenty years ago. But it is not the South Koreans—or the Japanese, the West Germans, or anyone else—who have decided that the human costs of this wrenching transition should be borne by the most vulnerable Americans. We have done that to ourselves.

One reason is that this economic upheaval did not simply strike at the poor. It had an enormous impact on everyone else and, among many other things, changed the very eyes of the society. In the sixties there was economic growth, political and social movement, hope. What was shocking was that poverty existed at all, and the very fact that it did was an incitement to abolish it. I simplify, of course. Even then, as I pointed out in *The Other America,* suburbanization was removing the middle class from daily contact with the poor. In our geography, as in our social structure, we were becoming two nations....

In the eighties it is not simply that structural economic change has created new poverties and given old poverties a new lease on life. That very same process has impaired the national vision; misery has simultaneously become more intractable and more difficult to see....

...More broadly, where the sixties spoke of possibilities, the eighties were forced to become aware of limits, which some assumed, wrongly, were ugly necessities to be imposed on those at the bottom of the society. In the process, America has lost its own generous vision of what it might be.

That is why, among many other things, this book cannot be *The Other America Revisited....*

...The next time we will have to be as innovative in fact as the sixties were in rhetoric. If we are not, when we are faced with a much more difficult battle than that of the sixties, we will fail again. And once more it will be poverty that wins the war....

...The Chinese ideograph for crisis is composed of the symbols for two words: danger and hope.

That accurately describes these times. The old poverty—the pace of social and economic time is accelerated and I am talking of the ancient days twenty and thirty years ago—seemed to be an exception to the basic trends of the society. Everyone was progressing steadily; a minority had been left behind. Therefore it would be a rather simple matter to deduct some few billions as they poured out of our industrial cornucopia and to use them to abolish the "pockets" of poverty. But the new poverty I have described in this book is quite different. It is, in complex ways, precisely the extreme consequence of tendencies that are transforming the entire society. To repeat, one reason why young men in the winter of 1983 had to ask New York City for beds for the night was that there were steel mills in South Korea, a fact that also menaced relatively well-paid trade unionists and even corporate executives.

This is the great danger confronting the new poor. If their plight is not an anomaly of the affluent society but the outcome of massive economic trends, why will the majority undertake the fairly radical changes that are needed in order to help a minority that is either not seen, despised, or feared? In the sixties, people thought that the struggle against poverty was going to be a lovely little war. But if, in the eighties, the poor and their friends explain that it is going to be a difficult and arduous struggle, who will respond, particularly when everyone is concerned about how it will affect him personally?

In that very real danger there is also hope. The majority of the people of the United States cannot possibly make themselves secure unless they also help the poor. That is, the very measures that will most benefit the working people and the middle class—the rich will take care of themselves, as they always have—will also strike a blow against poverty. That is by no means an automatic process; there are specific measures that have to be worked out to deal with particular problems of the poor. But basically the programs that are in the self-interest of the majority are always in the special interest of the poor....

...An increase in compassion and caring is essential, and for all of the simplifications of the early sixties, those were generous years, which does them credit. But in addition to affirming that we are indeed our sisters' and our brothers' keepers, it must also be said that the abolition of poverty requires programs—above all, full employment—that will probably do more for the nonpoor than for the poor. One is not asking men and women who have troubles enough of their own to engage in a noblesse oblige that is, in any case, patronizing. One appeals to both their decency and their interest....

...The nation is in a structural economic crisis, the most severe that we have known in almost a century. The overwhelming majority of the nonpoor are at least threatened by the same massive trends that have done so much to create a new poverty. The programs that are in their interest, above all full employment, are profoundly in the interest of the new poor. At the same time, there is no single group in the country that can, by its own unaided effort, resolve the crisis for itself. If all of the trade unionists (20 percent of the work force) or all of the blacks (12 percent of the population) or all of the poor (15 to 20 percent of the nation) mobilized independently, they would clearly fail. On the other hand, there is a community of interest between middle-class feminist activists and impoverished female heads of families: both need the transformation of an occupational structure that, in radically different ways, penalizes both. The building-trades worker, the underclass member, and even the distraught former mental patient have a common interest in affordable housing....

...So long as those at the bottom and middle of the society squabble over insufficient resources, all lose. There has to be genuine cooperation and a commitment to generating sufficient resources that will allow all to win.

This is one of the many political reasons why full employment is such a critical demand. It will not automatically eliminate all of the structures of misery that have grown up in the past two decades. But it is clearly the precondition for doing just that.

It is wrong, however, to put all of this simply in economic terms, with an emphasis on the intersecting self-interests of different groups. There is a moral dimension to the issue as well. As noted, the idealism of the sixties and the cynicism of the eighties are, in considerable measure, social products. Economics and ethics are not located in separate and sealed compartments. If there are economic policies that make moral concerns more likely, then a powerful lever for the organization of people in the battle against the new poverty is human solidarity. . . .

An antipoverty politics must be coalitional, with full employment as a central goal, and must awaken the latent moral idealism of the nation in the service of a very specific program.

Will it happen? The danger that it will not is great; the structures of misery are much more menacing today than they were in the sixties. There could be a revolution without revolutionaries, an unwitting transformation of the conditions of human existence that would preserve the worst of the past in a fantasy future. There would be custodial care for the suffering of increasing numbers of superfluous people, and electronic security would become a growth industry, protecting the elite from the sporadic, unorganized violence of a disconsolate, demoralized stratum at the bottom of the society. The gulf between the two nations—that of the rich and that of the poor—would deepen, since there would be an occupational void in what had once been the middle ground of the economy. . . .

. . . The danger in that Chinese ideograph of crisis is palpable, already here.

But there is reason for hope. In the sixties, the best people thought they were doing something for "them"—the blacks, the Appalachians, the truly *other* Americans. But now, more and more people are discovering that they, too, are "them." I do not mean to imply for a moment that the majority of Americans have become poor or will do so in the near future. I merely but emphatically insist that there is a growing sense of insecurity in the society, and for good reason. The very trends that have helped to create the new structure of misery for the poor are the ones that bewilder that famous middle of the American society, the traditional bastion of our complacency. And perhaps that middle will learn one of the basic lessons this book has tried to impart: A new campaign for social decency is not simply good and moral, but is also a necessity if we are to solve the problems that bedevil not just the poor, but almost all of us.

If we do understand that point, perhaps we will do something more profound than simply to discover an enlightened self-interest. Perhaps in the process we will discover a new vision of ourselves that rises above our individual needs and unites us in a common purpose. Perhaps that pilgrimage toward the fullness of our humanity will begin once again.

97

GEORGE GILDER

The Nature of Poverty

From *Wealth and Poverty*

—◆—

LIVING IN a world of wealth, the upper classes of Americans have long listened straight-faced and unboggled to the most fantastic tales from the world of the poor. Although inclined to accept Ernest Hemingway's assurances that the rich differ from us chiefly in having more money, we have been willing to suppose that the poor were some alien tribe, exotic in culture and motivation, who can be understood only through the channels of credentialed expertise.

It helped that many of the poor were black. They looked different; perhaps they were different. There came forth a series of authoritative fables: blacks are allegedly matriarchal by nature; like the Irish, the Jews, and other urban immigrants before them, their IQ's were shown to be genetically lower (possibly, in the case of blacks, because of cramped cranial spaces); and they were found to be markedly prone to violent crime and slovenly living. Nonetheless, we could not judge them, it was said by those of liberal spirit, without being guilty of ethnocentrism or cultural imperialism. A propensity for violence, low intelligence, and fatherless homes, it was implied, constitutes a reasonable adaptation to poverty from which we may all learn much.

This attitude, however, required a spirit of cultural relativism so heroic that it could not serve for long, particularly in political formulations. So new approaches emerged, allegedly more enlightened, but with implications equally farfetched. Slavery, discrimination, and deprivation, it was said, have so abused the black psyche that all sorts of new ministrations and therapies are needed to redeem it; racism and unemployment still inflict such liabilities that vast new programs of public employment and affirmative action are required to overcome them. The reasonable inference arises that even though blacks are not genetically inferior, science proves them to be so damaged by racism and poverty that they are inferior now.

Not only do these notions cause serious strain to the spirit of liberalism when confronting specific specimens of this maimed but deserving race, but such attitudes also perpetuate the idea that the poor, for whatever reason, are still very different from us. This belief permits a series of new fables to arise, some explicit, most implicit in government programs.

For example, most of us work for money and enjoy leisure. The poor, it is implied, despite their generally more onerous jobs, do not. They so lust for labor, so they tell all inquiring scholars, that their willingness to work is unaffected by levels of welfare and in-kind support substantially higher than the available wage; they even clamor to enter the work force in the face of effective tax rates on work (through reductions in welfare payments) of nearly 100 percent.

All American ethnic groups in the past rose out of poverty partly by learning English and downplaying their own languages. The current foreign poor, mostly Hispanic, are thought to require instruction chiefly in their native tongue, for reasons of ethnic pride.

Middle-class Americans are demonstrably devastated by divorce and separation: they leave their jobs, income plummets, health deteriorates; they drink and philander; their children behave badly in school. But the poor and their children are assumed to be relatively unshaken by a plague of family breakdowns; at least any resulting lower income and employment levels are said to be due to discrimination, and the behavior of the children is regarded to be little influenced by the absence of fathers.

Most American men earn more money than their wives; men that don't tend to leave, or be left, in large numbers. Yet poor men are assumed to be unaffected by the higher relative incomes available to their wives from welfare and affirmative action, which are alleged to have no relationship to high rates of unemployment and illegitimacy.

Perhaps most important of all, every successful ethnic group in our history rose up by working harder than other classes, in low-paid jobs, with a vanguard of men in entrepreneurial roles. But the current poor, so it is supposed, can leapfrog drudgery by education and credentials, or be led as a group from poverty, perhaps by welfare mothers trained for government jobs. These views depict the current poor as a race so alien to the entire American experience, so radically different in motive and character from whites, that one can speak in terms of a new form of bigotry....

...The prevailing expressed opinion is that racism and discrimination still explain the low incomes of blacks. This proposition is at once false and invidious. Not only does it slander white Americans, it deceives and demoralizes blacks. Not only does it obstruct the truth, it encourages, by its essential incredibility, the alternate falsehood, held in private by many blacks and whites, that blacks cannot now make it in America without vast federal assistance, without, indeed, the very government programs that in fact account for the worst aspects of black poverty and promise to perpetuate it. Finally, the liberal belief in bigotry as an explanation for the condition of blacks leads to still more preposterous theories about the alleged poverty of other groups, from women to Hispanics, and to a generally manic-depressive vision of the economy, in which poverty is seen both as more extreme and more remediable than it is.

The first thing to understand is that regardless of the affluence of the American economy, we live in a world full of poor people. Modern transport and communications ensure that increasing numbers will be both eager and able to reach our shores. Unless we wish to adopt an immoral and economically self-destructive policy of prohibiting immigration, there will be poverty in America for centuries to come. The policies and approaches we have adopted in our neurotic concern about blacks will likely be applied to many millions of others. The potential injury that could be inflicted on our economy and on the poor people in it is quite incalculable. But, on the basis of the long and thoroughly unambiguous experience of our government in blighting the lives of blacks and Indians, one can only predict that the damage will be tragically great.

To get a grip on the problems of poverty, one should also forget the idea of overcoming inequality by redistribution. Inequality may even grow at first as poverty declines. To lift the incomes of the poor, it will be necessary to increase the rates of investment, which in turn will tend to enlarge the wealth, if not the consumption, of the rich. The poor, as they move into the work force and acquire promotions, will raise their incomes by a greater percentage than the rich; but the upper classes will gain by greater absolute amounts, and the gap between the rich and the poor may grow. All such analyses are deceptive in the long run, however, because they imply a static economy in which the *numbers* of the rich and the middle class are not growing.

In addition, inequality may be favored by the structure of a modern economy as it interacts with demographic change. When the division of labor becomes more complex and refined, jobs grow more specialized; and the increasingly specialized workers may win greater rents for their rare expertise, causing their incomes to rise relative to common labor. This tendency could be heightened by a decline in new educated entrants to the work force, predictable through the 1990s, and by an enlarged flow of immigration, legal and illegal. Whatever the outcome of these developments, an effort to take income from the rich, thus diminishing their investment, and to give it to the poor, thus reducing their work incentives, is sure to cut American productivity, limit job opportunities, and perpetuate poverty....

The only dependable route from poverty is always work, family, and faith. The first principle is that in order to move up, the poor must not only work, they must work harder than the classes above them. Every previous generation of the lower class has made such efforts. But the current poor, white even more than black, are refusing to work hard. Irwin Garfinkel and Robert Haveman, authors of an ingenious and sophisticated study of what they call *Earnings Capacity Utilization Rates,* have calculated the degree to which various income groups use their opportunities—how hard they work outside the home. This study shows that, for several understandable reasons, the current poor work substantially less, for fewer hours and weeks a year, and earn less in proportion to their age, education, and other credentials (even *after* correcting the figures for unemployment, disability, and presumed discrimination) than either their predecessors in American cities or those now above them on the income scale.... The findings lend important confirmation to the growing body of evidence that work effort is the crucial unmeasured variable in American productivity and income distribution, and that current welfare and other subsidy programs substantially reduce work. The poor choose leisure not because of moral weakness, but because they are paid to do so....

...Because effective work consists not in merely fulfilling the requirements of labor contracts, but in "putting out" with alertness and emotional commitment, workers have to understand and feel deeply that what they are given depends on what they give—that they must supply work in order to demand goods. Parents and schools must inculcate this idea in their children both by instruction and example. Nothing is more deadly to achievement than the belief that effort will not be rewarded, that the world is a bleak and discriminatory place in which only the predatory and the specially preferred can get ahead. Such a view in the home discourages the work effort in school that shapes earnings capacity afterward. As with so many aspects of human performance, work effort begins in family experiences, and its sources can be best explored through an examination of family structure.

Indeed, after work the second principle of upward mobility is the maintenance of monogamous marriage and family. Adjusting for discrimination against women and for child-care responsibilities, the Wisconsin study indicates that married men work between two and one-third and four times harder than married women, and more than twice as hard as female family heads. The work effort of married men increases with their age, credentials, education, job experience, and birth of children, while the work effort of married women steadily declines. Most important in judging the impact of marriage, husbands work 50 percent harder than bachelors of comparable age, education, and skills.

The effect of marriage, thus, is to increase the work effort of men by about half. Since men have higher earnings capacity to begin with, and since the female capacity-utilization figures would be even lower without an adjustment for discrimination, it is manifest that the maintenance of families is the key factor in reducing poverty.

Once a family is headed by a woman, it is almost impossible for it to greatly raise its income even if the woman is highly educated and trained and she hires day-care or domestic help. Her family responsibilities and distractions tend to prevent her from the kind of all-out commitment that is necessary for the full use of earning power. Few women with children make earning money the top priority in their lives.

A married man, on the other hand, is spurred by the claims of family to channel his otherwise disruptive male aggressions into his performance as a provider for a wife and children. These sexual differences alone, which manifest themselves in all societies known to anthropology, dictate that the first priority of any serious program against poverty is to strengthen the male role in poor families....

The short-sighted outlook of poverty stems largely from the breakdown of family responsibilities among fathers. The lives of the poor, all too often, are governed by the rhythms of tension and release that characterize the sexual experience of young single men. Because female sexuality, as it evolved over the millennia, is psychologically rooted in the bearing and nurturing of children, women have long horizons within their very bodies, glimpses of eternity within their wombs. Civilized society is dependent upon the submission of the short-term sexuality of young men to the extended maternal horizons of women. This is what happens in monogamous marriage; the man disciplines his sexuality and extends it into the future through the womb of a woman. The woman gives him access to his children, otherwise forever denied him; and he gives her the product of his labor, otherwise dissipated on temporary pleasures. The woman gives him a unique link to the future and a vision of it; he gives her faithfulness and a commitment to a lifetime of hard work. If work effort is the first principle of overcoming poverty, marriage is the prime source of upwardly mobile work....

The key to the intractable poverty of the hardcore American poor is the dominance of single and separated men in poor communities. Black "unrelated individuals" are not much more likely to be in poverty than white ones. The problem is neither race nor matriarchy in any meaningful sense. It is familial anarchy among the concentrated poor of the inner city, in which flamboyant and impulsive youths rather than responsible men provide the themes of aspiration. The result is that male sexual rhythms tend to prevail, and boys are brought up without authoritative fathers in the home to instill in them the values of responsible paternity: the discipline and love of children and the dependable performance of the provider role....

An analysis of poverty that begins and ends with family structure and marital status would explain far more about the problem than most of the distributions of income, inequality, unemployment, education, IQ, race, sex, home ownership, location, discrimination, and all the other items usually multiply regressed and correlated on academic computers. But even an analysis of work and family would miss what is perhaps the most important of the principles of upward mobility under capitalism—namely, faith....

Faith in man, faith in the future, faith in the rising returns of giving, faith in the mutual benefits of trade, faith in the providence of God are all essential to successful capitalism. All are necessary to sustain the spirit of work and enterprise against the setbacks and frustrations it inevitably meets in a fallen world, to inspire trust and cooperation in an economy where they will often be betrayed; to encourage the forgoing of present pleasures in the name of a future that may well go up in smoke; to promote risk and initiative in a world where the rewards all vanish unless others join the game. In order to give without the assurance of return, in order to save without the certainty of future value, in order to work beyond the requirements of the job, one has to have confidence in a higher morality: a law of compensations beyond the immediate and distracting struggles of existence.... Faith, in all its multifarious forms and luminosities, can by itself move the mountains of sloth and depression that afflict the world's stagnant economies; it brought immigrants thousands of miles with pennies in their pockets to launch the American empire of commerce; and it performs miracles daily in our present impasse.

In general, however, upward mobility depends on all three principles—work, family, and faith—interdependently reaching toward children and future. These are the pillars of a free economy and a prosperous society....

These are the fundamental laws of economics, business, technology, and life. In them are the secret sources of wealth, and poverty.

98

THOMAS SOWELL
The Special Case of Blacks

From *Civil Rights: Rhetoric or Reality?*

———

BLACKS HAVE a history in the United States that is quite different from that of other American ethnic groups. The massive fact of slavery looms over more than half of that history. The Jim

Crow laws and policies, which not only segregated but discrimi-
nated, were still going strong in that part of the country where
most blacks lived, in the middle of the twentieth century. "Lynching" meant—almost invariably—the lynching of blacks by whites.
Blacks were widely believed to be genetically inferior in intelligence, both in the North and the South, long before Arthur Jensen's
writings on the subject appeared. James B. Conant's 1961 book,
Slums and Suburbs, reported a common assumption among school
officials around the country that black children were not capable
of learning as much as white children....

Given the unique—and uniquely oppressive—history of blacks,
it would follow almost inevitably from the civil rights vision that
blacks would today suffer far more than other groups from low
income, broken homes, and the whole litany of social pathology.
But like so many things that follow from the civil rights vision, it
happens not to be true in fact. Blacks do not have the lowest
income, the lowest educational level, or the most broken homes
among American ethnic groups. The habit of comparing blacks
with "the national average" conceals the fact that there are other
groups with very similar—and sometimes worse—social pathology. The national average is just one point on a wide-ranging
spectrum. It is not a norm showing where most individuals or
most groups are. The difference in income between Japanese Americans and Puerto Ricans is even greater than the difference between
blacks and whites, though most of the factors *assumed* to cause
black-white differences are not present in differences between Japanese Americans and Puerto Ricans....

In short, the historical uniqueness of blacks has not translated
into a contemporary uniqueness in incomes, occupations, I.Q.,
unemployment, female-headed households, alcoholism, or welfare
dependency, however much blacks may differ from the mythical
national average in these respects. All of these represent serious
difficulties (sometimes calamities) for blacks, and indirectly for the
larger society, but the question here is the *cause.* If that cause
is either a unique history or a unique genetics, blacks would
differ not only from the national average but also from other
groups that share neither that history nor the same genetic background....

Blacks and whites are not just people with different skin colors.
Nor is a history of slavery the only difference between them. Like

many other groups in contemporary America—and around the world and down through history—blacks and whites have different cultures that affect how they live individually and collectively. At the same time, there is sufficient overlap that some sets of blacks have a home life and family pattern very similar to those of most whites. Insofar as color is the over-riding factor in economic position, this will make relatively little difference in the incomes of such sets of blacks. Insofar as such cultural factors reflect traits that prove valuable and decisive in the marketplace, such sets of blacks should have incomes comparable to those of whites. . . .

A comparison of black and white male youths in 1969—again, before affirmative action—throws light on the role of color and culture. Harvard economist Richard Freeman compared blacks and whites whose homes included newspapers, magazines, and library cards, and who had also gone on to obtain the same number of years of schooling. There was no difference in the average income of these whites compared to these blacks. This had not always been true. In earlier periods, such cultural factors had little weight. But by 1969 it was true—during "equal opportunity" policies and before "affirmative action."

Home and family life differ in other ways between blacks and whites. Husband-wife families are more prevalent among whites than among blacks, though declining over time among both groups. About half of all black families with children are one-parent families, while more than four-fifths of all white families with children are two-parent families. But what of those black families that are two-parent families—more like the white families in this respect and perhaps in other respects as well? To the extent that racial discrimination is the crucial factor in depressing black income, there should be little difference between the incomes of these black families relative to their white counterparts than there is between the incomes of blacks and whites as a whole. But insofar as family structure reflects cultural values in general, those blacks whose family structure reflects more general norms of behavior should be more fortunate in the job market as well.

For more than a decade, young black husband-wife families outside the South have had incomes virtually identical to those of young white husband-wife families outside the South. In some years black families of this description have had incomes a few percentage points higher than their white counterparts. Today, where husbands and wives are both college-educated, and both working, black families of this description earn slightly *more* than white families of this description—nationwide and without regard to age.

The implication of all this is not, of course, that blacks as a group are doing as well as whites as a group—or are even close to doing as well. On the contrary. The average income of blacks as a group remains far behind the average income of whites as a group. What we are trying to find out is the extent to which this is due to cultural differences rather than color differences that call forth racism and discrimination....

Anyone who has been privileged to live through the past generation of changes among blacks knows that there have been many changes that cannot be quantified. One need only listen to an interview with a Bill Russell or an O. J. Simpson, or many other articulate black athletes today, and compare that with interviews with black athletes of a generation ago, to appreciate just one symptom of a profound transformation that has affected a wide segment of the black population.

It may be understandable that black politicans and civil rights organizations would want to claim the lion's share of the credit for the economic improvements that black people have experienced. But despite their constant attempts to emphasize the role of the demand side of the equation, and particularly discrimination and anti-discrimination laws, the fact is that enormous changes were taking place on the supply side. Blacks were becoming a different people. More were acquiring not only literacy but higher levels of education, skills, and broader cultural exposure. The advancement of blacks was not simply a matter of whites letting down barriers.

Much has been made of the fact that the numbers of blacks in high-level occupations increased in the years following passage of the Civil Rights Act of 1964. But the number of blacks in professional, technical, and other high-level occupations more than doubled in the decade *preceding* the Civil Rights Act of 1964. In other occupations, gains by blacks were greater during the 1940s—when there was practically no civil rights legislation—than during the 1950s. In various skilled trades, the income of blacks relative to whites more than doubled between 1936 and 1959. The trend was already under way. It may well be that both the economic and the legal advances were products of powerful social transformations taking place in the black population and beginning to make themselves felt in the consciousness of whites, as well as in the competition of the marketplace.

Knowledge of the strengths of blacks has been ignored or repressed in a different way as well. Few people today are aware that the ghettos in many cities were far safer places two generations ago than they are today, both for blacks and for whites. Incredulity often greets stories by older blacks as to their habit of sleeping out on fire escapes or on rooftops or in public parks on hot summer nights. Many of those same people would not dare to walk through those same parks today in broad daylight. In the 1930s whites went regularly to Harlem at night, stayed until the wee hours of the morning, and then stood on the streets to hail cabs to take them home. Today, not only would very few whites dare to do this, very few cabs would dare to be cruising ghetto streets in the wee hours of the morning.

Why should discussion of positive achievements by blacks ever be a source of embarrassment, much less resentment, on the part of black leaders? Because many of these positive achievements occurred in ways that completely undermine the civil rights vision. If crime is a product of poverty and discrimination as they say endlessly, why was there so much less of it when poverty and discrimination were much worse than today? If massive programs are the only hope to reduce violence in the ghetto, why was there so much less violence long before anyone ever thought of these programs? Perhaps more to the point, have the philosophies and policies so much supported by black leaders contributed to the decline in community and personal standards, and in family responsibility, so painfully visible today? For many, it may be easier to ignore past achievements than to face their implications for current issues....

The civil rights vision and the civil rights leadership continue pushing an approach which has proved counterproductive for the mass of disadvantaged blacks, beneficial primarily to those already advantaged, and which accumulates resentments against all blacks.

99

JOINT CENTER FOR POLITICAL STUDIES

The Black Community's Values as a Basis for Action

From *Black Initiative and Governmental Responsibility*

———

BLACK AMERICANS have been at the helm of a profound social revolution. Since World War II, we have engineered the demise of a rigidly segregated society, used nonviolent action and litigation to compel the protection of basic rights, expanded the American society's conception and application of equality, made dramatic gains in political participation and leadership, and secured notable improvements in our socioeconomic status. Today, American society remains far from colorblind, and race continues to be a powerful predictor of status; but viewed against the backdrop of history, blacks and the entire society have made genuine progress.

It is precisely these achievements that make untenable the condition of the large part of the black population that remains enmeshed in a crisis of poverty. While only one-tenth of white Americans are poor today, more than one-third of blacks are trapped in poverty, many with only dim prospects for escape. No stable democracy can afford to ignore such disparities.

Most of the black poor are concentrated in badly deteriorated inner cities, are poorly educated and without the skills and experience required in today's workplace, are plagued by extremely high rates of unemployment or underemployment, and are strained by a rapidly deteriorating family structure. Many of these poor blacks are part of what a number of analysts call an "urban underclass" that is increasingly isolated from the mainstream of society and its opportunities. The condition of this large population of urban poor casts a shadow over the gains made by the rest of society and by blacks themselves. This dilemma and appropriate responses to it are the concerns of this statement.

The causes of persistent urban black poverty are uncommonly complex, but some of the contributing factors are abundantly clear. Sweeping economic and technological changes in recent years have substantially altered the character and distribution of urban and rural labor markets. Even more sweeping changes in the global economy have resulted in a decline in the relative competitiveness of major segments of the U.S. economy, especially in well-paying jobs of modest skill that typically have brought other Americans into the middle class. Jobs that were plentiful in core cities when whites were residents have dispersed to the suburbs and outlying areas. Inadequate education and skill levels and damaged self-esteem and aspiration have often undermined the chances of poor blacks to compete successfully in the labor market. Finally, the cumulative effects of the long history of discrimination have impaired the capacity of many of the more disadvantaged to cope with a complex, rapidly changing economy and society.

These conditions of poverty have been allowed to fester for so long and are so difficult to eradicate that they will require the most determined and resourceful efforts by all who are implicated. The impacted network of economic and social problems is so novel and ferocious that it can be attacked effectively only by a judicious, concurrent, and sustained mix of *both* black self-help efforts *and* public and private assistance from the nation as a whole. Self-help can have only a limited impact on the economic environment, but it can encourage action and teach behavior that can pay handsome dividends for blacks and for the nation as a whole. However, the creation of a more robust economic environment and of greater equity in the distribution of its fruits is a public responsibility. Despite a vigorous continuing debate about the role of government in American life today, the mainstream American view remains that government should be an active agent for improving the quality of life of the people and for responding to community needs in times of crisis. Thus, even in the face of large budget cuts and huge deficits, farmers, children, veterans, immigrants, students, the elderly, small-business people, and others continue to be the focus of special attention and funding from government. The crisis of the black community deserves no less attention. . . .

The conditions associated with the profound urban poverty among blacks—declining male labor-force participation, very high rates of out-of-wedlock births and female-headed households, a high level of welfare dependency, poor educational performance, and high crime rates—inevitably prompt questions about the character and role of values in the black community. These questions have been raised in an effort both to account for current conditions and to search for the critical ingredients of a possible solution.

Blacks have always embraced the central values of the society, augmented those values in response to the unique experiences of slavery and subordination, incorporated them into a strong religious tradition, and espoused them fervently and persistently. These values—among them, the primacy of family, the importance of education, and the necessity for individual enterprise and hard work—have been fundamental to black survival. These community values have been matched by a strong set of civic values, ironic in the face of racial discrimination—espousal of the rights and responsibilities of freedom, commitment to country, and adherence to the democratic creed. Indeed, the country's democratic values defined black America's expectations of the society and formed the basis of our struggle for equality.

The value traditions of the black heritage are especially relevant to the needs of black people during this period. For example, commitment to the family historically has been one of the most powerful forces in black life. First as slaves, then as sharecroppers and farmers, and finally as urban workers, blacks always embraced a strong family ethic as central to our lives, and the great majority managed to maintain strong, intact families often in the face of enormous adversity....

While all along pressing the larger society for equity and fairness, we have continually drawn upon our own resources in order to define ourselves positively and to renew our strengths. This has been true particularly at moments—as in the case of the current black experience—when complex new problems were suddenly added to older ones and when opposition appeared in powerful new forms. The most basic resource of the black community is the special value structure that has sustained black people through the darkest of hours. The leadership of the black community must more forcefully articulate, reaffirm, and reinforce the black value heritage with renewed vigor and commitment as a basis for action today.

There are countless ways to do this. From our experience and history, black people have at hand an extraordinary store of values and traditions developed and honed through earlier battles that can be adapted to secure old gains as we fight up to higher ground.

We can begin by encouraging all of the black community's religious institutions, civic and social organizations, media, entertainers, educators, athletes, public officials, and other community leaders to make special efforts to emphasize black community values as a central feature of their service to the black community....

The black community always has been an agent for its own advancement. Action by government in addressing social and economic needs has been important, but it has been both recent and modest. Blacks made the transition from a largely impoverished mass of former slaves to a strong, vibrant community largely through individual effort and through the work of civil rights, cultural, fraternal, religious, social, professional, and service organizations in the black community. Thus, black Americans have an unusually rich history of self-initiated contributions to our own well-being. Indeed, without our own vigorous, creative, and persistent efforts, many of our needs would not have been met at all.

In spite of this proud history, blacks are often skeptical of assessments of black community responsibility as compared with government's proper role—and no wonder. The history of black people is the history of countless unsuccessful efforts to get government to allow blacks the ordinary privileges of citizenship that were routinely a matter of right for whites. That history has been characterized by a societal racial obsession replete with the most negative stereotypic attitudes that blamed blacks for problems that arose directly from oppressive and unequal treatment by the majority. As a result, blacks have a valiant history of protest and demands for equity from which we shall not retreat. But as so often in the past, black people and their leadership, armed with confidence from long years of struggle and angry at recent years of retreat, are also calling on the internal strengths of the community.

Recent salutary expansion of the government's role in assisting those in need has pushed to the background recognition of the black community's long history and continuing efforts of progress through self-reliance and has created misconceptions about historic and existing roles of community and of government in black socioeconomic advancement. Further, the very success of our civil rights movement in reducing many barriers to education, employment, housing, and economic opportunity has created a gap in socioeconomic status between those blacks who were in the best position to seize new opportunities and those who were not, facilitating physical and economic separation. This new diversity within the black community has sometimes altered community structures, dispersed leadership, and diminished the capacity for cohesive, effective initiatives....

This challenge does not underestimate the indisputable necessity of government action in addressing both the new and the lingering social and economic needs of the black community. To maximize—indeed, often to make community efforts bear fruit at all—government must play a principal role in the process. The complexity and magnitude of the task requires a judicious combination of public and private efforts and resources. At the same time, some of the problems blacks face cannot effectively be handled by government alone, as blacks know best of all. Moreover, community efforts, which have always been critical to black advancement, will be especially important today precisely because government has defaulted, failing altogether to act with the commitment or on the scale necessary to effect change. Blacks will never let government rest with its present posture of passivity and abdication. But as problems deepen, internal black community efforts must continue while we find ways to bring about the decent and committed governmental leadership we and the country deserve....

...Neither blacks nor any other group can create jobs on the scale needed; nor can we restore the economy to include more jobs of moderate skill and decent pay that created the white middle class. This is preeminently the work of government. The black community cannot restore the deteriorated infrastructure of the cities that provides the physical framework for the ghetto and for ghetto conditions and attitudes. This too is the job of government. In addition, initiatives by the community, many already in progress, cannot be fully effective if completely unaided by government. The continuing problems blacks face will require firm, responsive, long-term commitment by government at every level, led by the federal government.

In the past, the federal government has been responsible in many ways for policies that have brought important changes to the lives of blacks and other Americans. It reversed its historic position and moved to ensure basic civil rights and remove the most blatant racial discrimination. It acted more equivocally to alleviate severe poverty and expand economic opportunity. Since 1981 it has retreated on all fronts, deepening black problems, especially in employment, health, education, and family stability. Even in more vigorous periods, the actions of the government were belated and sometimes ambivalent. Thus, severe handicaps are still experienced by a large portion of the black community as a result of prolonged subordination that was government-sanctioned and of poverty from which most Americans have long been relieved.

What we propose is a new framework for eradicating the growing disparities between blacks and whites. We urge a concentrated effort by government to invest first in models and then in programs and strategies for human development that will facilitate economic independence and encourage the poor to take charge of their own lives. . . .

Pervasive and persistent poverty has eroded but not destroyed the strong, deep, value framework that for so long has sustained black people. These values—among them, family, education, and hard work—are so deeply held that they remain and can be explicitly tapped today. The black value system, together with the wonderful variety of historic and existing self-initiated activities, can be the basis for a newly energized and expanded effort from within the black community to tackle a new variety of unusually resistant social and economic problems. But the inexcusable disparities between whites and blacks that continue today were not created by blacks, and they cannot be addressed by blacks alone. These disparities would never have arisen at all if official and societal discrimination had not denied blacks earlier access to equality and to opportunity. They can be eradicated only if the government assumes its appropriate role in a democratic, humane, and stable society—its role of coming to the assistance of a community in crisis.

PART SEVENTEEN

Foreign and Defense Policy

F OR MORE THAN a hundred and fifty years, from the administration of George Washington until World War II, the United States was not a major actor on the world stage. Isolated from the power struggles of the great European nation-states by a vast ocean, America's major foreign policy before the twentieth century was an affirmation of Washington's idea that we should avoid being drawn into any kind of alliance with the European powers. Despite our flirtation with colonialism at the turn of the century and our participation in World War I, as late as the 1930s this was our normal posture. Everything changed in short order as the United States was required by circumstances beyond argument to fill the void created by the collapse of the major European powers at the end of World War II. From that moment on foreign and defense policies have been the foremost concerns of the federal government, and every president since Franklin Roosevelt has clearly understood the primacy of these concerns. Nothing whatever has more changed the conduct of American politics than our sudden emergence as the major world power in 1945.

Suddenly, the United States became the leader of the free world. (That phrase would not have made sense before the outcome of

World War II. So accustomed are we today to this kind of language, we are likely to forget that it is of very recent origin.) The presidency, already the focal point of activity as a result of fifteen years of depression and war, was permanently aggrandized as we began to see the chief executive in Clinton Rossiter's now-famous trinity of foreign policy roles as Chief Diplomat/Commander-in-Chief/ Leader of the Free World Coalition. Never again could a serious case be made for a national government of three coequal branches. For the first time in our history we would now be required to maintain a permanent military establishment of awesome dimensions and dedicate a major portion of the national treasury to its support. Through the Truman Doctrine, the Marshall Plan, and the formation of the North Atlantic Treaty Organization (NATO), a national bipartisan consensus was formed: The United States must spearhead action to "contain" the Soviet Union's expansionist tendencies in Europe and oppose other communist regimes throughout the world. At times in the late 1940s and early 1950s the "threat of communism" would become an obsession. By the time of John F. Kennedy's presidency, both political parties agreed that we must "go anywhere, do anything, pay any price" to defend the cause of freedom. In the brief period of twenty years, we had moved all the way from isolation to being a kind of policeman of the world order.

Then came the war in Vietnam with its own enormous repercussions on virtually all American institutions. The war subjected the American bipartisan foreign policy consensus to fractures that have not yet been fully healed. For better or worse, in the last twenty years, we have had to come to grips with a great many new realities. Clearly, we could not pay *any* price to achieve our objectives *everywhere;* there were indeed constraints on U.S. military-political action in many parts of the world. Our share of world economic markets, while still huge, had significantly declined. In the seventies it became painfully apparent that our energy needs placed us largely at the mercy of unstable world oil markets. A new Europe and the remarkable economic transformation of the Pacific rim were altering our economic and political relations with our allies. Perhaps most perplexing of all, in the last twenty years we have been forced to ponder the impact of nearly two centuries of industrialization on the global environment. On the plus side—for all but the most enthusiastic of cold warriors—we have learned over the last two decades that communism is not a unified world force and that the Marxist-Leninist regimes of the Soviet Union and China are much less potent than we had earlier supposed them to be.

Forced to be selective in our readings on the vast subject of foreign policy, we have opted to stress ideas rather than institutions and processes. The big questions of foreign policy—the strategic questions—are driven by particularly broad conceptualizations of national interest. It is appropriate that we begin with two selections from the work of one of the premier intellectuals of American foreign policy-making in the postward period, George Kennan. Kennan, a remarkable man, was (in his colleague Dean Acheson's nice phrase) "present at the creation" of the postwar world order, and he more than anyone else provided its theoretical basis. Our first reading is from his famous 1947 article in *Foreign Affairs* under the pseudonym "X," in which he advocated a careful and measured confrontation with the Soviet Union under the concept of "containment." Kennan, a Soviet specialist who had served in Moscow under Ambassador Averell Harriman, had first roughed out his argument in a widely circulated internal memo. Both ideology and circumstance, he argued, had generated a "Soviet psychology" to the effect that there could never be a "community of aims" between the Soviet Union and powers they regarded as capitalist. The Soviets would apply pressure against the West that could only be contained by "the adroit and vigilant application of counterforce at a series of constantly shifting geographical and political points, corresponding to the shifts and maneuvers of Soviet policy...." Note particularly the last paragraph of this article. Although Kennan is usually regarded as a hardheaded "realist," you will see here an interesting manifestation of American ideology. The Soviet challenge, properly understood, is "no cause for complaint." We should thank "a Providence" that has provided a challenge requiring us to accept "the responsibilities of moral and political leadership that history plainly intended ... [us] to bear." Here we have in a nutshell the thinking behind American strategic policy for many years to come.

Kennan's "Containment Then and Now," written in 1987, is no less fascinating. Today, he maintains, there is no real "ideological-political threat" to us from Moscow. Communism has lost its appeal outside the so-called peoples' democracies and "partially within that orbit as well." What remains is a military threat posed by the massive nuclear capabilities of both the Soviet Union and the United States. It is now the arms race that needs to be contained. Note again the closing paragraphs of his article. Kennan, always the philosopher, now extends the meaning of containment to a new world situation that he finds deeply worrying. Religious fundamentalism, terrorism, "the worldwide environmental crisis," and what he sees as our own profligate habits have created problems utterly unlike those we faced in 1947. In his most recent book, *Sketches From A Life* (1989), Kennan makes much more clear what he means here by saying that "the first thing we Americans need to contain is, in some ways, ourselves...." He has cultivated in his later years a deeply pessimistic view of industrial modernity in the United States. He now thinks that many of our most serious problems are of our own making, and that we now "have to develop a wider concept of what containment means—a concept more closely linked to the totality of the problems of Western civilization."

In our next readings, Senator Richard Lugar and Arthur Schlesinger briefly describe what they believe to be the major differences between Republican and Democratic foreign-policy perspectives in the 1980s. Here we see the legacy of the Vietnam years. As Lugar points out, Republicans see the Democrats as lacking in the confidence necessary to support "a strong, confident and globally engaged United States." Democrats, as Schlesinger shows, tend to see the Republicans (especially, Reagan Republicans) as ideological anticommunists driven by a "messianic conviction that the American destiny is to redeem a fallen world." How then, we might ask, can we make coherent foreign policy with a Republican president and a Democratic Congress? While we ought to dismiss some of these differences as the stuff of campaign rhetoric, we ought also to see that on questions like Central American policy, there is serious disagreement. That is how we got into the Iran-Contra affair. Nevertheless, it would be easy to overestimate real differences between the parties on overarching strategic questions like arms control and NATO. We do, after all, get by.

While the old postwar consensus is not what it once was, the thinking of the elite theorists of American foreign policy is still more bipartisan by far than comparable thinking in most other Western democracies. This is clearly apparent in our last selection, from a recent article by Henry Kissinger and Cyrus Vance. In what other nation could two former secretaries of state of major rival parties reach such wide areas of agreement? Could one imagine, for example, a British counterpart of this collaboration? Certainly not. There could only be a catfight. On the big questions there is still impressive agreement. Both parties' theorists believe that corporate capitalism is good, that we can make progress on arms control with the Soviets, that NATO must remain "the keystone of U.S. policy," that we must coordinate our economic and trade policies with our allies throughout the world, and that we need to get our own economic house in order. Kissinger and Vance agree that we live in a period of significant international transition, and that we can continue to prosper as a nation by incrementally adjusting policies that have been followed by administrations of both parties, despite the disagreements of the Vietnam years.

We leave off where we began, noting the remarkable agreement of Americans on the larger questions of politics. The American liberal consensus lives on in foreign policy as it does in all other aspects of American political life.

100

"X" [GEORGE KENNAN]

The Sources of Soviet Conduct

THE POLITICAL PERSONALITY of Soviet power as we know it today [in 1947] is the product of ideology and circumstances: ideology inherited by the present Soviet leaders from the movement in which they had their political origin, and circumstances of the power which they now have exercised for nearly three decades in Russia. There can be few tasks of psychological analysis more difficult than to try to trace the interaction of these two forces and the relative role of each in the determination of official Soviet conduct. Yet the attempt must be made if that conduct is to be understood and effectively countered....

Now the outstanding circumstance concerning the Soviet regime is that down to the present day this process of political consolidation has never been completed and the men in the Kremlin have continued to be predominantly absorbed with the struggle to secure and make absolute the power which they seized in November 1917. They have endeavored to secure it primarily against forces at home, within Soviet society itself. But they have also endeavored to secure it against the outside world. For ideology, as we have seen, taught them that the outside world was hostile and that it was their duty eventually to overthrow the political forces beyond their borders.... [The innate antagonism between capitalism and Socialism] has profound implications for Russia's conduct as a member of international society. It means that there can never be on Moscow's side any sincere assumption of a community of aims between the Soviet Union and powers which are regarded as capitalist. It must invariably be assumed in Moscow that the aims of the capitalist world are antagonistic to the Soviet regime, and therefore to the interests of the peoples it controls.... [However,] the Kremlin is under no ideological compulsion to accomplish its purposes in a hurry. Like the Church, it is dealing in ideological concepts which are of long-term validity, and it can afford to be patient. It has no right to risk the existing achievements of the revolution for the sake of vain baubles of the future. The very teachings of Lenin himself require great caution and flexibility in the pursuit of Communist purposes.... Thus the Kremlin has no compunction about retreating in the face of superior force. And being under the compulsion of no timetable, it does not get panicky under the necessity for such retreat. Its political action is a fluid stream which moves constantly, wherever it is permitted to move, toward a given goal. Its main concern is to make sure that it has filled every nook and cranny available to it in the basin of world power. But if it finds unassailable barriers in its path, it accepts these philosophically and accommodates itself to them. The main thing is that there should always be pressure, unceasing constant pressure, toward the desired goal. There is no trace of any feeling in Soviet psychology that that goal must be reached at any given time.

These considerations make Soviet diplomacy at once easier and more difficult to deal with than the diplomacy of individual aggressive leaders like Napoleon and Hitler. On the one hand it is more sensitive to contrary force, more ready to yield on individual sectors of the diplomatic front when that force is felt to be too strong, and thus more rational in the logic and rhetoric of power. On the other hand it cannot be easily defeated or discouraged by a single victory on the part of its opponents. And the patient persistence by which it is animated means that it can be effectively countered not by sporadic acts which represent the momentary whims of democratic opinion but only by intelligent long-range policies on the part of Russia's adversaries—policies no less steady in their purpose, and no less variegated and resourceful in their application, than those of the Soviet Union itself.

In these circumstances it is clear that the main element of any United States policy toward the Soviet Union must be that of a long-term, patient but firm and vigilant containment of Russian expansive tendencies. It is important to note, however, that such a policy has nothing to do with outward histrionics: with threats or blustering or superfluous gestures of outward "toughness." While the Kremlin is basically flexible in its reaction to political realities, it is by no means unamenable to considerations of prestige. Like almost any other government, it can be placed by tactless and threatening gestures in a position where it cannot afford to yield even though this might be dictated by its sense of realism. The Russian leaders are keen judges of human psychology, and as such they are highly conscious that loss of temper and of self-control is never a source of strength in political affairs. They are quick to exploit such evidences of weakness. For these reasons, it is a sine qua non of successful dealing with Russia that the foreign government in question should remain at all times cool and collected and that its demands on Russian policy should be put forward in such a manner as to leave the way open for a compliance not too detrimental to Russian prestige....

In the light of the above, it will be clearly seen that the Soviet pressure against the free institutions of the Western world is something that can be contained by the adroit and vigilant application of counterforce at a series of constantly shifting geographical and political points, corresponding to the shifts and maneuvers of Soviet policy, but which cannot be charmed or talked out of existence. The Russians look forward to a duel of infinite duration, and they see that already they have scored great successes....

Balanced against this are the facts that Russia, as opposed to the western world in general, is still by far the weaker party, that Soviet policy is highly flexible, and that Soviet society may well contain deficiencies which will eventually weaken its own total potential. This would of itself warrant the United States entering with reasonable confidence upon a policy of firm containment, designed to confront the Russians with unalterable counterforce at every point where they show signs of encroaching upon the interest of a peaceful and stable world.

But in actuality the possibilities for American policy are by no means limited to holding the line and hoping for the best. It is entirely possible for the United States to influence by its actions the internal developments, both within Russia and throughout the international Communist movement, by which Russian policy is largely determined. This is not only a question of the modest measure of informational activity which this government can conduct in the Soviet Union and elsewhere, although that, too, is important. It is rather a question of the degree to which the United States can create among the peoples of the world generally the impression of a country which knows what it wants, which is coping successfully with the problems of its internal life and with the responsibilities of a world power, and which has a spiritual vitality capable of holding its own among the major ideological currents of the time....

Thus the decision will really fall in large measure on this country itself. The issue of Soviet-American relations is in essence a test of the overall worth of the United States as a nation among nations. To avoid destruction the United States need only measure up to its own best traditions and prove itself worthy of preservation as a great nation.

Surely, there was never a fairer test of national quality than this. In the light of these circumstances, the thoughtful observer of Russian-American relations will find no cause for complaint in the Kremlin's challenge to American society. He will rather experience a certain gratitude to a Providence which, by providing the American people with this implacable challenge, has made their entire security as a nation dependent on their pulling themselves together and accepting the responsibilities of moral and political leadership that history plainly intended them to bear.

GEORGE KENNAN
Containment Then and Now

———

THE WORD "containment," of course, was not new in the year 1946. What was new, perhaps, was its use with relation to the Soviet Union and Soviet-American relations. What brought the word to public attention in this connection was its use in an article that appeared in 1947, in this magazine, under the title of "The Sources of Soviet Conduct," and was signed with what was supposed to have been an anonymous X. This piece was not originally written for publication; it was written privately for our first secretary of defense, James Forrestal, who had sent me a paper on communism and asked me to comment on it. It was written, as I recall, in December 1946, in the northwest corner room on the ground floor of the National War College building. At the time I was serving as deputy commandant for foreign affairs at the college. I suppose it is fitting that I, for my sins, should try to explain something about how the word "containment" came to be used in that document, and what it was meant to signify.

One must try to picture the situation that existed in that month of December 1946. The Second World War was only a year and some months in the past. U.S. armed forces were still in the process of demobilization; so, too, though to a smaller extent (because the Russians proposed to retain a much larger peacetime establishment than we did), were those of the Soviet Union.

In no way did the Soviet Union appear to me, at that moment, as a military threat to this country. Russia was at that time utterly exhausted by the exertions and sacrifices of the recent war....

In these circumstances, there was no way that Russia could appear to me as a military threat. It is true that even then the Soviet Union was credited—and credited by some of my colleagues at the War College—with the capability of overrunning Western Europe with its remaining forces, if it wanted to do so. But I myself regarded those calculations as exaggerated (I still do); and I was convinced that there was very little danger of anything of that sort. So when I used the word "containment" with respect to that country in 1946, what I had in mind was not at all the averting of the sort of military threat people talk about today.

What I *did* think I saw—and what explained the use of that term—was what I might call an ideological-political threat. Great parts of the northern hemisphere—notably Western Europe and Japan—had just then been seriously destabilized, socially, spiritually and politically, by the experiences of the recent war. Their populations were dazed, shell-shocked, uncertain of themselves, fearful of the future, highly vulnerable to the pressures and enticements of communist minorities in their midst. The world communist movement was at that time a unified, disciplined movement, under the total control of the Stalin regime in Moscow. Not only that, but the Soviet Union had emerged from the war with great prestige for its immense and successful war effort. The Kremlin was, for this and for other reasons, in a position to manipulate these foreign communist parties very effectively in its own interests. . . .

One must also remember that during that war, and to some extent into the post-hostilities period as well, the U.S. government had tried to win the confidence and the good disposition of the Soviet government by fairly extensive concessions to Soviet demands with respect to the manner in which the war was fought and to the prospects for the postwar international order. The United States had raised no serious objection to the extension of the Soviet borders to the west. Our government had continued to extend military aid to the Soviet Union even when its troops were overrunning most of the rest of Eastern Europe. We had complacently allowed its forces to take Prague and Berlin and surrounding areas even when there was a possibility that our forces could arrive there just as soon as theirs did. The Russians were refusing to give us even a look in their zone of occupation in Germany but were demanding a voice in the administration and reconstruction of the Ruhr industrial region in western Germany.

Now there seemed to be a danger that communist parties subservient to Moscow might seize power in some of the major Western European countries, notably Italy and France, and possibly in Japan. And what I was trying to say, in the *Foreign Affairs* article, was simply this: "Don't make any more unnecessary concessions to these people. Make it clear to them that they are not going to be allowed to establish any dominant influence in Western Europe and in Japan if there is anything we can do to prevent it. When we have stabilized the situation in this way, then perhaps we will be able to talk with them about some sort of a general political and military disengagement in Europe and in the Far East—not before." This, to my mind, was what was meant by the thought of "containing communism" in 1946.

One may wish to compare that situation with the one the United States faces today, and to take account of the full dimensions of the contrast—between the situation we then confronted and the one we confront today. I must point out that neither of the two main features of the situation we were confronting in 1946 prevails today; on the contrary, the situation is almost exactly the reverse.

I saw at that time, as just stated, an ideological-political threat emanating from Moscow. I see no comparable ideological-political threat emanating from Moscow at the present time. The Leninist-Stalinist ideology has almost totally lost appeal everywhere outside the Soviet orbit, and partially within that orbit as well. And the situation in Western Europe and Japan has now been stabilized beyond anything we at that time were able even to foresee. Whatever other dangers may today confront those societies, a takeover, politically, by their respective communist parties is simply not in the cards....

On the other hand, whereas in 1946 the military aspect of our relationship to the Soviet Union hardly seemed to come into question at all, today that aspect is obviously of prime importance. But here, lest the reader be left with a misunderstanding, a caveat must be voiced.

When I say that this military factor is now of prime importance, it is not because I see the Soviet Union as threatening the United States or its allies with armed force. It is entirely clear to me that Soviet leaders do not want a war with us and are not planning to initiate one. In particular, I have never believed that they have seen it as in their interests to overrun Western Europe militarily, or that they would have launched an attack on that region generally even if the so-called nuclear deterrent had not existed. But I recognize that the sheer size of their armed forces establishment is a disquieting factor for many of our allies. And, more important still, I see the weapons race in which we and they are now involved as a serious threat in its own right, not because of aggressive intentions on either side but because of the compulsions, the suspicions, the anxieties such a competition engenders, and because of the

very serious dangers it carries with it of unintended complications—
by error, by computer failure, by misread signals, or by mischief
deliberately perpetrated by third parties.

For all these reasons, there is now indeed a military aspect to
the problem of containment as there was not in 1946; but what
most needs to be contained, as I see it, is not so much the Soviet
Union as the weapons race itself. And this danger does not even
arise primarily from political causes. One must remember that
while there are indeed serious political disagreements between the
two countries, there is no political issue outstanding between them
which could conceivably be worth a Soviet-American war or which
could be solved, for that matter, by any great military conflict of
that nature.

The weapons race is not all there is in this imperfect world that
needs to be contained. There are many other sources of instability
and trouble. There are local danger spots scattered about in the
Third World. There is the dreadful situation in southern Africa.
There is the grim phenomenon of a rise in several parts of the
world of a fanatical and wildly destructive religious fundamentalism, and there is the terrorism to which that sort of fundamentalism
so often resorts. There is the worldwide environmental crisis, the
rapid depletion of the world's nonrenewable energy resources, the
steady pollution of its atmosphere and its waters—the general deterioration of its environment as a support system for civilized living.

And finally, there is much in our own life, here in this country,
that needs early containment. It could, in fact, be said that the first
thing we Americans need to learn to contain is, in some ways,
ourselves: our own environmental destructiveness, our tendency
to live beyond our means and to borrow ourselves into disaster,
our apparent inability to reduce a devastating budgetary deficit,
our comparable inability to control the immigration into our midst
of great masses of people of wholly different cultural and political
traditions.

In short, if we are going to talk about containment in the
context of today, then I think we can no longer apply that term
just to the Soviet Union.... We are going to have to recognize
that a large proportion of the sources of our troubles and dangers
lies outside the Soviet challenge, such as it is, and some of it even
within ourselves. And for these reasons we are going to have to
develop a wider concept of what containment means—a concept
more closely linked to the totality of the problems of Western

civilization at this juncture in world history—a concept, in other words, more responsive to the problems of our own time—than the one I so lightheartedly brought to expression, hacking away at my typewriter there in the northwest corner of the War College building in December of 1946.

102

RICHARD LUGAR
A Republican Looks at Foreign Policy

IF THE NEW administration is to develop a cohesive and coherent foreign policy, it cannot escape the changes in our nation's strategic position. It must recognize three fundamental new conditions. First, there is a potentially dangerous disparity developing between those vital security interests that the American people are prepared to support with force, and the degree and kind of force we are willing and able to employ to protect these interests. In short, our aims may exceed our resources.

The extent of American commitments abroad has not declined; in some parts of the world our obligations have even increased. This new reality has led some to argue once again that we must reduce our commitments and thereby decrease the risks our country must face. But it is far easier to demand a reduction in commitments than to define with clarity those commitments that can, in fact, be safely reduced....

This security dilemma, the growing gap between our objectives and our capabilities—sometimes described as a decline of relative American power—has been recognized in both parties, but the diversity of proposed remedies has accelerated the breakdown of the national consensus. The simultaneous end of any semblance of a national or bipartisan consensus in the country on foreign policy is the second new factor that the next administration must face....

It is clear that, as some of our strategic advantages have declined, a national consensus is all the more necessary in order to maximize the effective use of our residual power. But such a consensus cannot simply be wished into being. It can be restored only gradually over time, through the development of mutual trust and sustained credibility on the part of both the president and the Congress.

Reestablishing such trust, however, is all the more difficult in light of the third new factor: the revival of the struggle between the executive and legislative branches over foreign policy. This tension is inherent in the constitutional separation of powers but it has been exacerbated by new concerns over both the formulation as well as the implementation of policies—again, evident most recently in the debates over aid to the contras as well as the War Powers Act and its applicability in the Persian Gulf crisis.

Our nation must guarantee our essential interests at a reasonable risk through a judicious balancing of commitments and power: this means maintaining a credible deterrence and national defense as well as an ability and a willingness to use armed force, directly and indirectly. If we cannot achieve this, then a more restrictive interpretation of vital security interests must necessarily follow, at a cost to our national security that cannot be predicted. I believe that the Reagan Administration has succeeded in bringing our interests and power more into line, to the point that the inherent risks are approaching an acceptable level. The next Republican administration can build on this achievement. . . .

The Democratic Party has had great difficulty in reconciling its recent noninterventionist goal—"no more Vietnams"—with the need for a strong, confident and globally engaged United States. The Republican Party has sought to combine the twin imperatives of strength and prudence. A globally engaged great power is unlikely to be able to avoid involvements in peripheral conflicts.

Some Democrats continue to revert to moralistic arguments with a human rights content to criticize the foreign policy initiatives of the Reagan Administration. Still others adopt the language of "national interests" and "political realism" as a short-term political tactic to attack the Reagan Doctrine [support for anti-communist forces in countries currently dominated by Marxist regimes or clients of the Soviet Union]. For example, many Democrats continue to make largely moralistic arguments against the [Reagan] Administration's policy toward Nicaragua. Instead of directly addressing the Sandinista threat to U.S. interests in Central America, many Democrats concentrate on the [Reagan] Administration's tactics while simultaneously seeking to rebut the ideological rationale underlying the current policy.

Too many Democrats have focused their attention and criticisms on how the [Reagan] Administration has involved the country in Central American politics, and eschewed debate on how U.S. interests in effectively promoting peace and security in the region can be furthered. Too often, Democratic inputs to the debate on contra aid are confined to references to "slippery slopes," alleging that such aid constitutes the first step toward another Vietnam. While such dire warnings may carry some emotional appeal, they also reveal paucity in thinking about credible alternative policy directions.

Many Democrats attack the Reagan Doctrine for allegedly twisting anti-communist ideological objectives into the primary rationale for U.S. support of freedom fighters in Nicaragua, Angola, Cambodia and Afghanistan. Yet many of their calls for a change in emphasis in the direction of realistic self-interest betray an overriding concern for tactical expediency rather than strategic necessity. Oftentimes, there is less a calculation of national interest than an obvious political desire to avoid any intervention in situations where success may entail costs. But U.S. interests cannot be determined exclusively or in major part by assessed degrees of difficulty of U.S. involvement and/or tactical alternatives. Efforts to reduce national interests to simplify the task of maximizing gains while cutting costs merely avoid the difficult issue of defining U.S. interests in Third World countries. Calls for noninterventionism seldom reflect a clear appreciation of interests and power.

Regardless of party, however, the next president will have a unique opportunity. America's global position has changed radically since 1945, but a new administration can translate the rebuilding of the 1980s into a period of major and positive accomplishments. I would stress the following objectives.

We will need a general strategy that outlines clear-cut criteria for measuring Soviet actions against our legitimate security concerns. The test of our next president's policy will be his ability to define precise criteria for progress toward peace and stability, and to test Soviet intentions against those criteria. The test of Gorbachev's intentions must be his actions, not the growing sophistication of his public diplomacy.

Effective arms control will be an important element of that testing. It will remain both a necessary price of our continuing security, and a potential danger to it. It must not become a diversion from strategy or a substitute for defense planning, or be allowed to obscure the realities of the military balance, and the actions necessary to correct it.

Our alliance system must be sustained and strengthened as the basis for a coalition strategy; a new and more equitable distribution of burdens must be worked out. And we must obtain allied cooperation in attempting to relate concerns about arms control and the settlement of regional threats to our mutual security.

Both political parties have an obligation to participate in a continuous assessment of America's strategic interests. While no one can dispute the necessity of tactical caution, it alone cannot answer the policy dilemma as to the appropriate balance between strength and prudence. Many efforts to redefine or constrict our strategic interests merely mask a reluctance or unwillingness to contemplate the use of military power. A redefinition of or retreat from military commitments should not be confused with a policy designed to protect and promote U.S. national interests.

The administration that is sworn in on January 20, 1989, will inherit a far stronger, safer and more durable position in the world than Mr. Reagan did in January 1981, with the frustration of Iran and the shock of Afghanistan. Not only is our foreign policy sound and our international position greatly improved, but we are also pursuing an active dialogue with our adversary, on the basis of the strength necessary to defend our interests—and all without the agony of a foreign war.

103

ARTHUR SCHLESINGER
A Democrat Looks at Foreign Policy

——————

IN THE JUDGMENT of this free-lance Democrat, the foreign policy of the United States has been on a radically misconceived course since President Reagan took office in January 1981. This is not to lay all blame for foreign policy failure on the Reagan Administration nor to reject everything that Administration has done in its conduct of foreign relations. The continuities of U.S.

foreign policy are greater than European critics of the United States (and American critics of democracy) understand. Geopolitical imperatives fall impartially on Republican and Democrat alike. All American administrations, no matter how much they differ, will act to preserve a balance of power in Europe and to prevent extracontinental annexations in the Americas.

Even in the shorter run, the roots of Reagan's national security policy (misdirected, in this' writer's view) as well as of his human rights policy (steadily improving) lie in the Carter Administration. It was Carter who, for better or for worse, advanced the movement away from the concept of mutual assured destruction toward a war-prevailing strategy, who approved the MX missile, who expanded American security commitments in the Third World and whose Carter Doctrine defined the Persian Gulf as within the zone of U.S. vital interests. And it was Carter too who placed human rights on the world's conscience and agenda—for which Reagan roundly condemned him in the 1980 campaign, holding Carter's human rights preoccupation responsible for the "loss" of Iran and Nicaragua. In abandoning the Philippines' Ferdinand Marcos and Haiti's Jean-Claude Duvalier half a dozen years later, Reagan unabashedly adopted the policy for which he had so righteously denounced Carter in the cases of the shah and the Somozas....

Within this broad framework of bipartisan continuity, however, the Reagan Administration has carried forward historic differences between the Republican and Democratic parties[:] ... that the Republican Party has been in recent times the vehicle of unilateral action in world affairs and the Democratic Party the vehicle of international cooperation....

The Reagan Administration has now given the G.O.P.'s unilateralist tradition a global application. No administration in recent times has paid less heed to the views and interests of allies, has more systematically scorned multilateral forums or has taken greater pleasure in being able to say, as Reagan said after an American plane forced down Palestinian hijackers over Italy in 1985, that we did it "all by our little selves."

Reaganite unilateralism, moreover, is inspired by a messianic conviction that the American destiny is to redeem a fallen world. It is inspired by a crusading anti-communism of a sort not seen in the United States since the high noon of John Foster Dulles. Where presidents from Truman to Carter saw the cold war as a power struggle, Reagan saw it as a holy war. He regarded the Soviet

Union as unchanged, unchanging and unchangeable and found communist deviltry at the root of most of the world's troubles.

The presidential tone, it is true, has moderated as the years have passed. We hear less these days about the "evil empire," nor has the president recently repeated the remarks of his first press conference in 1981 ("The only morality they recognize is what will further their cause, meaning they reserve unto themselves the right to commit any crime, to lie, to cheat")—perhaps because people might think he was talking about his own National Security Council staff....

Global unilateralism driven by an anti-communist crusade wobbles the Administration's sense of reality. Local conflicts become tests of global resolve. Stakes are raised in situations that cannot be easily controlled, threatening to transmute limited into unlimited conflict. We are encouraged in the fallacy, one we share with the rival superpower, that we know the interests of other nations better than those nations know their own interests—that we understand remote and exotic problems more clearly than the countries most directly involved, most directly threatened and most familiar with the territory. Unilateralism breeds the arrogance of ignorance, and ignorance breeds bad policy....

The climax of the present Administration's self-arrogated right to intervene single-handedly everywhere in the world is the famous Reagan Doctrine. Once again unilateralism breeds bad policy. The Reagan Doctrine exhorts people to take up arms in order to overthrow communist regimes. "We must not break faith," Reagan said in 1985, "with those who are risking their lives on every continent, from Afghanistan to Nicaragua, to defy Soviet-supported aggression." Reagan's cry recalls the prizefight manager in the old cartoon urging his battered and bleeding pug into the ring for one more round: "Go on in there. They can't hurt us."

Obviously it is one thing to help people who, on their own, are resisting a foreign invasion, as in Afghanistan. Indeed, a Democratic administration initiated this policy. It is something quite different to create an insurgency in order to overthrow a government, such as Nicaragua's, recognized by most of the world, including ourselves....

Still worse, the Reagan Doctrine carries illegality from foreign relations into the domestic polity. Founded as it is on lawbreaking, deception and lies, covert action imports very bad habits into a constitutional democracy. There is no need here to rehearse the squalid story revealed in the Iran-contra hearings. One has only to note that the Reagan Doctrine led on to actions that violated both the Constitution President Reagan swore a solemn oath to uphold and the laws he was pledged to execute. Of course the "neat idea" advanced by Lieutenant Colonel Oliver North was a dumb policy. But the issue is not the Rube Goldberg scheme to get the ayatollah to subsidize the contras, nor even its mode of execution, which seems to have been devised by Inspector Clouseau. The issue is whether the president of the United States is above the Constitution and the laws....

...A Democratic president would aim at the resurrection of diplomacy, the revitalization of the State Department and the restoration of competence and coherence to the management of foreign relations. The process by which the government made foreign policy under Reagan could hardly have been worse. "Is it not your view," Senator Paul Sarbanes (Democratic of Maryland) asked the secretary of defense about the Iran-contra decisions, "that it's an inexcusable and deplorable way to conduct the policymaking process of the government?" Even the indefatigably loyal Caspar Weinberger responded, "Yes.".....

The Reagan method has been to treat foreign policy as the president's personal property, to be conducted without undue regard for the laws and the Constitution and to be concealed, if necessary, not only from Congress and the American people but even, on occasion, from his own secretaries of state and defense. A Democratic president would recognize the futility of trying to run foreign policy in a democracy on any other basis than consent. He would especially recognize the necessity of restoring Congress to its constitutional partnership in the making of foreign policy. As a great American—and Democratic—diplomat, Averell Harriman, once put it: "No foreign policy will stick unless the American people are behind it. And unless Congress understands it the American people aren't going to understand it.".....

The day of the messianic foreign policy, the United States as the redeemer nation commissioned by the Almighty to rescue fallen humanity, is coming to an end, for a while at least. A modesty more akin to the mood of the Founding Fathers may be taking over: "a decent respect to the opinions of mankind." Reaganism is running its course, the cycle is turning, and the time impends for a sharp change in the national direction.

Democrats will continue to stand, as they always have, for

national strength. They will never hesitate to use force when force is required to defend the national interest. But they will remind the nation that strength in the modern world has economic as well as military dimensions. The impending crisis for the United States is rather more likely to be in the banks than on the battlefield. . . . In the age ahead, economic power will be quite as significant as military power—a fact Gorbachev has recognized, though Reagan has not. . . .

Whether the question is diplomatic, military, political or economic, the choice today is not all that different from the choice of 1928: Republican unilateralism or Democratic internationalism. We have had seven years of a unilateralist, militarized, ideological, messianic foreign policy, and look where it has got us.

104

HENRY KISSINGER
CYRUS VANCE
Bipartisan Objectives for American Foreign Policy

WE HAVE DECIDED to write this article together because of our deep belief that the security of free peoples and the growth of freedom both demand a restoration of bipartisan consensus in American foreign policy. We disagree on some policy choices. But we are convinced that the American national purpose must at some point be fixed. If it is redefined—or even subject to redefinition—with every change of administration in Washington, the United States risks becoming a factor of inconstancy in the world. The national tendency to oscillate between exaggerated belligerence and unrealistic expectation will be magnified. Other nations— friends or adversaries—unable to gear their policies to American steadiness will go their own way, dooming the United States to growing irrelevance.

We hope the next president will appreciate the value of continuity in American foreign policy. He should know that the country has been well served by maintaining principles which have kept us strong and prosperous for almost half a century under Republican and Democratic presidents alike.

In this year of political transition, and in a foreign policy setting where major roles are changing at home and abroad, we believe it vital to identify several crucial bipartisan objectives for the next administration....

...Debate will continue past election day over specific policies and methods of implementation. However, if broad agreement on central foreign policy objectives can be achieved, the 41st president of the United States will be able to start his term with a strong popular mandate for leadership at home and abroad.

By the end of this century a number of the pillars on which the global order was rebuilt after World War II will have changed significantly. For the United States, our nuclear monopoly will have disappeared and our relative share of the world economy will be less than half of what it was forty years ago. Other countries, playing a variety of roles, already have had a major impact on U.S. interests: the economies of Japan, Western Europe and the "newly industrializing countries" are obvious examples; several countries have nuclear weapons capability and others are able to acquire it quickly. Old East-West security issues persist, but new issues such as state-sponsored terrorism and international drug trafficking have become urgent. At the same time, long-standing problems cannot be ignored: there will be a continuing need of the poorest countries and peoples for humanitarian assistance.

A growing list of constraints on American actions also must be considered: despite our vast military power, our ability to shape the world unilaterally is increasingly limited. Even with strong domestic support, we can no longer afford financially to do as much internationally by ourselves as was the case in the immediate postwar period. For many of our staunchest friends, the Soviet threat to the free world seems diminished, especially with the accession to power of a reform-minded leadership in the U.S.S.R. This perception tends to reduce Western dependence on America's dominant role. Thus the United States is called upon to exercise new, subtler and more comprehensive forms of leadership, and especially to play a major role in defining the threats to the alliance.

Since 1941, successive generations of Americans have accepted the global responsibilities thrust on the United States. It now appears that a growing number of Americans want the United States to be less active internationally than before. They urge that other nations assume greater risks, responsibilities and financial burdens for the maintenance of world order and international prosperity. We understand the frustration underlying this national mood, and agree that it must be dealt with constructively in the decades ahead. But we are also convinced that it is the duty of our national leadership to prevent international burdens from jeopardizing important American interests and the cause of freedom.

Our nation is on the eve of a new international era. At a time of political transition it is important to have a national debate on how and where the United States should spend its diplomatic, military and economic resources in the decades ahead. These discussions should involve Americans from a broad range of occupations, because citizens in all walks of life are vitally concerned not only about their survival, but about the shape of the world in which they will live....

As we define our choices we must consult with our closest allies and friends about the course of our deliberations, urge them to do likewise, and then share our findings. It is essential that we explore with our principal partners the pace and shape of the changes we envisage. Once common decisions are reached—as we believe it is possible to do—we should collectively manage change so as to enhance our long-term relations and our publics' confidence in our determination to remain close.

Over time we would anticipate that the American role in some areas of the world may become less conspicuous. For the foreseeable future, however, the United States must continue to play a major and often vital role. Far into the future, the United States will have the world's largest and most innovative economy, and will remain a nuclear superpower, a cultural and intellectual leader, a model democracy and a society that provides exceptionally well for the needs of its citizens. These are considerable strengths.

A United States that adjusts to new international realities and develops a broad consensus on its primary interests in the world will give cause for optimism. Only a combination of domestic ideological extremism, confusion between past and present, internal economic failings, xenophobia or loss of confidence can weaken the central role of the United States in world affairs....

For purposes of illustration we shall apply the principles we have discussed to some of the major foreign policy issues, beginning with the core issue of relations with the Soviet Union.

U.S.-Soviet relations. The possession of vast nuclear arsenals imposes on the two superpowers a special obligation to maintain world peace. Both have a moral and practical duty to prevent nuclear holocaust. But this common interest occurs in the context of ideological differences and geopolitical rivalry. America also has an obligation to ensure that the willingness to defend freedom and justice is not impaired by negotiations with the Soviet Union that raise unrealistic expectations.

Today the emergence of a rejuvenated Soviet leadership has raised new hopes for Soviet-American relations. We have both met several times with General Secretary Mikhail Gorbachev and have spent considerable time with some of his close advisers. We found Gorbachev highly intelligent and determined to remedy the failures of the Soviet economy with socialist solutions. He is eloquent in arguing that he prefers to live in peace with the West and that he wants to reduce Soviet defense spending so as to transfer resources into the civilian economy. At the same time, we have no doubt that Gorbachev is also firmly committed to defend Soviet international aims. . . .

No American president can base his policies for dealing with the U.S.S.R. on the presumed intentions of a Soviet general secretary. We cannot predict whether his intentions may radically change under domestic political pressure. A successor may change policies, as has happened before. Nor can we pretend to understand the inner workings of the Kremlin well enough to know whether Gorbachev will succeed or survive. Even *glasnost* and *perestroika,* which are intrinsically appealing to the West, should not by themselves fundamentally alter how we conduct our relations with the Soviet Union. . . .

Our overall conclusion is that there is a strategic opportunity for a significant improvement in Soviet-American relations. The issue is how to take advantage of what may be a favorable correlation of forces. This requires a concrete American and Western political program. . . .

Atlantic relations. Early in his term, the next president will preside over the 40th anniversary of the founding of the Atlantic alliance. NATO is one of the most successful treaty arrangements

in history. It has preserved the peace in Europe for four decades—
the longest such period since the European state system came into
being. It connects America with countries of similar cultural heritage. It must remain the keystone of U.S. policy.

But conditions have changed vastly since the early days of
NATO. The U.S. atomic monopoly of 1945 has given way to
nuclear parity with the U.S.S.R.; this situation, as well as other
aspects of East-West relations, has aroused doubts in some quarters
about America's continued commitment to the defense of Europe.
A second important change since the 1940s has been Europe's
economic recovery and the growing importance of the European
Community as an economic and political entity; this tempts more
intense economic competition with the United States and raises
some broader issues in European-American relations. On both
sides of the Atlantic a new generation has matured which shares
neither the sense of danger nor the emotional commitment to cooperation that characterized NATO's early years. Moreover, the era
of more active diplomacy with the East that involves both U.S.
and allied efforts creates new challenges and risks of competitive,
separate approaches to Moscow.

In sum, the state of the Atlantic alliance encourages a new
impetus in strategy, diplomacy and internal relations....

The world economy. America's role in the world has become
directly dependent on the strength and performance of the U.S.
economy. Foreign policy and economic policy have become increasingly interdependent.

When we served as secretaries of state, only a relatively small
portion of our time was spent on international economic issues.
Our successors do not have this luxury. Economic strength is
today even more central to the way America is perceived by its
friends and potential adversaries. U.S. political leadership in the
world cannot be sustained if confidence in the American economy continues to be undermined by substantial trade and budget
deficits.

For these reasons, the weaknesses of the U.S. economy may
be among the most serious and urgent foreign policy challenges to
the next president. Convincing economic discipline, clear and publicly supported long-term economic strategies, as well as equitable
budget reductions, must be applied quickly if we are to halt the
erosion of our international position....

To sum up: America's ability to influence events abroad and

ensure prosperity at home will be determined in large part by how rapidly we get our economic house in order. Fortunately we can still make these decisions ourselves. We must face the fact that our economy and consumption have become so overextended in recent years that the remedies will involve sacrifice and slower growth in our standard of living. If, however, we ignore these economic realities, American influence abroad will decline significantly and our children will pay the price of our inattention and excesses in weakened security and declining competitiveness....

Japan. The stunning economic success and political stability that Japan has achieved have placed it in a privileged, but also precarious, position. Tokyo is experiencing what can be fairly described as the "problems of success." Its major trading partners want Japan to modify its practices of emphasizing its national efforts above all other priorities....

We warn against any attempt to deal with the deficit by pressing Japan to step up its defense efforts. Of course, Japan has the right to determine its appropriate security requirements. The United States can have no interest in urging Japan to go beyond that. Such a course would generate the gravest doubts all over Asia. It might deflect Japan from a greater economic contribution to international stability, through a cooperative effort by all developed countries to infuse capital into the developing world....

China. No relationship has changed more dramatically over the past four administrations, of both parties, than America's relations with the People's Republic of China. Sino-U.S. friendship is one of few uncontested achievements of American policy in the past two decades of bitter debates. We are concerned that it not be neglected as we become more involved in a new phase of East-West negotiations. There is a strong bipartisan consensus in favor of developing the relationship further....

Central America. The most immediate political concerns that we have in the western hemisphere relate to ending the wars in Central America while strengthening democratic forces and reducing Soviet and Cuban influence in the area. Central America provides a conspicuous example of an area where U.S. policy has suffered because of a lack of clear-cut national objectives that could be publicly debated and congressionally mandated. Confusion remains over whether our principal aim should have been to overthrow the Nicaraguan government, halt Nicaraguan support for insurrections elsewhere in Central America, eliminate the Soviet-

Cuban presence and military assistance in Nicaragua or democratize the Sandinista regime. Now the presidents of five Central American nations have taken on the responsibility for making peace.

Is there anything left for the United States to do to promote an acceptable peace in the region?

First, it remains very much in the U.S. interest to obtain the withdrawal of Cuban and Soviet military advisers from Nicaragua, significant reductions in the armies and armaments in the region (especially in Nicaragua), a total ban on Sandinista help to guerrillas elsewhere, and the internal democratization of Nicaragua.

Second, the situation in Central America can be one measure of U.S.-Soviet relations: whether the Soviet Union is willing to suspend arms shipments into this area of our most traditional relationships. . . .

Also outstanding is the issue of the level and scope of our assistance to the area. . . .

Finally, the United States should also continue to support democracy within Nicaragua. Our diplomatic and material aid to those who work for a pluralistic economy and representative political process should be done openly. . . .

Latin American debt. One clear aim of the United States is to increase the likelihood that stable and democratic governments will survive in the region. To this end we must help them resolve critical problems of debt and development. . . .

Western commercial banks alone cannot resolve debt problems of this magnitude. Their governments must become more fully involved, together with international financial institutions. Some new public and private monies must be provided so that Latin America can begin to grow again—which would also make it possible for the region again to absorb significant quantities of U.S. exports. . . .

As is apparent from the foregoing, our next president will be severely challenged to guide us through a period of international transition and to secure a firm place for the United States in a changing configuration of nations. He must focus American resources and energies on areas where precisely defined U.S. national interests are at stake. He must not be reluctant to admit that there are important issues, even conflicts, in which the United States has no special role to play because our vital interests are not engaged. But he must not shrink from defending our interests.

It is true that this is a more restrictive approach to the defense of American objectives than that in the immediate postwar period. We believe, however, that America's international standing and national security need not be diminished because we adopt more selective and collaborative international strategies based on new realities.

PERMISSIONS
ACKNOWLEDGMENTS

12. Excerpt from *Inventing America* by Garry Wills, copyright © 1978 by Garry Wills. Used by permission of Doubleday, a division of Bantam, Doubleday, Dell Publishing Group, Inc.
13. From *A Machine That Would Go of Itself: The Constitution in American Culture* by Michael Kammen. Copyright © 1986 by Michael Kammen. Reprinted by permission of Alfred A. Knopf, Inc.
14. "What Americans Know about the Constitution" by Robert A. Goldwin from *Public Opinion,* Sept./Oct. 1987. Reprinted with the permission of the American Enterprise Institute for Public Policy Research.
15. *The Power Elite* by C. Wright Mills, published by Oxford University Press, 1959. Reprinted with permission from Yaraslova Mills.
16. *Who Governs?* by Robert Dahl, published by Yale University Press. Reprinted by permission of Yale University Press.
17. Copyright © 1988 by St. Martin's Press, Inc. From *Democracy for the Few* by Michael Parenti. Reprinted by permission of St. Martin's Press, Incorporated.
18. *Strong Democracy: Participatory Politics for a New Age* by Benjamin Barber, published by University of California Press. © 1984 The Regents of the University of California. Reprinted by permission.
19. *In Defence of Politics* by Bernard Crick, published by The University of Chicago Press. © The University of Chicago Press 1962. Reprinted by permission.
20. *The Federalist* number 51, by James Madison, published by Mentor, 1961.
21. *Congressional Government* by Woodrow Wilson, Peter Smith Publisher, Gloucester, Mass.: 1973. Reprinted by permission.
22. Report of the Congressional Committees Investigating the Iran-Contra Affair with the Supplemental, Minority and Additional Views, Nov. 1987.
23. "Reagan Vetoes *Grove City* Bill: Override Vote Set for March 22" and "Congress Overrides Reagan's *Grove City* Veto" by Nadine Cohodas and Mark Willen from *Congressional Quarterly Weekly Report,* March 19 and 26, 1988. Reprinted by permission.
24. *The Federalist* numbers 39 and 46, by James Madison, published by Mentor, 1961.
25. Excerpt from *American Federalism* by Daniel Elazar. Copyright © 1984 by Harper & Row, Publishers, Inc. Reprinted by permission of the publishers.
26. "Two Hundred Years of American Federalism" by David Walker. Reprinted by permission of author.
27. "The Bridge Is Out" by W. John Moore. Condensed from *National Journal,* April 2, 1988. Copyright 1988 by *National Journal* Inc. All Rights Reserved. Reprinted by permission.
28. James Young, *The Washington Community.* Copyright © 1987, 1966 Columbia University Press. Used by permission.
29. *Congress Against Itself* by Roger Davidson and Walter Oleszek, published by Indiana University Press, 1977. Permission granted by Walter Oleszek.

Herskowitz. (pp. 179–184, 186–189). Copyright © 1987 by Michael K. Deaver. Reprinted by permission of William Morrow and Co., Inc.

46. "Guess Who's Coming to Dinner at the White House" by Charlotte Hays from *Public Opinion*, May/June 1987. Reprinted with the permission of the American Enterprise Institute for Public Policy Research.

47. *A Government of Strangers* by Hugh Heclo, published by The Brookings Institution, 1977. Reprinted by permission.

48. Excerpted from *Politics, Position, and Power: From the Positive to the Regulatory State*, 4/e by Harold Seidman and Robert Gilmour. Copyright © 1986 by Oxford University Press, Inc. Reprinted by permission.

49. Scattered excerpts from *Revolution*, copyright © 1988 by Martin Anderson, reprinted by permission of Harcourt Brace Jovanovich, Inc.

50. "From Ouagadougou to Cape Canaveral: Why the Bad News Doesn't Travel Up" by Charles Peters, from *The Washington Monthly*, April 1986. Reprinted with permission from the Washington Monthly. Copyright 1986 by the Washington Monthly.

51. *The Federalist* number 78, by Alexander Hamilton, published by Mentor, 1961.

52. Reprinted from *Storm Center: The Supreme Court in American Politics* by David M. O'Brien, by permission of W. W. Norton & Company, Inc.

53. "The Democratic Character of Judicial Review" by Eugene Rostow from *Harvard Law Review*, Dec. 1952. Copyright © 1952 by The Harvard Law Review Association. Reprinted by permission.

54. "Towards an Imperial Judiciary?" by Nathan Glazer from *Public Interest*, Fall 1975, pp. 106, 109–11, 116–19.

55. "The Struggle Over the Role of the Court" by Robert Bork from *National Review*, Sept. 17, 1982. © by *National Review, Inc.*, 150 East 35 Street, New York, New York 10016. Reprinted with permission.

56. "On the Nomination of Robert Bork" from Testimony before the Senate Judiciary Committee, Sept. 22, 1987, by Laurence Tribe.

57. *The Brethren* by Bob Woodward and Scott Armstrong. Copyright © 1979 by Bob Woodward and Scott Armstrong. Reprinted by permission of Simon & Schuster, Inc.

58. *The American Commonwealth*, vol. III, by James Bryce, published by Macmillan, 1888.

59. Reprinted with permission of Macmillan Publishing Company from *The Phantom Public* by Walter Lippmann. Copyright 1925 by Walter Lippmann. Copyright renewed 1953 by Walter Lippmann.

60. *Silent Politics* by Leo Bogart, Copyright © 1972 by John Wiley & Sons, Inc. Reprinted by permission of John Wiley & Sons, Inc.

61. "The Use of Public Opinion Data by the Attorney General's Commission on Pornography" by Tom Smith in *Public Opinion Quarterly*, Summer, 1987, published by The University of Chicago Press. © The University of Chicago Press 1987. Reprinted by permission.

62. "Government as Villain" by Karlyn Keene and Everett Ladd from *Government Executive*, January 1988, pp. 11, 13–16.

63. *Public Opinion and American Democracy* by V. O. Key, published by Alfred A. Knopf, 1961. Permission granted by the executors of the Key Estate.

64. From *Democracy in America* by Alexis de Tocqueville, edited and abridged by Richard D. Heffner. Copyright © 1956 by Richard D. Heffner. Copyright © renewed 1984 by Richard D. Heffner. Reprinted by arrangement with New American Library, A Division of Penguin Books USA Inc., New York, New York.

65. Excerpts from *The Semisovereign People,* copyright © 1960 by E. E. Schattschneider, reprinted by permission of Holt, Rinehart andWinston, Inc.

66. Reprinted from *The End of Liberalism,* Second Edition, by Theodore J. Lowi, by permission of W. W. Norton & Company, Inc. Copyright © 1979, 1969 by W. W. Norton & Company, Inc.

67. "Public Interest Lobbies vs. Minority Faction" by Andrew McFarland, from Cigler and Loomis (eds.), *Interest Group Politics,* published by Congressional Quarterly Press, 1983. Reprinted by permission.

68. From *The Rise of Political Consultants: New Ways of Winning Elections,* by Larry J. Sabato. Copyright © 1981 by Larry J. Sabato. Reprinted by permission of Basic Books, Inc., Publishers.

69. *The Selling of the President 1968* by Joe McGinniss. Copyright © 1969 by JoeMac, Inc. Reprinted by permission of Simon & Schuster, Inc.

70. "Pocketbook Issues Still Matter the Most" by Stuart Rothenberg in *The Wall Street Journal,* March 28, 1989. Reprinted with permission of The Wall Street Journal © 1989 Dow Jones & Company, Inc. All rights reserved.

71. Reprinted with permission of Macmillan Publishing Company from *Politics and Money* by Elizabeth Drew. Copyright © 1983 by Elizabeth Drew.

72. *Money and Politics in the United States* by Michael Malbin, published by Chatham House, 1984. Reprinted by permission.

73. "Nice PAC You've Got Here ... A Pity if Anything Should Happen to It" by Amy Dockser, from *The Washington Monthly,* January 1987. Reprinted with permission from the Washington Monthly. Copyright 1987 by the Washington Monthly.

74. "What's in a Name? For Consultants, Much Cash" by Peter Bragdon from *Congressional Quarterly Weekly Report,* Dec. 19, 1987. Reprinted by permission.

75. "The Braintrusters" by Kirk Victor. Condensed from *National Journal,* Feb. 13, 1988. Copyright 1988 by *National Journal Inc.* All right reserved. Reprinted by permission.

76. "Political Humor: Who Are All Those Jokers?" by Mark Shields from *Public Opinion,* Sept./Oct. 1987. Reprinted with the permission of the American Enterprise Institute for Public Policy Research.

77. Reprinted from *Critical Elections and the Mainsprings of American Politics* by Walter Dean Burnham, by permission of W. W. Norton & Company, Inc. Copyright © 1970 by W. W. Norton & Company, Inc.

78. Excerpt from *The Party's Over* by David Broder. Copyright © 1971,